Journal Of George

Being An Historical Account Of The Life, Travels, Sufferings, Christian Experiences, And Labour Of Love, In The Work Of The Ministry, Of That Eminent And Faithful Servant Of Jesus Christ, Who Departed This Life, In Great Peace With The Lord, The 13Th Of The 11Th Month 1690 (Volume I)

George Fox
Wilson Armistead

Alpha Editions

This Edition Published in 2021

ISBN: 9789354501937

Design and Setting By
Alpha Editions
www.alphaedis.com
Email – info@alphaedis.com

A JOURNAL

LIFE, TRAVELS, SUFFERINGS, CHRISTIAN EXPERIENCES, AND LABOUR OF LOVE,

OF

GEORGE FOX.

JOURNAL

OF

GEORGE FOX;

BEING AN

HISTORICAL ACCOUNT

OF THE

LIFE, TRAVELS, SUFFERINGS, CHRISTIAN EXPERIENCES, AND LABOUR OF LOVE, IN
THE WORK OF THE MINISTRY, OF THAT EMINENT AND FAITHFUL SERVANT
OF JESUS CHRIST, WHO DEPARTED THIS LIFE, IN GREAT PEACE WITH
THE LORD, THE 13TH OF THE 11TH MONTH, 1690.

SEVENTH EDITION.—IN TWO VOLUMES.

WITH NOTES—BIOGRAPHICAL AND HISTORICAL, ETC.

BY

WILSON ARMISTEAD.

VOL. I.

"They that turn many to righteousness, shall shine as the stars for ever and ever," Dan. xii. 3.
"Many shall run to and fro; and knowledge shall be increased," Dan. xii. 4.
"If we suffer, we shall also reign with him" (i. e. with Christ), 2 Tim. ii. 12.

LONDON:

W. AND F. G. CASH (LATE GILPIN), BISHOPSGATE STREET:
AND JOSEPH SMITH, OXFORD STREET, WHITECHAPEL.
DUBLIN: J. B. GILPIN; CARLISLE: HUDSON SCOTT;
MANCHESTER: JOHN HARRISON AND SON, NEW MARKET CHAMBERS;
LIVERPOOL: PAUL SMITH, FRIENDS' MEETING-HOUSE, HUNTER ST.
YORK: JAMES HUNTON; BIRMINGHAM: WHITE & PIKE.
GLASGOW: W. & R. SMEAL, GALLOWGATE.
AND MAY BE HAD OF ALL BOOKSELLERS.

MDCCCLII.

INTRODUCTION

TO THE SEVENTH EDITION.

THE present re-issue of the *Journal of George Fox* has, in a great measure, resulted from the concern of a Friend lately deceased, who was actively engaged in the last edition, and who provided a handsome sum towards the further republication of this valuable Testimony to the Truth.

Assisted by the above bequest, and prompted by the encouragement of many Friends, the Editor of this Seventh Edition of the Journal has endeavoured to increase its usefulness by issuing it in a manner considerably more adapted, than heretofore, for general usefulness, and calculated, he hopes, to insure a still more extended circulation.

In printing from the last edition (which was collated with the first and third), some further slight improvements in the style have been made, and redundancies omitted, with an occasional transposition in the construction of a sentence, or the omission or insertion of a word to impart clearness to the sense of the author, care being taken in every instance not in the least to misrepresent his meaning. In addition to this, the work has now, for the first time, been divided into chapters; a general table of contents has been supplied; and a considerable number of Notes, chiefly biographical and historical, have been added, which must materially increase its interest.

Though highly approved as a standard work, there is reason to believe that the *Journal of George Fox* has not obtained that attention which its real worth justly demands, even from the members of the Society which the author was so eminently instrumental in forming. Let those who have not perused it be induced to make themselves acquainted with its contents; and may those who are of ability, be stimulated to expend a portion of their means in promoting the circulation of a work recording the labours of so eminent a servant of the Lord, concerning whom the following character was given by one of his contemporaries—not the less truthful and applicable from having been often quoted—that " He was indeed a heavenly-minded man, zealous for the name of the Lord, and preferred the honour of God before all things. He was valiant for the Truth, bold in asserting it, patient in suffering for it, unwearied in labouring in it, steady in his testimony to it, immovable as a rock."

The many and important truths unfolded in this work, though conveyed in a style not always suited to the taste of the present day, will, if patiently and seriously perused, amply compensate the reader, of whatever denomination, for the time and attention he may bestow upon it. Sir JAMES MACKINTOSH says, it "is one of the most extraordinary and instructive narratives in the world, which no reader of competent judgment can peruse without revering the virtue of the writer ;" and COLERIDGE in his *Biographia Literaria* observes: "There exist folios on the human understanding, and the nature of man, which would have a far juster claim to their high rank and celebrity, if, in the whole huge volume, there could be found as much fulness of heart and intellect, as bursts forth in many a simple page of George Fox."

In every point of view, George Fox was a character of no ordinary rank. Though a stranger to the polish of human learning, he possessed a truly enlightened mind, connected with sound practical knowledge ; and fearlessly inculcated, amongst persons of all ranks, sentiments and views on various points, equally conducive to the immediate comfort, and to the amelioration and advancement of the various classes of civil society. These views, though then rejected by many as visionary, have since met with very general acceptance, and in some cases have even obtained the favourable attention of government.

But what is of still more importance, he was well taught in the school of Christ. He was thoroughly versed in the Holy Scriptures, which, to use his own expression, were " very precious " to him, and he always held them in high estimation. He firmly believed in the Son of God—in the atoning efficacy of his sacrifice upon the cross, and in all his offices and works both *for* us, and *in* us; and, by obedience to the Light of Life, the illuminating, renovating power of the Holy Spirit—to Christ in his spiritual appearance, he realized in himself the benefits conferred upon mankind by the sufferings and death of the Saviour. By a variety of preparatory baptisms, he was, on the one hand, given to see the depths of Satan, and on the other, richly instructed in the mysteries of the everlasting kingdom of God. Thus trained and exercised he became abundantly furnished, and qualified to enter upon the arduous service, to which he believed himself Divinely called; and proved himself to be, as his *Journal* largely testifies, "a workman that needed not to be ashamed, rightly dividing the Word of Truth."

Contemplating the character of George Fox in this twofold light, the Editor may, in conclusion, say with his predecessors, that he "indulges a hope that the history of the author's life, written by his own hand, unfolding the energy and operation of that grace by which he was what he was, will be found interesting to persons of every class, especially to the really religious of whatever denomination, and still more peculiarly so to those who profess to believe in the same doctrines he was engaged so strenuously in preaching. To the promulgation of these doctrines he steadily devoted upwards of forty years of his life—a life which exhibited throughout 'an example of suffering affliction, and of patience;' evincing him to be, both in principle and in practice, a genuine disciple of his crucified LORD—a real CHRISTIAN." W. A.

P. S.—The Editor is also desirous of directing the special attention of the reader to the admirable Preface to this work, by William Penn.

LEEDS, 1852.

CONTENTS OF VOL. I.

PAGE

THE PREFACE; Being a summary account of the divers dispensations of God to men, from the beginning of the world to that of our present age, by the ministry and testimony of his faithful servant, George Fox, as an introduction to the ensuing Journal, ... 1

CHAPTER I.—1624–1647.—George Fox's birth and parentage—his gravity and piety in youth—apprenticed to a shoemaker, who is also a grazier, &c.—his integrity in dealing—refuses to drink healths—his exercises of mind commence—he lives retired—is tempted to despair—his sorrows continue for some years—has a sense of Christ's sufferings—confutes a people who held women to be devoid of souls—begins to travel on Truth's account—meets with Elizabeth Hooton—fasts often, and retires to solitary places with his Bible—his exercises intermit—sees why none but Christ could speak to his condition—visits a woman who had fasted twenty-two days—first declares the Truth at Duckingfield and Manchester—preaches at a great meeting at Broughton—his troubles wear off, and he weeps for joy—sees things which cannot be uttered—is reported to have a discerning spirit—overcomes his temptations through the power of Christ, ... 49

CHAPTER II.—1648–1649.—Begins to have great meetings—at Mansfield he is moved to pray—the Lord's power so great the house is shaken—cannot pray in his own will—a temptation besets him that there is no God, which is dissipated by an inward voice—he afterwards disputes with and confounds some Atheists—goes to courts and steeple-houses, &c., to warn against oppression and oaths—reproves a notorious drunkard, who is reformed—sees who are the greatest deceivers—shows how people read and understand the Scriptures—various mysteries are revealed to him—he is sent to turn people to the Inward Light, Spirit, and Grace, the Divine Spirit which he infallibly knew would not deceive—priests and professors rage at these innovations—he cries for justice in courts and against various wrong things—denounces the trade of preaching—is sent to preach freely, ... 63

CHAPTER III.—1649–1650.—George Fox is first imprisoned at Nottingham, where the sheriff is convinced—he is liberated and quiets a distracted woman—many miracles were wrought in those days, beyond what that unbelieving age would receive or bear—he is cruelly treated at Mansfield-Woodhouse—is taken before the magistrates at Derby—acknowledges that he is sanctified—is temptingly asked if he were Christ, which he denies, yet committed for blasphemy—his mittimus to Derby prison—writes to the priests of Derby against preaching for hire, &c.—also against persecution—to Barton and Bennet, justices, on the same subject—to Justice Bennet against covetousness—to Justice Barton, a preacher and a persecutor—to the Mayor of Derby against persecution and oppression—to the court of Derby against oaths and oppression—to the bell-ringers of Derby against vanities and

PAGE

worldly pleasures—his jailer is convinced—Justice Bennet first gives Friends
the name of Quakers in derision—writes to Friends and others, to open their
understandings, and to direct them to their true Teacher within themselves
—to the convinced people, directing them to internal silence and to true
obedience—an encouragement to the faithful—to the justices of Derby
against persecution, thrice repeated—to the priests of Derby, on the same
subject—to the justices of Derby, to prize their time, and to depart from evil
—the like to Colonel Barton, justice, and warning of the plagues and vengeance hanging over the oppressor, ...   75

CHAPTER IV.—1650–1651.—A trooper visits George Fox from an inward intimation—declines a commission in the army, and is put in the dungeon—
confutes one who denied Christ's outward appearance, from whence a slander
is raised against Friends—testifies against capital punishments for small
matters—writes for more speedy justice to prisoners—intercedes for the
life of a young woman, imprisoned for stealing, who is brought to the gallows
but reprieved, and afterwards convinced—again refuses to bear arms, and is
committed close prisoner—writes to Barton and Bennet, justices, against persecution—addresses the convinced and tender people against hirelings—to the
magistrates of Derby against persecution, and foretelling his own enlargement
and their recompense—is greatly exercised for the wickedness of Derby—
sees the visitation of God's love pass away from the town, and writes a lamentation over it—a great judgment fell upon the town—he is liberated after a
year's imprisonment—visits Lichfield—preaches repentance through Doncaster—many dread "the man with leather breeches"—goes to steeple-houses,
as the apostles did to the temples, to bring people off from them—is denied
entertainment, and ill-treated at some places—refuses to inform against his
persecutors—many are convinced in Yorkshire, amongst others, Richard
Farnsworth, James Naylor, William Dewsbury, Justice Hotham, and
Captain Pursloe, ...   93

CHAPTER V.—1652.—George Fox visits great men's houses, warning them to
repent—is accused of calling himself Christ—refutes the charge, and tells the
accuser that Judas's end would be his, which shortly came to pass, hence a
slander is raised against Friends—is stoned at Doncaster—a scoffing priest
made to tremble at the Lord's power—a slandering priest cut off in his wickedness—a murderous priest seeks George Fox, but misses him—he lays in a
wood all night—the influence of one man or woman, who lives in the same
spirit that the prophets and apostles were in, is to be felt within a circuit of
ten miles—George Fox ascends Pendle Hill, whence he sees the place of a
great gathering of people—on descending, refreshes himself at a spring of
water, having taken little sustenance for several days—foresees a great people
in white raiment about Wensleydale and Sedbergh—a wicked man designs to
injure him, but is prevented—many are convinced in Dent, and a meeting is
settled at Sedbergh, where he had seen a people in white raiment—preaches
for several hours in the steeple-house yard there—preaches on a rock, near
Firbank chapel, to 1000 people, for three hours—the family of Judge Fell
convinced, and a meeting settled at his house, and continued for forty years
—preaches through Lancaster streets—at a meeting of priests at Ulverstone
he speaks in great power, so that one of them said, "the church shook"—
disputes with priest Lampitt—Justice Sawrey is the first persecutor in the
north—forty priests appear against George Fox at Lancaster Sessions for
speaking blasphemy; they are confounded, and he is cleared of the charge—
James Naylor's account of George Fox's trial at Lancaster Sessions—priest
Jackus is reproved from the bench for his blasphemy—these priests are reproved by the populace—Colonel West defends and protects George Fox
against the machinations of the priests, and the design of Judge Windham,
at the risk of losing his place, ...   114

PAGE

CHAPTER VI.—1652–1653.—George Fox is branded by the priests as a witch
—writes to Justice Sawrey, prophesying of the judgments impending over
him—warning to priest Lampitt—exhortation to the people of Ulverstone—to
the followers of Lampitt, against a hireling ministry, &c.—a rebuke to Adam
Sands for his wickedness—to priest Tatham, against his hireling ministry and
his suing for tithes—foretells the dissolution of the Long Parliament—fasts
ten days—James Milner and Richard Myer create a schism, which is soon
healed—the latter is miraculously healed of his lameness, but afterwards disobeys the Lord, and dies not long after—Anthony Pearson, an opposer, is convinced—the priests are shown to be Antichrist—George Fox preaches at
John Wilkinson's steeple-house three hours—admonishes a professor *for
praising him*—reproves Wilkinson for speaking against his conscience—
many hundreds are convinced—discerns an unclean spirit in a woman, and
speaks sharply to her—the like of some other women—speaks sharply to an
envious Baptist—preaches in the steeple-house at Carlisle, where the Lord's
power was such that the people trembled—committed to Carlisle prison as a
blasphemer, heretic, and seducer—the priests who come to see him are exceedingly rude—Anthony Pearson's remonstrance to the Judges of assize
against the unjust imprisonment and detention of George Fox—he is put in
the dungeon, a filthy place, where a woman is found eaten to death with
vermin—here James Parnell visits him—a challenge to professors to declare
their objections to George Fox's ministry—it being reported that George
Fox was to die for religion, the Little Parliament write to the sheriff respecting him—he himself expostulates with Justices Craston and Studholm on their
imprisoning him—A. Pearson and the governor visit the prison, blame the
magistrates, require sureties of the jailer, and put the under-jailer in the
dungeon for his cruelty to George Fox, who is soon after liberated—George
Fox has great meetings, and *thousands* are convinced—visits Gilsland, a
noted country for thieving—has a glorious meeting of many thousands, near
Langlands, on the top of a hill—great convincement in the six northern
counties, ... 143

CHAPTER VII.—1653–1654.—George Fox disputes most of the day with
priest Wilkinson—Many Friends lose their business for declining the world's
salutations, but afterwards their tried faithfulness and integrity procure them
more than their neighbours—George Fox issues an address to Friends
everywhere—two persecuting justices at Carlisle are cut off, and a third disgraced—George Fox passes through Halifax, a rude town of professors—at
Synderhill-Green he has a mighty meeting of some thousands, and there was
a general convincement—about sixty ministers are now raised up in the north,
to travel towards the south, the east, and the west. in Truth's service—
George Fox's address to Friends in the ministry—Rice Jones and many
other false prophets rise up against Friends and are blasted—a wicked man
binds himself with an oath to kill George Fox, but is prevented—great convincement in Lincolnshire—at Swannington George Fox has much controversy with professors—has a great dispute with priest Stevens, and seven
other priests at Drayton—his father being present was convinced, and said,
" Truly I see he that will but stand to the truth it will carry him out"—
priest Stevens propagates lies respecting George Fox, which the Lord swept
away—is taken before Colonel Hacker, who sends him to the Protector—
speaks prophetically to the Colonel—has a friendly conference with the Protector—is dismissed by him very friendly—refuses his entertainment—
Captain Drury scoffs at trembling, but is made to tremble in a remarkable
manner—George Fox prays with some officers, who are greatly shaken by
the Lord's power—priests and professors greatly disturbed because many of
the people are convinced, and moved to declare against the rest,   . 169

CHAPTER VIII.—1654–1655.—Address to professors of Christianity against
persecution—to such as follow the world's fashions—to the Pope, and all

PAGE

kings, and rulers in Europe, against persecution—to the justices appointed
for trying ministers of religion, being a testimony against hireling ministers
—Samuel Fisher and others are convinced at a meeting at Romney, where
the Lord's power is marvellously displayed—a large meeting at Coggeshall
of about two thousand people, which lasted several hours—many reproaches
are cast upon the truth, and lying slanderous books published, which are
answered, and the truth set over the gainsayers—to those who scorn trembling and quaking—great rage is manifested against the truth and Friends, and
their plainness is contemned—to the churches gathered into outward forms,
opening their state and warning of the woes coming upon them—to the
Protector, respecting the imprisonment of Friends for refusing to take oaths
and pay tithes, &c.—to friends to offer themselves to lie in prison for a
brother or sister—an encouragement to Friends in their several exercises,   . 190

CHAPTER IX.—1655-1656.—Friends slandered by Presbyterians and Independents, suffer much from them and the Baptists for refusing to pay tithes—
the priests hunt after a fallen benefice like crows after carrion—great miracles
wrought through several—an Independent preacher convinced, but relapses
—address to the convinced in Ireland—a sick woman at Baldock restored—
George Fox parts and reconciles two furious combatants—to the seven
parishes at the Land's End, recommending attention to the Inward Light—
George Fox parts with James Naylor, and has a presentiment of his fall—
Major Ceely places George Fox and Edward Pyot under arrest—they are
sent to Launceston jail—put into Doomsdale, and suffer a long and cruel imprisonment—a paper against swearing—Peter Ceely's mittimus—George
Fox has great service in jail—many are convinced, and opposers are confounded—experiences some remarkable preservations—Edward Pyot writes
an excellent letter to Judge Glynne on the liberty of the subject, and on the
injustice and illegality of their imprisonment—Truth spreads in the west by
the very means taken to prevent it—exhortation and warning to magistrates
—answer to the Exeter general warrant for taking up and imprisoning
Friends—exhortation to Friends in the ministry—warning to priests and
professors—cruel jailer imprisoned in Doomsdale, and further judgments
upon him follow—a Friend offers to lie in prison instead of George Fox—
Edward Pyot to Major-General Desborough, in answer to his conditional
offer of liberty—George Fox to the same—he and his Friends are soon after
liberated, ... 215

CHAPTER X.—1656-1657.—Address to those who are given to pleasures and
wantonness—to the bowlers in Castle-Green at Launceston—George Fox
visits Friends imprisoned at Exeter, amongst whom is James Naylor, who
has apostatized, but afterwards returned into the Truth—at a meeting in the
orchard at Bristol about ten thousand persons are present—Paul Gwin, a
rude Baptist, creates a disturbance, but is reproved and silenced—meeting
of two or three thousand persons at N. Crips's—Justice Stooks prevents the
magistrates from apprehending George Fox—speaks to the Protector at
Hyde Park, who invites him to his house—accordingly goes to Whitehall,
and speaks to the Protector about Friends sufferings'—travels through most
parts of the nation after his liberation from Launceston jail—this year, 1656,
there were seldom fewer than one thousand Friends in prison—to Friends on
the schism of J. Naylor—to Friends to keep up their meetings—on judging
the ministry, &c.—an answer to a high-flown professor—to professors,
priests, and teachers on immediate revelation and universal grace, &c. &c.—
at Cardiff, George Fox sends word to some who had run out that "the day
of their visitation was over"—at Brecknock, his companion, John-ap-John,
preaches in the streets—at night, there is a great uproar, like that of Diana's
craftsmen—at William Gandy's has a large meeting of two or three thousand
persons—Cromwell proclaims a fast for rain, and is told by George Fox that
the drought was a sign of their barrenness—concerning the true fast and the

PAGE

false—preaches three hours at a great meeting in Radnorshire, and many are convinced—their horses are twice robbed of their oats—from a high hill sounds the day of the Lord, and foretells where God would raise up a people to himself, which came to pass—travels through every county in Wales, where there is a brave people, who sit under Christ's teaching—has a large meeting on the top of a hill near Liverpool—at Manchester is taken into custody, but soon released, ... 265

CHAPTER XI.—1657.—Exhortation to Friends to take heed to the Light of Christ—an expostulation with persecutors—to Friends to be valiant for the truth—in parts of Cumberland the priests are so forsaken that some steeple-houses stand empty—John Wilkinson, the priest, is so deserted, that he sets up a meeting in his own house—then a silent meeting, and at last joins Friends, and becomes an able minister—George Fox travels into Scotland with Colonel Osburn and Robert Widders—the latter was a thundering man against the rottenness of the priests' hypocrisy and deceit—Lady Hamilton is convinced—the Scotch priests raise the war-cry, and draw up their curses, which George Fox answers—they are in a rage and panic when he comes there, thinking " that all was gone"—some Baptists, with their logic and syllogisms, are confuted by George Fox's logic—he is banished from Scotland by the council, but disregards their order—George Fox and William Osburn are waylaid by thieves, who are admonished by the former, and overawed by the Lord's power—the Highlanders run at them with pitchforks—at Johnstons they are banished the town—on hearing that the council of Edinburgh had issued warrants against him, George Fox goes thither, and is not molested, ... 307

CHAPTER XII.—1657-1659.—George Fox journeys from Scotland to England —dissuades a person from setting up a college at Durham to make ministers —has a meeting with Rice Jones and his people—attends a general Yearly Meeting for the whole nation, held at John Crook's, which continued three days—address to Friends in the ministry—disputes with a Jesuit—writes to Lady Claypole—writes to Cromwell respecting the fast on account of persecution abroad, whilst there was much of it at home—writes a reproof to Parliament for their hypocrisy—speaks to the Protector in Hampton-Court Park about Friends' sufferings—the Protector invites Fox to his house—he goes next day, but the Protector being sick he does not see him—the Protector died soon after—writes to encourage Friends to faithfulness—has a foresight of the King's restoration long before the event occurred, as well as several others—Friends are disseized of their copyhold lands for refusing to swear—cautions Friends to avoid plots, &c.—against bearing arms—great places in the army are offered to Friends, but invariably refused—priest Townsend fails to substantiate his charge of error and blasphemy against George Fox, and is signally defeated—George Fox's vision of the city of London is realized—he gives a final warning to those in authority before their overthrow, ... 326

CHAPTER XIII.—1659-1660.—Address to the Cornish people, respecting shipwrecks—the soldiers at Bristol are punished for disturbing Friends' meetings —several thousands attend a general meeting at Edward Pyot's—General Monk also restrains his soldiers—great drunkenness at elections for Parliament-men—the Yearly Meeting is held at Balby—and a general meeting of discipline for several counties held at Skipton—a Friend goes naked (divested of the upper garments) through the town, declaring truth, and is much abused—general meeting at Arnside for three counties—George Fox is committed to Lancaster Castle by Major Porter—writes an answer to his mittimus—Margaret Fell writes to the magistrates thereon—address on true religion—against persecution—to Friends, on the change of government—to Charles II., exhorting him to exercise mercy and forgiveness towards his

PAGE

enemies, and to restrain profaneness—the sheriff of Lancashire's return to
George Fox's writ of *Habeas Corpus*—M. Fell and Ann Curtis speak to the
King on the subject—the King orders his removal to London by Habeas
Corpus, and there sets him at liberty, ... 355

CHAPTER XIV.—1660–1662.—George Fox writes an epistle of consolation to
Friends unjustly imprisoned in consequence of the insurrection of the Fifth-
Monarchy Men—Friends' declaration against war and plots—John Perrot
and Charles Bailie create a schism—some Friends in New England are put
to death, a sense whereof is given to George Fox at the time—the King's
mandamus to the Governor of New England and others, to restrain them from
executing Friends—the *Battledore* is published, showing by examples from
thirty languages, that "Thou" and "Thee" are proper to one person—on
true worship—George Fox disputes with some Jesuits, and with *all* other
sects—John Perrot's heresy condemned—on judicial swearing—George Fox
and Richard Hubberthorn write to the King, showing the number of Friends
imprisoned prior to, and during the first year of the Restoration, and the
number who died in prison during the Commonwealth—Thomas Sharman,
jailer at Derby, convinced, and writes to George Fox—George Fox applies
to Lord D'Aubeny on behalf of two Friends imprisoned in the Inquisition
at Malta, who procures their liberation—the ground and rise of persecution
set forth—great service at *Bristol*, where also he has a vision—visits Capt.
Brown and his wife; the former had fled from persecution, and was judged
in himself, but afterwards convinced—George Fox and several others are
arrested by Lord Beaumont, and sent to Leicester jail—they are suddenly
liberated—to Friends on the death of Edward Burrough—escapes from persecutors—Friends established on Christ, the Rock of Ages,   .   .   . 377

THE PREFACE;

BEING

A SUMMARY ACCOUNT OF THE DIVERS DISPENSATIONS OF GOD TO MEN,

FROM THE BEGINNING OF THE WORLD TO THAT OF OUR PRESENT AGE, BY THE MINISTRY AND TESTIMONY OF HIS FAITHFUL SERVANT, GEORGE FOX, AS AN INTRODUCTION TO THE ENSUING JOURNAL.

DIVERS have been the dispensations of God since the creation of the world unto the sons of men; but the great end of all of them has been the renown of his own excellent name in the creation and restoration of man: man, the emblem of himself, as a God on earth, and the glory of all his works. The world began with innocency: all was then good that the good God had made: and as he blessed the works of his hands, so their natures and harmony magnified Him their Creator. Then the morning stars sang together for joy, and all parts of his works said Amen to his law; not a jar in the whole frame, but man in paradise, the beasts in the field, the fowl in the air, the fish in the sea, the lights in the heavens, the fruits of the earth; yea the air, the earth, the water, and fire worshipped, praised, and exalted his power, wisdom, and goodness! O holy sabbath! O holy day to the Lord.

But this happy state lasted not long: for man, the crown and glory of the whole, being tempted to aspire above his place, unhappily yielded against command and duty, as well as interest and felicity; and so fell below it, lost the divine image, the wisdom, power, and purity he was made in. By which, being no longer fit for paradise, he was expelled that garden of God, his proper dwelling and residence, and was driven out, as a poor vagabond, from the presence of the Lord, to wander in the earth, the habitation of beasts.

Yet God that made him, had pity on him; for He seeing he was deceived, and that it was not of malice, or an original presumption in him, but through the subtilty of the serpent (that had first fallen from his own state), and by the mediation of the woman, man's own nature and companion (whom the serpent had first deluded), in his infinite goodness and wisdom found out a way to repair the breach, recover the loss, and restore fallen man again by a nobler and more excellent Adam, promised to be born of a woman; that as by means of a woman the evil one had prevailed upon man, by a woman also He should come into the world, who would prevail against him and bruise his head, and deliver man from his power; and which, in a signal manner, by the dispensation of the Son of God in the flesh, in the fulness of time, was personally and fully accomplished by him, and in him, as man's Saviour and Redeemer.

But his power was not limited, in the manifestation of it, to that time; for both before and since his blessed manifestation in the flesh, He has been the light and life, the rock and strength of all that ever feared God: present with them in their temptations, He followed them in their travels and afflictions, and supported and carried them through and over the difficulties that have attended them in their earthly pilgrimage. By this, Abel's heart excelled Cain's, Seth obtained the pre-eminence, and Enoch walked with God. It was this that strove with the old world, and which they rebelled against, and which sanctified and instructed Noah to salvation.

But the outward dispensation that followed the benighted state of man, after his fall, especially among the patriarchs, was generally that of angels; as the Scriptures of the Old Testament do in many places express, as to Abraham, Jacob, &c. The next was that of the law by Moses, which was also delivered by angels, as the apostle tells us. This dispensation was much outward, and suited to a low and servile state; called therefore that of a schoolmaster, to point out and prepare that people to look and long for the Messiah, who would deliver them from the servitude of a ceremonious and imperfect dispensation, by knowing the realities of those mysterious representations in themselves. In this time the law was written on stone, the temple built with hands, attended with an outward priesthood, and external rites and ceremonies, that were shadows of the good things that were to come, and were only to serve till the Seed came, or the more excellent and general manifestation of Christ, to whom was the promise, and to all men only in him, in whom it was Yea and Amen; even life from death, immortality and eternal life.

This the prophets foresaw, and comforted the believing Jews in the certainty of it; which was the height of the Mosaical dispensation, and which ended in John's ministry, the forerunner of the Messiah, as John's was finished in him, the fulness of all. And God, that at sundry times and in divers manners, had spoken to the fathers by his servants the prophets, spoke then by his Son Christ Jesus, who is heir of all things; being the gospel day, which is the dispensation of sonship; bringing in thereby a nearer testament and a better hope; even the beginning of the glory of the latter days, and of the restitution of all things; yea, the restoration of the kingdom unto Israel.

Now, the Spirit, that was more sparingly communicated in former dispensations, began to be "poured forth upon all flesh," according to the prophet Joel; and the light that shined in darkness, or but dimly before, the most gracious God caused to shine out of darkness: and the day-star began to arise in the hearts of believers, giving unto them the knowledge of God in the face (or appearance) of his Son Christ Jesus.

Now, the poor in spirit, the meek, the true mourners, the hungry and thirsty after righteousness, the peace-makers, the pure in heart, the merciful, and the persecuted, came more especially in remembrance before the Lord, and were sought out and blessed by Israel's true Shepherd. Old Jerusalem with her children grew out of date, and the New Jerusalem into request, the mother of the sons of the gospel day. Wherefore no more at old Jerusalem, nor at the mountain of Samaria, will God be worshipped, above other places; for, behold, he is declared and preached a Spirit, and he will be known as such, and worshipped in the Spirit and in the Truth. He will come nearer than of old time, and he will write his law in the heart, and put his fear and Spirit in the inward parts, according to his promise. Then signs, types, and shadows flew away, the day having discovered their insufficiency in not reaching to the inside of the cup, to the cleansing of the conscience; and all elementary services were expired in and by Him that is the substance of all.

And to this great and blessed end of the dispensation of the Son of God, did the apostles testify, whom he had chosen and appointed by his Spirit, to turn the Jews from their prejudice and superstition, and the Gentiles from their vanity and idolatry, to Christ's Light and Spirit that shined in them; that they might be quickened from the sins and trespasses in which they were dead, to serve the living God in the newness of the Spirit of life, and walk as children of the light, and of the day, even the day of holiness: for such "put on Christ," the light of the world, "and make no more provision for the flesh, to fulfil the lusts thereof." So that the Light, Spirit, and Grace that comes by Christ, and appears in man, was what the apostles ministered from, and turned people's minds unto, and in which they gathered and built up the churches of Christ in their day. For which cause they advised them not to quench the Spirit, but wait for the Spirit, and speak by the Spirit, and pray by the Spirit, and walk in the Spirit too, as that which approved them the truly begotten children of God; "born, not of flesh and blood, or of the will of man, but of the will of God;" by doing his will, and denying their own; by drinking of Christ's cup, and being baptized with his baptism of self-denial : the way and path that all the heirs of life have trod to blessedness. But alas! even in the apostles' days, those bright stars of the first magnitude of the Gospel light, some clouds, foretelling an eclipse of this primitive glory, began to appear, and several of them gave early caution of it to the Christians of their time; that even then there was, and yet would be more and more, a falling away from the power of godliness, and the purity of that spiritual dispensation, by such as sought to make a fair show in the flesh, but with whom the offence of the Cross ceased : yet with this comfortable conclusion, that they saw beyond it a more glorious time than ever, to the true church. Their sight was true, and what they foretold to the churches, gathered by them in the name and power of Jesus, came so to pass : for Christians degenerated apace into outsides, as days, and meats, and divers other ceremonies. And which was worse, they fell into strife and contention about them, separating one from another, then envying, and, as they had power, persecuting one another, to the shame and scandal of their common Christianity, and grievous stumbling and offence of the heathen, among whom the Lord had so long and so marvellously preserved them. And having got at last the worldly power into their hands, by kings and emperors embracing the Christian profession, they changed what they could, the kingdom of Christ, which is not of this world, into a worldly kingdom ; or at least styled the worldly kingdom that was in their hands the kingdom of Christ, and so they became worldly, and not true Christians. Then human inventions and novelties, both in doctrine and worship, crowded fast into the church ; a door being opened thereunto by the grossness and carnality that appeared then among the generality of Christians; who had long since left the guidance of God's meek and heavenly Spirit, and given themselves up to superstition, will-worship, and voluntary humility. And as superstition is blind, so it is heady and furious; for all must stoop to its blind and boundless zeal, or perish by it : in the name of the Spirit, persecuting the very appearance of the Spirit of God in others, and opposing that in them which they resisted in themselves, viz., the Light, Grace, and Spirit of the Lord Jesus Christ ; but always under the notion of innovation, heresy, schism, or some such plausible name. Though Christianity allows of no name or pretence whatever for persecuting any man for matters of mere religion ; religion being in its very nature, meek, gentle, and forbearing ; and consists of faith, hope, and charity, which no persecutor can have, whilst he remains a persecutor ; in that a man cannot believe well, or hope well, or have a charitable or tender regard to another, whilst he would violate his mind or persecute his body for matters of faith or worship towards his God.

Thus the false church sprang up, and mounted the chair. But though she lost her nature, she would keep her good name of the Lamb's bride, the true church and mother of the faithful; constraining all to receive her mark, either in the forehead, or right hand, publicly or privately: but in deed and in truth she was Mystery, Babylon, the mother of harlots: mother of those that, with all their show and outside of religion, were adulterated and gone from the Spirit, nature, and life of Christ, and grown vain, worldly, ambitious, covetous, cruel, &c., which are the fruits of the flesh, and not of the Spirit.

Now it was that the true church fled into the wilderness, that is, from superstition and violence, to a retired, solitary, and lonely state; hidden, and as it were out of sight of men, though not out of the world: which shows that her wonted visibility was not essential to the being of a true church in the judgment of the Holy Ghost; she being as true a church in the wilderness, though not as visible and lustrous, as when she was in her former splendour of profession. In this state many attempts she made to return, but the waters were yet too high, and her way blocked up, and many of her excellent children, in several nations and centuries, fell by the cruelty of superstition, because they would not fall from their faithfulness to the truth.

The last age did set some steps towards it, both as to doctrine, worship, and practice. But practice quickly failed, for wickedness flowed in a little time, as well among the professors of the Reformation, as those they reformed from; so that by the fruits of conversation they were not to be distinguished. And the children of the reformers, if not the reformers themselves, betook themselves very early to earthly policy and power to uphold and carry on their reformation, that had been begun with spiritual weapons; which I have often thought has been one of the greatest reasons the Reformation made no better progress, as to the life and soul of religion; for whilst the reformers were lowly and spiritually minded, and trusted in God, and looked to him, and lived in his fear, and consulted not with flesh and blood, nor sought deliverance in their own way, there were daily added to the church such as, one might reasonably say, should be saved. For they were not so careful to be safe from persecution, as to be faithful under it, being more concerned to spread the truth by their faith and patience in tribulation, than to get the worldly power out of their hands, that inflicted their sufferings upon them; and it will be well if the Lord suffer them not to fall by the very same way they took to stand. In doctrine, they were in some things short; in other things, to avoid one extreme they ran into another; and for worship, there was, for the generality, more of man than of God. They owned the Spirit, Inspiration, and Revelation indeed, and grounded their separation and reformation upon the sense and

understanding they received from it, in the reading of the Scriptures of
Truth; and this was their plea, the Scripture was the text, the Spirit the
interpreter, and that to every one for himself. But yet there was too much
of human invention, tradition, and art, that remained both in praying and
preaching, and of worldly authority and worldly greatness in their ministers,
especially in this kingdom, Sweden, Denmark, and some parts of Germany.
God was therefore pleased among us, to shift from vessel to vessel: and
the next remove humbled the ministry, so that they were more strict in
preaching, devout in praying, and zealous for keeping the Lord's day, and
catechising children and servants, and repeating at home in their families
what they had heard in public.

But even as these grew into power, they were not only for whipping
some out, but others into the temple; and they appeared rigid in their
spirits, rather than severe in their lives, and more for a party than for
piety, which brought forth another people, that were yet more retired and
select. They would not communicate at large, or in common with others;
but formed churches among themselves of such as could give some account
of their conversion, at least, of very promising experiences of the work of
God's grace upon their hearts, and under mutual agreements and covenants
of fellowship they kept together. These people were somewhat of a softer
temper, and seemed to recommend religion by the charms of its love, mercy,
and goodness, rather than by the terror of its judgments and punishments;
by which the former party would have terrified people into religion.

They also allowed greater liberty to prophesy than those before them;
for they admitted any member to speak or pray, as well as their pastor
(whom they always chose, and not the civil magistrate), if such found anything pressing upon them to either duty, even without the distinction of
clergy or laity; persons of any trade, be it never so low and mechanical.
But alas! even these people suffered great loss: for tasting of worldly
empire, and the favour of princes, and the gain that ensued, they degenerated but too much. For though they had cried down national churches,
and ministry, and maintenance too, some of them, when it was their own
turn to be tried, fell under the weight of worldly honour and advantage,
got into profitable parsonages too much, and outlived and contradicted
their own principles: and which was yet worse, turned some of them
absolute persecutors of other men for God's sake, that but so lately came
themselves out of the furnace; which drove many a step farther, and that
was into the water—another baptism, as believing they were not scriptu-
rally baptized; and hoping to find that presence and power of God in submitting to that ordinance, which they desired and wanted.

These people made also profession of neglecting, if not renouncing and censuring, not only the necessity but use of all human learning as to the ministry; and all other qualifications to it, besides the helps and gifts of the Spirit of God, and those natural and common to men; and for a time they seemed like John of old, a burning and a shining light to other societies.

They were very diligent, plain, and serious, strong in Scripture, and bold in profession, bearing much reproach, and contradiction: but that which others fell by, proved their hurt. For worldly power spoiled them too; who had enough of it to try them, what they would do if they had more; and they rested also too much upon their watery dispensation, instead of passing on more fully to the fire and Holy Ghost, which was his baptism, who came with a "fan in his hand, that he might thoroughly (and not in part only) purge his floor," and take away the dross and the tin of his people, and make a man finer than gold. Withal, they grew high, rough, and self-righteous, opposing further attainment; too much forgetting the day of their infancy and littleness, which gave them something of a real beauty; insomuch that many left them, and all visible churches and societies, and wandered up and down, as sheep without a shepherd, and as doves without their mates; seeking their beloved, but could not find Him (as their souls desired to know him) whom their souls loved above their chiefest joy.

These people were called Seekers by some, and the Family of Love by others; because, as they came to the knowledge of one another, they sometimes met together, not formally to pray or preach, at appointed times or places, in their own wills, as in times past they were accustomed to do; but waited together in silence, and as anything rose in any one of their minds that they thought savoured of a divine spring, so they sometimes spoke. But so it was, that some of them not keeping in humility, and in the fear of God, after the abundance of revelation, were exalted above measure; and for want of staying their minds in an humble dependence upon Him that opened their understandings to see great things in his law, they ran out in their own imaginations, and mixing them with those divine openings, brought forth a monstrous birth, to the scandal of those that feared God, and waited daily in the temple, not made with hands, for the consolation of Israel; the Jew inward, and circumcision in spirit.

This people obtained the name of Ranters, from their extravagant discourses and practices. For they interpreted Christ's fulfilling of the law for us, to be a discharging of us from any obligation and duty the law required, instead of the condemnation of the law for sins past, upon faith and repentance; and that now it was no sin to do that which before it was a sin to commit, the slavish fear of the law being taken off by Christ, and all things good that man did, if he did but do them with the mind and persuasion that it was so. Insomuch that divers fell into gross and enormous practices; pretending in excuse thereof that they could, without evil, commit the same act which was sin in another to do; thereby distinguishing between the action and the evil of it, by the direction of the mind, and intention in the doing of it. Which was to make sin superabound by the aboundings of grace, and to turn from the grace of God into wantonness, a securer way of sinning than before; as if Christ came not to take away sin, but that we might sin more freely at his cost, and with less danger to ourselves. I say, this ensnared divers, and brought them to an utter and lamentable loss, as to their eternal state; and they grew very troublesome to the better sort of people, and furnished the looser with an occasion to profane.

It was about that very same time, as you may see it in the ensuing annals, that the eternal, wise, and good God was pleased, in his infinite love, to honour and visit this benighted and bewildered nation with his glorious day-spring from on high; yea, with a most sure and certain sound of the Word of Light and Life, through the testimony of a chosen vessel, to an effectual and blessed purpose, can many thousands say, Glory be to the name of the Lord for ever!

For as it reached the conscience and broke the heart, and brought many to a sense and search, so what people had been vainly seeking *without*, with much pains and cost, they by this ministry found *within*; where it was they wanted what they sought for, viz., the right way to peace with God. For they were directed to the Light of Jesus Christ within them, as the seed and leaven of the kingdom of God; near all, because *in* all, and God's talent to all; a faithful and true witness and just monitor *in* every bosom; the gift and grace of God to life and salvation, that appears to all, though few regard it. This, the traditional Christian, conceited of himself, and strong in his own will and righteousness, and overcome with blind zeal and passion, either despised as a low and common thing, or opposed as a novelty, under many hard names or opprobrious terms; denying, in his ignorant and angry mind, any fresh manifestation of God's power and Spirit in man in these days, though never more needed to make true Christians: not unlike those Jews of old, that rejected the Son of God at the very same time that they blindly professed to wait for the Messiah to come; because, alas, he appeared not among them according to their carnal mind and expectation.

This brought forth many abusive books, which filled the greater sort with envy, and lesser with rage, and made the way and progress of this blessed testimony strait and narrow indeed to those that received it. However, God owned his own work, and this testimony did effectually reach, gather, comfort, and establish, the weary and heavy laden, the hungry and thirsty, the poor and needy, the mournful and sick of many maladies, that had spent all upon physicians of no value, and waited for relief from heaven; help only from above: seeing, upon a serious trial of all things, nothing else would do but Christ himself, the light of his countenance, a touch of his garment, and help from his hand, who cured the poor woman's issue, raised the centurion's servant, the widow's son, the ruler's daughter, and Peter's mother; and like her, they no sooner felt his power and efficacy upon their souls, than they gave up to obey him in a testimony to his power, and with resigned wills and faithful hearts, through all mockings, contradictions, beatings, prisons, and many other jeopardies that attended them for his blessed name's sake.

And truly, they were very many and very great; so that in all human probability they must have been swallowed up quick of the proud and boisterous waves that swelled and beat against them; but that the God of all their tender mercies was with them in his glorious authority, so that the hills often fled and the mountains melted before the power that filled them; working mightily for them, as well as in them, one ever following the other. By which they saw plainly, to their exceeding great confirmation and comfort, "that all things were possible with Him with whom they had to do." And that the more that which God required seemed to cross man's wisdom, and expose them to man's wrath, the more God appeared to help and carry them through all to his glory; insomuch that if ever any people could say in truth, "Thou art our sun and our shield, our rock and sanctuary, and by thee we have leaped over a wall, and by thee we have run through a troop, and by thee we have put the armies of the aliens to flight," these people had right to say it. And as God had delivered their souls of the wearisome burthens of sin and vanity, and enriched their poverty of spirit, and satisfied their great hunger and thirst after eternal righteousness, and filled them with the good things of his own house, and made them stewards of his manifold gifts; so they went forth to all quarters of these nations, to declare to the inhabitants thereof, what God had done for them; what they had found, and where and how they had found it; viz., the way to peace with God; inviting them to come and see and taste for themselves, the truth of what they declared unto them.

And as their testimony was to the principle of God *in* man, the precious pearl and leaven of the kingdom, as the only blessed means appointed of God to quicken, convince, and sanctify man; so they opened to them what it was in itself, and what it was given to them for; how they might know it from their own spirit, and that of the subtle appearance of the evil one; and what it would do for all those, whose minds are turned off from the vanity of the world and its lifeless ways and teachers, and adhere to this blessed light *in* themselves, which discovers and condemns sin in all its appearances, and shows how to overcome it, if minded and obeyed in its holy manifestations and convictions; giving power to such to avoid and resist those things that do not please God, and to grow strong in love, faith, and good works; that so man, whom sin hath made as a wilderness, overrun with briers and thorns, might become as the garden of God, cultivated by his Divine power, and replenished with the most virtuous and beautiful plants of God's own right hand planting, to his eternal praise.

But these experimental preachers of glad tidings of God's truth and kingdom, could not run when they list, or pray or preach when they pleased, but as Christ their Redeemer prepared and moved them by his own blessed Spirit, for which they waited in their services and meetings, and spoke as that gave them utterance, and which was as those having authority, and not like the dreaming, dry, and formal Pharisees. And so it plainly appeared to the serious-minded, whose spiritual eye the Lord Jesus had in any measure opened; so that to one was given the word of exhortation, to another the word of reproof, to another the word of consolation, and all by the same Spirit and in the good order thereof, to the convincing and edifying of many.

And truly they waxed strong and bold through faithfulness; and by the power and Spirit of the Lord Jesus became very fruitful; thousands, in a short time, being turned to the Truth through their testimony in ministry and sufferings, insomuch as in most counties, and many of the considerable towns of England, meetings were settled, and daily there were added such as should be saved. For they were diligent to plant and to water, and the Lord blessed their labours with an exceeding great increase; notwithstanding all the opposition made to their blessed progress, by false rumours, calumnies, and bitter persecutions; not only from the powers of the earth, but from every one that listed to injure and abuse them; so that they seemed indeed to be as poor sheep appointed to the slaughter, and as a people killed all the day long.

It were fitter for a volume than a preface, but so much as to repeat the contents of their cruel sufferings from professors as well as from profane, and from magistrates as well as from the rabble, that it may well be said of this abused and despised people, they went forth weeping and sowed in tears, bearing testimony to the precious seed, the seed of the kingdom, which stands not in words, the finest, the highest that man's wit can use, but in power; the power of Christ Jesus, to whom God the

Father hath given all power in heaven and in earth, that he might rule angels above, and men below; who empowered them, as their work witnesseth, by the many that were turned through their ministry from darkness to the light, and out of the broad into the narrow way, bringing people to a weighty, serious, and god-like conversation; the practice of that doctrine which they taught.

And as without this secret Divine power there is no quickening and regenerating of dead souls, so the want of this generating and begetting power and life, is the cause of the little fruit that the many ministries that have been, and are in the world, bring forth. O that both ministers and people were sensible of this! My soul is often troubled for them, and sorrow and mourning compass me about for their sakes. O that they were wise! O that they would consider, and lay to heart the things that truly and substantially make for their lasting peace!

Two things are to be briefly touched upon; the doctrine they taught, and the example they led among the people. I have already touched upon their fundamental principle, which is as the corner-stone of their fabric; and to speak eminently and properly, their characteristic, or main distinguishing point or principle, viz., the Light of Christ within, as God's gift for man's salvation. This, I say, is as the root of the goodly tree of doctrines that grew and branched out from it, which I shall now mention in their natural and experimental order.

First, Repentance from dead works to serve the living God; which comprehends three operations, first, a sight of sin; secondly, a sense and godly sorrow for it; thirdly, an amendment for the time to come. This was the repentance they preached and pressed, and a natural result from the principle they turned all people unto. For of light came sight; and of sight came sense and sorrow; and of sense and sorrow came amendment of life; which doctrine of repentance leads to justification; that is, forgiveness of the sins that are past, through Christ, the alone propitiation; and to the sanctification or purgation of the soul from the defiling nature and habits of sin present; which is justification in the complete sense of that word; comprehending both justification from the guilt of the sins that are past, as if they had never been committed, through the love and mercy of God in Christ Jesus; and the creature's being made inwardly just through the cleansing and sanctifying power and Spirit of Christ revealed in the soul, which is commonly called sanctification.

From hence sprang a second doctrine they were led to declare, as the mark of the prize of the high calling of all true Christians, viz., perfection from sin, according to the Scriptures of Truth, which testify it to be the end of Christ's coming, the nature of his kingdom, and for which his Spirit was given. But they never held a perfection in wisdom and glory in this life, or from natural infirmities or death, as some have with a weak or ill mind, imagined and insinuated against them.

This they called a redeemed state, regeneration, or the new birth; teaching everywhere, according to their foundation, that unless this work were known, there was no inheriting of the kingdom of God.

Third, to an acknowledgment of eternal rewards and punishments, as they have good reason; for else of all people, certainly they must be the most miserable; who for about forty years have been exceedingly great sufferers for their profession, and in some cases, treated worse than the worst of men, yea, as the refuse and offscouring of all things.

This was the purport of their doctrine and ministry; which, for the most part, is what other professors of Christianity pretend to hold in words and forms, but not in the *power* of godliness; that has been long lost by men's departing from that principle and Seed of Life that is in man, and which man has not regarded, but lost the sense of; and in and by which only he can be quickened in his mind to serve the living God in newness of life. For as the life of religion was lost, and the generality lived and worshipped God after their own wills, and not after the will of God, nor the mind of Christ, which stood in the works and fruits of the Holy Spirit; so that which they pressed, was not notion, but experience, not formality, but godliness; as being sensible in themselves, through the work of God's righteous judgments, that without holiness no man should ever see the Lord with comfort.

Besides these doctrines, and out of them, as the larger branches, there sprang forth several particular doctrines, that did exemplify and further explain the truth and efficacy of the general doctrine before observed, in their lives and examples. As,

I. Communion and loving one another. This is a noted mark in the mouth of all sorts of people concerning them. "They will meet, they will help and stick one to another." Whence it is common to hear some say, "Look how the Quakers love and take care of one another." Others less moderate will say, "The Quakers love none but themselves;" and if loving one another, and having an intimate communion in religion, and constant care to meet to worship God and help one another, be any mark of primitive Christianity, they had it, blessed be the Lord, in an ample manner.

II. To love enemies. This they both taught and practised; for they did not only refuse to be revenged for injuries done them, and condemned it as of an unchristian spirit, but they did freely forgive, yea, help and relieve those that had been cruel to them, when it was in their power to have been even with them; of which many and singular instances might be given; endeavouring, through patience, to overcome all injustice and oppression, and preaching this doctrine as Christian for others to follow.

III. The sufficiency of truth-speaking, according to Christ's own form of words, of Yea, Yea, and Nay, Nay, among Christians without swearing, both from Christ's express prohibition, "Swear not at all," Matt. v.; and for that they being under the tie and bond of truth in themselves, there was both no necessity for an oath, and it would be a reproach to their Christian veracity to assure their truth by such an extraordinary way of speaking; but offering at the same time, to be punished to the full, for false speaking, as others for perjury, if ever guilty of it; and hereby they exclude, with all true, all false and profane swearing; for which the land did and doth mourn, and the great God was and is not a little offended with it.

IV. Not fighting but suffering, is another testimony peculiar to this people; they affirm that Christianity teacheth people "to beat their swords into plough-shares, and their spears into pruning-hooks, and to learn war no more, so that the wolf may lie down with the lamb, and the lion with the calf, and nothing that destroys be entertained in the hearts of people;" exhorting them to employ their zeal against sin, and turn their anger against Satan, and no longer war one against another; because all wars and fightings come of men's own hearts' lusts, according to the apostle James, and not of the meek spirit of Christ Jesus, who is captain of another warfare, and which is carried on with other weapons. Thus, as truth-speaking succeeded swearing, so faith and truth succeeded fighting, in the doctrine and practice of this people. Nor ought they for this to be obnoxious to civil government, since if they cannot fight for it, neither can they fight against it; which is no mean security to the state; nor is it reasonable that people should be blamed for not doing more for others than they can do for themselves. And Christianity set aside, if the costs and fruits of war were well considered, peace, with its inconveniences, is generally preferable. But though they were not for fighting, they were for submitting to government; and that, not only for fear, but for conscience' sake, where government doth not interfere with conscience; believing it to be an ordinance of God, and where it is justly administered, a great benefit to mankind; though it has been their lot, through blind zeal in some, and interest in others, to have felt the strokes of it with greater weight and rigour than any other persuasion in this age; whilst they, of all others (religion set aside) have given the civil magistrate the least occasion of trouble in the discharge of his office.

V. Another part of the character of this people is, they refuse to pay tithes, or maintenance to a national ministry, and that for two reasons; the one is, that they believe all compelled maintenance, even to gospel ministers, to be unlawful, because expressly contrary to Christ's command, who said, "Freely you have received, freely give;" at least, that the maintenance of gospel ministers should be free, and not forced. The other reason of their refusal is, because those ministers are not gospel ones, in that the Holy Ghost is not their foundation, but human arts and parts; so that it is not matter of humour or sullenness, but pure conscience towards God, that they cannot help to support national ministries where they dwell, which are but too much and too visibly become ways of worldly advantage and preferment.

VI. Not to respect persons, was another of their doctrines and practices, for which they were often buffeted and abused. They affirmed it to be sinful to give flattering titles, or to use vain gestures and compliments of respect; though to virtue and authority they ever made a difference, but after their plain and homely manner, yet sincere and substantial way; well remembering the example of Mordecai and Elihu, but more especially the command of their Lord and Master Jesus Christ, who forbade his followers to call men Rabbi, which implies lord and master, also the fashionable greetings and salutations of those times; that so self-love and honour, to which the proud mind of man is incident, in his fallen estate, might not be indulged but rebuked.

VII. They also used the plain language of Thou and Thee to a single person, whatever was his degree among men. And indeed the wisdom of God was much seen, in bringing forth this people in so plain an appearance; for it was a close and distinguishing test upon the spirit of those they came among; showing their insides and what predominated, notwithstanding their high and great profession of religion. This, among the rest, sounded so harsh to many of them, and they took it so ill, that they would say, "Thou me, thou my dog; if thou thouest me, I'll thou thy teeth down thy throat," forgetting the language they use to God in their own prayers, and the common style of the Scriptures, and that it is an absolute and essential propriety of speech; and what good had their religion done them, who were so sensibly touched with indignation for the use of this plain, honest, and true speech?

VIII. They recommended silence by their example, having very few words upon all occasions; they were at a word in dealing; nor could their customers with many words tempt them from it; having more regard to truth than custom, to example than gain. They sought solitude; but when in company, they would neither use, nor willingly hear, unnecessary as well as unlawful discourses; whereby they preserved their minds pure and undisturbed from unprofitable thoughts and diversions; nor could they humour the custom of "Good night, Good morrow, God speed;" for they knew the night was good, and the day was good, without wishing of either; and that in the other expression, the holy name of God was too lightly and unthinkingly used, and therefore taken in vain. Besides, they were words and wishes of course, and are usually as little meant, as are love and service in the custom of cap and knee; and superfluity in those, as well as in other things, was burthensome to them; and therefore they did not only decline to use them, but found themselves often pressed to reprove the practice.

IX. For the same reason they forbore drinking to people, or pledging of them, as the manner of the world is; a practice that is not only unnecessary, but they thought evil in the tendencies of it; being a provocation to drinking more than did people good, as well as that it was in itself vain and heathenish.

X. Their way of marriage is peculiar to them; and is a distinguishing practice from all other societies professing Christianity. They say that marriage is an ordinance of God, and that God only can rightly join man and woman in marriage. Therefore they use neither priest nor magistrate, but the man and woman concerned, take each other as husband and wife, in the presence of divers credible witnesses, "promising unto each other, with God's assistance, to be loving and faithful in that relation, till death shall separate them." But, antecedent to all this, they first present themselves to the Monthly Meeting for the affairs of the church, where they reside, there declaring their intentions to take one another as man and wife, if the said meeting have nothing material to object against it. They are constantly asked the necessary questions,* as in case of parents, or guardians, if they have acquainted them with their intention, and have their consent, &c. The method of the meeting is to take a minute thereof, and to appoint proper persons to inquire of their conversation and clearness from all others, and whether they have discharged their duty to their parents or guardians; and make report thereof to the next Monthly Meeting; where the same parties are desired to give their attendance.† In case it appears they proceeded orderly, the meeting passes their proposal, and so records it in their meeting book; and in case the woman is a widow and hath children, due care is there taken, that provision also be made by her for the orphans before the said marriage; advising the parties concerned to appoint a convenient time and place, and to give fitting notice to their relations,

---

* Instead of being asked those questions, the present practice is to produce the needful certificates of consent.

† This second attendance is not now required.

and such friends and neighbours, as they desire should be the witnesses of their marriage: where they take one another by the hand, and by name promising reciprocally after the manner before expressed. Of all which proceedings, a narrative, in a way of certificate, is made, to which the said parties first set their hands, thereby making it their act and deed; and then divers of the relations, spectators, and auditors set their names as witnesses of what they said and signed; which certificate is afterward registered in the record belonging to the meeting where the marriage is solemnized. Which regular method has been, as it deserves, adjudged in courts of law a good marriage where it has been disputed and contested, for want of the accustomed formality of priest and ring, &c., which ceremonies they have refused, not out of humour, but conscience reasonably grounded, inasmuch as no Scripture example tells us, that the priest had any other part of old time, than that of a witness among the rest, before whom the Jews used to take one another: and therefore this people look upon it as an imposition, to advance the power and profits of the clergy. And for the use of the ring, it is enough to say, that it was a heathenish and vain custom, and never in practice among the people of God, Jews, or primitive Christians. The words of the usual form, as "With my body I thee worship," &c. are hardly defensible: in short, they are more careful, exact, and regular than any form now used, and it is free from the inconveniences other methods are attended with; their care and checks being so many, and such, that no clandestine marriages can be performed among them.

XI. It may not be unfit to say something here of their births and burials, which make up so much of the pomp and solemnity of too many called Christians. For births, the parents name their own children, which is usually some days after they are born, in the presence of the midwife (if she can be there) and those that were at the birth, &c., who afterward sign a certificate, for that purpose prepared, of the birth and name of the child, or children, which is recorded in a proper book, in the Monthly Meeting, to which the parents belong; avoiding the accustomed ceremonies and festivals.

XII. Their burials are performed with the same simplicity. If the corpse of the deceased be near any public meeting place, it is usually carried thither, for the more convenient reception of those that accompany it to the ground they bury in, and it so falls out sometimes, that while the meeting is gathering for the burial, some or other have a word of exhortation, for the sake of the people there met together: after which, the body is borne away by the young men, or those that are of their neighbourhood, or that were most intimate with the deceased party: the corpse being in a plain coffin, without any covering or furniture upon it. At the ground, they pause some time before they put the body into its grave, that if any there should have anything upon them to exhort the people, they may not be disappointed, and that the relations may the more retiredly and solemnly take their last leave of the corpse of their departed kindred, and the spectators have a sense of mortality, by the occasion then given them to reflect upon their own latter end. Otherwise, they have no set rites or ceremonies on those occasions; neither do the kindred of the deceased ever wear mourning,* they looking upon it as a worldly ceremony and piece of pomp; and that what mourning is fit for a Christian to have, at the departure of a beloved relation or friend, should be worn in the mind, which is only sensible of the loss; and the love they had to them, and remembrance of them, to be outwardly expressed by a respect to their advice, and care of those they have left behind them, and their love of that they loved. Which conduct of theirs, though unmodish or unfashionable, leaves nothing of the substance of things neglected or undone; and as they aim at no more, so that simplicity of life is what they observe with great satisfaction, though it sometimes happens not to be without the mockeries of the vain world they live in.

These things gave them a rough and disagreeable appearance with the generality; who thought them turners of the world upside down, as indeed in some sense they were; but in no other than that wherein Paul was so charged, viz., to bring things back into their primitive and right order again. For these, and such like practices of theirs, were not the result of humour, as some have fancied, but a fruit of inward sense, which God, through his fear, had begotten in them. They did not consider how to contradict the world, or distinguish themselves; being none of their business, as it was not their interest; no, it was not the result of consultation, or a framed design to declare or recommend schism or novelty. But God having given them a sight of themselves, they saw the whole world in the same glass of truth; and sensibly discerned the affections and passions of men, and the rise and tendency of things; what gratified " the lust of the flesh, the lust of the eye, and the pride of life, which are not of the Father, but of the world." And from thence sprang, in that night of darkness and apostacy, which hath been over people, through their degeneration from the Light and Spirit of God, these and many other vain customs; which are seen, by the heavenly day of Christ which dawns in the soul, to be, either wrong in their original, or, by time and abuse, hurtful in their practice. And though these things seemed trivial to some, and rendered this people stingy and conceited in such persons' opinions; there was and

* The collective sense and judgment of the church, herein, remains the same, as is manifest by the frequent advices given forth from their yearly and other meetings.

is more in them than they were aware of. It was not very easy to our
primitive Friends to make themselves sights and spectacles, and the scorn
and derision of the world; which they easily foresaw must be the consequence of so unfashionable a conversation in it. But herein was the wisdom of God seen in the foolishness of these things; first, that they discovered the satisfaction and concern that people had in and for the fashions
of this world, notwithstanding their pretences to another; in that any dis-
appointment about them came so very near them, that the greatest honesty,
virtue, wisdom, and ability were unwelcome without them. Secondly, it
seasonably and profitably divided conversation; for making their society
uneasy to their relations and acquaintance, it gave them the opportunity of
more retirement and solitude, wherein they met with better company, even
the Lord God, their Redeemer, and grew strong in his love, power, and
wisdom, and were thereby better qualified for his service; and the success
abundantly showed it : blessed be the name of the Lord.

And though they were not great and learned in the esteem of this
world (for then they had not wanted followers upon their own credit and
authority), yet they were generally of the most sober of the several persua-
sions they were in, and of the most repute for religion; and many of them
of good capacity, substance, and account among men.

And also some among them neither wanted for parts, learning, nor
estate; though then, as of old, not many wise, nor noble, &c. were called,
or at least received the heavenly call; because of the cross that attended
the profession of it in sincerity; but neither do parts or learning make
men the better Christians, though the better orators and disputants; and
it is the ignorance of people about the divine gift that causes that
vulgar and mischievous mistake. Theory and practice, expression and
enjoyment; words and life; are two things. O! it is the penitent, the
reformed, the lowly, the watchful, the self-denying and holy soul that is
the Christian; and that frame is the fruit and work of the Spirit, which
is the life of Jesus; whose life, though hid in God the Father, is shed
abroad in the hearts of them that truly believe. O! that people did
but know this to cleanse them, to circumcise them, to quicken them,
and to make them new creatures indeed; re-created, or regenerated
after Christ Jesus unto good works; that they might live to God and
not to themselves; and offer up living prayers and living praises to the
living God, through his own living Spirit, in which he is only to be worshipped in this gospel day. O! that they that read me could but feel
me; for my heart is affected with this merciful visitation of the Father of
Lights and Spirits, to this poor nation, and the whole world, through the
same testimony. Why should the inhabitants thereof reject it ? Why

should they lose the blessed benefit of it ? Why should they not turn to the Lord with all their hearts, and say, from the heart, "Speak, Lord, for now thy poor servants hear ? O ! that thy will may be done, thy great, thy good and holy will, in earth as it is in heaven : do it in us, do it upon us, do what thou wilt with us, for we are thine and desire to glorify thee our Creator, both for that, and because thou art our Redeemer ; for thou art redeeming us from the earth ; from the vanities and pollutions of it, to be a peculiar people unto thee." O ! this were a brave day for England, if so she could say in truth. But alas, the case is otherwise, for which some of thine inhabitants, O land of my nativity ! have mourned over thee with bitter wailing and lamentation. Their heads have been indeed as waters, and their eyes as fountains of tears, because of thy transgression and stiffneckedness ; because thou wilt not hear and fear, and return to the Rock, even thy Rock, O England ! from whence thou wert hewn. But be thou warned, O land of great profession, to receive Him into thy heart ; behold at that door it is, He hath stood so long knocking, but thou wilt yet have none of Him. O ! be thou awakened, lest Jerusalem's judgments do swiftly overtake thee, because of Jerusalem's sins that abound in thee. For she abounded in formality, but made void the weighty things of God's law, as thou daily doest.

She withstood the Son of God in the flesh, and thou resistest the Son of God in the Spirit. He would have gathered her as a hen gathereth her chickens under her wings, and she would not ; so would he have gathered thee out of thy lifeless profession, and have brought thee to inherit substance, to have known his power and kingdom, for which he often knocked within by his grace and Spirit, and without, by his servants and witnesses ; but thou wouldst not be gathered. On the contrary, as Jerusalem of old persecuted the manifestation of the Son of God in the flesh, and crucified him, and whipped and imprisoned his servants ; so hast thou, O land, crucified to thyself afresh the Lord of life and glory, and done despite to his Spirit of grace ; slighting the fatherly visitation, and persecuting the blessed dispensers of it by the laws and magistrates ; though they have early and late pleaded with thee in the power and Spirit of the Lord ; in love and meekness, that thou mightest know the Lord and serve him, and become the glory of all lands.

But thou hast evilly entreated and requited them. Thou hast set at naught all their counsel, and wouldst have none of their reproof, as thou shouldst have done. Their appearance was too strait, and their qualifications were too mean for thee to receive them ; like the Jews of old, that cried, " Is not this the carpenter's son, and are not his brethren among us ; which of the scribes, of the learned (the orthodox) believe in him ?" prophesying their fall in a year or two, and making and executing severe laws to bring it to pass; by endeavouring to terrify them out of their holy way, or destroying them for abiding faithful to it. But thou hast seen how many governments that rose against them, and determined their downfall, have been overturned and extinguished, and that they are still preserved, and become a great and a considerable people among the middle sort of thy numerous inhabitants. And notwithstanding the many difficulties, without and within, which they have laboured under, since the Lord God Eternal first gathered them, they are an increasing people, the Lord still adding unto them, in divers parts, such as shall be saved, if they persevere to the end. And to thee were they, and are they lifted up as a standard, and as a city set upon a hill, and to the nations round about thee, that in their light thou mayest come to see light, even in Christ Jesus, the Light of the world; and therefore thy Light, and Life too, if thou wouldst but turn from thy many evil ways, and receive and obey it. For in the "Light of the Lamb, must the nations of them that are saved walk," as the Scriptures testify.

Remember, O nation of great profession! how the Lord has waited upon thee since the days of reformation, and the many mercies and judgments with which he has pleaded with thee; awake and arise out of thy deep sleep, and yet hear his Word in thy heart, that thou mayest live.

Let not this thy day of visitation pass over thy head, nor neglect thou so great salvation as is this which is come to thy house, O England! For why shouldst thou die, O land that God desires to bless? Be assured it is He that has been in the midst of this people, in the midst of thee, and no delusion, as thy mistaken teachers have made thee believe. And this thou shalt find by their marks and fruits, if thou wilt consider them in the spirit of moderation.

I. They were changed men themselves before they went about to change others. Their hearts were rent as well as their garments; and they knew the power and work of God upon them. And this was seen by the great alteration it made, and their stricter course of life, and more godly conversation, that immediately followed upon it.

II. They went not forth, or preached in their own time or will, but in the will of God, and spoke not their own studied matter, but as they were opened and moved of his Spirit, with which they were well acquainted in their own conversion; which cannot be expressed to carnal men so as to give them any intelligible account; for to such it is as Christ said, "like the blowing of the wind, which no man knows whence it cometh, or whether it goeth:" yet this proof and seal went along with their ministry, that many were turned from their lifeless professions, and the evil of their ways, to the knowledge of God, and a holy life, as thousands can witness. And as they freely received what they had to say from the Lord, so they freely administered it to others.

III. The bent and stress of their ministry was conversion to God, regeneration, and holiness; not schemes of doctrines and verbal creeds, or new forms of worship; but a leaving off in religion the superfluous, and reducing the ceremonious and formal part, and pressing earnestly the substantial, the necessary and profitable part; as all upon a serious reflection must and do acknowledge.

IV. They directed people to a principle by which all that they asserted, preached, and exhorted others to, might be wrought in them, and known to them, through experience, to be true; which is a high and distinguishing mark of the truth of their ministry: both that they knew what they said, and were not afraid of coming to the test. For as they were bold from certainty, so they required conformity upon no human authority, but upon conviction, and the conviction of this principle, which they asserted was in them that they preached unto, and unto that they directed them, that they might examine and prove the reality of those things which they had affirmed of it, and its manifestation and work in man. And this is more than the many ministers in the world pretended to. They declare of religion, say many things true, in words of God, Christ, and the Spirit, of holiness and heaven; that all men should repent and mend their lives, or they will go to hell, &c. But which of them all pretend to speak of their own knowledge and experience? or ever directed men to a divine principle, or agent, placed of God in man, to help him; and how to know it, and wait to feel its power to work that good and acceptable will of God in them?

Some of them indeed have spoken of the Spirit, and the operations of it to sanctification, and the performance of worship to God; but *where* and *how* to find it, and wait in it to perform this duty, was yet as a mystery reserved for this further degree of reformation. So that this people did not only in words more than equally press repentance, conversion, and holiness, but did it knowingly and experimentally; and directed those to whom they preached to a sufficient principle, and told them where it is, and by what tokens they might know it, and which way they might experience the power and efficacy of it to their soul's happiness; which is more than theory and speculation, upon which most other ministries depend; for here is certainty,—a bottom upon which man may boldly appear before God in the great day of account.

V. They reached to the inward state and condition of people, which is an evidence of the virtue of their principle, and of their ministering from it, and not from their own imaginations, glosses, or comments upon Scripture. For nothing reaches the heart, but what is from the heart, or pierces the conscience, but what comes from a living conscience: insomuch that as it hath often happened, where people have under secrecy revealed their state or condition to some choice friends for advice or ease, they have been so particularly directed, in the ministry of this people, that they have challenged their friends with discovering their secrets, and telling the preachers their cases. Yea, the very thoughts and purposes of the hearts of many have been so plainly detected, that they have, like Nathaniel, cried, out of this inward appearance of Christ, "Thou art the Son of God, thou art the King of Israel." And those that have embraced this divine principle have found this mark of its truth and divinity (that the woman of Samaria did of Christ when in the flesh, to be the Messiah), viz., "it had told them all that ever they had done;" shown them their insides, the most inward secrets of their hearts; and laid judgment to the line and righteousness to the plummet; of which thousands can at this day give in their witness. So that nothing has been affirmed by this people of the power and virtue of this heavenly principle, that such as have turned to it have not found true, and more; and that one half had not been told to them of what they have seen of the power, purity, wisdom, mercy, and goodness of God herein.

VI. The accomplishments with which this principle fitted, even some of the meanest of this people, for their work and service; furnishing some of them with an extraordinary understanding in divine things, and an admirable fluency and taking way of expression, which gave occasion to some to wonder, saying of them, as of their Master, "Is not this such a mechanic's son; how came he by this learning?" As from thence others took occasion to suspect and insinuate they were Jesuits in disguise, who have had the reputation of learned men for an age past, though there was not the least ground of truth for any such reflection.

VII. That they came forth, low, and despised, and hated, as the primitive Christians did, and not by the help of worldly wisdom or power, as former reformations in part did: but in all things, it may be said, this people were brought forth in the cross, in a contradiction to the ways, worships, fashions, and customs of this world; yea, against wind and tide, that so no flesh might glory before God.

VIII. They could have no design to themselves in this work, thus to expose themselves to scorn and abuse, to spend and be spent; leaving wife and children, house and land, and all that can be accounted dear to men, with their lives in their hands, being daily in jeopardy, to declare this primitive message, revived in their spirits by the good Spirit and power of God, viz., "That God is light, and in him is no darkness at all; and that He has sent his Son a light into the world to enlighten all men in order to salvation; and that they that say they have fellowship with God and are his children and people, and yet walk in darkness, viz., in disobedience to the light in their consciences, and after the vanity of this world, lie, and do not the truth. But that all such as love the light, and bring their deeds to it, and walk in the light, as God is in the light, the blood of Jesus Christ His Son should cleanse them from all sin."

IX. Their known great constancy and patience in suffering for their testimony, in all the branches of it, and that, sometimes unto death, by beatings, bruisings, long and crowded imprisonments, and noisome dungeons. Four of them in New England dying by the hands of the executioner, purely for preaching amongst that people; besides banishments and excessive plunders and sequestrations of their goods and estates, almost in all parts, not easily to be expressed, and less to be endured, but by those that have the support of a good and glorious cause; refusing deliverance by any indirect ways or means, as often as it was offered to them.

X. That they did not only not show any disposition to revenge, when it was at any time in their power, but forgave their cruel enemies; showing mercy to those that had none for them.

XI. Their plainness with those in authority; not unlike the ancient prophets, not fearing to tell them to their faces of their private and public sins; and their prophecies to them of their afflictions and downfall, when in the top of their glory : also of some national judgments, as of the plague, and fire of London, in express terms, and likewise particular ones to divers persecutors, which accordingly overtook them, and which were very remarkable in the places where they dwelt, and in time they may be made public for the glory of God.

Thus, reader, thou seest this people in their rise, principles, ministry, and progress, both their general and particular testimony, by which thou mayest be informed how and upon what foot they sprung, and became so considerable a people. It remains next that I show also their care, conduct, and discipline, as a Christian and reformed Society, that they might be found living up to their own principles and profession. And this, the rather, because they have hardly suffered more in their character from the unjust charge of error, than by the false imputation of disorder; which calumny indeed has not failed to follow all the true steps that were ever made to reformation, and under which reproach none suffered more than the primitive Christians themselves, that were the honour of Christianity, and the great lights and examples of their own and succeeding ages.

This people increasing daily, both in town and country, a holy care fell upon some of the elders among them, for the benefit and service of the church. And the first business in their view, after the example of the primitive saints, was the exercise of charity; to supply the necessities of the poor, and answer the like occasions. Wherefore collections were early and liberally made for that and divers other services in the church, and entrusted with faithful men, fearing God, and of good report, who were not weary in well-doing; adding often of their own, in large proportions, which they never brought to account, or desired should be known, much less restored to them, that none might want, nor any service be retarded or disappointed.

They were also very careful that every one that belonged to them, answered their profession in their behaviour among men upon all occasions; that they lived peaceably, and were in all things good examples. They found themselves engaged to record their sufferings and services; and in case of marriage, which they could not perform in the usual methods of the nation, but among themselves, they took care that all things were clear between the parties and all others. And it was rare then, that any one entertained such inclinations to a person on that account, till he or she had communicated it secretly to some very weighty and eminent friends among them, that they might have a sense of the matter; looking to the counsel and unity of their brethren as of great moment to them. But because the charge of the poor, the number of orphans, marriages, sufferings, and other matters multiplied, and that it was good that the churches were in some way and method of proceeding in such affairs among them, to the end they might the better correspond upon occasion, where a member of one meeting might have to do with one of another; it pleased the Lord, in his wisdom and goodness, to open the understanding of the first instrument of this dispensation of life, about a good and orderly way of proceeding; and he felt a holy concern to visit the churches in person throughout this nation, to begin and establish it among them; and by his epistles the like was done in other nations and provinces abroad; which he also afterwards visited, and helped in that service, as shall be observed when I come to speak of him.

Now the care, conduct, and discipline I have been speaking of, and which are now practised among this people, are as followeth :—

This godly elder, in every county where he travelled, exhorted them, that some out of every meeting of worship, should meet together once in the month, to confer about the wants and occasions of the church. And as the case required, so those monthly meetings were fewer or more in number in every respective county; four or six meetings of worship usually making one monthly meeting of business. And accordingly the brethren met him from place to place, and began the said meetings, viz., for the Poor; Orphans; Orderly Walking; Integrity to their Profession; Births, Marriages, Burials, Sufferings, &c. And that these monthly meetings should, in each county, make up one quarterly meeting, where the most zealous and eminent friends of the county should assemble to communicate, advise, and help one another, especially when any business seemed difficult, or a monthly meeting was tender of determining a matter.

Also these quarterly meetings should digest the reports of the monthly meetings, and prepare one for the county, against the yearly meeting, in which the quarterly meetings resolve, which is held yearly in London; where the churches in this nation and other nations * and provinces meet, by chosen members of their respective counties, both mutually to communicate their church affairs, and to advise, and be advised in any depending case to edification; also to provide a requisite stock for the discharge of general expenses for general services in the church, not needful to be here particularized.†

At these meetings any of the members of the churches may come, if they please, and speak their minds freely, in the fear of God, to any matter; but the mind of each meeting therein represented is chiefly understood, as to particular cases, in the sense delivered by the persons deputed or chosen for that service.

During their yearly meeting, to which their other meetings refer in their order and resolve themselves, care is taken by a select number, for that service chosen by the general assembly, to draw up the minutes ‡ of the said meeting, upon the several matters that have been under consideration therein, to the end that the respective quarterly and monthly meetings may be informed of all proceedings, together with a general exhortation to holiness, unity, and charity. Of all which proceedings in yearly, quarterly, and monthly meetings, due record is kept by some one appointed for that service, or that hath voluntarily undertaken it. These meetings are opened, and usually concluded, in their solemn waiting upon God, who is sometimes graciously pleased to answer them with as signal evidences of his love and presence, as in any of their meetings for worship.

It is further to be noted, that in these solemn assemblies for the church's service, there is no one who presides among them after the manner of the assemblies of other people; Christ only being their president, as he

* At present (1836), there are eight Yearly Meetings on the American continent, which correspond with the Yearly Meeting in London, and mutually with each other; they are united in doctrine, and their discipline is similar.

† They are thus particularised in a more recent publication of the Society:— "This is an occasional voluntary contribution, expended in printing books; house-rent for a clerk, and his wages for keeping records; the passage of ministers who visit their brethren beyond sea; and some small incidental charges; but not, as has been falsely supposed, the re-imbursement of those who suffer distraint for tithes, and other demands, with which they scruple to comply."

‡ This is not now quite correct. A committee still draws up the General Epistle; but the minutes of the transactions of the meeting are made as matters occur during its several sittings.

is pleased to appear in life and wisdom in any one or more of them, to whom, whatever be their capacity or degree, the rest adhere with a firm unity, not of authority but conviction, which is the divine authority and way of Christ's power and Spirit in his people: making good his blessed promise, "that he would be in the midst of his, where and whenever they were met together in his name, even to the end of the world." So be it.

Now it may be expected, I should here set down what sort of authority is exercised by this people, upon such members of their society, as correspond not in their lives with their profession, and that are refractory to this good and wholesome order settled among them; and the rather, because they have not wanted their reproach and suffering from some tongues, upon this occasion, in a plentiful manner.

The power they exercise is such as Christ has given to his own people, to the end of the world, in the persons of his disciples, viz., "to oversee, exhort, reprove," and after long suffering and waiting upon the disobedient and refractory, "to disown them, as any more of their communion, or that they will any longer stand charged in the sight and judgment of God or men, with their conversation or behaviour as one of them until they repent." The subject matter about which this authority, in any of the foregoing branches of it, is exercised, is first, in relation to common and general practice; and secondly, about those things that more strictly refer to their own character and profession, and distinguish them from all other professors of Christianity; avoiding two extremes upon which many split, viz., persecution and libertinism; that is, a coercive power to whip people into the temple; that such as will not conform, though against faith and conscience, shall be punished in their persons or estates; or leaving all loose and at large, as to practice, unaccountable to all but God and the magistrate. To which hurtful extreme nothing has more contributed than the abuse of church power, by such as suffer their passions and private interests to prevail with them to carry it to outward force and corporal punishment—a practice they have been taught to dislike, by their extreme sufferings, as well as their known principle for an universal liberty of conscience.

On the other hand, they equally dislike an independency in society, an unaccountableness in practice and conversation to the terms of their own communion, and to those that are the members of it. They distinguish between imposing any practice that immediately regards faith or worship (which is never to be done, nor suffered, or submitted unto), and requiring Christian compliance with those methods that only respect church-business in its more civil part and concern, and that regard the discreet and orderly maintenance of the character of the society, as a sober and religious community. In short, what is for the promotion of holiness and charity, that men may practice what they profess, live up to their own principles, and not be at liberty to give the lie to their own profession, without rebuke, is their use and limit of church power. They compel none to them, but oblige those that are of them to walk suitably, or they are denied by them; that is all the mark they set upon them, and the power they exercise, or judge a Christian society can exercise, upon those that are the members of it.

The way of their proceeding against one who has lapsed or transgressed is this. He is visited by some of them, and the matter of fact laid home to him, be it any evil practice against known and general virtue, or any branch of their particular testimony, which he, in common, professeth with them. They labour with him in much love and zeal for the good of his soul, the honour of God, and reputation of their profession, to own his fault and condemn it, in as ample a manner as the evil or scandal was given by him; which, for the most part, is performed by some written testimony under the party's hand; and if it so happen that the party proves refractory, and is not willing to clear the truth they profess from the reproach of his or her evil-doing or unfaithfulness, they, after repeated entreaties and due waiting for a token of repentance, give forth a paper to disown such a fact, and the party offending; recording the same as a testimony of their care for the honour of the truth they profess.

And if such shall clear their profession and themselves, by sincere acknowledgment of their fault, and godly sorrow for so doing, they are received and looked upon again as members of their communion. For as God, so his true people, upbraid no man after repentance.

This is the account I had to give of the people of God called Quakers, as to their rise, appearance, principles, and practices, in this age of the world, both with respect to their faith and worship, discipline and conversation. And I judge it very proper in this place, because it is to preface the Journal of the first blessed and glorious instrument of this work, and for a testimony to him in his singular qualifications and services, in which he abundantly excelled in this day, and which are worthy to be set forth as an example to all succeeding times; to the glory of the most high God, and for a just memorial to that worthy and excellent man, his faithful servant and apostle to this generation of the world.

I am now come to the third head or branch of my Preface, viz., the instrumental author. For it is natural for some to say, Well, here is the people and work, but where and who was the man, the instrument? he that in this age was sent to begin this work and people? I shall, as God shall enable me, declare who and what he was, not only by report of others, but from my own long and most inward converse, and intimate knowledge of him; for which my soul blesseth God, as it hath often done; and I doubt not, that by the time I have discharged myself of this part of my Preface, my serious readers will believe I had good cause so to do.

The blessed instrument of this work in this day of God, of whom I am now about to write, was GEORGE FOX, distinguished from another of that name, by that other's addition of Younger to his name in all his writings; not that he was so in years, but that he was so in the truth; but he was also a worthy man, witness, and servant of God in his time.

But this George Fox was born in Leicestershire, about the year 1624. He descended of honest and sufficient parents, who endeavoured to bring him up, as they did the rest of their children, in the way and worship of the nation; especially his mother, who was a woman accomplished above most of her degree in the place where she lived. But from a child he appeared of another frame of mind than the rest of his brethren; being more religious, inward, still, solid, and observing, beyond his years, as the answers he would give, and the questions he would put upon occasion, manifested to the astonishment of those that heard him, especially in divine things.

His mother taking notice of his singular temper, and the gravity, wisdom, and piety that very early shined through him, refusing childish and vain sports and company, when very young, she was tender and indulgent over him, so that from her he met with little difficulty. As to his employment, he was brought up in country business; and as he took most delight in sheep, so he was very skilful in them; an employment that very well suited his mind in several respects, both from its innocency and solitude; and was a just figure of his after ministry and service.

I shall not break in upon his own account, which is by much the best that can be given, and therefore desire, what I can, to avoid saying any thing of what is said already, as to the particular passages of his coming forth; but, in general, when he was somewhat above twenty, he left his friends, and visited the most retired and religious people in those parts; and some there were, short of few, if any, in this nation, who waited for the consolation of Israel night and day; as Zacharias, Anna, and good old Simeon did of old time. To these he was sent, and these he sought out in the neighbouring counties, and among them he sojourned till his more ample ministry came upon him. At this time he taught, and was an example of silence, endeavouring to bring them from self-performances, testifying and turning to the Light of Christ within them, and encouraging them to wait in patience to feel the power of it to stir in their hearts, that their knowledge and worship of God might stand in the power of an endless life, which was to be found in the Light, as it was obeyed in the manifestation of it in man. "For in the Word was Life, and that Life is the Light of men," Life in the Word, Light in men—and Life in men too, as the Light is obeyed; the children of the Light living in the Life of the Word, by which the Word begets them again to God, which is the regeneration and new birth, without which there is no coming unto the kingdom of God; and which, whoever comes to, is greater than John, that is, than John's dispensation, which was not that of the kingdom, but the consummation of the legal, and forerunning of the gospel dispensation. Accordingly, several meetings were gathered in those parts; and thus his time was employed for some years.

In 1652, he being in his usual retirement to the Lord upon a very high mountain, in some of the higher parts of Yorkshire, as I take it, his mind exercised towards the Lord, he had a vision of the great work of God in the earth, and of the way that he was to go forth to begin it. He saw people as thick as motes in the sun, that should in time be brought home to the Lord; that there might be but one shepherd and one sheepfold in all the earth. There his eye was directed northward, beholding a great people that should receive him and his message in those parts. Upon this mountain he was moved of the Lord to sound forth his great and notable day, as if he had been in a great auditory, and from thence went north, as the Lord had shown him; and in every place where he came, if not before he came to it, he had his particular exercise and service shown to him, so that the Lord was his leader indeed; for it was not in vain that he travelled, God in most places sealing his commission with the convincement of some of all sorts, as well publicans as sober professors of religion. Some of the first and most eminent of them which are at rest, were Richard Farnsworth, James Naylor, William Dewsbury, Francis Howgill, Edward Burrough, John Camm, John Audland, Richard Hubberthorn, T. Taylor, John Aldam, T. Holmes, Alexander Parker, William Simpson, William Caton, John Stubbs, Robert Widders, John Burnyeat, Robert Lodge, Thomas Salthouse, and many more worthies, that cannot be well here named, together with divers yet living of the first and great convincement, who, after the knowledge of God's purging judgments in themselves, and some time of waiting in silence upon him, to feel and receive power from on high to speak in his name (which none else rightly can, though they may use the same words), felt the divine motions, and were frequently drawn forth, especially to visit the public assemblies, to reprove, inform, and exhort them; sometimes in markets, fairs, streets, and by the highway-side, calling people to repentance, and to turn to the Lord with their hearts as well as their mouths; directing them to the Light of Christ within them, to see, examine, and consider their ways by, and to eschew the evil, and do the good and acceptable will of God. They suffered great hardships for this their love and good-will, being often put in the stocks, stoned, beaten, whipped, and imprisoned, though honest men and of good report where they lived, that had left wives and children, and houses and lands, to visit them with a living call to repentance. And though the priests generally set themselves to oppose them, and write against them, and insinuated most false and scandalous stories to defame them, stirring up the magistrates to suppress them, especially in those northern parts; yet God was pleased so to fill them with his living power, and give them such an open door of utterance in his service, that there was a mighty convincement over those parts.

And through the tender and singular indulgence of Judge Bradshaw and Judge Fell, who were wont to go that circuit in the infancy of things, the priests were never able to gain the point they laboured for, which was to have proceeded to blood, and, if possible, Herod-like, by a cruel exercise of the civil power, to have cut them off and rooted them out of the country. Especially Judge Fell, who was not only a check to their rage in the course of legal proceedings, but otherwise upon occasion, and finally countenanced this people; for his wife receiving the truth with the first, it had that influence upon his spirit, being a just and wise man, and seeing in his own wife and family a full confutation of all the popular clamours against the way of truth, that he covered them what he could, and freely opened his doors, and gave up his house to his wife and her friends, not valuing the reproach of ignorant or evil-minded people, which I here mention to his and her honour, and which will be, I believe, an honour and a blessing to such of their name and family, as shall be found in that tenderness, humility, love, and zeal for the truth and people of the Lord.

That house was for some years at first, till the truth had opened its way in the southern parts of this island, an eminent receptacle of this people. Others of good note and substance in those northern counties, had also opened their houses with their hearts, to the many publishers, that in a short time the Lord had raised to declare his salvation to the people, and where meetings of the Lord's messengers were frequently held, to communicate their services and exercises, and comfort and edify one another in their blessed ministry.

But lest this may be thought a digression, having touched upon this before, I return to this excellent man; and for his personal qualities, both natural, moral, and divine, as they appeared in his converse with his brethren, and in the church of God, take as follows :—

I. He was a man that God endued with a clear and wonderful depth, a discerner of others' spirits, and very much a master of his own. And though the side of his understanding which lay next to the world, and especially the expression of it, might sound uncouth and unfashionable to nice ears, his matter was nevertheless very profound; and would not only bear to be often considered, but the more it was so, the more weighty and instructing it appeared. And as abruptly and brokenly as sometimes his sentences would fall from him, about divine things, it is well known they were often as texts to many fairer declarations. And indeed it showed, beyond all contradiction, that God sent him; that no arts or parts had any share in the matter or manner of his ministry; and that so many great, excellent, and necessary truths as he came forth to preach to mankind, had therefore nothing of man's wit or wisdom to recommend them; so that as to man he was an original, being no man's copy. And his ministry and writings show they are from one that was not taught of man, nor had learned what he said by study. Nor were they notional or speculative, but sensible and practical truths, tending to conversion and regeneration, and the setting up of the kingdom of God in the hearts of men; and the way of it was his work. So that I have many times been overcome in myself, and been made to say, with my Lord and Master upon the like occasion; "I thank thee, O Father, Lord of heaven and earth, that thou hast hid these things from the wise and prudent of this world, and revealed them to babes." For many times hath my soul bowed in an humble thankfulness to the Lord, that he did not choose any of the wise and learned of this world to be the first messenger, in our age, of his blessed truth to men; but that he took one that was not of high degree, or elegant speech, or learned after the way of this world, that his message and work he sent him to do, might come with less suspicion or jealousy of human wisdom and interest, and with more force and clearness upon the consciences of those that sincerely sought the way of truth in the love of it. I say, beholding with the eye of my mind, which the God of heaven had opened in me, the marks of God's finger and hand visibly, in this testimony, from the clearness of the principle, the power and efficacy of it, in the exemplary sobriety, plainness, zeal, steadiness, humility, gravity, punctuality, charity, and circumspect care in the government of church affairs, which shined in his and their life and testimony that God employed in this work, it greatly confirmed me that it was of God, and engaged my soul in a deep love, fear, reverence, and thankfulness for his love and mercy therein to mankind; in which mind I remain, and shall, I hope, to the end of my days.

II. In his testimony or ministry, he much laboured to open truth to the people's understandings, and to bottom them upon the principle and principal, Christ Jesus, the Light of the world, that by bringing them to something that was of God in themselves, they might the better know and judge of him and themselves.

III. He had an extraordinary gift in opening the Scriptures. He would go to the marrow of things, and show the mind, harmony, and fulfilling of them with much plainness, and to great comfort and edification.

IV. The mystery of the first and second Adam, of the fall and restoration, of the law and gospel, of shadows and substance, of the servant's and Son's state, and the fulfilling of the Scriptures in Christ, and by Christ, the true Light, in all that are his through the obedience of faith, were much of the substance and drift of his testimonies. In all which he was witnessed to be of God, being sensibly felt to speak that which he had received of Christ, and which was his own experience, in that which never errs nor fails.

V. But above all he excelled in prayer. The inwardness and weight of his spirit, the reverence and solemnity of his address and behaviour, and the fewness and fulness of his words, have often struck, even strangers, with admiration, as they used to reach others with consolation. The most awful, living, reverent frame I ever felt or beheld, I must say, was his in prayer. And truly it was a testimony he knew and lived nearer to the Lord than other men; for they that know Him most, will see most reason to approach him with reverence and fear.

VI. He was of an innocent life, no busy-body, nor self-seeker, neither touchy, nor critical; what fell from him was very inoffensive, if not very edifying. So meek, contented, modest, easy, steady, tender, it was a pleasure to be in his company. He exercised no authority but over evil, and that everywhere and in all; but with love, compassion, and long-suffering. A most merciful man, as ready to forgive, as unapt to take or give an offence. Thousands can truly say, he was of an excellent spirit and savour among them, and because thereof, the most excellent spirits loved him with an unfeigned and unfading love.

VII. He was an incessant labourer; for in his younger time, before his many great and deep sufferings and travels had enfeebled his body for itinerant services, he laboured much in the word, and doctrine, and discipline in England, Scotland, and Ireland, turning many to God, and confirming those that were convinced of the truth, and settling good order as to church affairs among them. And towards the conclusion of his travelling services, between the years seventy-one and seventy-seven, he visited the churches of Christ in the plantations in America, and in the United Provinces, and Germany, as his following Journal relates, to the convincement and consolation of many. After that time he chiefly resided in and about the city of London; and besides the services of his ministry, which were frequent and serviceable, he wrote much, both to them that are within, and those that are without, the communion. But the care he took of the affairs of the church in general was very great.

VIII. He was often where the records of the affairs of the church are kept, and the letters from the many meetings of God's people over all the world, where settled, come upon occasions; which letters he had read to him, and communicated them to the meeting that is weekly* held there for such services; and he would be sure to stir them up to discharge them, especially in suffering cases, showing great sympathy and compassion upon all such occasions, carefully looking into the respective cases, and endeavouring speedy relief, according to the nature of them. So that the churches, or any of the suffering members thereof, were sure not to be forgotten or delayed in their desires, if he were there.

IX. As he was unwearied, so he was undaunted in his services for God and his people; he was no more to be moved to fear than to wrath. His behaviour at Derby, Lichfield, Appleby, before Oliver Cromwell, at Launceston, Scarborough, Worcester, and Westminster-Hall, with many other places and exercises, did abundantly evidence it to his enemies as well as his friends.

But as in the primitive times, some rose up against the blessed apostles of our Lord Jesus Christ, even from among those that they had turned to the hope of the gospel, who became their greatest trouble; so this man of God had his share of suffering from some that were convinced by him, who through prejudice or mistake ran against him, as one that sought dominion over conscience; because he pressed, by his presence or epistles, a ready and zealous compliance with such good and wholesome things as tended to an orderly conversation about the affairs of the church, and in their walking before men. That which contributed much to this ill work, was, in some, a begrudging of this meek man the love and esteem he had and deserved in the hearts of the people; and weakness in others, that were taken with their groundless suggestions of imposition and blind obedience.

They would have had every man independent; that as he had the principle in himself, he should only stand and fall to that, and nobody else; not considering that the principle is one in all; and though the measure of light or grace might differ, yet the nature of it was the same; and being so, they struck at the spiritual unity, which a people, guided by the same principle, are naturally led into; so that what is an evil to one, is so to all, and what is virtuous, honest, and of good report to one, is so to all, from the sense and savour of the one universal principle which is common to all, and, which the disaffected also profess to be, the root of all true Christian fellowship, and that Spirit into which the people of God drink, and come to be spiritually-minded, and of one heart and one soul.

Some weakly mistook good order in the government of church affairs,

* Called the Meeting for Sufferings, and now held monthly, except exigencies require more frequent sittings.

for discipline in worship, and that it was so pressed or recommended by him and other brethren. And they were ready to reflect the same things that Dissenters had very reasonably objected upon the national churches, that have coercively pressed conformity to their respective creeds and worships. Whereas these things related wholly to conversation, and the outward (and as I may say) civil part of the church, that men should walk up to the principles of their belief, and not be wanting in care and charity. But though some have stumbled and fallen through mistakes, and an unreasonable obstinacy, even to a prejudice; yet, blessed be God, the generality have returned to their first love, and seen the work of the enemy, that loses no opportunity or advantage by which he may check or hinder the work of God, disquiet the peace of his church, and chill the love of his people to the truth and one to another; and there is hope of divers of the few that are yet at a distance.

In all these occasions, though there was no person the discontented struck so sharply at as this good man, he bore all their weakness and prejudice, and returned not reflection for reflection; but forgave them their weak and bitter speeches, praying for them that they might have a sense of their hurt, see the subtilty of the enemy to rend and divide, and return into their first love that thought no ill.

And truly, I must say, that though God had visibly clothed him with a divine preference and authority, and indeed his very presence expressed a religious majesty, yet he never abused it; but held his place in the church of God with great meekness, and a most engaging humility and moderation. For upon all occasions, like his blessed Master, he was a servant to all; holding and exercising his eldership, in the invisible power that had gathered them, with reverence to the Head and care over the body; and was received only in that spirit and power of Christ, as the first and chief elder in this age; who, as he was therefore worthy of double honour, so for the same reason it was given by the faithful of this day; because his authority was inward and not outward, and that he got it and kept it by the love of God, and power of an endless life. I write my knowledge and not report, and my witness is true, having been with him for weeks and months together on divers occasions, and those of the nearest and most exercising nature, and that by night and by day, by sea and by land, in this and in foreign countries: and I can say I never saw him out of his place, or not a match for every service or occasion. For in all things he acquitted himself like a man, yea, a strong man, a new and heavenly-minded man; a divine and a naturalist, and all of God Almighty's making. I have been surprised at his questions and answers in natural things; that whilst he was ignorant of useless and sophistical science, he had in him the foundation of useful and commendable knowledge, and cherished it every where. Civil, beyond all forms of breeding, in his behaviour; very temperate, eating little, and sleeping less, though a bulky person.

Thus he lived and sojourned among us: and as he lived, so he died; feeling the same eternal power, that had raised and preserved him, in his last moments. So full of assurance was he, that he triumphed over death; and so even in his spirit to the last, as if death were hardly worth notice or a mention; recommending to some with him, the despatch and dispersion of an epistle, just before written to the churches of Christ throughout the world, and his own books; but, above all, Friends, and, of all Friends, those in Ireland and America, twice over saying, "Mind poor Friends in Ireland and America."

And to some that came in and inquired how he found himself, he answered, "Never heed, the Lord's power is over all weakness and death; the Seed reigns, blessed be the Lord:" which was about four or five hours before his departure out of this world. He was at the great meeting near Lombard Street on the first day of the week, and it was the third following, about ten at night, when he left us, being at the house of Henry Goldney in the same court. In a good old age he went, after having lived to see his children's children, to many generations, in the truth. He had the comfort of a short illness, and the blessing of a clear sense to the last; and we may truly say, with a man of God of old, that "being dead, he yet speaketh;" and though absent in body, he is present in spirit; neither time nor place being able to interrupt the communion of saints, or dissolve the fellowship of the spirits of the just. His works praise him, because they are to the praise of Him that wrought by him; for which his memorial is, and shall be blessed. I have done, as to this part of my Preface, when I have left this short epitaph to his name: "Many sons have done virtuously in this day; but, dear George, thou excellest them all."

And now, Friends, you that profess to walk in the way this blessed man was sent of God to turn men into, suffer, I beseech you, the word of exhortation, as well fathers as children, and elders as young men. The glory of this day, and foundation of the hope that has not made us ashamed since we were a people, you know, is that blessed principle of Light and Life of Christ which we profess, and direct all people to, as the great instrument and agent of man's conversion to God. It was by this we were first touched, and effectually enlightened as to our inward state, which put us upon the consideration of our latter end, causing us to set the Lord before our eyes, and to number our days, that we might apply our hearts to wisdom. In that day we judged not after the sight of the eye, or after the hearing of the ear; but according to the light and sense this blessed principle gave us, we judged and acted in reference to things and persons, ourselves and others, yea, towards God our Maker. For being quickened by it in our inward man, we could easily discern the difference of things; and feel what was right and what was wrong, and what was fit and what not, both in reference to religious and civil concerns. That being the ground of the fellowship of all saints, it was in that our fellowship stood. In this we desired to have a sense one of another, and acted towards one another, and all men, in love, faithfulness, and fear.

In the feeling of the motions of this principle we drew near to the Lord, and waited to be prepared by it, that we might feel those drawings and movings before we approached the Lord in prayer, or opened our mouths in ministry. And, in our beginning and ending, with this stood our comfort, service, and edification. And as we ran faster, or fell short, we made burthens for ourselves to bear; our services finding in ourselves a rebuke instead of an acceptance, and in lieu of " Well done," " Who has required this at your hands?"   In that day we were an exercised people ; our very countenances and deportment declared it.

Care for others was then much upon us, as well as for ourselves, especially the young convinced.   Often had we the burthen of the word of the Lord to our neighbours, relations, and acquaintance; and sometimes strangers also.   We were in travail for one another's preservation; not seeking, but shunning occasions of any coldness or misunderstanding, treating one another as those that believed and felt God present; which kept our conversation innocent, serious, and weighty, guarding ourselves against the cares and friendships of the world.   We held the truth in the Spirit of it, and not in our own spirits, or after our own wills and affections. They were bowed and brought into subjection, insomuch that it was visible to them that knew us.   We did not think ourselves at our own disposal, to go where we list, or say or do what we list, or when we list.   Our liberty stood in the liberty of the Spirit of Truth; and no pleasure, no profit, no fear, no favour, could draw us from this retired, strict, and watchful frame.   We were so far from seeking occasions of company, that we avoided them what we could, pursuing our own business with moderation, instead of meddling with other people's unnecessarily.

Our words were few and savoury, our looks composed and weighty, and our whole deportment very observable.   True it is, that this retired and strict sort of life from the liberty of the conversation of the world, exposed us to the censures of many, as humourists, conceited and self-righteous persons, &c.; but it was our preservation from many snares, to which others were continually exposed from the prevalency of the lust of the eye, the lust of the flesh, and the pride of life, that wanted no occasions or temptations to excite them abroad in the converse of the world.

I cannot forget the humility and chaste zeal of that day. O how constant at meetings, how retired in them, how firm to Truth's life, as well as Truth's principles! and how entire and united in our communion, as indeed became those that profess One Head, even Christ Jesus the Lord!

This being the testimony and example the man of God before mentioned was sent to declare and leave amongst us, and we having embraced the same as the merciful visitation of God to us, the word of exhortation at this time is, that we continue to be found in the way of this testimony with all zeal and integrity, and so much the more, by how much the day draweth near.

And first, as to you, my beloved and much honoured brethren in Christ, that are in the exercise of the ministry: Oh, feel Life in your ministry! Let Life be your commission, your well-spring and treasury on all such occasions, else, you well know, there can be no begetting to God, since nothing can quicken or make people alive to God, but the Life of God: and it must be a ministry in and from Life, that enlivens any people to God. We have seen the fruit of all other ministries, by the few that are turned from the evil of their ways. It is not our parts or memory, the repetition of former openings in our own will and time, that will do God's work. A dry, doctrinal ministry, however sound in words, can reach but the ear, and is but a dream at the best. There is another soundness, that is soundest of all, viz., Christ the power of God. This is the key of David, that opens and none shuts, and shuts, and none can open; as the oil to the lamp, and the soul to the body, so is that to the best of words: which made Christ to say, "My words they are spirit, and they are life;" that is, they are from life, and therefore they make you alive, that receive them. If the disciples that had lived with Jesus were to stay at Jerusalem till they received it, so must we wait to receive before we minister, if we will turn people from darkness to light, and from Satan's power to God.

I fervently bow my knees to the God and Father of our Lord Jesus Christ, that you may always be like-minded, that you may ever wait reverently for the coming and opening of the Word of Life, and attend upon it in your ministry and service, that you may serve God in his Spirit. And be it little, or be it much, it is well; for much is not too much, and the least is enough, if from the motion of God's Spirit; and without it, verily, ever so little is too much, because to no profit.

For it is the Spirit of the Lord immediately, or through the ministry of his servants, that teacheth his people to profit; and to be sure, so far as we take him along with us in our services, so far we are profitable, and no farther. For if it be the Lord that must work all things in us, and for our salvation, much more is it the Lord, that must work in us, for the conversion of others. If therefore it was once a cross to us to speak, though the Lord required it at our hands, let it never be so to be silent, when he does not.

It is one of the most dreadful sayings in the book of God, that "he that adds to the words of the prophecy of this book, God will add the plagues written in this book." To keep back the counsel of God is as terrible; for "he that takes away from the words of the prophecy of this book, God shall take away his part out of the book of life." And truly, it has great caution in it to those that use the name of the Lord, to be well assured the Lord speaks, that they may not be found of the number of those that add to the words of the testimony of prophecy, which the Lord giveth them to bear; nor yet to mince or diminish the same, both being so very offensive to God.

Wherefore, brethren, let us be careful neither to out-go our Guide, nor yet loiter behind him; since he that makes haste may miss his way, and he that stays behind, lose his Guide: for even those that have received the word of the Lord, had need wait for wisdom, that they may see how to divide the word aright; which plainly implieth, that it is possible for one that hath received the word of the Lord, to miss in the division and application of it, which must come from an impatiency of spirit, and a self-working, which makes an unsound and dangerous mixture; and will hardly beget a right-minded, living people to God.

I am earnest in this, above all other considerations, as to public brethren, well knowing how much it concerns the present and future state, and preservation of the church of Christ Jesus, that has been gathered and built up by a living and powerful ministry, that the ministry be held, preserved, and continued in the manifestations, motions, and supplies, of the same life and power, from time to time.

And wherever it is observed that any one does minister more from gifts and parts than life and power, though they have an enlightened and doctrinal understanding, let them in time be advised and admonished for their preservation, because insensibly such will come to depend upon a self-sufficiency; to forsake Christ the living Fountain, and to hew out unto themselves cisterns that will hold no living waters; and by degrees to draw others from waiting upon the gift of God in themselves, to feel it in others, in order to their strength and refreshment, to wait upon them, and to turn from God to man again, and so to make shipwreck of the faith once delivered to the saints, and of a good conscience towards God; which are only kept by that Divine gift of life, that begat the one, and awakened and sanctified the other in the beginning.

Nor is it enough that we have known the Divine gift, and in it have reached to the spirits in prison, and been the instruments of the convincing of others of the way of God, if we keep not as low and poor in ourselves, and as depending upon the Lord as ever; since no memory, no repetitions of former openings, revelations, or enjoyments, will bring a soul to God, or afford bread to the hungry, or water to the thirsty, unless life go with what we say; and that must be waited for.

O that we may have no other fountain, treasury, or dependence! that none may presume at any rate to act of themselves for God! because they have long acted from God, that we may not supply want of waiting with our own wisdom, or think that we may take less care, and more liberty in speaking, than formerly; and that where we do not feel the Lord by his power to open us and enlarge us, whatever be the expectation of the people, or has been our customary supply and character, we may not exceed or fill up the time with our own.

I hope we shall ever remember who it was that said, "Of yourselves you can do nothing;" our sufficiency is in Him. And if we are not to speak our own words, or take thought what we should say to men in our defence, when exposed for our testimony, surely we ought to speak none of our own words, or take thought what we shall say in our testimony and ministry in the name of the Lord to the souls of the people; for then of all times, and of all other occasions, should it be fulfilled in us, "for it is not you that speak, but the Spirit of my Father that speaketh in you."

And indeed, the ministry of the Spirit must and does keep its analogy and agreement with the birth of the Spirit; that as no man can inherit the kingdom of God unless he be born of the Spirit, so no ministry can beget a soul to God but that which is from the Spirit. For this, as I said before, the disciples waited before they went forth; and in this our elder brethren, and messengers of God in our day, waited, visited, and reached to us. And having begun in the Spirit, let none ever hope or seek to be made perfect in the flesh. For what is the flesh to the Spirit, or the chaff to the wheat? And if we keep in the Spirit, we shall keep in the unity of it, which is the ground of true fellowship. For by drinking into that one Spirit, we are made one people to God, and by it we are continued in the unity of the faith, and the bond of peace. No envying, no bitterness, no strife, can have place with us. We shall watch always for good, and not for evil, over one another, and rejoice exceedingly, and not begrudge one another's increase in the riches of the grace with which God replenisheth his faithful servants.

And, brethren, as to you is committed the dispensation of the oracles of God, which give you frequent opportunities, and great place with the people among whom you travel, I beseech you that you would not think it sufficient to declare the word of life in their assemblies, however edifying and comfortable such opportunities may be to you and them. But, as was the practice of the man of God before mentioned, in great measure, when among us, inquire the state of the several churches you visit; who among them are afflicted or sick, who are tempted, and if any are unfaithful or obstinate; and endeavour to issue those things in the wisdom and power of God, which will be a glorious crown upon your ministry. As that prepares your way in the hearts of the people to receive you as men of God, so it gives you credit with them to do them good by your advice in other respects. The afflicted will be comforted by you; the tempted, strengthened; the sick, refreshed; the unfaithful, convicted and restored; and such as are obstinate, softened and fitted for reconciliation : which is clenching the nail, and applying and fastening the general testimony by that particular care of the several branches of it, in reference to them more immediately concerned in it.

For though good and wise men, and elders too, may reside in such places, who are of worth and importance in the general, and in other places; yet it does not always follow, that they may have the room they deserve in the hearts of the people they live among; or some particular occasion may make it unfit for him or them to use that authority. But you that travel as God's messengers, if they receive you in the greater, shall they refuse you in the less? And if they own the general testimony, can they withstand the particular application of it in their own cases? Thus ye will show yourselves workmen indeed, and carry your business before you to the praise of His name that hath called you from darkness to light, that you might turn others from Satan's power unto God and his kingdom, which is *within*. And O that there were more of such faithful labourers in the vineyard of the Lord!—Never more need since the day of God.

Wherefore I cannot but cry and call aloud to you, that have been long professors of the truth, and know the truth in the convincing power of it, and have had a sober conversation among men, yet content yourselves only to know truth for yourselves, to go to meetings, and exercise an ordinary charity in the church, and an honest behaviour in the world, and limit yourselves within those bounds; feeling little or no concern upon your spirits for the glory of the Lord in the prosperity of his truth in the earth, more than to be glad that others succeed in such service. Arise ye in the name and power of the Lord Jesus! Behold how white the fields are unto harvest, in this and other nations, and how few able and faithful labourers there are to work therein! Your country folks, neighbours, and kindred, want to know the Lord and his truth, and to walk in it. Does nothing lie at your door upon their account? Search and see, and lose no time, I beseech you, for the Lord is at hand. I do not judge you, there is one that judgeth all men, and his judgment is true. You have mightily increased in your outward substance; may you equally increase in your inward riches, and do good with both, while you have a day to do good. Your enemies would once have taken what you had from you, for his name's sake, in whom you have believed; wherefore he has given you much of the world in the face of your enemies. But, O let it be your servant and not your master—your diversion rather than your business! Let the Lord be chiefly in your eye, and ponder your ways, and see if God has nothing more for you to do; and if you find yourselves short in your account with him, then wait for his preparation, and be ready to receive the word of command, and be not weary of well-doing, when you have put your hand to the plough; and assuredly you shall reap (if you faint not) the fruit of your heavenly labour in God's everlasting kingdom.

And you, young convinced ones, be you entreated, and exhorted to a diligent and chaste waiting upon God, in the way of his blessed manifestation and appearance of himself to you. Look not out, but within. Let not another's liberty be your snare. Neither act by imitation, but sense and feeling of God's power in yourselves. Crush not the tender buddings of it in your souls, nor overrun in your desires, and warmness of affections, the holy and gentle motions of it. Remember it is a still voice that speaks to us in this day, and that it is not to be heard in the noises and hurries of the mind; but it is distinctly understood in a retired frame. Jesus loved and chose solitudes; often going to mountains, to gardens, and sea-sides, to avoid crowds and hurries, to show his disciples it was good to be solitary, and sit loose to the world. Two enemies lie near your states, imagination and liberty; but the plain, practical, living, holy truth, that has convinced you, will preserve you, if you mind it in yourselves, and bring all thoughts, imaginations, and affections to the test of it, to see if they are wrought in God, or of the enemy, or your ownselves. So will a true taste, discerning, and judgment, be preserved to you, of what you should do and leave undone. And in your diligence and faithfulness in this way you will come to inherit substance; and Christ, the eternal wisdom, will fill your treasury. And when you are converted, as well as convinced, then confirm your brethren, and be ready to every good word and work, that the Lord shall call you to; that you may be to his praise, who has chosen you to be partakers, with the saints in light, of a kingdom that cannot be shaken, an inheritance incorruptible, in eternal habitations.

And now, as for you that are the children of God's people, a great
concern is upon my spirit for your good; and often are my knees bowed to
the God of your fathers for you, that you may come to be partakers of the
same divine life and power, that has been the glory of this day; that a
generation you may be to God, a holy nation and a peculiar people, zealous
of good works, when all our heads are laid in the dust. O you young men
and women, let it not suffice you, that you are the children of the people
of the Lord! you must also be born again, if you will inherit the kingdom
of God. Your fathers are but such after the flesh, and could but beget
you in the likeness of the first Adam; but you must be begotten into the
likeness of the second Adam by a spiritual generation. And therefore look
carefully about you, O ye children of the children of God! consider your
standing, and see what you are in relation to this divine kindred, family,
and birth. Have you obeyed the Light, and received and walked in the
Spirit, that is the incorruptible Seed of the Word and kingdom of God, of
which you must be born again? God is no respecter of persons. The
father cannot save or answer for the child, or the child for the father, but
" in the sin thou sinnest, thou shalt die; and in the righteousness thou
doest, through Christ Jesus, thou shalt live;" for it is the willing and
obedient that shall eat the good of the land. Be not deceived, God is not
mocked; such as all nations and people sow, such they shall reap at the
hand of the just God. And then your many and great privileges, above
the children of other people, will add weight in the scale against you, if
you choose not the way of the Lord. For you have had line upon line,
and precept upon precept, and not only good doctrine, but good example;
and which is more, you have been turned to, and acquainted with, a principle in yourselves, which others have been ignorant of; and you know,
you may be as good as you please, without the fear of frowns and blows,
or being turned out of doors and forsaken of father and mother for God's
sake, and his holy religion, as has been the case of some of your fathers,
in the day they first entered into this holy path. If you, after hearing and
seeing the wonders that God has wrought in the deliverance and preservation of them, through a sea of troubles, and the manifold temporal, as well
as spiritual blessings, that he has filled them with, in the sight of their
enemies, should neglect and turn your backs upon so great and so near a
salvation, you would not only be most ungrateful children to God and them,
but must expect that God will call the children of those that knew him
not, to take the crown out of your hands, and that your lot will be a dreadful judgment at the hand of the Lord. But O, that it may never be so
with any of you! The Lord forbid, saith my soul.

Wherefore, O ye young men and women, look to the rock of your fathers! choose the God of your fathers. There is no other God but he; no other Light but his; no other grace but his, nor Spirit but his, to convince you, quicken, and comfort you; to lead, guide, and preserve you to God's everlasting kingdom. So will you be possessors, as well as professors, of the truth; embracing it not only by education, but judgment and conviction, from a sense begotten in your souls, through the operation of the eternal Spirit and power of God in your hearts, by which you may come to be the seed of Abraham through faith, and the circumcision not made with hands, and so heirs of the promise made to the fathers of an incorruptible crown; that (as I said before) a generation you may be to God, holding up the profession of the blessed truth in the life and power of it. For formality in religion is nauseous to God and good men; and the more so, where any form or appearance has been new and peculiar, and begun and practised upon a principle, with an uncommon zeal and strictness. Therefore, I say, for you to fall flat and formal, and continue the profession, without that salt and savour, by which it is come to obtain a good report among men, is not to answer God's love, nor your parents' care, nor the mind of truth in yourselves, nor in those that are without; who, though they will not obey the truth, have sight and sense enough to see if they do, that make a profession of it. For where the divine virtue of it is not felt in the soul, and waited for, and lived in, imperfections will quickly break out, and show themselves, and detect the unfaithfulness of such persons, and that their insides are not seasoned with the nature of that holy principle which they profess.

Wherefore, dear children, let me entreat you to shut your eyes at the temptations and allurements of this low and perishing world, and not suffer your affections to be captivated by those lusts and vanities that your fathers, for truth's sake, long since turned their backs upon. But as you believe it to be the truth, receive it into your hearts, that you may become the children of God; so that it may never be said of you, as the Evangelist writes of the Jews of his time, that Christ, the true Light, "came to his own, but his own received him not; but to as many as received him, to them he gave power to become the children of God: which were born, not of blood, nor of the will of the flesh, nor of the will of man, but of God." A most close and comprehensive passage to this occasion. You exactly and peculiarly answer to those professing Jews, in that you bear the name of God's people, by being the children and wearing the form of God's people: so that he, by his light in you, may be said to come to his own, and if you obey it not, but turn your back upon it, and walk after the vanities of your minds, you will be of those that receive him not, which, I pray God, may never be your case and judgment; but that you may be thoroughly sensible of the many and great obligations you lie under to the Lord for his love, and to your parents for their care; and with all your heart, and all your soul, and all your strength, turn to the Lord, to his gift and Spirit in you, and hear his voice, and obey it, that you may seal to the testimony of your fathers, by the truth and evidence of your own experience; that your children's children may bless you, and the Lord for you, as those that delivered a faithful example, as well as record of the truth of God unto them. So will the gray hairs of your dear parents yet alive, go down to the grave with joy, to see you the posterity of truth, as well as theirs, and that not only their nature but spirit shall live in you when they are gone.

I shall conclude this Preface with a few words to those that are not of our communion, into whose hands this may come; especially those of our own nation.

Friends, as you are the sons and daughters of Adam, and my brethren after the flesh, many and earnest have been my desires and prayers to God on your behalf, that you may come to know your Creator to be your Redeemer and Restorer to the image that, through sin, you have lost, by the power and Spirit of his Son Jesus Christ, whom he hath given for the light and life of the world. And O that you who are called Christians, would receive him into your heart! for there it is you want him, and at that door he stands knocking, that you should let him in, but you do not open to him; you are full of other guests, so that a manger is his lot among you now, as well as of old. Yet you are full of profession, as were the Jews when he came among them, who knew him not, but rejected and evilly entreated him. So that if you come not to the possession and experience of what you profess, all your formality in religion will stand you in no stead in the day of God's judgment.

I beseech you ponder with yourselves your eternal condition, and see what title, what ground and foundation you have for your Christianity; if more than a profession, and an historical belief of the gospel. Have you known the baptism of fire, and the Holy Ghost, and the fan of Christ that winnows away the chaff,—the carnal lusts and affections?—that divine leaven of the kingdom, that, being received, leavens the whole lump of man, sanctifying him throughout, in body, soul, and spirit? If this be not the ground of your confidence, you are in a miserable state.

You will say, perhaps, that though you are sinners, and live in the daily commission of sin, and are not sanctified, as I have been speaking, yet you have faith in Christ, who has borne the curse for you, and in him you are complete by faith; his righteousness being imputed to you.

But, my friends, let me entreat you not to deceive yourselves in so important a point as is that of your immortal souls. If you have *true* faith in Christ, your faith will make you clean, it will sanctify you; for the saints' faith was their victory. By this they overcame sin within, and sinful men without. And if thou art in Christ, thou walkest not after the flesh, but after the Spirit, whose fruits are manifest. Yea, thou art a new creature, new made, new fashioned after God's will and mould; old things are done away, and, behold, all things are become new; new love, desires, will, affections, and practices. It is not any longer thou that livest, thou disobedient, carnal, worldly one; but it is Christ that liveth in thee; and to live is Christ, and to die is thy eternal gain; because thou art assured, that "thy corruptible shall put on incorruption, and thy mortal, immortality;" and that thou hast a glorious house, eternal in the heavens, that will never wax old or pass away. All this follows being in Christ, as heat follows fire, and light the sun.

Therefore have a care how you presume to rely upon such a notion, as that you are in Christ, whilst in your old fallen nature. For what communion hath light with darkness, or Christ with Belial? Hear what the beloved disciple tells you; "If we say we have fellowship with God, and walk in darkness, we lie, and do not the truth." That is, if we go on in a sinful way, are captivated by our carnal affections, and are not converted to God, we walk in darkness, and cannot possibly have any fellowship with God. Christ clothes them with his righteousness, that receive his grace in their hearts, and deny themselves, and take up his cross daily, and follow him. Christ's righteousness makes men inwardly holy, of holy minds, wills, and practices. It is nevertheless Christ's, because we have it; for it is ours, not by nature, but by faith and adoption. It is the gift of God. But still, though not ours, as of or from ourselves, for in that sense it is Christ's, for it is of and from him; yet it is ours, and must be ours in possession, efficacy, and enjoyment, to do us any good, or Christ's righteousness will profit us nothing. It was after this manner that he was made to the primitive Christians, righteousness, sanctification, justification, and redemption; and if ever you will have the comfort, kernel, and marrow of the Christian religion, thus you must come to learn and obtain it.

Now, my friends, by what you have read, and will read in what follows, you may perceive that God has visited a poor people among you with this saving knowledge and testimony; whom he has upheld and increased to this day, notwithstanding the fierce opposition they have met withal. Despise not the meanness of this appearance; it was, and yet is (we know) a day of small things, and of small account with too many; and many hard and ill names are given to it; but it is of God; it came from Him because it leads to Him. This we know, but we cannot make another know it, as we know it, unless he will take the same way to know it that we took. The world talks of God; but what do they do? They pray for power, but reject the principle in which it is. If you would know God, and worship and serve God as you should do, you must come to the means he has ordained and given for that purpose. Some seek it in books, some in learned men, but what they look for is *in themselves*, yet they overlook it. The voice is too still, the Seed too small, and the Light shineth in darkness. They are abroad, and so cannot divide the spoil; but the woman that lost her silver, found it at home, after she had lighted her candle and swept her house. Do you so too, and you shall find what Pilate wanted to know, viz., Truth.

The Light of Christ within, who is the Light of the world (and so a light to you, that tells you the truth of your condition), leads all that take heed unto it, out of darkness into God's marvellous light; for light grows upon the obedient. It is sown for the righteous, and their way is a shining light, that shines forth more and more to the perfect day.

Wherefore, O friends, turn in, turn in, I beseech you! Where is the poison, there is the antidote; there you want Christ, and there you must find him; and, blessed be God, there you may find him. "Seek and you shall find," I testify for God; but then you must seek aright, with your whole heart, as men that seek for their lives, yea, for their eternal lives; diligently, humbly, patiently, as those that can taste no pleasure, comfort, or satisfaction in anything else, unless you find him whom your souls want, and desire to know and love above all. O, it is a travail, a spiritual travail! let the carnal, profane world think and say as it will. And through this path you must walk to the city of God, that has eternal foundations, if ever you will come there.

And what does this blessed Light do for you? 1. It sets all your sins in order before you; it detects the spirit of this world in all its baits and allurements, and shows how man came to fall from God, and the fallen estate he is in. 2. It begets a sense and sorrow, in such as believe in it, for this fearful lapse. You will then see Him distinctly whom you have pierced, and all the blows and wounds you have given him by your disobedience; and how you have made him to serve with your sins, and you will weep and mourn for it, and your sorrow will be a godly sorrow. 3. After this it will bring you to the holy watch, to take care that you do so no more, that the enemy surprise you not again. Then thoughts as well as words and works, will come to judgment, which is the way of holiness, in which the redeemed of the Lord do walk. Here you will come to love God above all, and your neighbours as yourselves. Nothing hurts, nothing harms, nothing makes afraid on this holy mountain; now you come to be

Christ's indeed, for you are his in nature and spirit, and not your own. And when you are thus Christ's, then Christ is yours, and not before; and here communion with the Father and with the Son you will know, and the efficacy of the blood of cleansing, even the blood of Jesus Christ, that immaculate Lamb, which speaketh better things than the blood of Abel, and which cleanseth from all sin the consciences of those that, through the living faith, come to be sprinkled with it from dead works to serve the living God.

To conclude; behold the testimony and doctrine of the people called Quakers! Behold their practice and discipline! and behold the blessed man and men that were sent of God in this excellent work and service! all which will be more particularly expressed in the ensuing annals of the man of God; which I do heartily recommend to my reader's most serious perusal, and beseech Almighty God, that his blessing may go along with it, to the convincing of many, as yet strangers to this holy dispensation, and also to the edification of the church of God in general; who, for his manifold and repeated mercies and blessings to his people, in this day of his great love, is worthy ever to have the glory, honour, thanksgiving, and renown; and be it rendered and ascribed, with fear and reverence, through Him in whom he is well pleased, his beloved Son and Lamb, our Light and Life, that sits with him upon the throne, world without end. Amen,

Says one whom God has long since mercifully favoured with his fatherly visitation, and who was not disobedient to the heavenly vision and call; to whom the way of Truth is more lovely and precious than ever, and who knowing the beauty and benefit of it above all worldly treasure, has chosen it for his chiefest joy; and therefore recommends it to thy love and choice, because he is with great sincerity and affection thy soul's friend,

WILLIAM PENN.

[For the Testimonies respecting George Fox, which were here inserted in the last edition of this work, see Appendix at the conclusion of Vol. II.]

JOURNAL OF GEORGE FOX.

CHAPTER I.

1624–1647.—George Fox's birth and parentage—his gravity and piety in youth. Apprenticed to a shoemaker, who is also a grazier, &c.—his integrity in dealing. Refuses to drink healths—his exercises of mind commence—he lives retired—is tempted to despair. His sorrows continue for some years—has a sense of Christ's sufferings. Confutes a people who held women to be devoid of souls—begins to travel on Truth's account—meets with Elizabeth Hooton—fasts often, and retires to solitary places with his Bible—his exercises intermit. Sees why none but Christ could speak to his condition. Visits a woman who had fasted twenty-two days—first declares the Truth at Duckingfield and Manchester. Preaches at a great meeting at Broughton. His troubles wear off, and he weeps for joy—sees things which cannot be uttered—is reported to have a discerning spirit—overcomes his temptations through the power of Christ.

THAT all may know the dealings of the Lord with me, and the various exercises, trials, and troubles through which he led me, in order to prepare and fit me for the work unto which he had appointed me, and may thereby be drawn to admire and glorify his infinite wisdom and goodness, I think fit (before I proceed to set forth my public travels in the service of Truth) briefly to mention how it was with me in my youth, and how the work of the Lord was begun, and gradually carried on in me, even from my childhood.

I was born in the month called July, 1624, at DRAYTON-IN-THE-CLAY, in LEICESTERSHIRE. My father's name was Christopher Fox: he was by profession a weaver, an honest man; and there was a seed of God in him. The neighbours called him Righteous Christer. My mother was an upright woman; her maiden name was Mary Lago, of the family of the Lagos, and of the stock of the martyrs.

In my very young years I had a gravity and stayedness of mind and spirit, not usual in children; insomuch, that when I saw old men behave lightly and wantonly towards each other, I had a dislike thereof raised in my heart, and said within myself, "If ever I come to be a man, surely I shall not do so, nor be so wanton."

When I came to eleven years of age, I knew pureness and righteousness; for while a child I was taught how to walk to be kept pure. The Lord taught me to be faithful in all things, and to act faithfully two ways, viz., inwardly to God, and outwardly to man; and to keep to Yea and Nay in all things. For the Lord showed me, that though the people of the

world have mouths full of deceit, and changeable words, yet I was to keep
to Yea and Nay in all things; and that my words should be few and
savoury, seasoned with grace; and that I might not eat and drink to make
myself wanton, but for health, using the creatures in their service, as
servants in their places, to the glory of Him that created them; they being
in their covenant, and I being brought up into the covenant, and sanctified
by the Word which was in the beginning, by which all things are upheld;
wherein is unity with the creation.

But people being strangers to the covenant of life with God, they eat
and drink to make themselves wanton with the creatures, wasting them
upon their own lusts, and living in all filthiness, loving foul ways, and
devouring the creation; and all this in the world, in the pollutions thereof,
without God: therefore I was to shun all such.

Afterwards, as I grew up, my relations thought to make me a priest;
but others persuaded to the contrary: whereupon I was put to a man, a
shoemaker by trade, but who dealt in wool, and was a grazier, and sold
cattle; and a great deal went through my hands. While I was with him,
he was blessed; but after I left him he broke, and came to nothing.   I
never wronged man or woman in all that time; for the Lord's power was
with me, and over me to preserve me. While I was in that service, I used
in my dealings the word Verily, and it was a common saying among people
that knew me, "If George says Verily, there is no altering him."   When
boys and rude people would laugh at me, I let them alone, and went my
way; but people had generally a love to me for my innocency and honesty.

When I came towards nineteen years of age, being upon business at a
fair, one of my cousins, whose name was *Bradford*, a professor, and having
another professor with him, came to me and asked me to drink part of a
jug of beer with them, and I, being thirsty, went in with them; for I loved
any that had a sense of good, or that sought after the Lord.   When we
had drunk each a glass, they began to drink healths, calling for more, and
agreeing together, that he that would not drink should pay all.   I was
grieved that any who made profession of religion, should do so.   They
grieved me very much, having never had such a thing put to me before, by
any sort of people; wherefore I rose up to go, and putting my hand into
my pocket, laid a groat on the table before them, and said, "If it be so, I
will leave you."   So I went away; and when I had done what business I
had to do, I returned home, but did not go to bed that night, nor could I
sleep, but sometimes walked up and down, and sometimes prayed and cried
to the Lord, who said unto me, "Thou seest how young people go together
into vanity, and old people into the earth; thou must forsake all, both
young and old, and keep out of all, and be a stranger unto all."

Then at the command of God, on the ninth day of the seventh month,
1643, I left my relations, and broke off all familiarity or fellowship with
old or young.   I passed to LUTTERWORTH, where I stayed some time; and
thence to NORTHAMPTON, where also I made some stay: then to NEWPORT-
PAGNELL, whence, after I had stayed a while, I went to BARNET, in the fourth
month, called June, in 1644.   As I thus travelled through the country,
professors took notice, and sought to be acquainted with me; but I was

afraid of them, for I was sensible they did not possess what they professed. Now during the time that I was at BARNET, a strong temptation to despair came upon me. Then I saw how Christ was tempted, and mighty troubles I was in; sometimes I kept myself retired in my chamber, and often walked solitary in the chace,* to wait upon the Lord.

I wondered why these things should come to me; and I looked upon myself and said, "Was I ever so before?" Then I thought, because I had forsaken my relations, I had done amiss against them; so I was brought to call to mind all the time that I had thus spent, and to consider whether I had wronged any. But temptations grew more and more, and I was tempted almost to despair; and when Satan could not effect his design upon me that way, he laid snares for me, and baits to draw me to commit some sin, whereby he might take advantage to bring me to despair. I was about twenty years of age when these exercises came upon me; and I continued in that condition some years, in great trouble, and fain would have put it from me. I went to many a priest to look for comfort, but found no comfort from them.

From BARNET I went to LONDON, where I took a lodging, and was under great misery and trouble there; for I looked upon the great professors of the city, and I saw all was dark and under the chain of darkness. I had an uncle there, one Pickering, a Baptist (and they were tender then), yet I could not impart my mind to him, nor join with them; for I saw all, young and old, where they were. Some tender people would have had me stay, but I was fearful, and returned homewards into LEICESTERSHIRE again, having a regard upon my mind unto my parents and relations, lest I should grieve them; who, I understood, were troubled at my absence.

When I was come down into Leicestershire, my relations would have had me marry, but I told them I was but a lad, and I must get wisdom. Others would have had me into the auxiliary band among the soldiery, but I refused; and I was grieved that they proffered such things to me, being a tender youth. Then I went to COVENTRY, where I took a chamber for a while at a professor's house, till people began to be acquainted with me; for there were many tender people in that town. After some time I went into my own country again, and was there about a year, in great sorrows and troubles, and walked many nights by myself.

Then the priest of DRAYTON, the town of my birth, whose name was Nathaniel Stevens, came often to me, and I went often to him; and another priest sometimes came with him; and they would give place to me to hear me, and I would ask them questions, and reason with them. And this priest Stevens asked me a question, viz., Why Christ cried out upon the cross, "My God, my God, why hast thou forsaken me?" and why he said, "If it be possible, let this cup pass from me; yet not my will, but thine be done?" I told him that at that time the sins of all mankind were upon him, and their iniquities and transgressions with which he was wounded, which he was to bear, and to be an offering for, as he was man, but he died not as he was God; and so, in that he died for all men, and

---

* Open fields.

tasted death for every man, he was an offering for the sins of the whole world. This I spoke, being at that time in a measure sensible of Christ's sufferings, and what he went through. And the priest said, "It was a very good, full answer, and such a one as he had not heard." At that time he would applaud and speak highly of me to others; and what I said in discourse to him on the week-days, he would preach on the first-days; for which I did not like him. This priest afterwards became my great persecutor.

After this I went to another ancient priest at MANCETTER, in Warwickshire, and reasoned with him about the ground of despair and temptations; but he was ignorant of my condition; he bade me take tobacco and sing psalms. Tobacco was a thing I did not love, and psalms I was not in a state to sing; I could not sing. Then he bid me come again, and he would tell me many things; but when I came he was angry and pettish, for my former words had displeased him. He told my troubles, sorrows, and griefs to his servants; which grieved me that I had opened my mind to such a one. I saw they were all miserable comforters; and this brought my troubles more upon me. Then I heard of a priest living about TAMWORTH, who was accounted an experienced man, and I went seven miles to him; but I found him only like an empty hollow cask. I heard also of one called Dr. Cradock, of COVENTRY, and went to him. I asked him the ground of temptations and despair, and how troubles came to be wrought in man? He asked me, Who was Christ's father and mother? I told him, Mary was his mother, and that he was supposed to be the Son of Joseph, but he was the Son of God. Now, as we were walking together in his garden, the alley being narrow, I chanced, in turning, to set my foot on the side of a bed, at which the man was in a rage, as if his house had been on fire. Thus all our discourse was lost, and I went away in sorrow, worse than I was when I came. I thought them miserable comforters, and saw they were all as nothing to me; for they could not reach my condition. After this I went to another, one Macham, a priest in high account. He would needs give me some physic, and I was to have been let blood; but they could not get one drop of blood from me, either in arms or head (though they endeavoured to do so), my body being, as it were, dried up with sorrows, grief and troubles, which were so great upon me that I could have wished I had never been born, or that I had been born blind, that I might never have seen wickedness or vanity; and deaf, that I might never have heard vain and wicked words, or the Lord's name blasphemed. When the time called Christmas came, while others were feasting and sporting themselves, I looked out poor widows from house to house, and gave them some money. When I was invited to marriages (as I sometimes was), I went to none at all, but the next day, or soon after, I would go and visit them; and if they were poor, I gave them some money; for I had wherewith both to keep myself from being chargeable to others, and to administer something to the necessities of those who were in need.

About the beginning of the year 1646, as I was going to COVENTRY, and approaching towards the gate, a consideration arose in me, how it was

said that "all Christians are believers, both Protestants and Papists;" and
the Lord opened to me that, if all were believers, then they were all born
of God, and passed from death to life, and that none were true believers
but such; and though others said they were believers, yet they were not.
At another time, as I was walking in a field on a first-day morning, the
Lord opened unto me, "that being bred at Oxford or Cambridge was not
enough to fit and qualify men to be ministers of Christ;" and I wondered
at it, because it was the common belief of people. But I saw it clearly
as the Lord opened it to me, and was satisfied, and admired the goodness
of the Lord who had opened this thing unto me that morning. This
struck at priest Steven's ministry, namely, "that to be bred at Oxford or
Cambridge was not enough to make a man fit to be a minister of Christ."
So that which opened in me, I saw struck at the priest's ministry. But
my relations were much troubled that I would not go with them to hear
the priest; for I would get into the orchards, or the fields, with my Bible,
by myself. I asked them, Did not the apostle say to believers, that
"they needed no man to teach them, but as the anointing teacheth them?"
And though they knew this was Scripture, and that it was true, yet they
were grieved because I could not be subject in this matter, to go to hear
the priest with them. I saw that to be a true believer was another thing
than they looked upon it to be: and I saw that being bred at Oxford or
Cambridge did not qualify or fit a man to be a minister of Christ: what
then should I follow such for? So neither these, nor any of the Dissenting
people, could I join with, but was a stranger to all, relying wholly upon
the Lord Jesus Christ.

At another time it was opened in me, "That God, who made the world,
did not dwell in temples made with hands." This at first seemed a strange
word, because both priests and people used to call their temples or churches,
dreadful places, holy ground, and the temples of God. But the Lord
showed me clearly, that he did not dwell in these temples which men had
commanded and set up, but in people's hearts: for both Stephen and the
apostle Paul bore testimony, that he did not dwell in temples made with
hands, not even in that which he had once commanded to be built, since
he put an end to it; but that his people were his temple, and he dwelt in
them. This opened in me as I walked in the fields to my relations' house.
When I came there, they told me that Nathaniel Stevens, the priest, had
been there, and told them "he was afraid of me, for going after new lights."
I smiled in myself, knowing what the Lord had opened in me concerning
him and his brethren; but I told not my relations, who though they saw
beyond the priests, yet they went to hear them, and were grieved because
I would not go also. But I brought them Scriptures, and told them, there
was an anointing within man to teach him, and that the Lord would teach
his people himself. I had also great openings concerning the things written in the Revelations; and when I spoke of them, the priests and professors would say that was a sealed book, and would have kept me out of it:
but I told them, Christ could open the seals, and that they were the nearest things to us; for the epistles were written to the saints that lived in
former ages, but the Revelations were written of things to come.

After this, I met with a sort of people that held, women have no souls, (adding in a light manner,) no more than a goose. But I reproved them, and told them that was not right; for Mary said, "My soul doth magnify the Lord, and my spirit hath rejoiced in God my Saviour."

Removing to another place, I came among a people that relied much on dreams. I told them, except they could distinguish between dream and dream, they would confound all together; for there were three sorts of dreams; multitude of business sometimes caused dreams; and there were whisperings of Satan in man in the night-season; and there were speakings of God to man in dreams. But these people came out of these things, and at last became Friends.

Now though I had great openings, yet great trouble and temptation came many times upon me; so that when it was day, I wished for night, and when it was night, I wished for day: and by reason of the openings I had in my troubles, I could say as David said, "Day unto day uttereth speech, and night unto night showeth knowledge." When I had openings, they answered one another, and answered the Scriptures; for I had great openings of the Scriptures: and when I was in troubles, one trouble also answered to another.

About the beginning of the year 1647, I was moved of the Lord to go into DERBYSHIRE, where I met with some friendly people, and had many discourses with them. Then passing further into the PEAK-COUNTRY, I met with more friendly people, and with some in empty, high notions. Travelling on through some parts of LEICESTERSHIRE and into NOTTINGHAMSHIRE, I met with a tender people, and a very tender woman, whose name was Elizabeth Hooton;* and with these I had some meetings and discourses. But my troubles continued, and I was often under great temptations; I fasted much, and walked abroad in solitary places many days, and often took my Bible, and went and sat in hollow trees and lonesome places till night came on; and frequently, in the night, walked mournfully about by myself: for I was a man of sorrows in the times of the first workings of the Lord in me.

---

* Elizabeth Hooton was born at Nottingham about the year 1600; was the wife of a person who occupied a respectable position in society. In 1647, when George Fox first met with her, she formed one of a company of serious persons, who occasionally met together. Little is known of her, but "the meetings and discourses" she had with George Fox appear to have been the means of convincing her of the spiritual views of Friends. Sewel says in 1650—"From a true experience of the Lord's work in man, she felt herself moved publicly to preach the way of salvation to others." She was therefore not only the first of her sex, but the second individual who appeared in the character of a minister amongst the newly-gathered society. The preaching of women was not at this period considered singular, several being thus engaged among the various religious sects then in England. Elizabeth Hooton had not long publicly testified as a minister, before her sincerity and faithfulness were tested by persecution. Besides suffering in other ways, she endured several imprisonments, sometimes for months together. As a gospel minister, she stood high in the estimation of her friends, and in advanced life performed two religious visits to America and the West Indies, the latter of which occupied her several years. She was one who travelled with George Fox amongst the West India Islands, as related elsewhere in these volumes, being suddenly taken ill in Jamaica, where she died the day following, aged about 71 years, a minister 21 years.

During all this time I was never joined in profession of religion with any, but gave myself up to the Lord, having forsaken all evil company, and taken leave of father and mother and all other relations, and travelled up and down as a stranger in the earth, which way the Lord inclined my heart; taking a chamber to myself in the town where I came, and tarrying sometimes a month, more or less in a place; for I durst not stay long in any place, being afraid both of professor and profane, lest, being a tender young man, I should be hurt by conversing much with either. For which reason I kept myself much as a stranger, seeking heavenly wisdom and getting knowledge from the Lord; and was brought off from outward things, to rely wholly on the Lord alone. Though my exercises and troubles were very great, yet were they not so continual but that I had some intermissions, and was sometimes brought into such a heavenly joy, that I thought I had been in Abraham's bosom. As I cannot declare the misery I was in, it was so great and heavy upon me; so neither can I set forth the mercies of God unto me in all my misery. O, the everlasting love of God to my soul, when I was in great distress! when my troubles and torments were great, then was his love exceedingly great. "Thou, Lord, makest a fruitful field a barren wilderness, and a barren wilderness a fruitful field; thou bringest down and settest up; thou killest and makest alive; all honour and glory be to thee, O Lord of glory; the knowledge of thee in the Spirit, is life; but that knowledge which is fleshly, works death." While there is this knowledge in the flesh, deceit and self-will conform to anything, and will say yes, yes, to that it doth not know. The knowledge which the world hath of what the prophets and apostles spoke, is a fleshly knowledge; and the apostates from the life, in which the prophets and apostles were, have gotten their words, the Holy Scriptures, in a form, but not in their life nor Spirit that gave them forth. So they all lie in confusion, and are making provision for the flesh, to fulfil the lusts thereof; but not to fulfil the law and command of Christ in his power and Spirit: this, they say, they cannot do; but to fulfil the lusts of the flesh, that they can do with delight.

Now after I had received that opening from the Lord, that "to be bred at Oxford or Cambridge was not sufficient to fit a man to be a minister of Christ," I regarded the priests less, and looked more after the Dissenting people. Among them I saw there was some tenderness; and many of them came afterwards to be convinced, for they had some openings. But as I had forsaken the priests, so I left the separate preachers also, and those esteemed the most experienced people; for I saw there was none among them all that could speak to my condition. When all my hopes in them and in all men, were gone, so that I had nothing outwardly to help me, nor could I tell what to do; then, O! then I heard a voice which said, "There is one, even Christ Jesus, that can speak to thy condition;" and when I heard it, my heart did leap for joy. Then the Lord let me see why there was none upon the earth that could speak to my condition, namely, that I might give Him all the glory; for all are concluded under sin, and shut up in unbelief, as I had been, that Jesus Christ might have the pre-eminence, who enlightens, and gives grace, and faith, and power. Thus when

God doth work, who shall hinder it? and this I knew experimentally. My desires after the Lord grew stronger, and zeal in the pure knowledge of God, and of Christ alone, without the help of any man, book, or writing. For though I read the Scriptures that spoke of Christ and of God; yet I knew Him not, but by revelation, as He who hath the key did open, and as the Father of Life drew me to his Son by his Spirit. Then the Lord gently led me along, and let me see his love, which was endless and eternal, surpassing all the knowledge that men have in the natural state, or can obtain from history or books; and that love let me see myself, as I was without him. I was afraid of all company, for I saw them perfectly where they were, through the love of God, which let me see myself. I had not fellowship with any people, priests or professors, or any sort of separated people, but with Christ, who hath the key, and opened the door of Light and Life unto me. I was afraid of all carnal talk and talkers, for I could see nothing but corruptions, and the life lay under the burthen of corruptions. When I myself was in the deep, shut up under all, I could not believe that I should ever overcome; my troubles, my sorrows, and my temptations were so great, that I thought many times I should have despaired, I was so tempted. But when Christ opened to me, how He was tempted by the same devil, and overcame him and bruised his head, and that through him and his power, light, grace, and Spirit, I should overcome also, I had confidence in him; so He it was that opened to me, when I was shut up, and had no hope nor faith. Christ, who had enlightened me, gave me his light to believe in; he gave me hope, which he himself revealed in me, and he gave me his Spirit and grace, which I found sufficient in the deeps and in weakness. Thus, in the deepest miseries, and in the greatest sorrows and temptations, that many times beset me, the Lord in his mercy did keep me. I found that there were two thirsts in me; the one after the creatures, to get help and strength there; and the other after the Lord, the Creator, and his Son Jesus Christ. I saw all the world could do me no good; if I had had a king's diet, palace, and attendance, all would have been as nothing; for nothing gave me comfort, but the Lord by his power. I saw professors, priests, and people, were whole and at ease in that condition which was my misery; and they loved that which I would have been rid of. But the Lord stayed my desires upon himself, from whom came my help, and my care was cast upon him alone. Therefore, all wait patiently upon the Lord, whatsoever condition you be in; wait in the grace and truth that came by Jesus: for if ye so do, there is a promise to you, and the Lord God will fulfil it in you. Blessed are all they that do indeed hunger and thirst after righteousness, they shall be satisfied with it. I have found it so, praised be the Lord who filleth with it, and satisfieth the desires of the hungry soul. O let the house of the spiritual Israel say, "His mercy endureth for ever!" It is the great love of God to make a wilderness of that which is pleasant to the outward eye and fleshly mind; and to make a fruitful field of a barren wilderness. This is the great work of God. But while people's minds run in the earthly, after the creatures and changeable things, changeable ways and religions, and changeable, uncertain teachers, their minds are in bondage, they are changeable, tossed up and down with windy doctrines and thoughts, and notions and things; their minds being out of the unchangeable truth in the inward parts, the Light of Jesus Christ, which would keep them to the unchangeable. He is the way to the Father; and in all my troubles he preserved me by his Spirit and power; praised be his holy name for ever!

Again, I heard a voice which said, "Thou serpent! thou dost seek to destroy the life, but canst not; for the sword which keepeth the tree of life, shall destroy thee." So Christ, the Word of God, that bruised the head of the serpent, the destroyer, preserved me; my inward mind being joined to his good Seed, that bruised the head of this serpent, the destroyer. This inward life sprung up in me, to answer all the opposing professors and priests, and brought Scriptures to my memory to refute them with.

At another time, I saw the great love of God, and I was filled with admiration at the infinitude of it; I saw what was cast out from God, and what entered into God's kingdom; and how by Jesus, the opener of the door, with his heavenly key, the entrance was given; and I saw death, how it had passed upon all men, and oppressed the seed of God in man, and in me; and how I in the seed came forth, and what the promise was to. Yet it was so with me, that there seemed to be two pleading in me; questionings arose in my mind about gifts and prophecies; and I was tempted again to despair, as if I had sinned against the Holy Ghost. I was in great perplexity and trouble for many days; yet I gave up myself to the Lord still. One day when I had been walking solitarily abroad, and was come home, I was wrapped up in the love of God, so that I could not but admire the greatness of his love. While I was in that condition, it was opened unto me by the eternal light and power, and I saw clearly therein, "that all was done, and to be done, in and by Christ; and how he conquers and destroys this tempter, the Devil, and all his works, and is above him; and that all these troubles were good for me, and temptations for the trial of my faith, which Christ had given me." The Lord opened me, that I saw through all these troubles and temptations; my living faith was raised, that I saw all was done by Christ, the life, and my belief was in Him. When at any time my condition was veiled, my secret belief was stayed firm, and hope underneath held me, as an anchor in the bottom of the sea, and anchored my immortal soul to its Bishop, causing it to swim above the sea, the world, where all the raging waves, foul weather, tempests, and temptations are. But, O! then did I see my troubles, trials, and temptations, more clearly than ever I had done. As the light appeared, all appeared that is out of the light; darkness, death, temptations, the unrighteous, the ungodly; all was manifest and seen in the light. After this, a pure fire appeared in me; then I saw how he sat as a refiner's fire and as fullers' soap;—then the spiritual discerning came into me, by which I did discern my own thoughts, groans, and sighs; and what it was that veiled me, and what it was that opened me. That which could not abide in the patience, nor endure the fire, in the light I found it to be the groans of the flesh, that could not give up to the will of God; which had so veiled me, that I could not be patient in all trials, troubles, and perplexities;— could not give up self to die by the cross, the power of God, that the

living and quickened might follow him; and that that which would cloud
and veil from the presence of Christ—that which the sword of the Spirit
cuts down, and which must die, might not be kept alive.   I discerned also
the groans of the Spirit, which opened me, and made intercession to God;
in which Spirit is the true waiting upon God, for the redemption of the
body and of the whole creation.   By this Spirit, in which the true sighing is,
I saw over the false sighings and groanings.   By this invisible Spirit I
discerned all the false hearing, the false seeing, and the false smelling
which was above the Spirit, quenching and grieving it; and that all they
that were there, were in confusion and deceit, where the false asking and
praying is, in deceit, in that nature and tongue that takes God's holy name
in vain, wallows in the Egyptian sea, and asketh, but hath not; for they
hate his light and resist the Holy Ghost; turn grace into wantonness, and
rebel against the Spirit; and are erred from the faith they should ask in,
and from the Spirit they should pray by.   He that knoweth these things
in the true Spirit, can witness them.   The divine light of Christ manifesteth all things; the spiritual fire trieth all things, and severeth all things.
Several things did I then see as the Lord opened them to me; for he
showed me that which can live in his holy refining fire, and that can live
to God under his law.   He made me sensible how the law and the prophets
were until John; and how the least in the everlasting kingdom of God is
greater than John.   The pure and perfect law of God is over the flesh, to
keep it and its works, which are not perfect, under, by the perfect law;
and the law of God that is perfect, answers the perfect principle of God in
every one.   This law the Jews, and the prophets, and John were to perform and do.   None know the giver of this law but by the Spirit of God;
neither can any truly read it, or hear its voice, but by the Spirit of God;
he that can receive it, let him.   John, who was the greatest prophet that
was born of a woman, did bear witness to the light, which Christ, the
great heavenly prophet, hath enlightened every man that cometh into the
world withal; that they might believe in it, and become the children of
light, and so have the light of life, and not come into condemnation.   For
the true belief stands in the light that condemns all evil, and the Devil,
who is the prince of darkness, and would draw out of the light into condemnation.   They that walk in this light, come to the mountain of the
house of God, established above all mountains, and to God's teaching, who
will teach them his ways.   These things were opened to me in the light.

I saw also the mountains burning up; and the rubbish, the rough and
crooked ways and places, made smooth and plain, that the Lord might come
into his tabernacle.   These things are to be found in man's heart.   But to
speak of these things being within, seemed strange to the rough, and
crooked, and mountainous ones.   Yet the Lord saith, "O Earth, hear the
word of the Lord!"   The law of the Spirit crosseth the fleshly mind,
spirit, and will, which lives in disobedience, and doth not keep within the
law of the Spirit.   I saw this law was the pure love of God, which was
upon me, and which I must go through though I was troubled while I was
under it; for I could not be dead to the law, but through the law which
did judge and condemn that, which is to be condemned.   I saw many

talked of the law, who had never known the law to be their schoolmaster; and many talked of the gospel of Christ, who had never known life and immortality brought to light in them by it. You that have been under that schoolmaster, and the condemnation of it, know these things; for though the Lord in that day opened these things unto me in secret, they have since been published by his eternal Spirit, as on the house top. And as you are brought into the law, and through the law to be dead to it, and witness the righteousness of the law fulfilled in you, ye will afterwards come to know what it is to be brought into the faith, and through faith from under the law; and abiding in the faith, which Christ is the author of, ye will have peace and access to God. But if ye look out from the faith, and from that which would keep you in the victory, and look after fleshly things or words, ye will be brought into bondage to flesh again, and to the law, which takes hold upon the flesh and sin, and worketh wrath, and the works of the flesh will appear again. The law of God takes hold upon the law of sin and death; but the law of faith, or the law of the Spirit of life, which is the love of God, and which comes by Jesus (who is the end of the law for righteousness' sake), makes free from the law of sin and death. This law of life fleshly-minded men do not know; yet they will tempt you, to draw you from the Spirit into the flesh, and so into bondage. Therefore ye, who know the love of God, and the law of his Spirit, and the freedom that is in Jesus Christ, stand fast in him, in that divine faith which he is the author of in you; and be not entangled with the yoke of bondage. For the ministry of Christ Jesus, and his teaching, bring into liberty and freedom; but the ministry that is of man, and by man, and which stands in the will of man, bringeth into bondage, and under the shadow of death and darkness. Therefore none can be ministers of Christ Jesus but in the eternal Spirit, which was before the Scriptures were given forth; for if they have not his Spirit, they are none of his. Though they may have his light to condemn them that hate it, yet they can never bring any into unity and fellowship in the Spirit, except they be in it; for the Seed of God is a burthensome stone to the selfish, fleshly, earthly will, which reigns in its own knowledge and understanding that must perish, and in its wisdom that is devilish. And the Spirit of God is grieved, and vexed, and quenched with that which brings into the fleshly bondage; and that which wars against the Spirit of God, must be mortified by it; for the flesh lusteth against the Spirit, and the Spirit against the flesh; and these are contrary the one to the other. The flesh would have its liberty, and the Spirit would have its liberty; but the Spirit is to have its liberty and not the flesh. If therefore ye quench the Spirit, and join to the flesh, and be servants of it, then ye are judged and tormented by the Spirit; but if ye join to the Spirit and serve God in it, ye have liberty and victory over the flesh and its works. Therefore keep in the daily cross, the power of God, by which ye may witness all that to be crucified which is contrary to the will of God, and which shall not come into his kingdom. These things are here mentioned and opened for information, exhortation, and comfort to others, as the Lord opened them unto me in that day. In that day I wondered that the children of Israel should murmur for water and victuals, for I could have fasted long without murmuring or minding victuals. But I was judged at other times, that I was not contented to be sometimes without the water and bread of life, that I might learn to know how to want, and how to abound.

I heard of a woman in LANCASHIRE, that had fasted two and twenty days, and I travelled to see her; but when I came to her I saw that she was under a temptation. When I had spoken to her what I had from the Lord, I left her, her father being one high in profession. Passing on, I went among the professors at DUCKINGFIELD and MANCHESTER, where I stayed a while, and declared truth among them. There were some convinced, who received the Lord's teaching, by which they were confirmed and stood in the truth. But the professors were in a rage, all pleading for sin and imperfection, and could not endure to hear talk of perfection, and of a holy and sinless life. But the Lord's power was over all; though they were chained under darkness and sin, which they pleaded for, and quenched the tender thing in them.

About this time there was a great meeting of the Baptists, at BROUGHTON, in Leicestershire, with some that had separated from them; and people of other notions went thither, and I went also. Not many of the Baptists came, but many others were there. The Lord opened my mouth, and the everlasting truth was declared amongst them, and the power of the Lord was over them all. For in that day the Lord's power began to spring, and I had great openings in the Scriptures. Several were convinced in those parts, and were turned from darkness to light, from the power of Satan unto God; and many were raised up to praise God. When I reasoned with professors and other people, some became convinced.

I was still under great temptations sometimes, and my inward sufferings were heavy; but I could find none to open my condition to but the Lord alone, unto whom I cried night and day. I went back into NOTTINGHAMSHIRE, and there the Lord showed me that the natures of those things, which were hurtful without, were within, in the hearts and minds of wicked men. The natures of dogs, swine, vipers, of Sodom and Egypt, Pharaoh, Cain, Ishmael, Esau, &c.; the natures of these I saw within, though people had been looking without. I cried to the Lord, saying, "Why should I be thus, seeing I was never addicted to commit those evils?" and the Lord answered, "That it was needful I should have a sense of all conditions, how else should I speak to all conditions!" and in this I saw the infinite love of God. I saw also, that there was an ocean of darkness and death; but an infinite ocean of light and love, which flowed over the ocean of darkness. In that also I saw the infinite love of God, and I had great openings. And as I was walking by the steeple-house,* in MANSFIELD,

---

* The term "steeple-house" occurs not unfrequently in this *Journal*, and in the early writings and records of Friends. Though it may sound harsh, and appear to savour of the scurrility and intolerance of that zealous age, yet this, or any other mode of speech adopted by Friends, was by no means taken up for the purpose of opprobrium, but rather significantly to discover the little veneration or distinction they could show for these buildings more than others; believing that the Almighty is equally present

the Lord said unto me, "That which people trample upon, must be thy food." And as the Lord spoke he opened it to me, that people and professors trampled upon the life, even the life of Christ; they fed upon words, and fed one another with words; but they trampled upon the life; trampled underfoot the blood of the Son of God, which blood was my life, and lived in their airy notions, talking of him. It seemed strange to me at first, that I should feed on that which the high professors trampled upon; but the Lord opened it clearly to me by his eternal Spirit and Power.

Then came people from far and near to see me; but I was fearful of being drawn out by them; yet I was made to speak, and open things to them. There was one Brown, who had great prophecies and sights upon his death-bed of me. He spoke only of what I should be made instrumental by the Lord to bring forth. And of others he spoke, that they should come to nothing, which was fulfilled on some, who then were something in show. When this man was buried, a great work of the Lord fell upon me, to the admiration of many, who thought I had been dead; and many came to see me for about fourteen days. I was very much altered in countenance and person, as if my body had been new moulded or changed. While I was in that condition, I had a sense and discerning given me by the Lord, through which I saw plainly, that when many people talked of God and of Christ, &c., the serpent spoke in them; but this was hard to be borne. Yet the work of the Lord went on in some, and my sorrows and troubles began to wear off, and tears of joy dropped from me, so that I could have wept night and day with tears of joy to the Lord, in humility and brokenness of heart. I saw into that which was without end, things which cannot be uttered, and of the greatness and infinitude of the love of God, which cannot be expressed by words. For I had been brought through the very ocean of darkness and death, and through and over the power of Satan, by the eternal, glorious power of Christ; even through that darkness was I brought, which covered over all the world, and which chained down all, and shut up all in death. The same eternal power of God, which brought me through these things, was that which afterwards shook the nations, priests, professors, and people. Then could I say I had been in spiritual Babylon, Sodom, Egypt, and the grave; but by the eternal power of God I was come out of it, and was

everywhere, to bless and to sanctify every place and everything to those that walk uprightly on the earth, his footstool.

One of the chief points of George Fox's ministry was to overturn that insidious reverence for names and things which is too frequently substituted for the worship that is "in spirit and in truth." Few instances more distinctly exhibit this sort of covert idolatry, than the general notion of *sanctity* which is attached to the building called a "*church*." The word "church" is, in the Holy Scriptures, never applied to an outward temple or building, but to a company of believers, whether generally or particularly. The use of this term appears to have crept in among Christians, and with it a superstitious consecration of those places, as possessing some latent quality not affecting other works of art or nature. To this Stephen the martyr evidently alluded when he said, "Howbeit the Most High dwelleth not in temples made with hands," &c., Acts vii. 48. Clemens of Alexandria says, "Not the place, but the congregation of the elect, I call a church," Stromat. vii., 715 B.

brought over it, and the power of it, into the power of Christ. I saw the harvest white, and the seed of God lying thick in the ground, as ever did wheat that was sown outwardly, and none to gather it; for this I mourned with tears. A report went abroad of me, that I was a young man that had a discerning spirit; whereupon many came to me, from far and near, professors, priests, and people. The Lord's power broke forth; and I had great openings and prophecies; and spoke unto them of the things of God, which they heard with attention and silence, and went away, and spread the fame thereof. Then came the tempter, and set upon me again, charging me, that I had sinned against the Holy Ghost; but I could not tell in what. Then Paul's condition came before me, how, after he had been taken up into the third heavens, and seen things not lawful to be uttered, a messenger of Satan was sent to buffet him. Thus, by the power of Christ, I got over that temptation also.

CHAPTER II.

1648-1649.—Begins to have great meetings—at Mansfield he is moved to pray—the Lord's power so great the house is shaken—cannot pray in his own will—a temptation besets him that there is no God, which is dissipated by an inward voice—he afterwards disputes with and confounds some Atheists—goes to courts and steeple-houses, &c., to warn against oppression and oaths—reproves a notorious drunkard, who is reformed—sees who are the greatest deceivers—shows how people read and understand the Scriptures—various mysteries are revealed to him—he is sent to turn people to the Inward Light, Spirit, and Grace, the Divine Spirit which he infallibly knew would not deceive—priests and professors rage at these innovations—he cries for justice in courts and against various wrong things—denounces the trade of preaching—is sent to preach freely.

In the year 1648, as I was sitting in a friend's house in Nottinghamshire (for by this time the power of God had opened the hearts of some to receive the word of life and reconciliation), I saw there was a great crack to go throughout the earth, and a great smoke to go as the crack went; and that after the crack there should be a great shaking: this was the earth in people's hearts, which was to be shaken before the seed of God was raised out of the earth. And it was so; for the Lord's power began to shake them, and great meetings we begun to have, and a mighty power and work of God there was amongst people, to the astonishment of both people and priests.

And there was a meeting of priests and professors at a justice's house, and I went among them. Here they discoursed how Paul said, "He had not known sin, but by the law, which said, Thou shalt not lust:" and they held that to be spoken of the outward law. But I told them, Paul spoke that after he was convinced; for he had the outward law before, and was brought up in it, when he was in the lust of persecution; but this was the law of God in his mind, which he served, and which the law in his members warred against; for that which he thought had been life to him, proved death. So the more sober of the priests and professors yielded, and consented that it was not the outward law, but the inward, which showed the inward lust which Paul spoke of after he was convinced: for the outward law took hold upon the outward action; but the inward law upon the inward lust.

After this I went again to Mansfield, where was a great meeting of professors and people; here I was moved to pray; and the Lord's power was so great, that the house seemed to be shaken. When I had done, some of the professors said it was now as in the days of the apostles, when the house was shaken where they were. After I had prayed, one of the professors would pray, which brought deadness and a veil over them: and others of the professors were grieved at him and told him, it was a temptation upon him. Then he came to me, and desired that I would pray again; but I could not pray in man's will.

Soon after there was another great meeting of professors, and a captain, whose name was Amor Stoddard, came in. They were discoursing of the blood of Christ; and as they were discoursing of it, I saw, through the immediate opening of the invisible Spirit, the blood of Christ. And I cried out among them, and said, "Do ye not see the blood of Christ? See it in your hearts, to sprinkle your hearts and consciences from dead works, to serve the living God:" for I saw it, the blood of the New Covenant, how it came into the heart. This startled the professors, who would have the blood only without them, and not in them. But Captain Stoddard was reached, and said, "Let the youth speak; hear the youth speak;" when he saw they endeavoured to bear me down with many words.

There was also a company of priests, that were looked upon to be tender; one of their names was Kellett; and several people that were tender, went to hear them. I was moved to go after them, and bid them mind the Lord's teaching in their inward parts. That priest Kellett was against parsonages then; but afterwards he got a great one, and turned a persecutor.

Now, after I had had some service in these parts, I went through DERBYSHIRE into my own county, LEICESTERSHIRE, again, and several tender people were convinced. Passing thence, I met with a great company of professors in WARWICKSHIRE, who were praying, and expounding the Scriptures in the fields. They gave the Bible to me, and I opened it on the fifth of Matthew, where Christ expounded the law; and I opened the inward state to them, and the outward state; upon which they fell into a fierce contention, and so parted; but the Lord's power got ground.

Then I heard of a great meeting to be at LEICESTER, for a dispute, wherein Presbyterians, Independents, Baptists, and Common-prayer-men were said to be all concerned. The meeting was in a steeple-house; and thither I was moved by the Lord God to go, and be amongst them. I heard their discourse and reasonings, some being in pews, and the priest in the pulpit; abundance of people being gathered together. At last one woman asked a question out of Peter, What that birth was, viz., a being born again of incorruptible seed, by the Word of God, that liveth and abideth for ever? And the priest said to her, "I permit not a woman to speak in the church;" though he had before given liberty for any to speak. Whereupon I was wrapped up, as in a rapture, in the Lord's power; and I stepped up and asked the priest, "Dost thou call this (the steeple-house) a church? Or dost thou call this mixed multitude a church?" For the woman asking a question, he ought to have answered it, having given liberty for any to speak. But, instead of answering me, he asked me what a church was? I told him, "The church was the pillar and ground of truth, made up of living stones, living members, a spiritual household, which Christ was the head of: but he was not the head of a mixed multitude, or of an old house made up of lime, stones, and wood." This set them all on fire: the priest came down out of his pulpit, and others out of their pews, and the dispute there was marred. But I went to a great inn, and there disputed the thing with the priests and professors of all sorts; and they were all on a fire. But I maintained the true church, and the true head thereof, over the heads of them all, till they all gave out and fled away. One man seemed loving, and appeared for a while to join with me; but he soon turned against me, and joined with a priest, in pleading for infants' baptism, though he himself had been a Baptist before; and so left me alone. Howbeit, there were several convinced that day; and the woman that asked the question was convinced, and her family; and the Lord's power and glory shone over all.

After this I returned into Nottinghamshire, and went into the VALE OF BEAVOR. As I went, I preached repentance to the people; and there were many convinced in the Vale of Beavor, in many towns; for I stayed some weeks amongst them. One morning, as I was sitting by the fire, a great cloud came over me, and a temptation beset me; but I sat still. And it was said, "All things come by nature;" and the elements and stars came over me, so that I was in a manner quite clouded with it. But as I sat still, and silent, the people of the house perceived nothing. And as I sat still under it, and let it alone, a living hope arose in me, and a true voice, which said, "There *is* a living God who made all things." And immediately the cloud and temptation vanished away, and life rose over it all; my heart was glad, and I praised the living God. After some time, I met with some people who had a notion that there was no God, but that all things came by nature. I had a great dispute with them, and overturned them, and made some of them confess that there is a living God. Then I saw that it was good that I had gone through that exercise. We had great meetings in those parts, for the power of the Lord broke through in that part of the country. Returning into NOTTINGHAMSHIRE, I found there a company of shattered Baptists, and others; and the Lord's power wrought mightily, and gathered many of them. Afterwards I went to MANSFIELD and thereaway, where the Lord's power was wonderfully manifested both at Mansfield and other neighbouring towns. In Derbyshire the mighty power of God wrought in a wonderful manner. At ETON, a town near Derby, there was a meeting of Friends, where there was such a mighty power of God that they were greatly shaken, and many mouths were opened in the power of the Lord God. Many were moved by the Lord to go to steeple-houses, to the priests and to the people, to declare the everlasting truth unto them.

At a certain time, when I was at MANSFIELD, there was a sitting of the justices about hiring of servants; and it was upon me from the Lord to go and speak to the justices, that they should not oppress the servants in their wages. So I walked towards the inn where they sat; but finding a company of fiddlers there, I did not go in, but thought to come in the morning, when I might have a more serious opportunity to discourse with them, not thinking that a seasonable time. But when I came again in the morning, they were gone, and I was struck even blind, that I could not see. I inquired of the innkeeper where the justices were to sit that day; and he told me, at a town eight miles off. My sight began to come to me again; and I went and ran thitherward as fast as I could. When I was come to the house where they were, and many servants with them, I exhorted the justices not to oppress the servants in their wages, but to do that which was right and just to them; and I exhorted the servants to do their duties, and serve honestly, &c. They all received my exhortation kindly; for I was moved of the Lord therein.

Moreover, I was moved to go to several courts and steeple-houses at Mansfield, and other places, to warn them to leave off oppression and oaths, and to turn from deceit to the Lord, and do justly. Particularly at Mansfield, after I had been at a court there, I was moved to go and speak to one of the most wicked men in the country, one who was a common drunkard, a noted whore-master, and a rhyme-maker; and I reproved him in the dread of the mighty God, for his evil courses. When I had done speaking, and left him, he came after me, and told me, that he was so smitten when I spoke to him, that he had scarcely any strength left in him. So this man was convinced, and turned from his wickedness, and remained an honest, sober man, to the astonishment of the people who had known him before. Thus the work of the Lord went forward, and many were turned from the darkness to the light, within the compass of these three years, 1646, 1647, and 1648. Divers meetings of Friends, in several places, were then gathered to God's teaching, by his light, Spirit, and power; for the Lord's power broke forth more and more wonderfully.

Now was I come up in Spirit through the flaming sword, into the paradise of God. All things were new; and all the creation gave another smell unto me than before, beyond what words can utter. I knew nothing but pureness, and innocency, and righteousness, being renewed into the image of God by Christ Jesus, to the state of Adam, which he was in before he fell. The creation was opened to me; and it was showed me how all things had their names given them, according to their nature and virtue. I was at a stand in my mind, whether I should practise physic for the good of mankind, seeing the nature and virtues of things were so opened to me by the Lord. But I was immediately taken up in Spirit, to see into another or more steadfast state than Adam's innocency, even into a state in Christ Jesus, that should never fall. And the Lord showed me that such as were faithful to him, in the power and light of Christ, should come up into that state in which Adam was before he fell; in which the admirable works of creation, and the virtues thereof, may be known, through the openings of that divine Word of wisdom and power, by which they were made. Great things did the Lord lead me into, and wonderful depths were opened unto me, beyond what can by words be declared; but as people come into subjection to the Spirit of God, and grow up in the image and power of the Almighty, they may receive the Word of Wisdom, that opens all things, and come to know the hidden unity in the Eternal Being.

Thus I travelled on in the Lord's service, as the Lord led me. And when I came to NOTTINGHAM, the mighty power of God was there among Friends. From thence I went to CLAWSON in Leicestershire, in the VALE of BEAVOR, and the mighty power of God was there also, in several towns and villages where Friends were gathered. While I was there, the Lord opened to me three things, relating to those three great professions in the world, physic, divinity (so called), and law. He showed me that the physicians were out of the wisdom of God, by which the creatures were made; and so knew not their virtues, because they were out of the Word of Wisdom; by which they were made. He showed me that the priests were out of the true faith, which Christ is the author of; the faith which purifies and gives victory, and brings people to have access to God, by which they please God; which mystery of faith is held in a pure conscience. He showed me also, that the lawyers were out of the equity, and out of the true justice, and out of the law of God, which went over the first transgression, and over all sin, and answered the Spirit of God, that was grieved and transgressed in man. And that these three, the physicians, the priests, and the lawyers, ruled the world out of the wisdom, out of the faith, and out of the equity and law of God; the one pretending the cure of the body, the other the cure of the soul, and the third the property of the people. But I saw they were all out of the wisdom, out of the faith, out of the equity and perfect law of God. And as the Lord opened these things unto me, I felt his power went forth over all, by which all might be reformed, if they would receive and bow unto it. The priests might be reformed, and brought into the true faith, which was the gift of God. The lawyers might be reformed, and brought into the law of God, which answers that of God, which is transgressed, in every one, and brings to love one's neighbour as himself. This lets man see, if he wrongs his neighbour he wrongs himself; and this teaches him to do unto others as he would they should do unto him. The physicians might be reformed, and brought into the wisdom of God, by which all things were made and created; that they might receive a right knowledge of them, and understand their virtues, which the Word of Wisdom, by which they were made and are upheld, hath given them. Abundance was opened concerning these things; how all lay out of the wisdom of God, and out of the righteousness and holiness that man at the first was made in. But as all believe in the light, and walk in the light, which Christ hath enlightened every man that cometh into the world withal, and so become children of the light, and of the day of Christ; in his day all things are seen, visible and invisible, by the divine light of Christ, the spiritual, heavenly man, by whom all things were made and created.

Then I saw concerning the priests, that although they stood in deceit, and acted by the dark power, which both they and their people were kept under; yet they were not the greatest deceivers spoken of in the Scriptures; for these were not come so far as many of them had come. But the Lord opened to me who the greatest deceivers were, and how far they might come; even such as came as far as Cain, to hear the voice of God; and such as came out of Egypt, and through the Red Sea, and to praise God on the banks of the sea-shore; such as could speak by experience of God's miracles and wonders; such as were come as far as Korah and Dathan, and their company; such as were come as far as Balaam, who could speak the word of the Lord, who heard his voice and knew it, and knew his Spirit, and could see the star of Jacob, and the goodliness of Israel's tent; the second birth, which no enchantment could prevail against: these that could speak so much of their experiences of God, and yet turned from the Spirit and the Word, and went into the gainsaying; these were,

and would be, the great deceivers, far beyond the priests. Likewise among
the Christians, such as should preach in Christ's name, and should work
miracles, cast out devils, and go as far as a Cain, a Korah, and a Balaam,
in the gospel times, these were and would be the great deceivers. They
that could speak some experiences of Christ and God, but lived not in the
life: these were they that led the world after them, who got the form of
godliness, but denied the power; who inwardly ravened from the Spirit,
and brought people into the form, but persecuted them that were in the
power, as Cain did; and ran greedily after the error of Balaam, through
covetousness, loving the wages of unrighteousness, as Balaam did. These
followers of Cain, Korah, and Balaam have brought the world, since the
apostles' days, to be like a sea. And such as these, I saw, might deceive
now, as they had in former ages: but it is impossible for them to deceive
the elect, who are chosen in Christ, who was before the world began, and
before the deceiver was; though others may be deceived in their openings
and prophecies, not keeping their minds to the Lord Jesus Christ, who doth
open and reveal to his.

I saw the state of those, both priests and people, who, in reading the
Scriptures, cry out much against Cain, Esau, and Judas, and other wicked
men of former times, mentioned in the Holy Scriptures; but do not see the
nature of Cain, of Esau, of Judas, and those others, in themselves. These
said, it was they, they, they, that were the bad people; putting it off from
themselves: but when some of these came, with the light and Spirit of
truth, to see into themselves, then they came to say, I, I, I, it is I myself,
that have been the Ishmael, and the Esau, &c. For then they came to
see the nature of wild Ishmael in themselves; the nature of Cain, of Esau,
of Korah, of Balaam, and of the son of perdition in themselves, sitting
above all that is called God in them. Thus I saw it was the fallen man
that was got up into the Scriptures, and was finding fault with those before mentioned; and, with the backsliding Jews, calling them the sturdy oaks,
and tall cedars, and fat bulls of Bashan, wild heifers, vipers, serpents, &c.;
and charging them that it was they that closed their eyes, and stopped their
ears, and hardened their hearts, and were dull of hearing: that it was they
that hated the light, and rebelled against it; that quenched the Spirit,
and vexed, and grieved it; that walked despitefully against the Spirit of grace,
and turned the grace of God into wantonness: and that it was they that
resisted the Holy Ghost, that got the form of godliness, and turned against
the power: and they were the inwardly ravening wolves, that had got the
sheep's clothing; they were the wells without water, and clouds without
rain, and trees without fruit, &c. But when these, who were so much
taken up with finding fault with others, and thought themselves clear from
these things, came to look into themselves, and, with the light of Christ,
thoroughly to search themselves, they might see enough of this in themselves; and then the cry could not be, it is he, or they, as before; but I,
and we are found in these conditions.

I saw also, how people read the Scriptures without a right sense of
them, and without duly applying them to their own states. For, when they
read that death reigned from Adam to Moses; that the law and the pro-

phets were until John; and that the least in the kingdom is greater than John; they read these things and applied them to others, but they did not turn in to find the truth of these things in themselves. As these things came to be opened in me, I saw death reigned over them from Adam to Moses; from the entrance into transgression, till they came to the ministration of condemnation, which restrains people from sin, that brings death. Then, when the ministration of Moses is passed through, the ministry of the prophets comes to be read and understood, which reaches through the figures, types, and shadows unto John, the greatest prophet born of a woman; whose ministration prepares the way of the Lord, by bringing down the exalted mountains, and making straight paths. And as this ministration is passed through, an entrance comes to be known into the everlasting kingdom. Thus I saw plainly that none could read Moses aright, without Moses' spirit, by which Moses saw how man was in the image of God in Paradise, and how he fell, how death came over him, and how all men have been under this death. I saw how Moses received the pure law, that went over all transgressors; and how the clean beasts, which were figures and types, were offered up, when the people were come into the righteous law that went over the first transgression. Both Moses and the prophets saw through the types and figures, and beyond them, and saw Christ, the great prophet, that was to come to fulfil them. I saw that none could read John's words aright, and with a true understanding of them, but in and with the same divine Spirit by which John spoke them; and by his burning, shining light, which is sent from God.* For by that Spirit their crooked natures might be made straight, and their rough natures smooth, and the exacter and violent doer in them might be cast out; and they that had been hypocrites might come to bring forth fruits meet for repentance, and their mountain of sin and earthliness might be laid low, and their valley exalted in them, that there might be a way prepared for the Lord in them: then the least in the kingdom is greater than John. But all must first know the voice crying in their wilderness, in their hearts, which, through transgression, were become as a wilderness. Thus I saw it was an easy matter to say death reigned from Adam to Moses; and that the law and the prophets were until John; and that the least in the kingdom is greater than John; but none could know *how* death reigned from Adam to Moses, &c., but by the same Holy Spirit that Moses, the prophets, and John were in. They could not know the spiritual meaning of Moses', the prophets', and John's words, nor see their path and travels, much less see through them, and to the end of them into the kingdom, unless they had the Spirit and light of Jesus; nor could they know the words of Christ and of his apostles, without his Spirit. But as man comes through, by the Spirit and power of God, to Christ, who fulfils the types, figures, shadows, promises, and prophecies that were of him, and is led by the Holy Ghost into the truth and substance of the Scriptures, sitting down in him who is the author and end of them; then are they read, and understood, with profit and great delight.

* Archbishop Secker says, "Before any one can peruse the sacred Scriptures to profit, the Lamb must open the seven seals."

Moreover, when I was brought up into his image in righteousness and holiness, and into the paradise of God, He let me see how Adam was made a living soul: and also the stature of Christ, the mystery that had been hid from ages and generations; which things are hard to be uttered, and cannot be borne by many. For, of all the sects in Christendom (so called) that I discoursed withal, I found none that could bear to be told that any should come to Adam's perfection, into that image of God, that righteousness and holiness that Adam was in before he fell; to be clear and pure without sin, as he was. Therefore, how should they be able to bear being told that any should grow up to the measure of the stature of the fulness of Christ, when they cannot bear to hear that any should come, whilst upon earth, into the same power and Spirit that the prophets and apostles were in? Though it is a certain truth, that none can understand their writings aright, without the same Spirit by which they were written.

Now the Lord God opened to me by his invisible power, "that every man was enlightened by the divine light of Christ;" and I saw it shine through all; and that they that believed in it came out of condemnation to the light of life, and became the children of it; but they that hated it, and did not believe in it, were condemned by it, though they made a profession of Christ. This I saw in the pure openings of the light, without the help of any man; neither did I then know where to find it in the Scriptures, though afterwards, searching the Scriptures, I found it. For I saw in that Light and Spirit which was before the Scriptures were given forth, and which led the holy men of God to give them forth, that all must come to that Spirit, if they would know God, or Christ, or the Scriptures aright, which they that gave them forth were led and taught by.

But I observed a dulness and drowsy heaviness upon people, which I wondered at: for sometimes, when I would set myself to sleep, my mind went over all to the beginning, in that which is from everlasting to everlasting. I saw death was to pass over this sleepy, heavy state; and I told people they must come to witness death to that sleepy, heavy nature, and a cross to it in the power of God, that their minds and hearts might be on things above.

On a certain time, as I was walking in the fields, the Lord said unto me: "Thy name is written in the Lamb's book of life, which was before the foundation of the world;" and, as the Lord spoke it, I believed, and saw it in the new birth. Then, some time after, the Lord commanded me to go abroad into the world, which was like a briery, thorny wilderness; and when I came, in the Lord's mighty power, with the word of life into the world, the world swelled, and made a noise, like the great raging waves of the sea. Priests and professors, magistrates and people, were all like a sea, when I came to proclaim the day of the Lord amongst them, and to preach repentance to them.

I was sent to turn people from darkness to the light, that they might receive Christ Jesus: for, to as many as should receive him in his light, I saw that he would give power to become the sons of God; which I had obtained by receiving Christ. I was to direct people to the Spirit, that gave forth the Scriptures, by which they might be led into all truth, and so up to Christ and God, as they had been who gave them forth. I was to turn them to the grace of God, and to the truth in the heart, which came by Jesus; that by this grace they might be taught, which would bring them salvation, that their hearts might be established by it, and their words might be seasoned, and all might come to know their salvation nigh. I saw that Christ died for all men, and was a propitiation for all; and enlightened all men and women with his divine and saving light; and that none could be a true believer, but who believed in it. I saw that the grace of God, which bringeth salvation, had appeared to all men, and that the manifestation of the Spirit of God was given to every man, to profit withal. These things I did not see by the help of man, nor by the letter, though they are written in the letter, but I saw them in the light of the Lord Jesus Christ, and by his immediate Spirit and power, as did the holy men of God, by whom the Holy Scriptures were written. Yet I had no slight esteem of the Holy Scriptures, but they were very precious to me, for I was in that Spirit by which they were given forth : and what the Lord opened in me, I afterwards found was agreeable to them. I could speak much of these things, and many volumes might be written, but all would prove too short to set forth the infinite love, wisdom, and power of God, in preparing, fitting, and furnishing me for the service he had appointed me to; letting me see the depths of Satan on the one hand, and opening to me, on the other hand, the divine mysteries of his own everlasting kingdom.

Now, when the Lord God and his Son Jesus Christ sent me forth into the world, to preach his everlasting gospel and kingdom, I was glad that I was commanded to turn people to that inward light, Spirit, and grace, by which all might know their salvation, and their way to God; even that Divine Spirit which would lead them into all truth, and which I infallibly knew would never deceive any.

But with and by this divine power and Spirit of God, and the light of Jesus, I was to bring people off from all their own ways, to Christ, the new and living way; and from their churches, which men had made and gathered, to the church in God, the general assembly written in heaven, which Christ is the head of : and off from the world's teachers, made by men, to learn of Christ, who is the way, the truth, and the life, of whom the Father said, "This is my beloved Son, hear ye Him;" and off from all the world's worships, to know the Spirit of Truth in the inward parts, and to be led thereby; that in it they might worship the Father of spirits, who seeks such to worship him; which Spirit they that worshipped not in, knew not what they worshipped. And I was to bring people off from all the world's religions, which are vain; that they might know the pure religion, might visit the fatherless, the widows, and the strangers, and keep themselves from the spots of the world; then there would not be so many beggars, the sight of whom often grieved my heart, as it denoted so much hard-heartedness amongst them that professed the name of Christ. I was to bring them off from all the world's fellowships, and prayings, and singings, which stood in forms without power; that their fellowship might be in the Holy Ghost, and in the Eternal Spirit of God; that they might pray in the Holy Ghost, and sing in the Spirit, and with the grace that comes by Jesus; making melody in their hearts to the Lord, who hath sent his beloved Son to be their Saviour, and caused his heavenly sun to shine upon all the world, and through them all, and his heavenly rain to fall upon the just and the unjust (as his outward rain doth fall, and his outward sun doth shine on all), which is God's unspeakable love to the world.   I was to bring people off from Jewish ceremonies, and from heathenish fables, and from men's inventions and worldly doctrines, by which they blew the people about this way and the other way, from sect to sect; and from all their beggarly rudiments, with their schools and colleges for making ministers of Christ, who are indeed ministers of their own making, but not of Christ's; and from all their images and crosses, and sprinkling of infants, with all their holy-days (so called) and all their vain traditions, which they had instituted since the apostles' days, which the Lord's power was against : in the dread and authority of which, I was moved to declare against them all, and against all that preached and not freely, as being such as had not received freely from Christ.

Moreover, when the Lord sent me forth into the world, he forbade me to "put off my hat" to any, high or low; and I was required to Thee and Thou all men and women, without any respect to rich or poor, great or small.   And as I travelled up and down, I was not to bid people Good morrow, or Good evening; neither might I bow or scrape with my leg to any one; and this made the sects and professions to rage.   But the Lord's power carried me over all to his glory, and many came to be turned to God in a little time; for the heavenly day of the Lord sprung from on high, and broke forth apace, by the light of which many came to see where they were.

But O! the rage that then was in the priests, magistrates, professors, and people of all sorts; but especially in priests and professors! for, though Thou, to a single person, was according to their own learning, their accidence, and grammar rules, and according to the Bible, yet they could not bear to hear it : and as to the hat-honour, because I could not put off my hat to them, it set them all into a rage.   But the Lord showed me that it was an honour below, which he would lay in the dust, and stain;—an honour which proud flesh looked for, but sought not the honour which came from God only;—an honour invented by men in the fall, and in the alienation from God, who were offended if it were not given them; and yet they would be looked upon as saints, church-members, and great Christians : but Christ saith, "How can ye believe, who receive honour one of another, and seek not the honour that cometh from God only?"   "And I (saith Christ) receive not honour of men :" showing that men have an honour, which men will receive and give; but Christ will have none of it.   This is the honour which Christ will not receive, and which must be laid in the dust.   O! the rage and scorn, the heat and fury that arose!   O! the blows, punchings, beatings, and imprisonments that we underwent, for not putting off our hats to men! for that soon tried all men's patience and sobriety what it was.   Some had their hats violently plucked off and thrown away, so that they quite lost them.   The bad language and evil usage we received on this account are hard to be expressed, besides the danger we were sometimes in, of losing our lives for this matter, and that by the great professors of Christianity, who thereby evinced that they were not true believers. And though it was but a small thing in the eye of man, yet a wonderful confusion it brought among all professors and priests : but, blessed be the Lord, many came to see the vanity of that custom of putting off the hat to men, and felt the weight of Truth's testimony against it.

About this time I was sorely exercised in going to their courts to cry for justice, and in speaking and writing to judges and justices to do justly ; in warning such as kept public-houses for entertainment, that they should not let people have more drink than would do them good ; and in testifying against their wakes or feasts, may-games, sports, plays, and shows, which trained up people to vanity and looseness, and led them from the fear of God ; and the days they had set forth for holy-days were usually the times wherein they most dishonoured God by these things.* In fairs, also, and in markets, I was made to declare against their deceitful merchandise, cheating, and cozening ; warning all to deal justly, to speak the truth, to let their yea be yea, and their nay be nay ; and to do unto others as they would have others do unto them ; forewarning them of the great and terrible day of the Lord, which would come upon them all. I was moved also to cry against all sorts of music, and against the mountebanks playing tricks on their stages, for they burthened the pure life, and stirred up people's minds to vanity. I was much exercised, too, with schoolmasters and school-mistresses, warning them to teach their children sobriety in the fear of the Lord, that they might not be nursed and trained up in lightness, vanity, and wantonness. Likewise I was made to warn masters and mistresses, fathers and mothers in private families, to take care that their children and servants might be trained up in the fear of the Lord ; and that they themselves should be therein examples and patterns of sobriety and virtue to them. For I saw that as the Jews were to teach their children the law of God and the old covenant, and to train them up in it, and their servants, yea, the very strangers were to keep the Sabbath amongst them, and be circumcised, before they eat of their sacrifices ; so

---

* By a royal proclamation of James I., issued in 1618 (for Lancashire), these pastimes were made lawful recreations for the First-day of the week, provided they did not interfere with the times appointed for worship. Many of the clergy at first refused to promulgate the proclamation, though by so doing they acted contrary to their canonical obedience, and laid themselves open to penalties. In the seventh year of Charles I., this proclamation, at the instigation of Archbishop Laud, was revived, and extended to the whole nation, and was enjoined to be published and advocated from the pulpit by all ministers, to their disgrace. By the revival of this offensive proclamation, these disorderly revels had arrived to such a height of licentious depravity, that some well-disposed justices, in the county of Somerset, petitioned the judges on the western circuit, Sir Thomas Richardson, Lord Chief Justice, and Baron Denham, to suppress them. For so doing, they were summoned before the King and Council, by Archbishop Laud, for illegally interfering with the ecclesiastical jurisdiction, and the council rescinded the prohibitions, and cashiered the judges.— (See Fuller's *Church Hist.* Book x. p. 74 ; and Book xi. p. 147.)

all Christians, and all that made a profession of Christianity, ought to train up their children and servants in the new covenant of light, Christ Jesus, who is God's salvation to the ends of the earth, that all may know their salvation : and they ought to train them up in the law of life, the law of the Spirit, the law of love and of faith ; that they might be made free from the law of sin and death. And all Christians ought to be circumcised by the Spirit, which puts off the body of the sins of the flesh, that they may come to eat of the heavenly sacrifice, Christ Jesus, that true spiritual food, which none can rightly feed upon but they that are circumcised by the Spirit. Likewise, I was exercised about the star-gazers, who drew people's minds from Christ, the bright and the morning-star ; and from the Sun of righteousness, by whom the sun, and moon, and stars, and all things else were made, who is the wisdom of God, and from whom the right knowledge of all things is received.

But the earthly spirit of the priests wounded my life ; and when I heard the bell toll to call people together to the steeple-house, it struck at my life ; for it was just like a market-bell, to gather people together, that the priest might set forth his ware to sale. O ! the vast sums of money that are gotten by the trade they make of selling the Scriptures, and by their preaching, from the highest bishop to the lowest priest ! What one trade else in the world is comparable to it ? notwithstanding the Scriptures were given forth freely, and Christ commanded his ministers to preach freely, and the prophets and apostles denounced judgment against all covetous hirelings and diviners for money. But in this free Spirit of the Lord Jesus was I sent forth to declare the Word of life and reconciliation freely, that all might come to Christ, who gives freely, and who renews up into the image of God, which man and woman were in before they fell, that they might sit down in heavenly places in Christ Jesus.

CHAPTER III.

1649–1650.—George Fox is first imprisoned at Nottingham, where the sheriff is convinced—he is liberated and quiets a distracted woman—many miracles were wrought in those days, beyond what that unbelieving age would receive or bear—he is cruelly treated at Mansfield-Woodhouse—is taken before the magistrates at Derby—acknowledges that he is sanctified—is temptingly asked if he were Christ, which he denies, yet is committed for blasphemy—his mittimus to Derby prison—writes to the priests of Derby against preaching for hire, &c.—also against persecution—to Barton and Bennet, justices, on the same subject—to Justice Bennet against covetousness—to Justice Barton, a preacher and a persecutor—to the mayor of Derby against persecution and oppression—to the court of Derby against oaths and oppression—to the bell-ringers of Derby against vanities and worldly pleasures—his jailer is convinced—Justice Bennet first gives Friends the name of Quakers in derision—writes to Friends and others, to open their understandings, and to direct them to their true Teacher within themselves—to the convinced people, directing them to internal silence and to true obedience—an encouragement to the faithful—to the justices of Derby against persecution, thrice repeated—to the priests of Derby, on the same subject—to the justices of Derby, to prize their time, and to depart from evil—the like to Colonel Barton, justice, and warning of the plagues and vengeance hanging over the oppressor.

Now as I went towards NOTTINGHAM on a First-day in the morning, with Friends to a meeting there, when I came on the top of a hill in sight of the town, I espied the great steeple-house; and the Lord said unto me, "thou must go cry against yonder great idol, and against the worshippers therein." I said nothing of this to the Friends that were with me, but went on with them to the meeting, where the mighty power of the Lord was amongst us; in which I left Friends sitting in the meeting, and I went away to the steeple-house. When I came there, all the people looked like fallow-ground, and the priest (like a great lump of earth) stood in his pulpit above. He took for his text these words of Peter, "We have also a more sure Word of prophecy, whereunto ye do well that ye take heed, as unto a light that shineth in a dark place, until the day dawn, and the day-star arise in your hearts." And he told the people that this was the Scriptures, by which they were to try all doctrines, religions, and opinions. Now the Lord's power was so mighty upon me, and so strong in me, that I could not hold, but was made to cry out and say, "O no, it is not the Scriptures;" and I told them what it was, namely, the Holy Spirit, by which the holy men of God gave forth the Scriptures, whereby opinions, religions, and judgments were to be tried; for it led into all truth, and so gave the knowledge of all truth. The Jews had the Scriptures, and yet resisted the Holy Ghost, and rejected Christ, the bright morning-star. They persecuted Christ and his apostles, and took upon them to try their doctrines by the Scriptures, but erred in judgment, and did not try them aright, because they tried without the Holy Ghost. As I spoke thus amongst them, the officers came and took me away, and put me into a nasty, stinking prison; the smell whereof got so into my nose and throat, that it very much annoyed me.

But that day the Lord's power sounded so in their ears, that they were amazed at the voice; and could not get it out of their ears for some time after, they were so reached by the Lord's power in the steeple-house. At night they took me before the mayor, aldermen, and sheriffs of the town; and when I was brought before them, the mayor was in a peevish, fretful temper, but the Lord's power allayed him. They examined me at large; and I told them how the Lord had moved me to come. After some discourse between them and me, they sent me back to prison again; but some time after the head sheriff, whose name was John Reckless, sent for me to his house. When I came in, his wife met me in the hall, and said, "Salvation is come to our house." She took me by the hand, and was much wrought upon by the power of the Lord God; and her husband, and children, and servants were much changed, for the power of the Lord wrought upon them. I lodged at the sheriff's, and great meetings we had in his house. Some persons of considerable condition in the world came to them, and the Lord's power appeared eminently amongst them. This sheriff sent for the other sheriff, and for a woman they had had dealings with in the way of trade; and he told her before the other sheriff, that they had wronged her in their dealings with her (for the other sheriff and he were partners), and that they ought to make her restitution. This he spoke cheerfully; but the other sheriff denied it; and the woman said she knew nothing of it. But the friendly sheriff said it was so, and that the other knew it well enough; and having discovered the matter, and acknowledged the wrong done by them, he made restitution to the woman, and exhorted the other sheriff to do the like. The Lord's power was with this friendly sheriff, and wrought a mighty change in him, and great openings he had. The next market-day, as he was walking with me in the chamber, in his slippers, he said, "I must go into the market, and preach repentance to the people;" and accordingly he went into the market, and into several streets, and preached repentance to the people. Several others also in the town were moved to speak to the mayor and magistrates, and to the people, exhorting them to repent. Hereupon the magistrates grew very angry, and sent for me from the sheriff's house, and committed me to the common prison. When the assize came on, there was one moved to come and offer up himself for me, body for body; yea, life also: but when I should have been brought before the judge, the sheriff's man being somewhat long in fetching me to the sessions-house, the judge was risen before I came. At which I understood the judge was somewhat offended, and said, "he would have admonished the youth, if he had been brought before him;" for I was then imprisoned by the name of A YOUTH. So I was returned to prison again, and put into the common jail. The Lord's power was great among Friends; but the people began to be very rude; wherefore the governor of the castle sent down soldiers, and dispersed them; and after that they were quiet. But both priests and people were astonished at the wonderful power that broke forth; and several of the priests were made tender, and some did confess to the power of the Lord.

Now, after I was released from Nottingham jail, where I had been kept prisoner some time, I travelled as before, in the work of the Lord. Coming to MANSFIELD-WOODHOUSE, there was a distracted woman under a doctor's hand, with her hair loose all about her ears. He was about to bleed her, she being first bound, and many people being about her, holding her by violence; but he could get no blood from her. I desired them to unbind her, and let her alone, for they could not touch the spirit in her, by which she was tormented. So they unbound her; and I was moved to speak to her, and in the name of the Lord to bid her be quiet and still; and she was so. The Lord's power settled her mind, and she mended; and afterwards she received the truth, and continued in it to her death. The Lord's name was honoured; to whom the glory of all his works belongs. Many great and wonderful things were wrought by the heavenly power in those days; for the Lord made bare his omnipotent arm, and manifested his power to the astonishment of many, by the healing virtue whereof many have been delivered from great infirmities, and the devils were made subject through his name; of which particular instances might be given, beyond what this unbelieving age is able to receive or bear. But blessed for ever be the name of the Lord, and everlastingly honoured, and over all exalted and magnified be the arm of his glorious power, by which he hath wrought gloriously; let the honour and praise of all his works be ascribed to him alone.

Now while I was at Mansfield-Woodhouse, I was moved to go to the steeple-house there, and declare the truth to the priest and people; but the people fell upon me in great rage, struck me down, and almost stifled and smothered me; and I was cruelly beaten and bruised by them with their hands, Bibles, and sticks. Then they haled me out, though I was hardly able to stand, and put me into the stocks, where I sat some hours; and they brought dog-whips and horse-whips, threatening to whip me. After some time they had me before the magistrate, at a knight's house, where were many great persons; who, seeing how evilly I had been used, after much threatening, set me at liberty. But the rude people stoned me out of the town, for preaching the word of life to them. I was scarcely able to move or stand, by reason of the ill usage I had received; yet with considerable effort I got about a mile from the town, and then I met with some people who gave me something to comfort me, because I was inwardly bruised; but the Lord's power soon healed me again. That day some people were convinced of the Lord's truth, and turned to his teaching, at which I rejoiced.

Then I went into LEICESTERSHIRE, several Friends accompanying me. There were some Baptists in that country whom I desired to see and speak with, because they were separated from the public worship. So one Oates, who was one of their chief teachers, and others of the heads of them, with several others of their company, came to meet us at BARROW; and there we discoursed with them. One of them said, "What was not of faith was sin." Whereupon I asked them, What faith was? and how it was wrought in man? But they turned off from that, and spoke of their baptism in water. Then I asked them, Whether their mountain of sin was brought down and laid low in them? and their rough and crooked ways made smooth and straight in them? for they looked upon the Scriptures as meaning outward mountains and ways. But I told them they must find them in their own hearts; which they seemed to wonder at. We asked them who baptized John the Baptist? and who baptized Peter, John, and the rest of the apostles? and put them to prove by Scripture that these were baptized in water; but they were silent. Then I asked them, "Seeing Judas, who betrayed Christ, and was called the Son of Perdition, had hanged himself, what Son of Perdition was that which Paul spoke of, that sat in the temple of God, exalted above all that is called God? and what temple of God that was in which this Son of Perdition sat? and whether he, that betrays Christ within in himself, be not one in nature with that Judas, that betrayed Christ without?" But they could not tell what to make of this, nor what to say to it. So after some discourse we parted; and some of them were loving to us.

On the First-day following we came to BAGWORTH, and went to a steeple-house, where some Friends were got in; and the people locked them in, and themselves too, with the priest. But after the priest had done, they opened the door, and we went in also, and had a service for the Lord amongst them. Afterwards we had a meeting in the town, amongst several people that were in high notions. Passing from thence, I heard of a people in prison in COVENTRY for religion. And as I walked towards the jail, the word of the Lord came to me saying, "MY LOVE WAS ALWAYS TO THEE, AND THOU ART IN MY LOVE." And I was ravished with the sense of the love of God, and greatly strengthened in my inward man. But when I came into the jail, where the prisoners were, a great power of darkness struck at me, and I sat still, having my spirit gathered into the love of God. At last these prisoners began to rant, and vapour, and blaspheme, at which my soul was greatly grieved. They said they were God; but we could not bear such things. When they were calm, I stood up and asked them, whether they did such things by motion, or from Scripture; and they said, from Scripture. A Bible being at hand, I asked them to point out that Scripture; and they showed me the place where the sheet was let down to Peter, and it was said to him, what was sanctified he should not call common or unclean. When I had showed them that that Scripture proved nothing for their purpose, they brought another, which spoke of God's reconciling all things to himself, things in heaven, and things in earth. I told them I owned that Scripture also, but showed them that that was nothing to their purpose either. Then seeing they said they were God, I asked them, if they knew whether it would rain to-morrow? they said they could not tell. I told them, God could tell. Again, I asked them if they thought they should be always in that condition, or should change? and they answered they could not tell. Then said I unto them, God can tell, and God doth not change. You say you are God; and yet you cannot tell whether you shall change or not. So they were confounded, and quite brought down for the time. After I had reproved them for their blasphemous expressions, I went away; for I perceived they were Ranters. I had met with none before; and I admired the goodness of the Lord in appearing so unto me before I went amongst them. Not long after this, one of these Ranters, whose name was Joseph Salmon, put forth a paper, or book of recantation; upon which they were set at liberty.

From Coventry I went to ATHERSTONE; and it being their lecture-day, I was moved to go to their chapel to speak to the priests and people. They were generally pretty quiet; only some few raged, and would have had my relations to have me bound. I declared largely to them, how that God was come to teach his people himself, and to bring them off from all their man-made teachers to hear his Son. Some were convinced there.

Then I went to MARKET-BOSWORTH, and there was a lecture there also. He that preached that day was Nathaniel Stevens, who was priest of the town where I was born. He raged much when I spoke to him and to the people, and told them I was mad. He had said before, to one Colonel Purfoy, that there was never such a plant bred in England; and he bid the people not to hear me. So the people, being stirred up by this deceitful priest, fell upon us, and stoned us out of the town; yet they did not do us much hurt. Howbeit, some people were made loving that day, and others were confirmed, seeing the rage of both priests and professors; and some cried out, that the priest durst not stand to prove his ministry.

As I travelled through markets, fairs, and divers places, I saw death and darkness in all people, where the power of the Lord God had not shaken them. As I was passing on in Leicestershire, I came to TWY-CROSS, where there were excise-men. I was moved of the Lord to go to them, and warn them to take heed of oppressing the poor; and people were much affected with it. There was in that town a great man, that had long lain sick, and was given up by the physicians; and some Friends in the town desired me to go to see him. I went up to him in his chamber, and spoke the word of life to him, and was moved to pray by him; and the Lord was entreated, and restored him to health. But when I was come down stairs, into a lower room, and was speaking to the servants, and to some people that were there, a serving-man of his came raving out of another room, with a naked rapier in his hand, and set it just to my side. I looked steadfastly on him, and said, "Alack for thee, poor creature! what wilt thou do with thy carnal weapon: it is no more to me than a straw." The standers-by were much troubled, and he went away in a rage, and full of wrath. But when the news of it came to his master, he turned him out of his service. Thus the Lord's power preserved me, and raised up the weak man, who afterwards was very loving to Friends; and when I came to that town again, both he and his wife came to see me.

After this I was moved to go into Derbyshire, where the mighty power of God was among Friends. And I went to CHESTERFIELD, where one Britland was priest. He saw beyond the common sort of priests, for he had been partly convinced, and had spoken much on behalf of Truth, before he was priest there; but when the priest of that town died, he got the parsonage, and choked himself with it. I was moved to speak to him and the people in the great love of God, that they might come off from all men's teaching unto God's teaching; and he was not able to gainsay. But they had me before the Mayor, and threatened to send me, with some others, to the House of Correction; and kept us in custody till it was late in the night. Then the officers, with the watchmen, put us out of the town, leaving us to shift as we could. So I bent my course towards Derby, having a friend or two with me. In our way we met with many professors; and at KIDSEY-PARK many were convinced.

Then coming to DERBY, I lay at a doctor's house, whose wife was convinced; and so were several more in the town. As I was walking in my chamber, the [steeple-house] bell rung, and it struck at my life at the very hearing of it; so I asked the woman of the house what the bell rung for? She said there was to be a great lecture there that day, and many of the officers of the army, and priests, and preachers were to be there, and a colonel, that was a preacher. Then was I moved of the Lord to go up to them; and when they had done I spoke to them what the Lord commanded me, and they were pretty quiet. But there came an officer and took me by the hand, and said I must go before the magistrates, and the other two that were with me. It was about the first hour after noon that we came before them. They asked me, Why we came thither; I said, God moved us so to do; and I told them, "God dwells not in temples made with hands." I told them also, All their preaching, baptism, and sacrifices, would never sanctify them; and bid them look unto Christ in them, and not unto men; for it is Christ that sanctifies. Then they ran into many words; but I told them they were not to dispute of God and Christ, but to obey him. The power of God thundered amongst them, and they flew like chaff before it. They put me in and out of the room often, hurrying me backward and forward; for they were from the first hour till the ninth at night in examining me. Sometimes they would tell me, in a deriding manner, that I was taken up in raptures. At last they asked me, Whether I was sanctified? I answered, Yes; for I was in the paradise of God. Then they asked me, If I had no sin? I answered, "Christ, my Saviour, has taken away my sin, and in him there is no sin." They asked, How we knew that Christ did abide in us? I said, By his Spirit, that he has given us. They temptingly asked, If any of us were Christ? I answered, Nay, we were nothing, Christ is all. They said, If a man steal, is it no sin? I answered, All unrighteousness is sin. So when they had wearied themselves in examining me, they committed me and one other man to the House of Correction in Derby for six months, as blasphemers; as appears by the following mittimus :—

"*To the Master of the House of Correction in Derby, greeting.*

"WE have sent you herewithal the bodies of George Fox, late of Mansfield, in the county of Nottingham, and John Fretwell, late of Staniesby, in the county of Derby, husbandman, brought before us this present day, and charged with the avowed uttering and broaching of divers blasphemous opinions contrary to a late act of Parliament, which, upon their examination before us, they have confessed. These are therefore to require you forthwith, upon sight hereof, to receive them, the said George Fox and

John Fretwell, into your custody, and them therein safely to keep during the space of six months, without bail or mainprize, or until they shall find sufficient security to be of good behaviour, or be thence delivered by order from ourselves. Hereof you are not to fail. Given under our hands and seals this 30th day of October, 1650.　　Ger. Bennet,
Nath. Barton."

Now did the priests bestir themselves in their pulpits to preach up sin for term of life; and much of their work was to plead for it; so that people said, never was the like heard. After some time, he that was committed with me, not standing faithful in his testimony, got in with the jailer, and by him made way to the justice to have leave to go to see his mother; and so got his liberty. It was then reported, that he said I had bewitched and deceived him; but my spirit was strengthened when he was gone. The priests and professors, the justices and the jailer, were all in a great rage against me. The jailer watched my words and actions, and would often ask me questions to ensnare me; and sometimes asked me such silly questions as, Whether the door was latched, or not? thinking to draw some sudden, unadvised answer from me, whence he might take advantage to charge sin upon me; but I was kept watchful and chaste, so that they could get no advantage of me, which they wondered at.

Not long after my commitment, I was moved to write both to the priests and magistrates of Derby. And first to the priests.

"O friends, I was sent unto you to tell you, that if you had received the gospel freely, you would minister it freely without money or price: but you make a trade and sale of what the prophets and the apostles have spoken; and so you corrupt the truth. And you are the men that lead silly women captive, who are ever learning, and never able to come to the knowledge of the truth; you have a form of godliness, but you deny the power. Now as Jannes and Jambres withstood Moses, so do you resist the truth, being men of corrupt minds, reprobate concerning the faith. But you shall proceed no further; for your folly shall be made manifest to all men as theirs was. Moreover, the Lord sent me to tell you, that he doth look for fruits. You asked me, If Scripture was my rule? but it is not your rule, to rule your lives by, but to talk of in words. You are the men that live in pleasures, pride, and wantonness, in fulness of bread, and abundance of idleness: see if this be not the sin of Sodom. Lot received the angels, but Sodom was envious. You show forth the vain nature; you stand in the steps of them that crucified my Saviour, and mocked him; you are their children; you show forth their fruit. They had the chief place in the assemblies, and so have you; they loved to be called Rabbi, and so do you."　　G. F.

I wrote to the magistrates who committed me to this effect:—
"Friends,
"I am forced, in tender love unto your souls, to write unto you, and to beseech you to consider what you do, and what the commands of God

call for. He requires justice and mercy, to break every yoke, and to let the oppressed go free. But who calleth for justice, or loveth mercy, or contendeth for the truth? Is not judgment turned backward, and doth not justice stand afar off? Is not truth silenced in the streets, or can equity enter? And do not they that depart from evil make themselves a prey? Oh! consider what ye do in time, and take heed whom ye imprison; for the magistrate is set for the punishment of evil-doers, and for the praise of them that do well. Now, I entreat you, in time take heed what you do; for surely the Lord will come, and will make manifest both the builders and the work. If it be of man, it will fail; but if it be of God, nothing will overthrow it. Therefore I desire and pray, that you would take heed, and beware what you do, lest ye be found fighters against God."   G. F.

Now, after I had thus far cleared my conscience to them, I waited in holy patience, leaving the event to God, in whose will I stood. After some time I was moved to write again to the justices that had committed me, to lay their evils before them, that they might repent. One of them, Nathaniel Barton, was a colonel, a justice, and a preacher.

"FRIENDS,

"You spoke of the good old way which the prophet spoke of; but the prophet cried against the abominations which you hold up. Had you the power of God, ye would not persecute the good way. He that spoke of the good way was set in the stocks. The people cried, 'Away with him to the stocks,' for speaking the truth. Ah! foolish people, who have eyes and see not, ears and hear not, without understanding! 'Fear ye not me,' saith the Lord, 'and will ye not tremble at my presence?' O your pride and abominations are odious in the eyes of God! You that are preachers have the chief place in the assemblies, and are called of men, Master. Such were and are against my Saviour and Maker: they shut up the kingdom of heaven from men, and neither go in themselves, nor suffer others. Therefore ye shall receive the greater damnation, who have their places, and walk in their steps. You may say, if you had been in the days of the prophets, or Christ, you would not have persecuted them; wherefore be ye witnesses against yourselves, that ye are the children of them, seeing ye now persecute the way of truth. O consider, there is a true judge, that will give every one of you a reward according to your works. O mind where you are, you that hold up the abominations which the true prophet cried against! O come down, and sit in the dust! The Lord is coming with power, and he will throw down every one that is lifted up, that he alone may be exalted."

As I had thus written unto them jointly, so, after some time, I wrote to each of them by himself. To Justice Bennet thus:—

"FRIEND,

"Thou that dost profess God and Christ in words, see how thou followest him. To take off burthens, to visit them that are in prison, to show mercy, clothe thy own flesh, and deal thy bread to the hungry; these are God's commandments. To relieve the fatherless, and to visit the widows in their afflictions, and to keep thyself unspotted of the world; this is pure religion before God. But if thou dost profess Christ, and follow covetousness, and greediness, and earthly-mindedness, thou deniest him in life, and deceivest thyself and others, and takest him for a cloak. Woe be to you, greedy and rich men; weep and howl, for your misery that shall come. Take heed of covetousness and extortion; God doth forbid that. Woe be to the man that coveteth an evil covetousness, that he may set his nest on high, and cover himself with thick clay. O! do not love that which God forbids. His servant thou art, whom thou dost obey, whether it be of sin unto death, or of obedience unto righteousness. Think of Lazarus and Dives; the one fared sumptuously every day, the other was a beggar. See if thou be not Dives: be not deceived, God is not mocked with vain words; evil communication corrupteth good manners; awake to righteousness, and sin not." G. F.

That to Justice Barton was in these words :—
"FRIEND,
"Thou that preachest Christ, and the Scriptures in words, when any come to follow that which thou hast spoken of, and to live the life of the Scriptures, then they that speak the Scriptures, but do not lead their lives according thereunto, persecute them that do. Mind the prophets, and Jesus Christ, and his apostles, and all the holy men of God; what they spoke was from the life; but they that had not the life, but the words, persecuted and imprisoned them that lived in the life, which those had backslidden from." G. F.

Having written to the justices and to the priests, it was upon me to write to the Mayor of Derby also; who, though he did not sign the mittimus, had a hand with the rest in sending me to prison. To him I wrote after this manner :—
"FRIEND,
"Thou art set in place to do justice; but, in imprisoning my body, thou hast done contrary to justice, according to your own law. O take heed of pleasing men more than God, for that is the way of the Scribes and Pharisees; they sought the praise of men more than God. Remember who said, 'I was a stranger, and ye took me not in; I was in prison, and ye visited me not.' O friend, thy envy is not against me, but against the power of truth. I had no envy to you, but love. O take heed of oppression, 'for the day of the Lord is coming, that shall burn as an oven; and all the proud, and all that do wickedly, shall be as stubble; and the day that cometh, shall burn them up, saith the Lord of Hosts; it shall leave them neither root nor branch.' O friend, if the love of God were in thee, thou wouldst love the truth, hear the truth spoken, and not imprison unjustly. The love of God beareth, and suffereth, and envieth no man. If the love of God had broken your hearts, you would show mercy; but you show forth what ruleth you. Every tree doth show forth its fruit; you do show forth your fruits openly. For drunkenness, swearing, pride, and

vanity, rule among you, from the teacher to the people. O friend, mercy, and true judgment, and justice, are cried for in your streets! Oppression, unmercifulness, cruelty, hatred, pride, pleasures, wantonness, and fulness, are in your streets; but the poor are not regarded. O! take heed: 'Woe be to the crown of pride! Woe be to them that drink wine in bowls, and the poor is ready to perish.' O! remember Lazarus and Dives! One fared deliciously every day, and the other was a beggar. O friend, mind these things, for they are near; and see whether thou be not in Dives' state."

I wrote also to the court at Derby thus :—

"I AM moved to write unto you, to take heed of oppressing the poor in your courts, or laying burthens upon poor people, which they cannot bear; and of imposing false oaths, or making them to take oaths which they cannot perform. The Lord saith, 'I will come near to judgment, and will be a swift witness against the sorcerers, against the false swearers, and against the idolaters, and against those that oppress widows and fatherless.' Therefore take heed of all these things betimes. The Lord's judgments are all true and righteous; and he delighteth in mercy. So love mercy, dear people, and consider in time."

Likewise to the ringers of the bells in the steeple-house, called St. Peter's, in Derby, I sent these few lines :—

" FRIENDS,

"Take heed of pleasures, and prize your time now, while you have it, and do not spend it in pleasures, or earthliness. The time may come, that you will say you had time, when it is past. Therefore look at the love of God now, while you have time; for it bringeth to loathe all vanities and worldly pleasures. O consider! Time is precious. Fear God, and rejoice in him, who hath made heaven and earth."

While I was in prison, divers professors came to discourse with me; and I had a sense, before they spoke, that they came to plead for sin and imperfection. I asked them, Whether they were believers, and had faith? and they said, Yes. I asked them, In whom? and they said, In Christ. I replied, If ye are true believers in Christ, you are passed from death to life; and if passed from death, then from sin that bringeth death. And if your faith be true, it will give you victory over sin and the devil, purify your hearts and consciences (for the true faith is held in a pure conscience), and bring you to please God, and give you access to him again. But they could not endure to hear of purity, and of victory over sin and the devil; for they said they could not believe that any could be free from sin on this side the grave. I bid them give over babbling about the Scriptures, which were holy men's words, whilst they pleaded for unholiness. At another time a company of professors came, and they also began to plead for sin. I asked them, Whether they had hope? and they said, Yes: God forbid but we should have hope. I asked them, What hope is it that you have? Is Christ *in* you the hope of your glory? Doth it purify you, as he is pure? But they could not abide to hear of being made pure here. Then I bid them forbear talking of the Scriptures, which were holy men's words. For the holy men, that wrote the Scriptures, pleaded for holiness in heart, life, and conversation here; but since you plead for impurity and sin, which is of the devil, what have you to do with the holy men's words?

Now the keeper of the prison, being a high professor, was greatly enraged against me, and spoke very wickedly of me: but it pleased the Lord one day to strike him so, that he was in great trouble and under great terror of mind. As I was walking in my chamber I heard a doleful noise; and standing still, I heard him say to his wife, "Wife, I have seen the day of judgment, and I saw George there, and I was afraid of him, because I had done him so much wrong, and spoken so much against him to the ministers and professors, and to the justices, and in taverns and ale-houses." After this, towards the evening, he came up into my chamber, and said to me, "I have been as a lion against you; but now I come like a lamb, and like the jailer that came to Paul and Silas trembling." And he desired that he might lodge with me; I told him that I was in his power, he might do what he would: but he said nay, he would have my leave, and he could desire to be always with me, but not to have me as a prisoner; and he said "he had been plagued, and his house had been plagued for my sake." So I suffered him to lodge with me; and then he told me all his heart, and said he believed what I had said of the true faith and hope to be true; and he wondered that the other man that was put into prison with me did not stand to it; and said, "That man was not right, but I was an honest man." He confessed also to me, that at times when I had asked him to let me go forth to speak the word of the Lord to the people, and he had refused to let me, and I had laid the weight thereof upon him, that he used to be under great trouble, amazed, and almost distracted for some time after; and in such a condition that he had little strength left him. When the morning came, he rose, and went to the justices, and told them, "that he and his house had been plagued for my sake:" and one of the justices replied (as he reported to me), that the plagues were on them too for keeping me. This was Justice Bennet of Derby, who was the first that called us Quakers, because I bid them tremble at the word of the Lord. This was in the year 1650.*

After this the justices gave leave that I should have liberty to walk a mile. I perceived their end, and told the jailer if they would show me how far a mile was, I might walk it sometimes; for I believed they thought I would go away. And the jailer confessed afterwards, that they did it with that intent, to have me escape, to ease them of their plague; but I told him I was not of that spirit.

This jailer had a sister, a sickly young woman. She came up into my chamber to visit me; and after she had stayed some time, and I had

---

* The designation "Quakers," which was at first applied in scorn, has ever since been used by the world to distinguish Friends from other professors of religion. The first use of the term in the records of Parliament, occurs in the journals of the House of Commons in 1654.

spoken the words of truth to her, she went down, and told them that "we were an innocent people, and did none any hurt, but did good to all, even to them that hated us;" and she desired them to use kindness towards me.

As my restraint prevented my travelling about, to declare and spread truth through the country, it came upon me to write a paper, and send it forth to be spread abroad both amongst Friends and other tender people, for the opening of their understandings in the way of truth, and directing them to the true teacher in themselves. It was as follows:—

"THE LORD doth show unto man his thoughts, and discovereth all the secret workings in man. A man may be brought to see his evil thoughts, running mind, and vain imaginations, and may strive to keep them down, and to keep his mind in; but he cannot overcome them, nor keep his mind within, to the Lord. In this state and condition submit to the Spirit of the Lord, which will discover them, and will bring to wait upon Him, and destroy them. Therefore stand in the faith of the Lord Jesus Christ, who is the author of the true faith, and mind Him; for he will discover the root of lusts, evil thoughts, and vain imaginations, and how they are begotten, conceived, and bred; then how they are brought forth, and how every evil member doth work. He will discover every principle from its own nature and root.

"So mind the faith of Christ, and the anointing which is in you, to be taught by it, which will discover all workings in you; and as he teacheth you, so obey and forsake; else you will not grow up in the faith, nor in the life of Christ, where the love of God is received. Now love begetteth love, its own nature and image: and when mercy and truth meet, what joy there is! Mercy triumphs in judgment; and love and mercy bear the judgment of the world in patience. That which cannot bear the world's judgment is not the love of God; for love beareth all things, and is above the world's judgment; for the world's judgment is but foolishness. Though it is the world's judgment and practice to cast all the world's filthiness that is among themselves upon the saints, yet their judgment is false. Now the chaste virgins follow Christ, the Lamb that takes away the sins of the world; but they that are of that spirit which is not chaste, will not follow Christ the Lamb in his steps, but are disobedient to him in his commands. So the fleshly mind doth mind the flesh, and talketh of the flesh: its knowledge is fleshly and not spiritual; and savours of death and not of the Spirit of life. Some men have the nature of swine wallowing in the mire. Some the nature of dogs to bite both the sheep and one another. Some of lions, to tear, devour, and destroy. Some of wolves, to tear and devour the lambs and sheep of Christ; and some men have the nature of the serpent (that old adversary), to sting, envenom, and poison. 'He that hath an ear to hear, let him hear,' and learn these things *within* himself. Some men have the natures of other beasts and creatures, minding nothing but earthly and visible things, and feeding without the fear of God. Some have the nature of a horse, to prance and vapour in their strength, and to be swift in doing evil; and some have the nature of tall, sturdy oaks, to flourish and spread in wisdom and strength; who are strong in evil, which must perish and come to the fire. Thus the evil is but one in all, but worketh many ways; and whatsoever a man's or woman's nature is addicted to, that is outward, the evil one will fit him with that, and will please his nature and appetite to keep his mind in his inventions, and in the creatures from the Creator. O! therefore, let not the mind go forth from God; for if it do, it will be stained, venomed, and corrupted. If the mind go forth from the Lord it is hard to bring it in again; therefore take heed of the enemy, and keep in the faith of Christ. O! therefore mind that which is eternal and invisible, and Him who is the Creator and Mover of all things; for the things that are made are not made of things that do appear; for the visible covereth the invisible sight in you. But as the Lord, who is invisible, opens you by his invisible Power and Spirit, and brings down the carnal mind in you, so the invisible and immortal things are brought to light in you. O! therefore you, that know the light, walk in the light! for there are children of darkness, that will talk of the light and of the truth, and not walk in it. The children of the light love the light, and walk in the light; but the children of darkness walk in darkness, and hate the light; and in these the earthly lust, and the carnal mind choke the seed of faith; and this bringeth oppression on the seed and death over themselves. O! therefore, mind the pure Spirit of the everlasting God, which will teach you to use the creatures in their right place, and which judgeth the evil. 'To thee, O God, be all glory and honour, who art Lord of all, visible and invisible! To thee be all praise, who bringest out of the deep, to thyself; O powerful God, who art worthy of all glory!' For the Lord, who created all, and gives life and strength to all, is over all, and merciful to all. 'So thou, who hast made all, and art over all, to thee be all glory! In thee is my strength, my refreshment, and life, my joy and my gladness, my rejoicing and glorying for evermore!' * To live and walk in the Spirit of God is joy, and peace, and life; but the mind going forth into the creatures, or into any visible things from the Lord, this bringeth death. Now when the mind is got into the flesh, and into death, the accuser gets within, and the law of sin and death gets into the flesh. Then the life suffers under the law of sin and death; and then there is straitness and failings. For then the good is shut up, and the self-righteousness is exalted. Then man doth work in the outward law, though he cannot justify himself by the law, but is condemned by the light; for he cannot get out of that state, but by abiding in the light, resting in the mercy of God and believing in him, from whom all mercy flows. For there is peace in resting in the Lord Jesus. This is the narrow way that leads to him, the life; but few will abide in it; keep therefore in the innocency, and be obedient to the faith in him; and take heed of conforming to the world, and of reasoning with flesh and blood, for that bringeth disobedience; and then imaginations and questionings arise to draw from obedience to the truth of Christ. But the obedience of faith destroyeth imaginations, and questionings, and all the

* How vain are bonds and imprisonments, or any other human infliction, to the soul thus magnifying the Lord in a strain of thanksgiving, affectingly fervent. To the soul that can thus rejoice in God, its Saviour, there is but one language, "It is well!" 2 Kings iv. 26.

temptations in the flesh, and buffetings, and lookings forth, and fetching up things that are past. By not keeping in the life and light, and not crossing the corrupt will by the power of God, the evil nature grows up in man, and then burdens will come, and man will be stained with that nature. But Esau's mountain shall be laid waste, and become a wilderness, where the dragons lie: but Jacob, the second birth, shall be fruitful, and shall arise. For Esau is hated, and must not be lord: but Jacob, the second birth, which is perfect and plain, shall be lord; for he is beloved of God."

G. F.

I wrote another paper about the same time, and sent it forth amongst the convinced people as follows :—

"THE LORD IS KING over all the earth! Therefore, all people, praise and glorify your King in true obedience, in uprightness, and in the beauty of holiness. O! consider, in true obedience, the Lord is known, and an understanding from him is received. Mark and consider in silence, in lowliness of mind, and thou wilt hear the Lord speak unto thee in thy mind. His voice is sweet and pleasant; his sheep hear his voice, and they will not hearken to another. When they hear his voice, they rejoice and are obedient; they also sing for joy. O, their hearts are filled with everlasting triumph! They sing, and praise the eternal God in Sion; their joy man shall never take from them. Glory to the Lord God for evermore!"

But many that had been convinced of the truth, turned aside, because of the persecution that arose; whereupon I wrote a few lines for the comfort and encouragement of the faithful, thus :—

"COME, ye blessed of the Lord, and rejoice together! keep in unity and oneness of spirit; triumph above the world! be joyful in the Lord, reigning above the world, and above all things that draw from the Lord; that in clearness, righteousness, pureness, and joy, you may be preserved to the Lord. O hear! O hearken to the call of the Lord! Come out of the world, and keep out of it for evermore! Come, sing together, ye righteous ones, the song of the Lord, the song of the Lamb; which none can learn, but they who are redeemed from the earth, and from the world."

While I was in the House of Correction, my relations came to see me; and being troubled for my imprisonment, they went to the justices that cast me into prison, and desired to have me home with them; offering to be bound in one hundred pounds, and others of Derby with them in fifty pounds each, that I should come no more thither to declare against the priests. So I was had up before the justices; and because I would not consent, that they, or any should be bound for me (for I was innocent from any ill behaviour, and had spoken the word of life and truth unto them), Justice Bennet rose up in a rage; and as I was kneeling down to pray to the Lord to forgive him, he ran upon me, and struck me with both his hands, crying, "Away with him, jailer, take him away, jailer." Whereupon I was had again to prison, and there kept, until the time of my commitment for six months was expired. But I had now the liberty of walking a mile by myself, which I made use of, as I felt freedom. Sometimes I went into the market, and streets, and warned the people to repent of their wickedness; and so returned to prison again. And there being persons of several sorts of religion in the prison, I sometimes went and visited them in their meetings on first-days.

After I had been before the justices, and they had required sureties for my good behaviour (which I could not consent should be given, to blemish my innocency), it came upon me to write to the justices again; which I did as follows :—

"FRIENDS,

"See what it is in you that doth imprison; see, who is head in you; and see, if something do not accuse you? Consider, you must be brought to judgment. Think of Lazarus and Dives; the one fared sumptuously every day, the other was a beggar. Now you have time, prize it, while you have it. Would you have me to be bound to my good behaviour? I am bound to my good behaviour; and cry for good behaviour of all people, to turn from the vanities and pleasures, the oppression and deceits, of this world; and there will come a time that you shall know it. Therefore take heed of pleasures, and deceits, and pride; and look not at man, but at the Lord; for 'Look unto me, all ye ends of the earth, and be ye saved, saith the Lord.' "

Some little time after I wrote to them again :—

"FRIENDS,

"Would you have me to be bound to my good behaviour from drunkenness, or swearing, or fighting, or adultery, and the like? The Lord hath redeemed me from all these things; and the love of God hath brought me to loathe all wantonness, blessed be his name! Drunkards, and fighters, and swearers, have their liberty without bonds; and you lay your law upon me, whom neither you, nor any other can justly accuse of these things; praised be the Lord! I can look to no man for my liberty, but to the Lord alone, who hath all men's hearts in his hand."

And after some time, not finding my spirit clear of them, I wrote to them again, as follows :—

"FRIENDS,

"Had you known who sent me to you, ye would have received me; for the Lord sent me to warn you of the woes that are coming upon you; and to bid you look at the Lord, and not at man. But when I told you my experience, what the Lord had done for me, then your hearts were hardened, and you sent me to prison, where you have kept me many weeks. If the love of God had broken your hearts, then would ye see what ye have done; ye would not have imprisoned me, had not my Father suffered you; and by his power I shall be loosed; for he openeth and shutteth; to him be all glory! In what have I misbehaved myself, that any should be bound for me? All men's words will do me no good, nor their bonds either, to keep my heart, if I had not a guide *within*, to keep me in the upright life to God. But I believe in the Lord, that through his strength and power, I shall be preserved from ungodliness and worldly lusts. The Scripture saith, 'receive strangers,' but you imprison such. As you are in authority, take heed of oppression and oaths, of injustice, and gifts or rewards, for God doth loathe all such. But love mercy, and true judgment, and justice, for that the Lord delights in. I do not write with hatred to you; but to keep my conscience clear; take heed how you spend your time."

I was moved also to write again to the priests of Derby :—

"FRIENDS,

"You profess to be the ministers of Jesus Christ in words, but you show by your fruits what your ministry is. Every tree shows its fruit; the ministry of Jesus Christ is in mercy and love, to loose them that are bound, to bring out of bondage, and to let them that are in captivity go free. Where is your example, if the Scriptures be your rule, to imprison for religion? Have you any command for it from Christ? If that were in you, which you profess, you would walk in their steps, who wrote the Scriptures, 'But he is not a Jew who is one outwardly, whose praise is of men; but he is a Jew who is one inwardly, whose praise is of God.' But if you build upon the prophets and apostles in words, and pervert their life, remember the woes which Jesus Christ spoke against such. They that spoke the prophets' words, but denied Christ, they professed a Christ to come; but had they known him they would not have crucified him. The saints, whom the love of God did change, were brought thereby to walk in love and mercy; for he that dwelleth in love, dwelleth in God. But where envy, pride, and hatred rule, the nature of the world rules, and not the nature of Jesus Christ. I write with no hatred to you; but that you may weigh yourselves, and see how you pass your time."

Thus having cleared my conscience to the priests, it was not long before a concern came upon me to write again to the justices, which I did as follows :—

"I AM moved to warn you to take heed of giving way to your own wills. Love the cross; and satisfy not your own minds in the flesh; but prize your time, while you have it, and walk up to that you know, in obedience to God; then you shall not be condemned for that you know not; but for that you do know, and do not obey. Consider betimes, weigh yourselves, and see where you are, and whom you serve. For if ye blaspheme God, and take his name in vain; if ye swear and lie; if ye give way to envy and hatred, to covetousness and greediness, to pleasures and wantonness, or any other vices, be assured that ye do serve the Devil. But if ye fear the Lord, and serve him, ye will loathe all these things. He that loveth God, will not blaspheme his name; but where there is opposing God, and serving the Devil, that profession is sad and miserable. O prize your time, and do not love that which God forbids; lying, wrath, malice, envy, hatred, greediness, covetousness, oppression, gluttony, drunkenness, whoredom, and all unrighteousness God doth forbid. So consider, and be not deceived; 'Evil communication corrupts good manners.' Be not deceived, God will not be mocked with vain words; the wrath of God is revealed from heaven against all ungodliness. Therefore obey that which convinces you of all evil, and tells you that you should do no evil; it will lead you to repentance, and keep you in the fear of the Lord. O look at the mercies of God, and prize them, and do not turn them into wantonness. O eye the Lord, and not earthly things!"

Besides this, I wrote the following to Colonel Barton, who was both a justice and a preacher, as was hinted before :—

"FRIEND,

"Do not cloak and cover thyself; there is a God, who knoweth thy heart, and will uncover thee; he seeth thy way. 'Woe be to him that covereth, and not with my Spirit,' saith the Lord. Dost thou do contrary to the law, and then put it from thee? Mercy and true judgment thou neglectest; look what was spoken against such. My Saviour said to such, 'I was sick and in prison, and ye visited me not; I was hungry, and ye fed me not; I was a stranger, and ye took me not in.' And when they said, 'When saw we thee in prison, and did not come to thee,' &c., he replied, 'Inasmuch as ye did it not to one of these little ones, ye did it not to me.' Thou hast imprisoned me for bearing witness to the life and power of truth, and yet thou professest to be a minister of Christ; but if Christ had sent thee, thou wouldst bring out of prison, and out of bondage, and wouldst receive strangers. Thou hast been wanton upon earth, thou hast lived plenteously, and nourished thy heart, as in a day of slaughter; thou hast killed the Just. O look where thou art, and how thou hast spent thy time! O remember thyself, and now, whilst thou hast time, prize it. Do not slight the free mercy, or despise the long-suffering of God, which is great salvation; but mind that in thee which doth convince, and would not let thee swear, nor lie, nor take God's name in vain. Thou knowest thou shouldst do none of these things; thou hast learned that which will condemn thee; therefore obey the light, which doth convince thee, forsake thy sins, and look at the mercies of God; and prize his love in sparing thee till now. The Lord saith, 'Look unto me, all ye ends of the earth, and be ye saved; cease from man, whose breath is in his nostrils.' Prize thy time, and see whom thou servest; for his servant thou art whom thou dost obey, whether of sin unto death, or of obedience unto righteousness. If thou serve God, and fear him, thou wilt not blaspheme his name, or curse, or swear, or take his name in vain, or follow pleasures and wantonness, whoredom, and drunkenness, or wrath, or malice, or revenge, or rashness, or headiness, pride or gluttony, greediness, oppression, or covetousness, or foolish jestings, or vain songs. God doth forbid these things, and all unrighteousness. If thou profess God, and act any of these things, thou takest him for a cloak, and servest the Devil. Consider with thyself, and do not love that which God hateth. He that loveth God, keepeth his commandments. The Devil will tell thee, it is a hard thing to keep God's commandments; but it is an easy thing to keep the Devil's commandments, and to live in all unrighteousness and ungodliness, turning the grace of God into wantonness. But let the unrighteous man forsake his ways, and turn unto me, saith the Lord, and I will have mercy. 'Turn ye, why will ye die? saith the Lord.'

"Howl, ye great ones, for the plagues are pouring out upon you! Howl, ye oppressors, for recompense and vengeance is coming upon you! Woe unto them that covetously join one house to another; and bring one field so nigh unto another that the poor can get no more ground, and that ye may dwell upon the earth alone; these things are in the ears of the Lord of Hosts. Woe unto him that covetously getteth evil-gotten goods into his house, that he may set his nest on high, to escape from the power of evil."

CHAPTER IV.

1650-1651.—A trooper visits George Fox from an inward intimation—declines a commission in the army, and is put in the dungeon—confutes one who denied Christ's outward appearance, from whence a slander is raised against Friends—testifies against capital punishments for small matters—writes for more speedy justice to prisoners—intercedes for the life of a young woman, imprisoned for stealing, who is brought to the gallows but reprieved, and afterwards convinced—again refuses to bear arms, and is committed close prisoner—writes to Barton and Bennet, justices, against persecution—addresses the convinced and tender people against hirelings—to the magistrates of Derby against persecution, and foretelling his own enlargement and their recompense—is greatly exercised for the wickedness of Derby—sees the visitation of God's love pass away from the town, and writes a lamentation over it—a great judgment fell upon the town —he is liberated after a year's imprisonment—visits Lichfield—preaches repentance through Doncaster—many dread "the man with leather breeches"—goes to steeple-houses, as the apostles did to the temples, to bring people off from them —is denied entertainment, and ill-treated at some places—refuses to inform against his persecutors—many are convinced in Yorkshire, amongst others, Richard Farnsworth, James Naylor, William Dewsbury, Justice Hotham, and Captain Pursloe.

WHILE I was yet in the House of Correction, there came unto me a trooper, and said, as he was sitting in the steeple-house, hearing the priest, exceeding great trouble came upon him; and the voice of the Lord came to him saying, "Dost thou not know that my servant is in prison? Go to him for direction." So I spoke to his condition, and his understanding was opened. I told him, that which showed him his sins, and troubled him for them, would show him his salvation; for he that shows a man his sin, is the same that takes it away. While I was speaking to him, the Lord's power opened him, so that he began to have a good understanding in the Lord's truth, and to be sensible of God's mercies; and began to speak boldly in his quarters amongst the soldiers, and to others, concerning truth (for the Scriptures were very much opened to him), insomuch that he said, "his colonel was as blind as Nebuchadnezzar, to cast the servant of the Lord into prison." Upon this his colonel had a spite against him; and at Worcester fight, the year after, when the two armies were lying near one another, two came out from the king's army, and challenged any two of the Parliament army to fight with them; his colonel made choice of him and another to answer the challenge. And when in the encounter his companion was slain, he drove both his enemies within musket-shot out of the town, without firing a pistol at them. This, when he returned, he told me with his own mouth. But when the fight was over, he saw the deceit and hypocrisy of the officers; and being sensible how wonderfully the Lord had preserved him, and seeing also to the end of fighting, he laid down his arms.

Now the time of my commitment to the house of correction being nearly ended, and there being many new soldiers raised, the commissioners would have made me captain over them; and the soldiers said they would have none but me.* So the keeper of the house of correction was commanded to bring me before the commissioners and soldiers in the market-place; and there they offered me that preferment, as they called it, asking me, if I would not take up arms for the Commonwealth against Charles Stuart? I told them, I knew from whence all wars arose, even from the lust, according to James's doctrine; and that I lived in the virtue of that life and power that took away the occasion of all wars. But they courted me to accept their offer, and thought I did but compliment them. But I told them, I was come into the covenant of peace, which was before wars and strifes were. They said, they offered it in love and kindness to me, because of my virtue; and such like flattering words they used. But I told them, if that was their love and kindness, I trampled it under my feet. Then their rage got up, and they said, "Take him away, jailer, and put him into the dungeon amongst the rogues and felons." So I was had away and put into a lousy, stinking place, without any bed, amongst thirty felons, where I was kept almost half a year, unless it were at times; for they would sometimes let me walk in the garden, having a belief that I would not go away. Now when they had got me into Derby dungeon, it was the belief and saying of people that I should never come out; but I had faith in God, and believed I should be delivered in his time; for the Lord had said to me before, that I was not to be removed from that place yet, being set there for a service which he had for me to do.

After it was noised abroad that I was in Derby dungeon, my relations came to see me again; and they were much troubled that I should be in prison; for they looked upon it to be a great shame to them for me to be imprisoned for religion; and some thought I was mad, because I advocated purity, and righteousness, and perfection.

Among others that came to see, and discourse with me, was a person from Nottingham, a soldier, that had been a Baptist (as I understood), and with him came several others. In discourse he said to me, "Your faith stands in a man that died at Jerusalem, and there never was any such thing." I was exceedingly grieved to hear him say so: and I said to him, "How! did not Christ suffer without the gates of Jerusalem through the professing Jews, and chief priests, and Pilate?" And he denied that ever Christ suffered there outwardly. Then I asked him whether there were not chief priests, and Jews, and Pilate there outwardly? and when he could not deny that, then I told him, as certainly as there was a chief priest, and Jews, and Pilate there outwardly, so certainly was Christ persecuted by

---

* The English nation at this period was much engrossed with the great subjects of religion and politics, and both were mingled together in strange conjunction. The chief rulers of the Commonwealth, more especially Oliver Cromwell, had contrived to interweave their own views on spiritual matters into the minds of the soldiers; who, in those days, commonly united, with the profession of arms, the profession also of Christianity. The unsettled state of the country caused them to be stationed in considerable numbers in most of the principal towns of the north, where several of them had made acquaintance with George Fox during his imprisonment, and were so much impressed in his favour, that it appears they were desirous, as the time of his release drew near, to engage him in the capacity of their captain.

them, and did suffer there outwardly under them. Yet from this man's words was a slander raised upon us, that the Quakers denied Christ that suffered and died at Jerusalem; which was all utterly false, and the least thought of it never entered our hearts; but it was a mere slander cast upon us, and occasioned by this person's words. The same person also said, that never any of the prophets, or apostles, or holy men of God, suffered any thing outwardly; but all their sufferings were inward. But I instanced to him how many of them suffered, and by whom they suffered: and so was the power of the Lord brought over his wicked imaginations.

There came also another company to me, that pretended they were triers of spirits; I asked them what was the first step to peace, and what it was by which a man might see his salvation? and they were presently up in the airy mind, and said I was mad. Thus they came to try spirits, who did not know themselves, nor their own spirits.

In this time of my imprisonment, I was exceedingly exercised about the proceedings of the judges and magistrates in their courts of judicature. I was moved to write to the judges concerning their putting men to death for cattle, and money, and small matters; and to show them how contrary it was to the law of God in old time; for I was under great suffering in my spirit because of it, and under the very sense of death; but standing in the will of God, a heavenly breathing arose in my soul to the Lord. Then did I see the heavens opened, and I rejoiced, and gave glory to God. So I wrote to the judges as follows:—

"I AM moved to write unto you to take heed of putting men to death for stealing cattle or money, &c.; for thieves in the old time were to make restitution; and if they had not wherewith, they were to be sold for their theft. Mind the laws of God in the Scriptures, and the Spirit that gave them forth; let them be your rule in executing judgment; and show mercy, that you may receive mercy from God, the judge of all. Take heed of gifts and rewards, and of pride; for God doth forbid them; they blind the eyes of the wise. I do not write to give liberty to sin; God hath forbidden it; but that you should judge according to his laws, and show mercy: for he delighteth in true judgment and in mercy. I beseech you to mind these things, and prize your time, now you have it: fear God, and serve him; for he is a consuming fire.'

Besides this, I wrote another letter to the judges, to this effect:—

"I AM moved to write unto you that ye do true justice to every man; and see that none be oppressed, or wronged, or any oaths imposed; for the land mourneth because of oaths, and adulteries, and sorceries, and drunkenness, and profaneness. O consider, ye that are men set in authority: be moderate, and in lowliness consider these things. Show mercy to the fatherless, to the widows, and to the poor; and take heed of rewards or gifts, for they blind the eyes of the wise; the Lord doth loathe all such. Love mercy and true judgment, justice, and righteousness, for the Lord delighteth therein. Consider these things in time, and take heed how ye spend your time. Now ye have time, prize it; and show mercy, that ye may receive mercy from the Lord; for he is coming to try all things, and will plead with all flesh, as by fire."

Moreover, I laid before the judges what an hurtful thing it was, that prisoners should lie so long in jail; showing how they learned wickedness one of another in talking of their bad deeds: and therefore speedy justice should be done. For I was a tender youth, and dwelt in the fear of God, and being grieved to hear their bad language, I was often made to reprove them for their wicked words, and evil conduct towards each other. People admired that I was so preserved and kept; for they could never catch a word or action from me, to make any thing of against me, all the time I was there; for the Lord's infinite power upheld and preserved me all that time; to him be praises and glory for ever!

While I was here in prison, there was a young woman in the jail for robbing her master of some money. When she was to be tried for her life, I wrote to the judge and to the jury about her, showing them how it was contrary to the law of God in old time to put people to death for stealing, and moving them to show mercy. Yet she was condemned to die, and a grave was made for her; and at the time appointed she was carried forth to execution. Then I wrote a few words, warning all people to beware of greediness or covetousness, for it leads from God; and exhorting all to fear the Lord, to avoid all earthly lusts, and to prize their time while they have it: this I gave to be read at the gallows. And though they had her upon the ladder, with a cloth bound over her face, ready to be turned off, yet they did not put her to death, but brought her back again to prison: and in the prison she afterwards came to be convinced of God's everlasting truth.

There was also in the jail, while I was there, a prisoner, a wicked, ungodly man, who was a reputed conjuror. He threatened how he would talk with me, and what he would do to me; but he never had power to open his mouth to me. And once the jailer and he falling out, he threatened that he would raise the Devil, and break his house down, so that he made the jailer afraid. Then I was moved of the Lord to go in his power, and rebuke him, and say unto him, "Come let us see what thou canst do; do thy worst:" and I told him the Devil was raised high enough in him already, but the power of God chained him down: so he slunk away from me.

Now the time of Worcester fight coming on, Justice Bennet sent the constables to press me for a soldier, seeing I would not voluntarily accept of a command. I told them that I was brought off from outward wars. They came down again to give me press-money, but I would take none. Then I was brought up to Sergeant Holes, kept there a while, and then taken down again. After a while the constables fetched me up again, and brought me before the commissioners, who said I should go for a soldier; but I told them that I was dead to it. They said I was alive. I told them, where envy and hatred are, there is confusion. They offered me money twice, but I would not take it: then they were angry, and committed me close prisoner, without bail or mainprize. Whereupon I wrote to them again, directing my letter to Colonel Barton (who was a preacher), and the rest that were concerned in my commitment.   I wrote thus :—

"You who are without Christ, and yet use the words which he and his saints have spoken ; consider, neither he nor his apostles did ever imprison any ; but my Saviour is merciful even to the unmerciful and rebellious. He brings out of prison and bondage ; but men, while the carnal mind rules, oppress and imprison.   My Saviour saith, 'Love your enemies, and do good to them that hate you, and pray for them that despitefully use you and perse-cute you ;' for the love of God doth not persecute any, but loveth all where it dwelleth.   'He that hateth his brother is a murderer.'   You profess to be Christians, and one of you a minister of Jesus Christ ; yet you have im-prisoned me, who am a servant of Jesus Christ.   The apostles never imprisoned any, but were imprisoned themselves.   Take heed of speaking of Christ in words, and denying him in life and power.   O friends, the imprisoning of my body is to satisfy your wills ; but take heed of giving way to your wills, for that will hurt you.   If the love of God had broken your hearts, ye would not have imprisoned me ; but my love is to you, as to all my fellow-creatures ; and that you may weigh yourselves, and see how you stand, is this written."

About this time I was moved to give forth the following, to go amongst the convinced and tender people, to manifest the deceits of the world, and how the priests have deceived the people :—

To all you that love the Lord Jesus Christ with a pure and naked heart, and the generation of the righteous.

"CHRIST was ever hated ; and the righteous for his sake.   Mind who they were that did ever hate them : he that was born after the flesh did persecute him that was born after the Spirit ; and so it is now.   Mind who were the chiefest against Christ ; even the great, learned men, the heads of the people, rulers and teachers, that professed the law and the prophets, and looked for Christ.   They looked for an outwardly glorious Christ, to hold up their outward glory ; but Christ spoke against the works of the world, and against the priests, and scribes, and Pharisees, and their hypocritical profession.   He that is a stranger to Christ, is a hireling ; but the servants of Jesus Christ are free men.   The false teachers always laid burthens upon the people ; and the true servants of the Lord spoke against them.   Jeremiah spoke against hirelings, and said, It was a horrible thing ; What will ye do in the end ? for the people and priests were given to covetousness.   Paul spoke against such as made gain upon the people ; and exhorted the saints to turn away from such as were covetous men and proud, such as loved pleasures more than God—such as had a form of god-liness, but denied the power thereof ; 'for of this sort,' said he, 'are they that creep into houses, and lead captive silly women, who are ever learning, but never able to come to the knowledge of the truth ; men of corrupt minds, reprobate concerning the faith ; and as Jannes and Jambres with-stood Moses, so,' said he, 'do these resist the truth ; but they shall proceed no further, for their folly shall be made manifest unto all men.'   Moses forsook honours and pleasures which he might have enjoyed. The apostle in his time saw this corruption entering, which now is spread over the world, of having a form of godliness, but denying the power. Ask any of your teachers whether you may ever overcome your corruptions or sins? None of them believe that; but, 'as long as man is here, he must,' they say, 'carry about with him the body of sin.' Thus pride is kept up, and that honour and mastership, which Christ denied, and all unrighteousness; yet multitudes of teachers! heaps of teachers! the golden cup full of abominations! Paul did not preach for wages, but laboured with his hands, that he might be an example to all them that follow him. O people, see who follow Paul! The prophet Jeremiah said, 'The prophets prophesy falsely, and the priests bear rule by their means;' but now the priests bear rule by the means they get from the people: take away their means, and they will bear rule over you no longer. They are such as, the apostle said, 'intruded into those things which they never saw, being vainly puffed up with a fleshly mind;' and as the Scriptures declare of some of old, 'They go in the way of Cain, who was a murderer, and in the way of Balaam, who coveted the wages of unrighteousness.' The prophet Micah also cried against the judges that judged for reward, and the priests that taught for hire, and the prophets that prophesied for money; and yet leaned on the Lord, saying, 'Is not the Lord amongst us?' Gifts blind the eyes of the wise. The gift of God was never purchased with money. All the holy servants of God did ever cry against deceit; and where the Lord hath manifested his love, they do loathe it, and that nature which holdeth it up."

Again a concern came upon me to write to the magistrates of Derby; which I did as follows:—

"FRIENDS,

"I desire you to consider in time whom ye do imprison; for the magistrate is set for the punishment of evil-doers, and for the praise of them that do well. But when the Lord doth send his messengers unto you, to warn you of the woes that will come upon you, except you repent, then you persecute them, and put them in prison; and say, 'We have a law, and by our law we may do it.' For you indeed justify yourselves before men; but God knoweth your hearts. He will not be worshipped with your forms and professions, and shows of religion. Therefore consider, ye that talk of God, how ye are subject to him; for they are his children that do his will. What doth the Lord require of you but to do justice, to love and show mercy, to walk humbly with him, and to help the widows and fatherless to their right? But instead thereof ye oppress the poor. Do not your judges judge for rewards, and your priests teach for hire? The time is coming, that he who seeth all things, will discover all your secrets: and know this assuredly, the Lord will deliver his servants out of your hands, and he will recompense all your unjust dealings towards his people. I desire you to consider of these things; search the Scriptures, and see whether any of the people of God did ever imprison any for religion. They were themselves imprisoned. I desire you to consider, that it is written, 'When the church is met together, ye may all prophesy one by one, that

all may learn, and all may be comforted;' and then, 'if anything be revealed
to another that sitteth by, let the first hold his peace.'   Thus it was in the
true church; and thus it ought to be now.   But it is not so in your assemblies; he that teaches for hire may speak, and none may contradict him.
Again, consider the liberty that was given to the apostles, even among the
unbelieving Jews; when after the reading of the law and the prophets, the
rulers of the synagogue said unto them, 'Ye men and brethren, if ye have
any word of exhortation for the people, say on.'   I desire you to consider
in stillness, and strive not against the Lord; for he is stronger than you.
Though ye hold his people fast for a time, yet when he cometh, he will
make known who are his; for his coming is like the refiner's fire and like
fuller's soap.   Then the stone that is set at nought by you builders, shall
be the headstone of the corner.   O friends, lay these things to heart, and
let them not seem light things to you.   I write to you in love, to mind the
laws of God and your own souls, and to do as the holy men of God did."

Great was my exercise and travail in spirit, during my imprisonment
here, because of the wickedness that was in this town; for though some
were convinced, yet the generality were a hardened people; and I saw the
visitation of God's love pass away from them.   I mourned over them; and
it came upon me to give forth the following lamentation for them :—

"O DERBY! as the waters run away when the flood-gates are up, so
doth the visitation of God's love pass away from thee, O Derby!   Therefore look where thou art, and how thou art grounded; and consider, before
thou art utterly forsaken.   The Lord moved me twice, before I came to cry
against the deceits and vanities that are in thee, and to warn all to look at
the Lord, and not at man.   The woe is against the crown of pride; the
woe is against drunkenness and vain pleasures, and against them that make
a profession of religion in words, yet are high and lofty in mind, and live
in oppression and envy.   O Derby! thy profession and preaching stink
before the Lord.   Ye profess a Sabbath in words, and meet together,
dressing yourselves in fine apparel; you uphold pride.   Thy women go with
stretched-forth necks and wanton eyes, &c., which the true prophet of old
cried against.   Your assemblies are odious, and an abomination to the
Lord: pride is set up, and bowed down to; covetousness abounds; and he
that doeth wickedly is honoured: so deceit bears with deceit; and yet they
profess Christ in words.   O the deceit that is within thee! it doth even
break my heart to see how God is dishonoured in thee, O Derby!"

After I had seen the visitation of God's love pass away from this
place, I knew that my imprisonment here would not continue long; but I
saw that when the Lord should bring me forth, it would be as the letting
of a lion out of a den amongst the wild beasts of the forest.   For all professions stood in a beastly spirit and nature, pleading for sin, and for the
body of sin and imperfection, as long as they lived.   They all raged, and
ran against the life and Spirit which gave forth the Scriptures, which they
professed in words.   And so it was, as will appear hereafter.

There was a great judgment upon the town, and the magistrates were uneasy about me; but they could not agree what to do with me. One while they would have me sent up to the parliament; another while they would have banished me to Ireland. At first they called me a deceiver, and a seducer, and a blasphemer: afterwards, when God had brought his plagues upon them, they said I was an honest, virtuous man. But their good report or bad report, their well speaking or their ill speaking, was nothing to me; for the one did not lift me up, nor the other cast me down: praised be the Lord! At length they were made to turn me out of jail, about the beginning of Winter in the year 1651, after I had been a prisoner in Derby almost a year; six months in the House of Correction, and the rest of the time in the common jail and dungeon.

Thus being set at liberty again, I went on, as before, in the work of the Lord, passing through the country, first, into my own country of LEICESTERSHIRE, and had meetings as I went; and the Lord's Spirit and power accompanied me. Afterwards I went near to BURTON-ON-TRENT, where some were convinced; and so to BUSHEL-HOUSE, where I had a meeting. I went up into the country, where there were friendly people; yet an outrageous wicked professor had an intent to do me a mischief, but the Lord prevented him. Blessed be the Lord!

As I was walking along with several Friends, I lifted up my head, and I saw three steeple-house spires, and they struck at my life. I asked them what place that was? and they said, LICHFIELD. Immediately the word of the Lord came to me, that I must go thither. Being come to the house we were going to, I wished the Friends that were with me, to walk into the house, saying nothing to them whether I was to go. As soon as they were gone, I stepped away, and went by my eye over hedge and ditch, till I came within a mile of Lichfield; where, in a great field, there were shepherds keeping their sheep. Then I was commanded by the Lord to pull off my shoes. I stood still, for it was Winter; and the word of the Lord was like a fire in me. So I put off my shoes, and left them with the shepherds; and the poor shepherds trembled and were astonished. Then I walked on about a mile, and as soon as I was within the city, the word of the Lord came to me again, saying, "Cry, Woe unto the bloody city of Lichfield." So I went up and down the streets, crying with a loud voice, "WOE TO THE BLOODY CITY OF LICHFIELD!" It being market-day, I went into the market-place, and to and fro in the several parts of it, and made stands, crying as before, "WOE TO THE BLOODY CITY OF LICHFIELD!" And no one laid hands on me; but as I went thus crying through the streets, there seemed to me to be a channel of blood running down the streets, and the market-place appeared like a pool of blood. When I had declared what was upon me, and felt myself clear, I went out of the town in peace; and returning to the shepherds, gave them some money, and took my shoes of them again. But the fire of the Lord was so in my feet, and all over me, that I did not matter to put on my shoes any more, and was at a stand whether I should or not, till I felt freedom from the Lord so to do; and then, after I had washed my feet, I put on my shoes again. After this a deep consideration came upon me, why, or for what reason, I should be sent to cry against that city, and call it THE BLOODY CITY.   For though the parliament had the minster one while, and the king another, and much blood had been shed in the town, during the wars between them, yet that was no more than had befallen many other places.   But afterwards I came to understand, that in the Emperor Dioclesian's time, a thousand Christians were martyred in Lichfield.   So I was to go, without my shoes, through the channel of their blood, and into the pool of their blood in the market-place, that I might raise up the memorial of the blood of those martyrs which had been shed above a thousand years before, and lay cold in their streets.   So the sense of this blood was upon me, and I obeyed the word of the Lord.   Ancient records testify how many of the Christian Britons suffered there.   Much I could write of the sense I had of the blood of the martyrs that hath been shed in this nation for the name of Christ, both under the ten persecutions and since; but I leave it to the Lord, and to his book, out of which all shall be judged; for his book is a most certain record, and his Spirit a true recorder.*

Then I passed up and down through the countries, having meetings amongst friendly people in many places; but my relations were offended at me.   After some time I returned into Nottinghamshire, to MANSFIELD, and went into Derbyshire, visiting Friends.   Then passing into Yorkshire, I preached repentance through DONCASTER, and several other places; and after came to BALBY, where Richard Farnsworth† and some others were convinced.   So travelling through several places, preaching repentance, and the word of life to the people, I came into the parts about WAKEFIELD, where James Naylor lived; he and Thomas Goodyear came to me, and were both convinced, and received the truth.   William Dewsbury‡ also and his

* Various constructions have been put upon the act here recorded.   It appears to have afforded a feeling of satisfaction to the mind of the actor, in having performed a service which he believed required of him, which may have been a test of his faith and obedience.   It certainly affords a striking example of that undaunted courage George Fox evinced on all occasions, where his sense of religious duty called upon him to yield implicit obedience to its injunctions.

† Richard Farnsworth became an eminent minister, and many were turned to God by him.   He was mighty in discourses with priests and professors, and laboured much in the gospel.   He was twelve months imprisoned at Banbury in 1655, and after great sufferings and persecutions, he finished his testimony in London, in 1666.   A short time before his death, sitting up in bed, he spoke in as much power and strength of spirit as he had done at any time in his health, testifying that he was filled with the love of God more than he was able to express.   He published many small works in defence of truth.

‡ William Dewsbury, often mentioned in this Journal, became a valiant minister of the gospel, travelling extensively in its advocacy.   Whiting says, "he was an extraordinary man many ways, and I thought as exact a pattern of a perfect man as ever I knew."   His health became impaired through the sharp persecutions he passed through, consisting of many long imprisonments, beatings, and bruisings. In 1688, going up to London to visit the brethren, he was taken ill of a distemper contracted in prison.   Returning home, he died shortly after, leaving a heavenly testimony behind him, expressed about a week before he died.   This, with other information, is recorded in *Piety Promoted,* vol. i. pp. 163–168, and further particulars in Whiting's *Memoirs,* p. 25, and at pp. 376–387.   His works were published in 1 vol. quarto, in 1689.

wife, with many more, came to me, who were convinced, and received the truth. From thence I passed through the country towards Captain Pursloe's house by SELBY, and visited John Leek, who had been to visit me in Derby prison, and was convinced. I had a horse, but was fain to leave him, not knowing what to do with him; for I was moved to go to many great houses, to admonish and exhort the people to turn to the Lord. Thus passing on, I was moved of the Lord to go to BEVERLEY steeple-house, which was then a place of high profession; and being very wet with rain, I went first to an inn, and as soon as I came to the door, a young woman of the house came to the door, and said, " What, is it you? come in," as if she had known me before; for the Lord's power bowed their hearts. So I refreshed myself and went to bed; and in the morning, my clothes being still wet, I got ready, and having paid for what I had had in the inn, I went up to the steeple-house, where was a man preaching. When he had done, I was moved to speak to him, and to the people, in the mighty power of God, and turned them to their teacher, Christ Jesus. The power of the Lord was so strong, that it struck a mighty dread amongst the people. The mayor came and spoke a few words to me; but none of them had any power to meddle with me. So I passed away out of the town, and in the afternoon went to another steeple-house about two miles off. When the priest had done, I was moved to speak to him, and to the people very largely, showing them the way of life and truth, and the ground of election and reprobation. The priest said, he was but a child, and could not dispute with me; I told him I did not come to dispute, but to hold forth the word of life and truth unto them, that they might all know the one Seed, which the promise of God was to, both in the male and in the female. Here the people were very loving, and would have had me come again on a week-day, and preach among them; but I directed them to their teacher, Christ Jesus, and so passed away. The next day I went to CRANTSICK, to Captain Pursloe's, who accompanied me to Justice Hotham's. This Justice Hotham was a tender man, one that had some experience of God's workings in his heart. After some discourse with him of the things of God, he took me into his closet; where, sitting together, he told me he had known that principle these ten years, and was glad that the Lord did now publish it abroad to the people. After a while there came a priest to visit him, with whom also I had some discourse concerning Truth. But his mouth was quickly stopped, for he was nothing but a notionist, and not in possession of what he talked of.

While I was here, there came a great woman of Beverley to speak to Justice Hotham about some business; and in discourse she told him, that the last Sabbath-day (as she called it) there came an angel or spirit into the church at Beverley, and spoke the wonderful things of God, to the astonishment of all that were there; and when it had done, it passed away, and they did not know whence it came, nor whither it went; but it astonished all, both priest, professors, and magistrates of the town. This relation Justice Hotham gave me afterwards, and then I gave him an account how I had been that day at Beverley steeple-house, and had declared truth to the priest and people there.

There were in the country thereabouts some noted priests and doctors, with whom Justice Hotham was acquainted. He would fain have them speak with me, and offered to send for them, under pretence of some business he had with them, but I wished him not to do so.

When the First-day of the week was come, Justice Hotham walked out with me into the field; and Captain Pursloe coming up after us, Justice Hotham left us and returned home, but Captain Pursloe went with me into the steeple-house. When the priest had done, I spoke both to priest and people; declared to them the word of life and truth, and directed them where they might find their teacher, the Lord Jesus Christ. Some were convinced, received the truth, and stand fast in it; and have a fine meeting to this day.

In the afternoon I went to another steeple-house about three miles off, where preached a great high-priest, called a doctor, one of them whom Justice Hotham would have sent for to speak with me. I went into the steeple-house, and stayed till the priest had done. The words which he took for his text were these, "Ho, every one that thirsteth, come ye to the waters; and he that hath no money, come ye, buy and eat, yea come, buy wine and milk without money and without price." Then was I moved of the Lord God to say unto him, "Come down, thou deceiver; dost thou bid people come freely, and take of the water of life freely, and yet thou takest three hundred pounds a-year of them, for preaching the Scriptures to them. Mayest thou not blush for shame? Did the prophet Isaiah, and Christ do so, who spoke the words, and gave them forth freely? Did not Christ say to his ministers, whom he sent to preach, 'Freely ye have received, freely give?'" The priest, like a man amazed, hastened away. After he had left his flock, I had as much time as I could desire to speak to the people; and I directed them from the darkness to the light, and to the grace of God, that would teach them, and bring them salvation; to the Spirit of God in their inward parts, which would be a free teacher unto them.

Having cleared myself amongst the people, I returned to Justice Hotham's house that night, who, when I came in, took me in his arms, and said his house was my house, for he was exceedingly glad at the work of the Lord, and that his power was revealed. Then he told me why he went not with me to the steeple-house in the morning, and what reasonings he had in himself about it; for he thought, if he had gone with me to the steeple-house, the officers would have put me to him; and then he should have been so put to it, that he should not have known what to do. But he was glad, he said, when Captain Pursloe came up to go with me; yet neither of them was dressed, nor had his band about his neck. It was a strange thing then to see a man come into a steeple-house without a band; yet Captain Pursloe went in with me without his band, the Lord's power and truth had so affected him that he minded it not.

From hence I passed on through the country, and came at night to an inn where was a company of rude people. I bid the woman of the house, if she had any meat, to bring me some; but because I said Thee and Thou to her she looked strangely on me. Then I asked her if she had any milk; and she said, No. I was sensible she spoke falsely, and being willing to try her further, I asked her if she had any cream; she denied that she had any. Now there stood a churn in the room, and a little boy playing about it, put his hands into it, and pulled it down, and threw all the cream on the floor before my eyes. Thus was the woman manifested to be a liar. She was amazed, and blessed herself, and taking up the child, whipped it sorely; but I reproved her for her lying and deceit. After the Lord had thus discovered her deceit and perverseness, I walked out of the house, and went away till I came to a stack of hay, and lay in the hay-stack that night in rain and snow, it being but three days before the time called Christmas.

The next day I came into YORK, where were several people that were very tender. Upon the First-day of the week following, I was commanded of the Lord to go to the great minster, and speak to priest Bowles and his hearers in their great cathedral. Accordingly I went: and when the priest had done, I told them I had something from the Lord God to speak to the priest and people. "Then say on quickly," said a professor that was among them, for it was frost and snow, and very cold weather. Then I told them, This was the word of the Lord God unto them, that they lived in words; but God Almighty looked for fruits amongst them. As soon as the words were out of my mouth, they hurried me out, and threw me down the steps; but I got up again without hurt, and went to my lodgings. Several were convinced there: for the very groans that arose from the weight and oppression that was upon the Spirit of God in me, would open people, and strike them, and make them confess that the groans which broke forth through me did reach them; for my life was burthened with their profession without possession, and words without fruit.

After I had done my present service in York, and several were convinced there, received the truth of God, and were turned to his teaching, I passed out of York, and looking towards Cleveland, I saw there was a people that had tasted of the power of God. I saw then there was a seed in that country, and that God had an humble people there. Passing onwards that night, a Papist overtook me, and talked to me of his religion, and of their meetings; and I let him speak all that was in his mind. That night I stayed at an ale-house. The next morning I was moved of the Lord to speak the word of the Lord to this Papist. So I went to his house, and declared against his religion, and all their superstitious ways; and told him that God was come to teach his people himself. This put the Papist into such a rage, that he could not then endure to stay in his own house.

The next day I came to BURRABY, where a priest and several friendly people met together. Many of the people were convinced, and have continued faithful ever since; and there is a great meeting of Friends in that town. The priest also was forced to confess to the truth, though he came not into it.

The day following I went into CLEVELAND, amongst those people that had tasted of the power of God. They had formerly had great meetings, but were then all shattered to pieces, and the heads of them turned Rant-

ers.   I told them that after they had had such meetings, they did not
wait upon God to feel his power, to gather their minds inward, that they
might feel his presence and power amongst them in their meetings, to sit
down therein, and wait upon him; for they had spoken themselves dry;
they had spent their portions, and not living in that which they spoke of,
they were now become dry.   They had some kind of meetings still; but
they took tobacco and drank ale in their meetings, and were grown light
and loose.   But my message unto them from the Lord was, That they
should all come together again, and wait to feel the Lord's power and
Spirit in themselves, to gather them to Christ, that they might be taught
of him who says, " Learn of me."   For when they had declared that which
the Lord had opened to them, then the people were to receive it; and both
the speakers and hearers were to live in that themselves.   But when these
had no more to declare, but went to seek forms without life, that made
themselves dry and barren, and the people also; and from thence came all
their loss : for the Lord renews his mercies and his strength to them that
wait upon him.   The heads of these people came to nothing : but most of
them came to be convinced, and received God's everlasting truth, and continue a meeting to this day, sitting under the teaching of the Lord Jesus
Christ their Saviour.

Upon the First-day of the next week, the word of the Lord came to me
to go to the steeple-house there, which I did.   When the priest had done I
spoke the truth to him and the people, and directed them to their teacher
within, Christ Jesus, their free teacher, that had bought them.   The priest
came to me, and I had a little discourse with him ; but he was soon stopped,
and silent.   Then being clear of the place, I passed away, having had
several meetings amongst those people.

Though at this time the snow was very deep, I kept travelling; and
going through the country, came to a market-town, where I met with many
professors, with whom I had much reasoning.   I asked them many questions, which they were not able to answer; saying, they had never had
such deep questions put to them in all their lives.

From them I went to STATH, where also I met with many professors,
and some Ranters.   I had large meetings amongst them, and a great convincement there was.   Many received the truth ; amongst whom, one was
a man of an hundred years of age; another was a chief constable; and
a third was a priest, whose name was Philip Scafe.   Him the Lord, by
his free Spirit, did afterwards make a free minister of his free gospel.

The priest of this town was a lofty one, who much oppressed the
people for his tithes.   If they went a-fishing many leagues off, he would
make them pay the tithe-money of what they made of their fish, though
they caught them at a great distance, and carried them as far as Yarmouth
to sell.   I was moved to go to the steeple-house there, to declare the truth,
and expose the priest.   When I had spoken to him, and laid his oppression
of the people before him, he fled away.   The chief of the parish were very
light and vain; so after I had spoken the word of life to them, I turned
away from them, because they did not receive it, and left them.   But the
word of the Lord, which I had declared amongst them, remained with

some of them; so that at night some of the heads of the parish came to
me, and most of them were convinced and satisfied, and confessed to the
truth. Thus the truth began to spread in that country, and great meetings
we had; at which the priest began to rage, and the Ranters to be stirred;
and they sent me word that they would have a dispute with me, both the
oppressing priest, and the leaders of the Ranters. A day was fixed, and
the Ranter came with his company; and another priest, a Scotchman, came;
but not the oppressing priest of Stath. Philip Scafe, who had been a
priest, and was convinced, was with me; and a great number of people
met. When we were settled, the Ranter, whose name was T. Bushel, told
me he had had a vision of me; that I was sitting in a great chair, and that
he was to come and put off his hat, and bow down to the ground before
me; and he did so: and many other flattering words he spoke. I told
him it was his own figure, and said unto him, "Repent, thou beast." He
said it was jealousy in me to say so. Then I asked him the ground of
jealousy, and how it came to be bred in man? and the nature of a beast,
what made it, and how it was bred in man? For I saw him directly
in the nature of the beast; and therefore I wished to know of him how
that nature came to be bred in him? I told him he should give me an
account of the things done in the body, before we came to discourse of
things done out of the body. So I stopped his mouth, and all his fellow
Ranters were silenced; for he was the head of them. Then I called for
the oppressing priest, but he came not; only the Scotch priest came, whose
mouth was soon stopped with a very few words; he being out of the life
of what he professed. Then I had a good opportunity with the people.
I laid open the Ranters, ranking them with the old Ranters in Sodom.
The priests I manifested to be of the same stamp with their fellow-hirelings,
the false prophets of old, and the priests that then bore rule over the people
by their means, seeking for their gain from their quarter, divining for
money, and teaching for filthy lucre. I brought all the prophets, and
Christ, and the apostles, over the heads of the priests, showing how the
prophets, Christ, and the apostles, had long since discovered them by their
marks and fruits. Then I directed the people to their inward teacher,
Christ Jesus their Saviour; and I preached up Christ in the hearts of his
people, when all these mountains were laid low. The people were all quiet,
and the gainsayers' mouths were stopped; for though they broiled inwardly,
yet the power bound them down, that they could not break out.

After the meeting, this Scotch priest desired me to walk with him on
the top of the cliffs; whereupon I called a brother-in-law of his, who was in
some measure convinced, and desired him to go with me, telling him I
desired to have somebody by to hear what was said, lest the priest, when
I was gone, should report anything of me which I did not say. We went
together; and as we walked, the priest asked me many things concerning
the light, and concerning the soul; to all which I answered him fully.
When he had done questioning, we parted, and he went his way; and meeting with Philip Scafe, he broke his cane against the ground in madness,
and said, if ever he met with me again, he would have my life, or I should
have his; adding, that he would give his head, if I was not knocked down

within a month. By this, Friends suspected that his intent was, in desiring me to walk with him alone, either to thrust me down from off the cliff, or to do me some other mischief; and that when he saw himself frustrated in that, by my having one with me, it made him rage. I feared neither his prophecies nor his threats; for I feared God Almighty. But some Friends, through their affection for me, feared much that this priest would do me some mischief, or set on others to do it. Yet after some years this very Scotch priest, and his wife also, came to be convinced of the truth; and about twelve years after this, I was at their house.

After this, there came another priest to a meeting where I was, one that was in repute above all the priests in the country. As I was speaking in the meeting, that the gospel was the power of God, and how it brought life and immortality to light in men, and was turning people from darkness to the light, this high-flown priest said the gospel was mortal. I told him, the true minister said, the gospel was the power of God, and would he make the power of God mortal? Upon that the other priest, Philip Scafe, that was convinced, and had felt the immortal power of God in himself, took him up and reproved him; so a great dispute arose between them; the convinced priest holding that the gospel was immortal, and the other priest that it was mortal. But the Lord's power was too hard for this opposing priest, and stopped his mouth; and many people were convinced, seeing the darkness that was in the opposing priest, and the light that was in the convinced priest.

Then another priest sent to have a dispute with me, and Friends went with me to the house where he was: but when he understood we were come, he slipped out of the house, and hid himself under a hedge. The people went to seek him, and found him, but could not get him to come to us. Then I went to a steeple-house hard by, where the priest and people were in a great rage: this priest had threatened Friends what he would do; but when I came he fled; for the Lord's power came over him and them. Yea, the Lord's everlasting power was over the world, and reached to the hearts of people, and made both priests and professors tremble. It shook the earthly and airy spirit, in which they held their profession of religion and worship, so that it was a dreadful thing unto them, when it was told them, "The man in leather breeches is come."* At the hearing

---

* The leathern garments worn by George Fox were chosen by him for their simplicity and durability; and though they often subjected their wearer to ridicule and abuse, he had no motive beyond the above-mentioned for chosing such a garb. Many persons have been amused, if not offended at him for having worn such a dress when he was a young man. In those days leathern garments for working men may not have been so singular as some suppose. It is a well authenticated fact, that an eminent merchant of the city of London, about 150 years ago, travelled on foot from Newcastle, in search of a livelihood, clad in a *coat of leather*. He opened a warehouse in London for the sale of heavy articles of iron, which were manufactured in the neighbourhood of Newcastle. In a few years he became prosperous, accumulated a large fortune, and ranked with the magnates of the city, sharing in all the civic honours of the corporation. The firm which he established still continues to conduct a flourishing business, at a warehouse in Thames Street, which is familiarly known in the trade by "The Leathern Doublet;" a representation of the founder's original dress being fixed as a sign in front of the building.

thereof the priests, in many places, would get out of the way; they were so struck with the dread of the eternal power of God; and fear surprised the hypocrites.

From this place we passed to WHITBY and SCARBOROUGH, where we had some service for the Lord; there are large meetings settled there since. From thence I passed over the WOLDS to MALTON, where we had great meetings; as we had also at the towns thereabouts. At one town a priest sent me a challenge to dispute with me; but when I came, he would not come forth; so I had a good opportunity with the people, and the Lord's power came over them. One, who had been a wild, drunken man, was so reached therewith, that he came to me as lowly as a lamb; though he and his companions had before sent for drink, to make the rude people drunk, on purpose that they might abuse us. When I found the priest would not come forth, I was moved to go to the steeple-house; the priest was confounded, and the Lord's power came over all.

On the First-day following, came one of the highest Independent professors, a woman, who had let in such a prejudice against me, that she said before she came, she could willingly go to see me hanged: but when she came, she was convinced, and remains a Friend.

Then I turned to MALTON again, and very great meetings there were; to which more people would have come, but durst not for fear of their relations; for it was thought a strange thing then to preach in houses, and not go to the church, as they called it; so that I was much desired to go and speak in the steeple-houses. One of the priests wrote to me, and invited me to preach in the steeple-house, calling me his brother. Another priest, a noted man, kept a lecture there. Now the Lord had showed me, while I was in Derby prison, that I should speak in steeple-houses, to gather people from thence; and a concern sometimes would come upon my mind about the pulpits that the priests lolled in. For the steeple-houses and pulpits were offensive to my mind, because both priests and people called them the house of God, and idolized them; reckoning that God dwelt there in the outward house. Whereas they should have looked for God and Christ to dwell *in* their hearts, and their bodies to be made the temples of God; for the apostle said, "God dwelleth not in temples made with hands:" but by reason of the people's idolizing those places, it was counted a heinous thing to declare against them. When I came into the steeple-house, there were not above eleven hearers, and the priest was preaching to them. But after it was known in the town that I was in the steeple-house, it was soon filled with people. When the priest that preached that day had done, he sent the other priest that had invited me thither, to bring me up into the pulpit; but I sent word to him, that I needed not to go into the pulpit. Then he sent to me again, desiring me to go up into it; for, he said, it was a better place, and there I might be seen of the people. I sent him word again, I could be seen and heard well enough where I was; and that I came not there to hold up such places, nor their maintenance and trade. Upon my saying so, they began to be angry, and said, "these false prophets were to come in the last times." Their saying so grieved many of the people; and some began to murmur at it. Whereupon I stood up, and desired all to be quiet; and stepping upon a high seat, I declared unto them the marks of the false prophets, and showed that they were already come; and set the true prophets, and Christ, and his apostles over them; and manifested these to be out of the steps of the true prophets, and of Christ and his apostles. I directed the people to their inward teacher, Christ Jesus, who would turn them from darkness to the light. And having opened divers Scriptures to them, I directed them to the Spirit of God in themselves, by which they might come to him, and by which they might also come to know who the false prophets were. So having had a large opportunity among them, I departed in peace.

After some time, I came to PICKERING, where in the steeple-house the justices held their sessions, Justice Robinson being chairman. I had a meeting in the school-house at the same time; and abundance of priests and professors came to it, asking questions, which were answered to their satisfaction. It being sessions-time, four chief constables and many other people were convinced that day; and word was carried to Justice Robinson that his priest was overthrown and convinced, whom he had a love to, more than to all the priests besides. After the meeting, we went to an inn. Justice Robinson's priest was very lowly and loving, and would have paid for my dinner, but I would by no means suffer it. Then he offered that I should have his steeple-house to preach in, but I refused it, and told him and the people, that I came to bring them off from such things to Christ.

The next morning I went with the four chief constables, and others, to visit Justice Robinson, who met me at his chamber door. I told him, I could not honour him with man's honour. He said he did not look for it. So I went into his chamber, and opened to him the state of the false prophets, and of the true prophets; and set the true prophets, and Christ, and the apostles over the other; and directed his mind to Christ his teacher. I opened to him the parables, and how election and reprobation stood; as that reprobation stood in the first birth, and election stood in the second birth. I showed also what the promise of God was to, and what the judgment of God was against. He confessed to it all; and was so opened with the truth, that when another justice that was present, made some little opposition, he informed him. At our parting, he said it was very well that I exercised that gift, which God had given me. He took the chief constables aside, and would have given them some money for me, saying, he would not have me at any charge in their country; but they told him that they could not persuade me to take any; and so accepting his kindness, I refused his money.

From thence I passed up into the country, and the priest that called me brother (in whose school-house I had the meeting at Pickering), went along with me. When we came into a town to bait, the bells rang. I asked what they rang for: and they said, for me to preach in the steeple-house. After some time I felt drawings that way; and as I walked to the steeple-house, I saw the people were gathered together in the yard. The old priest would have had me to go into the steeple-house; but I said, it was no matter. It was something strange to the people, that I would not go into that which they called the house of God. I stood up in the steeple-house yard, and declared to the people, that I came not to hold up their idol temples, nor their priests, nor their tithes, nor their augmentations, nor their priests' wages, nor their Jewish and heathenish ceremonies and traditions (for I denied all these), and told them that that piece of ground was no more holy than another piece of ground. I showed them that the apostles' going into the Jews' synagogues and temples, which God had commanded, was to bring people off from that temple, and those synagogues, and from the offerings, and tithes, and covetous priests of that time; that such as came to be convinced of the truth, and converted to it, and believed in Jesus Christ, whom the apostles preached, met together afterwards in dwelling-houses; and that all who preach Christ, the Word of life, ought to preach freely, as the apostles did, and as he had commanded. So I was sent of the Lord God of heaven and earth to preach freely, and to bring people off from these outward temples made with hands, which God dwelleth not in; that they might know their bodies to become the temples of God and of Christ: and to draw people off from all their superstitious ceremonies, and Jewish and heathenish customs, traditions, and doctrines of men; and from all the world's hireling teachers, that take tithes and great wages, preaching for hire, and divining for money, whom God and Christ never sent, as themselves confess, when they say they never heard God's voice, nor Christ's voice. Therefore I exhorted the people to come off from all these things, and directed them to the Spirit and grace of God in themselves, and to the light of Jesus in their own hearts, that they might come to know Christ, their free teacher, to bring them salvation, and to open the Scriptures to them. Thus the Lord gave me a good opportunity amongst them to open things largely unto them. All was quiet, and many were convinced; blessed be the Lord!

I passed on to another town, where there was another great meeting, the old priest before mentioned going along with me; and there came professors of several sorts to it. I sat on a haystack, and spoke nothing for some hours; for I was to famish them from words. The professors would ever and anon be speaking to the old priest, and asking him when I would begin, and when I would speak. He bade them wait; and told them, that the people waited upon Christ a long while before he spoke. At last I was moved of the Lord to speak; and they were struck by the Lord's power; the word of life reached to them, and there was a general convincement amongst them.

From hence I passed on, the old priest being still with me, and several others. As we went along, some people called to him, and said, "Mr. Boyes, we owe you some money for tithes, pray come and take it." But he threw up his hands, and said, he had enough, he would have none of it; they might keep it; and he praised the Lord he had enough.

At length we came to this old priest's steeple-house in the Moors; and when we were come into it, he went before me, and held open the pulpit door; but I told him I should not go into it. This steeple-house was very much painted. I told him and the people, that the painted beast had a painted house. Then I opened to them the rise of all those houses, and their superstitious ways; showing them, that as the end of the apostles' going into the temple and synagogues, which God had commanded, was not to hold them up, but to bring the people to Christ, the substance; so the end of my coming there, was not to hold up these temples, priests, and tithes, which God had never commanded, but to bring themselves off from all these things, to Christ the substance. I showed them the true worship, which Christ had set up; and distinguished Christ the true way, from all the false ways, opening the parables to them, and turning them from darkness to the true light, that by it they might see themselves, their sins, and Christ their Saviour; that believing in him, they might be saved from their sins.

After this we went to one Birdet's house, where I had a great meeting, and this old priest accompanied me still, leaving his steeple-house; for he had been looked upon as a famous priest, above Common-Prayermen, and Presbyters, and Independents too. Before he was convinced, he went sometimes into their steeple-houses and preached; for he had been a zealous man in his way. And when they complained of him to Justice Hotham, he bid them distrain his horse for travelling on the Lord's day (as he called it); but Hotham did that only to put them off, for he knew the priest used no horse, but travelled on foot.

Now I came towards CRANTSICK, to Captain Pursloe's and Justice Hotham's, who received me kindly, being glad that the Lord's power had so appeared; that truth was spread, and so many had received it; and that Justice Robinson was so civil. Justice Hotham said, If God had not raised up this principle of light and life, which I preached, the nation had been overrun with Ranterism, and all the justices in the nation could not have stopped it with all their laws; because (said he) they would have said as we said, and done as we commanded, and yet have kept their own principle still. But this principle of truth, said he, overthrows their principle, and the root and ground thereof; and therefore, he was glad the Lord had raised up this principle of life and truth.

From thence I travelled up into HOLDERNESS, and came to a justice's house, whose name was Pearson, where there was a very tender woman, that believed in the truth, and was so affected therewith, that she said she could have left all and have followed me.

Thence I went to ORAM, to one George Hartise's, where many of that town were convinced. On the First-day I was moved to go into the steeple-house, where the priest had got another to help him; and many professors and contenders were assembled together. But the Lord's power was over all; the priests fled away, and much good service I had for the Lord amongst the people. Some of those great professors were convinced, and became honest, faithful Friends, being men of account in the place.

The next day, Friends and friendly people having left me, I travelled alone, declaring the day of the Lord amongst people in the towns where I came, and warning them to repent. One day, I came towards night into a town called PATRINGTON; and as I walked along the town, I warned both priest and people (for the priest was in the street) to repent, and turn to the Lord. It grew dark before I came to the end of the town; and a multitude of people gathered about me, to whom I declared the word of life. When I had cleared myself, I went to an inn, and desired them to let me have a lodging; but they would not. Then I desired them to let me have a little meat, or milk, and I would pay them for it; but they would not. So I walked out of the town, and a company of fellows followed me, and asked me, what news? I bid them repent, and fear the Lord. After I had gone some distance, I came to another house, and desired the people to let me have a little meat and drink, and lodging for my money; but they denied me. Then I went to another house, and desired the same; but they refused me also. By this time it was grown so dark, that I could not see the highway; but I discerned a ditch, and got a little water and refreshed myself. Then I got over the ditch, and being weary with travelling, sat down among the furze-bushes till it was day. About break of day I got up and passed over the fields. A man came after me with a great pike-staff, and went along with me to a town; and he raised the town upon me, with the constable and chief constable, before the sun was up. I declared God's everlasting truth amongst them, warning them of the day of the Lord, that was coming upon all sin and wickedness; and exhorted them to repent. But they seized me, and had me back to Patrington, about three miles, guarding me with pikes, staves, and halberds. Now when I was come back to Patrington, all the town was in an uproar, and the priest and people were consulting together; so I had another opportunity to declare the word of life amongst them, and warn them to repent. At last a professor, a tender man, called me into his house, and there I took a little milk and bread, not having eaten for some days before. Then they guarded me about nine miles to a justice. When I was come near his house, a man came riding after us, and asked me whether I was the man that was apprehended? I asked him wherefore he asked? He said, for no hurt; and I told him I was; so he rode away to the justice before us. The men that guarded me said, It was well if the justice was not drunk, before we got to him; for he used to be drunk early. When I was brought in before him, because I did not put off my hat, and said Thou to him, he asked the man that rode thither before me, whether I was not mazed or fond; but the man told him, no, it was my principle. Then I warned him to repent, and come to the light, which Christ had enlightened him with, that by it he might see all his evil words and actions; and to return to Christ Jesus whilst he had time; and that whilst he had time, he should prize it. "Ay, ay," said he, "the light, that is spoken of in the third of John." I desired him that he would mind it, and obey it. As I admonished him, I laid my hand upon him, and he was brought down by the power of the Lord; and all the watchmen stood amazed. Then he took me into a little parlour with the other man, and desired to see what I had in my pockets, of letters or intelligence. I plucked out my linen, and showed him that I had no letters. He said, He is not a vagrant by his linen; and then he set me at liberty. I went back to Patrington, with the man that had ridden before me to the justice; for he lived at Patrington. When I came there, he would have had me have a meeting at the Cross; but I said, it was no matter, his house would serve. He desired me to go to bed, or lie down upon a bed; which he did, that they might say, they had seen me in a bed, or upon a bed; for a report had been raised that I would not lie on any bed, because at that time I lay many times out of doors. Now when the First-day of the week was come, I went to the steeple-house, and declared the truth to the priest and people; and the people did not molest me, for the power of God was come over them. Presently after I had a great meeting at the man's house where I lay, and many were convinced of the Lord's everlasting truth, who stand faithful witnesses of it to this day. They were exceedingly grieved that they did not receive me, nor give me lodging, when I was there before.

From hence I travelled through the country, even to the furthest part thereof, warning people, in towns and villages, to repent, and directing them to Christ Jesus, their teacher.

On the First-day of the week I came to one Colonel Overton's house, and had a great meeting of the prime of the people of that country; where many things were opened out of the Scriptures, which they had never heard before. Many were convinced, and received the word of life, and were settled in the truth of God.

Then I returned to PATRINGTON again, and visited those Friends that were convinced there; by whom I understood that a tailor, and some wild blades in that town, had occasioned my being carried before the justice. The tailor came to ask my forgiveness, fearing I would complain of him. The constables also were afraid, lest I should trouble them. But I forgave them all, and warned them to turn to the Lord, and to amend their lives. Now that which made them the more afraid was this: when I was in the steeple-house at Oram not long before, there came a professor, who gave me a push on the breast in the steeple-house, and bid me get out of the church; "Alas, poor man!" said I, "dost thou call the steeple-house the church? The church is the people, whom God hath purchased with his blood, and not the house." It happened that Justice Hotham came to hear of this man's abuse, sent his warrant for him, and bound him over to the sessions; so affected was he with the truth, and so zealous to keep the peace. And indeed this Justice Hotham had asked me before, whether any people had meddled with me, or abused me; but I was not at liberty to tell him anything of that kind, but was to forgive all.

CHAPTER V.

1652.—George Fox visits great men's houses, warning them to repent—is accused of calling himself Christ—refutes the charge, and tells the accuser that Judas's end would be his, which shortly came to pass; hence a slander is raised against Friends—is stoned at Doncaster—a scoffing priest made to tremble at the Lord's power—a slandering priest cut off in his wickedness—a murderous man seeks George Fox, but misses him—he lays in a wood all night—the influence of one man or woman, who lives in the same spirit that the prophets and apostles were in, is to be felt within a circuit of ten miles—George Fox ascends Pendle Hill, whence he sees the place of a great gathering of people—on descending, refreshes himself at a spring of water, having taken little sustenance for several days—foresees a great people in white raiment about Wensleydale and Sedbergh—a wicked man designs to injure him, but is prevented—many are convinced in Dent, and a meeting is settled at Sedbergh, where he had seen a people in white raiment—preaches for several hours in the steeple-house yard there—preaches on a rock, near Firbank chapel, to 1000 people, for three hours—the family of Judge Fell convinced, and a meeting settled at his house, and continued for forty years—preaches through Lancaster streets—at a meeting of priests at Ulverstone he speaks in great power, so that one of them said, " the church shook "—disputes with priest Lampitt—Justice Sawrey is the first persecutor in the north—forty priests appear against George Fox at Lancaster Sessions for speaking blasphemy; they are confounded, and he is cleared of the charge—James Naylor's account of George Fox's trial at Lancaster Sessions—priest Jackus is reproved from the bench for his blasphemy—these priests are reproved by the populace—Col. West defends and protects George Fox against the machinations of the priests, and the design of Judge Windham, at the risk of losing his place.

FROM PATRINGTON I went to several great men's houses, warning them to repent. Some received me lovingly, and some slighted me. Thus I passed on, and at night came to another town, where I desired lodging and meat, and I would pay for it; but they would not lodge me, except I would go to the constable, which was the custom (they said) of all lodgers at inns, if strangers. I told them I should not go; for that custom was for suspicious persons, but I was an innocent man. After I had warned them to repent, declared unto them the day of their visitation, and directed them to the light of Christ and Spirit of God, that they might come to know salvation, I passed away; and the people were something tendered, and troubled afterwards. When it grew dark, I spied a hay-stack, and went and sat under it all night, till morning.

The next day I passed into HULL, admonishing and warning people, as I went, to turn to Christ Jesus that they might receive salvation. That night I got a lodging, but was very sore with travelling on foot so far.

Afterwards, I came to BALBY, and visited Friends up and down in those parts; and then passed into the edge of NOTTINGHAMSHIRE, visiting Friends there; and so into LINCOLNSHIRE, and visited Friends there. And on the First-day of the week I went to a steeple-house on this side of Trent; and in the afternoon to one on the other side of Trent, declaring the word of life to the people, and directing them to their teacher, Christ Jesus, who died for them that they might hear him, and receive salvation by him. Then I went further into the country, and had several meetings. To one meeting came a great man, and a priest, and many professors; but the Lord's power came over them all, and they went their ways peaceably. There came a man to that meeting, who had been at one before, and raised a false accusation against me, and made a noise up and down the country, reporting that I had said, I was Christ; which was utterly false. And when I came to GAINSBOROUGH, where a Friend had been declaring truth in the market, the town and market-people were all in an uproar. I went into a friendly man's house, and the people rushed in after me; so that the house was filled with professors, disputers, and rude people. This false accuser came in, and charged me openly before all the people, that I had said, I was Christ, and he had got witnesses to prove it. This set the people into such a rage, that they had much to do to keep their hands off me. Then was I moved of the Lord God to stand up on the table, and, in the eternal power of God, to tell the people "That Christ was *in* them, except they were reprobates; and that it was Christ the eternal power of God, that spoke in me at that time unto them; not that I was Christ." And the people were generally satisfied, except himself, a professor, and his own false-witnesses. I called the accuser Judas, and was moved to tell him, that Judas's end would be his; and that that was the word of the Lord and of Christ, through me, to him. So the Lord's power came over all, and quieted the minds of the people, and they departed in peace. But this Judas went away, and shortly after hanged himself, and a stake was driven into his grave. Afterwards the wicked priests raised a scandal upon us, and reported that a Quaker had hanged himself in Lincolnshire, and had a stake driven through him. This falsehood they printed to the nation, adding sin to sin; which the truth and we were clear of: for he was no more a Quaker than the priest that printed it, but was one of their own people. But notwithstanding this wicked slander, by which the adversary designed to defame us, and turn people's minds against the truth we held forth, many in Lincolnshire received the gospel, being convinced of the Lord's everlasting truth, and sat down therein under the Lord's heavenly teaching.

After this I passed, in the Lord's power, into YORKSHIRE, came to WARMSWORTH, and went to the steeple-house in the forenoon,* but they

---

* The circumstance of Friends entering the public places of worship in the times of the Commonwealth, is one which has been much misunderstood, and greatly misrepresented. For these acts of dedication they have been calumniated as disturbers of religious congregations, and as outraging the peace and order of the churches. This estimate, doubtless, has been formed with reference to usages of more modern date; but to decide upon the conduct of Friends in this particular, from a consideration of present circumstances, would be exceedingly erroneous. In preaching in the national places of worship, they did but avail themselves of a common liberty, in a period of extraordinary excitement on religious things. There were numerous other religious meetings held in those times, but into none of these did Friends obtrude themselves. Some probably will argue, that the fact of their being so severely punished for persisting in this practice, may be adduced in support of its irregularity; but it may be answered, that the preaching of Friends almost everywhere, at that

shut the door against me; yet after a while they let in Thomas Aldam, and then shut it again; and the priest fell upon him, asking him questions. At last they opened the door, and I went in. As soon as I was in the priest's sight, he discontinued preaching, though I said nothing to him, and asked me, "What have you to say?" and presently cried out, "Come, come, I will prove them false prophets in Matthew;" but he was so confounded, he could not find the chapter. Then he fell on me, asking me many questions, and I stood still all this while, not saying any thing amongst them. At last I said, "Seeing here are so many questions asked, I may answer them." But as soon as I began to speak, the people violently rushed upon me, and thrust me out of the steeple-house again, and locked the door on me. As soon as they had done their service, and were come forth, the people ran upon me, and knocked me sorely with their staves, threw clods and stones at me, and abused me much; the priest also, being in a great rage, laid violent hands on me himself. But I warned them and him of the terrible day of the Lord, and exhorted them to repent, and turn to Christ. Being filled with the Lord's refreshing power, I was not sensible of much hurt I had received by their blows. In the afternoon I went to another steeple-house, but the priest had done before I got thither; so I preached repentance to the people that were left, and directed them to their inward teacher, Jesus Christ.

From hence I went to BALBY, and so to DONCASTER, where I had formerly preached repentance on the market-day; which had made a noise and alarm in the country. On the First-day I went to the steeple-house, and after the priest had done, I spoke to him and the people what the Lord had commanded me; and they were in a great rage, hurried me out, threw me down, and haled me before the magistrates. A long examination they made of me, and much work I had with them. They threatened my life if ever I came there again; and that they would leave me to the mercy of

---

time, whether in steeple-houses or private houses, in-doors or out of doors, equally called down the rigour of ecclesiastical vengeance. It was not, in fact, because Friends preached in these places so much as for what they preached that they suffered. When George Fox was committed to Derby prison in 1650, after preaching in the steeple-house at "a great lecture," the mittimus states his offence was, for "uttering and broaching of divers blasphemous opinions." In 1659, Gilbert Latey went to Dunstan's steeple-house in the west, where the noted Dr. Manton preached. At the conclusion of the sermon, Gilbert Latey addressed the assembly relative to some errors in Manton's sermon, for which he was seized by a constable and taken before a magistrate; who, however, gave G. Latey leave to speak for himself. The statement he made satisfied the justice, and he replied, that he had heard the people called Quakers, were a sort of mad, whimsical folks; "but," said he, "for this man, he talks very rationally, and I think, for my part, you should not have brought him before me." To which the constable replied, "Sir, I think so too." This occurred eleven years after G. Fox first visited a steeple-house, and, during that time, Friends had suffered very much for speaking in them, yet now a magistrate declares, that speaking rationally after the preacher had finished in a steeple-house, is not an offence for which a man ought to be brought before him. But the ministry of Friends struck at the very foundation of all hierarchical systems, and the discovery of this circumstance prompted the priests to call in the aid of the civil power, to suppress the promulgation of views so opposed to ecclesiastical domination.

the people. Nevertheless, I declared truth amongst them, and directed them to the light of Christ *in* them; testifying unto them that "God was come to teach his people himself, whether they would hear or forbear." After a while they put us out (for some Friends were with me) among the rude multitude, and they stoned us down the street. An innkeeper, that was a bailiff, came and took us into his house; and they broke his head, that the blood ran down his face, with the stones that they threw at us. We stayed a while in his house, and showed the more sober people the priest's fruits. Then we went to Balby, about a mile off, and the rude people laid wait for us, and stoned us down the lane; but, blessed be the Lord, we did not receive much hurt.

The next First-day I went to TICKHILL, whither the Friends of that side gathered together, and in the meeting a mighty brokenness by the power of God was amongst the people. I went out of the meeting, being moved of God to go to the steeple-house; and when I came there, I found the priest and most of the chief of the parish together in the chancel. So I went up to them, and began to speak; but they immediately fell upon me; and the clerk took up his Bible, as I was speaking, and struck me on the face with it, so that it gushed out with blood, and I bled exceedingly in the steeple-house. Then the people cried, "Let us have him out of the church;" and when they had got me out, they beat me exceedingly, and threw me down, and over a hedge; and afterwards they dragged me through a house into the street, stoning and beating me as they drew me along, so that I was besmeared all over with blood and dirt. They got my hat from me, which I never obtained again. Yet when I was got upon my legs again, I declared to them the word of life, and showed them the fruits of their teacher, and how they dishonoured Christianity. After a while I got into the meeting again amongst Friends; and the priest and people coming by the house, I went forth with Friends into the yard, and there I spoke to the priest and people. The priest scoffed at us, and called us Quakers. But the Lord's power was so over them, and the word of life was declared in such authority and dread to them, that the priest began trembling himself; and one of the people said, "Look how the priest trembles and shakes, he is turned a Quaker also." When the meeting was over, Friends departed; and I went without my hat to BALBY, about seven or eight miles. Friends were much abused that day by the priest and his people; insomuch that some moderate justices hearing of it, two or three of them came, and sat at the town, to hear and examine the business. And he that had shed my blood was afraid of having his hand cut off, for striking me in the church (as they called it); but I forgave him, and would not appear against him.

In the beginning of this year 1652 great rage got up in priests and people, and in some of the magistrates of the West-Riding of Yorkshire, against the truth and Friends; insomuch that the priest of WARMSWORTH procured a warrant from the justices against me and Thomas Aldam, to be executed in any part of the West-Riding of Yorkshire. At the same time I had a vision of a bear and two great mastiff dogs; that I should pass by them, and they should do me no hurt; and it proved so: for the constable took Thomas Aldam and carried him to York. I went with Thomas Aldam twenty miles towards York: and the constable had the warrant for me also, and said, "he saw me, but he was loath to trouble men that were strangers; but Thomas Aldam was his neighbour." So the Lord's power restrained him, that he had not power to meddle with me. We came to Lieutenant Roper's, where we had a great meeting of many considerable men; and the truth was powerfully declared amongst them, and the Scriptures wonderfully opened, and the parables and sayings of Christ were expounded, and the state of the church in the apostles' days was plainly set forth, and the apostacy since from that state discovered. The truth had great dominion that day, so that those great men that were present did generally confess to it, saying, "they believed that this principle must go over the whole world." There were at this meeting James Naylor, Thomas Goodyear,* and William Dewsbury, who had been convinced the year before; and Richard Farnsworth also. And the constable stayed with Thomas Aldam till the meeting was over, and then went towards York prison; but did not meddle with me.

From hence I went to WAKEFIELD; and on the First-day after, I went to a steeple-house, where James Naylor had been a member of an Independent church; but upon his receiving truth, he was excommunicated. When I came in, and the priest had done, the people called upon me to come up to the priest, which I did; but when I began to declare the word of life to them, and to lay open the deceit of the priest, they rushed upon me suddenly, thrust me out at the other door, punching and beating me, and cried, "Let us have him to the stocks." But the Lord's power restrained them, that they were not suffered to put me in. So I passed away to the meeting, where were a great many professors and friendly people gathered, and a great convincement there was that day; for the people were mightily satisfied that they were directed to the Lord's teaching *in themselves.* Here we got some lodging; for four of us had lain under a hedge the night before, there being then few Friends in that place.

The same day Richard Farnsworth went to another great steeple-house, belonging to a high priest, and declared the word of truth unto the people; and a great service he had amongst them; for the Lord's dread and power was mightily over all.

The priest of that church which James Naylor had been a member of, whose name was Marshall, raised many wicked slanders about me, as, "that I carried bottles with me, and made people drink of them, which made them follow me;" and, "that I rode upon a great black horse, and was seen in one country upon it in one hour, and at the same hour in another country threescore miles off;" and, "that I would give a fellow money to

---

* Thomas Goodyear became a faithful minister, and suffered much persecution and imprisonment. When in Oxford jail (for refusing to swear), the jailer put irons on his legs, which being too small hurt him, and besides other abuse, would not let him and other Friends have straw to lie on. The jailer also told the other prisoners if they wanted coats, they might take those of the Friends off their backs; but one of the prisoners answered he would go naked first.

Thomas Goodyear was the author of *A Plain Testimony to the Ancient Truth and Work of God.* He died at Selby, in 1693.

follow me, when I was on my black horse." With these lies he fed his people, to make them think evil of the truth which I had declared amongst them. But by these lies he preached many of his hearers away from him; for I was then travelling on foot, and had no horse at that time ; which the people generally knew. The Lord soon after cut off this envious priest in his wickedness.

After this I came to HIGH-TOWN, where dwelt a woman who had been convinced a little before. We went to her house, and had a meeting ; and the people gathered together, and we declared the truth to them, and had some service for the Lord amongst them ; they passed away again peaceably. But there was a widow woman, named Green, who, being filled with envy, went to one that was called a gentleman in the town, (who was reported to have killed two men and one woman,) and informed him against us, though he was no officer. The next morning we drew up some queries to be sent to the priest. When we had done, and were just going away, some of the friendly people of the town came running up to the house where we were, and told us that this murdering man had sharpened a pike to stab us, and was coming up with his sword by his side. We were just passing away, and so missed him. But we were no sooner gone, than he came to the house where we had been ; and the people generally concluded if we had not been gone, he would have murdered some of us. That night we lay in a wood, and were very wet, for it rained exceedingly. In the morning I was moved to return to the town, when they gave us a full relation of this wicked man.

From hence we passed to BRADFORD, where we met with Richard Farnsworth again, from whom we had parted a little before. When we came in, they set meat before us ; but as I was going to eat, the word of the Lord came to me, saying, "Eat not the bread of such as have an evil eye." Immediately I arose from the table, and ate nothing. The woman of the house was a Baptist. After I had exhorted the family to turn to the Lord Jesus Christ, and hearken to his teachings in their own hearts, we departed thence.

As we travelled through the country, preaching repentance to the people, we came into a town on the market-day. There was a lecture there that day ; and I went into the steeple-house, where were many priests, professors, and people. The priest that preached, took for his text those words of Jeremiah, chap. v. ver. 31 : "My people love to have it so ;" leaving out the foregoing words, viz., "The prophets prophesy falsely, and the priests bear rule by their means." So I showed the people his deceit, and directed them to Christ, the true teacher *within ;* declaring, "that God was come to teach his people himself, and to bring them off from all the world's teachers and hirelings, that they might come to receive freely from him." Then warning them of the day of the Lord, that was coming upon all flesh, I passed from thence without much opposition.

At night we came to a country place, where there was no public-house near. The people desired us to stay all night ; which we did, and had good service for the Lord, declaring his truth amongst them.

The next day we passed on ; for the Lord had said unto me, "If but one man or woman were raised up by his power, to stand and live in the same Spirit that the prophets and apostles were in, who gave forth the Scriptures, that man or woman should shake all the country in their profession for ten miles round." For people had the Scriptures, but were not in that same light, and power, and Spirit, which they were in that gave forth the Scriptures; and so they neither knew God, nor Christ, nor the Scriptures aright; nor had they unity one with another, being out of the power and Spirit of God. Therefore as we passed along we warned all people, wherever we met them, of the day of the Lord that was coming upon them.

As we travelled we came near a very great hill, called PENDLE-HILL, and I was moved of the Lord to go up to the top of it; which I did with difficulty, it was so very steep and high. When I was come to the top, I saw the sea bordering upon Lancashire. From the top of this hill the Lord let me see in what places he had a great people to be gathered. As I went down, I found a spring of water in the side of the hill, with which I refreshed myself, having eaten or drunk but little for several days before.*

At night we came to an inn, and declared truth to the man of the house, and wrote a paper to the priests and professors, declaring "the day of the Lord, and that Christ was come to teach people himself, by his power and Spirit in their hearts, and to bring people off from all the world's ways and teachers, to his own free teaching, who had bought them, and was the Saviour of all them that believed in him." The man of the house spread the paper abroad, and was mightily affected with the truth. Here the Lord opened unto me, and let me see a great people in white raiment by a river side, coming to the Lord; and the place that I saw them in was about WENSLEYDALE and SEDBERGH.

The next day we travelled on, and at night got a little fern or brackens to put under us, and lay upon a common. Next morning we reached a town, where Richard Farnsworth parted from me; and then I travelled alone again. I came up Wensleydale, and at the market-town in that Dale, there was a lecture on the market-day. I went into the steeple-house; and after the priest had done, I "proclaimed the day of the Lord to the priest and people, warning them to turn from darkness to the light, and from the power of Satan unto God, that they might come to know God and Christ aright, and to receive his teaching, who teacheth freely." Largely and freely did I declare the word of life unto them, and had not much persecution there. Afterwards I passed up the Dales, warning people to fear God, and preaching the everlasting gospel to them. In my way I came to a great house, where was a schoolmaster; and they got me into the house. I asked them questions about their religion and worship; and afterwards I declared the truth to them. They had me into a parlour, and locked me in, pretending that I was a young man that was mad, and had run away from my relations; and that they would keep me till they could send to them. But I soon convinced them of their mistake, and they let me forth, and would have had me to stay; but I was not to stay there. Then having exhorted them to repentance, and directed them to the light of Christ

---

* The spring here alluded to is called George Fox's well to this day.

Jesus, that through it they might come unto him and be saved, I passed from them, and came in the night to a little ale-house on a common, where there was a company of rude fellows drinking. Because I would not drink with them, they struck me with their clubs; but I reproved them, and brought them to be somewhat cooler; and then I walked out of the house upon the common in the night. After some time one of these drunken fellows came out, and would have come close up to me, pretending to whisper to me; but I perceived he had a knife; and therefore I kept off him, and bid him repent, and fear God. So the Lord by his power preserved me from this wicked man; and he went into the house again. The next morning I went on through other Dales, warning and exhorting people everywhere as I passed, to repent and turn to the Lord: and several were convinced. At one house that I came to, the man of the house (whom I afterwards found to be a kinsman of John Blakelin's) would have given me money, but I would not receive it.

As I travelled through the Dales, I came to a man's house, whose name was Tennant. I was moved to speak to the family, and declare God's everlasting truth to them; and as I was turning away from them, I was moved to turn again, and speak to the man himself; and he was convinced, and his family, and lived and died in the truth. Thence I came to Major Bousfield's, who received me, as did also several others; and some that were then convinced have stood faithful ever since. I went also through GRISDALE, and several others of those Dales, in which some were convinced. And I went into DENT, where many were convinced also. From Major Bousfield's I came to Richard Robinson's, and declared the everlasting truth to him.

The next day I went to a meeting at Justice Benson's, where I met a people that were separated from the public worship. This was the place I had seen, where a people came forth in white raiment. A large meeting it was, and the people were generally convinced, and continue a large meeting still of Friends near Sedbergh; which was then first gathered through my ministry in the name of Jesus.

In the same week there was a great fair, at which servants used to be hired; and I declared the day of the Lord through the fair. After I had done so, I went into the steeple-house yard, and many of the people of the fair came thither to me, and abundance of priests and professors. There "I declared the everlasting truth of the Lord, and the word of life for several hours, showing that the Lord was come to teach his people himself, and to bring them off from all the world's ways and teachers, to Christ the true teacher, and the true way to God. I laid open their teachers, showing that they were like them that were of old condemned by the prophets, and by Christ, and by the apostles. I exhorted the people to come off from the temples made with hands; and wait to receive the Spirit of the Lord, that they might know themselves to be the temples of God." Not one of the priests had power to open his mouth against what I declared: but at last a captain said, "Why will you not go into the church? this is not a fit place to preach in." I told him, I denied their church. Then stood up one Francis Howgill, who was a preacher to a congregation: he had not seen me before, yet he undertook to answer that captain, and soon put him to silence. Then said Francis Howgill of me, "This man speaks with authority, and not as the scribes." After this I opened to the people, that that ground and house was no holier than another place; and that that house was not the church, but the people, whom Christ is the head of. After a while the priests came up to me, and I warned them to repent. One of them said I was mad, and so they turned away. But many people were convinced there that day, and were glad to hear the truth declared, and received it with joy. Amongst these was one Captain Ward, who received the truth in the love of it, and lived and died in it.

The next First-day I came to FIRBANK CHAPEL, in Westmorland, where Francis Howgill, before named, and John Audland,* had been preaching in the morning. The chapel was full of people, so that many could not get in. Francis Howgill said, he thought I looked into the chapel, and his spirit was ready to fail, the Lord's power did so surprise him; but I did not look in. They made haste, and had quickly done, and they and some of the people went to dinner, but abundance stayed till they came again. Now John Blakelin and others came to me, and desired me not to reprove them publicly; for they were not parish teachers, but pretty tender men. I could not tell them whether I should or not (though I had not at that time any drawings to declare publicly against them), but I said they must leave me to the Lord's movings. While the others were gone to dinner, I went to a brook and got a little water; and then came and sat down on the top of a rock hard by the chapel. In the afternoon the people gathered about me, with several of their preachers. It was judged there were above a thousand people; "amongst whom I declared God's everlasting truth and word of life freely and largely, for about the space of three hours, directing all to the Spirit of God in themselves, that they might be turned from darkness to the light, and believe in it, that they might become the children of it; and might be turned from the power of Satan, which they had been under, unto God; and by the Spirit of truth might be led into all truth, and sensibly understand the words of the prophets, and of Christ, and of the apostles; and might all come to know Christ to

---

* Francis Howgill and John Audland were both religiously inclined, and were convinced during the present year. They became eminent ministers, travelling in the gospel, and suffering fines and imprisonments for its sake, turning many to God. Howgill, for refusing to swear, was sent to Appleby jail, the following sentence being passed against him:—"You are put out of the king's protection and the benefit of the law; your lands are confiscated to the king during your life, and your goods and chattels for ever; and you to be a prisoner during your life." He praised God for the many sweet enjoyments and refreshments he received on his prison bed, whereon he lay, freely forgiving all. His end was in great peace, in 1676. See *Piety Promoted*, i. 64-67.

Audland also laboured much in the gospel, for which he suffered persecution and imprisonments. In his last sickness he was exceedingly filled with high praises to God, being overcome with a sense of his love and joy. When he grew weaker he was helped on his knees, and upon his bed fervently supplicated the Lord on behalf of all his people that "they might be preserved in the truth out of the evil of the world." See *Piety Promoted*, i. 41-44; and *Memoirs of F. Howgill*, by James Backhouse.

be their teacher to instruct them, their counsellor to direct them, their shepherd to feed them, their bishop to oversee them, and their prophet to open divine mysteries to them ; and might know their bodies to be prepared, sanctified, and made fit temples for God and Christ to dwell in. In the openings of heavenly life, I explained unto them the prophets, and the figures, and shadows, and directed them to Christ, the substance. Then I opened the parables and sayings of Christ, and things that had been long hid, showing the intent and scope of the apostles' writings, and that their epistles were written to the elect. When I had opened that state, I showed also the state of the apostacy since the apostles' days ; that the priests have got the Scriptures, but are not in that Spirit which gave them forth, and have put them into chapter and verse, to make a trade of holy men's words ; and that the teachers and priests now are found in the steps of the false prophets, chief priests, scribes, and Pharisees of old, and are such, as the true prophets, Christ, and his apostles cried out against, and so are judged and condemned by the Spirit of the true prophets, and of Christ, and of his apostles ; and that none, who are in that Spirit, and guided by it now, can own them.*

Now there were many old people, who went into the chapel and looked out at the windows, thinking it a strange thing to see a man preach on a hill, and not in their church, as they called it ; whereupon "I was moved to open to the people, that the steeple-house, and the ground whereon it stood, were no more holy than that mountain ; and that those temples, which they called the dreadful houses of God, were not set up by the command of God and of Christ ; nor their priests called, as Aaron's priesthood was ; nor their tithes appointed by God, as those amongst the Jews were ; but that Christ was come, who ended both the temple and its worship, and the priests and their tithes ; and that all should now hearken unto him ; for he said, 'Learn of me ;' and God said of him, 'This is my beloved Son, in whom I am well pleased, hear ye him.' I declared unto them that the Lord God had sent me to preach the everlasting gospel and word of life amongst them, and to bring them off from all these temples, tithes, priests, and rudiments of the world, which had been instituted since the apostles'

* If these remarks appear harsh and unqualified, we must bear in mind, that one of the strongest features of this period was a time-serving spirit amongst the priesthood ; a trait in the character of too many of them, which was curiously exhibited by the fact that several veered round with all the changes of those inconstant times ; being Episcopalians with the first Charles and his bishops ; Presbyterians with Oliver and the Parliament ; again on the side of the Episcopacy at the Restoration ; and probably would have been as ready to unite with the Papists, if Charles II. had established Popery instead of Protestantism. Some of these instances are recorded in Neale's *History of the Puritans.* After the Restoration of Charles II. so general was the flood of riotous dissipation spread over the land, that Bishop Burnet complains of the unworthy lives of many of the clergy ; and states that in Scotland more particularly, their conduct was so flagrantly bad, that they were even despised by the drunken and licentious troopers, who, under their orders, spread rapine and distress throughout the western provinces of that country. One of their commanders, Sir John Turner, "confessed it often went against the grain with him to serve such a debauched and worthless company, as the clergy generally were."—Burnet's *Own Times.*

days, and had been set up by such as had erred from the Spirit and power
the apostles were in." Very largely was I opened at this meeting, and
the Lord's convincing power accompanied my ministry, and reached the
hearts of the people, whereby many were convinced; and all the teachers
of that congregation (who were many), were convinced of God's everlasting
truth.

After the meeting was over I went to John Audland's, and from thence
to PRESTON-PATRICK chapel, where a great meeting was appointed; to
which I went, and had a large opportunity amongst the people to preach
the everlasting gospel, opening to them (as to others on the like occasion),
that the end of my coming into that place was, not to hold it up, no more
than the apostles' going into the Jewish synagogues and temple was, to
uphold those; but to bring them off from all such things, as the apostles
brought the saints of old from off the Jewish temple and Aaron's priesthood, that they might come to witness their bodies to be the temples of
God, and Christ *in* them to be their teacher.

From this place I went to KENDAL, where a meeting was appointed
in the town-hall; in which I declared the word of life amongst the people,
showing them "how they might come to the saving knowledge of Christ,
and have a right understanding of the Holy Scriptures; opening to them
what it was that would lead them into the way of reconciliation with God,
and what would be their condemnation." After the meeting I stayed a
while in the town; several were convinced there, and many appeared loving.
One, whose name was Cock, met me in the street, and would have given
me a roll of tobacco, for people then were much given to smoking: I
accepted his love, but did not receive the tobacco.

From thence I went to UNDERBARROW, to one Miles Bateman's; and
several people going along with me, great reasonings I had with them,
especially with Edward Burrough.* At night the priest and many professors came to the house, and much disputing I had with them. Supper
being provided for the priest and the rest of the company, I had not freedom
to eat with them, but told them, if they would appoint a meeting for the
next day at the steeple-house, and acquaint the people with it, I might meet
them. They had a great deal of reasoning about it; some being for it,
and some against it. In the morning I went out, after I had spoken again

---

* Edward Burrough was a religious and promising young man, had left the Episcopal
church, for which he had been educated as a minister, and joined the Presbyterians,
with whom he was a preacher of great account. After several discussions with George
Fox, he became fully convinced, and joined Friends, to the great displeasure of his
parents and relatives. He became a most active and zealous gospel labourer, being
both a great writer, and a powerful and awakening preacher. In 1662, he was taken
from a meeting in London, and for "testifying to the name of the Lord Jesus," was
committed to prison, where he lay with above 100 of his friends imprisoned on the
same account, being shut up among felons in nasty places, so that, for want of room,
many of them sickened and died. Amongst these was Edward Burrough, whose
sickness increased daily. He was heard often in prayer, day and night, not forgetting
to intercede for his persecutors. The morning before he died, he said, "Now my
soul and spirit is entered into its own being with God, and this form of person must
return from whence it was taken." His works were collected and printed in 1672,
and have recently been republished.

to them concerning the meeting; and as I walked upon a bank by the house, there came several poor people, travellers, asking relief, who I saw were in necessity; and they gave them nothing, but said they were cheats. It grieved me to see such hard-heartedness amongst professors; so, when they were gone in to their breakfast, I ran after the poor people about a quarter of a mile, and gave them some money.   Meanwhile some of them that were in the house, coming out again, and seeing me a quarter of a mile off, said I could not have gone so far in such an instant, if I had not had wings.   Hereupon the meeting was like to have been put by; for they were filled with such strange thoughts concerning me, that many of them were against having a meeting with me.   I told them I ran after those poor people to give them some money, being grieved at their hard-heartedness, who gave them nothing.   Then came Miles and Stephen Hubbersty, who being more simple-hearted men, would have the meeting held.   So to the chapel I went, and the priest came.   A great meeting there was, and the way of life and salvation was opened; and after a while the priest fled away.   Many of Crook and Underbarrow were convinced that day, received the word of life, and stood fast in it under the teaching of Christ Jesus.   After I had declared the truth to them for some hours, and the meeting was ended, the chief-constable, and some other professors fell to reasoning with me in the chapel-yard; whereupon I took a Bible, and opened to them the Scriptures, and dealt tenderly with them, as one would do with a child.   They that were in the light of Christ, and Spirit of God, knew when I spoke Scripture, though I did not mention chapter and verse, after the priest's form unto them.

From hence I went along with an aged man, whose heart the Lord had opened, and he invited me to his house; his name was James Dickinson; he was convinced that day, received the truth, and lived and died in it.

I came the next day to James Taylor's, of NEWTON, in Cartmell, in Lancashire.   And on the First-day of the week I went to the chapel, where one priest Camelford used to preach; and after he had done I began to speak the word of life to the people.   But this priest was in such a rage, and was so peevish, that he had no patience to hear; but stirred up the rude multitude, who haled me out, struck and punched me, and threw me headlong over a stone wall; yet, blessed be the Lord, his power preserved me.   He that did this violence to me was a wicked man, one John Knipe, whom afterwards the Lord cut off.   There was a youth in the chapel, writing after the priest; I was moved to speak to him, and he came to be convinced, and received a part of the ministry of the gospel; his name was John Braithwaite.

Then went I up to an ale-house, to which many people resorted between the time of their morning and afternoon preaching.   I had much reasoning with the people there, declaring to them, that " God was come to teach his people himself, and to bring them off from all false teachers, such as the prophets, Christ, and the apostles cried against."   Many received the word of life at that time, and abode in it.

In the afternoon I went about two or three miles to another steeple-house or chapel, called LYNDAL.   When the priest had done, I spoke to him and the people what the Lord commanded me; and there were great opposers; but afterwards they came to be convinced. After this I went to one Captain Sands, who with his wife seemed somewhat affected with truth; and if they could have held the world and truth together they would have received it; but they were hypocrites, and he a very chaffy light man. Wherefore I reproved him for his lightness, and for his jesting, telling him it was not seemly in a great professor, as he was. He told me he had a son, who upon his death-bed had also reproved him for it, and warned him of it. But he neither regarded the admonition of his dying son, nor the reproofs of God's Spirit in himself.

From hence I went to ULVERSTONE, and so to SWARTHMORE to Judge Fell's; whither came up one Lampitt, a priest, who was a high notionist. With him I had much reasoning; for he talked of high notions and perfection, and thereby deceived the people. He would have owned me, but I could not own nor join with him, he was so full of filth. He said, he was above John; and made as though he knew all things. But I told him, "Death reigned from Adam to Moses, that he was under death, and knew not Moses, for Moses saw the paradise of God; but he knew neither Moses nor the prophets, nor John." For that crooked and rough nature stood in him, and the mountain of sin and corruption; and the way was not prepared in him for the Lord. He confessed he had been under a cross in things; but now he could sing psalms, and do anything: I told him, "now he could see a thief, and join hand in hand with him, but he could not preach Moses, nor the prophets, nor John, nor Christ, except he were in the same Spirit that they were in." Margaret Fell had been absent in the day-time; and at night her children told her, that priest Lampitt and I had disagreed; which somewhat troubled her, because she was in profession with him; but he hid his dirty actions from them. At night we had much reasoning, and I declared the truth to her and her family. The next day Lampitt came again, and I had much discourse with him before Margaret Fell, who then clearly discerned the priest. A convincement of the Lord's truth came upon her and her family. Soon after a day was to be observed for a humiliation, and Margaret Fell asked me to go with her to the steeple-house at Ulverstone, for she was not wholly come off from them; I replied, "I must do as I am ordered by the Lord." So I left her, and walked into the fields; and the word of the Lord came to me, saying, "Go to the steeple-house after them." When I came, Lampitt was singing with his people; but his spirit was so foul, and the matter they sung so unsuitable to their states, that after they had done singing, I was moved of the Lord to speak to him and the people. The word of the Lord to them was, "He is not a Jew that is one outwardly, but he is a Jew that is one inwardly, whose praise is not of man, but of God." Then, as the Lord opened further, I showed them, "that God was come to teach his people by his Spirit, and to bring them off from all their old ways, religions, churches, and worships; for all their religions, worships, and ways, were but talking with other men's words; but they were out of the life and Spirit which they were in who gave them forth." Then cried out one, called Justice Sawrey, "Take him away;" but Judge

Fell's wife said to the officers, "Let him alone, why may not he speak as well as any other?" Lampitt also, the priest, in deceit said, "Let him speak." So at length, when I had declared some time, Justice Sawrey caused the constable to put me out; and then I spoke to the people in the grave-yard.

The First-day after, I was moved to go to ALDENHAM steeple-house; and when the priest had done, I spoke to him; but he got away. Then I declared the word of life to the people, and warned them to turn to the Lord.

From thence I passed to RAMPSIDE, where was a chapel, in which Thomas Lawson used to preach, who was an eminent priest. He very lovingly acquainted his people in the morning of my coming in the after-noon; by which means very many people were gathered together. When I came, I saw there was no place so convenient as the chapel; so I went into it, and all was quiet. Thomas Lawson went not up into his pulpit, but left all the time to me. The everlasting day of the eternal God was proclaimed that day, and the everlasting truth was largely declared, which reached and entered into the hearts of people, and many received the truth in the love of it. This priest came to be convinced, left his chapel, threw off his preaching for hire, and came to preach the Lord Jesus and his kingdom freely. After that some rude people cast scandals upon him, and thought to have done him a mischief; but he was preserved over all, grew in the wisdom of God mightily, and proved very serviceable in his place.

I returned to Swarthmore again, and on the next First-day went to DALTON steeple-house; where, after the priest had done, I declared the word of life to the people, that they might be turned from darkness to light, and from the power of Satan to God, and might come off from their superstitious ways, and from their teachers made by man, to Christ, the true and living way, to be taught of him.

From thence I went into the island of WALNEY; and after the priest had done, I spoke to him, but he got away. Then I declared the truth to the people, but they were rude. I went to speak with the priest at his house, but he would not be seen. The people said he went to hide him-self in the haymow; and they went to look for him there, but could not find him. Then they said he was gone to hide himself in the standing corn, but they could not find him there either. I went to James Lancas-ter's, who was convinced in the island; and thence I returned to SWARTH-MORE, where the Lord's power came upon Margaret Fell and her daughter Sarah, and several others.

Then I went to BECLIFF, where Leonard Fell was convinced, and became a minister of the everlasting gospel. Several others were con-vinced there, and came into obedience to the truth. Here the people said, they could not dispute, and would fain have put some other to con-verse with me; but I bid them "fear the Lord, and not in a light way talk of the Lord's words, but put the things in practice. I directed them to the divine light of Christ and his Spirit in their hearts, which would discover to them all the evil thoughts, words and actions, they had thought, spoken, and acted; by which light they might see their sin, and also their Saviour, Christ Jesus, to save them from their sins. This, I told them, was their first step to peace, even to stand still in the light that showed them their sins and transgressions; by which they might come to see how they were in the fall of old Adam, in darkness and death, strangers to the covenant of promise, and without God in the world; and by the same light they might see Christ, that died for them, to be their Redeemer and Saviour, and their way to God."

After this I went to a chapel beyond GLEASTON, which was built, but no priest had ever preached in it. Thither the country people came, and a quiet, peaceable meeting it was, in which the word of life was declared, and many were convinced of the truth about Gleaston.

From thence I returned to SWARTHMORE. After I had stayed a few days, and most of the family were convinced, I went again into Westmorland, where priest Lampitt had been amongst the professors on Kendal side, and had mightily incensed them against me; telling them I held many strange things; I met with those he had so incensed, and sat up all night with them at James Dickinson's, and answered all their objections. They were both thoroughly satisfied with the truth that I had declared, and dissatisfied with him and his lies, so that he clearly lost the best of his hearers and followers, who thus came to see his deceit, and forsook him.

I passed on to John Audland's and Gervase Benson's, and had great meetings amongst those people that had been convinced before; then to John Blakelin's* and Richard Robinson's, and had mighty meetings there; and so up towards GRISDALE.

Soon after, Judge Fell being come home, Margaret Fell his wife sent to me, desiring me to return thither; and, feeling freedom from the Lord so to do, I went back to SWARTHMORE. I found the priests and professors, and that envious Justice Sawrey, had much incensed Judge Fell and Captain Sands against the truth by their lies; but when I came to speak with him, I answered all his objections; and so thoroughly satisfied him by the Scriptures, that he was convinced in his judgment. He asked me if I was that George Fox, whom Justice Robinson spoke so much in commendation of amongst many of the parliament men. I told him, I had been with Justice Robinson, and with Justice Hotham in Yorkshire, who were very civil and loving to me, and that they were convinced in their judgment by the Spirit of God, that the principle which I bore testimony to, was the truth, and they saw over and beyond the priests of the nation; so that they, and many others, were now come to be wiser than their teachers. After we had discoursed some time together, Judge Fell himself was satisfied also, and came to see, by the openings of the Spirit of God in his heart, over all the priests and teachers of the world, and did

---

* John Blakelin, mentioned elsewhere in this Journal, became a faithful minister of the gospel, travelling much on truth's account, for which he also suffered imprisonments, and great loss of goods. He died without sigh or groan, in 1705, aged about 80. He expressed, in his old age, "the comfort he had in the Lord's peace and presence with him, that his day's work was nigh done, and his reward and rest with God sure." See *Piety Promoted*, ii., 42–46.

not go to hear them for some years before he died; for he knew it was the truth that I declared, and that Christ was the teacher of his people, and their Saviour. He sometimes wished that I were a while with Judge Bradshaw to discourse with him. There came to Judge Fell's, Captain Sands before-mentioned, endeavouring to incense the judge against me; for he was an evil-minded man, and full of envy against me; and yet he could speak high things, and use the Scripture words, and say, "Behold, I make all things new." But I told him, then he must have a new God, for his God was his belly. Besides him, came also that envious justice, John Sawrey. I told him "his heart was rotten, and he was full of hypocrisy to the brim." Several other people also came, whose states the Lord gave me a discerning of; and I spoke to their conditions. While I was in those parts, Richard Farnsworth and James Naylor came to see me and the family; and Judge Fell, being satisfied that it was the way of truth, notwithstanding all their opposition, suffered the meeting to be kept at his house; and a great meeting was settled there in the Lord's power, which continued near forty years, until the year 1690, that a new meeting-house was erected near it.

After I had stayed a while, and the meeting there was well settled, I went to UNDERBARROW, where I had a great meeting. From thence to KELLET, and had a great meeting at Robert Widders's, to which several came from Lancaster, and some from York; and many were convinced there. On the market-day I went to LANCASTER, and spoke through the market in the dreadful power of God, declaring the day of the Lord to the people, and crying out against all their deceitful merchandize. I preached righteousness and truth unto them, which they should all follow after, and walk and live in; directing them how and where they might find and receive the Spirit of God to guide them thereinto. After I had cleared myself in the market, I went to my lodging, whither several people came, and many were convinced, who have stood faithful to the truth.

On the First-day following, in the forenoon, I had a great meeting in the street at Lancaster, amongst the soldiers and people, unto whom I declared the word of life, and the everlasting truth. I opened unto them, "that all the traditions they had lived in, and all their worships and religions, and the profession they made of the Scriptures, were good for nothing, while they lived out of the life and power which they were in who gave forth the Scriptures. I directed them to the light of Christ, the heavenly Man, and to the Spirit of God in their own hearts, that they might come to be acquainted with God and with Christ, receive him for their teacher, and know his kingdom set up in them."

In the afternoon I went to the steeple-house at Lancaster, and declared the truth both to the priest and people; laying open before them the deceits they lived in, and directing them to the power and Spirit of God, which they wanted. But they haled me out, and stoned me along the street, till I came to John Lawson's house.

Another First-day I went to a steeple-house by the water side, where one Whitehead was priest, to whom, and to the people, I declared the truth in the dreadful power of God. There came to me a doctor, who was so full of envy, that he said he could find in his heart to run me through with his rapier, though he should be hung for it the next day; yet this man came afterwards to be convinced of the truth, so far as to be loving to Friends. Some people were convinced thereabouts, who willingly sat down under the ministry of Christ their teacher : and a meeting was settled there in the power of God, which has continued to this day.

After this I returned into Westmorland, and spoke through KENDAL, on a market-day. So dreadful was the power of God upon me, that people flew like chaff before me into their houses. I warned them of the mighty day of the Lord, and exhorted them to hearken to the voice of God in their own hearts, who was now come to teach his people himself. When some opposed, many others took my part, insomuch, that at last some of the people fell to fighting about me ; but I went and spoke to them, and they parted again. Several were convinced.

On the First-day after I had a very large meeting in UNDERBARROW, at Miles Bateman's house, where I was moved to declare, " that all people in the fall were gone from the image of God, righteousness, and holiness, and were become as wells without the water of life, as clouds without the heavenly rain, as trees without the heavenly fruit, and were degenerated into the nature of beasts, and of serpents, and of tall cedars, and of oaks, and of bulls, and of heifers : so that they might read the natures of these creatures within, as the prophet described them to the people of old that were out of truth. I opened to them how some were in the nature of dogs and swine, biting and rending ; some in the nature of briars, thistles, and thorns ; some like the owls and dragons in the night ; some like wild asses and horses, snuffing up the wind ; and some like mountains and rocks, and crooked and rough ways. Wherefore I exhorted them to read these things within, in their own natures, as well as without ; and that, when they read without of the wandering stars, they should look within, and see how they wandered from the bright and morning star. And they should consider, that as the fallow ground in their fields must be ploughed up, before it would bear seed to them, so must the fallow ground of their hearts be ploughed up, before they could bear seed to God. Now all these names and things I showed them, were spoken of, and to man and woman, since they fell from the image of God ; but as they come to be renewed again into the image of God, they come out of the natures of these things, and so out of the names thereof." Many more such things were declared to them, and they were turned to the light of Christ, by which they might come to know Christ, to receive him, and to witness him to be their substance and their way, their salvation and true teacher. Many were convinced at that time.

After I had travelled up and down in those countries, and had had great meetings, I came to SWARTHMORE again. And when I had visited Friends in those parts, I heard of a great meeting the priests were to have at ULVERSTONE, on a lecture-day. I went to it, and into the steeple-house in the dread and power of the Lord. When the priest had done, I spoke among them the word of the Lord, which was as a hammer, and as a fire amongst them. And though Lampitt, the priest of the place, had been at variance with most of the priests before, yet against the truth they all joined together. But the mighty power of the Lord was over all; and so wonderful was the appearance thereof, that priest Bennett said "the church shook," insomuch that he was afraid and trembled. And when he had spoken a few confused words, he hastened out, for fear it should fall on his head. Many priests got together there; but they had no power as yet to persecute.

When I had cleared my conscience towards them, I went up to SWARTHMORE again, whither came four or five of the priests. Coming to discourse, I asked them, "whether any one of them could say he ever had the word of the Lord to go and speak to such or such a people?" None of them durst say he had; but one of them burst out into a passion, and said, "he could speak his experiences as well as I." I told him experience was one thing; but to receive and go with a message, and to have a word from the Lord, as the prophets and apostles had and did, and as I had done to them, this was another thing. And therefore I put it to them again, "could any of them say he had ever had a command or word from the Lord immediately at any time?" but none of them could say so. Then I told them, the false prophets, the false apostles, and antichrists, could use the words of the true prophets, the true apostles, and of Christ, and would speak of other men's experiences, though they themselves never knew or heard the voice of God or Christ; and such as they might obtain the good words and experiences of others; this puzzled them much, and laid them open. At another time, when I was discoursing with several priests at Judge Fell's house, and he was by, I asked them the same question, "whether any of them ever heard the voice of God or Christ, to bid him go to such and such a people, to declare his word or message unto them?" for any one, I told them, that could but read, might declare the experiences of the prophets and apostles, which were recorded in the Scriptures. Hereupon Thomas Taylor,* an ancient priest, did ingenuously confess before Judge Fell, "that he had never heard the voice of God, nor of Christ, to send him to any people, but he spoke his experiences, and the experiences of the saints in former ages, and that he preached." This very much confirmed Judge Fell in the persuasion he had, "that the priests were wrong;" for he had thought formerly, as the generality of people then did, "that they were sent from God."

Thomas Taylor was convinced at this time, and travelled with me into Westmorland. Coming to CROSSLAND steeple-house, we found the people gathered together; and the Lord opened Thomas Taylor's mouth (though he was convinced but the day before), so that he declared amongst them, "how he had been before he was convinced;" and like the good scribe that was converted to the kingdom, he brought forth things new and old

---

* Thomas Taylor, born in 1616, was educated at Oxford university, and became a preacher among the Puritans, at or near Skipton, and also at Richmond. He discontinued preaching for hire, and joined Friends, becoming a valiant minister of Christ. He also wrote much in support of the truth. He suffered many imprisonments, but the Lord was with him, and upheld him by his mighty power, in the hardships and opposition he met with for truth's sake. He died in peace at Stafford, in 1681.

to the people, and showed them how "the priests were out of the way;" which tormented the priest. Some little discourse I had with them, but they fled away; and a precious meeting there was, wherein the Lord's power was over all; and the people were directed to the Spirit of God, by which they might come to know God and Christ, and to understand the Scriptures aright. After this I passed on, visiting Friends, and had very large meetings in Westmorland.

Now began the priests to rage more and more, and as much as they could, to stir up persecution. James Naylor and Francis Howgill were cast into prison in Appleby jail, at the instigation of the malicious priests; some of whom prophesied "that within a month we should be all scattered again, and come to nothing." But, blessed for ever be the worthy name of the Lord, the work of the Lord went on and prospered. For about this time John Audland, Francis Howgill, John Camm,* Edward Burrough, Richard Hubberthorn,† Miles Hubbersty, and Miles Halhead,‡ with several others, being endued with power from on high, came forth in the work of

---

* John Camm, after joining Friends, became an eminent minister, travelling in the service of truth. He was a man of weak constitution, but richly furnished with the gifts of the Holy Spirit, clear in judgment, and a sharp reprover of wickedness. His ministry was deep and weighty. Having an estate of his own, he suffered the spoiling of his goods joyfully. He often called his children together, and exhorted them to fear the Lord, and would wonderfully praise God for his goodness, counting his bodily weakness a happiness, saying, "How great a benefit do I enjoy beyond many, I have such a large time of preparation for death, being daily dying, that I may live forever with my God, in that kingdom that is unspeakably full of glory. My outward man daily wastes and moulders down, and draws towards its place and centre; but my inward man revives and mounts upwards, towards its place and habitation in the heavens." See *Piety Promoted*, i., 3-6.

† Richard Hubberthorn, who is frequently mentioned in this *Journal*, and whose name often occurs in the early part of the history of Friends, became an able gospel minister, and patient sufferer for the truth. He was a native of Lancashire, the only son of a yeoman of good repute. In his youth he obtained a post in the Parliamentary army, which, on his embracing the truth, he quitted, and testified publicly against it; becoming a valiant soldier under the banner of the Prince of peace. After passing through many inward probations, he became qualified to direct others in their way to the kingdom of heaven, and was one of the first of our Society who travelled in the work of the ministry.

Richard Hubberthorn was a man of much meekness, humility, patience, and brotherly kindness, clear in judgment, and quick of understanding; and, although he was of low stature, and had an infirm constitution and weak voice, he was a powerful and successful minister, and great numbers were convinced by him, and brought over to the faith and practice which he preached. He travelled in the exercise of his gift nine years, and shared at different times in the sufferings to which the early Friends were exposed. In 1662, he was violently haled from a meeting in London, and taken before that implacable persecutor, Alderman Brown, who, after abusing him with his own hands, committed him to Newgate. Here the throng was so great, and the air so impure, that he soon fell sick. His disorder increased upon him, and, within two months from the time of his commitment, with an unclouded prospect of a resting-place "where the wicked cease from troubling," he was released by death. He wrote many treatises, which were collected and published in 1 vol. quarto, in 1663.

‡ This is the only mention of Miles Halhead in this Journal. His name occurs frequently in Sewell's *History*, from which it appears he travelled largely and suffered much on Truth's account, being the first of the Quakers imprisoned at Kendal.

the ministry, and approved themselves faithful labourers therein, travelling up and down, and preaching the gospel freely ; by means whereof multitudes were convinced, and many effectually turned to the Lord. Amongst these, Christopher Taylor* was one, brother to Thomas Taylor before-mentioned ; and who had been a preacher to a people as well as his brother ; but after they had received a knowledge of the truth, they soon came into obedience thereunto, and left their preaching for hire or rewards. And having received a part of the ministry of the gospel, they preached Christ freely ; being often sent by the Lord to declare his word in steeple-houses and in markets ; and great sufferers they were.

After I had visited Friends in Westmorland, I returned into Lancashire, and went to ULVERSTONE, where W. Lampitt was priest ; who, though he had preached of a people that should own the teachings of God, and had said, "that men and women should come to declare the gospel ;" yet afterwards, when it came to be fulfilled, he persecuted both it and them. To this priest's house I went, where abundance of priests and professors were got together after their lecture, with whom I had great disputings concerning Christ and the Scriptures ; for they were loath to let their trade go down, which they made of preaching Christ's, and the apostles' and prophets' words. But the Lord's power went over the heads of them all, and his word of life went forth amongst them ; though many of them were exceedingly envious and devilish. Yet after this many priests and professors came to me from far and near ; of whom, they that were innocent and simple-minded were satisfied, and went away refreshed ; but the fat and full were fed with judgment, and sent empty away : for that was the word of the Lord to be divided to them.

Now when meetings were set up, and we met in private houses, Lampitt the priest began to rage ; and he said, " we forsook the temple, and went to Jeroboam's calves' houses ;" so that many professors began to see how he had declined from that which he had formerly held and preached. Hereupon the case of Jeroboam's calves was opened to the professors, priests, and people ; and it was manifested unto them, " that their houses (which they called churches) were more like Jeroboam's calves' houses, even the old mass-houses which were set up in the darkness of Popery ; and which they, who called themselves Protestants, and professed to be more enlightened than the Papists, did still hold up ; although God had never commanded them : whereas that temple, which God had commanded at Jerusalem, Christ came to end the service of ; and they that received and believed in him, their bodies came to be the temples of God, and of Christ, and of the Holy Ghost, to dwell in them, and to walk in them. And all such were gathered into the name of Jesus, whose name is above every name, and there is no salvation by any other name under the whole heaven, but by the name of Jesus. And they that were thus gathered met together in several dwelling-houses, which were not called the temple,

* Christopher Taylor, after writing and preaching much on Truth's account, removed to America about the year 1683, and died at Philadelphia in 1686. See account of him in Whiting's *Memoirs*, pp. 352-55.

nor the church; but their bodies were the temples of God, and the believers were the church, which Christ was the head of. So that Christ was not called the head of an old house, which was made by men's hands, neither did he come to purchase and sanctify, and redeem with his blood, an old house, which they called their church, but the people of whom he is the head." Much work I had in those days with priests and people, concerning their old mass-houses, which they called their churches; for the priests had persuaded the people that it was the house of God; whereas the apostle says, "whose house we are," &c. Heb. iii. 6. So the people are God's house, in whom he dwells. And the apostle saith, "Christ purchased his church with his own blood;" and Christ calls his church his spouse, his bride, and the Lamb's wife; so that this title, church and spouse, was not given to an old house, but to his people, the true believers.

After this, on a lecture-day, I was moved to go to the steeple-house at ULVERSTONE, where were abundance of professors, priests, and people. I went up near to priest Lampitt, who was blustering on in his preaching; and after the Lord had opened my mouth to speak, John Sawrey the justice came to me and said, "if I would speak according to the Scriptures, I should speak." I wondered at his speaking so to me, for I did speak according to the Scriptures, and I told him, "I should speak according to the Scriptures, and bring the Scriptures to prove what I had to say; for I had something to speak to Lampitt and to them." Then he said, I should not speak, contradicting himself who had said just before, "I should speak, if I would speak according to the Scriptures." The people were quiet, and heard me gladly, until this Justice Sawrey (who was the first stirrer up of cruel persecution in the North) incensed them against me, and set them on to hale, beat, and bruise me. Suddenly the people were in a rage, and fell upon me in the steeple-house before his face; knocked me down, kicked me, and trampled upon me; and so great was the uproar, that some tumbled over their seats for fear. At last he came and took me from the people, led me out of the steeple-house, and put me into the hands of the constables and other officers, bidding them whip and put me out of the town. They led me about a quarter of a mile, some taking hold of my collar, and some by my arms and shoulders, and shook and dragged me along. Many friendly people being come to the market, and some of them to the steeple-house to hear me, divers of these they knocked down also, and broke their heads, so that the blood ran down from several of them; and Judge Fell's son running after, to see what they would do with me, they threw him into a ditch of water, some of them crying, "knock the teeth out of his head." Now when they had haled me to the common moss-side, a multitude of people following, the constables and other officers gave me some blows over my back with their willow-rods, and so thrust me among the rude multitude, who, having furnished themselves, some with staves, some with hedge-stakes, and others with holm or holly-bushes, fell upon me, and beat me on my head, arms, and shoulders, till they had deprived me of sense; so that I fell down upon the wet common. When I recovered again, and saw myself lying in a watery common, and the people standing about me, I lay still a little while; and the power of the Lord sprang through me, and the Eternal Refreshings refreshed me, so that I stood up again in the strengthening power of the Eternal God; and stretching out my arms amongst them, I said with a loud voice, "Strike again; here are my arms, my head, and my cheeks." There was in the company a mason, a professor, but a rude fellow; he with his walking rule-staff gave me a blow with all his might, just over the back of my hand, as it was stretched out; with which blow my hand was so bruised, and my arm so benumbed, that I could not draw it unto me again; so that some of the people cried out, "he hath spoiled his hand for ever having the use of it any more." But I looked at it in the love of God (for I was in the love of God to them all, that had persecuted me), and after a while the Lord's power sprang through me again, and through my hand and arm, so that in a moment I recovered strength in my hand and arm, in the sight of them all. Then they began to fall out among themselves, and some of them came to me, and said, if I would give them money, they would secure me from the rest. But I was moved of the Lord to declare to them the word of life, and showed them their false Christianity, and the fruits of their priest's ministry; telling them they were more like heathens and Jews, than true Christians. Then was I moved of the Lord to come up again through the midst of the people, and go into Ulverstone market. As I went, there met me a soldier, with his sword by his side; "Sir," said he to me, "I see you are a man, and I am ashamed and grieved that you should be thus abused;" and he offered to assist me in what he could. But I told him the Lord's power was over all; so I walked through the people in the market, and none of them had power to touch me then. But some of the market-people abusing some Friends in the market, I turned me about and saw this soldier among them with his naked rapier, whereupon I ran in amongst them, and catching hold of his hand that his rapier was in, I bid him put up his sword again, if he would go along with me; for I was willing to draw him out from the company, lest some mischief should be done. A few days after seven men fell upon this soldier, and beat him cruelly, because he had taken part with Friends and me; for it was the manner of the persecutors of that country, for twenty or forty people to run upon one man. And they fell so upon Friends in many places, that they could hardly pass the highways, stoning, beating, and breaking their heads. When I came to SWARTHMORE, I found the friends there dressing the heads and hands of Friends and friendly people, which had been broken or hurt that day by the professors and hearers of Lampitt, the priest. My body and arms were yellow, black, and blue, with the blows and bruises I received amongst them that day. Now began the priests to prophesy again, that within half a year we should be all put down and gone.*

---

* The priests reckoned wrong in this, for, as Sewell justly observed, it fared with the early Friends as with trees, which grow best when most lopped. "Duris ut ilex tonsa bipennibus, per damna, per cædes, ab ipso, ducit opes animumque ferre."

"As by the lopping axe, the sturdy oak
Improves her shade, and thrives beneath the stroke;
Tho' present loss and wounds severe she feel,
She draws fresh vigour from the invading steel."

About two weeks after this I went into WALNEY island, and James Naylor went with me. We stayed one night at a little town on this side, called COCKAN, and had a meeting there, where one was convinced. After a while there came a man with a pistol, whereupon the people ran out of doors. He called for me; and when I came out to him, he snapped his pistol at me, but it would not go off. This caused the people to make a great bustle about him; and some of them took hold of him, to prevent his doing mischief; but I was moved in the Lord's power to speak to him; and he was so struck by the power of the Lord, that he trembled for fear, and went and hid himself. Thus the Lord's power came over them all, though there was a great rage in the country.

Next morning I went over in a boat to James Lancaster's. As soon as I came to land, there rushed out about forty men with staves, clubs, and fishing-poles, who fell upon me, beating and punching me, and endeavouring to thrust me backward into the sea. When they had thrust me almost into the sea, and I saw they would have knocked me down in it, I went up into the midst of them; but they laid at me again, and knocked me down, and stunned me. When I came to myself, I looked up and saw James Lancaster's wife throwing stones at my face, and her husband James Lancaster was lying over me, to keep the blows and the stones off me. For the people had persuaded James Lancaster's wife that I had bewitched her husband; and had promised her, that if she would let them know when I came thither, they would be my death. And having got knowledge of my coming, many of the town rose up in this manner with clubs and staves to kill me; but the Lord's power preserved me, that they could not take away my life. At length I got up on my feet, but they beat me down again into the boat; which James Lancaster observing, he presently came into it, and set me over the water from them; but while we were on the water within their reach, they struck at us with long poles, and threw stones after us. By the time we were come to the other side, we saw them beating James Naylor; for whilst they had been beating me, he walked up into a field, and they never minded him till I was gone; then they fell upon him, and all their cry was, "Kill him, kill him."

When I was come over to the town again, on the other side of the water, the townsmen rose up with pitchforks, flails, and staves, to keep me out of the town, crying, "Kill him, knock him on the head, bring the cart, and carry him away to the churchyard." So after they had abused me, they drove me some distance out of the town, and there left me. Then went James Lancaster back to look after James Naylor; and I being now left alone, went to a ditch of water, and having washed myself (for they had besmeared my face, hands, and clothes, with miry dirt), I walked about three miles to Thomas Hutton's house, where lodged Thomas Lawson, the priest that was convinced. When I came in, I could hardly speak to them, I was so bruised; only I told them where I left James Naylor; so they took each of them a horse, and went and brought him thither that night. The next day Margaret Fell hearing of it, sent a horse for me; but so sore I was with bruises, I was not able to bear the shaking of the

horse without much pain. When I was come to SWARTHMORE, Justice
Sawrey, and one Justice Thompson of Lancaster, granted a warrant against
me; but Judge Fell coming home, it was not served upon me; for he was
out of the country all this time, that I was thus cruelly abused. When
he came home, he sent forth warrants into the isle of Walney, to apprehend all those riotous persons; whereupon some of them fled the country.
James Lancaster's wife was afterwards convinced of the truth, and repented
of the evils she had done me; and so did others of those bitter persecutors
also; but the judgments of God fell upon some of them, and destruction
is come upon many of them since. Judge Fell asked me to give him a
relation of my persecution; but I told him they could do no otherwise in
the spirit wherein they were, and that they manifested the fruits of their
priest's ministry, and their profession and religion to be wrong. So he
told his wife I made light of it, and that I spoke of it as a man that had
not been concerned; for, indeed, the Lord's power healed me again.

After I was recovered, I went to YELLAND, where there was a great
meeting. In the evening there came a priest to the house, with a pistol
in his hand, under pretence to light a pipe of tobacco. The maid of the
house seeing the pistol, told her master; who, clapping his hands on the
door-posts, told him he should not come in there. While he stood there,
keeping the door-way, he looked up, and spied over the wall a company of
men coming, some armed with staves, and one with a musket. But the
Lord God prevented their bloody design; so that seeing themselves discovered, they went their way, and did no harm.

The time for the sessions at LANCASTER being come, I went thither
with Judge Fell; who on the way told me, he had never had such a matter
brought before him before, and he could not well tell what to do in the
business. I told him, when Paul was brought before the rulers, and the
Jews and priests came down to accuse him, and laid many false things to
his charge, Paul stood still all that while. And when they had done, Festus,
the governor, and king Agrippa, beckoned to him to speak for himself;
which Paul did, and cleared himself of all those false accusations; so he
might do with me. Being come to Lancaster, Justice Sawrey and Justice
Thompson having granted a warrant to apprehend me, though I was not
apprehended by it, yet hearing of it, I appeared at the sessions; where
there appeared against me about forty priests. These had chosen one
Marshall, priest of Lancaster, to be their orator; and had provided one
young priest, and two priests' sons, to bear witness against me, who had
sworn beforehand that I had spoken blasphemy. When the justices were
sat, they heard all that the priests and their witnesses could say and charge
against me; their orator Marshall, sitting by, and explaining their sayings
for them; but the witnesses were so confounded, that they discovered
themselves to be false witnesses; for when the court had examined one of
them upon oath, and then began to examine another, he was at such loss
he could not answer directly, but said the other could say it. Which made
the justices say to him, " have you sworn it, and given it in already upon
your oath, and now say that he can say it? It seems you did not hear
those words spoken yourself, though you have sworn it."

There were then in court several people who had been at that meeting, wherein the witnesses swore I spoke those blasphemous words, which the priests accused me of; and these being men of integrity and reputation in the country, declared and affirmed in court, that the oath, which the witnesses had taken against me, was altogether false; and that no such words as they had sworn against me, were spoken by me at that meeting. Indeed, most of the serious men of that part of the country, that were then at the sessions, had been at that meeting, and had heard me both at that and other meetings also. This was taken notice of by Colonel West, who, being a justice of the peace, was then upon the bench; and having long been weak in body, blessed the Lord, and said, "the Lord had healed him that day;" adding, that he never saw so many sober people and good faces together in all his life. And then, turning himself to me, he said in the open sessions, "George, if thou hast anything to say to the people, thou mayest freely declare it." I was moved of the Lord to speak; and as soon as I began, priest Marshall, the orator for the rest of the priests, went away. That which I was moved to declare was this: "that the Holy Scriptures were given forth by the Spirit of God, and all people must first come to the Spirit of God in themselves, by which they might know God and Christ, of whom the prophets and the apostles learnt; and by the same Spirit know the Holy Scriptures; for as the Spirit of God was in them that gave forth the Scriptures, so the same Spirit of God must be in all them that come to understand the Scriptures; by which Spirit they might have fellowship with the Son, and with the Father, and with the Scriptures, and with one another; and without this Spirit they can know neither God nor Christ, nor the Scriptures, nor have right fellowship one with another." I had no sooner spoken these words, than about half a dozen priests that stood behind me, burst out into a passion; and one of them, named Jackus, amongst other things that he spoke against the truth, said, that the Spirit and the letter were inseparable. I replied, "then every one that hath the letter hath the Spirit; and they might buy the Spirit with the letter of the Scriptures." This plain discovery of darkness in the priest, moved Judge Fell and Colonel West to reprove them openly, and tell them, that according to that position they might carry the Spirit in their pockets, as they did the Scriptures. Upon this the priests being confounded and put to silence, rushed out in a rage against the justices, because they could not have their bloody ends upon me. The justices, seeing the witnesses did not agree, and perceiving that they were brought to answer the priests' envy, and finding that all their evidences were not sufficient in law to make good their charge against me, discharged me. And after Judge Fell had spoken to Justice Sawrey and Justice Thompson concerning the warrant they had given forth against me, and showed them the errors thereof, he and Colonel West granted a supersedeas to stop the execution of it. Thus was I cleared in open sessions of all those lying accusations which the malicious priests had laid to my charge; and multitudes of people praised God that day, for it was a joyful day to many. Justice Benson* of West-

---

* Gervase Benson, once a colonel in the army, and, at this date, a Justice of the

morland, was convinced; and Major Ripan, mayor of Lancaster, also. It was a day of everlasting salvation to hundreds of people; for the Lord Jesus Christ, the way to the Father, and the free teacher, was exalted and set up, and his everlasting gospel was preached and the word of eternal life was declared over the heads of the priests, and all such money-preachers. For the Lord opened many mouths that day to speak his word to the priests, and several friendly people and professors reproved the priests in their inns, and in the streets; so that they fell, like an old rotten house; and the cry was among the people, that the Quakers had got the day, and the priests were fallen. Many people were convinced that day, amongst whom was Thomas Briggs, who before had been averse to Friends and truth, insomuch that discoursing with John Lawson, a Friend, concerning perfection, Thomas Briggs said to him, "dost thou hold perfection?" at the same time lifting up his hand to give the Friend a box on the ear. But this Thomas Briggs, being convinced of the truth that day, declared against his own priest, Jackus; and afterwards became a faithful minister of the gospel, and stood so to the end of his days.*

When the sessions were over, James Naylor, who was present, gave a brief account of the proceedings in a letter, which soon after he wrote to Friends; and which is here added for the reader's further satisfaction in this matter:—

"DEAR friends and brethren in the Lord Jesus Christ, my dear love unto you all, desiring you may be kept steadfast in the Lord Jesus Christ, and in the power of his love, boldly to witness forth the truth, as it is revealed in you by the mighty working of the Father: to whom alone be everlasting praise and honour for evermore! Dear friends, the Lord doth much manifest his love and power in these parts. On the Second-day of last week, my brother George and I were at Lancaster; there were abundance of Friends from all parts: and a high sort, which sided with the priests, giving out, they now hoped to see a stop put to that great work which had gone on so fast, and with such power, that their kingdom is much

---

peace, appears, from the burial register of Friends, to have been resident at Kendal. He died in 1679. In *Barclay's Letters, &c., of Early Friends*, is a letter from him to George Fox and James Naylor. It is dated at London, 11th Month, 29th, 1653. He appears to have gone up to that city under a sense of duty. "Pray to the Lord for me," he writes, "that I may be kept in all faithfulness, with boldness to bear witness to the truth, against all deceits as they are made manifest in me, to the praise of his free grace and love to me, which I find daily flowing into my soul, to the refreshing thereof."

* Thomas Briggs, from being a persecutor and an opposer, became an eminent minister amongst Friends, and his name occurs frequently in Sewell's *History*, and in Whiting's *Memoirs*, to which the reader is referred for some account of his labours. He was very instrumental in turning men from darkness to light, and from the power of Satan unto God. Not only did he suffer personally, by imprisonment and violence, but was fined five times, for having meetings in his house, to the extent of £50. He travelled much in Wales, and other places, often accompanying George Fox. He went with him to the West Indies in 1671. A short time before his death, he wrote to George Fox, in which he signified his perseverance in godliness. He bore "a large testimony the First-day before his decease," being aged about seventy-five; a minister thirty-two years.

shaken.   We were called before Judge Fell, Colonel West, Justice Sawrey, &c., to answer what was charged against George.   There were three witnesses to eight particulars, but they were much confused in themselves; which gave much light to the truth; whereby the justices did plainly see that it was envy; and they many times told them so.   One of the witnesses was a young priest, who confessed he should not have meddled, had not another priest sent for him, and set him to work.   The other witnesses were two priests' sons: it was proved there by many that heard one of them say, 'if he had power he would make George deny his profession, and that he would take away his life.'   This was a single witness to one of the greatest untruths that was charged against George; and the justices told him, that they saw, because he could not take away his life, he went about to take away his liberty.   There was one priest chosen out of the whole number, as an orator to plead against us; who spared no pains to show forth his envy against the truth: and when he could not prevail, he went down in a rage; and there came up a number of them into the room, among whom was one Jackus.   George was then speaking in the room, one of the justices having desired him, if he had anything to say, he would speak, at which priest Jackus was in such a rage, that he broke forth into many high expressions against the truth spoken by my dear brother George; amongst which this was one that the letter and the Spirit were inseparable. Hereupon the justices stood up, and bid him prove that, before he went any further.   Then seeing himself caught, he would have denied it; and when he could not get off so, the rest of the priests would have helped him to a meaning for his words; but the justices would admit no other meaning than the plain sense of the words, and told him he had laid down a position, and it was fit he should prove it; pressing the matter close upon him.   Whereupon the priests, being put to silence, went down in a greater rage than before; and some of them, after they were gone down, being asked what they had done, lied and said, they could not get into the room; thereby to hide their shame, and keep the people in blindness.   The justices, Judge Fell and Colonel West, were much convinced of the truth, and set up justice and equity; and have much silenced the rage of the people.   Many bitter spirits were at Lancaster to see the event, but went home and cried the priests had lost the day: everlasting praises be to him who fought the battle for us, who is our King for ever!   There were others called, whom the witnesses confessed were in the room when the things charged on George were said to have been spoken; but they all, as one man, denied that any such words were spoken; which gave much light to the justices, and they durst rely on what they witnessed; for they said they knew many of them to be honest men.   There was a warrant granted against us at Appleby; but Justice Benson told them it was not according to law, and so it ceased.   I hear he is a faithful man in the truth.   The priests began to preach against the justices, and said, they were not to meddle in these things, but to end controversy between neighbour and neighbour.   They are not pleased with the law, because it is not in the statute to imprison us, as the priest that pleaded against us said.   The justices bid him put it into the statute, if he could; he said, it should want no will of his. They are much afraid that they shall lose all; they are much discontented in these parts; and some of them cry, all 'is gone.' Dear Friends, dwell in patience, and wait upon the Lord, who will do his own work. Look not at man, in the work; nor at man, who opposeth the work; but rest in the will of the Lord, that so ye may be furnished with patience, both to do and to suffer what ye shall be called unto; that your end in all things may be his praise. Take up his cross freely, which keeps low the fleshly man; that Christ may be set up and honoured in all things, the light advanced in you, and the judgment set up, which must give sentence against all that opposeth the truth;—that the captivity may be led captive, and the prisoner set free to seek the Lord;—that righteousness may rule in you, and peace and joy may dwell in you, wherein consisteth the kingdom of the Father; to whom be all praise for ever! Dear Friends, meet often together; and take heed of what exalteth itself above its brother; but keep low, and serve one another in love for the Lord's sake. Let all Friends know how it is with us, that God may have the praise of all."   J. N.

Written from Kellet, the 30th
    of the 8th Month, 1652.

At this time I was in a fast, and was not to eat until this work of God, which then lay weighty upon me, was accomplished. But the Lord's power was wonderfully exalted, and gave truth and Friends dominion therein over all, to his glory. This gospel was freely preached that day, over the heads of about forty hireling priests. I stayed two or three days afterwards in Lancaster, and had some meetings there; and the rude and baser sort of people plotted together to draw me out of the house, and to throw me over Lancaster bridge, but the Lord prevented them. Then they invented another mischief, which was this: after a meeting at Lancaster they brought down a distracted man, and another with him with bundles of birchen rods, bound together like besoms, with which they would have whipped me: but I was moved to speak to them in the Lord's mighty power, which chained down the distracted man, and the other also, and made them calm and quiet. Then I bid him throw his rods into the fire, and burn them; and he did so. Thus the Lord's power being over them, they departed quietly.

But the priests, fretting to see themselves overthrown at the sessions at Lancaster, got some of the envious justices to join with them; and, at the following assize at Lancaster, informed Judge Windham against me. Whereupon the judge made a speech against me in open court; and commanded Colonel West, who was clerk of the assize, to issue forth a warrant for the apprehending of me: but Colonel West told the judge of my innocency, and spoke boldly in my defence. Yet the judge commanded him again, either to write a warrant, or go off from his seat: then he told the judge plainly that he would not do it; but that he would offer up all his estate, and his body also, for me. Thus he stopped the judge; and the Lord's power came over all: so that the priests and justices could not get their

envy executed. That same night I came into LANCASTER, it being the
assize time, and hearing of a warrant to be given out against me, I judged
it better to show myself openly, than for my adversaries to seek me. So
I went to Judge Fell's and Colonel West's chambers. As soon as I came
in they smiled on me; and Colonel West said, "What! are you come into
the dragon's mouth?" I stayed in town till the judge went out of town;
and I walked up and down the town, but no one meddled with me, or questioned me. Thus the Lord's blessed power, which is over all, carried me
through and over this exercise, gave dominion over his enemies, and enabled
me to go on in his glorious work and service for his great name's sake.
For though the beast maketh war against the saints, yet the Lamb hath
got, and will get, the victory.

CHAPTER VI.

1652–1653.—George Fox is branded by the priests as a witch—writes to Justice Sawrey, prophesying of the judgments impending over him—warning to priest Lampitt—exhortation to the people of Ulverstone—to the followers of Lampitt, against a hireling ministry, &c.—a rebuke to Adam Sands for his wickedness—to priest Tatham, against his hireling ministry and his suing for tithes—foretells the dissolution of the Long Parliament—fasts ten days—James Milner and Richard Myer create a schism, which is soon healed—the latter is miraculously healed of his lameness, but afterwards disobeys the Lord, and dies not long after—Anthony Pearson, an opposer, is convinced—the priests are shown to be Antichrist—George Fox preaches at John Wilkinson's steeple-house three hours—admonishes a professor *for praising him*—reproves Wilkinson for speaking against his conscience—many hundreds are convinced—discerns an unclean spirit in a woman, and speaks sharply to her—the like of some other women—speaks sharply to an envious Baptist—preaches in the steeple-house at Carlisle, where the Lord's power was such that the people trembled—committed to Carlisle prison as a blasphemer, heretic, and seducer—the priests who come to see him are exceedingly rude—Anthony Pearson's remonstrance to the Judges of assize against the unjust imprisonment and detention of George Fox—he is put in the dungeon, a filthy place, where a woman is found eaten to death with vermin—here James Parnell visits him—a challenge to professors to declare their objections to George Fox's ministry—it being reported that George Fox was to die for religion, the Little Parliament write to the sheriff respecting him—he himself expostulates with Justices Craston and Studholm on their imprisoning him—A. Pearson and the governor visit the prison, blame the magistrates, require sureties of the jailer, and put the under-jailer in the dungeon for his cruelty to George Fox, who is soon after liberated—George Fox has great meetings, and *thousands* are convinced—visits Gilsland, a noted country for thieving—has a glorious meeting of many thousands, near Langlands, on the top of a hill—great convincement in the six northern counties.

From Lancaster I returned to Robert Widders's, and from thence I went to Thomas Leper's to a meeting in the evening; and a very blessed meeting we had there; after which I walked in the evening to Robert Widders's again. No sooner was I gone than there came a company of disguised men to Thomas Leper's, with swords and pistols; who suddenly entering the house put out the candles, and swung their swords about amongst the people of the house, who held up the chairs before them to save themselves from being cut and wounded. At length they drove all the people out of the house, and then searched it for me; who, it seems, was the only person they looked for: for they had laid wait before on the highway, by which I should have gone had I rode to Robert Widders's. And not meeting with me on the way, they thought to find me in the house, but the Lord prevented them. Soon after I was come to Robert Widders's, some friends came from the town where Thomas Leper lived, and gave us a relation of this wicked attempt: and they were afraid lest they should come and search Robert Widders's house also for me, and do me a mischief; but the Lord restrained them that they came not. Though these men were in disguise the friends perceived some of them to be Frenchmen, and supposed them to be servants belonging to one called Sir Robert Bindlas; for some of them had said, that in their nation they used to tie the Protestants to trees, and whip and destroy them. His servants used often to abuse Friends, both in their meetings, and going to and from them. They once took Richard Hubberthorn and several others out of one, and carried them a good way off into the fields; and there bound them, and left them bound in the Winter season. At another time one of his servants came to Francis Fleming's house, and thrust his naked rapier in at the door and windows; but there being at the house a kinsman of Francis Fleming's, one who was not a Friend, he came with a cudgel in his hand, and bid the serving-man put up his rapier; which when the other would not, but vapoured at him with it, and was rude, he knocked him down with his cudgel, and took his rapier from him; and had it not been for Friends, he would have run him through with it. So the Friends preserved the life of him that would have destroyed theirs.

From Robert Widders's I went to visit Justice West, Richard Hubberthorn accompanying me. Not knowing the way, or the danger of the sands, we rode where, as we were afterwards told, no man ever rode before, swimming our horses over a very dangerous place. When we were come in, Justice West asked us if we did not see two men riding over the sands: "I shall have their clothes anon," said he, "for they cannot escape drowning, and I am the coroner." But when we told him that we were the men, he was astonished, and wondered how we escaped drowning. Upon this the envious priests and professors raised a slanderous report concerning me, that neither water could drown me, nor could they draw blood of me; and that therefore surely I was a witch; indeed, sometimes when they beat me with great staves, they did not much draw my blood, though they bruised my body ofttimes very sorely. But all these slanders were nothing to me with respect to myself, though I was concerned on the truth's behalf, which, I saw, they endeavoured by these means to prejudice people against; for I considered that their forefathers, the apostate Jews, called the master of the house Beelzebub; and these apostate Christians from the life and power of God, could do no less to his seed. But the Lord's power carried me over their slanderous tongues, and their bloody murderous spirits; who had the ground of witchcraft in themselves, which kept them from coming to God and to Christ.

Having visited Justice West, I went to SWARTHMORE, visiting Friends; and the Lord's power was over all the persecutors there. I was moved to write several letters to the magistrates, priests, and professors, thereabouts, who had raised persecution before; that which I sent to Justice Sawrey was after this manner:—

"FRIEND,

"Thou wast the first beginner of all the persecution in the North; thou wast the beginner and the maker of the people tumultuous. Thou wast the first stirrer of them up against the righteous seed, and against the truth of God; the first strengthener of the hands of evil-doers against the innocent and harmless; and thou shalt not prosper. Thou wast the first stirrer up of strikers, stoners, persecutors, stockers, mockers, and imprisoners in the North, and of revilers, slanderers, railers, and false accusers. This was thy work, and this thou stirredst up! so thy fruits declare thy spirit. Instead of stirring up the pure mind in people, thou hast stirred up the wicked, malicious, and envious, and taken hand with the wicked. Thou hast made the people's minds envious up and down the country; this was thy work. But God hath shortened thy days, and limited thee; hath set thy bounds, and broken thy jaws; discovered thy religion to the simple and babes, and brought thy deeds to light. How is thy habitation fallen, and become the habitation of devils! How is thy beauty lost, and thy glory withered! How hast thou showed thy evil, that thou hast served God but with thy lips, thy heart being far from him, and thou in hypocrisy! How hath the form of thy teaching declared itself to be the mark of the false prophets, whose fruit declares itself! for by their fruits they are known. How are the wise men turned backward! View thy ways, and take notice with whom thou hast taken part. That of God in thy conscience will tell thee; the Ancient of Days will reprove thee. How hath thy zeal appeared to be the blind zeal of a persecutor, which Christ and his apostles forbade Christians to follow! How hast thou strengthened the hands of evil-doers, and been a praise to them, and not to them that do well! How like a madman and blind man, didst thou turn thy sword backward against the saints, against whom there is no law! How wilt thou be gnawed and burned one day, when thou shalt feel the flame and have the plagues of God poured upon thee, and thou begin to gnaw thy tongue for pain, because of the plagues! Thou shalt have thy reward according to thy works. Thou canst not escape; the Lord's righteous judgment will find thee out, and the witness of God in thy conscience shall answer it. How hast thou caused the heathen to blaspheme, gone on with the multitude to do evil, and joined hand and hand with the wicked! How is thy latter end worse than thy beginning, who art come with the dog to bite, and art turned as a wolf, to devour the lambs! How hast thou discovered thyself to be a man more fit to be kept in a place to be nurtured, than to be set in a place to nurture! How wast thou exalted and puffed up with pride! and now art thou fallen down with shame, that thou comest to be covered with that which thou stirredst up and broughtest forth. Let not John Sawrey take the words of God into his mouth till he be reformed; let him not take his name into his mouth till he depart from iniquity; let not him and his teacher make a profession of the saints' words, except they intend to proclaim themselves hypocrites, whose lives are so contrary to the lives of the saints; whose church hath made itself manifest to be a cage of unclean birds. You, having a form of godliness, but not the power, have made them that are in the power your derision, your by-word, and talk at your feasts. Thy ill savour, John Sawrey, the country about have smelled, and of thy unchristian carriage all that fear God have been ashamed; and to them thou hast been a grief; in the day of account thou shalt know it, even in the day of thy condemnation. Thou wast mounted up, and hadst set thy nest on high, but never gottest higher than the fowls of the air. Now thou art run amongst the beasts of prey, and art fallen into the earth; so that earthliness and covetousness have swallowed thee up. Thy conceitedness would not carry thee through, in whom was found the selfish principle, which hath blinded thy eye. Thy back must be bowed down always; for thy table is already become thy snare."   G. F.

This Justice Sawrey, who was the first persecutor in that country, was afterwards drowned.

I wrote also to William Lampitt, the priest of Ulverstone, thus :—

"THE word of the Lord to thee, O Lampitt! who art a deceiver, surfeited and drunk with the earthly spirit, rambling up and down in the Scriptures, and blending thy spirit amongst the saints' conditions; who hadst a prophecy, as thy father Balaam had, but art erred from it, as thy father did; one whose fruit hath withered (of which I am a witness), and many who have known thy fruit, have seen the end of it, that it is withered, and do see where thou art in the blind world, a blind leader of the blind; as a beast wallowing and tumbling in the earth, and in the lust; one that is erred from the Spirit of the Lord, of old ordained for condemnation. Thou art in the seat of the Pharisees, art called of men master, standest praying in the synagogues, and hast the chief seat in the assemblies; a right hypocrite in the steps of the Pharisees, and in the way of thy fathers, the hypocrites, which our Lord Jesus Christ cried woe against. Such with the light thou art seen to be, and by the light art comprehended; which is thy condemnation, who hatest it, and will be so eternally, except thou repent. To thee this is the word of God; for in Christ's way thou art not, but in the Pharisees', as thou mayest read, Matt. xxiii., and all that own Christ's words may see thee there. Christ, who died at Jerusalem, cried woe against such as thou art; and Christ is the same yesterday, to-day, and for ever. The woe remains upon thee, and from under it thou canst never come, but through judgment, condemnation, and true repentance. To thee this is the word of God; to that of God in thy conscience I do speak, which will witness the truth of what I write, and will condemn thee. And when thou art in thy torment (though now thou swellest in thy vanity, and livest in wickedness), remember thou wast warned in thy lifetime. When the eternal condemnation is stretched over thee, thou shalt witness this to be the word of the Lord God unto thee; and if ever thy eye shall see repentance, thou wilt witness me to have been a friend of thy soul."   G. F.

Having thus cleared my conscience to the justice, and to the priest of Ulverstone, who had raised the first persecution in that country, it was upon me to send this warning in writing to the people of Ulverstone in general.

"CONSIDER, O people! who are within the parish of Ulverstone; I was moved of the Lord to come into your public places to speak among you, being sent of God to direct your minds to him, that you might know where you might find your teacher; that your minds might be staid alone upon God, and you might not gad abroad without you for a teacher; for the Lord God alone will teach his people; and he is coming to teach them, and to gather them from idols' temples, and from the customary worships, which all the world is trained up in. God hath given to every one of you a measure of his Spirit, according to your capacity; liars, drunkards, whoremongers, and thieves, and who follow filthy pleasures, you all have this measure in you. This is the measure of the Spirit of God, that shows you sin, and evil, and deceit; which lets you see that lying is sin; and theft, drunkenness, and uncleanness, all to be the works of darkness. Therefore mind your measure (for nothing that is unclean shall enter into the kingdom of God), and prize your time while you have it, lest the time come that you say with sorrow, we had time, but it is past. O! why will ye die? why will ye choose your own ways? why will ye follow the course of the world? and why will ye follow envy, malice, drunkenness, and foolish pleasures? know ye not in your consciences that all these are evil and sin? and that they who act such things, shall never enter into the kingdom of God? O! that ye would consider, and see how you have spent your time, and mind how ye do spend it, and observe whom you serve; for 'the wages of sin is death.' Do not ye know, that whatsoever is more than yea and nay, cometh of evil? O! ye drunkards, who live in drunkenness, do ye think to escape the fire and the judgment of God? Though ye swell in venom, and live in lust for a while, yet God will find you out, and bring you to judgment. Therefore love the light, which Christ hath enlightened you withal, who saith, 'I am the light of the world,' and who doth enlighten every one that cometh into the world. One loves the light, and brings his works to the light, and there is no occasion at all of stumbling; the other hates the light, because his deeds are evil, and the light will reprove him. Thou that hatest this light, thou hast it; thou knowest that lying, drunkenness, swearing, whoredom, theft, all ungodliness, and all unrighteousness, are evil. Christ Jesus hath given thee light enough to let thee see these are evil. This light, if thou lovest it, will teach thee holiness and righteousness, without which none shall see God; but if thou hatest this light, it is thy condemnation. Thus are Christ's words found to be true, and fulfilled among you; you that hate this light, set up hirelings, and idols' temples, and such priests as bear rule by their means; such .shepherds as hold up such things; who are called of men masters, and have the chiefest place in the assemblies, whom Christ cried woe against, Matt. xxiii.; such as go in the way of Cain in envy, and after the error of Balaam for wages, gifts, and rewards; these have been your teachers; and these you have held up. But they who love the light, are taught of God; and the Lord is coming to teach his people himself, and to gather his own from the hirelings, and from such as seek for their gain from their quarter, and from such as bear rule by their means. The Lord is opening the eyes of people, that they may see such as bear rule over them. But all, whose eyes are shut, are such as the prophet spoke of, that 'have eyes and see not,' but are foolish, upholding such things. Therefore, poor people, as ye love your own souls, consider the love of God to your souls, while ye have time, and do not turn the grace of God into wantonness. That which shows you ungodliness and worldly lusts, should and would be your teacher, if ye would hearken to it; for the saints of old witnessed the grace of God to be their teacher, which taught them to live soberly and godly in this present world. Ye that are not sober, this grace of God hath appeared unto you, but you turn it into wantonness, and so set up teachers, who are not sober, not holy, not godly. Here you are left without excuse, when the righteous judgment of God shall be revealed upon all who live ungodly. Therefore to the light in you I speak; and when the book of conscience shall come to be opened, then shall you witness what I say to be true, and you all shall be judged out of it. God Almighty direct your minds (such of you especially who love honesty and sincerity), that you may receive mercy in the time of need. Your teacher is *within you;* look not forth; it will teach you both lying in bed, and going abroad, to shun all occasion of sin and evil."   G. F.

As the foregoing was directed to all the inhabitants of Ulverstone in general, so it was upon me to write also to those more particularly, that most constantly followed W. Lampitt, the priest. To these I wrote thus:—

"THE word of the Lord God to all the people that follow priest Lampitt, who is a blind guide. Ye are such as are turned from the light of Christ within, which he hath enlightened you withal; ye are such as follow that which Christ cried woe against, that go not in Christ's way, but in the Pharisees' way, as ye may read, Matt. xxiii., which our Lord Jesus Christ cried woe against. He is the same yesterday, to-day, and for ever: but him ye own not, while ye follow such as he cried woe against; though under a colour ye make a profession, and Lampitt, your priest, makes a trade of Christ's and the saints' words, as his fathers, the Pharisees, made a profession of the prophets' and of Moses's words. Woe was unto them who had not the life, so woe is unto you who have not the life that gave forth the Scriptures, as your fruits have made manifest. For when the Lord hath moved some to come amongst you to preach the truth freely, you have knocked them down, beat, and punched, and haled them out of your assemblies. Such a people serve thee, O Lampitt, to make a prey upon, and these are thy fruits. O! let shame, shame, strike thee and you all in the faces, who make a profession of Christ's words, and yet are stoners, and strikers, and mockers, and scoffers. Let all see, if this be not a cage of unclean birds, spoken of in the Scriptures, by those who had the life of the Scriptures. Such a company of people thou deceivest, and feedest them with thy fancies; thou makest a trade of the Scriptures, and takest them for thy cloak. But thou art manifest to all the children of light; for that cloak will not cover thee; thy skirts are seen, and thy nakedness appears. The Lord made one to go naked among you, a figure of thy nakedness, and of your nakedness, and as a sign amongst you, before your destruction cometh; that you might see that you were naked, and not covered with the truth. To the light in all your consciences I speak, which Christ Jesus doth enlighten you withal. It will show you the time you have spent, and all the evil deeds you have done in that time; who follow such a teacher, that acts contrary to this light, and leads you into the ditch. When you are in the ditch together, both teacher and people, remember, ye were warned in your lifetime. If ever your eye come to see repentance, and you obey the light of Jesus Christ in you, you will witness me to have been a friend of your souls, and that I have sought your eternal good, and written this in dear love to you. Then will you own your condemnation; which you must all own, before you can come into that blessed life, of which there is no end. But ye, who hate the light, because your deeds are evil, this light is your condemnation. O! that ye would love this light, and hearken to it! It would teach you, both in your daily occupations, and as you lie upon your beds, and would never let you speak a vain word. In loving it, you love Christ; in hating it, you bring condemnation thereof upon yourselves. To you this is the word of God, from under which you can never pass, nor ever escape the terror of the Lord, in the state you are in, who hate the light." G. F.

Amongst the chief hearers and followers of this priest Lampitt of Ulverstone, was one Adam Sands, who was a very wicked, false man, and would have destroyed truth and its followers if he could. To him I was moved to write thus :—

"ADAM SANDS,

"To the light in thy conscience I appeal, thou child of the Devil, thou enemy of righteousness; the Lord will strike thee down, though now for a while in thy wickedness thou mayest reign. The plagues of God are due to thee, who hardenest thyself in thy wickedness against the pure truth of God. With the pure truth of God, which thou hast resisted and persecuted, thou art to be thrashed down, which is eternal, and doth comprehend thee; and with the light, which thou despisest, thou art seen; and it is thy condemnation. Thou as one brutish, and thy wife as an hypocrite, and you both as murderers of the just, in that which is eternal, are seen and comprehended; and your hearts searched, and tried, and condemned by the light. The light in thy conscience will witness the truth of what I write to thee; and will let thee see that thou art not born of God, but art from the truth, in the beastly nature. If ever thy eye see repentance, thou wilt witness me a friend of thy soul, and a seeker of thy eternal good." G. F.

This Adam Sands afterwards died miserably.

I was moved also to write to priest Tatham.

"THE word of the Lord to thee, priest Tatham, who art found out of the doctrine of Christ; having the chiefest place in the assembly, being called of men, master, and standing praying in the synagogue in the steps of the Pharisees, which our Lord Jesus Christ cried woe against. In his way thou art not, but in the way of the scribes and Pharisees, as thou mayest read, Matt. xxiii. There Christ's words judge thee, and the Scriptures of truth condemn thee. For thou art such a one as sues men at the law for tithes, and yet professest thyself to be a minister of Christ; which Christ never empowered his to do; neither did any of his apostles or ministers ever do so. Here I charge thee in the presence of the living God, to be out of their doctrine; and that as one of those evil beasts the Scripture speaks of, thou mindest earthly things, which the life of the Scriptures is against. Thou art for destruction in the state wherein thou standest; and it will be thy portion eternally, if thou dost not repent. To that of God in thy conscience I speak, which will witness the truth of what I say. Thou goest in Cain's way, in envy, an enemy to God, and from the command of God. Thou goest in Balaam's way, from the Spirit of God, for gifts and rewards, the wages of unrighteousness. Thou son of Balaam, thou art worse than thy father, for though he loved the wages of unrighteousness, yet he durst not take them; but thou not only takest them, but suest men at the law if they will not give them thee, which no true minister of Jesus Christ ever did; therefore stop thy mouth for ever, and never make mention of them, or profess thyself one of them. With the light thou art seen and comprehended, who art light and vain, and speakest a divination of thy own brain, and deceivest the people. That in thy conscience will witness what I say, and will condemn thee, who art one of those that bear rule by their means, which the Lord sent Jeremiah to cry against, Jer. v.; and so thou holdest up 'the horrible and filthy thing that is committed in the land.' They that do not tremble at the word of the Lord, are the foolish people that hold thee up; they are sottish children, and have no understanding; they are wise to do evil, but not to do good, who are deceived by thee. Thou art one of those that seek their gain from their quarter; a greedy dumb dog, that never hath enough, as thy practice makes manifest, which the Lord sent Isaiah to cry against, Isa. lvi. 11, 12. And thou art such a one as the Lord sent Ezekiel to cry against, who feedest of the fat, and clothest with the wool, and makest a prey of the people. But the Lord is gathering his sheep from thy mouth, that to thee they shall be a prey no longer. Thou enemy of God, here this prophecy is fulfilled upon thee, Ezek. xxxiv., and thou art one of them; I charge it upon thee in the presence of the living God; a hireling thou art, and they that put not into thy mouth, thou preparest war against them. Thou hatest the good, and lovest the evil, which the Lord sent Micah to cry against, Mic. iii. Cover thy lips, and stop thy mouth for ever, thou child of darkness; for with the light thou art comprehended, and seen to be among them which the holy men of God cried woe against; and by the Spirit of the Living God thou art judged. In the light, which is thy condemnation, thou art comprehended; thy race is seen, and thy compass known, who art out of the commands of Christ, and out of the doctrine and life of the apostles. Thou art proved and tried: to thee this is the word of the Lord, to thee it shall be as a hammer, a fire, and a sword, and from under it thou shalt never come, unless thou repent; who art with the light to be condemned in that state wherein thou standest: and if ever thy eye see repentance, this thy condemnation thou must own." G. F.

I wrote also to —— Burton, priest of Sedbergh, much to the same purpose, he being in the same evil ground, nature, and practice. Many other epistles also and papers I wrote about that time, as the Lord moved me thereunto, which I sent among the priests, professors, and people of all sorts, for the laying their evil ways open before them, that they might see and forsake them; and opening the way of truth unto them, that they might come to walk therein; which are too many and large to be inserted in this place.

After I had cleared my conscience at that time to the priests and people near Swarthmore, I went again into WESTMORLAND. A company of men with pikes and staves laid wait for me at a bridge in the way, and they met with some Friends, but missed me. Afterwards they came to the meeting with their pikes and staves: but Justice Benson being there, and many considerable people besides, they were prevented from doing the mischief they intended. So they went away in a great rage, without hurting any one.

I went from the meeting to GRAYRIGG, and had a meeting there at Alexander Dixon's house, to which the priest (who was a Baptist, and a chapel priest) came to oppose; but the Lord confounded him by his power. Some of the priest's people tumbled down some milk-pails which stood upon the side of the house, which was much crowded; whereupon the priest, after he and his company were gone away, raised a slander, "that the Devil frightened him, and took away a side of the house while he was in the meeting." And though this was a known falsehood, yet it served the priests and professors to feed on for a while; and so shameless they were, that they printed and published it.

Another time this priest came to a meeting, and fell to jangling. First he said, "the Scriptures were the word of God." I told him they were the words of God, but were not Christ, who is the Word; and bid him prove by Scripture what he said. Then he said it was not the Scripture that was the word; and setting his foot upon the Bible, he said it was but copies bound up together. Many unsavoury words came from him, but after he was gone we had a blessed meeting, and the Lord's power and presence was preciously manifested and felt amongst us. Soon after he sent me a challenge to meet me at Kendal. I sent him word he need not go so far as Kendal, for I would meet him in his own parish. The hour being fixed, we met, and abundance of rude people gathered together, besides the baptized people who were his own members; and they had intended to do mischief, but God prevented them. When we were met, I declared the day of the Lord to them, and directed them to Christ Jesus. Then the priest out with his Bible, and said it was the word of God. I told him it was the words of God, but not God, the Word. His answer was, he would prove the Scriptures to be the word before all the people. I let him go on, having a man there that could take down in writing both what he said, and what I said. When he could not prove it (for I kept him to Scripture proof, chapter and verse for it), the people gnashed their teeth for anger, and said he would have me anon; but in going about to prove that one error, he ran into many. And when at length he saw he could not prove it, then he said he would prove it to be a God: so he toiled himself afresh, till he perspired again, but could not prove what he had affirmed. And he and his company were full of wrath; for I kept his assertions on the head of him and them all, and told them I owned what the Scriptures said of themselves, namely, that they were the words of God, but Christ was the Word. So the Lord's power came over all, and they being confounded went away. The Lord disappointed their mischievous intentions against me; and Friends were established in Christ, and many of the priest's followers saw the folly of their teacher.

After this, priest Bennet, of CARTMEL, sent a challenge to dispute with me. Hereupon I came to his steeple-house on a First-day, and found him preaching. When he had done, I spoke to him and his people; but the priest would not stand the trial, but went his way. After he was gone, I had much discourse with the people; and when I was come out into the steeple-house yard, and was discoursing further with the professors, and declaring truth unto them, one of them set his foot behind me, and two of them ran against my breast, and threw me down backwards against a grave-stone, wickedly and maliciously seeking to hurt me; but I got up again, and was moved of the Lord to speak to them. Then I went up to the priest's house, and desired him to come forth that I might discourse with him, seeing he had challenged me; but he would not be seen. So the Lord's power came over them all, which was greatly manifested at that time. Amongst the priest's hearers was one Richard Roper, one of the bitterest professors the priest had: he was very fierce and hot in his contention; but afterwards he came to be convinced of God's eternal truth, became a minister thereof, and continued faithful to his death.

It was now about the beginning of the year 1653, when I returned to SWARTHMORE; and going to a meeting at Gleaston, a professor challenged a dispute with me. I went to the house where he was, and called him to come forth; but the Lord's power was over him, so that he durst not meddle. Then I departed thence, and visited the meetings of Friends in LANCASHIRE, and came back to Swarthmore. Great openings I had from the Lord, not only of divine and spiritual matters, but also of outward things, relating to the civil government. For being one day in Swarthmore-hall, when Judge Fell and Justice Benson were talking of the news, and of the parliament then sitting, which was called the Long Parliament, I was moved to tell them, that before that day two weeks the parliament should be broken up, and the speaker plucked out of his chair. And that day two weeks Justice Benson coming thither again, told Judge Fell, that now he saw George was a true prophet; for Oliver had broken up the parliament.

About this time I was in a fast for about ten days, my spirit being greatly exercised on truth's account; for James Milner and Richard Myer went out into imaginations, and a company followed them. This James Milner and some of his company, had true openings at first; but getting into pride and exaltation of spirit, they ran out from truth. I was sent for to them, and was moved of the Lord to go, and show them their outgoings: and they were brought to see their folly, and condemned it, and came into the way of truth again. After some time I went to a meeting at ARN-SIDE, where Richard Myer was, who had been long lame of one of his arms. I was moved of the Lord to say unto him, amongst all the people, "Stand up on thy legs" (for he was sitting down): and he stood up, and stretched out his arm that had been lame a long time, and said, "Be it known unto you, all people, that this day I am healed." Yet his parents could hardly believe it; but after the meeting was done, they had him aside, took off his doublet, and then saw it was true. He came soon after to Swarthmore meeting, and then declared how that the Lord had healed him. Yet after this the Lord commanded him to go to York with a message from him, but he disobeyed the Lord; and the Lord struck him again, so that he died about three-quarters of a year after.

Now were great threatenings given forth in Cumberland, that if ever I came there again, they would take away my life. When I heard it, I was drawn to go into Cumberland, and went to Miles Wennington's, in the same parish, from which those threatenings came; but they had not power to touch me.

About this time Anthony Pearson was convinced, who had been an opposer of Friends.[*] He came over to Swarthmore; and I being then at Colonel West's, they sent for me. Colonel West said, "Go, George, for it may be of great service to the man." So I went, and the Lord's power reached him.

About this time also the Lord opened several mouths to declare the truth to priests and people, so that many were cast into prison. I went again into CUMBERLAND, and Anthony Pearson and his wife, and several Friends, went with me to BOOTLE, where Anthony Pearson left me, and went to Carlisle sessions; for he was a Justice of the peace in three counties. On a First-day, I went into the steeple-house at Bootle; and when the priest had done, I began to speak. But the people were exceeding rude, and struck and beat me in the yard: one gave me a very great blow over my wrist, so that the people thought he had broken my hand to pieces. The constable was very desirous to keep the peace, and would have set some of them by the heels that struck me, if I would have given way to it. After my service amongst them was over, I went to Joseph Nicolson's house,[†] and the constable went a little way with us, to keep off the rude multitude. In the afternoon I went again; and then the priest had got another priest to help him, that came from London, and was highly accounted of. Before I went into the steeple-house, I sat a little upon the Cross, and Friends with me; but the Friends were moved to go into the steeple-house, and I went in after them. The London priest was preaching; who gathered up all the Scriptures he could think of, that spoke of false prophets, and antichrists, and deceivers, and threw them upon us: but when he had done I recollected all those Scriptures, and brought them back upon himself. Then the people fell upon me in a rude manner; but the constable charged them to keep the peace, and so made them quiet again. Then the

---

* Justice Pearson, who "was convinced as he sat on the bench," became the author of an approved work, *The Great Case of Tithes*. A striking letter from him, dated in 1653, respecting his religious state, is inserted in *Letters of Early Friends*, pages 10–12.

† Joseph Nicholson was one of those who, with his wife, suffered in the New England persecution, being imprisoned there and laid in irons. He was also immured within the walls of Dover Castle in 1661. See Bowden's *History of Friends in America*, vol. i., pp. 203–206, and 268, &c.

priest began to rage, and said I must not speak there : I told him he had
his hour-glass, by which he had preached, and he having done, the time was
free for me, as well as for him, for he was but a stranger there himself.
So I opened the Scriptures to them, and let them see "that those Scriptures, that spoke of the false prophets, and antichrists, and deceivers,
described them and their generation, and belonged to them who were found
walking in their steps, and bringing forth their fruits; and not unto us,
who were not guilty of such things." I manifested to them, that they
were out of the steps of the true prophets and apostles; and showed them
clearly, by the fruits and marks, that it was they of whom those Scriptures
spoke, and not we. And I declared the truth, and the word of life to the
people, and directed them to Christ their teacher. All was quiet while I
was speaking; but when I had done, and was come out, the priests were
both of them in such a rage, that they foamed at the mouth for anger
against me. The priest of the place made an oration to the people in the
steeple-house yard, and said, "This man hath gotten all the honest men
and women in Lancashire to him; and now," said he, "he comes here to
do the same." Then said I unto him, "What wilt thou have left? and
what have the priests left them, but such as themselves? For if it be the
honest that receive the truth, and are turned to Christ, then it must be the
dishonest that follow thee, and such as thou art." Some also of the priest's
people began to plead for their priest, and for tithes; but I told them it were
better for them to plead for Christ, who had ended the tithing-priesthood and
tithes, and had sent forth his ministers to give freely, as they had received
freely. So the Lord's power came over them all, put them to silence, and
restrained the rude people, that they could not do the mischief they intended.
When I came down again to Joseph Nicholson's house, I saw a great hole
in my coat, which was cut with a knife, but it was not cut through my
doublet, for the Lord had prevented their mischief. And the next day a
rude wicked man would have done violence to a Friend, but the Lord's
power stopped him.

Now was I moved to send James Lancaster to appoint a meeting at
John Wilkinson's steeple-house near COCKERMOUTH, who was a preacher
in great repute, and had three parishes under him; wherefore I stayed at
Millom-in-Bootle till he came back again. In the meantime some of those
called the gentry of the country had formed a plot against me, and had
given a little boy a rapier, to do me a mischief with it. They came with
the boy to Joseph Nicholson's house to seek me; but the Lord had so
ordered it, that I was gone into the fields. They met with James Lancaster, but did not much abuse him; and not finding me in the house, after
a while they went away again. So I walked up and down in the fields
that night, and did not go to bed as very often I used to do. The next
day we came to the steeple-house, where James Lancaster had appointed
the meeting. There were at this meeting twelve soldiers and their wives,
who were come thither from Carlisle; and the country people came in, as
if it had been to a fair. I lay at a house a short distance from the place,
so that many Friends were there before me. When I came, I found James
Lancaster speaking under a yew tree; which was so full of people that I

feared they would break it down. I looked about for a place to stand upon, to speak to the people; for they lay all up and down like people at a leaguer. After I was discovered, a professor came to me, and asked, if I would not go into the church; seeing no place convenient to speak to the people from, I told him, "Yes;" whereupon the people rushed in; so that when I came in, the house and even the pulpit was so full of people, that I had much ado to get in; and they that could not get in, stood about the walls. When the people were settled, I stood up on a seat; and the Lord opened my mouth "to declare his everlasting truth, and his everlasting day; and to lay open all their teachers, their rudiments, traditions, and inventions, that they had been in, in the night of apostacy since the apostles' days. I turned them to Christ the true teacher, and to the true spiritual worship; directing them where to find the Spirit and truth, that they might worship God therein. I opened Christ's parables unto them, and directed them to the Spirit of God in themselves, that would open the Scriptures unto them. And I showed them, how all might come to know their Saviour, and sit under his teaching;—might come to be heirs of the kingdom of God, and know both the voice of God and of Christ, by which they might discover all the false shepherds and teachers they had been under; and be gathered to the true shepherd, priest, bishop, and prophet, Christ Jesus, whom God commanded all to hear." So when I had largely declared the word of life unto them, for about three hours, I walked from amongst the people, and they passed away very well satisfied. Among the rest a professor followed me, praising and commending me; but his words were like a thistle to me. At last I turned about, and bid him "fear the Lord:" whereupon priest Larkham, of Cockermouth (for several priests were got together on the way who came after the meeting was over), said to me, "Sir, why do you judge so; you must not judge." But I turned to him and said, "Friend, dost not thou discern an exhortation from a judgment? I admonished him to fear God; and dost thou say I judge him?" So this priest and I falling into discourse, I manifested him to be amongst the false prophets and covetous hirelings. And several people being moved to speak to him, he and two others of the priests soon got away. When they were gone, John Wilkinson, who was preacher of that parish, and of two other parishes in Cumberland, began to dispute against his own conscience for several hours, till the people generally turned against him; for he thought to have tired me out, but the Lord's power tired him out, and the Lord's truth came over him and them all. Many hundreds were convinced that day, and received the Lord Jesus Christ, and his free teaching, with gladness; of whom some have died in the truth, and many stand faithful witnesses thereof. The soldiers also were convinced, and their wives, and continued with me till First-day.

On First-day I went to the steeple-house at COCKERMOUTH, where priest Larkham lived. When he had done, I began to speak, and the people began to be rude; but the soldiers told them we had broken no law, and they became quiet. Then I turned to the priest, and laid him open among the false prophets and hirelings; at which word the priest went his way, and said, "He calls me hireling;" which was true enough, and all the people knew it. Then some of the great men of the town came to me, and said, "Sir, we have no learned men to dispute with you." I told them I came not to dispute, but to show the way of salvation to them, the way of everlasting life. I declared largely the way of life and truth, and directed them to Christ their teacher, who had died for them, and bought them with his blood.

When I had done, I went about two miles to another great steeple-house of John Wilkinson's, called BRIGHAM; where the people, having been at the other meeting, were mightily affected, and would have put my horse into the steeple-house yard; but I said, "No, the priest claims that; take him to an inn." When I came into the steeple-house yard, I saw the people coming in great companies, as to a fair; and abundance were already gathered in the lanes, and about the steeple-house. I was very thirsty, and walked about a quarter of a mile to a brook, where I got some water, and refreshed myself. As I came up again, I met Wilkinson, who as I passed by him said, "Sir, will you preach to-day? If you will," said he, "I will not oppose you in word or thought." I replied, "Oppose if thou wilt; I have something to speak to the people." "And," said I, "thou carriedst thyself foolishly the other day, and spoke against thy conscience and reason; insomuch that thy hearers cried out against thee." So I left him, and went on; for he saw it was in vain to oppose, the people were so affected with the Lord's truth. When I came into the steeple-house yard, a professor came to me, and asked, if I would not go into the church, as he called it. And I seeing no convenient place to stand to speak to the people from, went in, and stood up on a seat, after they were settled. The priest came in also, but did not go up to his pulpit. "The Lord opened my mouth, and I declared his everlasting truth, and word of life to the people; directing them to the Spirit of God *in* themselves, by which they might know God and Christ, and the Scriptures, and come to have heavenly fellowship in the Spirit. I declared to them, that every one that cometh into the world, was enlightened by Christ the life; by which light they might see their sins, and Christ, who was come to save them from their sins, and died for them. And, if they came to walk in this light, they might therein see Christ to be the author of their faith, and the finisher thereof; their Shepherd to feed them, their Priest to teach them, and their great Prophet to open divine mysteries unto them, and to be always present with them. I explained also unto them, in the openings of the Lord, the first covenant, explaining to them the types, and the substance of those figures; and so bringing them on to Christ, the new covenant. I also manifested unto them, that there had been a night of apostacy since the apostles' days; but that now the everlasting gospel was preached again, which brought life and immortality to light; and the day of the Lord was come, and Christ was come to teach his people himself by his light, grace, power, and Spirit." A fine opportunity the Lord gave me to preach truth among the people that day for about three hours; and all was quiet. Many hundreds were convinced; and some of them praised God and said, "Now we know the first step to peace." The preacher also said privately to some of his hearers, that I had broken them and overthrown them.

After this I went to a village, and many people accompanied me. As I was sitting in a house full of people, declaring the word of life unto them, I cast mine eye upon a woman, and discerned an unclean spirit in her. And I was moved of the Lord to speak sharply to her, and told her she was under the influence of an unclean spirit; whereupon she went out of the room. Now, I being a stranger there, and knowing nothing of the woman outwardly, the people wondered at it, and told me afterwards that I had discovered a great thing; for all the country looked upon her to be a wicked person. The Lord had given me a spirit of discerning, by which I many times saw the states and conditions of people, and could try their spirits. For not long before, as I was going to a meeting, I saw some women in a field, and I discerned an evil spirit in them; and I was moved to go out of my way into the field to them, and declare unto them their conditions. At another time there came one into Swarthmore-hall in the meeting time; and I was moved to speak sharply to her, and told her she was under the power of an evil spirit; and the people said afterwards she was generally accounted so. There came also at another time another woman, and stood at a distance from me, and I cast mine eye upon her, and said, "Thou hast been an harlot;" for I perfectly saw the condition and life of the woman. The woman answered and said, many could tell her of her outward sins, but none could tell her of her inward. Then I told her her heart was not right before the Lord, and that from the inward came the outward. This woman came afterwards to be convinced of God's truth, and became a Friend.

From the aforesaid village we came up to Thomas Bewley's, near COLDBECK; and from thence, having had some service for the Lord there, I passed to a town, where I had a meeting at the Cross; and all was pretty quiet. When I had declared the truth unto them, and directed them to Christ their teacher, some received the truth. We had another meeting upon the borders, in a steeple-house yard, to which many professors and contenders came; but the Lord's power was over all; and when the word of life had been declared amongst them, some received the truth there also.

From thence we came to CARLISLE, and the pastor of the Baptists, with most of his hearers, came to me to the abbey, where I had a meeting, and declared the word of life amongst them; and many of the Baptists, and of the soldiers, were convinced. After the meeting, the pastor of the Baptists, a high notionist, and a flashy man, came to me, and asked me, "what must be damned;" I was moved immediately to tell him, "that which spoke in him was to be damned." This stopped his mouth; and the witness of God was raised up in him. I opened to him the states of election and reprobation, so that he said he never heard the like in his life. He also came afterwards to be convinced.

Then I went up to the castle among the soldiers, who beat a drum, and called the garrison together. I preached the truth amongst them, "directing them to the Lord Jesus Christ to be their teacher, and to the measure of his Spirit *in* themselves, by which they might be turned from darkness to the light, and from the power of Satan unto God. I warned them all, that they should do no violence to any man, but should show forth a Christian life; telling them, that he who was to be their teacher, would be their condemner, if they were disobedient to him." So I left them, having no opposition from any of them except the serjeants, who afterwards came to be convinced.

On the market-day I went up into the market to the market-cross. Now the magistrates had both threatened and sent their serjeants; and the magistrates' wives had said that if I came there, they would pluck the hair off my head; and that the serjeants should take me up. Nevertheless I obeyed the Lord God, and went upon the Cross, and there declared unto them, "that the day of the Lord was coming upon all their deceitful ways and doings, and deceitful merchandize; and that they should put away all cozening and cheating, and keep to yea and nay, and speak the truth one to another; so the truth and the power of God was set over them." After I had declared the word of life to the people, the throng being so great that the serjeants could not get to me, nor the magistrates' wives come at me, I passed away quietly. Many people and soldiers came to me, and some Baptists, that were bitter contenders; amongst whom one of their deacons, being an envious man, and finding the Lord's power was over them, cried out for very anger. Whereupon I set my eyes upon him, and spoke sharply to him in the power of the Lord; and he cried, "Do not pierce me so with thy eyes; keep thy eyes off me."

On the First-day following I went into the steeple-house; and after the priest had done, I preached the truth to the people, and declared the word of life amongst them. The priest got away, and the magistrates desired me to go out of the steeple-house. But I still declared the way of the Lord unto them, and told them, "I came to speak the word of life and salvation from the Lord amongst them." The power of the Lord was dreadful amongst them in the steeple-house, so that the people trembled and shook, and they thought the steeple-house shook; and some of them feared it would fall down on their heads. The magistrates' wives were in a rage, and strove mightily to be at me; but the soldiers and friendly people stood thick about me. At length the rude people of the city rose, and came with staves and stones into the steeple-house, crying "Down with these round-headed rogues;" and they threw stones. Whereupon the governor sent a file or two of musketeers into the steeple-house, to appease the tumult, and commanded all the other soldiers out. So those soldiers took me by the hand in a friendly manner, and said they would have me along with them. When we came forth into the street, the city was in an uproar, and the governor came down; and some of those soldiers were put in prison for standing by me, and for me, against the town's-people. A lieutenant, that had been convinced, came, and brought me to his house, where there was a Baptists' meeting, and thither came Friends also, and we had a very quiet meeting; they heard the word of life gladly, and many received it. The next day, the justices and magistrates of the town being gathered in the townhall, they granted a warrant against me, and sent for me to come before them. I was then gone to a Baptist's house; but hearing of it I went up to the hall to them, where many rude

people were; some of whom had sworn strange, false things against me.
I had much discourse with the magistrates, wherein I laid open the fruits
of their priests' preaching, and showed them how void they were of Christianity; and that, though they were such great professors (for they were
Independents and Presbyterians) they were without the possession of that
which they professed. After a large examination they committed me to
prison as a blasphemer, a heretic, and a seducer; though they could not
justly charge any such thing against me. The jail at Carlisle had two
jailers, an upper and an under, who looked like two great bear-wards.
Now when I was brought in, the upper jailer had me up into a great
chamber, and told me, I should have what I would in that room. But I
told him, he should not expect any money from me, for I would neither
lie in any of his beds, nor eat any of his victuals. Then he put me into
another room; where after a while, I got something to lie upon. There
I lay till the assizes came; and then all the talk was, that I was to be
hanged. The high sheriff, whose name was Wilfred Lawson, stirred them
much up to take away my life; and said, he would guard me to my execution himself. They were in a great rage, and set three musketeers for a
guard upon me; one at my chamber door, another at the stairs' foot, and
a third at the street door; and they would let none come at me, except one
sometimes, to bring me some necessary things. At night they would bring
up priests to me, sometimes as late as the tenth hour; who were exceedingly rude and devilish. There was a company of bitter Scotch priests,
Presbyterians, made up of envy and malice, who were not fit to speak of
the things of God, they were so foul-mouthed; but the Lord, by his power,
gave me dominion over them all, and I let them see both their fruits and
their spirits. Great ladies also (as they were called) came to see the man
that they said was to die. While both the judge, justices, and sheriff,
were contriving together how they might put me to death, the Lord disappointed their design by an unexpected way; for the judge's clerk (as I
was informed) started a question among them, which confounded all their
counsels; so that after that they had not power to call me before the judge.

Anthony Pearson being then in Carlisle, and perceiving that they did
not intend to bring me, as was expected, upon my trial, wrote a letter to
the judges, directed as follows:—

*To the Judges of Assize and Jail-delivery for the Northern Parts, sitting at
Carlisle.*

"You are raised up to do righteousness and justice, and sent forth to
punish him that doth evil, and to encourage him that doth well, and to set
the oppressed free. I am therefore moved to lay before you the condition
of George Fox, whom the magistrates of this city have cast into prison, for
words that he is accused to have spoken, which they call blasphemy. He was
sent to the jail, till he should be delivered by due course of law; and it was
expected he should have been proceeded against in the common-law course
at this assizes. The informations against him were delivered into court;
and the act allows and appoints that way of trial. How hardly and unchris-
tianly he hath been hitherto dealt with, I shall not now mention; but you

may consider, that nothing he is accused of is nice and difficult.   And, to my knowledge, he utterly abhors and detests every particular, which by the act against blasphemous opinions, is appointed to be punished; and differs as much from those people against whom the law was made, as light from darkness.   Though he is committed, judgment is not given against him; nor have his accusers been face to face, to affirm before him what they have informed against him; nor was he heard as to the particulars of their accusations; nor doth it appear, that any word they charge against him, is within the act.   But, indeed, I could not yet so much as see the information, no, not in court, though I desired it, both of the clerk of the assizes and of the magistrates' clerk; nor hath he had a copy of them.   This is very hard; and that he should be so closely restrained, that his friends may not speak with him, I know no law nor reason for.   I do therefore claim for him a due and lawful hearing, and that he may have a copy of his charge, and freedom to answer for himself; and that rather before you, than to be left to the rulers of this town, who are not competent judges of blasphemy, as by their mittimus appears; who have committed him upon an act of parliament, and mention words as spoken by him at his examination, which are not within the act, and which he utterly denies.   The words mentioned in the mittimus he denies to have spoken; and hath neither professed nor avowed them."   ANTHONY PEARSON.

Notwithstanding this letter, the judges were resolved not to suffer me to be brought before them; but reviling and scoffing at me behind my back, left me to the magistrates of the town; giving them what encouragement they could to exercise their cruelty upon me.   Whereupon (though I had been kept up so close in the jailer's house that Friends were not suffered to visit me, and Colonel Benson and Justice Pearson were denied to see me, yet) the next day, after the judges were gone out of town, an order was sent to the jailer to put me down into the dungeon among the moss-troopers,* thieves, and murderers, which accordingly he did.   A filthy nasty place it was, where men and women were put together in a very uncivil manner, and not even a house of convenience to it; and the prisoners so lousy that one woman was almost eaten to death with lice.   Yet, as bad as the place was, the prisoners were all made very loving and subject to me; and some of them were convinced of the truth, as the publicans and harlots were of old; so that they were able to confound any priest, that might come to the grates to dispute.   But the jailer was very cruel, and the under-jailer very abusive to me and to Friends that came to see me; for he would beat Friends with a great cudgel, that did but come to the window to look in upon me.   I could get up to the grate, where sometimes I took in my meat; at which the jailer was often offended.   One time he came in a great rage, and beat me with a great cudgel, though I was not at the grate at that time; and as he beat me, he cried, "Come out of the

---

* Moss-troopers were the remnant of a kind of freebooters, who infested the borders of England and Scotland in feudal times, making incursions on each other, less for the purpose of contention in arms, than for committing depredations on cattle and property.

window," though I was then far enough from it. While he struck me, I was made to sing in the Lord's power; and that made him rage the more. Then he fetched a fiddler, and brought him in where I was, and set him to play, thinking to vex me thereby; but while he played, I was moved in the everlasting power of the Lord God to sing; and my voice drowned the noise of the fiddle, and struck and confounded them, and made them give over fiddling and go their way.

Justice Benson's wife was moved of the Lord to come to visit me, and to eat no meat but what she ate with me at the bars of the dungeon window. She was afterwards herself imprisoned at York, when she was great with child, for speaking to a priest; and was kept in prison, and not suffered to go out, when the time of her travail was come; so she was delivered of her child in the prison. She was an honest, tender woman, and continued faithful to the truth until she died.

Whilst I was in the dungeon at Carlisle, James Parnell, a little lad of about sixteen years of age, came to see me, and was convinced: and the Lord quickly made him a powerful minister of the word of life, and many were turned to Christ by him, though he lived not long: for, travelling into Essex, in the work of the ministry, in the year 1655, he was committed to Colchester castle, where he endured very great hardships and sufferings; being put by the cruel jailer into a hole in the castle-wall, called the oven, so high from the ground, that he went up to it by a ladder; which being six feet too short, he was obliged to climb from the ladder to the hole by a rope that was fastened above. And when Friends would have given him a cord and a basket, to draw up his victuals in, the inhuman jailer would not suffer them, but forced him to go down and up by that short ladder and rope, to fetch his victuals, (which for a long time he did) or else he might have famished in the hole. At length, his limbs being much benumbed with lying in that place, yet being constrained to go down to take up some victuals, as he came up the ladder again with his victuals in one hand, and caught at the rope with the other, he missed the rope, and fell down from a very great height upon the stones; by which fall he was exceedingly wounded in his head and arms, and his body was so much bruised, that he died in a short time after.* When he was dead, the wicked professors, to cover their own cruelty, wrote a book of him, and said, "he fasted himself to death;" which was an abominable falsehood, and was manifested so to be by another book, which was written in answer to that, and was called "The Lamb's Defence against Lies."

---

* James Parnell, according to the historian Sewell, was trained up in the schools of literature. Though young, he became a valiant soldier of the Lamb;

"In age a stripling, but in service old;"

and died a true martyr in a dungeon's gloom. Particulars of his barbarous treatment, and consequent death in jail, may be found in Sewell's *History*, vol. i., under date 1655; and fuller information in his *Life* by Callaway. In Barclay's *Letters of Early Friends* is one from James Parnell, written from Colchester Castle, wherein he says, "They have laboured to make my bonds grievous, but my strength the Philistines know not: I am kept and nourished in the midst of mine enemies; glory be to God the Highest, who hath counted me worthy to bear the bonds of the gospel."

Now when I saw that I was not likely to be brought to a public hearing and trial (although I had before answered, in writing, the particular matters charged against me, at the time of my first examination and commitment), I was moved to send the following paper, as a public challenge to all those that belied the truth and me behind my back, to come forth and make good their charge :—

"IF any in Westmorland, or Cumberland, or elsewhere, that profess Christianity, and pretend to love God and Christ, are not satisfied concerning the things of God, which I, who am called George Fox, have spoken and declared, let them declare and publish their dissatisfaction in writing, and not back-bite, nor lie, nor persecute, in secret : this I demand of you all in the presence of the living God, as ye will answer it to him. For the exaltation of the truth, and the confounding of deceit, is this given forth. To that of God in your consciences I speak ; declare or write your dissatisfaction to any of them, whom you call Quakers, that truth may be exalted, and all may come to the light, with which Christ hath enlightened every one that cometh into the world : that nothing may be hid in darkness, in prisons, holes, or corners, but that all things may be brought to the light of Christ, and by the light of Christ may be tried. This am I moved of the Lord to write, and send forth to be set upon the market-crosses in Westmorland, and elsewhere. To the light of Christ in you I speak, that none of you may speak evil of the things of God, which you know not ; nor act contrary to the light, that gave forth the Scriptures ; lest you be found fighters against God, and the hand of the Lord be turned against you."　　　　　　　　　　　　　　　　　　　　G. F.

While I thus lay in the dungeon at Carlisle, the report raised at the time of the assize, "that I should be put to death," was gone far and near ; insomuch that the parliament then sitting, which, I think, was called the Little Parliament, hearing, that a young man at Carlisle was to die for religion, caused a letter to be sent to the sheriff and magistrates concerning me. About the same time I wrote also to the justices at Carlisle, that had cast me into prison, and that persecuted Friends at the instigation of the priests for tithes ; expostulating the matter with them thus :—

"FRIENDS, THOMAS CRASTON AND CUTHBERT STUDHOLM,

"Your noise is gone up to London before the sober people : what imprisoning, what gagging, what havoc and spoiling of the goods of people have you made within these few years ! Unlike men ; as though you had never read the Scriptures, or had not minded them ! Is this the end of Carlisle's religion ? is this the end of your ministry ; and is this the end of your church, and of your profession of Christianity ? you have shamed it by your folly, your madness, and blind zeal. Was it not always the work of the blind guides, watchmen, leaders, and false prophets, to prepare war against them that would not put into their mouths ? And have not you been the priests' pack-horses and executioners ? When they spur you up, to bear the sword against the just, do not you run on against the creatures, that cannot hold up such as the Scriptures did always testify against ? Yet will you lift up your unholy hands, and call upon God with your polluted lips, and pretend a fast, who are full of strife and debate. Did your hearts never burn within you? Did you never come to question your conditions? Are you wholly given up to do the Devil's lusts, to persecute? Where is your loving of enemies? Where is your entertaining of strangers? Where is your overcoming evil with good? Where are your teachers that can stop the mouths of gainsayers, and can convince gainsayers and such as oppose themselves? Have you no ministers of the Spirit, no soldiers with spiritual weapons displaying Christ's colours? But all the dragon's, the murderer's, the persecutor's arm of flesh; Cain's weapons, chief priests taking counsel; Judas and the multitude with swords and staves; Sodom's company raging about Lot's house, like the priests and princes against Jeremiah; like the dragon, beast, and great whore, and the false church, which John saw, should cast into prison, and kill, and persecute? Whose weapons are you bearing? doth not the false church, the whore, make merchandize of cattle, corn, wine, and oil, even to the very souls of men? And hath not all this been since the true church went into the wilderness? Read Revelations the xiith, with the xviiith: do you not read and see what a spirit you are of, and what a bottomless pit you are in? And have not you dishonoured the place of justice and authority? What! turned your sword backward like madmen, who are a praise to the evil-doer, and would be a terror to the good, with all force and might to stop the way of justice! Doth not the Lord, think you, behold your actions? How many have you wronged? how many have you imprisoned and persecuted, and put out of your synagogues? Are you they that must fulfil the prophecy of Christ, Matt. xxiii. John xvi.? Read the Scriptures, and see how unlike you are to the prophets, Christ, and his apostles; and what a visage you have, like unto them that persecuted the prophets, Christ and the apostles. You are found in their steps, wrestling with flesh and blood, and not with principalities, and powers, and spiritual wickedness, and your teachers imprisoning and persecuting for outward things, you being their executioners; the like whereof hath not been in all the nations. The havoc that hath been made, the spoiling of the goods of people, taking away their oxen and fatted beeves, their sheep, corn, wool, and household goods, and giving them to the priests, that have done no work for them; more like moss-troopers than ministers of the gospel, they take them from Friends; sueing them in your courts, and fining them, because they will not break the commands of Christ; that is, because they will not swear. Thus you act against them that do not lift up a hand against you; and as much as you turn against them, you turn against Christ. But he is risen that will plead their cause, and you cannot be hid; for your works are come to light, and the end of your ministry is seen, what it is for—for means. You have dishonoured the truth, the gospel, and are they that make it chargeable? You have lost your glory. You have dishonoured yourselves. Persecution was ever blind and mad. Read the apostle, what he saith of himself, when he was in your nature. Exaltation and pride, and your lifting up yourselves, hath brought you to this; not being humble, not doing justice, not loving mercy. When such as have been beaten and bruised by your rude company, to whom you are a praise and encouragement, have come, and laid things before you, that you might do justice, preserve and keep peace, you, knowing they could not swear, have put an oath to them. This hath been your trick and cover, that ye might not do justice to the just; but by this means you have gone on still further to encourage the evil-doer. But the Lord sees your hearts! If ye were not men past feeling, ye would fear and tremble before the God of the whole earth, who is risen, and will stain your glory, mar your pride, deface your beauty, and lay it in the dust. Though for a time you may swell in your pride, glory in your shame, and make a mock of God's messengers, who, for reproving sin in the gate, are become your prey, you will feel the heavy hand of God, and his judgments at the last. This is from a lover of the truth, and of righteousness, and of your souls; but a witness against all such as make a trade of the prophets', Christ's, and the apostles' words, and are found in the steps of them that persecuted the prophets', Christ's, and the apostles' life; who will persecute them, that will not hold you up, and put into your mouths, and give you means. Tithes were before the law, and tithes were in the law; but tithes, since the days of the apostles, have been only since the false church got up. Now Christ, who is come to end the law, and to end war, redeems men out of the tenths and out of the nines also. The redeemed of the Lord shall reign upon the earth, and know the election which was before the world began. Since the days of the apostles, tithes have been set up by the Papists, and by them that went forth from the apostles into the world; so set up by the false church, that made merchandize of people, since the true church went into the wilderness. But now is the judgment of the great whore come, and the beast and false prophet, the old dragon, shall be taken and cast into the fire, and the Lamb and his saints shall have the victory. Now is Christ come, who will make war in righteousness, and destroy with the sword of his mouth all these inventors and inventions, that have got up, and been set up since the days of the apostles, and since the true church went into the wilderness. And the everlasting gospel, which is the power of God, shall be preached again to all nations, and kindreds, and tongues, in this the Lamb's day, before whom you shall appear to judgment. You have no way to escape. For he hath appeared, who is 'the first and the last, the beginning and the ending, the Alpha and the Omega; he that was dead, is alive again, and lives for evermore!'"

I mentioned before, that Gervase Benson and Anthony Pearson, though they had been justices of the peace, were not permitted to come to me in the prison; whereupon they jointly wrote a letter to the magistrates, priests, and people at Carlisle, concerning my imprisonment; which was thus :—

"Him, who is called George Fox, who is persecuted by rulers and magistrates, by justices, by priests, and by people, and who suffers imprisonment of his body at this present, as a blasphemer, and a heretic, and a seducer, him do we witness, who in measure are made partakers of the same life, that lives in him, to be a minister of the eternal word of God, by whom the everlasting gospel is preached; by the powerful preaching whereof the eternal Father of the saints hath opened the blind eyes, hath unstopped the deaf ears, hath let the oppressed go free, and hath raised up the dead out of the graves. Christ is now preached in and among the saints, the same that ever he was; and because his heavenly image is borne up in this his faithful servant, therefore doth fallen man (rulers, priests, and people) persecute him. Because he lives up out of the fall, and testifies against the works of the world, that the deeds thereof are evil, he suffers by you magistrates; not as an evil-doer. For thus it was ever, where the seed of God was kept in prison under the cursed nature, that nature sought to imprison them in whom it was raised. The Lord will make him to you as a burthensome stone; for the sword of the Spirit of the Almighty is put into the hands of the saints, which shall wound all the wicked, and shall not be put up till it hath cut down all corrupt judges, justices, magistrates, priests, and professors; till he hath brought his wonderful thing to pass in the earth; which is to make new heavens and a new earth, wherein shall dwell righteousness; which now he is about to do. Therefore fear the Lord God Almighty, ye judges, justices, commanders, priests, and people; ye that forget God, suddenly will the Lord come, and destroy you with an utter destruction, and will sweep your names out of the earth, and will restore his people judges, as at the first, and counsellors, as at the beginning. And all persecutors shall partake of the plagues of the whore, who hath made the kings of the earth and the great men drunk with the wine of her fornications, and hath drunk the blood of the saints; and therefore shall you be partakers of her plagues. We are not suffered to see our friend in prison, whom we witness to be a messenger of the living God. Now, all people, consider whether this be according to law, or from the wicked, perverse, envious will of the envious rulers and magistrates, who are of the same generation that persecuted Jesus Christ; for, said he, 'as they have done to me, so will they do to you.' And as he took the love, the kindness, and service that was showed and performed to any of his afflicted ones in their sufferings and distress, as done unto himself, so the injuries and wrongs that were done by any to any of his little ones, he resented, as done unto himself also. Therefore you, who are so far from visiting him yourselves in his suffering servant, that ye will not suffer his brethren to visit him, ye must depart, ye workers of iniquity, into the lake that burns with fire. The Lord is coming to thrash the mountains, and will beat them to dust; and all corrupt rulers, corrupt officers, and corrupt laws, the Lord will take vengeance on, by which the tender consciences of his people are oppressed. He will give his people his law, and will judge his people himself, not according to the sight of the eye, and hearing of the ear, but with righteousness, and with equity. Now are your hearts made manifest to be full of envy against the living truth of God, which is made manifest in his people, who are contemned and despised of the world, and scornfully called Quakers. You are worse than the heathens, that put Paul in prison, for none of his friends or acquaintance were hindered to come to him by them; therefore they shall be witnesses against you. Ye are made manifest to the saints, to be of the same generation that put Christ to death, and that put the apostles in prison on the same pretence that you act under, in calling truth error, and the ministers of God blasphemers, as they did. But the day is dreadful and terrible, that shall come upon you, ye evil magistrates, priests, and people, who profess the truth in words outwardly, and yet persecute the power of truth, and them that stand in and for the truth. While ye have time prize it, and remember what is written Isa. liv. 17."

GERVASE BENSON.
ANTHONY PEARSON.

Not long after this, the Lord's power came over the justices, and they were made to set me at liberty. But some time previous, the governor, and Anthony Pearson, came down into the dungeon to see the place where I was kept, and understand what usage I had. They found the place so bad, and the savour so ill, that they cried shame on the magistrates for suffering the jailer to do such things. They called for the jailers into the dungeon, and required them to find sureties for their good behaviour; and the under-jailer, who had been such a cruel fellow, they put into the dungeon with me, amongst the moss-troopers.

After I was set at liberty, I went to Thomas Bewley's, where came a Baptist teacher to oppose me; but he was convinced. Robert Widders being with me, was moved to go to Coldbeck steeple-house, and the Baptist teacher went along with him the same day. The people fell upon them, and almost killed Robert Widders; and took the Baptist's sword from him, and beat him sorely. This Baptist had the inheritance of an impropriation of tithes; and he went home, and gave it up freely. Robert Widders was sent to Carlisle jail, where having lain a while, he was set at liberty again.* William Dewsbury also went to another steeple-house hard by, and the people almost killed him, they beat him so; but the Lord's power was over all, and healed him again. In that day many Friends went to the steeple-houses, to declare the truth to the priests and people, and great sufferings they underwent; but the Lord's power sustained them.

Now I went into the country, and had mighty great meetings. The everlasting gospel and word of life flourished, and thousands were turned to the Lord Jesus Christ, and to his teaching. Several that had taken tithes, as impropriators, denied the receiving of them any longer, and delivered them up freely to the parishioners. Passing on into WESTMORLAND, I had many great meetings. At STRICKLAND-HEAD I had a large meeting, where a justice of peace out of Bishoprick, whose name was Henry Draper,

---

* Robert Widders is often mentioned in this Journal, having travelled with George Fox in Scotland, as also in many parts of America. They went through great perils by sea and land, in the wilderness and in woods, in danger of wild beasts; yet, through all the Lord supported him, and kept him faithful to the end. He was valiant for God's truth, establishing many in the faith. He was a great sufferer from persecutors; once, at Coldbeck, he was thrown down on the ground, and kicked and beaten so cruelly, that blood gushed out of his mouth, and he was supposed to be dead. At Lamplugh, his clothes were torn on his back, and the hair from off his head; and, at Bishop-Auckland, he was stoned and sorely bruised. His cattle, corn, and household goods were also swept away by wholesale, yet he was not at all dejected or concerned, knowing well for what he suffered. He was much resigned during his last sickness, often saying on his death-bed, "his heart was filled with the love of God;" and he departed this life in great peace in 1686, aged sixty-eight years.

came, and many contenders were there. The priests and magistrates were in a great rage against me in Westmorland, and had a warrant to apprehend me, which they renewed from time to time, for a long time; yet the Lord did not suffer them to serve it upon me. I travelled on amongst Friends, visiting the meetings till I came to SWARTHMORE, where I heard that the Baptists and professors in Scotland had sent to have a dispute with me. I sent them word, that I would meet them in Cumberland, at Thomas Dewley's house, whither accordingly I went, but none of them came. Some dangers at this time I underwent in my travels; for at one time, as we were passing from a meeting, and going through WIGTON on a market-day, the people of the town had set a guard with pitch-forks; and although some of their own neighbours were with us, they kept us out of the town, and would not let us pass through it, under the pretence of preventing the sickness; though there was no occasion for any such thing. However, they fell upon us, and had like to have spoiled us and our horses; but the Lord restrained them, that they did not much hurt; and we passed away. Another time, as I was passing between two Friends' houses, some rude fellows lay in wait in a lane, and exceedingly stoned and abused us; but at last, through the Lord's assistance, we got through them, and had not much hurt. But this showed the fruits of the priest's teaching, which shamed their profession of Christianity.

After I had visited Friends in that county, I went through the county into DURHAM, having large meetings by the way. A very large one I had at Anthony Pearson's, where many were convinced. From thence I passed through Northumberland to DERWENT-WATER, where there were great meetings; and the priests threatened that they would come, but none came. The everlasting word of life was freely preached, and freely received; and many hundreds were turned to Christ, their teacher.

In Northumberland many came to dispute, of whom some pleaded against perfection; unto whom I declared, "that Adam and Eve were perfect before they fell; and all that God made was perfect; and that the imperfection came by the Devil, and the fall; but Christ, that came to destroy the Devil, said, 'Be ye perfect.'" One of the professors alleged that Job said, "Shall mortal man be more pure than his Maker? The heavens are not clean in his sight. God charged his angels with folly." But I showed him his mistake, and let him see, "that it was not Job that said so, but one of those that contended against Job; for Job stood for perfection, and held his integrity; and they were called miserable comforters." Then these professors said, the outward body was the body of death and sin. I showed them their mistake in that also; for "Adam and Eve had each of them an outward body, before the body of death and sin got into them; and that man and woman will have bodies, when the body of sin and death is put off again; when they are renewed up into the image of God again by Christ Jesus, which they were in before they fell." So they ceased at that time from opposing further; and glorious meetings we had in the Lord's power.

Then we passed on to HEXHAM, where we had a great meeting at the top of a hill. The priest threatened he would come, and oppose us, but he came not; so that all was quiet; and the everlasting day, and renowned truth of the everliving God was sounded over those dark countries, and his Son exalted over all. It was proclaimed amongst the people that "the day was now come, wherein all that made a profession of the Son of God, might receive him; and that to as many as would receive him, he would give power to become the sons of God, as he had done to me." And it was further declared, that "he that had the Son of God, had life eternal; but that he that had not the Son of God (though he professed all the Scriptures, from the first of Genesis to the last of the Revelations), had not life." After all were directed to the light of Christ, by which they might see him and receive him, and know where their true teacher was; and the everlasting truth had been largely declared amongst them, we passed away through Hexham peaceably, and came to GILSLAND, a country noted for thieving.

Here a Friend seeing the priest, went to speak to him; whereupon the latter came down to our inn, and the town's-people gathered about us. The priest said, he would prove us deceivers out of the Bible, but could find no Scripture for his purpose. Then he went into the inn; and after a while came out again, and brought some broken sentences of Scripture, that mention "the doctrines and commandments of men, &c., and, touch not, taste not, &c., for they perish with the using." All which, poor man! was his own condition; whereas we were persecuted, because we would not taste, nor touch, nor handle their doctrines and traditions, which we knew perished with the using. I asked him what he called the steeple-house? "O," said he, "the dreadful house of God, the temple of God." Then I showed him, and the poor dark people, that their bodies should be the temples of God; and that Christ never commanded these temples, but ended that temple at Jerusalem, which God had commanded. While I was speaking, the priest got away; and afterwards the people appeared as if they feared we would take their purses, or steal their horses; judging us like themselves, who are naturally given to thieving.

The next day we came through the country into CUMBERLAND again, where we had a general meeting of many thousands of people at the top of a hill near LANGLANDS. A glorious and heavenly meeting it was; for the glory of the Lord did shine over all; and there were as many as one could well speak over, the multitude was so great. Their eyes were fixed on Christ their teacher; and they came to sit under their own vine; insomuch that Francis Howgill, coming afterwards to visit them, found they had no need of words; for they were sitting under their teacher Christ Jesus; in the sense whereof, he sat down amongst them, without speaking anything. A great convincement there was in Cumberland, Durham, Northumberland, Westmorland, Lancashire, and Yorkshire; and the plants of God grew, and flourished, the heavenly rain descending, and God's glory shining upon them, so that many mouths were opened by the Lord to his praise; yea, to babes and sucklings he ordained strength.

CHAPTER VII.

1653-1654.—George Fox disputes most of the day with priest Wilkinson—many Friends lose their business for declining the world's salutations, but afterwards their tried faithfulness and integrity procure them more than their neighbours. —George Fox issues an address to Friends everywhere—two persecuting justices at Carlisle are cut off, and a third disgraced—George Fox passes through Halifax, a rude town of professors—at Synderhill-Green he has a mighty meeting of some thousands, and there was a general convincement—about sixty ministers are now raised up in the north, to travel towards the south, the east, and the west, in Truth's service—George Fox's address to Friends in the ministry—Rice Jones and many other false prophets rise up against Friends and are blasted—a wicked man binds himself with an oath to kill George Fox, but is prevented—great convincement in Lincolnshire—at Swannington George Fox has much controversy with professors—has a great dispute with priest Stevens, and seven other priests at Drayton—his father being present was convinced, and said, "Truly I see he that will but stand to the truth it will carry him out."—Priest Stevens propagates lies respecting George Fox, which the Lord swept away—is taken before Col. Hacker, who sends him to the Protector—speaks prophetically to the Colonel— has a friendly conference with the Protector—is dismissed by him very friendly— refuses his entertainment—Captain Drury scoffs at trembling, but is made to tremble in a remarkable manner—George Fox prays with some officers, who are greatly shaken by the Lord's power—priests and professors greatly disturbed because many of their people are convinced, and moved to declare against the rest.

AFTER my release from Carlisle prison, I was moved to go to priest Wilkinson's steeple-house again at BRIGHAM; and being got in before him, when he came in, I was declaring the truth to the people, though they were but few; for the most and the best of his hearers were turned to Christ's free teaching; and we had a meeting of Friends hard by, where Thomas Stubbs was declaring the word of life amongst them. As soon as the priest came in, he opposed me; and there we stayed most part of the day; for when I began, he opposed me; so if any law was broken, he broke it. When his people would be haling me out, I manifested his fruits to be such, as Christ spoke of, when he said, "they shall hale you out of their synagogues;" and then he would be ashamed, and they would let me alone. There he stood till it was almost night, jangling and opposing me, and would not go to his dinner; for he thought to weary me out. But at last, the Lord's power and truth came so over him, that he packed away with his people. When he was gone, I went to the meeting of Friends, who were turned to the Lord, and by his power established on Christ, the rock and foundation of the true prophets and apostles, but not of the false.

About this time the priests and professors fell to prophesying against us afresh. They had said long before, that we should be destroyed within a month; and after that, they prolonged the time to half a-year; but that time being long expired, and we mightily increased in number, they now gave forth, that we would eat out one another. For often after meetings, many tender people having a great way to go, tarried at Friends' houses by the way, and sometimes more than there were beds to lodge in; so that some have lain on the hay-mows; hereupon Cain's fear possessed the professors and world's people. For they were afraid, that when we had eaten one another out, we would all come to be maintained by the parishes, and be chargeable to them. But after a while, when they saw that the Lord blessed and increased Friends, as he did Abraham, both in the field and in the basket, at their goings forth, and comings in, at their risings up and lyings down, and that all things prospered with them; then they saw the falseness of all their prophecies against us; and that it was in vain to curse, where God had blessed. At the first convincement, when Friends could not put off their hats to people, or say You to a single person, but Thou and Thee;—when they could not bow, or use flattering words in salutations, or adopt the fashions and customs of the world, many Friends, that were tradesmen of several sorts, lost their customers at first; for the people were shy of them, and would not trade with them; so that for a time some Friends could hardly get money enough to buy bread. But afterwards, when people came to have experience of Friends' honesty and faithfulness, and found that their yea was yea, and their nay was nay; that they kept to a word in their dealings, and that they would not cozen and cheat them; but that if they sent a child to their shops for anything, they were as well used as if they had come themselves; the lives and conversation of Friends did preach, and reached to the witness of God in the people. Then things altered so, that all the inquiry was, "where is there a draper, or shopkeeper, or tailor, or shoemaker, or any other tradesman, that is a Quaker?" Insomuch that Friends had more trade than many of their neighbours, and if there was any trading, they had a great part of it. Then the envious professors altered their note, and began to cry out, "if we let these Quakers alone, they will take the trade of the nation out of our hands." This has been the Lord's doing to and for his people! which my desire is, that all, who profess his holy truth, may be kept truly sensible of, and that all may be preserved, in and by his power and Spirit, faithful to God and man; first to God, in obeying him in all things; and then in doing unto all men, that which is just and righteous, to all men and women, in all things, that they have to do or deal with them in; that the Lord God may be glorified in their practising truth, holiness, godliness, and righteousness, amongst people in all their lives and conversation.

Friends being now grown very numerous in the northern parts of the nation, and many young-convinced ones coming daily in among us, I was moved of the Lord to write the following epistle, and send it forth amongst them, in order to stir up the pure mind, and raise a holy care and watchfulness in them over themselves, and one another, for the honour of truth:—

"*To you all, Friends everywhere, scattered abroad.*

"In the measure of the life of God, wait for wisdom from God, even from Him, from whom it comes. And all ye, who are children of God, wait for living food from the living God, to be nourished up to eternal life, from the one fountain, from whence life comes; that ye may all be guided and walk in order; servants in your places, young men and women in your places, and rulers of families; that every one, in your respective places, may adorn the truth, in the measure of it. With it let your minds be kept up to the Lord Jesus, from whom it comes, that ye may be a sweet savour to God, and in wisdom ye may all be ordered and ruled;—that a crown and a glory ye may be one to another in the Lord. And that no strife, bitterness, or self-will, may appear amongst you; but with the Light, in which is unity, all these may be condemned. And that every one in particular, may see to, and take care of, the ordering and ruling of his own family; that in righteousness and wisdom it may be governed, the fear and dread of the Lord being set in every one's heart; that the secrets of the Lord every one may come to receive; that stewards of his grace you may come to be, to dispense it to every one as they have need; and so in savouring and right-discerning you may all be kept; that nothing, that is contrary to the pure life of God, may be brought forth in you, or among you; but all that is contrary to it, may be judged by it; so that in light, in life, and love, ye may all live, and all that is contrary to the light, and life, and love, may be brought to judgment, and by that light condemned. And that no fruitless trees be among you; but all cut down and condemned by the light, and cast into the fire; so that every one may bear and bring forth fruit unto God, and grow fruitful in his knowledge, and in his wisdom; and that none may appear in words beyond what they are in the life, that gave forth the words. Here none shall be as the untimely figs; none shall be of those trees whose fruit withers; such go in Cain's way, from the light, and by it are condemned. Let none amongst you boast yourselves above your measure; for if you do, out of God's kingdom you are excluded; for in that boasting part gets up the pride, and the strife, which is contrary to the light, that leads to the kingdom of God, and gives an entrance thereinto, and an understanding to know the things that belong to the kingdom of God. There the light and life of man every one receives, even Him who was, before the world was, by whom it was made, who is the righteousness of God, and his wisdom; to whom all glory, honour, thanks, and praise belong, who is God blessed for ever. Let no image or likeness be made; but wait in the light, which will bring condemnation on that part that would make the images; for that prisons the just. So to the lust yield not the eye, nor the flesh; for the pride of life stands in that which keeps out the love of the Father; and upon which his judgments and wrath remain, where the love of the world is sought after, and a crown that is mortal. In this ground the evil enters, which is cursed; which brings forth briars and thorns, where death reigns, and tribulation and anguish are upon every soul, and the Egyptian tongue is heard; all which is by the light condemned. There the earth is, which must be removed; by the light it is seen, and by the power it is removed, and out of its place it is shaken; to which the thunders utter their voices, before the mysteries of God be opened, and Jesus revealed. Therefore all ye, whose minds are turned to this light, wait upon the Lord Jesus for the crown that is immortal, and that fadeth not away."   G. F.

"This is to be sent amongst all Friends in the truth, the flock of God, to be read at their meetings."

While Friends abode in the northern parts, a priest of Wrexham, in Wales, whose name was Morgan Floyd, having heard reports concerning us, sent two of his congregation into the North to inquire concerning us, to try us, and bring him an account of us. But when these triers came down amongst us, the power of the Lord overcame them, and they were both convinced of the truth. So they stayed some time with us, and then returned into Wales; where afterwards one of them departed from his convincement; but the other, whose name was John-ap-John, abode in the truth, and received a part in the ministry, in which he continued faithful.

Now were the priests greatly disturbed at Newcastle, at Kendal, and in most of the northern counties. There being one Gilpin, that had sometimes come amongst us at Kendal, and soon run out from the truth into vain imaginations, the priests made what evil use they could of him against us; but the Lord's power confounded them all. And the Lord God cut off two of the persecuting justices at Carlisle; and the other, after a time, was turned out of his place, and left the town.

About this time the oath or engagement to OLIVER CROMWELL was tendered to the soldiers; many of whom were disbanded, because, in obedience to Christ, they could not swear. John Stubbs was one, who was convinced when I was in Carlisle prison, and became a good soldier in the Lamb's war, and a faithful minister of Christ Jesus, travelling much in the service of the Lord in Holland, Ireland, Scotland, Italy, Egypt, and America. And the Lord's power preserved him out of the hands of the Papists, though many times he was in great danger of the Inquisition. But some of the soldiers who had been convinced in their judgments, but had not come into obedience to the truth, took Cromwell's oath; and going afterwards into Scotland, and coming before a garrison there, the garrison thinking they had been enemies, fired at them, and killed many of them; which was a sad event.

When the churches were settled in the North, and Friends were sat down under Christ's teaching, and the glory of the Lord shone over them, I passed from Swarthmore to LANCASTER (about the beginning of the year 1654) and so through the counties, visiting Friends till I came to SYNDER-HILL-GREEN, where a meeting was appointed three weeks before; leaving the North fresh and green, under Christ their teacher. But before I came to Synderhill-Green, we passed through HALIFAX, a rude town of professors, and came to one Thomas Taylor's, who had been a captain, where we met with some janglers; but the Lord's power was over all; for I travelled in the motion of God's power. When I came to Synderhill-Green, there was a mighty meeting, some thousands of people (as it was supposed). Many persons of note were there, as captains and other officers; and there was a general convincement; for the Lord's power and truth was over all, and there was no opposition.

About this time did the Lord move upon the spirits of many, whom he had raised up, and sent forth to labour in his vineyard, to travel southwards, and spread themselves, in the service of the gospel, to the eastern, southern, and western parts of the nation; as Francis Howgill and Edward Burrough to London; John Camm and John Audland to Bristol; Richard Hubberthorn and George Whitehead* towards Norwich; Thomas Holmes† into Wales, and others different ways; for above sixty ministers had the Lord raised up, and now sent abroad out of the North country. The sense of their service being very weighty upon me, I was moved to give forth the following paper:—

"To Friends in the Ministry.

"ALL Friends everywhere, Know the Seed of God, which bruiseth the seed of the serpent, and is above the seed of the serpent; which Seed sins not, but bruiseth the serpent's head, that doth sin, and tempts to sin; which Seed God's promise and God's blessing is to; and which is one in the male and in the female. Where it is head, and hath bruised the head of the other, to the beginning you are come; and the younger is known, and he that is servant to the younger. And the promise of God, which is to the Seed, is fulfilled and fulfilling; the Scriptures come to be opened and owned; the flesh of Christ known, who took upon him the seed of Abraham according to the flesh; and the everlasting priesthood known, the everlasting covenant. Christ takes upon him the seed of Abraham, and is a priest after the order of Melchizedek; without father, without mother, without beginning of days (mark) or end of life; this is the priest that ever lives; the covenant of life, of light, and peace. And the everlasting offering here is known once for all, which offering overthrows that nature which offered; out of which the priesthood arose, that could not continue by reason of death. And here is the other offering known, the everlasting offering which perfects for ever them that are sanctified; which offering blotted out the hand-writing of ordinances, triumphs over them, and ascends above all principalities and powers. Now he that hath the Spirit of Jesus, sees this; and here is the love of God received, that doth not rejoice in iniquity, but leads to repent of it. This is the word of the

---

* George Whitehead, who was convinced when about seventeen years old, became a valiant minister for about sixty-eight years, till the time of his decease, which took place, in great peace, after an illness of some weeks. He waited, patiently resigned to the will of God, desiring to be dissolved and be with Christ; saying, "he felt the sting of death to be taken away." He was a preacher of the gospel in life and power, and turned many from darkness to light, being a chief instrument in gathering a people to the Lord in and about Norwich. At one meeting he had in those parts, it is recorded that "nearly the whole congregation was convinced by the mighty power of God, through his lively and piercing testimony and prayer." He suffered great hardships, long and sore imprisonments, and severe whipping for his testimony to the truth, much of which is recorded in his published Journal, with his travels and other services, to which the reader is referred.

† Thomas Holmes was serviceable in his day and generation, suffering imprisonment on Truth's account. In 1656, he was in jail, at Chester, with seven or eight other Friends. Some of his services in Wales are related, in a letter from him (probably to George Fox), in Barclay's *Letters of Early Friends*, p. 222.

Lord God to you all, Friends everywhere scattered abroad, Know the power of God in one another, and in that rejoice; for then you rejoice in the cross of Christ, who is not of the world; which cross is the power of God to all them that are saved. You, that know the power, and feel the power, you feel the cross of Christ, you feel the gospel, which is the power of God unto salvation to every one that believeth. Now, he that believes in the light, believes in the everlasting covenant, in the one offering; comes to the life of the prophets and Moses; comes to see Christ the hope, the mystery, which hope perisheth not, but lets you see the hope that perisheth, which is not that mystery; and the expectation in that perishing hope fades. Where this never-failing hope is witnessed, the Lord comes to be sanctified in the heart, and you come to the beginning, to Christ the hope, which perisheth not; but the other hope, and the other expectation perisheth. So all of you, know the perishing of the other, and the failing of the expectation therein; and know that which perisheth not; that you may be ready to give a reason of this hope with meekness and fear, to every man that asketh you. Christ the hope, the mystery, that perisheth not; the end of all perishing things, the end of all changeable things, the end of the decaying covenant, the end of that which waxeth old and doth decay; the end of the first covenant, of Moses, and of the prophets; the righteousness of God, Christ Jesus the Son; his throne ye will know, heirs with him ye will be; who makes his children kings and priests to him, and brings them to know his throne and his power. There is no justification out of the light, out of Christ; justification is in the light in Christ; here is the doer of the will of God, here is the entering into the kingdom. He that believes in the light, becomes a child of light; and here the wisdom is received that is justified of her children. Here believing in the light, you shall not abide in darkness, but shall have the light of life; and come every one to witness the light that shines in your hearts, which light will give you the light of the knowledge of the glory of God, in the face of Jesus Christ. With which light you will see him reign, who is the prince of life and of peace; which light turns from him, that is out of the truth, and abode not in it; where the true peace is not.

"Friends, be not hasty; for he that believes in the light, makes not haste. Here the grace is received, by which you come to be saved; the election is known, which obtains the promise; the will is seen that wills; the mind is known that runs and obtains not, but stops and becomes dull. Now, that with the light being seen, and judged, and stopped, the patience is here known which obtains the crown, and the immortality is come to light. So all they now that act contrary to the light, and do not believe in it, do not come to justification. And, all Friends, if you go from the light, from wanting to have the promise of God fulfilled to the Seed, whereby you may know Christ to reign, you thereby bring on yourselves changeable garments, and come to wear the changeable garments, and the strange flesh, which leads to adultery, which the law goes upon, which shuts out of the kingdom: and out of this will doth proceed the work or building, that is for the fire; whereby you may come to suffer loss. Therefore love the light, which doth condemn that, and receive the power from the Lord, with which you stand over that, and condemn it; feeling and seeing that which gives you the victory over the world, and to see out of time, to before time. Again, Friends, know Abraham, that must obey the voice of Sarah, that bears seed; which casts forth the bond-woman and her son: do not go forth, there will the wildness lodge. Know that which bears the wild son, and its mother, who is not Sarah; for the promise is to the Seed, not of many, but one, which seed is Christ: and this Seed now you come to witness stand above all, yea, on the head of the serpent. And so all, as I said before, who come to feel and witness this, come to the beginning; and this to all the seed of God, the church, that it you all may come to know, where there is no blemish, nor spot, nor wrinkle, nor any such thing. This is that which is purchased by the blood of Jesus, and to the Father presented out of all that defiles; which is the pillar and ground of truth. None come to this, but such as come to the light of Christ, who purchased this church. They who go from the light are shut out and condemned, though they profess all the Scriptures declared from it. Therefore walk in the light, that you may have fellowship with the Son, and with the Father; and come all to witness his image, his power, and his law, which is his light, which hath converted your souls, and brought them to submit to the higher power, above that which is out of the truth: that you may know here the mercy and truth, and the faith that works by love, which Christ is the author of, who lighteth every one of you; which faith gives the victory. Now that which gives the victory is perfect; and that which the ministers of God received from God, is that which is perfect; and that which they are to minister is for the perfecting of the saints, till they all come in the unity of the faith unto a perfect man. This is the word of the Lord God to you all; every one in the measure of life wait, that with it all your minds may be guided up to the Father of life, the Father of Spirits; to receive power from him, and wisdom, that with it you may be ordered to his glory; to whom be all glory for ever! All keep in the light and life, that judgeth down that which is contrary to the light and life. So the Lord God Almighty be with you all. And keep your meetings everywhere, being guided by that of God; by that you may see the Lord God among you, even him who lighteth every man that cometh into the world: by whom the world was made; that men, who are come into the world, might believe. He that believeth not, the light condemns him: he that believeth, cometh out of condemnation. So this light, which lighteth every man that cometh into the world, and which they that hate it stumble at, is the light of men.

"All Friends, that speak in public, see that it be in the life of God; for that begets to God: the fruits of that shall never wither. This sows to the Spirit, which is in prison, and of the Spirit reaps life; and the other sows to the flesh, and of the flesh reaps corruption. And this you may see all the world over, amongst these seeds-men, what may be reaped in the field, that is, the world. Therefore in the Spirit of the Lord God wait, which cuts down and casts out all this, the root and branches of it. In that wait to receive power, and the Lord God Almighty preserve you in it; whereby you may come to feel the light, that comprehends time and the world, and fathoms it; which, believed in, gives you victory over the world. And here the power of the Lord is received, which subdues all the contrary, and puts off the garments that will stain and pollute. With this light you come to reach the light in every man, which Christ enlightens every man that cometh into the world withal: and here the things of Christ come to be known, and the voice of Christ heard. Therefore keep in the light, the covenant of peace, and walk in the covenant of life. There is that which maketh merry over the witness of God; and there is that which maketh merry in the Lord; which rejoiceth over that which hath made merry over it: of that take notice, you who are in the light. Such the Lord doth beautify, whose trust is in his strength: and the Lord doth see such, and them that are in his light. But such as are from the light, whose eyes are after their abominations and idols, their eyes are to be blinded; and their beautiful idols, and their abominations to be destroyed, and by the light condemned, which they have made from the life, in their own strength; which with the light is seen, and overthrown by the power of God. 'If you can change my covenant,' saith the Lord, 'which keeps the day in its season, and the night in its season (mark, my covenant, the light); if you can change this, then may you change the covenant of God with his seed.' So all Friends, that are turned to the light, which cometh from him, by whom the world was made, who was, before it was made, Christ Jesus, the Saviour of your souls; abide in the light, and you will see your salvation to be walls and bulwarks against that, which the light discovers to be contrary to it. Waiting in the light, you will receive the power of God, which is the gospel of peace; that you may be shod with it, and know that in one another, which raiseth up the seed of God, sets it over the world and the earth, and crucifies the affections and lusts: then the truth comes to reign, which is the girdle."   G. F.

About this time Rice Jones of Nottingham (who had been a Baptist, and was turned Ranter), and his company, began to prophesy against me, giving out, that I was then at the highest, and that after that time I should fall down as fast. He sent a bundle of railing papers from Nottingham to Mansfield, Clawson, and the towns thereabouts, judging Friends for declaring the truth in the markets and in steeple-houses; which papers I answered. But his and his company's prophecies came upon themselves; for soon after they fell to pieces, and many of his followers became Friends, and continued so. And through the Lord's blessed power, truth and Friends have increased, and do increase in the increase of God: and I, by the same power, have been and am preserved, and kept in the everlasting Seed, that never fell, nor changes. But Rice Jones took the oaths that were put to him, and so disobeyed the command of Christ. Many such false prophets have risen up against me, but the Lord hath blasted them, and will blast all who rise against the blessed Seed, and me in that. My confidence is in the Lord; for I saw their end, and how the Lord would confound them, before he sent me forth.

I was now at SYNDERHILL-GREEN, where I had had a large meeting in the daytime; and at night we had a great meeting again in Thomas

Stacey's house; for people came from far, and could not soon depart. The high sheriff of the county told Captain Bradford, that he intended to come up with half a dozen of his troopers to the meeting; but the Lord prevented him. When I had attended some meetings thereabouts, I travelled up and down in Yorkshire, as far as HOLDERNESS, and to the land's end that way, visiting Friends and the churches of Christ; which were finely settled under Christ's teaching. At length I came to Captain Bradford's house, whither many Ranters came from York to wrangle; but they were confounded and stopped. Thither came also she who was called the Lady Montague, who was then convinced, and lived and died in the truth.

Then I came again to Thomas Taylor's, within three miles of HALIFAX, where was a meeting of about two hundred people; amongst which were many rude people, and divers butchers, several of whom had bound themselves with an oath before they came out, that they would kill me (as I was told); one of those butchers had been accused of killing a man and a woman. They came in a very rude manner, and made a great disturbance in the meeting. The meeting being in a field, Thomas Taylor stood up, and said unto them, "If you will be civil, you may stay, but if not, I charge you to be gone from off my ground." But they were the worse, and said they would make it like a common; and they yelled, and made a noise, as if they had been at a bear-baiting. They thrust Friends up and down; and Friends being peaceable, the Lord's power came over them. Several times they thrust me off from the place I stood on, by the crowding of the people together against me; but still I was moved of the Lord to stand up again, as I was thrust down. At last I was moved of the Lord to say unto them, "if they would discourse of the things of God, let them come up to me one by one; and if they had anything to say or to object, I would answer them all, one after another;" but they were all silent, and had nothing to say. And then the Lord's power came so over them all, and answered the witness of God in them, that they were bound by the power of God; and a glorious, powerful meeting we had, and his power went over all, and the minds of the people were turned by the Spirit of God in them to God, and to Christ their teacher. The powerful word of life was largely declared that day; and in the life and power of God we broke up our meeting; and that rude company went their way to Halifax. The people asked them, why they did not kill me, according to the oath they had sworn; and they maliciously answered, that I had so bewitched them, that they could not do it. Thus was the devil chained at that time. Friends told me, that they used to come at other times, and be very rude; and sometimes break their stools and seats, and make frightful work amongst them; but the Lord's power had now bound them. Shortly after this, the butcher, that had been accused of killing a man and a woman before, and who was one of them that had then bound himself by an oath to kill me, killed another man, and was sent to York jail. Another of those rude butchers, who had also sworn to kill me, having accustomed himself to thrust his tongue out of his mouth, in derision of Friends, when they passed by him, had it so swollen out of his mouth, that he could never draw it in again, but died so. Several strange and sudden judgments came upon many of these conspirators against me, which would be too large here to declare.   God's vengeance from heaven came upon the blood-thirsty, who sought after blood; for all such spirits I laid before the Lord, and left them to him to deal with them, who is stronger than all; in whose power I was preserved, and carried on to do his work.   The Lord hath raised a fine people in these parts, whom he hath drawn to Christ, and gathered in his name; who feel Christ amongst them, and sit under his teaching.

After this I came to BALBY; from whence several Friends went with me into LINCOLNSHIRE; of whom some went to the steeple-houses, and some to private meetings.   There came to the meeting where I was, the sheriff of Lincoln,* and several with him, who made great contention and jangling for a time.   But at length the Lord's power struck him, that he was convinced of the truth, and received the word of life, as did several others also that had opposed, and continued among Friends till they died. Great meetings there were, and a large convincement in those parts. Many were turned to the Lord Jesus, and came to sit under his teaching; leaving their priests, and their superstitious ways; and the day of the Lord flourished over all.   Amongst them that came to our meetings in that country, was one called Sir Richard Wrey, who was convinced; as was also his brother, and his brother's wife, who abode in the truth, and died therein, though he afterwards ran out.

Having visited these countries, I came into DERBYSHIRE; the sheriff of Lincoln, who was lately convinced, being with me.   In one meeting we had some opposition, but the Lord's glorious power gave dominion over all.   At night there came a company of bailiffs and serving-men, and called me out.   I went out to them, having some Friends with me.   They were exceedingly rude and violent; for they had plotted together, and intended to carry me away with them in the dark of the evening by force: and then to do me a mischief: but the Lord's power went over them, and chained them, so that they could not effect their design; and at last they went away.   The next day, Thomas Aldam understanding that the serving-men belonged to one called a knight, who lived not far off, went to his house, and laid before him the bad conduct of his servants.   The knight rebuked them, and did not allow of their evil carriage towards us.

After this we came into Nottinghamshire to SKEGBY, where we had a great meeting of divers sorts of people: and the Lord's power went over them, and all was quiet.   The people were turned to the Spirit of God, by which many came to receive his power, and to sit under the teaching of Christ, their Saviour.   A great people the Lord hath in those parts.

I passed towards KIDSLEY PARK, where came many Ranters; but the Lord's power checked them.   From thence I went into the PEAK COUNTRY towards Thomas Hammersley's, where came the Ranters of that country, and many high professors.   The Ranters opposed me, and began swearing.   When I reproved them for it, they would bring Scripture for it, and said, Abraham, and Jacob, and Joseph swore; and the priests,

* The sheriff of Lincoln, Richard Craven, was afterwards convinced, and travelled with George Fox.

Moses, the prophets, and the angels swore. Then I told them, "I confessed all these did so, as the Scripture records; but, said I, Christ (who said, 'Before Abraham was, I am') saith, 'Swear not at all.' And Christ ends the prophets, and the old priesthood, and the dispensation of Moses, and reigns over the house of Jacob and of Joseph; and he says, 'Swear not at all.' And God, when he bringeth in the first-begotten into the world, saith, 'Let all the angels of God worship him,' to wit, Christ Jesus, who saith, 'Swear not at all.' And as for the plea that men make for swearing to end their strife, Christ, who says, 'Swear not at all,' destroys the Devil and his works, who is the author of strife, for that is one of his works. And God said, 'This is my beloved Son, in whom I am well pleased; hear ye him.' So the Son is to be heard, who forbids swearing. And the apostle James, who heard the Son of God, followed him, and preached him, forbids all oaths,* James v. 12." So the Lord's power went over them: and his Son and his doctrine was set over them. The word of life was fully and richly preached, and many were convinced that day. This Thomas Hammersley being summoned to serve upon a jury, was admitted to serve without an oath; and when he, as foreman of the jury, brought in the verdict, the judge declared, "that he had been a judge many years, but never heard a more upright verdict than that Quaker had then brought in." Much might be written of things of this nature, which time would fail to declare. But the Lord's blessed power and truth was exalted over all, who is worthy of all praise and glory for ever!

Travelling through Derbyshire, I visited Friends till I came to SWAN-NINGTON in Leicestershire, where was a general meeting, to which many Ranters, Baptists, and other professors came; for great contests there had been with them, and with the priests in that town. To this meeting several Friends came from various parts, as John Audland, Francis Howgill, and Edward Pyot from Bristol, and Edward Burrough from London: and several were convinced in those parts. The Ranters made a disturbance, and were very rude, but at last the Lord's power came over them, and they were confounded. The next day Jacob Bottomley, a great Ranter, came from Leicester; but the Lord's power stopped him, and came over them all. There came a priest too, but he also was confounded by the mighty power of the Lord. About this time the priests, Baptists, Ranters, and other professors, were very rude, and stirred up the rude people against us. We sent to the Ranters to come forth, and try their God. Abundance of them came, who were very rude, and sung, and whistled, and danced; but the Lord's power so confounded them, that many of them came to be convinced.

After this I went to TWYCROSS, whither came some Ranters, who sung and danced before me. But I was moved in the dread of the Lord to reprove them; and the Lord's power came over them, so that some of them were convinced, and received the Spirit of God; and are become a fine people, living and walking soberly in the truth of Christ. I went to Anthony Brickley's in WARWICKSHIRE, where there was a great meeting;

* See Gurney on Oaths, p. 334.

several Baptists and other people came and jangled; but the Lord's power came over them.

Then I went to DRAYTON in Leicestershire to visit my relations. As soon as I was come in, Nathaniel Stephens the priest, having got another priest, and given notice to the country, sent to me to come to them, for they could not do anything till I came. Having been three years away from my relations, I knew nothing of their design. But at last I went into the steeple-house yard, where the two priests were; and they had gathered abundance of people. When I came there, they would have me go into the steeple-house. I asked them what I should do there; and they said, Mr. Stephens could not bear the cold. I told them, he might bear it as well as I. At last we went into a great hall, Richard Farnsworth being with me; and a great dispute we had with these priests, concerning their practices, how contrary they were to Christ and his apostles. The priests would know, where tithes were forbidden or ended. I showed them out of the seventh chapter to the Hebrews, "that not only tithes, but the priesthood that took tithes, was ended; and the law was ended and disannulled, by which the priesthood was made, and tithes were commanded to be paid." Then the priests stirred up the people to some lightness and rudeness. I had known Stephens from a child, therefore I laid open his condition, and the manner of his preaching; and "how that he, like the rest of the priests, did apply the promises to the first birth, which must die. But I showed that the promises were to the Seed, not to many seeds, but to one Seed, Christ; who was one in male and female; for all were to be born again before they could enter into the kingdom of God." Then he said, I must not judge so: but I told him, "he that was spiritual judged all things." Then he confessed, that that was a full Scripture; "but, neighbours," said he, "this is the business; George Fox is come to the light of the sun, and now he thinks to put out my star-light." I told him, "I would not quench the least measure of God in any, much less put out his star-light, if it were true star-light—light from the morning star." But I told him, "if he had anything from Christ or God, he ought to speak it freely, and not take tithes from the people for preaching, seeing Christ commanded his ministers to give freely, as they had received freely." So I charged him to preach no more for tithes, or any hire. But he said, he would not yield to that. After a while the people began to be vain and rude; so we broke up; yet some were made loving to the truth that day. Before we parted, I told them that, if the Lord would, I intended to be at the town again that day week. In the interim I went into the country, and had meetings, and came thither again that day week. Against that time this priest had got seven priests to help him: for priest Stephens had given notice at a lecture on a market-day at Adderston, that such a day there would be a meeting and a dispute with me. I knew nothing of it; but had only said, I should be in town that day week again. These eight priests had gathered several hundreds of people, even most of the country thereabouts, and they would have had me into the steeple-house; but I would not go in, but got on a hill, and there spoke to them and the people. There were with me Thomas Taylor, who had been a priest, James Parnell, and several other Friends. The priests thought that day to trample down truth; but the truth came over them. Then they grew light, and the people rude; and the priests would not stand trial with me; but would be contending here and there a little, with one Friend or other. At last one of the priests brought his son to dispute with me; but his mouth was soon stopped. When he could not tell how to answer, he would ask his father: and his father was confounded also, when he came to answer for his son. So, after they had toiled themselves, they went away in a rage to priest Stephen's house to drink. As they went away, I said, "I never came to a place where so many priests together would not stand the trial with me." Whereupon they and some of their wives came about me, laid hold of me, and fawningly said, "what might I have been, if it had not been for the Quakers!" Then they began to push Friends to and fro, to thrust them from me, and to pluck me to themselves. After a while several lusty fellows came, took me up in their arms, and carried me into the steeple-house porch, intending to carry me into the steeple-house by force; but the door being locked, they fell down on a heap, having me under them. As soon as I could, I got up from under them, and went to the hill again: then they took me from that place to the steeple-house wall, and set me on something like a stool; and all the priests being come back, stood under with the people. The priests cried, "Come, to argument, to argument:" I said, "I denied all their voices, for they were the voices of hirelings and strangers." And they cried, "Prove it, prove it." Then I directed them to the tenth of John, where they might see what Christ said of such; he declared, "he was the true shepherd that laid down his life for his sheep, and his sheep heard his voice, and followed him; but the hireling would fly, when the wolf came, because he was a hireling." I offered to prove that they were such hirelings. Then the priests plucked me off from the stool again; and they themselves got all upon stools under the steeple-house wall. Then I felt the mighty power of God arise over all, and told them, "if they would but give audience, and hear me quietly, I would show them by the Scriptures, why I denied those eight priests or teachers, that stood before me; and all the hireling teachers of the world whatsoever; and I would give them Scriptures for what I said." Whereupon both priests and people consented. Then I showed them out of the prophets Isaiah, Jeremiah, Ezekiel, Micah, Malachi, and others, that they were in the steps of such as God sent his true prophets to cry against; for, said I, "You are such as the prophet Jeremiah cried against, chap. v. when he said, 'The prophets prophesy falsely, and the priests bear rule by their means;' which he called a horrible filthy thing. You are such as they that used their tongues and said, Thus saith the Lord, when the Lord never spoke to them: and such as followed their own spirits, and saw nothing; but spoke forth a divination of their own brain; and by their lies and their lightness had caused the people to err, Jer. xiv. You are such as they were, that sought for their gain from their quarter; that were as greedy, dumb dogs, that could never have enough, whom the Lord sent his prophet Isaiah to cry against, Isaiah lvi. You are such, as they were, who taught for handfuls of barley, and pieces of bread; who sewed pillows under people's arm-holes, that they might lie soft in their sins, Ezek. xiii. You are such as they that taught for the fleece, and the wool, and made a prey of the people, Ezek. xxxiv. But the Lord is gathering his sheep from your mouths, and from off your barren mountains; and is bringing them to Christ, the one Shepherd, which he hath set over his flocks; as by his prophet Ezekiel he then declared he would do. You are such as they that divined for money, and preached for hire; and if a man did not put into their mouths, they prepared war against him, as the prophet Micah complained, chap. iii." Thus I went through the prophets, too largely to be here repeated. Then coming to the New Testament, I showed from thence, "that they were like the chief priests, and scribes, and Pharisees of old, such as Christ cried woe against, Matt. xxiii. And that they were such false apostles, as the true apostles cried against, such as taught for filthy lucre; such antichrists and deceivers, as they cried against, that minded earthly things, and served not the Lord Jesus Christ, but their own bellies: for they that served Christ gave freely, and preached freely, as he commanded them. But they that will not preach without hire, tithes, or outward means, serve their own bellies, and not Christ; and through the good words of the Scriptures, and feigned words of their own, they made merchandize of the people then, as (said I) ye do now." So when I had largely quoted the Scriptures, and showed them, wherein they were like the Pharisees, loving to be called of men masters, and to go in long robes, and to stand praying in the synagogues, and to have the uppermost rooms at feasts, and the like; and when I had thrown them out in the sight of the people amongst the false prophets, deceivers, scribes, and Pharisees, and showed at large, how such as they were judged and condemned by the true prophets, by Christ, and by the apostles, "I directed them to the light of Christ Jesus, who enlightens every man that cometh into the world; that by it they might see, whether these things were not true, as had been spoken." When I appealed to that of God in their consciences, the light of Christ Jesus in them, they could not bear to hear of it; they were all quiet till then; but then a professor said, "George, what! wilt thou never have done?" I told him, I should have done shortly. So I went on a little longer, and cleared myself of them in the Lord's power. When I had done, all the priests and people stood silent for a time: at last one of the priests said, they would read the Scriptures that I had quoted. I told them, with all my heart. They began to read the 23rd of Jeremiah, and there they saw the marks of the false prophets, that he cried against. When they had read a verse or two, I said, "Take notice, people:" but the priests said, "Hold thy tongue, George." I bid them read the whole chapter throughout; for it was all against them: then they stopped, and would read no further; but asked me a question. I told them, I would answer their question, the matter being first granted that I had charged them with, viz., that they were false prophets, false teachers, antichrists, and deceivers, such as the true prophets, Christ, and the apostles cried against. A professor said Nay to that; but I said, Yea; for you leaving the matter, and going to another thing, seem to consent to the proof of the former charge. Then I answered their question, which was this; Seeing those false prophets were adulterated, whether I did judge

Stephens to be an adulterer? To which I answered, he was adulterated from God in his practice, like those false prophets and the Jews. They would not stand to vindicate him, but broke up the meeting. Then the priests whispered together; and priest Stephens came to me, and desired that my father and brother and I might go aside with him, that he might speak to me in private; and the rest of the priests should keep the people from coming to us. I was very loath to go aside with him; but the people cried, "Go, George; do, George, go aside with him." I was afraid, if I did not go, they would say, I was disobedient to my parents; so I went, and the rest of the priests were to keep the people off; but they could not, for the people being willing to hear, drew close to us. I asked the priest what he had to say; and he said, "if he was out of the way, I should pray for him: and if I was out of the way, he would pray for me: and he would give me a form of words to pray for him by." I replied, "It seems thou dost not know whether thou art in the right way or not; neither dost thou know whether I am in the right way, or not: but I know that I am in the everlasting way, Christ Jesus, which thou art out of. And thou wouldest give me a form of words to pray by, and yet thou deniest the Common Prayer-Book to pray by, as well as I; and I deny thy form of words, as well as it. If thou wouldst have me pray for thee by a form of words, is not this to deny the apostle's doctrine and practice of praying by the Spirit, as it gave words and utterance?" Here the people fell a laughing: but I was moved to speak more to him. And when I had cleared myself to him and them, we parted, after I had told them, that I should (God willing) be in the town that day week again. So the priests packed away, and many people were convinced; for the Lord's power came over all. Though they thought to have confounded truth that day, many were convinced of it; and many that were convinced before, were by that day's work confirmed in the truth, and abode in it; and a great shake it gave to the priests. My father, though he was a hearer and follower of the priest, was so well satisfied, that he struck his cane upon the ground, and said, "Truly, I see, he that will but stand to the truth, it will carry him out." I passed about in the country till that day week, and then came again; for we had appointed a meeting at my relations' house. Now priest Stephens having had notice beforehand thereof, had got another priest to him; and they had a company of troopers with them, and sent for me to come to them. But I sent them word our meeting was appointed, and they might come to it, if they would. The priests came not; but the troopers came, and many rude people. They had laid their plot, that the troopers should take every one's name, and then command them to go home; and such as would not go, they should take, and carry them away with them. Accordingly they began, and took several names, charging them to go home; but when they came to take my name, my relations told them, I was at home already: so they could not take me away that time. Nevertheless they took my name: but the Lord's power was over them, and they went away, both professors and troopers, crossed and vexed, because they obtained not their end. But several were convinced that day, and admired the love and power of God. This was that priest Stephens, who once said of me, "never was such a plant bred in

England:" yet afterwards he reported, "that I was carried up into the clouds, and found again full of gold and silver;" and many lies, and false reports he raised respecting me: but the Lord swept them all away. The reason why I would not go into their steeple-house was, because I was to bear my testimony against it, and to bring all off from such places, to the Spirit of God; that they might know their bodies to be the temples of the Holy Ghost; and to bring them off from all the hireling teachers, to Christ their free teacher, who died for them, and purchased them with his blood.

After this I went into the country, and had several meetings, and came to SWANNINGTON, where the soldiers came again; but the meeting was quiet, the Lord's power was over all, and the soldiers did not interfere. Then I went to LEICESTER, and then to WHETSTONE. There came about seventeen troopers of Colonel Hacker's regiment, with his marshal, and took me up before the meeting, though Friends were beginning to gather together; for there were several Friends come from various parts. I told the marshal, "he might let all the Friends go, I would answer for them all;" so he took me, and let them go, except Alexander Parker, who went with me.* At night they had me before Colonel Hacker, his major, and captains, a great company of them; and much discourse we had about the priests, and meetings, for at this time there was a rumour of a plot against Oliver Cromwell. Much reasoning I had with them about the light of Christ, which enlighteneth every man that cometh into the world. Colonel Hacker asked, whether it was not this light of Christ that made Judas betray his master, and afterwards led him to hang himself? I told him, "No; that was the spirit of darkness, which hated Christ and his light." Then Colonel Hacker said, I might go home, and keep there, and not go abroad to meetings. I told him, "I was an innocent man, free from plots, and denied all such work." His son Needham said, "Father, this man hath reigned too long, it is time to have him cut off." I asked him, "For what? what had I done? or whom had I wronged from a child? for I was bred and born in that country, and who could accuse me of any evil from a child?" Then Colonel Hacker asked me again, if I would go home, and stay there? I told him, "if I should promise him that, it would manifest that I was guilty of something, to go home, and make my home a prison; and if I went to meetings, they would say, I broke their order. I told them, "I should go to meetings, as the Lord should order me, and therefore could not submit to their requirings;" but I said, "we were a peaceable people." "Well then," said Colonel Hacker, "I will send you to my Lord Protector, by Captain Drury, one of his life-guards." That

* "Alexander Parker," says Whiting, " was an eminent servant of God, and minister of Jesus Christ; born near Bolton, in Lancashire, well-educated, and had a gentleman-like carriage and deportment, for I knew him well." He travelled extensively in the service of the gospel, often in company with George Fox, being frequently mentioned in this Journal. He suffered fines, imprisonments, and persecution, being once pulled down as he was preaching in London, and fined for it £20. He died in great peace in 1689, having written many books and epistles, in which, though being dead, he yet speaketh.

night I was kept a prisoner at the Marshalsea; and the next morning by six o'clock, I was delivered to Captain Drury. I desired he would let me speak with Colonel Hacker before I went, and he had me to his bed-side. Colonel Hacker set upon me presently again, to go home and keep no more meetings. I told him, "I could not submit to that, but must have my liberty to serve God, and to go to meetings." "Then," said he, "you must go before the Protector." "Whereupon I kneeled by his bed-side, and besought the Lord to forgive him, for he was as Pilate, though he would wash his hands; and when the day of his misery and trial should come upon him, I bid him then remember what I had said to him." But he was stirred up, and set on by priest Stephens, and the other priests and professors, wherein their envy and baseness was manifest; who, when they could not overcome me by disputes and arguments, nor resist the Spirit of the Lord that was in me, then they got soldiers to take me up.

Afterwards, when this Colonel Hacker was in prison in London, a day or two before he was executed, he was put in mind of what he had done against the innocent; and he remembered it, and confessed to it to Margaret Fell, saying he knew well whom she meant; and he had a trouble upon him for it. So his son, who told his father I had reigned too long, and that it was time to have me cut off, might observe how his father was cut off afterwards, he being hanged at Tyburn.

Now was I carried up a prisoner by Captain Drury from Leicester; and when we came to HARBOROUGH, he asked me, if I would go home and stay a fortnight? "I should have my liberty," he said, "if I would not go to, nor keep meetings." I told him, "I could not promise any such thing." Several times upon the road did he ask, and try me after the same manner, and still I gave him the same answers. So he brought me to LONDON, and lodged me at the Mermaid over-against the Mews at Charing-Cross. As we travelled, I was moved of the Lord to warn people at the inns and places, where I came, of the day of the Lord that was coming upon them. William Dewsbury and Marmaduke Storr being in prison at Northampton, he let me go and visit them.

After Captain Drury had lodged me at the Mermaid, he left me there, and went to give the Protector an account of me. When he came to me again, he told me, the Protector required that I should promise not to take up a carnal sword or weapon against him or the government, as it then was, and that I should write it in what words I saw good, and set my hand to it. I said little in reply to Captain Drury. But the next morning I was moved of the Lord to write a paper to the Protector, Oliver Cromwell; "wherein I did in the presence of the Lord God declare, that I denied the wearing or drawing of a carnal sword, or any other outward weapon, against him or any man; and that I was sent of God to stand a witness against all violence, and against the works of darkness; and to turn people from darkness to light; and to bring them from the causes of war and fighting, to the peaceable gospel, and from evil-doers, which the magistrates' swords should be a terror to." When I had written what the Lord had given me to write, I set my name to it, and gave it to Captain Drury to hand to Oliver Cromwell, which he did. After some

time Captain Drury brought me before the Protector himself at Whitehall.
It was in a morning, before he was dressed, and one Harvey, who had
come a little among Friends, but was disobedient, waited upon him.
When I came in, I was moved to say, "Peace be in this house; and I
exhorted him to keep in the fear of God, that he might receive wisdom
from him, that by it he might be directed, and order all things under his
hand to God's glory." I spoke much to him of truth, and much discourse
I had with him about religion; wherein he carried himself very moderately.
But he said, we quarrelled with priests, whom he called ministers. I told
him, "I did not quarrel with them, but they quarrelled with me and my
friends. But," said I, "if we own the prophets, Christ, and the apostles,
we cannot hold up such teachers, prophets, and shepherds, as the prophets,
Christ, and the apostles declared against; but we must declare against
them by the same power and Spirit." Then I showed him, "that the
prophets, Christ, and the apostles declared freely, and against them that
did not declare freely; such as preached for filthy lucre, and divined for
money, and preached for hire, and were covetous and greedy, that can
never have enough; and that they that have the same Spirit, that Christ,
and the prophets, and the apostles had, could not but declare against all
such now, as they did then." As I spoke, he several times said, it was
very good, and it was truth. I told him, "that all Christendom (so called)
possessed the Scriptures, but wanted the power and Spirit that they had,
who gave forth the Scriptures, and that was the reason they were not in
fellowship with the Son, nor with the Father, nor with the Scriptures, nor
one with another." Many more words I had with him, but people coming
in, I drew a little back; and as I was turning, he caught me by the hand,
and with tears in his eyes, said, "Come again to my house, for if thou and
I were but an hour a day together, we should be nearer one to the other;"
adding, that he wished me no more ill than he did to his own soul. I told
him, "if he did, he wronged his own soul;" and I bid him "hearken to
God's voice, that he might stand in his counsel and obey it; and if he did
so, that would keep him from hardness of heart; but if he did not hear
God's voice, his heart would be hardened." He said, it was true. Then
I went out; and when Captain Drury came out after me, he told me, "his
lord Protector said, I was at liberty, and might go whither I would."
Then I was brought into a great hall, where the Protector's gentlemen
were to dine; and I asked them, what they brought me thither for? they
said, it was by the Protector's order, that I might dine with them. I bid
them let the Protector know, I would not eat of his bread, nor drink of
his drink. When he heard this, he said, "Now I see there is a people
risen and come up, that I cannot win either with gifts, honours, offices,
or places; but all other sects and people I can." It was told him again,
"that we had forsaken our own, and were not likely to look for such
things from him."

Being set at liberty I went to the inn again, where Captain Drury
had at first lodged me. This Captain Drury, though he sometimes carried
fairly, was an enemy to me and to truth, and opposed it; and when professors came to me (while I was under his custody) and he was by, he

would scoff at trembling, and call us Quakers, as the Independents and Presbyterians had nick-named us before. But afterwards he once came to me, and told me, that, as he was lying on his bed to rest himself in the day-time, a sudden trembling seized on him, that his joints knocked together, and his body shook so that he could not rise from his bed; he was so shaken, that he had not strength enough left to rise. But he felt the power of the Lord was upon him, and he fell off his bed, and cried to the Lord, and said, he never would speak against the Quakers more, or such as trembled at the word of God.

During the time I was prisoner at Charing-Cross, there came abundance to see me, people of almost all sorts, priests, professors, officers of the army, &c. And one time a company of officers being with me, desired me to pray with them. I sat still, with my mind retired to the Lord. At last I felt the power and Spirit of God move in me, and the Lord's power did so shake and shatter them, that they wondered, though they did not live in it.

Among those that came to see me, was one Colonel Packer, with several of his officers; and while they were with me, came in one Cobb, and a great company of Ranters with him. The Ranters began to call for drink and tobacco; but I desired them to forbear it in my room, telling them, if they had such a desire for it, they might go into another room. One of them cried, "all is ours;" and another said, "all is well." I replied, "how is all well, while thou art so peevish, and envious, and crabbed?" for I saw he was of a peevish nature. I spoke to their conditions, and they were sensible of it, and looked upon one another, wondering.

Then Colonel Packer began to talk with a light, chaffy mind, concerning God, and Christ, and the Scriptures; it was a great grief to my soul and spirit, when I heard him talk so lightly; so that I told him, "he was too light to talk of the things of God, for he did not know the solidity of a man." Thereupon the officers raged, and said, would I say so of their colonel. This Packer was a Baptist, and he and the Ranters bowed and scraped to one another very much; for it was the manner of the Ranters to be exceedingly complimental (as they call it), so that Packer bid them give over their compliments; but I told them, "they were fit to go together, for they were both of one spirit."

This Colonel Packer lived at Theobald's near Waltham, and was made a justice of peace. He set up a great meeting of the Baptists at Theobald's Park; for he and some other officers had purchased it. They were exceedingly high, and railed against Friends and truth, and threatened to apprehend me with their warrants if ever I came there. Yet after I was set at liberty, I was moved of the Lord God to go down to THEOBALD's, and appoint a meeting hard by them; to which many of his people came, and divers of his hearers were convinced of the way of truth, and received Christ, the free teacher, and came off from the Baptist; and that made him rage the more. But the Lord's power came over him, so that he had not power to meddle with me. Then I went to WALTHAM close by him, and had a meeting there; but the people were very rude, and gathered about the house and broke the windows. Whereupon I went out to them, with the Bible in my hand, and desired them to come in; and told them, "I would show them Scripture both for our principles and practices." And when I had done so, I showed them also, "that their teachers were in the steps of such, as the prophets, and Christ, and the apostles testified against." Then I directed them to the Light of Christ, and Spirit of God in their own hearts, that by it they might come to know their free teacher, the Lord Jesus Christ. The meeting being ended, they went away quieted and satisfied, and a meeting hath since been settled in that town. But this was some time after I was set at liberty by Oliver Cromwell.

When I came from Whitehall to the Mermaid at Charing-Cross, I stayed not long there; but went into the city of LONDON, where we had great and powerful meetings; so great were the throngs of people, that I could hardly get to and from the meetings for the crowds; and the truth spread exceedingly. Thomas Aldam and Robert Craven, who had been sheriff of Lincoln, and many Friends, came up to London after me; but Alexander Parker abode with me.

After a while I went to WHITEHALL again, and was moved " to declare the day of the Lord amongst them, and that the Lord was come to teach his people himself;" so I preached truth both to the officers, and to them that were called Oliver's gentlemen, who were of his guard. But a priest opposed, while I was declaring the word of the Lord amongst them; for Oliver had several priests about him, of which this was his news-monger; an envious priest, and a light, scornful, chaffy man. I bid him repent; and he put it in his newspaper the next week, that I had been at Whitehall, and had bid a godly minister there repent. When I went thither again, I met with him; and abundance of people gathered about me. I manifested the priest to be a liar in several things that he had affirmed; and so he was silenced. He put in the news, that I wore silver buttons, which was false, for they were but alchymy. Afterwards he said in the news, that I hung ribands on people's arms, which made them follow me; this was another of his lies, for I never wore or used ribands in my life. Three Friends went to examine this priest, that gave forth this false intelligence, and to know of him where he had that information. He said, it was a woman that told him so; and if they would come again, he would tell them her name. When they returned, he said, it was a man, but would not mention his name then; but if they would come again, he would tell them his name, and where he lived. They went the third time, and then he would not say who told him; but offered, if I would give it under my hand, that there was no such thing, he would put that into the news. Thereupon the Friends carried it to him under my hand; but when they came, he broke his promise, and would not insert it; but was in a rage, and threatened them with the constable. This was the deceitful doing of this forger of lies; which he spread over all the nation in the news, to render truth odious, and to put evil into people's minds against Friends and truth; of which a more large account may be seen in a book printed soon after this time, for the clearing of Friends and truth from the slanders, lies, and false reports raised and cast upon them. These priests, the news-mongers, were of the Independent sect, like those in Leicester; but the Lord's power came over all their lies, and swept them away; and many came to see the wickedness of these priests. The God of heaven carried me over all in his power, and his blessed power went over the nation: insomuch, that many Friends about this time were moved to go up and down, to sound forth the everlasting gospel in most parts of it, and also in Scotland; and the glory of the Lord was felt over all to his everlasting praise. A great convincement there was in LONDON, and some in the Protector's house and family; I went to see him again, but could not get access to him, the officers were grown so rude.

The Presbyterians, Independents, and Baptists, were greatly disturbed; for many of their people turned to the Lord Jesus Christ, and sat down under his teachings: they received his power, and felt it in their hearts: and then they were moved of the Lord to declare against the rest of them.

I appointed a meeting in the fields near Acton, in which the word of life, the saving truth, was declared freely. The Lord's power was eminently manifested, and his blessed day exalted over all.

CHAPTER VIII.

1654–1655.—Address to professors of Christianity against persecution—to such as follow the world's fashions—to the Pope, and all kings, and rulers in Europe, against persecution—to the justices appointed for trying ministers of religion, being a testimony against hireling ministers—Samuel Fisher and others are convinced at a meeting at Romney, where the Lord's power is marvellously displayed—a large meeting at Coggeshall of about two thousand people, which lasted several hours—many reproaches are cast upon the truth, and lying slanderous books published, which are answered, and the truth set over the gainsayers—to those who scorn trembling and quaking—great rage is manifested against the truth and Friends, and their plainness is contemned—to the churches gathered into outward forms, opening their state and warning of the woes coming upon them—to the Protector, respecting the imprisonment of Friends for refusing to take oaths and pay tithes, &c.—to Friends, to offer themselves to lie in prison for a brother or sister—an encouragement to Friends in their several exercises.

About this time I was moved to write a paper, and send it among the professors; as follows :—

" *To all professors of Christianity.*

"All they that professed Jesus Christ in words, and yet heard him not when he was come, said, he was a deceiver and a devil. The chief priests called him so. The Jews said, 'He hath a devil, and is mad; why do ye hear him?' But others said, 'These are not the words of him that hath a devil: can a devil open the eyes of the blind?' The Jews then doubted, whether he was the Christ or not; and so all, like the Jews, in the knowledge, in the notion, that profess Christ without only, where Christ is risen within, do not own him, but doubt of him; though Christ is the same now and for ever. Jesus Christ said, 'I and my Father are one;' then the Jews took up stones to stone him. And where Jesus Christ is now spiritually come and made manifest, such as are Christians in outward profession only, have the same hard hearts inwardly now, as the Jews had then; and cast stones at him where he is risen. Jesus said, 'For which of these good works do ye stone me?' The Jews answered, 'For thy good works we stone thee not; but for blasphemy, in that thou being a man, makest thyself God.' Jesus answered them, 'Is it not written in your law, I said, Ye are gods? and the Scripture cannot be broken. Say ye of him, whom the Father hath sanctified, and sent into the world, Thou blasphemest, because I said, I am the Son of God?' The Jews said to him, 'Say we not well, that thou hast a devil?' Jesus answered, 'I honour my Father, and ye dishonour me. And they that were in the synagogue rose up, and thrust him out of the city; and took him up to the edge of the hill whereon their city was built, to cast him down headlong. The Pharisees said of him, 'He casteth out devils, by the prince of devils.' Jesus Christ was called a glutton and a wine-bibber, a friend of publicans and sinners; but wisdom is justified of her children. The officers, when the high-priests and Pharisees asked them, 'Why have ye not brought him?' said, 'Never man spake like this man.' The Pharisees said, 'Are ye also deceived? Do any of the rulers or of the Pharisees believe on him?' but this people, which know not the law, are accursed. Nicodemus (he that came unto Jesus by night), said unto them, 'Doth our law judge any man, before it hear him?' When Stephen confessed Jesus, the substance of all figures and types, and was brought before the chief priests to his trial, he told them, 'The Most High dwelleth not in temples made with hands:' and brought the prophets' words to witness, and told them they were stiff-necked, and uncircumcised in heart and ears, and always resisted the Holy Ghost, as their fathers had done. Stephen was full of the Holy Ghost, and said he saw Jesus, and they ran upon him and stoned him to death, as he was calling upon the Lord. When Paul confessed Jesus Christ and his resurrection, Festus said he was mad. When Paul preached the resurrection, some mocked; the Jews persuaded the people, and they stoned him, and drew him out of the city, thinking he had been dead. They stirred up the Gentiles to make their minds evil-affected towards the brethren. They stirred up the devout and honourable women, and the chief of the city, and raised persecution against Paul and Barnabas, and expelled them out of their coasts; and there was an assault made both of the Gentiles and of the Jews with their rulers, to use them despitefully and to stone them. In like manner all in the nature of those Jews now, whose religion stands in notions, stir up the rulers, and ignorant people, and incense them against Jesus Christ, to stone all with one consent, in whom he is risen. This is, that the Scriptures might be fulfilled, and the blindness of the people discovered. The same power now is made manifest, and doth overturn the world, as did then overturn the world, to the exalting of the Lord, and to the pulling down of the kingdom of Satan and of this world, and setting up his own kingdom, to his everlasting praise. The Lord is now exalting himself, and throwing down man's self. The proud one's head is aloft, fearing he should lose his pride and his crown. The priests incense the ignorant people, for fear their trade should go down; and the professors show forth what is in them, being full of rage; which proves that Jesus Christ, the substance, is not there; but a stony heart to stone the precious, where it is risen. The carnal mind feeds upon the outward letter; earth feeds upon earth; and that vineyard is not dressed, but is full of briars and nettles; and ravenous beasts, swine and dogs, wolves and lions, and all venomous creatures lodge in that habitation. That house is not swept. These are the persecutors of the just, enemies of the truth, and of Christ; blasphemers of God and his truth. These call upon God with their lips, but their hearts are far from him. These feed on lies, priests and people. These incense the people, and stir up envy; for it begets its own, one like itself. These are as the waves of the sea, foaming out their own shame. These have double eyes, whose bodies are full of darkness. These paint themselves with the prophets', with Christ's, and with the apostles' words most fair. Whited walls ye are; painted sepulchres; murderers of the just. Your eyes, your minds, your hearts are

double. Ye flatterers, repent and turn from your carnal ends, who are full
of mischief, pretending God and godliness, taking him for your cloak; but
he will uncover you, and he hath uncovered you to his children. He will
make you bare, discover your secrets, and take off your crown; he will take
away your mantle and your veil, and strip you of your clothing, that your
nakedness may appear, and how you sit deceiving the nations. Your
abomination and your falseness is now made manifest to them, who are of
God; who in his power triumph over you, rejoice over you, the beast, the
dragon, the false prophet, the seducer, the hypocrite, the mother of all
harlots. Now thou must have thy cup double, give it to her double. Sing
over her, ye righteous ones, sing over them all ye saints; triumph in glory,
triumph over deceit; sing the song of the Lamb, triumph over the world;
spread the truth abroad. Come ye captive ones out of prison, and rejoice
with one accord, for the joyful days are coming. Let us be glad and
rejoice for ever! singleness of heart is come, pureness of heart is come, joy
and gladness is come. The glorious God is exalting himself; truth hath
been talked of, but now it is possessed. Christ hath been talked of; but
now he is come and is possessed. The glory hath been talked of; but now
it is possessed, and the glory of man is defacing. The Son of God hath
been talked of; but now he is come, and hath given us understanding.
Unity hath been talked of; but now it is come. Virgins have been talked
of; but now they are come with oil in their lamps. He will be glorified
alone. Where pride is thrown down, earth and the fleshly will is thrown
down, and the pure is raised up; there alone is the Lord exalted. Let
the heavens bow down to him, and the earth reel to and fro, and stagger
up and down. The Lord is setting up his throne and his crown, and
throwing down the crown of man, and he alone will be glorified; to whom
be all honour and glory, all praises and all thanks! Who gives his children wisdom and strength, knowledge and virtue, power and riches, blessings
and durable substance; an eye to discern, and an ear to hear things singly;
and brings down the pride of man's heart, and turns the wicked out of the
kingdom. The righteous inherit righteousness; the pure, pureness; the
holy, holiness. Praises, praises be to the Lord, whose glory now shines,
whose day is broken forth; which is hid from the world, hid from all worldly-
wise ones, and from all the prudent of this world; hid from the fowls of
the air, hid from all vultures' eyes, all venomous beasts, all liars, all dogs,
and all swine. But to them that fear his name, the secrets of the Lord
are made manifest, the treasures of wisdom are opened, and the fulness of
knowledge: for thou, O Lord, dost make thyself manifest to thy children."   G. F.

My spirit was greatly burdened to see the pride, that existed in the
nation, even among professors, and in the sense thereof I was moved to
give forth the following paper,* directed—

---

* The address of George Fox, "to such as follow the world's fashions," a popular
writer observes, "draws a vivid picture of a fine lady and gentleman of the Commonwealth, in which their habiliments, vanities, and pastimes are minutely depicted."

"To such as follow the World's Fashions.

"WHAT a world is this! how doth the devil garnish himself! and how obedient are people to do his will and mind! They are altogether so carried away with fooleries and vanities, both men and women, that they have lost the hidden man of the heart, and the meek and quiet spirit; which with the Lord is of great price. They have lost the adorning of Sarah; they are putting on gold and gay apparel; women plaiting the hair, men and women powdering it; making their backs look like bags of meal. They look so strange, that they can scarce look at one another, they are so lifted up in pride. Pride is flown up into their head, and hath so lifted them up, that they snuff up, like wild asses; like Ephraim, they feed upon wind; and are like wild heifers, who feed upon the mountains. Pride hath puffed up every one of them: they are out of the fear of God, men and women, young and old: one puffs up another. They must be in the fashion of the world, else they are not in esteem; else they shall not be respected, if they have not gold or silver upon their backs, or if the hair be not powdered. But if he have store of ribands hanging about his waist, and at his knees, and in his hat, of divers colours, red, white, black, or yellow, and his hair be powdered, then he is a brave man; then he is accepted, he is no Quaker, because he has ribands on his back, and front, and knees, and his hair powdered. This is the array of the world. But is not this from the lust of the eye, the lust of the flesh, or the pride of life? Likewise the women having their gold, their patches on their faces, noses, cheeks, foreheads; having their rings on their fingers, wearing gold, having their cuffs double, under and above, like unto a butcher with his white sleeves; having their ribands tied about their hands, and three or four gold laces about their clothes; this is no Quaker, say they. This attire pleaseth the world: and if they cannot get these things, they are discontented. But this is not the attire of Sarah, whose adorning was the hidden man of the heart, the ornament of a quiet and meek spirit. This is the adorning of the heathen, not of the apostle, nor of the saints, whose adorning was, not wearing of gold, nor plaiting of hair, but a meek and quiet spirit; which was and is of great price with the Lord. Here was the sobriety and good ornament, which was accepted of the Lord. This was Paul's exhortation and preaching; but we see, the talkers of Paul's words live out of Paul's command, and out of the example of Sarah; and are found in the steps of the great heathen, who comes to examine the apostles in his gorgeous apparel. Now, are not these, that have got their ribands hanging about their arms, hands, back, waists, knees, hats, like unto fiddlers' boys? This shows that you are got into the basest and most contemptible life, who are in the fashion of the fiddlers' boys and stage-players, quite out of the paths and steps of solid men; and in the very steps and paths of the wild heads, who give themselves up to every invention and vanity of the world that appears, and are inventing how to get it upon their backs, heads, feet, and legs, and say, if it be out of the fashion it is nothing worth. Are not these the spoilers of the creation, who have the fat and the best of it, and waste and destroy it? Do not these cumber God's earth? Let that of God in all consciences

answer, and who are in the wisdom, judge. And further, if one get a pair
of trousers like a coat, and hang them about with points, and up almost to
the middle, a pair of double cuffs upon his hands, and a feather in his cap,
here is a gentleman; bow before him, put off your hats, get a company of
fiddlers, a set of music, and women to dance. This is a brave fellow. Up
in the chamber; up in the chamber without, and up in the chamber within.
Are these your fine Christians ? Yea, say they, they are Christians. Yea!
But, say the serious people, they are out of Christ's life, and out of the
apostles' command, and out of the saints' ornament. And to see such as
are before described, as are in the fashions of the world before-mentioned,
a company of them playing at bowls, or at tables, or at shuffle-board; or
each taking his horse, that has bunches of ribands on his head, as the rider
has on his own (who, perhaps, has a ring in his ear too) and so go to horse-
racing, to spoil the creatures; O, these are gentlemen indeed, these are
bred up gentlemen, these are brave fellows, and they must take their recrea-
tion ; for pleasures are lawful. These in their sports set up their shouts,
like wild asses. They are like the kine or beasts, when they are put to
grass, lowing when they are full. Here is the glorying of those before
mentioned; but it is in the flesh, not in the Lord. These are bad Christians, and show that they are gluttoned with the creatures, and then the
flesh rejoiceth. Here is bad breeding of youth and young women, who are
carried away with the vanities of the mind in their own inventions, pride,
arrogancy, lust, gluttony, uncleanness. They eat and drink, and rise up to
play. This is the generation which God is not well-pleased with; for their
eyes are full of adultery, and cannot cease from evil. These be they that
live in pleasures upon earth; these be they who are dead while they live;
who glory not in the Lord, but in the flesh. These be they that are out of
the life, that the Scriptures were given forth from; who live in the fashions
and vanities of the world, out of truth's adorning, in the devil's adorning
(who is out of the truth) ; and not in the adorning of the Lord, which is a
meek and quiet spirit, which is with the Lord of great price. But this
ornament and this adorning is not put on by them that adorn themselves,
and have the ornament of him that is out of the truth. That is not accepted
with the Lord, which is accepted in their eye."   G. F.

Moreover it came upon me about this time from the Lord, to write a
short paper and send forth, as an exhortation and warning to the Pope, and
all kings and rulers in Europe ; as follows :—

        " FRIENDS,
        "YE heads, and rulers, kings, and nobles of all sorts, be not bitter,
nor hasty in persecuting the lambs of Christ, neither turn yourselves against
the visitation of God, and his tender love and mercies from on high, who
sent to visit you; lest the Lord's hand, arm, and power, take hold swiftly
upon you; which is now stretched over the world. It is turned against
kings, and shall turn wise men backward, and will bring their crowns to the
dust, and lay them low and level with the earth. The Lord will be king,
who gives crowns to whomsoever obey his will. This is the age wherein
the Lord God of heaven and earth is staining the pride of man, and defacing

his glory. You that profess Christ, and do not love your enemies, but on the contrary shut up and imprison those who are his friends; these are marks that you are out of his life, and do not love Christ, who do not the things he commands. The day of the Lord's wrath is kindling, and his fire is going forth to burn up the wicked; which will leave neither root nor branch. They that have lost their habitation with God, are out of the Spirit, that gave forth the Scriptures, and from the light that Jesus Christ hath enlightened them withal; and so from the true foundation. Therefore be swift to hear, slow to speak, and slower to persecute: for the Lord is bringing his people to himself, from all the world's ways, to Christ the way; and from all the world's churches, to the church which is in God, the Father of our Lord Jesus Christ; and from all the world's teachers, to teach his people himself by his Spirit; from all the world's images, into the image of himself; and from their likenesses into his own likeness; and from all the world's crosses of stone or wood, into his power, which is the cross of Christ. For all these images, crosses, and likenesses, are among them, that are apostatized from the image of God, the power of God, the cross of Christ, which now fathoms the world, and is throwing down that which is contrary to it; which power of God never changes.

"Let this go to the kings of France, and of Spain, and to the Pope, for them to prove all things, and to hold that which is good. And first to prove, that they have not quenched the Spirit: for the mighty day of the Lord is come, and coming upon all wickedness, and ungodliness, and unrighteousness of men, who will plead with all flesh by fire and by sword. And the truth, the crown of glory, and the sceptre of righteousness over all shall be exalted; which shall answer that of God in every one upon the earth, though they be from it. Christ is come a light into the world, and doth enlighten every one that cometh into the world; that all through him might believe. He that feeleth the light that Christ hath enlightened him withal, he feeleth Christ in his mind, and the cross of Christ, which is the power of God; he shall not need to have a cross of wood or stone, to put him in mind of Christ, or of his cross, which is the power of God manifest in the inward parts."   G. F.

Besides this I was moved to write a letter to the Protector, to warn him of the mighty work the Lord hath to do in the nations, and of the shaking of them; and to beware of his own wit, craft, subtilty, and policy, or seeking any by-ends to himself.

There was about this time an order for the trying of ministers (so called), and for approving, or ejecting them out of their places or benefices; whereupon I wrote a paper to the justices, and other commissioners, who were appointed to that work, as follows:—

"FRIENDS,

"You that are justices, and in commission to try ministers, who have so long been in the vineyard of God, see whether they be such as are mentioned in the Scriptures, whom the prophets, Christ, and the apostles, disapproved of. And if they be such as they disapproved, see how ye can stand approved in the sight of God, to let such go into his vineyard, and approve of them who will admire your persons, because of advantage, and if you do not give them advantage, they will not admire your persons. Such Jude speaks of. See if they be not such as teach for filthy lucre, for the love of money, covetous, such as love themselves, who have a form of godliness, but deny the power; from such the apostles bid to 'turn away.' The apostle said their mouths should be stopped, who served not the Lord Jesus, but their own bellies, being evil, who mind earthly things. Paul gave Timothy a description to try ministers by; he said, 'they must not be covetous, nor given to wine, nor filthy lucre, nor novices; lest being lifted up into pride, they fall into the condemnation of the devil:' these he was to try and prove without partiality. Now take heed of approving such as he disapproved; for since the apostles' days such as he disapproved have had their liberty; and they have told us, the tongues were their original, and that they were orthodox men; and that the steeple-house, with a cross on the top of it, was the church (the Papist's mass-house, you may look on the top of it, and see the sign). But the Scriptures tell us, 'all the earth was of one language before the building of Babel;' and when Pilate crucified Christ, he set the tongues, Hebrew, Greek, and Latin, over his head. And John tells us, that the beast had power over the tongues, kindreds, and nations; and that the whore sits upon the tongues, of whose cup all nations have drunk, and the kings of the earth have committed fornication with her. John also said the tongues are waters. Christ gives marks to his disciples, and to the multitude, how to try such as these that you are to try. They are called of men master; they love the chiefest seat in the assemblies; they are sayers but not doers; and, said he, they shall put you out of the synagogues. Seven woes he denounced against them, and so disapproved them. Christ said, false prophets should come; and John saw they were come; for they went forth from them, and the world since hath gone after them. But Babylon must be confounded, the mother of harlots; and the Devil must be taken; and with him the beast, and the false prophet must be cast into the lake of fire; for the Lamb and his saints over all must reign, and have the victory. The Lord God sent his prophets of old, to cry against the shepherds, that sought for the fleece, Ezek. xxxiv., and to cry against such shepherds as seek for their gain from their quarter, and never have enough, Isa. v. 6; and to cry against the prophets that prophesied falsely, and the priests that bore rule by their means; which was the filthy and horrible thing, Jer. v. And if you would forbear to give them means, you would see how long they would bear rule. There was in old time a storehouse for the fatherless, strangers, and widows, to come to and be filled; and they did not prosper then who did not bring their tithes to the storehouse. But did not Christ put an end to that priesthood, tithes, temple, and priests? And doth not the apostle say, that the priesthood is changed, the law is changed, and the commandment disannulled? Might not they have pleaded the law of God that gave them tithes? Have ever any of the priests prospered that take tithes since, by the law of man? Was not the first author of them, since Christ's time, the Pope, or some of his church? Did the apostles cast men into prison for tithes, as your ministers do now? As instance; Ralph Hollingworth, priest of Phillingham, for petty tithes, not exceeding six shillings, has cast into Lincoln prison a poor thatcher, named Thomas Bromby; where he has been about eight and thirty weeks, and still remains a prisoner. And the priest petitioned the judge that the poor man might not labour in the city, to get a little money towards his maintenance in prison. Is this a good savour amongst you, that are in commission to choose ministers? Is this glad tidings, to cast into prison a man that is not his hearer, because he could not put into his mouth? Can such as are in the fear of God, and in his wisdom, own such things. The ministers of Christ are to plant a vineyard, and then eat of the fruit; to plough, sow, and thrash, and get the corn; and then let them reap; but not cast them into prison for whom they do no work. Christ, when he sent forth his ministers, bid them give freely, as they had received freely; and into what city or town soever they came, inquire who were worthy and there abide; and what they set before you, said he, that eat. And when these came back again to Christ, and he asked them if they wanted anything, they said No. They did not go to a town, and call the people together, to know how much they might have by the year, as these that are in the apostacy do now. The apostle said, 'have I not power to eat and to drink?' But he did not say, to take tithes, Easter-reckonings, Midsummer-dues, augmentations, and great sums of money; but 'have I not power to eat and to drink?' Yet he did not use that power among the Corinthians. But they that are apostatized from him, will take tithes, great sums of money, Easter-reckonings, and Midsummer-dues; and cast them into prison that will not give it them, whom they do no work for. The ox's mouth must not be muzzled that treads out the corn; but see if the corn be trodden out in you, and the wheat be in the garner. This is from a lover of your souls, and one that desires your eternal good." G. F.

After I had made some stay in the city of London, and cleared myself of what service lay upon me at that time there, I was moved of the Lord to go down into BEDFORDSHIRE to John Crook's house, at LUTON, where there was a great meeting, and people generally convinced of the Lord's truth. When I was come thither, John Crook told me that next day several of those that were called the gentlemen of the country, would come to dine with him and to discourse with me. They came, and I declared to them God's eternal truth. Several Friends went to the steeple-houses that day. And there was a meeting in the country, which Alexander Parker went to; and towards the middle of the day it came upon me to go to it, though it was several miles off. John Crook went with me. When we arrived, there was one —— Gritton, who had been a Baptist, but was got higher than they, and called himself a trier of spirits. He told people their fortunes, and pretended to discover to them when their goods were stolen or houses broken up, who the persons were that did it; by which he had got into the affections of many people thereabouts. This man was in that meeting, speaking, and making a hideous noise over the young-convinced Friends, when I came in; and he bid Alexander Parker give a reason of his hope. Alexander Parker told him, Christ was his hope; but because he did not answer him so soon as he expected, he boastingly cried, "his mouth is stopped." Then Gritton directed his speech to me, for I stood still and heard him express many things, which were not agreeable to Scripture. I asked him, whether he could make those things out by Scripture which he had spoken, and he said, Yes, yes. Then I bid the people take out their Bibles to search the places he should quote for proof of his assertions; but he could not make good by Scripture that which he had said. So he was ashamed and fled out of the house, and his people were generally convinced; for his spirit was discovered, and he came no more amongst them. When his people were convinced and settled in God's truth, they gave forth a book against him, and denied his spirit and his false discoveries. Many were turned to Christ Jesus that day, and came to sit under his teaching; insomuch that the judges were in a great rage, and many of the magistrates in Bedfordshire, because there were so many turned from the hireling priests to the Lord Jesus Christ's free teaching. But John Crook was kept by the power of the Lord; yet he was discharged from being a justice.*

After some time I returned to LONDON again, where Friends were finely established in the truth, and great comings-in there were. About this time several Friends went beyond sea to declare the everlasting truth of God. When I had stayed a while in the city, I went into KENT. When we came to ROCHESTER, there was a guard kept to examine passengers, but we passed by, and were not stopped. So I went to CRANBROOK, where there was a great meeting; several soldiers were at it, and many were turned to the Lord that day. After the meeting, some of the soldiers were somewhat rude, but the Lord's power came over them. Thomas Howsigoe, an Independent preacher, who lived near Cranbrook, was convinced, and became a faithful minister for the Lord Jesus. Some Friends had travelled into Kent before, as John Stubbs and William Caton, and the priests and professors had stirred up the magistrates at Maidstone to whip them, for declaring God's truth unto them; as may be seen at large in the Journal of William Caton's life. Captain Dunk was also convinced in Kent. He went with me to RYE, where we had a meeting; to which the mayor and officers, and several captains came. They took down what I said in writing, which I was well pleased with. All was quiet, and the people affected with the truth.

From Rye I went to ROMNEY, where, the people having had notice of my coming some time before, there was a very large meeting. Thither came Samuel Fisher, an eminent preacher among the Baptists, who had

---

* John Crook was a Justice of the Peace, and a man of note in the county of Bedford. He became an eminent preacher of the gospel, in which he laboured extensively, and many were the seals of his ministry. He suffered many imprisonments, which he bore with patience, as also his bodily infirmities, often expressing the inward joy and peace he had with the Lord. He died in 1699, in the eighty-second year of his age, having been a minister about forty-four years, and his writings were published in 1701, entitled, *The design of Christianity testified in the Books, Epistles, and MSS. of John Crook.*

had a parsonage reputed worth about two hundred pounds a year, which for conscience sake he had given up. There was also the pastor of the Baptists, and abundance of their people. The power of the Lord was so mightily over the meeting, that many were reached thereby, and one greatly shaken, and the life sprung up in many. One of the pastors of the Baptists, being amazed at the work of the Lord's power, bid one of our friends that was so wrought upon, have a good conscience; whereupon I was moved of the Lord to bid him take heed of hypocrisy and deceit; and he was silent. A great convincement there was that day; many were turned from darkness to the divine light of Christ, and came to see their teachers' errors, and to sit under the Lord Jesus Christ's teaching, to know him their way, and the covenant of light, which God had given to be their salvation; and they were brought to the one baptism, and to the one baptizer, Christ Jesus. When the meeting was over, Samuel Fisher's wife said, "Now we may discern this day between flesh and spirit, and distinguish spiritual teaching from fleshly." The people were generally well satisfied with what had been declared; but the two Baptist teachers and their company, when they were gone from the meeting, fell to reasoning amongst the people. Samuel Fisher, with many others, reasoned for the word of life, which had been declared that day; and the other pastor and his party reasoned against it; so it divided them asunder, and cut them in the midst. A friend came and told me, that the Baptists were disputing one with another; and desired me to go up to them; but I said "let them alone, the Lord will divide them; and they that reason for truth, will be too hard for the other;" and so it was. Samuel Fisher received the truth in the love of it, became a faithful minister, preached Christ freely, and laboured much in the service of the Lord, being moved to go and declare the word of life at Dunkirk and in Holland, and in divers parts of Italy, as Leghorn, and Rome itself; yet the Lord preserved him and his companion John Stubbs, out of their Inquisitions.*

From Romney I passed to DOVER, and had a meeting, where several were convinced. Near Dover a governor and his wife were convinced, who had been Baptists; and the Baptists thereabouts were much offended, and grew very envious; but the Lord's power came over all. Luke

---

* Sewell states that Samuel Fisher and John Stubbs, when at Rome, conversed with some of the cardinals, and testified against Popish superstitions. They also spread books among the friars, some of whom expressed their contents to be true; but, said they, if we should acknowledge this publicly, we might expect to be burned for it.

Whiting records the death of Samuel Fisher in 1665. "Other Friends," he says, "were transported; and many died in Newgate, and on shipboard, in order to transportation, to the number of 122, in London, Westminster, and Southwark; particularly Samuel Fisher, &c., faithful ministers and labourers in the work of the Lord, taken at meetings died in the White Lion prison, Southwark, 1665, in the time of the pestilence [plague], which began in the time of the persecution of Friends under the Conventicle Act, as a signal token of the Lord's displeasure. It broke out first in a house next to that of the first man that was banished, who lived to return to London, and died at a great age."

Howard of Dover was convinced some time before, and became a faithful minister of Christ.*

Returning from Dover I went to CANTERBURY, where a few honest-hearted people were turned to the Lord, who sat down under Christ's teaching. Thence I passed to CRANBROOK again, where I had a great meeting. A friend went to the steeple-house, and was cast into prison; but the Lord's power was manifested, and his truth spread.

From thence I passed into Sussex, and lodged near HORSHAM, where there was a great meeting, and many were convinced. Also at STEYNING we had a great meeting in the market-house, and several were convinced; for the Lord's power was with us. I had several meetings in the neighbourhood; and among the rest, one was appointed at a great man's house, and he and his son went to fetch several priests that had threatened to come and dispute. But none of them came; for the Lord's power was mighty in us; a glorious meeting we had. The man of the house and his son were vexed, because none of the priests would come. So the hearts of people were opened by the Spirit of God, and they were turned from the hirelings to Christ Jesus their shepherd, who had purchased them without money, and would feed them without money or price. Many that came, expecting to hear a dispute, were convinced; amongst whom Nicholas Beard was one.†

Thus the Lord's power came over all, and his day many came to see. There were abundance of Ranters in those parts, and professors that had been so loose in their lives, that they began to be weary of it, and had thought to go into Scotland to live privately. But the Lord's net caught them, and their understandings were opened by his light, Spirit, and power, through which they came to receive the truth, and to be settled upon the Lord; and so became very sober men, and good friends in the truth. Great blessing and praising of the Lord there was amongst them, and great admiration in the country.

Out of Sussex I travelled to READING, where I found a few that were

---

* For some account of Luke Howard, see *Piety Promoted*, Part ix. He was several times imprisoned; once in Dover Castle, for sixteen months, for going to meetings. At this time, he employed six men in his trade, but was obliged to shut up his shop for six months. He obtained the use of an entry to the prison grate, where meat was drawn up with a cord, and he worked a little there. He suffered another long confinement in 1684. Speaking of his imprisonments, he says, "I had perfect peace, joy, and content in it all; the Lord made it good unto me, both within and without."

† Nicholas Beard was an early seeker of the Lord in his youth, and would often travel many miles to hear the best reputed teachers of the times. He became a faithful minister of Christ, and a large sufferer for his sake. For one year's tithes he had taken from him twelve oxen, six cows, and one bull, which were sold for £111, 5s., but worth more. For worshipping God, and refusing to swear or bear arms, he was prosecuted on the statute for £20 a month, and underwent imprisonment several years, and loss of goods to more than £1000. Yet it pleased the Lord to support and bless him and a large family, so that on his deathbed he was heard to say, "O Lord, my soul blesseth thee, and all that is within me magnifieth thy holy name!" He often desired to depart and be with Christ, and died in great peace, in 1702, aged eighty, a minister about thirty years.

convinced of the way of the Lord. There I stayed till First-day, and had a meeting in George Lamboll's orchard; and a great part of the town came to it. A glorious meeting it proved; a great convincement there was, and the people were mightily satisfied. Thither came two of Judge Fell's daughters to me, and George Bishop, of Bristol, with his sword by his side, for he was a captain.* After the meeting many Baptists and Ranters came privately, reasoning and discoursing; but the Lord's power came over them. The Ranters pleaded, that God made the Devil; I denied it, and told them, " I was come into the power of God, the seed Christ, which was before the Devil was, and bruised the head of him; and he became a Devil by going out of truth, and so became a murderer and a destroyer. So I showed them that God did not make the Devil; for God is a God of truth, and he made all things good, and blessed them; but God did not bless the Devil. And the Devil is bad, and was a liar and a murderer from the beginning, and spoke of himself and not from God." And so the truth stopped them, and bound them, and came over all the highest notions in the nation, and confounded them. For by the power of the Lord God I was manifest, and sought to be made manifest to the Spirit of God in all; that by it (which they vexed, and quenched, and grieved) they might be turned to God; as many were turned to the Lord Jesus Christ by the Holy Spirit, and were come to sit under his teaching.

After this meeting at Reading I passed up to LONDON, where I stayed a while, and had large meetings, then into ESSEX, and came to COGGESHALL, where was a meeting of about two thousand people, as it was supposed, which lasted several hours, and a glorious meeting it was; for the word of life was freely declared, and people were turned to the Lord Jesus Christ, their teacher and their Saviour, the way, the truth, and the life.

On the sixth day of that week I had a meeting near COLCHESTER, to which many professors and the Independent teachers came. After I had done speaking, and was stepped down from the place on which I stood, one of the Independent teachers began to make a jangling; which Amor Stoddart perceiving, said to me, Stand up again, George; for I was going away, and did not at first hear them. But when I heard the jangling Independent, I stood up again; and after a while the Lord's power came over him and his company; and they were confounded, and the Lord's truth went over all. A great flock of sheep hath the Lord Jesus Christ in that country, that feed in his pastures of life. On the First-day following we had a very large meeting, near Colchester, wherein the Lord's power was eminently manifested, and the people were very well satisfied; for they were turned to Christ's free teaching, and received it gladly. Many of these people had been of the stock of the martyrs.

As I passed through Colchester, I went to visit James Parnell in prison, but the cruel jailer would hardly let us come in, or stay with him.

* This Captain Bishop, who is mentioned as wearing his sword, soon discontinued it, being convinced, and joining Friends. He was the author of *An Account of the Persecution in New England,* and he issued a prophetic warning to the King and Parliament, in 1664, for banishing Friends, which was fulfilled. See Sewell's *History;* Index.

Very cruel they were to him; the jailer's wife threatened to have his blood; and in that jail they destroyed him, as the reader may see in a book printed soon after his death, giving an account of his life and death; and also in an epistle printed with his collected books and writings.

From Colchester I went to IPSWICH, where we had a little meeting, and very rude; but the Lord's power came over them. After the meeting I said, "if any had a desire to hear further, they might come to the inn;" and there came in a company of rude butchers, that had abused Friends; but the Lord's power so chained them that they could not do mischief. Then I wrote a paper, and gave it forth to the town, "warning them of the day of the Lord, that they might repent of the evils they lived in; directing them to Christ, their teacher, and way; and exhorting them to forsake their hireling teachers."

We passed from Ipswich to MENDLESHAM, in SUFFOLK, where Robert Duncan lived. There we had a large quiet meeting, and the Lord's power was preciously felt amongst us. Then we passed to a meeting at Captain Lawrence's in NORFOLK; where, it was supposed, were above a thousand people; and all was quiet. Many persons of note were present, and a great convincement there was; for they were turned to Christ, their way and their teacher, and many of them received him, and sat down under him, their vine. Here we parted with Amor Stoddart and some other Friends, who intended to meet us again in Huntingdonshire.

About two in the morning we took horse for NORWICH, where Christopher Atkins had run out, and brought dishonour upon the blessed truth and name of the Lord. But he had been denied by Friends; and afterwards he gave forth a paper of condemnation of his sin and evil. We came to YARMOUTH, and there stayed a while; where there was a Friend, Thomas Bond, in prison for the truth of Christ. There we had some service; and some were turned to the Lord in that town. From thence we rode to another town, about twenty miles off, where were many tender people; and I was moved of the Lord to speak to them, as I sat on my horse, in several places as I passed along. We went to another town about five miles from thence, and set up our horses at an inn, Richard Hubberthorn and I having travelled five and forty miles that day. There were some friendly people in the town; and we had a tender, broken meeting amongst them, in the Lord's power, to his praise.

We bid the hostler have our horses ready by three in the morning; for we intended to ride to Lynn, about three and thirty miles, next morning. But when we were in bed at our inn, about eleven at night, the constable and officers came, with a great rabble of people, into the inn, and said they were come with a hue and cry from a justice of peace, that lived near the town about five miles off, where I had spoken to the people in the streets, as I rode along, to search for two horsemen, that rode upon gray horses, and in gray clothes; a house having been broken up on the Seventh-day before at night. We told them "we were honest, innocent men, and abhorred such things;" yet they apprehended us, and set a guard with halberts and pikes upon us that night; making some of those friendly people, with others, to watch us. Next morning we were up betimes, and the constable with his guard carried us before a justice of peace about five miles off. We took two or three of the sufficient men of the town with us, who had been with us at the great meeting at Captain Lawrence's, and could testify that we lay both the Seventh-day night, and the First-day night, at Captain Lawrence's; and it was the Seventh-day night that they said the house was broken up. The reader is to be informed, that during the time that I was a prisoner at the Mermaid at Charing-Cross, this Captain Lawrence brought several Independent justices to see me there, with whom I had much discourse; which they took offence at. For they pleaded for imperfection, and to sin as long as they lived; but did not like to hear of Christ teaching his people himself, and making people as clear, whilst here upon the earth, as Adam and Eve were before they fell. These justices had plotted together this mischief against me in the country, pretending a house was broken up; that they might send their hue and cry after me. They were vexed also, and troubled, to hear of the great meeting at John Lawrence's aforesaid; for a colonel was convinced there that day, who lived and died in the truth. But Providence so ordered, that the constable carried us to a justice about five miles onward in our way towards Lynn, who was not an independent justice, as the rest were. When we were brought before him, he began to be angry, because we did not put off our hats to him. I told him, I had been before the Protector, and he was not offended at my hat; and why should he be offended at it, who was but one of his servants? Then he read the hue and cry; and I told him, "that that night, wherein the house was said to be broken up, we were at Captain Lawrence's house; and that we had several men present who could testify the truth thereof." Thereupon the justice, having examined us and them, said, "he believed we were not the men that had broken the house; but he was sorry," he said, "that he had no more against us." We told him, "he ought not to be sorry for not having evil against us; but rather to be glad; for to rejoice, when he got evil against people, as for housebreaking, or the like, was not a good mind in him." It was a good while yet, before he could resolve, whether to let us go, or send us to prison; and the wicked constable stirred him up against us, telling him, "we had good horses, and that if it pleased him, he would carry us to Norwich jail." But we took hold of the justice's confession, that "he believed we were not the men that had broken the house;" and after we had admonished him to fear the Lord in his day, the Lord's power came over him, so that he let us go; so their snare was broken. A great people were afterwards gathered to the Lord in that town, where I was moved to speak to them in the street; and from whence the hue and cry came.

Being set at liberty, we travelled to LYNN; where we arrived about three in the afternoon. Having set up our horses, we met with Joseph Fuce,* who was an ensign; and we wished him to speak to as many of the people of the town as he could that feared God; and to the captains and

---

* Joseph Fuce was one of those faithful ministers who died in White Lion prison, Southwark, in 1665, during the time of the plague.

officers to come together: which he did. We had a very glorious meeting amongst them, and turned them to the Spirit of God, by which they might know God and Christ, and understand the Scriptures; and so learn of God and of Christ, as the prophets and apostles did. Many were convinced there; and a fine meeting there is, of them that are come off from the hirelings' teaching, and sit under the teaching of the Lord Jesus Christ.

Lynn being then a garrison, we desired Joseph Fuce to get us the gate opened by three next morning, for we had forty miles to ride next day. By that means getting out early, we came next day by eleven or twelve to SUTTON, near the Isle of Ely, where Amor Stoddart, and the Friends with him, met us again. A multitude of people was gathered there, and no less than four priests. The priest of the town made a great jangle; but the Lord's power so confounded him, that he went away: the other three stayed; and one of them was convinced. One of the other two, whilst I was speaking, came to lean upon me; but I bid him sit down, seeing he was so slothful. A great convincement there was that day; and many hundreds were turned from darkness to the light, from the power of Satan unto God, and from the spirit of error to the Spirit of truth, to be led thereby into all truth. People came to this meeting from Huntingdon, and beyond; and the mayor's wife of Cambridge was there also. A glorious meeting it was, and many were settled under Christ's teaching, and knew him, their Shepherd, to feed them; for the word of life was freely declared, and gladly received by them. The meeting ended in the power of the Lord, and in peace; and after it I walked out and went into a garden; where I had not been long, before a Friend came to me, and told me several justices were come to break up the meeting. But many of the people were gone away; so they missed of their design: and after they had stayed a while, they went away also, in a fret.

That evening I passed to CAMBRIDGE. When I came into the town, the scholars hearing of me, were up, and were exceedingly rude. I kept on my horse's back, and rode through them in the Lord's power; but they unhorsed Amor Stoddard before he could get to the inn. When we were in the inn, they were so rude in the courts, and in the streets, that miners, colliers, and carters could never be ruder. The people of the house asked us "what we would have for supper." "Supper!" said I, "were it not that the Lord's power is over them, these rude scholars look as if they would pluck us in pieces, and make a supper of us." They knew I was so against the trade of preaching, which they were there as apprentices to learn, that they raged as much as ever Diana's craftsmen did against Paul. At this place John Crook met us. When it was within night, the mayor of the town, being friendly, came and fetched me to his house; and as we walked through the streets, there was a bustle in the town; but they did not know me, it being darkish. They were in a rage, not only against me, but against the mayor also; so that he was almost afraid to walk the streets with me, for the tumult. We sent for the friendly people, and had a fine meeting there in the power of God; and I stayed there all night. Next morning, having ordered our horses to be ready by six, we passed peaceably out of town; and the destroyers were disappointed; for they thought I would have stayed longer, and intended to do us mischief; but our passing away early in the morning frustrated their evil purposes against us.

Then we rode to BISHOP-STORTFORD, where some were convinced: and so to HERTFORD, where also there were some convinced; and where there is now a large meeting. From thence we returned to LONDON, where Friends received us gladly; the Lord's power having carried us through many snares and dangers. Great service we had for the Lord; for many hundreds were brought to sit under the teaching of the Lord Jesus Christ, their Saviour, and to praise the Lord through him. James Naylor also was come up to London; and Richard Hubberthorn and I stayed some time in the city, visiting Friends and answering gainsayers; for we had great disputes with professors of all sorts. Many reproaches they cast upon truth; and lying slanderous books they gave forth against us: but we answered them all, cleared God's truth, and set it over them; and the Lord's power was over all.

Amongst other services for the Lord, which then lay upon me in the city, I was moved to give forth a paper to those that made a scorn of trembling and quaking; which is as follows :—

"THE word of the Lord to all you that scorn trembling, and quaking; who scoff at, scorn, stone, and belch forth oaths against, those who are trembling and quaking; threatening them, and beating them. Strangers ye are to all the apostles and prophets; and are of the generation that stoned them, and mocked them in those ages. Ye are the scoffers of whom they spoke, that are come in the last times. Be ye witnesses against yourselves. To the light in all your consciences I speak, that with it you may see yourselves to be out of the life of the holy men of God.

"Moses, who was judge over all Israel, trembled, feared, and quaked: when the Lord said unto him, 'I am the God of Abraham, the God of Isaac, and the God of Jacob, then Moses trembled, and durst not behold.' This, which makes to tremble now, ye teachers and people scoff at, and scorn them in your streets who witness the power of the Lord. Moses forsook the pleasures of the world, which he might have enjoyed for a season. He might have been called the son of Pharaoh's daughter; he refused it, and forsook Pharaoh's house; yet was no vagabond. David, a king, trembled; he was mocked; they made songs on him; they wagged their heads at him. Will you profess David's words, and Moses's words, who are in the generation of your fathers, mockers, scoffers, wonderers, and despisers, who are to perish? O blush! be ashamed of all your profession, and be confounded! Job trembled, his flesh trembled, and they mocked him: so do you now mock them in whom the same power of God is made manifest; and yet you profess Job's words. O deceitful hypocrites! will ye not own Scripture? O shame! never profess Scripture words, and deny the power, which, according to Scripture, makes the keepers of the house to tremble, and the strong man to bow himself. These things both priests, magistrates, and people scoff at; but with the power ye are judged, and by the power and life condemned.

"The prophet Jeremiah trembled, he shook, his bones quaked, he reeled to and fro, like a drunken man, when he saw the deceits of the priests and prophets, who were turned from the way of God; they were not ashamed, neither could they blush. Such were gone from the light; and such were they that ruled over the people. But he was brought to cry, O foolish people! that had eyes, and could not see; that had ears, and could not hear; that did not fear the Lord, and tremble at his presence, who placed the sands for bounds to the sea, by a perpetual decree, that the waves thereof cannot pass! And he said, 'A horrible thing is committed in the land; the prophets prophesy falsely, and the priests bear rule by their means. Shall not I visit for these things, saith the Lord? Shall not my soul be avenged upon such a nation as this?' They were such as did not tremble at the word of the Lord; therefore he called them a foolish people. Hear all ye the word of the Lord, ye foolish people, who scorn trembling and quaking. Give over professing the prophet Jeremiah's words, and making a trade of them; for with his words you are judged to be among the scoffers, scorners, and stockers. For he was stocked by your generation; and you now stock them that tremble at the word of the Lord, at the power of the mighty God, which raises up the seed of God, and throws down the earth which hath kept it down. So, you who are in the fall where death reigneth, who are enemies of the truth, despising the power of God, as those of your generation ever did, woe and misery is your portion, except you speedily repent.

"Isaiah saith, 'Hear the word of the Lord, ye that tremble at his word.' Again, 'To this man will I look, even to him that is poor, and of a contrite spirit, and trembleth at my word.' Isa. lxv. 2. 'Your brethren that hated you, that cast you out for my name's sake, said, Let the Lord be glorified; but he shall appear to your joy, and they shall be ashamed.' Isa. lxvi. 5. Now all ye scoffers and scorners, that despise trembling, you regard not the word of the Lord; they are not regarded by you, that tremble at the word; who are regarded by the Lord: therefore you are contrary to Isaiah's words. Profess him and his words no more, for shame, nor make a trade of his words, ye that seek for your gain from your quarter, ye greedy, dumb dogs, that never have enough; ye are they that despise trembling; ye are such as Isaiah cried against, who himself witnessed trembling. Here therefore be ye witnesses against yourselves, that with the light in your consciences ye may see ye are out of the prophet Isaiah's spirit, and are haters of them that tremble, whom the Lord regards; such you regard not, but hate and persecute, mock and rail against them. It is manifest that you walk in the steps of your forefathers, that persecuted the prophets.

"Habakkuk, the prophet of the Lord, trembled. And Joel, the prophet of the Lord, said, 'Blow the trumpet in Zion, and let all the inhabitants of the earth tremble: the people shall tremble, and all faces shall gather blackness, and the people shall be much pained.' And now this trembling is witnessed by the power of the Lord. This power of the Lord is come; the trumpet is sounding; the earth is shaking, the inhabitants of the earth are trembling; the dead are arising, and the living are praising

God; the world is raging, and the scoffers are scorning; and they that witness trembling and quaking wrought in them by the power of the Lord, can scarcely pass up and down the streets, but with stones and blows, fists and sticks, or dogs set at them; or they are pursued with mockings and reproaches. Thus you vent forth your malice against them that witness the power of the Lord, as the prophets did; who are come to the broken heart and contrite spirit, who tremble at the word of the Lord, and whom the Lord regards: these you stone and stock, and set your dogs at; these you scoff and scorn, these you revile and reproach: but these reproaches are our riches; praised be the Lord who hath given us power over them. If you see one, as Habakkuk, whose 'lips quivered,' whose 'belly shook,' who said, 'rottenness was entered into his bones,' and who 'trembled in himself;' if you see such a one in this condition now, ye say, he is bewitched. Here again you show yourselves strangers to that power, to that life, that was in the prophet: therefore, for shame, never make a profession of his words, nor a trade of his words; nor of Joel's, who witnessed trembling, which ye scorn and scoff at. Ye proud scoffers and scorners, misery, misery is your end, except you speedily repent.

"Daniel, a servant of the most high God, trembled; his strength and his breath were gone: he was imprisoned, he was hated, he was persecuted. They laid baits and snares for him, in whom the Holy Spirit of God was. Now for shame, you that make a profession of Daniel's words, give over your profession; priests and people, who scorn and scoff at trembling, with the light you are seen to be out of Daniel's life, and by the same power you are judged, at which you scorn and scoff. Here again be ye witnesses against yourselves, that ye are scorners and scoffers against the truth; and with the Scripture ye are judged to be contrary to the life of the holy men of God.

"Paul, a minister of God, made, by the will of God, a messenger of the Lord Jesus, a vessel of the Lord, to carry his name abroad into several nations, trembled; and when the dark, blind world, having got some of his words and epistles, you teachers make a trade of them, and obtain great sums of money by it, and so destroy souls for dishonest gain; making a trade of his words, and of the rest of the apostles' and prophets', and of Christ's words, but denying the Spirit and life that they were guided by; and that power which shook the flesh and the earth, which the apostle witnessed, who said, when he came among the Corinthians, that 'he was with them in weakness, and in fear, and in much trembling,' that their faith might not stand in the wisdom of men, but in the power of God; in that power which made him to tremble. This power it is that the world, and all the scoffing teachers, scoff at and scorn in your towns, in your villages, in your assemblies, in your ale-houses. For shame, lay aside all your profession of the apostle's words and conditions! Some of them that scoff at this power, call it the power of the devil. Some persecute, stone and stock, imprison and whip them, in whom that power is made manifest, and load them with reproaches, as not worthy to walk on the earth; hated and persecuted, as the off-scouring of all things. Here you may see you are in the steps of your forefathers, who persecuted the apostles, and acted so against them; stocked them, mocked them, imprisoned them, stoned them, whipped them, haled them out of the synagogues, reproached them, and shamefully entreated them. Do not you here fulfil the Scripture, and Christ's saying, who said, 'If they kill you, they will think they do God service?' Yet you make a profession of Christ's words, of the prophets' and apostles' words, and call yourselves churches, and ministers of the gospel. I charge you, in the presence of the living God, to be silent who act such things! Mind the light in your consciences, ye scoffers and scorners, which Christ hath enlightened you withal: that with it ye may see yourselves, what ye act, and what ye have acted; for they who act such things shall not inherit the kingdom of God: all such things are by the light condemned.

"You who have come to witness trembling and quaking, the powers of the earth to be shaken, the lustful nature to be destroyed, the scorning and scoffing nature judged by the light; wait in it to receive power from him who shakes the earth. That power we own, and our faith stands in it, which all the world scoffs at; the lofty ones, the proud, the presumptuous, who live in presumption, and yet make a profession of the Scriptures, as your fathers the Pharisees did, who were painted sepulchres and serpents; and as the scribes did, who had the chiefest places in the assemblies, stood praying in the synagogues, and were called of men masters, which Christ cried woe against. These are not come so far as the trembling of devils, who believed and trembled. Let that judge you. The light and life of the Scripture is seen and made manifest, and with it all you scoffers and scorners, all you persecutors and railers are seen.

"Take warning, all ye powers of the earth, how ye persecute them whom the world nickname and call Quakers, who dwell in the eternal power of God; lest the hand of the Lord be turned against you, and ye be all cut off. To you this is the word of God. Fear and tremble, and take warning! for this is the man whom the Lord doth regard, who trembles at his word; whom you, who are of the world, scoff and scorn, stock, persecute, and imprison. Here ye may see ye are contrary to God and to the prophets; and are such as hate what the Lord regards; which we, whom the world scorns, and calls Quakers, own. We exalt and honour that power, that makes the devils tremble, shakes the earth, and throws down the loftiness and the haughtiness of man; which makes the beasts of the field to tremble, and the earth to reel to and fro; which cleaves the earth asunder, and overturneth the world. This power we own, and honour, and preach; but all scoffers and persecutors, railers and scorners, stockers and whippers, we deny by that power which throweth down all that nature; seeing that all who act such things, without repentance, shall not inherit the kingdom of God, but are for destruction.

"Rejoice all ye righteous ones, who are persecuted for righteousness' sake; for great is your reward in heaven. Rejoice, ye that suffer for well-doing; for ye shall not lose your reward. Wait in the light, that you may grow up in the life that gave forth the Scriptures; that with it you may see the saints' conditions, and all that which they testified against; and there with it ye will see the state of those that reproached and scoffed at them; that mocked and persecuted them; that whipped and stocked them, and haled them out of the synagogues before magistrates. To you, who are in the same light and life, the same things do they now; that they may fill up the measure of their fathers. With the light now they are seen, where the light, and life, and power of God is made manifest; for as they did unto them, so they will do unto you. Here is our joy; the Scripture is fulfilled, and fulfilling; and with the light, which was before the world was, which is now made manifest in the children of light, they see the world, and comprehend it, and the actions of it; for he that loves the world, and turns from the light, is an enemy to God; he turneth into wickedness; for the whole world lieth in wickedness. He who turns from the light, turns into the works of evil, which the light of Christ testifies against; and by this light, where it is made manifest, all the works of the world are seen and made manifest.''   G. F.

This is to go abroad among the scattered
    ones, and among the world.

Great was the rage and enmity of professors, as well as profane, against the truth and people of God at this time; and great the contempt and disdain they showed of Friends' plainness. Wherefore I was moved to write the following, and sent it forth:—

"*An Epistle to Churches gathered into outward forms, upon the earth.*

"ALL ye churches gathered into outward forms upon the earth, the Son of God is come to reign; he will tread and trample, will shake and make you quiver, you that are found out of his light, without his life and power. His day hath appeared; mortar and clay will you be found. Breaking, shaking, and quaking are coming among you! your high building is to be laid desolate; your professed liberty shall be your bondage; the mouth of the Lord of hosts hath spoken it. Tremble, ye hypocrites, ye notionists! the fenced cities shall be laid desolate, the fruitful fields shall become a wilderness; your false joy shall become your heaviness; the time of weeping and desolation draweth nigh! Come, ye witty ones, see how ye can stand before the Almighty, who is now come to plead with you; you will fall like leaves, and wither like weeds! Come, you that have boasted of my name, saith the Lord, and have gloried in the flesh, ye shall fade like a flower; who have slain my witness, yet boast of my words, which have been as a song unto you. Come, ye novelists, who love novelties, changeable suits of apparel, who are in the fashions, outward and inward, putting on one thing this day, and another the other day. 'I will strip thee,' saith the Lord, 'I will make thee bare, I will make thee naked, and thou shalt know that I am the Lord. What! hast thou professed the prophets' words? hast thou professed the apostles' words, and my Son's words? hast thou covered thyself with their expressions? thinkest thou not that I see thee out of my life? thinkest thou, thou witty one, to hide thyself where none can see thee? thinkest thou, if thou fliest to the uttermost parts of the earth, that I am not there? Is not the earth mine, and the fulness of it, saith the Lord?' Come, all ye that have trusted in your own conceited notions, and knowledge, and wisdom, who were never yet out of the earth, and the lusts of it; never yet got the load of thick clay off you; never were out of the drunken spirit, whose imperfection appears, which must be come upon, as a potter's vessel; broken cisterns; ye that have been made wise in your own conceit, wise in your own eyes, in which pride hath lifted you up, and not the humility; you must be abased. You have run on, every one after his own invention; every man hath done the thing that was right in his own eyes, that which pleased himself. This hath been the course of people upon earth. Ye have run on without a king, without Christ, the light of the world, which hath enlightened every one that is come into the world. But now is truth risen, now are your fruits withering.

"And you that are fortified, and have fortified your strong houses, called your churches, make ye your cords strong, the Lord will break you asunder, ye that are gathering in, and ye that are gathered. For the Lord is risen to scatter you; his witness is risen in the hearts of his people, they will not be fed with dead words, nor with that which dies of itself; nor will they be satisfied with the husks which the swine feed upon. All ye priests in the nation, and teachers, that now stand against the light, your envy shows that ye are in Cain's way; your greediness shows that ye are in Balaam's way; your standing against the light which hath enlightened every man that cometh into the world, doth manifest that you are in Korah's way, that spoke the great high words of vanity; ye, whose consciences are seared as with a hot iron, whose judgment doth not linger, whose damnation doth not slumber, who serve not the Lord Jesus Christ, but your own bellies; who are the evil beasts spoken of, which have destroyed many families, taken away their cattle, their horses, their goods, even their household goods; destroyed many poor men, even whole families, taking their whole estates from them, whom you do no work for. O! the grievous actions that are done by you, the ministers of unrighteousness; whose fruits declare to the whole nation that you are the devil's messengers! your actions declare it; your taking tithes, augmentations, treble damages, Midsummer-dues (as ye call them), of them ye do no work for, nor minister to.

"All ye powers of the earth, beware of holding such up as are unrighteous. Let not the words of the unrighteous overcome you, lest God, the righteous judge of heaven and earth, take hold upon you; whose judgment is according to that of God in you, which will let you see when you transgress. Come you proud and lofty ones, who have not considered the handy-works of the Lord, but have destroyed them; nor have regarded the way of the Lord, but have had plenty of the creatures, and have therewith fattened yourselves, and forgotten the Lord and his way: O let shame cover your faces here upon earth! Come, ye that are given to pleasures, and spend your time in sports, and idleness, and fulness; your fruits declare the sins of Sodom; yet you will talk of my name, and of my saints' words. 'But I behold you afar off,' saith the Lord; you are proud and lofty; you are evil patterns, bad examples, full, rich, and idle; who say, others are idle, that cannot maintain your lusts. O! the unrighteous balances that are among people! O! the iniquity in measuring! O! the oppression in ruling and governing! Because of these things my hand shall come upon you, saith the Lord. For the oppression is entered into the ears of the Lord, who gives rest to the wearied, to the burthened, to the oppressed; who feeds the hungry, and clothes the naked; who brings the mighty from their seats, beats the lofty to the ground, and makes the haughty bend.

"Come, saith the Lord, ye mockers, scorners, and rebellious ones, light and wild people, vain and heady; you have had your day of joy, you have scoffed, you have mocked and derided my messengers and my ambassadors, who have preached in your streets, and cried in your synagogues and temples; a day of trembling and lamentation shall come upon you, when you are not aware. I will take away your pride and your height; I will shake you as a leaf, and bring you to be as men distracted. I will distract you, and make you that you shall not trust one another in the earth, who have joined hand in hand against my servants in the truth. I will smite you with terrors, and bring fear upon you; the cup of my indignation and fury shall you drink. Where will you appear when repentance is hid from your eyes, when profane Esau, your father, is set before you, and Ishmael and Cain, wild and envious, whose fruits declare the stock?

"Come, ye proud priests, who have eaten up the fat of the nation, who by violence have taken other men's goods, whose envy hath slain many, whose wickedness and darkness hath abounded, and whose unrighteousness daily appears; your fruits every day declare it, in summoning up by writs and subpœnas from most parts of the nation for wages and tithes, such as you do no work for. O abominable unrighteousness! how is the state of man lost, that they do not take these things to heart to feel them! what havoc is made in most parts of the nation with such! And all ye priests and teachers, who are railing and brawling in the pulpit, setting people at variance one against another, haters and hateful, provoking people to hate one another, here is the seed of enmity seen, which you have sown and are sowing, whose seed must be bruised by the seed of the woman, which above your heads is set."   G. F.

This year came out the oath of abjuration, by which many Friends suffered; and several went to speak to the Protector about it; but he began to harden. And sufferings increasing upon Friends, by reason that envious magistrates made use of that oath as a snare to catch Friends in, who, they knew, could not swear at all; I was moved to write to the Protector, as follows:—

"The magistrate is not to bear the sword in vain, who ought to be a terror to evil-doers; but as the magistrate that doth bear the sword in vain, is not a terror to evil-doers, so he is not a praise to them that do well. Now hath God raised up a people by his power, whom people, priests, and magistrates, who are out of the fear of God, scornfully call Quakers, who cry against drunkenness (for drunkards destroy God's creatures), and against oaths (for because of oaths the land mourns), and these drunkards and swearers, to whom the magistrate's sword should be a terror, are, we see, at liberty; but for crying against such, many are cast into prison; as also for testifying against their pride and filthiness, their deceitful merchandize in markets, their cozening and their cheating, their excess and naughtiness, their playing at bowls and shuffle-boards, at cards and at dice, and their other vain and wanton pleasures. They who live in pleasures, are dead while they live; and they who live in wantonness, kill the just. This we know by the Spirit of God, which gave forth the Scriptures, which the Father has given to us, and hath placed his righteous law in our hearts; which law is a terror to evil-doers, and answers that which is of God in every man's conscience. They who act contrary to the measure of God's Spirit in every man's conscience, cast the law of God behind their backs, and walk despitefully against the Spirit of grace. The magistrate's sword, we see, is borne in vain, whilst the evil-doers are at liberty to do evil; and they that cry against such, are for so doing punished by the magistrate, who hath turned his sword backward against the Lord. Now the wicked one fenceth himself, and persecutes the innocent as vagabonds and wanderers, for crying against sin, and against unrighteousness and ungodliness openly, in the markets and in the highways; or as railers, because they tell them what judgment will come upon them that follow such practices. Here they that depart from iniquity are become a prey, and few lay it to heart. But God will thrash the mountains, beat the hills, cleave the rocks, and cast into his press, which is trodden without the city, and will bathe his sword in the blood of the wicked and unrighteous. You that have drunk the cup of abominations, a hard cup have you had to drink; you are the enemies of God, and of you he will be avenged.

"Now ye, in whom something of God is remaining, consider; if the sword was not borne in vain, but turned against the evil-doers, then the righteous would not suffer, and be cast into holes, dungeons, corners, prisons, and houses of correction, as peace-breakers, for testifying against sin openly, as they are commanded of the Lord, and against the covetousness of the priests, and their false worships; who exact money of poor people, whom they do no work for. O! where will you appear in the day of the Lord? or how will you stand in the day of his righteous judgment? How many jails and houses of correction are now made places to put the lambs of Christ in, for following him, and obeying his commands, which are too numerous to mention. The royal law of Christ, 'to do as ye would be done by,' is trodden down under foot; so that men can profess him in words, but crucify him wheresoever he appears, and cast him into prison, as the talkers of him always did in the generations and ages past. The labourers, which God, the master of the harvest, hath sent into his vineyard, do the chief of the priests, and the rulers now take counsel together against, to cast them into prison: and here are the fruits of priests, and people, and rulers, without the fear of God. The day is come and coming, that every man's work doth appear, and shall appear; glory be to the Lord God for ever. So see, and consider the days you have spent, and do spend; for this is your day of visitation. Many have suffered great fines, because they could not swear, but obey Christ's doctrine, who saith, 'Swear not at all:' and are made a prey upon for abiding in the command of Christ. Many are cast into prison because they cannot take the oath of abjuration, though they denied all that is abjured in it; and by that means many of the messengers and ministers of the Lord Jesus Christ are cast into prison because they will not swear, nor go out of Christ's command. Therefore, O man, consider; to the measure of the life of God in thee I speak. Many also lie in jails, because they cannot pay the priest's tithes; many have their goods spoiled, and treble damages taken of them; and many are whipped and beaten in the house of correction, without breach of any law. These things are done in thy name, in order to protect them in these actions. If men fearing God bore the sword, if covetousness were hated, and men of courage for God were set up, then they would be a terror to evil-doers, and a praise to them that do well; and not cause them to suffer. Here equity would be heard in our land, and righteousness would stand up and take place; which giveth not place to the unrighteous, but judgeth it. To the measure of God's Spirit in thee I speak, that thou mayest consider, and come to rule for God; that thou mayest answer that which is of God in every man's conscience; for this is that, which bringeth to honour all men in the Lord. Therefore consider for whom thou dost rule, that thou mayest come to receive power from God to rule for him; and all that is contrary to God may by his light be condemned.

"From a lover of thy soul, who desires thy eternal good."   G. F.

But sufferings and imprisonments continuing and increasing, and the Protector (under whose name they were inflicted), hardening himself against the complaints that were made to him, I was moved to issue the following amongst Friends, to bring the weight of their sufferings more heavy upon the heads of the persecutors :—

"Who is moved by the power of the Lord to offer himself to the justice for his brother or sister, that lies in prison, and to go lie there in their stead, that his brother or sister may come out of prison, and so offer his life for his brother or sister? Where any lie in prison for tithes, witnessing the priesthood changed, that took tithes, and the unchangeable priesthood come; if any brother in the light, who witnesseth a change of the old priesthood that took tithes, and a disannulling of the commandment for tithes, be moved of the Lord to go to the priest or impropriator, to offer himself to lie in prison for his brother, and to lay down his life, that he may come forth, he may cheerfully do it, and heap up coals of fire upon the head of the adversary of God. Likewise where any suffer for the truth by them who are in the untruth, if any Friends be moved of the Lord to go to the magistrate, judge, general, or protector, and offer up themselves to lay down their lives for the brethren; as Christ hath laid down his life for you, so lay down your lives one for another. Here you may go over the heads of the persecutors, and reach the witness of God in all. And this shall rest a judgment upon them all for ever, and be witnessed to by that which is of God in their consciences. Given forth from the Spirit of the Lord through   G. F."

Besides this, I wrote also a short epistle to Friends, as an encouragement to them in their several exercises; which was as follows :—

"MY DEAR FRIENDS,

"In the power of the everlasting God, which comprehends the power of darkness, and all temptation, and that which comes out of it, in this power of God dwell. It will bring and keep you to the Word in the beginning; it will keep you up to the life, to feed thereupon, in which you are over the power of darkness, and in which you will find and feel dominion and life. And that will let you see, before the tempter was, and over him; and into that the tempter cannot come; for the power and truth he is out of. Therefore in that life dwell, in which you will know dominion; and let your faith be in the power, and over the weakness and temptations, and look not at them: but in the light and power of God look at the Lord's strength, which will be made perfect in your weakest state. In all temptations look at the grace of God to bring your salvation, which is your teacher to teach you: for when you look or hearken to the temptations, you go from your teacher, the grace of God; and so are darkened in going from that teacher, the grace of God, which is sufficient in all temptations, to lead out of them, and to keep over them."   G. F.

CHAPTER IX.

1655-1656.—Friends slandered by Presbyterians and Independents, suffer much from them and the Baptists for refusing to pay tithes—the priests hunt after a fallen benefice like crows after carrion—great miracles wrought through several —an Independent preacher convinced, but relapses—address to the convinced in Ireland—a sick woman at Baldock restored—George Fox parts and reconciles two furious combatants—to the seven parishes at the Land's End, recommending attention to the Inward Light—George Fox parts with James Naylor, and has a presentiment of his fall—Major Ceely places George Fox and Edward Pyot under arrest—they are sent to Launceston jail—put into Doomsdale, and suffer a long and cruel imprisonment—a paper against swearing—Peter Ceely's mittimus— George Fox has great service in jail—many are convinced, and opposers are confounded—experiences some remarkable preservations—Edward Pyot writes an excellent letter to Judge Glynne on the liberty of the subject, and on the injustice and illegality of their imprisonment—Truth spreads in the west by the very means taken to prevent it—exhortation and warning to magistrates—answer to the Exeter general warrant for taking up and imprisoning Friends—exhortation to Friends in the ministry—warning to priests and professors—cruel jailer imprisoned in Doomsdale, and further judgments upon him follow—a Friend offers to lie in prison instead of George Fox—Edward Pyot to Major-General Desborough, in answer to his conditional offer of liberty—George Fox to the same—he and his Friends are soon after liberated.

AFTER clearing myself of those services for the Lord, which lay upon me in London, I passed into Bedfordshire and Northamptonshire. At WELLINGBOROUGH, I had a great meeting, in which the Lord's everlasting power and truth was over all; and many in that country were turned to the Lord. Great rage was amongst the professors, for the wicked priests, Presbyterians, and Independents, falsely reported "that we carried bottles about with us, which we gave people to drink of; which made them follow us:" but the Power, and Spirit, and Truth of God kept Friends over the rage of the people. Great spoiling also there was of Friends' goods for tithes, by the Independent and Presbyterian priests, and some Baptist priests, that had got into the steeple-houses.

From Wellingborough I went into Leicestershire, where Colonel Hacker had threatened, that if I came there he would imprison me again, though the Protector had set me at liberty: but when I was come to WHETSTONE (the meeting from which he took me before) all was quiet there. Colonel Hacker's wife, and his marshal came to the meeting, and were convinced: for the glorious powerful day of the Lord was exalted over all, and many were convinced that day. There were at that meeting two justices of the peace, that came out of Wales, whose names were Peter Price and Walter Jenkin; who came both to be ministers of Christ.

I went from thence to SILEBY, to William Smith's, where was a great meeting, to which several Baptists came; one of them, a Baptist teacher, was convinced, and came to sit under the Lord's teaching by his Spirit and power. This Baptist said, he had baptized thirty in a day.

From thence I went to DRAYTON, my native town, where so many priests and professors had formerly gathered together against me; but now not a priest or professor appeared. I asked some of my relations where all the priests and professors were? They said, the priest of Nun-Eaton was dead, and eight or nine of them were seeking to get his benefice. "They will let you alone now," said they, "for they are like a company of crows, when a sheep is dead, they all gather together to pull out the puddings; so do the priests for a fallen benefice." These were some of their own hearers that said so of them; but they had spent their venom against me, and the Lord delivered me by his power out of their snares.

Then I went to BADGLEY, where was a great meeting. Many came far to it; and were convinced and turned to the Lord; who came under Christ's teaching, and were settled upon him, their foundation and their rock.

From thence I passed into NOTTINGHAMSHIRE, and had large meetings there; and into DERBYSHIRE, where the Lord's power came over all; and many were turned from darkness to light, and from the power of Satan unto God, and came to receive the Holy Ghost. Great miracles were wrought in many places by the power of the Lord through several.

In Derbyshire James Naylor met me, and told me, seven or eight priests had challenged him to a dispute. I had a travail in my spirit for him, and the Lord answered me, and I was moved to bid him go on, and God Almighty would be with him, and give him the victory in his power. And the Lord did so; insomuch that the people saw the priests were foiled, and they cried, "a Nailer, a Nailer hath confuted them all." After the dispute, he came to me again, praising the Lord. Thus was the Lord's day proclaimed and set over all their heads, and people began to see the apostacy and slavery they had been under to their hireling teachers for means; and they came to know their teacher, the Lord Jesus, who had purchased them, and made their peace between God and them. While we were here, Friends came out of Yorkshire to see us, and were glad of the prosperity of truth.

After this I passed into Warwickshire, through Friends, visiting their meetings; and so into Worcestershire. I had a meeting at BIRMINGHAM, as I went, where several were convinced and turned to the Lord. At length I came to one Cole's house in Worcestershire, near CHATTAN. This Cole had given an Independent preacher a meeting-place, and the Independent came to be convinced, and after he was convinced he laid aside his preaching; whereupon the old man —— Cole gave him a hundred pounds a-year. I had a meeting there, and a very great one it was, inasmuch that the meeting-place would not hold the people: and many were turned to the Lord that day. Afterwards, when the time of trials came, this Independent did not stand to that which had convinced him, but turned back, whereupon the old man took away his hundred pounds a-year from him again. But Cole himself died in God's truth.

I heard that at Evesham the magistrates had cast several Friends into prison; and that, hearing of my coming, they made a pair of high stocks. I sent for Edward Pittaway, a Friend that lived near Evesham, and asked him the truth of the thing; and he said it was so. I went that night with him to EVESHAM, and in the evening we had a large, precious meeting, wherein Friends and people were refreshed with the word of life, and with the power of the Lord. Next morning I rode to one of the prisons, and visited Friends there, and encouraged them. Then I rode to the other prison, where there were several prisoners; and amongst them was Humphrey Smith,* who had been a priest, but was now become a free minister of Christ. When I had visited the Friends at both prisons, and was turned away from the prison to go out of town, I espied the magistrates coming to seize me. But the Lord frustrated their intent, the innocent escaped their snare, and God's blessed power came over them all. But exceedingly rude and envious were the priests and professors about this time in those parts.

I went from Evesham to WORCESTER, and had a precious meeting there, and quiet. But after it, as we came down the street towards our inn, some of the professors fell to discourse with Friends, and were like to have made a tumult in the city. As we went into the inn, they all cluttered into the yard; but I went among them, and got them quieted. Next day I walked into the town, and had much discourse with some of the professors, concerning Christ and the way of truth. One of them denied that Christ was of Abraham, according to the flesh, and that he was declared to be the Son of God, according to the Spirit; but I proved from Rom. i. that he was of the seed of Abraham, being made of the seed of David according to the flesh; and that according to the Spirit he was declared to be the Son of God. Afterwards I wrote a paper concerning it.

From Worcester we went to TEWKESBURY, where in the evening we had a great meeting; to which came the priest of the town with a great rabble of rude people. He boasted, that he would see whether he or I should have the victory. "I turned the people to the divine light, which Christ, the heavenly and spiritual man, enlighteneth them withal; that with that light they might see their sins, and that they were in death and darkness, and without God in the world; and that with the same light they might also see Christ from whom it comes, their Saviour and Redeemer, who shed his blood and died for them, and who is the way to God, the truth, and the life." Here the priest began to rage against the Light, and denied it; for neither priest nor professor could endure to hear the Light

---

* Humphrey Smith became an able gospel minister, turning many to righteousness. He had a vision of the destruction of London by fire, six years before it happened, which vision he made known as a warning to the people to repent. (See *Piety Promoted*, vol. i. p. 39 and his published works). He had also a clear foresight of his own sufferings and death thereby. He died a prisoner for the testimony of Jesus in Winchester jail, in 1663, where he fell ill after a year's imprisonment. Whilst he was very ill in prison, he said, "My heart is filled with the power of God;" and then added, "It is good for a man at such a time as this, to have the Lord to be his friend." Near his departure, he prayed earnestly, saying, "Hear me, O Lord, uphold and preserve me. I know that my Redeemer liveth: Thou art strong and mighty, O Lord;" and prayed, "that the Lord would deliver his people from their cruel oppressors;" and for those who had been convinced by him, "that the Lord would be their teacher."

spoken of. So the priest having railed at the Light went away, and left his rude company amongst us; but the Lord's power came over them, though mischief was in their hearts.

Leaving Tewkesbury, we came to WARWICK, where in the evening we had a meeting at a widow's house, with many sober people. A precious meeting we had in the Lord's power, and several were convinced and turned to the Lord. After it, as I was walking out, a Baptist in the company began to jangle; and the bailiff of the town with his officers came in, and said, "What do these people here at this time of night?" So he secured John Crook, Amor Stoddart, Gerrard Roberts,* and myself, but we had leave to go to our inn, and to be forth-coming in the morning. Next morning many rude people came to the inn and into our chambers, desperate fellows; but the Lord's power gave us dominion over them. Gerrard Roberts and John Crook went up to the bailiff to speak with him, and to know what he had to say to us. He said we might go our ways, for he had little to say to us. As we rode out of town, it lay upon me to ride to his house to let him know, "that the Protector having given forth an instrument of government, in which liberty of conscience was granted, it was very strange that, contrary to that instrument of government, he would trouble peaceable people that feared God." The Friends went with me, but the rude people gathered about us with stones; and one of them took hold of my horse's bridle and broke it; but the horse drawing back threw him under him. Though the bailiff saw this, yet he did not stop, nor so much as rebuke the rude multitude, so that it was much we were not slain or hurt in the streets; for the people threw stones, and struck at us, as we rode along the town.

When we were quite out of the town, I told Friends, "it was upon me from the Lord, that I must go back into it again; and if any one of them felt any thing upon him from the Lord, he might follow me, and the rest that did not, might go on to Dun-Cow." So I passed up through the market in the dreadful power of God, declaring the word of life to them, and John Crook followed me. Some struck at me; but the Lord's power was over them, and gave me dominion over all. I showed them their unworthiness of the name of Christians, and the unworthiness of their teachers who had not brought them into more sobriety; and what a shame they were to Christianity!

Having cleared myself, I turned back out of the town again, and passed to COVENTRY; where we found the people closed up with darkness. I went to a professor's house that I had formerly been at, and he was drunk, which grieved my soul so, that I did not go into any house in the town; but rode into some of the streets, and into the market-place. I felt the power of the Lord God was over the town.

Then I went on to DUN-COW, and had a meeting there in the evening, and some were turned to the Lord by his Spirit, as also at Warwick

---

* Gerrard Roberts, a merchant of London, was one of the most active members of the Society in making the needful arrangements for the visits of its ministers to foreign parts.

and Tewkesbury. We lay at Dun-Cow that night, and there we met with John Camm, a faithful minister of the everlasting gospel. In the morning there gathered a rude company of priests and people, who behaved more like beasts than men; for some of them came riding on horseback into the room where we were; but the Lord gave us dominion over them.

From thence we passed into LEICESTERSHIRE, where we had a great meeting at the place where I had been taken formerly; and after that we came to BADGLEY in Warwickshire. Here William Edmundson,* a Friend who lived in Ireland, having some drawings upon his spirit to come over

---

* William Edmundson was the first person who publicly espoused the principles of Friends in Ireland. He was some time a soldier in Cromwell's army, but the strivings of the Holy Spirit drew him out of the corruptions of the world, to a nearer acquaintance with God. He left the army, and joined the people called Quakers, though they were much spoken against. His life and property were given up to the service of the gospel, and many were his trials and sufferings on its account, which he bore with exemplary patience. During the civil wars, he had on one occasion twenty of his cows driven away from him. His house was also beset by some hundreds of banditti, and the shots they fired into the house were heard at two miles' distance. After it was plundered and burned, himself and two sons were led away prisoners, bareheaded, and barefooted, and nearly naked, except they gave William Edmundson an old blanket of his own to wrap about him.

After a toilsome night, journeying through bushes, rough stones, mire, and water knee-deep, they were taken to a wood, and, after a mock show of justice, condemned to death; the young men to be hanged, and their father, in compliment to his courage, to be shot. Though death was no terror to this pious man, he expostulated with his persecutors; reminding them of his services in behalf of their countryfolk. Several of them confessed they knew him to be an honest man; yet justice and mercy were disregarded, and they prepared to execute their purpose. The youths were hoodwinked, in order to hang them; and two firelocks made ready to shoot their father, whom they were about to hoodwink also; but he told them they need not, for he could look them in the face, and was not afraid to die.

At this juncture arrived a lieutenant, a brother of one whose life William Edmundson had saved, when the English soldiers were about to hang him. Thus the Lord interposed, and would not suffer them to take their lives. The officer released the prisoners from death, but did not restore them to liberty, taking them to Athlone, not from a grateful sense of remembered services, but from a hope of preferment thereby. On entering the town, the high sheriff, soldiers, and rabble, gave them abusive language; and their lives were endangered, had not a lieutenant of the Irish army who recognized William Edmundson, declared aloud his knowledge of him, and of his worth, and thus quieted the tumult. They were then brought to the Irish colonel, before whom he appeared, wrapped in his blanket. Though the colonel was personally acquainted with him, he did not, in these circumstances, know him; but when he said, I am old William Edmundson, the colonel rose, and with tears in his eyes, expressed his sorrow to see him in that condition. After reprimanding the lieutenant, he committed them to the care of one of his captains, sent them food and money, and they met with better treatment.

Great sufferings was it the lot of this faithful man to endure; who was unwearied in his Master's service for upwards of fifty years of his life, counting nothing too near or dear to part with, or too great to suffer, if he could but win Christ and the souls of his fellow-men. Yet in these and many other great exercises and straits, the Lord's arm and generous providence, says he, have preserved and supported me. He spared not himself, even to old age, in performing travels and services as a gospel minister, beyond the ordinary course of nature, often saying the Lord was his song and his strength, and had carried him through many and various exercises and perils. As a

into England to see me, met with me; by whom I wrote to the few Friends then convinced in the north of Ireland, as follows :—

"FRIENDS,

"In that which convinced you, wait; that you may have that removed you are convinced of. And all my dear Friends, dwell in the life, and love, and power, and wisdom of God, in unity one with another, and with God; and the peace and wisdom of God fill all your hearts, that nothing may rule in you but the life, which stands in the Lord God."   G. F.

When these few lines were read amongst the Friends in Ireland at their meeting, the power of the Lord came upon all in the room.

From Badgley we passed to SWANNINGTON and HIGHAM, and so into Northamptonshire and Bedfordshire, having great meetings; and many were turned to the Lord by his power and Spirit. When we came to BALDOCK in Hertfordshire, I asked, if there was nothing in that town, no profession; and it was answered me, there were some Baptists and a Baptist woman sick. John Rush of Bedfordshire went with me to visit her. When we came in, there were many tender people about her. They told me she was not a woman for this world, but if I had any thing to comfort her concerning the world to come, I might speak to her. I was moved of the Lord God to speak to her; and the Lord raised her up again to the astonishment of the town and country. This Baptist woman and her husband, whose name was Baldock, came to be convinced, and many hundreds of people have met at their house since. Great meetings and convincements were in those parts afterwards; many received the word of life, and sat down under the teaching of Christ, their Saviour.

When we had visited this sick woman, we returned to our inn, where were two desperate fellows fighting so furiously, that none durst come nigh to part them. But I was moved, in the Lord's power, to go to them; and when I had loosed their hands, I held one of them by one hand, and the other by the other, showed them the evil of their doings, and reconciled them one to the other, and they were so loving and thankful to me, that people admired at it.*

fixed star in the firmament of God's power did he continue to hold his integrity to the last, being enabled to say, "O death! where is thy sting? O grave! where is thy victory?"

* The circumstance above related is reminding of a somewhat similar one recorded of Edward Burrough.

"At London," says Sewell the historian, "there is a custom in summer-time, when the evening approaches, and tradesmen leave off working, that many lusty fellows meet in the fields, to try their skill and strength in wrestling, where generally a multitude of people stand gazing in a ring.

"Now it so fell out, that Edward Burrough passed by the place where they were wrestling, and standing still among the spectators, saw how a strong and dexterous fellow had already thrown three others, and was waiting for a fourth champion, if any durst venture to enter the lists. At length, none being bold enough to try, Edward Burrough stepped into the ring, which was commonly made up of all sorts of people; and having looked upon the wrestler with a serious countenance, the man was not a little surprised, instead of an airy antagonist, to meet with a grave and awful young man; and all stood amazed as it were at this sight, eagerly expecting what would be

From thence I passed to Market-Street, where God had a people, and through Alban's to London, where Friends were glad of the prosperity of truth, and the manifestation of the Lord's glorious power which had delivered us, and carried us through many dangers and difficulties. I also rejoiced to find truth prosper in the city, and all things well amongst Friends there. Only there was one John Toldervey, who had been convinced of truth, and run out from it, and the envious priests took occasion from thence to write a wicked book against Friends, which they stuffed with many lies, to render truth and Friends odious. They entitled their book, "The Foot out of the Snare." But this poor man came to see his folly and returned, condemned his backsliding, answered the priest's book, and exposed all their lies and wickedness. Thus the Lord's power came over them, and his everlasting Seed reigned, and reigns to this day.

Now after I had tarried some time in London, and had visited Friends in their meetings, I went out of town, leaving James Naylor in the city. As I passed from him I cast my eyes upon him, and a fear struck me concerning him; but I went away, and rode down to Ryegate in Surrey, where I had a little meeting. There the Friends told me of one Thomas Moore, a justice of peace, that lived not far from Ryegate, a friendly, moderate man; I went to visit him at his house, and he came to be a serviceable man in truth.

We passed on to Thomas Patchings', of Binscombe in Godalming, where we had a meeting, to which several Friends came from London, and John Bolton and his wife came on foot in frost and snow. After this we went towards Horsham-Park; and having visited Friends, passed on to Arundel and Chichester, where we had meetings. At Chichester many professors came in, and made some jangling, but the Lord's power was over them. The woman of the house where the meeting was, though convinced of truth, yet not keeping her mind close to that which convinced her, fell in love with a man of the world, who was there that time. When I knew it, I took her aside, and was moved to speak to her, and to pray for her; but a light thing got up in her mind, and she slighted it. Afterwards she married the man, and soon after went distracted; for he was greatly in debt, and she greatly disappointed. Then was I sent for to her, and the

the issue of this combat. But it was quite another fight Edward Burrough aimed at. For having already fought against spiritual wickedness, that had once prevailed over him, and having overcome in measure, by the grace of God, he now endeavoured also to fight against it in others, and to turn them from the evil of their ways. With this intention, he began very seriously to speak to the bystanders, and that with such a heart-piercing power, that he was heard by the mixed multitude, with no less attention than admiration; for his speech tended to turn them from darkness to the light, and from the power of Satan unto God. To effect this, he laboured with convincing words, showing how God had not left himself without a witness, but had given to man a measure of his grace, and enlightened every one with the light of Christ.

"Thus zealously he preached; and though many might look upon this as a novelty, yet it was of such effect, that some were convinced of the truth; for Burrough was a breaker of stony hearts, and therefore by a certain author not unjustly called 'a son of thunder;' though he omitted not in due season to speak a word of consolation to those that were of a broken heart, and of a contrite spirit."

Lord was entreated, raised her up again, and settled her mind by his power. Afterwards her husband died; and she acknowledged the just judgments of God were come upon her, for slighting the exhortation and counsel I had given her.

After we left Chichester, we travelled to PORTSMOUTH. There the soldiers had us to the governor's house. After some examination, the Lord's power came over them, and we were set at liberty, and had a meeting in the town. After which we came to RINGWOOD, where in the evening we had a meeting, at which several were convinced, and turned to the Spirit of the Lord, and to the teaching of Christ Jesus, their Saviour.

From Ringwood we came to POOLE; and having set up our horses at an inn, we sent into the town to inquire for such as feared the Lord, and such as were worthy; and had a meeting with several sober people. William Baily, a Baptist teacher, was convinced there at that time.* The people received the truth in the inward parts, and were turned to the Lord Jesus Christ, their rock and foundation, their teacher and Saviour; and there is become a great gathering in the name of Jesus of a very tender people, who continue under Christ's teaching.

We went also to SOUTHAMPTON and had a meeting; several were convinced there also. Edward Pyot of Bristol travelled with me all this western journey.

From thence we went to DORCHESTER, and alighted at an inn, a Baptist's house; we sent into the town to the Baptists, to let us have their meeting-house to meet in, and to invite the sober people to the meeting; but they denied it us. We sent to them again, to know why they would deny us their meeting-house; so the thing was noised in the town. Then we sent them word, if they would not let us come to their house, they, or any people that feared God, might come to our inn, if they pleased. They were in a great rage; and their teacher and many of them came up, and slapped their Bibles on the table. I asked them, why they were so angry; were they angry with the Bible? But they fell into a discourse about their water-baptism. I asked them, whether they could say, they were sent of God to baptize people, as John was; and whether they had the same Spirit and power that the apostles had? They said, they had

---

* William Baily (or Bayley) whose writings were published in one volume, 4to, in 1676, and of whom there is a brief account in *Piety Promoted*, vol. i. p. 83, is stated to have been "mighty in the Scriptures," and not only a believer and preacher of the word of faith, but a sufferer for the same. On one occasion, he was thrown down and dragged upon the ground by the hair of his head, his persecutors endeavouring to rend and break asunder his jaws, so that the ground whereon he lay was besmeared with his blood. As if this butchering had not been enough to make him a sacrifice, a heavy man stamped on his breast with his feet, endeavouring to beat the breath out of his body. When this persecutor had done his pleasure, he told the jailer to take him away and put him in some nasty hole, for his entertainment and cure.

William Bailey, being master of a ship, often crossed the mighty waters for the maintenance of his family, and many beyond the seas were comforted by his ministry. He was taken ill at sea on his return from visiting Friends in Barbadoes, and died on board the *Samuel* of London, in latitude 46° 36′ N. He died in great peace, as if he had fallen asleep, exhorting those around him to fear God.

not. Then I asked them, how many powers there are; whether there are
any more than the power of God, and the power of the devil? They said,
there was not any other power than those two. Then said I, "if you have
not the power of God that the apostles had, then you act by the power of the
devil." Many sober people were present, who said, "they have thrown
themselves on their backs." Many substantial people were convinced that
night; a precious service we had there for the Lord, and his power came
over all. Next morning, as we were passing away, the Baptists, being in
a rage, began to shake the dust off their feet after us. "What," said I,
"in the power of darkness! We, who are in the power of God, shake off
the dust of our feet against you."

Leaving Dorchester, we came to WEYMOUTH; where also we enquired
after the sober people; and about four score of them gathered together at a
priest's house. Most of them received the word of life, and were turned
to their teacher Christ Jesus, who had enlightened them with his divine
light, by which they might see their sins, and him who saveth from sin.
A blessed meeting we had with them of several hours, and they received the
truth in the love of it, with gladness of heart. The state of their teachers
and the apostacy was opened to them; and the state of the apostles, and
of the church in their days; and the state of the law, and of the prophets
before Christ, and how Christ came to fulfil them; how he was their
teacher in the apostles' days, and how he was come now to teach his
people himself by his power and Spirit. All was quiet, the meeting broke
up peaceably, and the people were very loving; and a meeting is continued
in that town to this day. Many are added to them; and some that had
been Ranters came to own the truth, and to live very soberly.

There was a captain of horse in the town, who sent to me, and would
fain have had me to stay longer; but I was not to stay. He and his man
rode out of town with me about seven miles, Edward Pyot also being with
me. This captain was the fattest, merriest man, the most cheerful, and
the most given to laughter, that ever I met with; insomuch that I was
several times moved to speak in the dreadful power of the Lord to him;
and yet it was become so customary to him, that he would presently laugh
at any thing he saw. But I still admonished him to come to sobriety,
sincerity, and the fear of the Lord. We staid at an inn that night; and
in the morning I was moved to speak to him again, when he parted from
us. Next time I saw him, he told me, that when I spoke to him at
parting, the power of the Lord so struck him, that before he got home
he was serious enough, and had discontinued his laughing. He afterwards was convinced, and became a serious and good man, and died in
the truth.

Parting from him we went to HONITON; and at our inn inquired what
people there were in the town that feared God, and sent for them. There
came to us some of the Particular Baptists, with whom we had much
reasoning. I told them, "they held their doctrine of particular election in
Esau's, Cain's, and Ishmael's nature; not in Jacob, the second birth; but
they must be born again, before they could enter the kingdom of God.
And that as the promise of God was to the Seed, not as many, but as one,

which is Christ; so the election stands *in Christ;* and they must be such as walk in his light, grace, Spirit, and truth."

From thence we passed to TOPSHAM, and stayed over the First-day; but the innkeeper and his people were rude. Next morning we gave forth some queries to the priests and professors; whereupon some rude professors came into our inn; and had we not gone when we did, they would have stopped us. I wore a girdle, which through forgetfulness I left behind me at the inn, and afterwards sent to the innkeeper for, but he would not let me have it again. Afterwards, when he was tormented in his mind about it, he took it and burnt it, lest he should be bewitched by it, as he said; yet when he had burnt it, he was more tormented than before. Some, notwithstanding the rudeness of the place, were convinced; and a meeting was afterwards settled in that town, which has continued ever since.

After this we passed to TOTNESS, a dark town. We lodged at an inn, and at night Edward Pyot was sick, but the Lord's power healed him, so that next day we got to KINGSBRIDGE, and at our inn inquired for the sober people of the town. They directed us to Nicholas Tripe and his wife, and we went to their house. They sent for the priest, with whom we had some discourse; but he being confounded, quickly left us. Nicholas Tripe and his wife were convinced; and there is since a good meeting of Friends in that country. In the evening we returned to our inn; and there being many people drinking in the house, I was moved of the Lord to go amongst them, and to direct them to the light, which Christ, the heavenly Man, had enlightened them withal; by which they might see all their evil ways, words, and deeds, and by the same light they might also see Jesus Christ their Saviour. The innkeeper stood uneasy, seeing it hindered his guests from drinking; and as soon as the last words were out of my mouth, he snatched up the candle, and said, "Come, here is a light for you to go into your chamber." Next morning, when he was cool, I represented to him "what an uncivil thing it was for him to do so;" then warning him of the day of the Lord, we got ready and passed away.

We came next day to PLYMOUTH, and after having refreshed ourselves at our inn, we went to Robert Cary's house, where we had a very precious meeting. At this meeting was one Elizabeth Trelawny, daughter to a baronet; she being somewhat dull of hearing came close to me, and placed her ear very near me while I spoke; and she was convinced. After the meeting some jangling Baptists came in, but the Lord's power came over them, and Elizabeth Trelawny gave testimony thereto. A fine meeting was settled there in the Lord's power, which has continued ever since; where many faithful Friends have been convinced.

From thence we passed into CORNWALL, and came to an inn in the parish of MENHENIOT. At night we had a meeting at Edward Hancock's house, to which came one Thomas Mounce, and a priest, with many people. We made the priest confess he was a minister made and maintained by the state; and he was confounded and went his way; but many of the people stayed. I directed them to the "light of Christ, by which they might see their sins, and their Saviour Christ Jesus, the way to God, and their Mediator to make peace between God and them; their Shepherd to feed them, and their Prophet to teach them. I directed them also to the Spirit of God *in* themselves, by which they might know the Scriptures, and be led into all truth; by which they might know God, and in it have unity one with another." Many were convinced at that time, and came under Christ's teaching, and there are fine gatherings in the name of Jesus in those parts at this day.

We travelled thence through PENRYN to HELSTON; but could not obtain knowledge of any sober people, through the badness of the inn-keepers. At length we came to a village where some Baptists and sober people lived, with whom we had some discourse; and some of them were brought to confess, that they stumbled at the light of Christ. They would have had us to stay with them, but we passed thence to MARKET-JEW; and having taken up our lodging at an inn, we went out over-night to inquire for such as feared the Lord. Next morning the mayor and aldermen gathered together, with the high-sheriff of the county; and they sent first the constables to bid us come before them. We asked them for their warrant, and they saying they had none, we told them we should not go along with them without. Upon the return of the constables without us, they sent their serjeants, and we asked them for their warrant. They said, they had none; but they told us, the mayor and aldermen stayed for us. We told them, the mayor and his company did not well to trouble us in our inn, and we should not go with them without a warrant. So they went away and came again; and when we asked them for their warrant, one of them pulled his mace from under his cloak; we asked them whether this was their custom to molest and trouble strangers in their inns and lodgings? After some time Edward Pyot went to the mayor and aldermen, and had much discourse with them; but the Lord's power gave him dominion over them all. When he returned, several of the officers came to us, and we laid before them the incivility and unworthiness of their conduct towards us, who were the servants of the Lord God, thus to stop and trouble us in our lodgings; and what an unchristian act it was. Before we left the town I wrote a paper, to be sent to the seven parishes at the Land's End. A copy of which follows:—

"THE mighty day of the Lord is come, and coming, wherein all hearts shall be made manifest, and the secrets of every one's heart shall be revealed by the light of Jesus, who lighteth every man that cometh into the world, that all men through him might believe, and that the world might have life through him, who saith, 'Learn of me,' and of whom God saith, 'This is my beloved Son, hear ye him.' Christ is come to teach his people himself; and every one that will not hear this Prophet, which God hath raised up, and which Moses spoke of, when he said, 'Like unto me will God raise you up a Prophet, him shall you hear;' every one (I say) that will not hear this Prophet, is to be cut off. They that despised Moses's law, died under the hand of two or three witnesses; but how much greater punishment will come upon them that neglect this great salvation, Christ Jesus, who saith, 'Learn of me: I am the way, the truth, and the life;' who lighteth every man that cometh into the world; and by his light lets him see his evil ways

and his evil deeds. But if you hate this light, and go on in evil, this light will be your condemnation. Therefore, now ye have time, prize it; for this is the day of your visitation, and salvation offered to you. Every one of you hath a light from Christ, which lets you see you should not lie, nor do wrong to any, nor swear, nor curse, nor take God's name in vain, nor steal. It is the light that shows you these evil deeds; which if you love, and come unto it and follow it, will lead you to Christ, who is the way to the Father, from whom it comes; where no unrighteousness enters, nor ungodliness. If you hate this light, it will be your condemnation; but if you love it and come to it, you will come to Christ; and it will bring you off from all the world's teachers and ways, to learn of Christ, and will preserve you from the evils of the world, and all the deceivers in it." G. F.

This paper a Friend who was then with me had; and when we were gone three or four miles from Market-Jew towards the West, he meeting with a man upon the road, gave him a copy of the paper. This man proved to be a servant to one Peter Ceely, major in the army, and a justice of peace in that county; and he riding before us to a place called St. Ives, showed the paper to his master, Major Ceely. When we came to IVES, Edward Pyot's horse having cast a shoe, we stayed to have it set; and while he was getting his horse shod, I walked down to the sea-side. When I returned I found the town in an uproar; and they were haling Edward Pyot and the other Friend before Major Ceely. I followed them into the justice's house, though they did not lay hands upon me. When we came in, the house was full of rude people; whereupon I asked whether there were not an officer among them to keep the people civil? Major Ceely said, he was a magistrate. I told him, " he should show forth gravity and sobriety then, and use his authority to keep the people civil; for I never saw any people ruder: the Indians were more like Christians than they." After a while they brought forth the paper aforesaid, and asked whether I would own it? I said, Yes. Then he tendered the oath of abjuration to us; whereupon I put my hand in my pocket and drew forth the answer to it, which had been given to the Protector. After I had given him that, he examined us severally, one by one. He had with him a silly, young priest, who asked us many frivolous questions; and amongst the rest he desired to cut my hair, which then was pretty long; but I was not to cut it though many times many were offended at it. I told them, "I had no pride in it, and it was not of my own putting on." At length the justice put us under a guard of soldiers, who were hard and wild, like the justice himself; nevertheless " we warned the people of the day of the Lord, and declared the truth to them." The next day he sent us, guarded by a party of horse with swords and pistols, to REDRUTH. On First-day the soldiers would have taken us away; but we told them it was their Sabbath, and it was not usual to travel on that day. Several of the town's-people gathered about us, and whilst I held the soldiers in discourse, Edward Pyot spoke to the people; and afterwards he held the soldiers in discourse, whilst I spoke to the people; and in the mean time the other Friend got out the back way, and went to the steeple-house to speak to the priest and people. The people were exceedingly desperate, in a mighty rage against him, and abused him. The soldiers also missing him, were in a great rage, ready to kill us; but I declared the day of the Lord, and the word of eternal life to the people that gathered about us. In the afternoon the soldiers were resolved to have us away, so we took horse. When we were got to the town's-end, I was moved of the Lord to go back again, to speak to the old man of the house; the soldiers drew out their pistols, and swore I should not go back. I heeded them not, but rode back, and they rode after me. I cleared myself to the old man and the people, and then returned with them, and reproved them for being so rude and violent.

At night we were brought to a town called Smethick then, but since FALMOUTH. It being the evening of the First-day, there came to our inn the chief constable of the place, and many sober people, some of whom began to inquire concerning us. We told them we were prisoners for truth's sake; and much discourse we had with them concerning the things of God. They were very sober, and loving to us. Some were convinced, and stood faithful ever after.

After the constable and these people were gone, other people came in, who also were very civil, and went away very loving. When all were gone we went to our chamber to go to bed, and about eleven o'clock Edward Pyot said, "I will shut the door, it may be some may come to do us a mischief." Afterwards we understood that Captain Keat, who commanded the party, had purposed to do us some mischief that night; but the door being bolted, he missed his design. Next morning Captain Keat brought a kinsman of his, a rude, wicked man, and put him into the room, he himself standing without. This evil-minded man, walking huffing up and down the room, I bid him fear the Lord; whereupon he ran upon me, struck me with both his hands; and placing his leg behind me, would fain have thrown me down, but he could not, for I stood stiff and still, and let him strike. As I looked towards the door, I saw Captain Keat look on and see his kinsman thus beat and abuse me. Whereupon I said, "Keat, dost thou allow this?" and he said, he did; "Is this manly or civil," said I, "to have us under a guard and put a man to abuse and beat us? is this manly, civil, or christian?" I desired one of our friends to send for the constables, and they came. Then I desired the captain to let the constables see his warrant or order, by which he was to carry us; which he did; and his warrant was to conduct us safe to Captain Fox, governor of Pendennis Castle; and if the governer should not be at home, he was to convey us to Launceston jail. I told him, he had broken his order concerning us; for we, who were his prisoners, were to be safely conducted, but he had brought a man to beat and abuse us; so he having broken his order, I wished the constable to keep the warrant. Accordingly he did, and told the soldiers they might go, for he would take charge of the prisoners; and if it cost twenty shillings in charges to carry us up, they should not have the warrant again. I showed the soldiers the baseness of their carriage towards us; and they walked up and down the house, being pitifully blank and down. The constables went to the castle, and told the officers what they had done. The officers showed great dislike of Captain Keat's base carriage towards us; and told the constables that Major-General Desborough was coming to Bodmin, and that we should meet him; and it was likely he would free us. Meanwhile our old guard of soldiers came by way of entreaty to us, and promised that they would be civil to us, if we would go with them. Thus the morning was spent till it was about eleven o'clock; and then upon the soldiers' entreaty, and promise to be more civil, the constables gave them the order again, and we went with them. Great was the civility and courtesy of the constables and people of that town towards us, who kindly entertained us; and the Lord rewarded them with his truth; for many of them have since been convinced thereof, and are gathered into the name of Jesus, and sit under Christ, their teacher and Saviour.

Captain Keat, who commanded our guard, understanding that Captain Fox, who was the governor of Pendennis Castle, was gone to meet Major-General Desborough, did not take us thither; but went with us directly to Bodmin. We met Major-General Desborough on the way; the captain of his troop that rode before him, knew me, and said, "O, Mr. Fox, what do you here?" I replied, "I am a prisoner." "Alack," said he, "for what?" I told him, "I was taken up as I was travelling." "Then," said he, "I will speak to my lord, and he will set you at liberty." So he came from the head of his troop, rode up to the coach, and spoke to the major-general. We also told him how we were taken. He began to speak against the light of Christ, for which I reproved him; then he told the soldiers they might carry us to Launceston; for he could not stay to talk with us, lest his horses should take cold.

So to BODMIN we were conveyed that night; and when we were come to our inn, Captain Keat, who was in before us, put me into a room, and went his way. When I was come in, there stood a man with a naked rapier in his hand. Whereupon I turned out again, called for Captain Keat, and said unto him, "What now, Keat, what trick hast thou played now, to put me into a room where there is a man with his naked rapier? what is thy end in this?" "O," said he, "pray hold your tongue; for if you speak to this man we cannot all rule him, he is so devilish." "Then," said I, "Dost thou put me into a room where there is such a man with a naked rapier, that thou sayest, you cannot rule him? What an unworthy, base trick is this! and to put me singly into this room from the rest of my friends, that were my fellow-prisoners with me!" Thus his plot was discovered, and the mischief they intended was prevented. Afterwards we got another room, where we were together all night; and in the evening we declared the truth to the people; but they were hardened and dark people. The soldiers also, notwithstanding their fair promises, were very rude and wicked to us again, and sat up drinking and roaring all night.

Next day we were brought to LAUNCESTON, where Captain Keat delivered us to the jailer. Now was there no friend, nor friendly people near us; and the people of the town were dark and hardened. The jailer required us to pay seven shillings a-week for our horse-meat, and seven for our diet a-piece. But after some time, several sober people came to see us, and some of the town were convinced; and many friendly people, out of several parts of the country, came to visit us, and were convinced. Then arose a great rage among the professors and priests against us; and they said, this people Thou and Thee all men without respect, and they will not put off their hats, nor bow the knee to any man: this made them fret. But, said they, we shall see, when the assize comes, whether they will dare to Thou and Thee the judge, and keep on their hats before him. They expected we should be hanged at the assize. But all this was little to us; for we saw how God would stain the world's honour and glory, and were commanded not to seek that honour, nor give it; but we knew the honour that comes from God only, and sought that.

It was nine weeks from the time of our commitment to the assizes, to which abundance of people came from far and near to hear the trial of the Quakers. Captain Bradden lay with his troop of horse there, whose soldiers and the sheriff's men guarded us up to the court through the multitude of people that filled the streets; and much ado they had to get us through them. Besides, the doors and windows were filled with people looking out upon us. When we were brought into the court, we stood sometime with our hats on, and all was quiet; and I was moved to say, "Peace be amongst you!" Judge Glynne, a Welchman, then chief justice of England, said to the jailer, "what be these you have brought here into the court?" "Prisoners, my Lord," said he. "Why do you not put off your hats?" said the judge to us: we said nothing. "Put off your hats," said the judge again. Still we said nothing. Then said the judge, "The court commands you to put off your hats." Then I spoke, and said, "Where did ever any magistrate, king, or judge, from Moses to Daniel, command any to put off their hats, when they came before them in their courts, either amongst the Jews, the people of God, or amongst the heathens? and if the law of England doth command any such thing, show me that law either written or printed." Then the judge grew very angry, and said, "I do not carry my law-books on my back." "But," said I, "tell me where it is printed in any statute-book, that I may read it." Then said the judge, "Take him away, prevaricator! I'll *ferk* him." So they took us away, and put us among the thieves. Presently after he calls to the jailer, "Bring them up again." Come, said he, where had they hats from Moses to Daniel; come, answer me: I have you fast now," said he. I replied, "Thou mayest read in the third of Daniel, that the three children were cast into the fiery furnace by Nebuchadnezzar's command, with their coats, their hose, and their hats on." This plain instance stopped him: so that not having any thing else to say to the point, he cried again, "Take them away, jailer." Accordingly we were taken away, and thrust in among the thieves, where we were kept a great while; and then, without being called again, the sheriff's men and the troopers made way for us (but we were almost spent) to get through the crowd of people, and guarded us to the prison again, a multitude of people following us, with whom we had much discourse and reasoning at the jail. We had some good books to set forth our principles, and to inform people of the truth; which the judge and justices hearing of, they sent Captain Bradden for them, who came into the jail to us, and violently took our books from us, some out of Edward Pyot's hands, and carried them away; so we never got them again.

In the afternoon we were had up again into the court by the jailer and sheriff's men, and troopers, who had a mighty toil to get us through the crowd of people. When we were in the court, waiting to be called, I seeing both the jurymen, and such a multitude of others swearing, it grieved my life, that such as professed Christianity should so openly disobey and break the command of Christ and the apostle. And I was moved of the Lord to give forth a paper against swearing, which I had about me, to the grand and petty juries; which was as follows:—

"*Concerning Swearing.*

"TAKE heed of giving people oaths to swear: for Christ our Lord and Master saith, 'Swear not at all; but let your communications be yea yea, and nay nay; for whatsoever is more than these cometh of evil.' If any man was to suffer death, it must be by the hand of two or three witnesses; and the hands of the witnesses were to be first put upon him, to put him to death. And the apostle James saith, "My brethren, above all things swear not, neither by heaven, nor by earth, nor by any other oath, lest ye fall into condemnation.' Hence you may see, those that swear fall into condemnation, and are out of Christ's and the apostle's doctrine. Therefore, every one of you having a light from Christ, who saith, ' I am the light of the world,' and doth enlighten every man that cometh into the world; who also saith, 'Learn of me,' whose doctrine is, not to swear; and the apostle's doctrine is, not to swear; ' let your yea be yea, and your nay be nay, in all your communications; for whatsoever is more, cometh of evil.' Then, they that go into more than yea and nay, go into evil, and are out of the doctrine of Christ.

"Now if you say, 'that the oath was the end of controversy and strife,' they who are in strife, are out of Christ's doctrine; for he is the covenant of peace: and they who are in it, are in the covenant of peace. And the apostle brings that but as an example: as, men swearing by the greater; and the oath was the end of controversy and strife among men; and said, verily, men swear by the greater: but God could not find a greater, but swears by himself, concerning Christ; who, when he was come, taught not to swear at all. So such as are in him, and follow him, cannot but abide in his doctrine.

"If you say, 'they swore under the law, and under the prophets,' Christ is the end of the law, and of the prophets, to every one that believeth for righteousness' sake. Now mark; if you believe, ' I am the light of the world, which doth enlighten every man that cometh into the world,' saith Christ, by whom it was made; and every man of you that is come into the world is enlightened with a light that comes from Christ, by whom the world was made, that all of you through him might believe; that is the end for which he doth enlighten you. Now if you do believe in the light, as Christ commands, and saith, 'believe in the light, that you may be children of light,' you believe in Christ, and come to learn of him who is the way to the Father. This is the light which shows the evil actions you have all acted, the ungodly deeds you have committed, and all the ungodly speeches you have spoken; and all your oaths, cursed speaking, and ungodly actions.   Now if you attend to this light, it will let you see all that you have done contrary to it; and loving it, it will turn you from your evil deeds, evil actions, evil ways, evil words, to Christ, who is not of the world; who is the light which lighteth every man that cometh into the world;— who testifies against the world, that the deeds thereof are evil.   So doth the light in every man, that he hath received from him, testify against his works and deeds that are evil, that they are contrary to the light; and each shall give an account at the day of judgment for every idle word that is spoken.   This light shall bring every tongue to confess, yea, and every knee to bow at the name of Jesus; in which light, if you believe, you shall not come into condemnation, but come to Christ, who is not of the world; —to him by whom it was made; but if you believe not in the light, this, the light, is your condemnation, saith Christ."   G. F.

This paper passing among them from the jury to the justices, they presented it to the judge; so that when we were called before the judge, he bade the clerk give me that paper; and then asked me, " whether that seditious paper was mine;" I told him, " If they would read it up in open court, that I might hear it, if it was mine I would own it, and stand by it."   He would have had me to take it, and look upon it in my own hand; but " I again desired that it might be read, that all the country might hear it, and judge whether there was any sedition in it or not; for if there were I was willing to suffer for it."   At last the clerk of the assize read it with an audible voice, that all the people might hear it: and when he had done, I told them, " it was my paper; I would own it; and so might they too, except they would deny the Scripture: for was not this Scripture language, and the words and commands of Christ, and the apostle, which all true Christians ought to obey?" then they let fall that subject; and the judge fell upon us about our hats again, bidding the jailer take them off, which he did, and gave them to us; and we put them on again.   Then we asked the judge and the justices, what we had lain in prison for these nine weeks, seeing they now objected nothing to us but about our hats; and as for putting off our hats, I told them, that was the honour which God would lay in the dust, though they made so much to do about it; the honour which is of men, and which men seek one of another, and is the mark of unbelievers.   For " how can ye believe," saith Christ, " who receive honour one of another, and seek not the honour that cometh from God only?" and Christ saith, " I receive not honour from men;" and all true Christians should be of his mind.   Then the judge began to make a great speech, how he represented the lord Protector's person; who had made him lord chief justice of England, and sent him to come that circuit, &c.   We desired him then, that he would do us justice for our false imprisonment, which we had suffered nine weeks wrongfully.   But instead of that, they brought in an indictment, that they had framed against us; so strange a thing, and so full of lies, that I thought it had been against some of the thieves; that we came " by force and arms, and in a hostile manner into the court;" who were brought, as aforesaid.   I told them, " it was false:" and still we cried for justice for our false imprisonment, being taken up in our journey without cause by Major Ceely. Then Peter Ceely spoke to the judge, and said, "May it please you, my lord, this man (pointing to me, went aside with me, and told me how serviceable I might be for his design; that he could raise forty thousand men at an hour's warning, and involve the nation in blood, and so bring in King Charles. I would have aided him out of the country, but he would not go. If it please you, my lord, I have a witness to swear it." So he called upon his witness; but the judge not being forward to examine the witness, I desired that he would be pleased to let my mittimus be read in the face of the court and country, in which my crime was signified, for which I was sent to prison. The judge said, "it should not be read;" I said, "it ought to be, seeing it concerned my liberty and my life." The judge said again, "It shall not be read;" but I said, "it ought to be read; for if I have done anything worthy of death, or of bonds, let all the country know it." Then seeing they would not read it, I spoke to one of my fellow-prisoners, "Thou hast a copy of it, read it up," said I. "It shall not be read," said the judge; "Jailer," said he, "take him away, I will see whether he or I shall be master." So I was taken away; and a while after called for again. I still cried to have my mittimus read; for that signified the cause of my commitment: wherefore I again spoke to the friend, my fellow-prisoner, to read it. He did read it, and the judge, justices, and whole court were silent; for the people were eager to hear it. It was as follows:—

Peter Ceely, one of the Justices of the Peace of this County, to the Keeper of His Highness's Jail at Launceston, or his lawful Deputy in that behalf, Greeting :—

"I send you herewithal by the bearers hereof, the bodies of Edward Pyot of Bristol, and George Fox of Drayton-in-the-Clay, in Leicestershire, and William Salt of London, which they pretend to be the places of their habitations, who go under the notion of Quakers, and acknowledge themselves to be such; who have spread several papers, tending to the disturbance of the public peace, and cannot render any lawful cause of coming into these parts, being persons altogether unknown, and having no pass for their travelling up and down the country, and refusing to give sureties of their good behaviour, according to the law in that behalf provided; and refuse to take the oath of abjuration, &c. These are therefore, in the name of his Highness the lord Protector, to will and command you, that when the bodies of the said Edward Pyot, George Fox, and William Salt, shall be unto you brought, you them receive, and in his highness's prison aforesaid you safely keep them, until by due course of law they shall be delivered. Hereof fail you not, as you will answer the contrary at your perils. Given under my hand and seal, at St. Ives, the eighteenth day of January, 1655."

P. CEELY.

When it was read I spoke thus to the judge and justices: "Thou that sayest thou art chief justice of England, and you justices know, that if I had put in sureties, I might have gone whither I pleased; and have carried on the design (if I had had one), which Major Ceely hath charged

me with : and if I had spoken those words to him, which he hath here
declared, judge ye, whether bail or mainprize could have been taken in that
case." Then, turning my speech to Major Ceely, I said, "When or where
did I take thee aside? Was not thy house full of rude people, and thou
as rude as any of them at our examination : so that I asked for a constable
or some other officer, to keep the people civil? But if thou art my accuser,
why sittest thou on the bench? This is not a place for thee to sit in; for
accusers do not use to sit with the judge : thou oughtest to come down,
and stand by me, and look me in the face. Besides, I would ask the
judge and justices whether or not Major Ceely is not guilty of this treason,
which he charges against me, in concealing it so long as he hath done?
Does he understand his place either as a soldier or a justice of the peace?
For he tells you here, that I went aside with him, and told him what a
design I had in hand, and how serviceable he might be for my design : that
I could raise forty thousand men in an hour's time, and bring in King
Charles, and involve the nation in blood. He saith, moreover, he would
have aided me out of the country, but I would not go; and therefore he
committed me to prison for want of sureties for the good behaviour, as the
mittimus declares. Now do not you see plainly that Major Ceely is guilty
of this plot and treason that he talks of, and hath made himself a party to
it, by desiring me to go out of the country, and demanding bail of me, and
not charging me with this pretended treason till now, nor discovering it?
But I deny and abhor his words, and am innocent of his devilish design."
So that business was let fall : for the judge saw clearly enough, that instead
of ensnaring me, he had ensnared himself.

Major Ceely then got up again and said, "If it please you, my lord,
to hear me : this man struck me, and gave me such a blow, as I never had
in my life." At this I smiled in my heart, and said, "Major Ceely, thou
art a justice of peace, and a major of a troop of horse, and tells the judge
here in the face of the court and country, that I (who am a prisoner) struck
thee, and gave thee such a blow, as thou never hadst the like in thy life?
What! art thou not ashamed? Prithee, Major Ceely?" said I, "where
did I strike thee? and who is thy witness for that? who was by?" He
said it was in the Castle-Green, and that Captain Bradden was standing
by, when I struck him. "I desired the judge to let him produce his witness for that, and I called again upon Major Ceely to come down from off
the bench, telling him, it was not fit that the accuser should sit as judge
over the accused." When I called again for his witnesses, he said Captain
Bradden was his witness. Then, I said, "Speak, Captain Bradden, didst
thou see me give him such a blow, and strike him, as he saith?" Captain
Bradden made no answer; but bowed his head towards me. I desired him
to speak up, if he knew any such thing : but he only bowed his head again.
"Nay," said I, "speak up, and let the court and country hear, and let not
bowing of the head serve the turn. If I have done so, let the law be
inflicted on me; I fear not sufferings, nor death itself, for I am an innocent
man concerning all this charge." But Captain Bradden never testified to
it : and the judge finding those snares would not hold, cried, "Take him
away, jailer:" and then, when we were taken away, he fined us twenty

marks a-piece for not putting off our hats; and to be kept in prison till we paid it: so he sent us back to the jail.

At night Captain Bradden came to see us, and seven or eight justices with him, who were very civil to us, and told us, they believed neither the judge nor any in the court gave credit to the charges which Major Ceely had brought forward against me in the face of the country. And Captain Bradden said, Major Ceely had an intent to take away my life if he could have got another witness. "But," said I, "Captain Bradden, why didst not thou witness for me, or against me, seeing Major Ceely produced thee for a witness, that thou saw me strike him?' and when I desired thee to speak either for me or against me, according to what thou saw or knew, thou wouldst not speak." "Why," said he, "when Major Ceely and I came by you, as you were walking in the Castle-Green, he put off his hat to you, and said, ' How do you do, Mr. Fox? Your servant, Sir.' Then you said to him, 'Major Ceely, take heed of hypocrisy, and of a rotten heart: for when came I to be thy master, and thou my servant? Do servants cast their masters into prison?' This was the great blow he meant you gave him." Then I called to mind that they walked by us, and that he spoke so to me, and I to him; which hypocrisy and rotten-heartedness he manifested openly, when he complained of this to the judge in open court, and in the face of the country; and would have made them all believe, that I struck him outwardly with my hand.

Now we were kept in prison, and many came from far and near, to see us; of whom some were people of account in the world; for the report of our trial was spread abroad, and our boldness and innocency in our answers to the judge and court were talked of in town and country. Among others came Humphrey Lower to visit us, a grave, sober, old man, who had been a justice of peace; he was very sorry we should lie in prison; telling us how serviceable we might be if we were at liberty. We reasoned with him concerning swearing; and having acquainted him how they tendered the oath of abjuration to us, as a snare, because they knew we could not swear, we showed him that no people could be serviceable to God, if they disobeyed the command of Christ; and that they that imprisoned us for the hat-honour, which was of men, and which men sought for, prisoned the good, and vexed and grieved the Spirit of God in themselves, which should have turned their minds to God. So we directed him to the Spirit of God in his heart, and to the light of Christ Jesus; and he was thoroughly convinced, and continued so to his death, and became very serviceable to us.*

* Humphrey Lower, who resided near Bodmin, in Cornwall, was an influential magistrate, his name appearing as such in the history of the county, under Charles I. He could, however, say with Paul, "What things were gain unto me, those I counted loss for Christ." In 1658, for not attending the national worship, and refusing to enter into bond to appear at the assizes, on a presentment made against him by the constable of the parish, H. Lower was, on his non-appearance, committed, notwithstanding his age and high character, to Launceston jail, where he continued till the assizes; and then was put forth without examination or trial, or any satisfaction for such rough treatment. In 1660, he was sent for by a warrant, to appear before two justices at Wadebridge, when one of them, Rosearrock, tendered him the oath of su-

There came also to see us one Colonel Rouse, a justice of peace, with a great company with him. He was as full of words and talk as ever I heard any man in my life, so that there was no speaking to him. At length I asked him, "whether he had ever been at school, and knew what belonged to questions and answers;" (this I said to stop him). "At school!" said he, "Yes." "At school!" said the soldiers; "doth he say so to our colonel, that is a scholar?" Then said I, "If he be so, let him be still, and receive answers to what he hath said." Then I was moved to speak the word of life to him in God's dreadful power; which came so over him that he could not open his mouth: his face swelled and was red like a turkey; his lips moved, and he mumbled something; but the people thought he would have fallen down. I stepped to him, and he said he was never so in his life before: for the Lord's power stopped the evil power in him; so that he was almost choked. The man was ever after very loving to Friends, and not so full of airy words to us; though he was full of pride; but the Lord's power came over him, and the rest that were with him.

Another time there came an officer of the army, a very malicious, bitter professor, whom I had known in London. He was full of his airy talk also, and spoke slightingly of the light of Christ, and against the truth, and against the Spirit of God being in men, as it was in the apostles' days; till the power of God that bound the evil in him, had almost choked him as it did Colonel Rouse: for he was so full of evil that he could not speak, but blubbered and stuttered. But from the time that the Lord's power struck him, and came over him, he was ever after more loving to us.

The assize being over, and we settled in prison upon such a commitment, that we were not likely to be soon released, we discontinued giving the jailer seven shillings a-week each for our horses, and seven for ourselves; and sent our horses out into the country. Upon which he grew very wicked and devilish; and put us down into Doomsdale, a nasty, stinking place, where they put murderers, after they were condemned. The place was so noisome, that it was observed few that went in ever came out again in health. There was no house of office in it; and the excrements of the prisoners that from time to time had been left there, had not been carried out (as we were told) for many years. So that it was all like mire, and in some places to the top of the shoes in water and urine; and he would not let us cleanse it, nor suffer us to have beds or straw to lie on. At night some friendly people of the town brought us a candle and a little straw, and we burnt some of it to take away the stink. The thieves lay

premacy; and for his refusing to take it, a mittimus was made out and subscribed by him and two other magistrates, who acted very unwillingly. Thereupon he was again sent to Launceston jail, where he remained about two weeks, and then was freed by Sir J. Coryton and E. Hearle. It is stated that H. Lower, when himself in the commission of the peace, had more obliged the said Rosearrock than any other man, by doing him many singular offices of justice and courtesy. The return was a very ungrateful one.

G. Fox mentions large and satisfactory meetings held at his house in 1663 and 1668, and says that he continued serviceable till his death, the date of which event is not recorded.

over our heads, and the head jailer in a room by them, over us also. It seems the smoke went up into the jailer's room; which put him into such a rage, that he took the pots of excrements of the thieves, and poured them through a hole upon our heads in Doomsdale; whereby we were so bespattered, that we could not touch ourselves nor one another. And the stink increased upon us, so that what with that, and what with smoke, we had nearly been choked and smothered. We had the stink under our feet before, but now we had it on our heads and backs also; and he having quenched our straw with the filth he poured down, had made a great smother in the place. Moreover he railed at us most hideously, calling us hatchet-faced dogs, and such strange names as we had never heard. In this manner were we fain to stand all night, for we could not sit down, the place was so full of filthy excrements.* A great while he kept us in this manner, before he would let us cleanse it, or suffer us to have any victuals brought in but what we had through the grate. Once a girl brought us a little meat, and he arrested her for breaking his house, and sued her in the town-court for breaking the prison. Much trouble he put her to, whereby others were so discouraged, that we had much to do to get water or victuals. Near this time we sent for a young woman, Ann Downer, from London, that could write, and take things well in short-hand, to buy and dress our meat for us, which she was very willing to do, it being also upon her spirit to come to us in the love of God; and she was very serviceable to us.

This head-jailer, we were informed, had been a thief, and was branded in the hand and in the shoulder: his wife too had been branded in the hand. The under-jailer had been branded in the hand and shoulder; and his wife in the hand also. Colonel Bennet, who was a Baptist teacher, having purchased the jail and lands belonging to the castle, had placed this head-jailer therein. The prisoners, and some wild people, talked of spirits that haunted Doomsdale, and how many had died in it; thinking perhaps to terrify us therewith. But I told them, that if all the spirits and devils in hell were there, I was over them in the power of God, and feared no such

---

* We who live in the middle of the 19th century, when the impartial administration of justice extends to all ranks of society, and when the accommodations of our prisons are so vigilantly looked into, can scarcely credit that respectable Englishmen should be subjected to such gross abuse in pestilential dungeons. But the early annals of Friends abound with similar cases, many of them still more aggravated. Take the following example:—

During the close imprisonment of Friends at Aberdeen, Patrick Livingstone often preached to the people through the prison windows, exhorting them to fear God. This practice was highly displeasing to the magistrates. They, therefore, sought to prevent it, by causing some of them to be separated from the rest of their companions, and violently thrust into a close-vaulted cell, on the top of the jail, called the "iron-house," where the worst of felons and murderers were usually confined. They had neither light nor air, except through a long hole in the thick wall, which had a double grating of iron on the outside, and another within. Here they were kept night and day, in the heat of the summer of 1678, when the filthiness of the place, and the corruption of the air so closely pent-up, produced a multitude of worms, called *white maggots,* and *other vermin,* which swarmed about even upon their beds and victuals, and manifestly tended to the extreme danger of their health and lives.

thing; for Christ, our priest, would sanctify the walls and the house to us, he who bruised the head of the devil. The priest was to cleanse the plague out of the walls of the house under the law, which Christ, our priest, ended; who sanctifies both inwardly and outwardly the walls of the house, the walls of the heart, and all things to his people.

By this time the general quarter-sessions drew nigh; and the jailer still carrying himself basely and wickedly towards us, we drew up our suffering case, and sent it to the sessions at Bodmin. On the reading of which the justices gave order, "that Doomsdale door should be opened, and that we should have liberty to cleanse it, and to buy our meat in the town." We also sent a copy of our sufferings to the Protector, setting forth how we were taken and committed by Major Ceely; and abused by Captain Keat as aforesaid, and the rest in order. The Protector sent down an order to Captain Fox, governor of Pendennis Castle, to examine the matter about the soldiers abusing us, and striking me. There were at that time many of the gentry of the country at the castle; and Captain Keat's kinsman, that struck me, was sent for before them, and much threatened. They told him "that if I should change my principle, I might take the extremity of the law against him, and might recover sound damages of him." Captain Keat also was checked, for suffering the prisoners under his charge to be abused. This was of great service in the country; for afterwards Friends might have spoken in any market or steeple-house thereabouts, and none would meddle with them. I understood that Hugh Peters, one of the Protector's chaplains, told him they could not do George Fox a greater service for the spreading of his principles in Cornwall, than to imprison him there. And indeed my imprisonment there was of the Lord, and for his service in those parts; for after the assizes were over, and it was known we were likely to continue prisoners, several Friends from most parts of the nation came into the country to visit us. Those parts of the West were very dark countries at that time; but the Lord's light and truth broke forth, shone over all, and many were turned from darkness to light, and from Satan's power unto God. Many were moved to go to the steeple-houses; and several were sent to prison to us; and a great convincement began in the country. For now we had liberty to come out, and to walk in the Castle-Green; and many came to us on first-days, to whom we declared the word of life. Great service we had among them, and many were turned to God, up and down the country; but great rage got up in the priests and professors against the truth and us. One of the envious professors had collected many Scripture sentences, to prove that we ought to put off our hats to the people; and he invited the town of Launceston to come into the castle-yard to hear him read them: amongst other instances that he there brought, one was, that Saul bowed to the witch of Endor. When he had done, we got a little liberty to speak; and we showed both him and the people, "that Saul was gone from God, and had disobeyed God, like them, when he went to the witch of Endor: that neither the prophets, nor Christ, nor the apostles ever taught people to bow to a witch." The man went away with his rude people; but some stayed with us, and we showed them that this was not gospel instruction, to teach people to bow to a witch.

For now people began to be affected with the truth, and the devil's rage increased; so that we were often in great danger.

One time there came a soldier to us; and whilst one of our friends was admonishing and exhorting him to sobriety, &c., I saw him begin to draw his sword. Whereupon I stepped to him, and told him what a shame it was to offer to draw his sword upon a naked man, and a prisoner; and how unfit and unworthy he was to carry such a weapon; and that if he should have offered such a thing to some men, they would have taken his sword from him, and have broken it to pieces. So he was ashamed, and went his way; and the Lord's power preserved us.

Another time, about eleven at night, the jailer being half drunk, came and told me he had got a man now to dispute with me (this was when we had leave to go a little into the town.) As soon as he spoke these words, I felt there was mischief intended to my body. All that night and the next day I lay down on a grass-plat to slumber, and I felt something still about my body; and I started up, and struck at it in the power of the Lord, and yet still it was about my body. Then I arose and walked into the Castle-Green, and the under-keeper came to me, and told me there was a maid would speak with me in the prison. I felt a snare in his words too, therefore I went not into the prison, but to the grate, and looking in, I saw a man that was lately brought to prison for being a conjuror, and he had a knife in his hand. I spoke to him, and he threatened to cut my chaps; but being within the jail, he could not come at me. This was the jailer's great disputant. I went soon after into the jailer's house, and found him at breakfast; and he had then got his conjuror out with him. I told the jailer his plot was discovered. Then he got up from the table, and cast his napkin away in a rage; and I left them and went away to my chamber; for at this time we were out of Doomsdale. At the time the jailer had said the dispute should be, I went down and walked in the court (the place appointed) till about eleven, but nobody came. Then I went up to my chamber again, and after a while I heard one call for me. I stepped to the stairs' head, and there I saw the jailer's wife upon the stairs, and the conjuror at the bottom of the stairs, holding his hand behind his back, and in a great rage. I asked him, "Man, what hast thou in thy hand behind thy back? Pluck thy hand before thee," said I; "let us see thy hand, and what thou hast in it." Then in a rage he plucked forth his hand with a naked knife in it. I showed the jailer's wife the wicked design of her husband and herself against me; for this was the man they had brought to dispute of the things of God. But the Lord discovered their plot, and prevented their evil design; they both raged, and the conjuror threatened. Then I was moved to speak sharply to him in the dreadful power of the Lord, which bound him down, so that he never after durst appear before me to speak to me. I saw it was the Lord alone that preserved me out of their bloody hands; for the devil had a great enmity to me, and stirred up his instruments to seek my hurt. But the Lord prevented them; and my heart was filled with thanksgivings and praises unto him.

Now while I was exercised with people of divers sorts, that came some out of good will to visit us, some out of an envious, carping mind to wrangle and dispute, and some out of curiosity to see us, Edward Pyot, who before his convincement had been a captain in the army, and had a good understanding in the laws and rights of the people, being sensible of the injustice and envy of Judge Glynne to us at our trial, and willing to lay the weight thereof upon him, and make him sensible thereof also, wrote an epistle to him on behalf of us all, thus :—

" *To John Glynne, Chief Justice of England.*

" Friend,

" We are free men of England, free born ; our rights and liberties are according to law, and ought to be defended by it : and therefore with thee, by whose hand we have so long suffered, and still suffer, let us reason a little plainly concerning thy proceedings against us, whether they have been according to law, and agreeable to thy duty and office, as chief minister of the law, or justice of England. And in meekness and lowliness abide, that the witness of God in thy conscience may be heard to speak and judge in this matter : for thou and we must all appear before the judgment-seat of Christ, that every one may receive according to what he hath done, whether it be good or bad. Therefore, friend, in moderation and soberness, weigh what is herein laid before thee.

" In the afternoon, before we were brought before thee at the assize at Launceston, thou didst cause many scores of our books to be violently taken from us by armed men without due process of law ; which being perused to see if any thing in them could be found to be laid to our charge, who were innocent men, and then upon our legal issue, thou hast detained from us to this very day. Now our books are our goods, and our goods are our property ; and our liberty is to have and enjoy our property ; and of our liberty and property the law is the defence, which saith, ' No free man shall be disseized of his freehold, liberties, or free customs, &c., nor any way otherwise destroyed : and we shall not pass upon him, but by lawful judgment of his peers, or by the law of the land.' Magna Charta, cap. 29. Now friend, consider, is not the taking away of a man's goods violently, by force of arms, as aforesaid, contrary to the law of the land ? Is not the keeping of them so taken away, a disseizing him of his property, and a destroying of it and his liberty, yea, his very being, so far as the invading of the guard the law sets about him, is in order thereunto ? Calls not the law this, a destroying of a man ? Is there any more than one common guard or defence to property, liberty, and life, viz. the law ? And can this guard be broken on the former (viz. property and liberty), and the latter (viz. life), be sure ? Doth not he that makes an invasion upon a man's property and liberty (which he doth, who, contrary to law, which is the guard, acts against either), make an invasion upon a man's life ; since that which is the guard of the one, is also of the other ? If a penny, or a penny's-worth, be taken from a man contrary to law, may not by the same rule all that a man hath be taken away ? If the bond of the law be broken upon a man's property, may it not on the same ground be broken upon his person ? And by the same reason, as it is broken on one man, may it not be broken upon all, since the liberty, and property, and beings of all men under a government are relative, a communion of wealth, as the members in the body, but one guard and defence to all, the law? One man cannot be injured therein, but it redounds to all. Are not such things in order to the subversion and dissolution of government? Where there is no law, what is become of government? And of what value is the law made, when the ministers thereof break it at pleasure upon men's properties, liberties, and persons? Canst thou clear thyself of these things, as to us? To that of God in thy conscience, which is just, do I speak. Hast thou acted like a minister, the chief minister, of the law, who hast taken our goods, and yet detainest them, without so much as going by lawful warrant, grounded upon due information, which in this our case thou couldst not have; for none had perused them, whereby to give thee information? Shouldst thou exercise violence and force of arms on prisoners' goods, in their prison-chamber, instead of proceeding orderly and legally, which thy place calls upon thee, above any man, to tender, defend, and maintain against wrong, and to preserve entire the guard of every man's being, liberty, life, and livelihood? Shouldst thou, whose duty it is to punish the wrong-doer, do wrong thyself? who ought to see that the law is kept and observed, break the law, and turn aside the due administration thereof? Surely from thee, considering thou art chief justice of England, other things were expected, both by us and by the people of this nation.

"And when we were brought before thee, and stood upon our legal issue, and no accuser or accusation came in against us, as to what we had been wrongfully imprisoned, and in prison detained for nine weeks, shouldst not thou have caused us to be acquitted by proclamation? Saith not the law so? Oughtest thou not to have examined the cause of our commitment? And there not appearing a lawful cause, oughtest thou not to have discharged us? Is it not the substance of thy office and duty, to do justice according to the law and custom of England? Is not this the end of the administration of the law? of the general assizes? of the jail delivery? of the judges going the circuits? Hast not thou by doing otherwise, acted contrary to all these, and to Magna Charta? which, cap. 29, saith, 'We shall sell to no man, we shall deny or defer to no man, either justice or right.' Hast thou not both deferred and denied to us, who had been so long oppressed, this justice and right? And when of thee justice we demanded, saidst thou not, 'If we would be uncovered, thou wouldst hear us, and do us justice?'—'We shall sell to no man, we shall deny or defer to no man, either justice or right,' saith Magna Charta, as aforesaid. Again, 'We have commanded all our justices, that they shall henceforth do even law, and execution of right to all our subjects, rich and poor, without having regard to any man's person; and without letting to do right for any letters or commandments, which may come to them from us, or from any other, or by any other cause, &c., upon pain to be at our will, body, lands, and goods, to do therewith as shall please us, in case they do contrary,' saith Stat. 20. Edw. III. cap. 1. Again, 'Ye shall swear that ye shall do even law and execution of right to all, rich and poor, without having regard to any person; and that ye deny to no man common right by the king's letters, or other man's, nor for any other cause. And in case any letter come to you contrary to the law, that ye do nothing by such letter, but certify the king thereof, and go forth to do the law notwithstanding those letters. And in case ye be from henceforth found in default in any of the points aforesaid, ye shall be at the king's will of body, lands, and goods, thereof to be done, as shall please him,' saith the oath, appointed by the statute to be taken by all the judges, Stat. 18. Edw. III. But none of these, nor any other law hath such an expression or condition in it as this, viz., 'provided he will put off his hat to you, or be uncovered:' nor doth the law of God so say, or that your persons be respected; but the contrary. From whence then comes this new law, 'If ye will be uncovered, I will hear you, and do you justice?' This hearing complaint of wrong, this doing of justice, upon condition, wherein lies the equity and reasonableness of that? When were these fundamental laws repealed, which were the issue of much blood and war; to uphold which cost the miseries and blood of the late wars, that we shall now be heard, as to right, and have justice done us but upon condition, and that too such a trifling one as putting off the hat? Doth thy saying so, who art commanded, as aforesaid, repeal them, and make them of none effect, and all the miseries undergone, and the blood shed for them of old, and of late years? Whether it be so or not indeed, and to the nation, thou hast made it so to us, to whom thou hast denied the justice of our liberty (when we were before thee, and no accuser, nor accusation came in against us), and the hearing of the wrong done to us, who are innocent, and the doing us right. And bonds hast thou cast, and continued upon us until this day, under an unreasonable and cruel jailer, for not performing that thy condition, for conscience-sake. But thinkest thou that this thine own conditional justice maketh void the law? or can it do so? or absolve thee before God or man? or acquit the penalty mentioned in the laws aforesaid? unto which hast thou not consented and sworn? viz., 'And in case ye be from henceforth found in default, in any of the points aforesaid, ye shall be at the king's will, of body, lands, and goods, thereof to be done as shall please him.' And is not thy saying, 'If ye will be uncovered (or put off your hats), I will hear you, and do you justice;' and because we could not put them off for conscience-sake, thy denying us justice, and refusing to hear us, as to wrong, who had so unjustly suffered, a default in thee against the very essence of those laws, yea, an overthrow thereof, for which thing's sake (being of the highest importance to the well-being of men), so just, so equal, so necessary, those laws were made, and all the provisions therein? To make a default in any one point of which provisions, exposeth to the said penalty. Dost not thou by this time see where thou art? Art thou sure thou shalt never be made to understand and feel the justice thereof? Is thy seat so high, and thy fence so great, and art thou so certain of thy time and station, above all that have gone before thee, whom justice hath cut down, and given them their due, that thou shalt never be called to an account, nor with its long and sure stroke be reached? Deceive not thyself, God is come nearer to judgment than the workers of iniquity in this age imagine; who persecute and evil-entreat those that witness the Just and Holy One, for their witnessing of him who is come to reign for ever and ever. Saith he not, he will be a swift witness against the false swearers? God is not mocked.

"Surely, friend, that must needs be a very great offence which deprives a man of justice, of being heard as to wrong, of the benefit of the law, and of those laws afore-rehearsed; to defend the justice and equity of which a man hath adventured his blood and all that is dear to him. But to stand covered (or with the hat on), in conscience to the command of the Lord, is made by thee such an offence (which is none in law), and rendered upon us (who are innocent, serving the living God), effectual to deny us justice, though the laws of God, and of man, and the oath, equity and reason, say the contrary, and on it pronounce such a penalty. 'If ye will be uncovered (uncovered, saidst thou), I will hear you, and do you justice;' but justice we had not, nor were we heard, because Jesus Christ, who is the higher power, the lawgiver of his people, in our consciences commanded us not to respect persons, whom we choose to obey rather than man. And for our obedience unto him hast thou cast us into prison, and continue us there till this very day, having showed us neither law for it, nor Scripture, nor instances of either, nor example of heathens nor others. Friend, come down to that of God, that is just in thee, and consider, was ever such a thing as this heard of in this nation? What is become of seriousness, of true judgment, and of righteousness? An unrighteous man, standing before thee with his hat off, shall be heard; but an innocent man, appearing with his hat on in conscience to the Lord, shall neither be heard nor have justice. Is not this regarding of persons contrary to the laws aforesaid, and the oath and the law of God? Understand and judge: Did we not own authority and government oftentimes before the court? Didst not thou say in the court, thou wast glad to hear so much from us of our owning magistracy? Pleaded we not to the indictment, though it was such a new-found one as England never heard of before? Came we not when thou sent for us? Went we not when thou bade us go? And are we not still prisoners at thy command and at thy will? If the hat had been such an offence to thee, couldst not thou have caused it to be taken off, when thou heard us so often declare, we could not do it in conscience to the commands of the Lord, and that for that cause we forbore it, not in contempt of thee or of authority, nor in disrespect to thine, or any man's person (for we said, we honoured all men in the Lord, and owned authority, which was a terror to evil-doers, and a praise to them that do well; and our souls were subject to the higher powers for conscience-sake): as thou caused them to be taken off, and to be kept so, when thou called the jury to find us transgressors without a law? What ado hast thou made to take away the righteousness of the righteous from him, and to cause us to suffer further, whom thou knew to have been so long wrongfully in prison contrary to law? Is not liberty of conscience a natural right? Had there been a law in this case, and we bound up in our consciences that we could not have obeyed it, was not liberty of conscience there to take place? For where the law saith not against, there needs no plea of liberty of conscience; but the law have we not offended, yet in thy will hast thou caused, and dost thou yet cause us to suffer for our consciences, where the law requires no such thing; and yet for liberty of conscience hath all the blood been spilt, and the miseries of the late wars undergone, and (as the Protector saith), this government undertakes to preserve it; and a natural right, he saith, it is; and he that would have it, he saith, ought to give it. And if it be a natural right, as is undeniable, then to attempt to force it, or to punish a man for not doing contrary to it, is to act against nature; which, as it is unreasonable, so it is the same as to offer violence to a man's life. And what an offence that is in the law thou knowest; and how, by the common law of England, all acts, agreements, and laws, that are against nature, are mere nullities; and all the judges cannot make one case to be law that is against nature. But put the case, had our standing with our hats on been an offence in law, and we wilfully, and in contempt, and not out of conscience had stood so (which we deny as aforesaid), yet that is not a ground wherefore we should be denied justice, or be heard as to the wrong done to us. 'If ye will not offend in one case, I will do you justice in another;' this is not the language of the law, or of justice, which distributes to every one right; justice to whom justice is due, punishment to whom punishment is due. A man who does wrong may also have wrong done to him; shall he not have right wherein he is wronged, unless he right him whom he hath wronged? The law saith not so; but the wrong-doer is to suffer, and the sufferer of wrong to be righted. Is not to do otherwise a denying, letting, or stopping of even law and execution of justice, and a bringing under the penalties aforesaid? Mind and consider.

"And shouldst thou have accused, when no witness appeared against us, as in the particulars of striking Peter Ceely, and dispersing books (as thou saidst) against magistracy and ministry, with which thou didst falsely accuse one of us? Saith not the law, 'the judge ought not to be the accuser?' much less a false accuser? And wast not thou such a one, in affirming, that he dispersed books against magistracy and ministry, when as the books were violently taken out of our chamber (as hath been said,) undispersed by him, or any of us? Nor didst thou make it appear in one particular, wherein those books thou didst so violently cause to be taken away, were against magistracy or ministry? or gave one instance, or reply, when he denied what thou charged therein, and spoke to thee to bring forth those books and make thy charge appear. Is not the sword of the magistrate of God to pass upon such evil-doing? And according to the administration of the law, ought not accusations to be by way of indictment, wherein the offence is to be charged, and the law expressed against which it is? Can there be an issue without an indictment? Or can an indictment be found before proof be made of the offence charged therein? And hast thou not herein acted contrary to the law and the administration thereof, and thy duty as a judge? What just cause of offence gave George Fox to thee, when, upon thy producing a paper concerning swearing, sent by him (as thou said) to the grand jury, and requiring him to say, whether it was his handwriting? he answered, 'read it up before the country, and when he heard it read, if it were his, he would own it?' Is it not equal, and according to law, that what a man is charged with before the country, should be read in the hearing of him and of the country? When a paper is delivered out of a man's hand, alterations may be made in it to his prejudice, which, on a sudden looking over it, may not presently be discerned, but by hearing it read up, may be better understood, whether any such alterations have been made therein? Couldst thou in justice have expected or required him to do otherwise? Considering also, that he was not insensible how much he had suffered already, being innocent, and what endeavours were used to cause him further to suffer? Was not what he said, as aforesaid, a plain and single answer, and sufficient in the law? Though (as hath been demonstrated) thou didst act contrary to law, and to thy office, in being his accuser therein, and producing the paper against him. And his liberty it was, whether he would have made thee any answer at all, to what thou didst exhibit, or demand, out of the due course of law; for to the law answer is to be made, not to thy will. Wherefore then wast thou so filled with rage and fury at his reply? Calmly, and in the fear of the Lord, consider, wherefore didst thou revile him, particularly with the reproachful names of juggler and prevaricator? Wherein did he juggle? wherein did he prevaricate? Wherefore didst thou use such threatening language, and such menacings to him and us, saying, thou wouldst *ferk* us, with such like? Doth not the law forbid reviling, and rage, and fury, threatening, and menacing of prisoners? Soberly mind, is this to act like a judge or a man? Is not this transgression? Is not the sword of the magistrate of God to pass on this as evil-doing, which the righteous law condemns, and the higher power is against, which judgeth for God? Take heed what ye do, for ye judge not for man, but for the Lord, who is with you in the judgment. 'Wherefore now, let the fear of the Lord be upon you; take heed, and do it: for there is no iniquity with the Lord our God, nor respect of persons, nor taking of gifts,' said Jehoshaphat to the judges of Judah. Pride and fury, passion and rage, reviling and threatening, are not the Lord's; these, and the principle out of which they spring, are for judgment, and must come under the sword of the magistrate of God; and it is of an ill savour, especially such an expression, as to threaten to *ferk* us. Is not such a saying more becoming a schoolmaster with his rod and ferula in his hand, than thee, who art the chief justice of the nation, who sittest in the highest seat of judgment, who ought to give a good example, and so to judge that others may hear and fear? Weigh it soberly and consider, doth not threatening language demonstrate an inequality, and partiality in him, who sits as judge? Is it not a deterring of a prisoner from standing to, and pleading the innocency of his cause? Provides not the law against it? Saith it not, that irons and all other bonds shall be taken from the prisoner, that he may plead without fear, and with such freedom of spirit, as if he were not a prisoner? But when he, who is to judge according to the law, shall beforehand threaten and menace the prisoner contrary to the law, how can the mind of the prisoner be free to plead his innocency before him? or expect equal judgment from him who, before he hears him, threatens what he will do unto him? Is not this the case between thee and us?

Is not this the measure we have received at thy hands? Hast thou herein dealt according to law? or to thy duty? or as thou wouldst be done unto? Let that of God in thy conscience judge.

"And didst thou not say, there was a law for putting off the hat, and that thou wouldst show a law? and didst not thou often so express thyself? But didst thou produce any law, or show where that law might be found? or any judicial precedent, or in what king's reign, when we so often desired it of thee, having never heard of, nor known any such law, by which thou didst judge us? Was not what we demanded of thee reasonable and just? Was that a savoury answer, and according to law, which thou gave us, viz., 'I am not to carry the law-books at my back, up and down the country; I am not to instruct you?' Was ever such an expression heard before these days to come out of a judge's mouth? Is he not to be of counsel in the law for the prisoner, and to instruct him therein? Is it not for this cause that the prisoner, in many cases, is not allowed counsel by the law? In all courts of justice in this nation, has it not been known so to have been? And to the prisoner has not this been often declared when he demanded counsel, alleging his ignorance in the law, by reason of which his cause might miscarry, though it were righteous, viz., 'the court is of counsel for you?' Ought not he that judgeth in the law, to be expert in the law? Couldst thou not tell by what act of parliament it was made, or by what judicial precedent, or in what king's reign, or when it was adjudged so by the common law (which are all the grounds the law of England has), had there been such a law, though the words of the law thou couldst not remember? Surely, to inform the prisoner when he desired it, especially as to a law which was never heard of, by which he proceeds to judge him, that he may know what law it is by which he is to be judged, becomes him who judgeth for God; for so the law was read to the Jews by which they were to be judged, yea, every Sabbath-day; this was the commandment of the Lord. But instead thereof to say, 'I am not to carry the law-books at my back up and down the country; I am not to instruct you:' to say, 'there is a law,' and to say, 'thou wilt show it,' and yet not to show it, nor to tell where it is to be found; consider whether it be consistent with truth or justice?

"Have not thy whole proceedings against us made it evidently appear, that thy desire was to cause us to suffer, not to deliver us, who, being innocent, suffered; to have us aspersed and reproached before the country, not to have our innocency cleared and vindicated? Doth not thy taking away our books as aforesaid, and perusing them in such haste before our trial, and accusing us with something, which thou said was contained in them, make it to appear, that matter was sought out of them, wherewithal to charge us, when the Et Cetera warrant would not stand in law, by which we stood committed, and were then upon our delivery, according to due course of law? Doth it not further appear, by thy refusing to take from our hands a copy of the strange Et Cetera warrant, by which we were committed, and of the paper for which we were apprehended, to read it or cause it to be read, that so our long sufferings by reason of both might be looked into, and weighed in the law, whether just or righteous, and the country might as well see our innocency and sufferings without a cause, and the manner of dealing with us as to hear such reports as went of us, as great offenders, when we called upon thee often so to do, and which thou ought to have done, and said, thou would do, but did it not; or so much as take notice before the country that we had been falsely imprisoned, and had wrongfully suffered? But what might asperse and charge us, thou brought in thyself, contrary to law, and called to have us charged therewith. Is not this further manifest, in that thou didst cause us on a sudden to be withdrawn, and the petty jury to be called in with their verdict, whereupon Peter Ceely's falsely accusing George Fox with telling him privately of a design, and persuading him to join therein, it was by G. Fox made so clear to be a manifest falsehood, and so plainly to be perceived, that the cause of our sufferings was not any evil we had done, or law that we had transgressed, but malice and wickedness? And is it not abundantly clear from thy not permitting us to answer, and clear ourselves of the many foul slanders charged upon us in the new-found indictment, of which no proof was made; but when we were answering thereunto, and clearing ourselves thereof, thou didst stop us, saying, 'thou minded not those things, but only the putting off the hat;' when as, before the country, the new-found indictment, charged us with those things, and the petty jury brought in their verdict, 'guilty of the trespasses and contempts mentioned therein; of which (except as to the hat) not one witness or evidence was produced; and as to the hat, not any law, or judicial precedent, upon the transgression of which all legal indictments are only to be grounded? Now the law seeks not for causes whereby to make the innocent suffer, but helps him to right who suffers wrong, relieves the oppressed, and searches out the matter, whether that, of which a man stands accused, be so or not, seeking judgment, and hastening righteousness; and it saith, 'the innocent and the righteous slay thou not.' But whether thou hast done so to us, or the contrary, let the witness of God in thee search and judge, as these thy fruits do also make manifest.

"And, friend, consider how abominably wicked, and how highly to be abhorred, denied, and witnessed against, and how contrary to the laws such a proceeding is, to charge a man with many offences in an indictment, which they who draw the indictment, they who prosecute, and they who find the bill, know to be false, and to be inserted purposely to reproach and wound his good name, whom with some small matter which they can prove, they charge and indict; as is the common practice at this day. Prove but one particular charge in the indictment, and it must stand (say they) for a true bill, though there be ever so many falsehoods therein, purposely to wrong him, who is maliciously prosecuted: this is known to the judges, and almost every man who has to do with, and attends, their courts. How contrary is this to the end and righteousness of the law, which clears the innocent, and condemns the guilty, and condemns not the righteous with the wicked? Much it is cried out against; but what reformation is there thereof? How else shall clerks of assize, and other clerks of courts, fill up their bags (out of which perhaps their master must have a secret consideration), and be heightened in pride and impudence; that even in open court they take upon them to check and revile men; men without reproof, when a few lines might serve instead of a hundred? How else shall the spirit that is in men, that lusteth unto envy, malice, strife, and contention, be cherished and nourished to feed the lawyers, and dependents on courts, with the bread of men's children, and the ruin of their families, to maintain their long suits and malicious intentions. For a judge to say, 'I mind not these things; I will not hear you clear yourselves of what you are falsely accused: one thing I mind in your charge, the rest are but matter of form, set there to render you such wicked men before the country, as the thing that is to be proved against you is not sufficient to make out.' O! abominable wickedness, and perverting of the righteous end of the law, which is so careful and tender of every man's peace and innocency. How is the law in the administration thereof adulterated by lawyers, as the Scriptures are mangled by priests! And that which was made to preserve the righteous, and to punish the wicked, perverted to the punishing of the righteous, and the preserving of the wicked! An eye for an eye; a tooth for a tooth; life for life; burning for burning; wound for wound; a stripe for a stripe; he that accuseth a man falsely to suffer the same as he should have suffered, who was falsely accused, if he had been guilty; this saith the righteous law of God, which is agreeable to that of God in every man's conscience. Are not such forms of iniquity to be denied, which are so contrary to the law of God and man? which serve for gendering strife, and kindling contention? and of this nature was not that, with which thou didst cause us to be indicted? and this form didst thou not uphold, in not permitting us to answer to the many foul slanders therein; saying, 'Those things thou mindest not.' Will not the wrath of God be revealed from heaven against all ungodliness and unrighteousness of men, who hold the truth in unrighteousness; who are so far from the power of godliness, that they have not the form, but the form of iniquity, which is set and held up, instead of, and as a law, to overthrow and destroy the righteousness of the righteous, and so to shut him up, as by the law he can never get out? Is not the cry, thinkest thou, gone up? 'It is time for thee to set to thine hand, O Lord, for thine enemies have made void thy law!' Draws not the hour nigh? Fills not up the measure of iniquity apace? Surely the day is coming, and hasteneth. Ye have been warned from the presence, and by the mouth of the Lord; and clear will he be when he cometh to judgment, and upright when he giveth sentence. That of God in every one of your consciences shall so to him bear witness and confess, and your mouths shall be stopped, and before your judge shall ye be silent, when he shall divide you your portion, and render unto you according to your deeds. Therefore, whilst thou hast time, prize it, and repent: for verily 'Our God shall come, and shall not keep silence; a fire shall devour before him, and it shall be very tempestuous round about him. He shall call to the heavens from above, and to the earth that he may judge his people; and the heavens shall declare his righteousness: for God is judge himself. Consider this, ye that forget God, lest he tear you in pieces, and there be none to deliver.'

"And, friend, shouldst thou have given judgment against us (wherein thou didst fine us twenty marks a-piece, and imprisonment till payment), without causing us, being prisoners, to be brought before thee, to hear the judgment, and to move what we had to say in arrest of judgment? Is not this contrary to the law, as is manifest to those who understand the proceedings thereof? Is not the prisoner to be called before judgment be given? and is not the indictment to be read? and the verdict thereupon? And is not liberty to be given him to move in arrest of judgment? And if it be a just exception in the law, ought not there to be an arrest of judgment? For the indictment may not be drawn up according to law, and may be wrong placed, and the offence charged therein may not be a crime in law; or the jury may have been corrupted, or menaced, or set on by some of the justices; with other particulars, which are known to be legal and just exceptions. And the judgment ought to be in the prisoner's hearing, not behind his back, as if the judge were so conscious of the error thereof, that he dare not give it to the face of the prisoner. But these privileges of the law, this justice, we (who had so long and so greatly suffered contrary to law), received not, nor could have at thy hands; no, not so much as a copy or sight of that long and new-found indictment (which in England was never heard of before, nor that the matter contained therein was an offence in law, nor ever was there any law, or judicial precedent, that made it so); though two friends of ours in our names and our behalf, that night, next day, and day following, often desired it of the clerk of the assize, his assistants, and servants; but they could not have it, nor so much liberty as to see it. And it is likely not unknown, or unperceived by thee, that, had we been called, as we ought to have been, or known when it was to be given, three or four words might have been a sufficient, legal arrest, of the judgment given on that new-found indictment, and the verdict thereupon. Therefore, as our liberties, who are innocent, have not (in thy account) been worth the minding, and esteemed fit for nothing but to be trampled under foot and destroyed, so, if we find fault with what thou hast done, thou hast taken care that no door be left open to us in the law, but a writ of error; the consideration whereof, and the judgment to be given thereon, is to be had only where thyself art chief; of whom such complaint is to be made, and the error assigned for the reverse of thy judgment. And what the fruit of that may be well expected to be, by what we have already mentioned, as having received at thy hands, thou hast given us to understand. And here thou mayest think thou hast made thyself secure, and sufficiently barred up our way of relief, against whom (though thou knew we had done nothing contrary to the law, or worthy of bonds, much less of the bonds and sufferings we had sustained): thou hast proceeded as has been rehearsed; notwithstanding that thou art (as are all the judges of the nation) entrusted, not with a legislative power, but to administer justice, and to do even law and execution of right to all, high and low, rich and poor, without having regard to any man's person; and art sworn so to do, as has been said: and wherein thou dost contrary art liable to punishment, as ceasing from being a judge, and becoming a wrongdoer and an oppressor; which what it is to be, many of thy predecessors have understood, some by death, others by fine and imprisonment. And of this thou mayest not be ignorant, that to deny a prisoner any of the privileges the law allows him, is to deny him justice, to try him in an arbitrary way, to rob him of that liberty which the law gives him, which is his inheritance as a free man; to do which is in effect to subvert the fundamental laws and government of England, and to introduce an arbitrary and tyrannical government against law; which is treason by the common law; and treasons by the common law are not taken away by the statutes of 25 Edw. III. 1 Henry IV. 1, 2, m. See O. St. Johns, now chief justice of the common pleas, his argument against Strafford, fol. 65, in the case.

"These things we have laid before thee in all plainness, that (with the light of Jesus Christ, who lighteth every one that cometh into the world, a measure of which thou hast, which showeth the evil, and reproveth thee for sin, for which thou must be accountable) thou mayest consider and see what thou hast done against the innocent; that shame may overtake thee, and thou mayest turn unto the Lord, who now calleth thee to repentance by his servants, whom, for witnessing his living truth in them, thou hast cast into, and yet continues under, cruel bonds and sufferings." EDW. PYOT.

From the Jail in Launceston, the 14th
    day of the 5th Month, 1656.

By this letter the reader may observe how contrary to law we were made to suffer: but the Lord, who saw the integrity of our hearts to him, and knew the innocency of our cause, was with us in our sufferings, bore up our spirits, and made them easy to us; and gave us opportunities of publishing his name and truth amongst the people; so that several of the town came to be convinced, and many were made loving to us. Friends from many parts came to visit us; amongst whom were two out of Wales, who had been justices of peace. Also Judge Hagget's wife, of Bristol, who was convinced, with several of her children; and her husband was very kind and serviceable to Friends, and had a love to God's people, which he retained to his death.

Now in Cornwall, Devonshire, Dorsetshire, and Somersetshire, truth began to spread mightily, and many were turned to Christ Jesus and his free teaching: for many Friends that came to visit us, were drawn forth to declare the truth in those countries; which made the priests and professors rage, and they stirred up the magistrates to ensnare Friends. They placed watches in the streets and highways, on pretence of taking up all suspicious persons; under which colour they stopped and took up the Friends that travelled in and through those countries, coming to visit us in prison; which they did, that they might not pass up and down in the Lord's service. But that by which they thought to stop the truth, was the means of spreading it so much the more; for then Friends were frequently moved to speak to one constable, and to the other officer, and to the justices they were brought before; and this caused the truth to spread the more amongst them in all their parishes. And when Friends got among the watches, it would be a fortnight or three weeks before they could get out of them again; for no sooner had one constable taken them and carried them before the justices, and they had discharged them, than another would take them up, and carry them before other justices; which put the country to much needless trouble and charges.

As Thomas Rawlinson was coming out of the north to visit us, a constable in Devonshire took him up, and at night took twenty shillings out of his pocket; and after being thus robbed, he was cast into Exeter jail. They cast Henry Pollexfen also into prison in Devonshire for being a Jesuit, who had been a justice of peace for nearly forty years before. Many Friends were cruelly beaten by them; nay, some clothiers that were going to the mill with their cloth, and others about their occupations, were taken up and whipped, though men of about eighty or a hundred pounds a year, and not above four or five miles from their families.

The mayor of Launceston, too, was a very wicked man, for he took up all he could get, and cast them into prison; and he would search substantial grave women, their petticoats and their head-clothes. A young man having come to see us, who came not through the town, I drew up all the gross, inhuman, and unchristian actions of the mayor (for his carriage was more like a heathen than a Christian), to him I gave it, and bid him seal it up, and go out again the back way; and then come into the town through the gates. He did so; and the watch took him up, and carried him before the mayor, who presently searched his pockets and found the letter, wherein he saw all his actions characterized. This shamed him so, that from that time he meddled little with the servants of the Lord.

Now from the sense I had of the snare that was laid, and mischief intended, in setting up those watches at the time to stop and take up Friends, it came upon me to give forth the following, as—

"An Exhortation and Warning to the Magistrates.

"All ye powers of the earth, Christ is come to reign, and is among you, and ye know him not; who doth enlighten every one of you, that ye all through him might believe in him, who is the light, who treads the wine-press alone without the city, and whose feet are upon it. Therefore see all, and examine with the light, what ye are ripe for; for the press is ready for you.

"Before honour is humility. You that would have honour before ye have humility (mark, before ye have humility), are ye not as the heathen are? Ye would have honour before ye have humility; did not all the persecutors that ever were upon the earth want this humility? They wanted the honour, and yet would have the honour before they had the humility, and had learned that. So ye that are out of the humility, are out of the honour; and ye are not to have the honour, who have not the humility; for before honour is humility; mark, before it.

"Now ye pretend liberty of conscience; yet one shall not carry a letter to a friend, nor men visit their friends, nor prisoners, nor carry a book about them, either for their own use, or for their friends. Men shall not see their friends; but watches are set up to catch and stop them; and these must be well-armed men too, against an innocent people, that have not so much as a stick in their hands, who are in scorn called Quakers. Yet by such as set up these watches is pretended liberty of conscience; who take up them, whose consciences are exercised towards God and men, who worship God in spirit and in truth; which they that are out of the light call heresy. Now these set up the watches against them, whom they in scorn call Quakers, because they confess and witness the true light, that lighteth every one that cometh into the world, amongst people, as they pass through the country, or among their friends. This is the dangerous doctrine which watchmen are set up against, to subdue error, as they call it, which is the light that doth enlighten every man that cometh into the world—Him, by whom the world was made; who was glorified with the Father before the world began. For those whom they in scorn call Quakers, have they set their watches, able men, well-armed; to take up such as bear this testimony either in words, books, or letters. So that is the light you hate, which enlightens every man that cometh into the world; and these that witness to this light you put in prison; and after you have imprisoned them, you set your watches to take up all that go to visit them, and imprison them also; so that by setting up your watches, ye would stop all relief from coming to prisoners. Therefore this is the word of the Lord God to you, and a charge to you all, in the presence of the living God of heaven and earth; every man of you being enlightened with a light that cometh from Christ, the Saviour of people's souls; to this light, all take heed, that with it you may see Christ, from whom the light cometh, to be your Saviour, by whom the world was made, who saith, 'Learn of me.' But if ye hate this light, ye hate Christ, who doth enlighten you all, that through him you might believe. But not believing in, nor bringing your deeds to the light, which will make them manifest and reprove them, this is your condemnation, even the light. Remember, you are warned in your life-time, for this light is your way to salvation, if you walk in it; and your condemnation, if you reject and hate it. You can never come to Christ, the Second Priest, unless you come to the light, which the Second Priest hath enlightened you withal. So ye that come not to the light, ye go to the priests that take tithes, as did the first priesthood; and hale out of your synagogues and temples (as some call them), as that priesthood did that took tithes; which they that were of the second priesthood did not. Was there ever such a generation! or did ever such a generation of men appear, as in this age, who are so full of madness, envy, and persecution, that they stand up in watches, with weapons against the truth, to persecute it, as the towns and countries do declare; which rings as Sodom, and like Gomorrah! And this hath its liberty, and truth is stood against; and to reprove sin is accounted a breach of the peace, as they say who are out of the truth, and set up their watches against it." G. F.

Besides this general warning, there coming to my hand a copy of a warrant issued from the Exeter sessions, in express terms, "for apprehending all Quakers," wherein truth and Friends were reproached and vilified, I was moved to write an answer thereunto, and send it abroad, for clearing truth and Friends from the slanders therein cast upon them, and to manifest the wickedness of that persecuting spirit from whence it proceeded; which was after this manner:—

" Whereas a warrant was granted last sessions, held at Exeter, on the eighteenth day of the fifth month, 1656, which warrant is 'for apprehending and taking up all such as are Quakers, or call themselves Quakers, or go under the notion of Quakers; and is directed to the chief constables, to be sent by them to the petty constables, requiring them to set watches, able men with bills, to take up all such Quakers as aforesaid.' And whereas in your said warrant, you speak of the Quakers spreading seditious books and papers; I answer, They whom ye in scorn call Quakers, have no seditious books or papers; but their books are against sedition, and seditious men, and seditious books, and seditious teachers, and seditious ways. Thus ye have numbered them, who are honest, godly, and holy men, that fear God, amongst beggars, rogues, and vagabonds; thus putting no difference between the precious and the vile. You are not fit to judge, who have set up your bills, and armed your men, to stand up together in battle against innocent people, the lambs of Christ, who have not lifted up a hand against you. But if ye were sensible of the state of your own country, your cities, your towns, your villages, how the cry of them is like Gomorrah, and the ring like Sodom, and the sound like the old world, where all flesh had corrupted its way, which God overthrow with the flood;—if you did consider this with yourselves, you would find something to turn the sword against, and not against the lambs of Christ;—you would not make a mock of the innocent, that stand a witness against all sin and unrighteousness in your towns and steeple-houses. Noah, the eighth person, a preacher of righteousness, was grieved with the filthy conversation of the wicked; so are we now. So likewise just Lot was grieved with their unmerciful deeds, and the filthy conversation of Sodom. And were not these hated of the world, and of them that lived in filthiness? And whereas you speak of those, whom you in scorn call Quakers, that they are a grief to those whom you call pious and religious people, and their religion. To such as are in the religion that is vain, whose tongues are not bridled, I believe the Quakers are a grief; but they are not a grief to such as are in the pure religion, which keepeth unspotted from the world; which sets not up bills, nor watches, to maintain it by the world; for they are not of the world who are in the pure religion, which keeps them unspotted of the world; mark, the 'pure religion, which keeps unspotted of the world.' But to such as are in the religion that is not pure, who have a form of godliness, and not the power—to such as you call pious, the truth itself was always a grief; and so it is in this age. And now your fruits appear, the end of your religion and profession, and what you possess; but you are in error, and have been but in the profession, out of the possession of the Spirit, who are not in the Spirit of truth. For where did that ever set stints and bounds, and number the just and innocent with the wicked? But the wicked set stints, and bounds, and limits to the just, and number them among the wicked; yea, they spoke all manner of evil of them, as ye are doing now of us. Nay, according as it was foretold in the Scripture, such as tremble at the word of God, you cast out and hate, you that have your temple-worship. You say, the Quakers come to disturb you in your churches (as you call them); was it not the practice of the apostles to go into the synagogues and temples, to witness against the priesthood that took tithes, and was it not the practice of the Jews to hale them out, persecute and stone them, that witnessed Christ the second priest, and went to bring people off from the first priesthood? Was it not the practice of the prophets, to go and cry against the high places? And was it not the practice of the Jews, when they were backslidden, and of the heathen, to imprison and persecute the prophets, and send after them into other countries? And is this not the practice of you now, who are holding up your high places, which the Papists erected, which ye now call your churches; where ye beat and persecute? What kind of religious people are you, that are filled with so much madness? Did not Paul confess he was mad, while he was in your practice, haling, beating, imprisoning, putting out of the synagogues, having his authority from the chief priests? And are not the chief priests the cause of this? Was there ever such a cry made in any age past, as there is now in the pulpits, railing against an innocent people, whom in scorn ye call Quakers, who lift not up a hand against you; but who are indeed the pious, that are of the pure religion, who fear God, worship him in Spirit and in truth, and cannot join with you in your religion? And do not the ministers of God say, that the Scriptures are a declaration, which you call the word? Do you not rob Christ of his title, and of his honour, and give it to the letter, and show yourselves out of the doctrine of the ministers of God, who call the Scriptures by the name of writings and treatises, and declarations; and who said, Christ's name is called the Word of God? Are not you here in the error you speak of, which is your common talk among you? There was talk among some of you of your gospel-shining; doth your gospel which you profess persecute? Did ever any of them, that did possess it, cast into prison and not suffer others to go to visit them? Are you like Christians in this, or like heathens, who set bounds and watches over the land, that they should not pass to visit them that are in prison? Was ever the like heard in any age? Search and see, if you have not outstripped them all in your watches, in your persecution, and imprisonments. O! never talk, that we are a grief to them that are in the pure religion.

"And whereas in your warrant we are represented as disaffected to government; I say, the law, which is a terror to the evil-doer, we own, the higher power to which the soul must be subject; but we deny the evil-doer, the malicious man reigning, and the envious man seeking for his prey, whose envy is against the innocent; who raiseth up the country against honest men, and so becomes a trouble to the country, in raising them up to take the innocent; but that we leave to the Lord to judge. Your false accusations of heresy and blasphemy we deny. You should have laid them down in particulars, that people might have seen them, and not have slandered us behind our backs. The law saith, the crime should be mentioned in the warrant. Then for your saying, 'we deny the godly ministers to be a true ministry of Christ,' that is false; for we say, that the godly ministers are the ministers of Christ. But which of your ministers dare say, that they are truly godly? And your charging us with seducing many weak people, is false also; we seduce none; but you, that deny the light, which lighteth every man that cometh into the world, are seduced from the anointing which should teach you; and if ye would be taught by it, ye would not need that any man should teach you. But such as are taught by the anointing, which abideth in them, and deny man's teaching, these ye call seducers, quite contrary to John's doctrine, 1 John ii. You speak quite contrary to him; that which is truth, ye call seducing; and that which he calls seducing, you call truth; read the latter part of the chapter. Beware, I warn you all from the Lord God of glory, set not any bound against him; stint him not; limit not the Holy One of Israel; for the Lord is rising in power and great glory, who will rule the nations with a rod of iron, which to him are but as the drop of a bucket. He that measures the waters in the hollow of his hand, will dash the nations together as a potter's vessel. And know, you that are found in this his day blaspheming his work, that God hath brought forth, calling it blasphemy, fighting against it, setting up your carnal weapons, making your bonds strong; God will break asunder that which your carnal policy hath invented, and which by your carnal weapons ye would uphold; and make you to know there is a God in heaven, who carries his lambs in his arms, which are come among wolves, and are ready to be torn in pieces in every place, yea, in your steeple-houses; where people have appeared without reason, and natural affection. Therefore all ye petty constables, sheriffs, and justices, take warning; take heed, what ye do against the lambs of Christ; for Christ is come, and coming, who will give to every one of you a reward according to your works, you who have the letter, which speaks of Christ; but now ye are persecuting that which the Scripture speaks of; as your fruits make manifest. Therefore every one, sheriffs, justices, constables, &c., consider what ye do possess, and what a profession ye are now in, that all these carnal weapons are now set up against the innocent, yea, against the truth; which shows that ye have not the spiritual weapons, and that ye want the counsel of Gamaliel, yea, ye want the counsel of such a man among you, who said, ‘Let the apostles alone; if it be of God, it will stand; if it be not, it will come to nought.' But ye may see yourselves on the contrary, in the spirit of them that came with Judas, with swords and staves from the chief priests against Christ; still it is against Christ, where he is made manifest. Paul (while Saul) went against him, though he professed a Christ that was to come; and the Jews professed a Christ that was to come; yet Paul persecuted him, where he was manifested in his saints. So ye profess a Christ that is come, but persecute him where he is manifest. You that have the letter, the high places, the synagogues, you persecute him, where he is made manifest in his saints, as the Jews did. They who were in the letter, out of the life, persecuted them that were in the life of that which they profess in the letter; so now do you persecute them that are in the life, and are yourselves strangers to it, as your fruits make appear. You have numbered the people of God amongst transgressors; but have you imprisoned any of the rogues and transgressors you speak of? You have imprisoned the innocent, and let the others go free."   G. F.

When I had sent abroad the foregoing, so great a sense came upon me of the veil of darkness that was over the priests and professors of Christianity, that I was moved to give forth the following, as an awakening warning to them :—

"Blindness hath happened to the professed Christians of the letter now-a-days, as blindness happened to the Jews, who professed the letter, but owned not the life which the letter speaks of; as the Christians now, to whom this blindness hath happened, who profess the Scripture, but own not the life, which the Scripture speaks of. For against the life the Jews stood, who professed the letter of the Scripture, but they were blind; they gathered counsel against the life; they were in an uproar when the babe was born in Bethlehem, Herod and all the chief priests. And Herod sought to destroy all the young children in Bethlehem, yet missed the babe; Herod, that fox, though he put John to death. You may here see how the literal professors stood up, not for the truth, but quite against it. Furthermore, the chief priests consulted together how they might take Jesus by subtilty, and put him to death; mark, by their subtilty. The professors of a Christ that was to come, preached of a Messiah, of a Christ, of a Saviour; but denied the life, when he was made manifest. The chief priests, when they were assembled with the elders, and had taken counsel, gave large money unto the soldiers, to declare that 'his disciples came by night, and stole him away.' Likewise in the day, when the children of Israel were in Egypt, and they with their children began to spread and multiply, 'Come,' said the Egyptians, 'let us deal wisely with them to afflict them, and tax them;' which held, until the Lord overthrew their oppressors, and brought out his seed by his mighty power from under the oppressor, and exalted his Son above all, though the heathen raged, and the people imagined vain things. He made his power known, that all might see that there was no God upon the earth but himself. This power now hath brought forth the work of the Lord! Many who are turned to Christ, the light, have received the power of God, and are thereby become the sons of God. Now this birth, that is born of God, are all the powers of the world joined together to crucify; to put to death those Jews in the Spirit, as they put Christ to death in the flesh formerly. This is the birth that all the wicked world is enraged against; against this they set their watches,—this birth, brought forth by the Mighty God of Jacob, who rides upon the high places of the earth. This is the birth that the professed Christians without the life in our days rage against, and lay out all their wisdom about. Are not the chief priests and wise men of the earth consulting together how they may destroy this birth? Is not this the birth, that is banished out of your hearts, you that profess the Scripture, and are talkers of it, but do not own the light and life which the Scripture speaks of, as the Jews would not; and so you will not have Christ to reign over you, as they would not? Do you not hale out of your synagogues, and before magistrates? Do you not herein fulfil Christ's words, who said to his disciples, They should be haled out of the synagogues, and before rulers? Do you not persecute them from city to city? Do you not almost fill your prisons with them? And now set your watches, that none may visit them, whom ye have put into

prison? Is not this an unchristian spirit? How can you for shame say
you are upholders of truth? Or how can you for shame say that truth
hath been professed among you? Yet we grant that you have talked of
it. And how can you for shame say the gospel shines among you, when
you will not own the life of it; when you call it error, and the evil seed?
Yea, the very truth, the very life of truth ye have blasphemed against now,
as the Jews did against Christ, calling him a devil; you now call it error,
and the evil seed, and stand up against it, and turn the sword against it.
As in the days of the Jews, it was the Jews outward in the flesh, not the
Jews in the Spirit, who turned the sword against Christ; so in these days
it is those Christians who profess the Scripture, but are out of the Life of
it. And is it not a shame to all the ministers of the Gospel (as they are
called), that they can find no better way to maintain that which they call
the truth and their Gospel, than by carnal weapons, stocks and prisons,
whips, watches, and wards, and powers of the earth? Were these the
apostles' weapons? Carnal watches and wards, stocks and prisons, and
haling out of the synagogues, when they came to speak? Judge yourselves,
what an antichristian spirit you have. Never talk of defending truth with
that which is against truth. For are you not setting up the rabble of the
world against it? Do they not join with you with swords and staves
against it? Is this the life of Christians? Is not this the life of error,
and of the evil seedsman? Surely, ye would find work enough, if ye were
in the fear of the Lord, to turn your swords against profaneness, the oaths
and wickedness that are in your streets and highways. How do they ring
like Sodom, and give a sound like Gomorrah! But these are become a
prey in this your age, that reprove in your gates sin, wickedness, and profaneness; they are become your by-word. Against them your councils are
gathered, them you cast into prison, and hale out of your synagogues; and
cast them likewise into prison that write and speak against it, and set
your guards to stop and hinder any from visiting them whom you cast
into prison, and give them the names of vagabonds and wanderers. Was
ever the like heard, in the days of the heathen, against the apostles who
witnessed the gospel? Did they set guards and watches in every town, in
every city, to take the disciples, the brethren, the believers, that heard that
the apostles were cast into prison, and came to see what they wanted? Show
ye not as much rage and fury now in your age, as was in those in that age?
And how can you talk of the gospel, and of defending the gospel, when you
are setting guards and watches against it, and are defending that which
stands against it; and the lambs of Christ are almost torn to pieces amongst
you, who are like wolves? for the Lord hath now sent his lambs amongst
wolves. Have not you professed the words of Christ, of the prophets and
apostles, as the Jews had long professed the Scriptures, the words of Moses
and of the prophets, that prophesied of Christ that was to come, and stood
against him when he was come? as you do in this day of his reign, in this
day of his glorious gospel, who are persecuting the messengers of it, imprisoning them, persecuting them in your streets and highways; and are
setting up your watches against them, who bring you the glad tidings of
peace to your souls, whose feet are beautiful on the top of the mountains;

mark, on the top of the mountains, that against which the mountains rage and swell. But God will make them melt; the sun is risen, which will make them melt. God will cleave the rocks and mountains asunder, and make the hills to bow perpetually; for his Son he will exalt, and his glory he will give to HIM and not to another.

"Therefore be awakened, ye rulers of the earth, and take counsel of the Lord; take not counsel together against him. Make not your bonds strong; set not yourselves in battle against him, for ye will be found but as briars and thorns before him, which the fire shall consume. Therefore be awakened, all ye talkers of the Scripture, that gather yourselves together by your multitudes and meetings, and have had your teachers; but not having the Spirit that gave forth the Scriptures, the Lord God of glory, the Father of spirits, will scatter you. All your bonds will not hold you together, who are out of the Spirit, which is the bond of peace. The thrashing instrument is gone forth, which will beat the hills to pieces. Sion is risen to thrash. Out of the holy mountain is the trumpet sounded. Stand not up against the Lord; for all nations are with the Lord as the drop of a bucket. He that measures the waters in the hollow of his hand, and weighs the earth in scales, the Lord of hosts is his name, who is now risen and rising to plead the cause of the innocent; who is exalting his Son, and bringing his sheep to him. Now are they seen and known that feed upon wind, that are lifted up, given up to believe lies; who report, and say, 'Report, and we will report it.' Now are they seen who have a form of godliness, but deny the power; so Christ is denied, the power itself is denied; for Christ is the power of God. And the power being denied by you, that have a form of godliness, that have the words of the Scriptures, the gospel is denied; for the gospel is the power of God. Thus it is among you, that have the knowledge and wisdom that is sensual, earthly, and devilish. Doth it not appear so? Let your jails and watches witness your fruits in every town. Your wisdom is earthly, sensual, and devilish; you have a knowledge and wisdom, but not that which is from above; for that is pure and gentle, so is not your knowledge; but to know Christ is life eternal. Now your fruits have manifested that you are not of this; and so out of the power of God, which is the cross of Christ; for you are found in the world, out of the power of God, out of the cross of Christ, persecuting. So that which doth persecute, and send forth writings and decrees to stop all, and take up all, and set watches, and prepare bonds to stint the Lord; to imprison and persecute, and suffer none to go to visit them; this shows you are not Christians, but stand against a Christian's life, which brings to love enemies. Where is your heaping up coals of fire; your love to your enemies; who are thus persecuting your friends? 'He came to his own, and his own received him not;' here is a turning of the sword against the just. Do you show here a Christian's life, or yourselves Christians, who are filling your jails with Christians in Spirit, you that are in the letter (in shadows), as the Jews in the letter put the Jews in the Spirit into prison? Is not this the fruit in our days of the Christians in the letter, to put the Christians in the Spirit into prison? Doth not this show that your decrees, which you have sent forth, proceed from death, who thus act against the life, and them that are in it; which the Scriptures were given forth from? Is it not here as it was with Saul, when he went to persecute, to hale to prison, and bind all that he could find calling upon that name, who were Christians in the life, the Spirit, such as you are now persecuting, because they are in the life, though you profess their words? Are not your decrees gone forth from the same spirit of envy, against the same Spirit of Christ they were in? Is it not manifest to all that fear God, and to the sober-minded and honest-hearted people that see your practices, your decrees, your letters, to stop, to molest, to hinder, to imprison them that are moved of the Lord to do his will, or to go to visit prisoners whom you have imprisoned? Doth this show you to have a spirit like Paul, yea or nay? or are you not quite contrary, like unto them that persecuted Paul? The day hath declared it. To that of God in you all I speak, which shall witness it at the last day,—the day of judgment. Persecution was blind in all ages; and madness and folly led it: yet persecution got always a form or pretence of godliness,—a talk of religion, as in the days of Moses, of Jeremiah, of Christ, and of the apostles. 'Come,' saith the council, 'let us crush them while they are young, they have almost overspread the nation in every corner.' This is as much as to say, 'Let us put this birth to death, as Pharaoh and Herod did the children.' But the Lord caused his truth the more to spread. For you may read, what numbers came out of Egypt! and what multitudes followed Christ! Therefore, with consideration read these lines, and not with fury. Let not foolishness appear; but consider in humility the paths you go in, what spirit you are of, and what the end of your conversation is; for in love to your souls I write, that in the day of your visitation you may consider it.

> "From him who loveth righteousness, and the establishing of it, and truth, peace, and faith, which is by Christ Jesus (Mercy and peace be multiplied among such!) but a witness against all hypocrites, and all who have a profession, but live out of the possession, in an hypocritical religion, in the lusts and fashions of the world, having a form of godliness, but standing against the power with might and main, sword and staff. Which things declare your conversation and practices to be out of Christ's life, against the gospel practice, and contrary to the manner and order of the saints."   G. F.

We continued in prison till the next assize; before which time divers Friends, both men and women, were sent to prison, that had been taken up by the watches. When the assize came on, several of these were called before the judge, and indicted; and though the jailer brought them into court, yet they indicted them, that they came in "by force of arms and in an hostile manner;" and the judge fined them, because they would not put off their hats. But we were not called before the judges any more.

Great work we had, and service for the Lord, both between the assizes and after, amongst professors and people of all sorts; for many came to see us and to reason with us. Elizabeth Trelawny of Plymouth (who was the daughter of a baronet) being convinced (as was formerly mentioned), the priests and professors, and some great persons of her kindred were exasperated, and wrote letters to her.   She being a wise and tender woman, and fearing to give them any advantage, sent their letters to me; and I answered them, and returned them to her again, for her to answer.   Which she did: till growing in the power, and Spirit, and wisdom of God, she came herself to be able to answer the wisest priest and professor of them all; and had a dominion over them in the truth, through the power of the Lord, by which she was kept faithful to her death.

While I was in prison here, the Baptists and Fifth-monarchy-men prophesied, "That this year Christ should come, and reign upon earth a thousand years."   And they looked upon this reign to be outward; when he was come inwardly in the hearts of his people, to reign and rule there, and these professors would not thus receive him.   So they failed in their prophecy and expectation, and had not the possession of him.   But Christ *is* come, and doth dwell in the hearts of his people, and reign there.   Thousands, at the door of whose hearts he hath been knocking, have opened to him; and he is come in, and doth sup with them and they with him; the heavenly supper with the heavenly and spiritual man.   So many of these Baptist and Monarchy-people turned the greatest enemies to the professors of Christ; but he reigns in the hearts of his saints over all their envy.

At the assize divers justices came to us and were pretty civil, and reasoned of the things of God soberly, expressing a pity towards us.   Captain Fox, governor of Pendennis Castle, came and looked me in the face, and said not a word; but went to his company, and told them, "he never saw a simpler man in his life."   I called after him, and said, "Stay, we will see who is the simpler man."   But he went his way; a light chaffy man.

Thomas Lower * also came to visit us, and offered us money, which we refused; accepting his love nevertheless.   He asked us many questions concerning our denying the Scriptures to be the word of God; and concerning the sacraments, and such like; to all which he received satisfaction.   I spoke particularly to him, and he afterwards said, "my words were as a flash of lightning, they ran so through him."   He said, "he never met with such men in his life; for they knew the thoughts of his heart, and were as the wise master-builders of the assemblies, that fastened their words like nails."   He came to be convinced of the truth, and remains a Friend to this day.   When he came home to his aunt Hambley's, where he then lived, and made report to her concerning us, she, with her sister Grace Billing, hearing the report of truth, came to visit us in prison, and was convinced also.   Great sufferings and spoiling of goods both he and his aunt have undergone for the truth's sake.

About this time I was moved to give forth the following exhortation to Friends in the ministry:—
      "FRIENDS,
      "In the power of life and wisdom, and dread of the Lord God of life, and heaven, and earth, dwell; that in the wisdom of God over all ye may

---

* Thomas Lower was son-in-law to Judge Fell, having married his daughter Mary.

be preserved, and be a terror to all the adversaries of God, and a dread, answering that of God in them all, spreading the truth, awakening the witness, confounding deceit, gathering out of transgression into the life, the covenant of light and peace with God. Let all nations hear the sound by word or writing. Spare no place, spare no tongue, nor pen; but be obedient to the Lord God; go through the work; be valiant for the truth upon earth; and tread and trample upon all that is contrary. Ye have the power, do not abuse it; and strength and presence of the Lord, eye it, and the wisdom; that with it you may all be ordered to the glory of the Lord God. Keep in the dominion; keep in the power over all deceit; tread over them in that which lets you see to the world's end, and the uttermost parts of the earth. Reign and rule with Christ, whose sceptre and throne are now set up, whose dominion is over all to the ends of the earth; whose dominion is an everlasting dominion; whose throne is an everlasting throne; whose kingdom is an everlasting kingdom; and whose power is above all powers. Therefore this is the word of the Lord God to you all: keep in the wisdom of God, that spreads over all the earth; the wisdom of the creation, that is pure, from above, not destructive. For now shall salvation go out of Zion, to judge the mount of Esau: and now shall the law go forth from Jerusalem, to answer the principle of God in all; to hew down all inventors and inventions. For all the princes of the earth are but as air to the power of the Lord God, which you are in, and have tasted of: therefore live in it; this is the word of the Lord God to you all, do not abuse it; keep down and low; and take heed of false joys, that will change.

"Bring all into the worship of God. Plough up the fallow ground. Thrash and get out the corn; that the seed, the wheat, may be gathered into the barn; that to the beginning all people may come—to Christ, who was, before the world was made. For the chaff is come upon the wheat by transgression; he that treads it out, is out of transgression, and fathoms transgression; puts a difference between the precious and the vile; and can pick out the wheat from the tares, and gather into the garner: so brings to the lively hope, the immortal soul into God, out of which it came. None worship God but who come to the principle of God, which they have transgressed. None are ploughed up but he who comes to the principle of God in him, that he hath transgressed. Then he doth service to God; then is the planting and the watering; and the increase from God cometh. So the ministers of the Spirit must minister to the Spirit that is in prison, which hath been in captivity in every one; that with the Spirit of Christ, people may be led out of captivity up to God, the Father of Spirits, do service to him, and have unity with him, with the Scriptures, and one with another. This is the word of the Lord God to you all, and a charge to you all in the presence of the living God; be patterns, be examples in all your countries, places, islands, nations, wherever you come; that your carriage and life may preach among all sorts of people, and to them: then you will come to walk cheerfully over the world, answering that of God in every one; whereby in them ye may be a blessing, and make the witness of God in them to bless you: then to the Lord God you will be a sweet savour, and a blessing.

"Spare no deceit. Lay the sword upon it; go over it: keep yourselves clear of the blood of all men, either by word, or writing; and keep yourselves clean, that you may stand in your throne, and every one have his lot, and stand in the lot in the Ancient of Days. The blessing of the Lord be with you, and keep you over all the idolatrous worships and worshippers. Let them know the living God; for teachings, churches, worships, set up by man's earthly understanding, knowledge, and will, must be thrown down by the power of the Lord God. All this must be overthrown by that which gave forth Scripture; and who are in that, reign over it all: that is the word of the Lord God to you all. In that is God worshipped, that brings to declare his will; and brings to the church in God, the ground and pillar of truth: for now has the mighty day of the Lord appeared, and the arrows of the Almighty are gone forth, which shall stick in the hearts of the wicked. Now will I arise, saith the Lord God Almighty, to trample and thunder down deceit, which hath long reigned, and stained the earth: now will I have my glory out of every one. The Lord God Almighty over all in his strength and power keep you, to his glory, that you may come to answer that of God in every one. Proclaim the mighty day of the Lord of fire and sword, who will be worshipped in spirit and in truth; and keep in the life and power of the Lord God, that the inhabitants of the earth may tremble before you; that the Lord's power and majesty may be admired among the hypocrites and heathens, and ye in the wisdom, dread, life, terror, and dominion preserved to his glory: that nothing may rule or reign, but power and life itself; and in the wisdom of God ye may be preserved in it. This is the word of the Lord God to you all. The call is now out of transgression; the Spirit bids, 'come.' The call is now from all false worships and gods, and from all inventions and dead works, to serve the living God. The call is to repentance, to amendment of life, whereby righteousness may be brought forth; which shall go throughout the earth. Therefore ye that are chosen and faithful, who are with the Lamb, go through your work faithfully, and in the strength and power of the Lord: and be obedient to the power; for that will save you out of the hands of unreasonable men, and preserve you over the world to himself. Hereby you may live in the kingdom, that stands in power, which hath no end; where glory and life is."

G. F.

After the assizes, the sheriff, with some soldiers, came to guard a woman to execution, that was sentenced to die; and we had much discourse with them. One of them wickedly said, that "Christ was as passionate a man as any that lived upon the earth;" for which we rebuked him. Another time we asked the jailer what doings there were at the sessions; and he said, "Small matters; only about thirty for bastardy." We thought it very strange, that they who professed themselves Christians should make small matters of such things. But this jailer was very bad himself; I often admonished him to sobriety; but he abused people that came to visit us. Edward Pyot had a cheese sent him from Bristol by his wife; and the jailer took it from him, and carried it to the mayor, to search it for treasonable letters, as he said; and though they found no treason in the cheese, they kept it from us. This jailer might have been rich if he had carried himself civilly; but he sought his own ruin; which soon after came upon him; for the next year he was turned out of his place, and for some wickedness cast into the jail himself; and there begged of our Friends. And for some unruliness in his conduct, he was, by the succeeding jailer, put into Doomsdale, locked in irons, and beaten; and bid to "remember how he had abused those good men, whom he had wickedly, without any cause, cast into that nasty dungeon;" and told, "that now he deservedly should suffer for his wickedness; and the same measure he had meted to others, should be meted out to himself." He became very poor, and died in prison; and his wife and family came to misery.

While I was in prison in Launceston, a friend went to Oliver Cromwell, and offered himself, body for body, to lie in Doomsdale in my stead; if he would take him, and let me have liberty. Which thing so struck him, that he said to his great men and council, "Which of you would do so much for me if I were in the same condition?" And though he did not accept of the Friend's offer, but said, "he could not do it, for that it was contrary to law;" yet the truth thereby came mightily over him. A good while after this he sent down Major-General Desborough, pretending to set us at liberty. When he came, he offered us our liberty, if we would say, "we would go home, and preach no more;" but we could not promise him. Then he urged, that we should promise "to go home, if the Lord permitted;" whereupon Edward Pyot wrote him the following letter:—

" To Major-General Desborough.

"FRIEND,

"Though much might be said as to the liberty of Englishmen to travel in any part of the nation of England, it being as the Englishman's house by the law, and he to be protected in any part of it; and if he transgress the law, the penalty upon the transgressor is to be inflicted. And as to liberty of conscience, which is a natural right, and a fundamental; the exercise of it, by those who profess faith in God by Jesus Christ, is to be protected; as by the instrument of government appears, though they differ in doctrine, worship, and discipline; provided the liberty extend not to Popery, to prelacy, nor to licentiousness. Where these rights, which are the price of much blood and treasure in the late wars, are denied us, our liberty is infringed. Yet in the power of God over all, by which all are to be ruled, are we, and in it dwell, and by it alone are guided to do the will of God; whose will is free; and we, in the freedom of his will, walk by the power, either as it commands or permits, without any condition or enforcement thereunto by men; but as the power moves either by command or permission. And although we cannot covenant or condition to go forth of these parts, or to do this or that thing, if the Lord permit (for that were to do the will of man by God's permission), yet it is probable we may pass forth from these parts in the liberty of the will of God, as we may be severally moved, guided by the pure power, and not of necessity. We, who were first committed, were passing homewards when we were apprehended; and, as far as I know, we might pass, if the prison doors were commanded to be opened, and we freed of our bonds. Should we stay, if the Lord commands us to go; or should we go, if the Lord commands us to stay; or having no command to stay, but being permitted to pass from hence, the pure power moving thereto, and yet we stay; or go, when as before commanded to stay; we should then be wanderers indeed; for such are wanderers, who wander out from the will and power of God, abroad, at large, in their own wills and earthly minds. And so, in the fear of the Lord God, well weigh and consider, with the just weight and just balance, that justice thou mayest do to the just and innocent in prison."   EDWARD PYOT.

Some time having elapsed after the foregoing was delivered him, and he not giving any order for our discharge, I also wrote to him, as follows:—

" To Major-General Desborough.

"FRIEND,

"We who are in the power of God, the ruler and upholder of all things, who know and dwell in his power, to it we must be obedient; which brings us to stand out of all men's wills, unlimited. To say, 'we will, if the Lord permit,' in a case of buying and selling to get gain, if the intent be so to do, may be done; but we standing in the power of God to do his will, and to stand out of man's will, if man propose, 'we shall have our liberty if we will say we will go to our outward home, if the Lord permit, or if it be the will of God;' and because we cannot say these words in this case, shall not have our liberty, when we know that the will of God is, we shall 'go to speak at some other place;' here we cannot say these words truly. For to say, 'we will go to our outward habitation, if it be according to the will of God,' when we know the will of God is otherwise, we cannot speak so truly and clearly. Neither can any man say so to him, that requires it of him; who stands in the power, and knows the power of God to lead him, according to God's will, when it leads him to another place than his outward home. But the Son of God, who came to do, and did, the will of God, had no place whereon to lay his head; and the apostles, and many of the followers of Christ, had no certain dwelling-place. Now, if these should have been restrained, because they could not say, they would go to their outward homes, if it were the will of God, when they knew it was the will of God they should not; and they could not do the will of God in doing so; and therefore could not speak those words to satisfy man's mind and will, would not such restraint have been evil? Abraham could not do the will of God, but in going from his native country; and who are of faith are of Abraham, of whom Christ came according to the flesh. Now, if you allege, 'this is to let all loose, and at liberty to idleness,' I say, no; such as are in the power of God, who do the will of God, come to receive his wisdom, by which all his creatures were created; and by which they are used to his glory. This I shall say; whoever are moved by the Lord God of glory and power, to go to their outward habitations, such of us may go to our outward homes, and there be diligent in serving the Lord, that they may be a blessing from the Lord

God in their generation; diligently serving him in life and doctrine, in manners, in conversation, in all things. And who are moved of the Lord to go to any other place, we standing in his will, and being moved by his power, which comprehends all things, and is not to be limited, we shall do his will, as we are commanded to do. So the Lord God open your understandings, that you may see this great power of the Lord, which he is now manifesting among his children in this his day; that ye may not withstand it in our Friends, that are come into the power of God, and to God, and know him by whom the world was made; by whom all things were created that were created; and there was not anything made, but what was made for him, and to him, and by him; who is the power of God, and doth enlighten every man that cometh into the world. Friends being come to this light, which cometh from Christ, and having received power from him, by whom all things were created, who hath all power in heaven and earth given to him, who is the wisdom of God, we have received wisdom and power from him; by which the Lord doth give us to know how to use and order the creatures to the glory of him who is the Creator of all things. Friends here are taught of the Lord to be diligent, serving him; and who come into the life, the Scriptures were given forth from, are given up to serve the Lord; and of this I have in all your consciences a witness. So, if thou open the prison door, we shall not stay there. If thou send a liberate, and set us free, we shall not stay in prison; for Israel is to go out free, whose freedom is purchased by the power of God, and the blood of Jesus. But who goeth out of the power of God, loseth his freedom.

"George Fox,

"The 13th of the 6th   And the rest who are sufferers for
Month, 1656."   the truth in Launceston jail."

After this Major Desborough came to the Castle-Green, and played at bowls with the justices and others. Several Friends were moved to go, and admonish them not to spend their time so vainly; desiring them to consider, that "though they professed themselves to be Christians, yet they gave themselves up to their pleasures, and kept the servants of God meanwhile in prison;" and telling them, "the Lord would plead with them, and visit them for such things." But notwithstanding what was written or said to him, he went away, and left us in prison. We understood afterwards, that he left the business to Colonel Bennet, who had the command of the jail. For sometime after Bennet would have set us at liberty, if we would have paid his jailer's fees. But we told him, "we could give the jailer no fees, for we were innocent sufferers; and how could they expect fees of us, who had suffered so long wrongfully?" After a while Colonel Bennet coming to town, sent for us to an inn, and insisted again upon fees, which we refused. At last the power of the Lord came so over him, that he freely set us at liberty on the 13th day of the seventh month, 1656. We had been prisoners nine weeks at the first assize, called the Lent-assize, which was in the spring of the year.

CHAPTER X.

1656-1657.—Address to those who are given to pleasures and wantonness—to the bowlers in the Castle-Green at Launceston—George Fox visits Friends imprisoned at Exeter, amongst whom is James Naylor, who has apostatized, but afterwards returned into the Truth—at a meeting in the orchard at Bristol about 10,000 persons are present—Paul Gwin, a rude Baptist, creates a disturbance, but is reproved and silenced—meeting of two or three thousand persons at N. Crips's— Justice Stooks prevents the magistrates from apprehending George Fox—speaks to the Protector at Hyde-Park, who invites him to his house—accordingly goes to Whitehall, and speaks to the Protector about Friends' sufferings—travels through most parts of the nation after his liberation from Launceston jail—this year, 1656, there were seldom fewer than one thousand Friends in prison—to Friends, on the schism of J. Naylor—to Friends, to keep up their meetings—on judging the ministry, &c.—an answer to a high-flown professor—to professors, priests, and teachers, on immediate revelation and universal grace, &c., &c.—at Cardiff, George Fox sends word to some who had run out that "the day of their visitation was over"—at Brecknock, his companion, John-ap-John, preaches in the streets—at night, there is a great uproar, like that of Diana's craftsmen—at William Gandy's has a large meeting of two or three thousand persons—Cromwell proclaims a fast for rain, and is told by George Fox that the drought was a sign of their barrenness—concerning the true fast and the false—preaches three hours at a great meeting in Radnorshire, and many are convinced—their horses are twice robbed of their oats—from a high hill sounds the day of the Lord, and foretells where God would raise up a people to himself, which came to pass—travels through every county in Wales, where there is a brave people, who sit under Christ's teaching—has a large meeting on the top of a hill near Liverpool—at Manchester is taken into custody, but soon released.

OBSERVING, while I was a prisoner at Launceston, how much the people (especially they who are called the gentry) were addicted to pleasures and vain recreations, I was moved, before I left the place, to give forth several papers as a warning to them, and all that so misspend their time. One of which was thus directed:—

" This is to go abroad among them who are given to pleasures and wantonness.

"THE sins of Sodom and Gomorrah were pride, fulness of bread, and abundance of idleness. Their filthy conversation vexed the righteous soul of just Lot day by day, and they would not take warning: on whom God therefore sent fire, and turned them into ashes. And in spiritual Sodom and Egypt was our Lord Jesus Christ crucified; and it is written, 'The people sat down to eat and to drink, and rose up to play; with whom God was not well pleased; and there fell three and twenty thousand in one day.' These the apostle commanded the saints they should not follow; for these things happened to them for examples, and are written for our admonition. God spared not the old world; but reserving Noah, a preacher of righteousness brought the flood upon the world of the ungodly, making them an example to all that after should live ungodly. Mark, ye ungodly ones, who are as natural brute beasts, who speak great swelling words of vanity, alluring through the lusts of the flesh, through much wantonness, as they that count it pleasure to riot in the day-time, sporting yourselves with your own deceivings; ye shall receive the reward of unrighteousness. Ye are as dogs and swine turned to the vomit, and wallowing in the mire, speaking evil of things that ye know not; and unless ye repent, ye shall utterly perish in your own corruptions. Ye have lived in pleasure on the earth, and been wanton; ye have nourished your hearts as in a day of slaughter: ye have condemned and killed the just, and he doth not resist you. Go to, weep and howl, for the misery that is coming upon you. She that liveth in pleasures, is dead while she liveth. God condemned the cities of Sodom and Gomorrah, making them an example to all those that after should live ungodly, in the wicked, filthy conversation: mark, here is your example. Hear this, ye that are given to pleasures, and read your examples."   G. F.

Another paper, upon my taking notice of the bowlers that came to sport themselves in the Castle-Green, was as follows:—

"The word of the Lord to all you vain and idle-minded people, who are lovers of sports, pleasures, foolish exercises, and recreations, as you call them; consider of your ways, what it is you are doing. Was this the end of your creation? Did God make all things for you, and you to serve your lusts and pleasures? Did not the Lord make all things for you, and you for himself, to fear and worship him in spirit and in truth, in righteousness and true holiness? But where is your service of God, so long as your hearts run after lusts and pleasures? Ye cannot serve God, and the foolish pleasures of the world, as bowling, drinking, hunting, hawking, and the like: if these have your hearts, God will not have your lips: consider, for it is true. Therefore from the Lord must you all witness woe and misery, tribulation and wrath, who continue in the love and practice of your vain sports, lusts, and pleasures. Now is the day, when all everywhere are exhorted to repentance. O foolish people, wicked and slow of heart to believe the threatenings of the great Jehovah against the wicked! What will ye do in the day of the Lord's fierce wrath, that makes haste to come upon the world of ungodly men! What good have your foolish sports and delights done you now they are past? Or what good will they do you, when the Lord calls for your souls? Therefore all now awake from sleep, and see where you are: and let the light of Jesus Christ, that shines in every one of your consciences, search you thoroughly; and it will let you clearly see, for all your profession of God, Christ, and the Scriptures, you are ignorant of them, and enemies to them all, and your own souls also: and being found living in pleasures, you are dead while you live. Therefore doth the Lord by many messengers forewarn you, and call you to repentance and deep humiliation, that you may forsake the evil of your doings, own this day of your visitation, and while you have time, prize it; lest the things which belong to your peace be hid from your eyes, for your disobedience and rebellion against the Holy One. And then had it been good that you never had been born. Repent, for the kingdom of heaven is at hand : again I say, repent !"

Given forth in Launceston Jail,

To the Bowlers in the Green. in Cornwall.

Being released from our imprisonment we got horses and rode towards Humphrey Lower's, and met him on the road. He told us, "he was much troubled in his mind concerning us, and could not rest at home, but was going to Colonel Bennet to seek our liberty." When we told him, "we were set at liberty, and were going to his house," he was exceedingly glad. To his house we went, and had a fine precious meeting ; many were convinced, and turned by the Spirit of the Lord to Christ's teaching.

From his house we went to Loveday Hambley's, where we also had a fine large meeting. The Lord's power was over all ; many were convinced there also, and turned to the Lord Jesus Christ, their teacher.

After we had tarried there two or three days, we came to Thomas Mounce's, where we had a general meeting for the whole county ; which, being very large, was held in his orchard. Friends from Plymouth were there, and from many places. The Lord's power was over all ; and a great convincement there was in many parts of the county. Their watches were down, and all was plain and open ; for the Lord had let me see, before I was set at liberty, that he would make all the country plain before us. Thomas and Ann Curtis, with an alderman of Reading, who was convinced, had come to Launceston to see us while I was a prisoner : and when Ann, and the other man returned, Thomas Curtis stayed behind in Cornwall, and had good service for the Lord at that time.*

From Thomas Mounce's we passed to LAUNCESTON again, and visited that little remnant of Friends that had been raised up there while we were in prison ; and the Lord's plants grew finely, and were established on Christ, their rock and foundation. As we were going out of town again, the constable of Launceston came running to us with the cheese that had been taken from Edward Pyot ; which they had kept from us all this while, and were tormented with it. But being now set at liberty, we would not receive it.

From Launceston we came to OKINGTON [Oakhampton], and lodged at an inn, which the mayor of the town kept. He had stopped and taken up several Friends, but was very civil to us ; and was convinced in his judgment.

From thence we came to EXETER, where many Friends were in prison ; and amongst the rest James Naylor. For a little before we were set at liberty, James had run out into imaginations, and a company with him ; which raised up a great darkness in the nation.† He came to Bristol, and

---

* Thomas Curtis became a faithful minister, and sufferer for Christ's sake. In 1666, he is mentioned in a letter from Alexander Parker to Margaret Fell as being a prisoner with thirty-two or thirty-three others. His wife, Ann Curtis, was a daughter of a sheriff of Bristol. See a letter of T. Curtis to George Fox, in *Letters of Early Friends,* p. 240.

† James Naylor was a monument of human frailty. His gift in the ministry was

made a disturbance there: and from thence he was coming to Launceston to see me; but was stopped by the way, and imprisoned at Exeter; as were also several others; one of whom, an honest tender man, died in prison there, whose blood lieth on the heads of his persecutors.

The night we came to Exeter, I spoke with James Naylor; for I saw he was out and wrong; and so was his company. Next day, being First-day, we went to visit the prisoners, and had a meeting with them in the prison; but James Naylor and some of them could not stay the meeting. There came a corporal of horse into the meeting, and was convined, and remained a very good Friend. The next day I spoke to James Naylor again; and he slighted what I said, and was dark, and much out; yet he would have come and kissed me. But I said, "since he had turned against the power of God, I could not receive his show of kindness;" the Lord moved me to slight him, and to "set the power of God over him." So after I had been warring with the world, there was now a wicked spirit risen up amongst Friends to war against. I admonished him and his company. When he was come to London, his resisting the power of God in me, and the truth that was declared to him by me, became one of his greatest burdens. But he came to see his out-going, and to condemn it; and after some time he returned to truth again; as in the printed relation of his repentance, condemnation, and recovery, may be more fully seen.

We passed from Exeter through COLLUMPTON and TAUNTON, visiting Friends; and had meetings amongst them. From thence we came to PUDDIMOOR, to William Beaton's; where on the First-day we had a very

---

eminent; his experience in divine things truly great. He fell through unwatchful-ness, but was restored through deep sufferings and unfeigned repentance. His own writings are the most clear and lively description of the various dispensations he under-went; some of them deserve to be transmitted to the latest posterity. His address to his brethren bespeaks the real repentance of his heart; in that he says, "My heart is broken this day for the offence I have occasioned to God's truth and people,—I be-seech you, forgive wherein I evilly requited your love in that day. God knows my sorrow for it!" &c. A few hours before his death, he spoke in the presence of several witnesses the following remarkable words:—

"There is a spirit which I feel, that delights to do no evil, nor to revenge any wrong; but delights to endure all things, in hope to enjoy its own in the end. Its hope is to outlive all wrath and contention, and to weary out all exaltation and cruelty, or whatever is of a nature contrary to itself. It sees to the end of all temptations; as it bears no evil in itself, so it conceives none in thought to any other. If it be betrayed, it bears it; for its ground and spring is the mercy and forgiveness of God. Its crown is meekness; its life is everlasting love unfeigned. It takes its kingdom with entreaty, and not with contention, and keeps it by lowliness of mind. In God alone it can rejoice, though none else regard it, or can own its life. It is conceived in sorrow, and brought forth without any to pity it; nor doth it murmur at grief and oppression. It never rejoiceth, but through sufferings; for with the world's joy it is murdered. I found it alone; being forsaken. I have fellowship therein, with those who lived in dens and desolate places in the earth; who through death obtained this resurrection, and eternal, holy life!"

Such was the end of James Naylor; who, in his forty-fourth year, "chastened, but not killed—cast down, but not destroyed"—through much tribulation, entered, we may humbly hope, "into the kingdom of God."—(For full particulars, see his Life by Joseph Gurney Bevan.)

large meeting.   A great convincement there was all through that country; many meetings we had, and the Lord's power was over all; many were turned, by the power and Spirit of God, to the Lord Jesus Christ, who died for them, and came to sit under his free teaching.

From thence we went to John Dander's, where we had another precious meeting.   The Lord's power was over all, and many were convinced of God's eternal truth.   Contention was raised by professors and Baptists in some places, but the Lord's power came over them.   From thence we came to Edward Pyot's house near Bristol.   It was the Seventh-day at night that we came thither; and it was quickly noised over the town that I was come.   I had never been there before.

On First-day morning I went to the meeting in Broadmead at BRISTOL; which was large and quiet.   Notice was given of a meeting to be in the afternoon in the orchard.   There was at Bristol a rude Baptist, named Paul Gwin, who had before made great disturbance in our meetings, being encouraged and set on by the mayor, who, it was reported, would sometimes give him his dinner to encourage him.   Such multitudes of rude people he gathered after him, that it was thought there had been sometimes ten thousand people at our meeting in the orchard.   As I was going into the orchard, the people told me, that Paul Gwin, the rude jangling Baptist, was going to the meeting.   " I bid them never heed, it was nothing to me who went to it."   When I was come into the orchard, I stood upon the stone that Friends used to stand on when they spoke; and I was moved of the Lord to put off my hat, and to stand a pretty while, and let the people look at me; for some thousands of people were there.   While I thus stood silent, this rude Baptist began to find fault with my hair; but I said nothing to him.   Then he ran on into words; and at last, " Ye wise men of Bristol," said he, " I strange at you, that you will stand here, and hear a man speak and affirm that which he cannot make good."   Then the Lord opened my mouth (for as yet I had not spoken a word), and I asked the people, " whether they ever heard me speak; or ever saw me before:" and I bid them " take notice what kind of man this was amongst them that should so impudently say, that I spoke and affirmed that which I could not make good; and yet neither he nor they had ever heard me or seen me before.   Therefore that was a lying, envious, malicious spirit, that spoke in him; and it was of the Devil, and not of God.   I charged him in the dread and power of the Lord to be silent: and the mighty power of God came over him, and all his company.   Then a glorious, peaceable meeting we had, and the word of life was divided amongst them; and they were turned from darkness to the light,—to Jesus their Saviour.   The Scriptures were largely opened to them; and the traditions, rudiments, ways, and doctrines of men were laid open before the people; and they were turned to the light of Christ, that with it they might see them, and see him to lead them out of them.   I opened also to them the types, figures, and shadows of Christ in the time of the law; and showed them that Christ was come, and had ended the types, shadows, tithes, and oaths, and put down swearing; and had set up yea and nay instead of it, and a free ministry; for he was now come to teach people himself, and his heavenly day was springing from on high." For many hours did I declare the word of life amongst them in the eternal power of God, that by him they might come up into the beginning, and be reconciled to him. And having turned them to the Spirit of God in themselves, that would lead into all truth, I was moved to pray in the mighty power of God; and the Lord's power came over all When I had done, this fellow began to babble again; and John Audland was moved to bid him repent, and fear God. So his own people and followers being ashamed of him, he passed away, and never came again to disturb the meeting. The meeting broke up quietly, and the Lord's power and glory shone over all: a blessed day it was, and the Lord had the praise. After a while this Paul Gwin went beyond the seas; many years after I met with him again at Barbadoes: of which in its place.

From Bristol we returned to Edward Pyot's, where we had a great meeting. The Lord's power was over all, truth was declared and spread abroad, and many were turned to Christ Jesus, their life, their prophet to teach them, their shepherd to feed them, and their bishop to oversee them. After the meeting, I had reasoning with some professors; and the Lord's truth and power came over them.

From Edward Pyot's we passed to SLATTENFORD, where we had a very large meeting (Edward Pyot and another Friend being still with me); great turning of people there was to the Lord Jesus Christ, their teacher: and people were glad that they were brought to know their way, their free teacher, and their Saviour, Christ Jesus.

The First-day following we went to Nathaniel Crips's house, who had been a justice of peace in Wiltshire, where it was supposed there were between two and three thousand people at a meeting; and all was quiet. The mighty power of God was manifest, and people were turned to the grace and truth in their hearts, that came by Jesus Christ, which taught them to deny all ungodliness and worldly lust, and to live soberly and godly in this present world; so that every man and woman might know the grace of God, which had appeared to all men, and which was saving, and sufficient to bring their salvation. This teacher, the grace of God, would teach them how to live, what to do, and what to deny; it would season their words, and establish their hearts. This was a free teacher to every one of them; that they might come to be heirs of this grace, and of Christ, by whom it came; who hath ended the prophets, and the priests that took tithes, and the Jewish temple. And as for the hireling priests that take tithes now, and their temples (which priests were made at schools and colleges of man's setting up, and not by Christ), they, with all their inventions, were to be denied. For the apostles denied the true priesthood and temple, which God had commanded, after Christ had put an end thereto. The Scriptures, and the truths therein contained, were largely opened, and the people turned to the Spirit of God in their hearts; that by it they might be led into all truth, and understand the Scriptures, and know God and Christ, and come to have unity with them, and one with another in the same Spirit. They went away generally satisfied, and were glad that they were turned to Christ Jesus, their teacher and Saviour.

Next day we went to MARLBOROUGH, where we had a little meeting.

The sessions being held that day, they were about to grant a warrant to send for me; but one Justice Stooks being at the sessions, stopped them, telling them there was a meeting at his house yesterday, at which were several thousands. So the warrant was stopped, and the meeting was quiet; and several received Christ Jesus their teacher, came into the new covenant, and abode in it.

From hence we went to NEWBURY, where we had a large, blessed meeting, and several were convinced. Then we passed to READING, where we had a large, precious meeting in the Lord's power, amongst the plants of God. Many of other professions came in, and were reached, and added to the meeting. All was quiet, and the Lord's power was over all. We went next to KINGSTON-ON-THAMES, where a few came in to us that were turned to the Lord Jesus Christ: but it is since become a larger meeting.

Leaving Kingston, we rode to LONDON. When we came near Hyde Park, we saw a great concourse of people, and looking towards them, espied the Protector coming in his coach. Whereupon I rode to his coach-side; and some of his life-guards would have put me away, but he forbade them. So I rode by with him, "declaring what the Lord gave me to say of his condition, and of the sufferings of Friends in the nation; showing him, how contrary this persecution was to Christ and his apostles, and to Christianity." When we arrived at James's Park-gate, I left him; and at parting he desired me to come to his house. Next day, one of his wife's maids, whose name was Mary Sanders, came to me at my lodging, and told me her master came to her, and said he would tell her some good news. When she asked him what it was, he told her, George Fox was come to town. She replied that was good news indeed (for she had received truth), but she said, she could hardly believe him, till he told her how I met him, and rode from Hyde Park to James's Park with him.

After a little time Edward Pyot and I went to Whitehall: and when we came before him, Dr. Owen, vice-chancellor of Oxford, was with him. We were moved "to speak to Oliver Cromwell concerning the sufferings of Friends, and laid them before him; and directed him to the light of Christ, who enlighteneth every man that cometh into the world." He said it was a natural light; but we "showed him the contrary, and manifested that it was divine and spiritual, proceeding from Christ, the spiritual and heavenly man; and that which was called the *life* in Christ the Word, was called the *light* in us." The power of the Lord God arose in me, and I was moved in it "to bid him lay down his crown at the feet of Jesus." Several times I spoke to him to the same effect. Now I was standing by the table, and he came and sat upon the table's side by me, and said he would be as high as I was; and so continued speaking against the light of Christ Jesus; and went away in a light manner. But the Lord's power came over him, so that when he came to his wife and other company, he said, "I never parted so from them before;" for he was judged in himself.

After he had left us, as we were going out, many great persons came about us; and one of them began to speak against the light, and against the truth; and I was made to slight him, for speaking so lightly of the things of God. Whereupon, one of them told me he was the Major-General of Northamptonshire. "What!" said I, "our old persecutor, that has persecuted and sent so many of our friends to prison, and is a shame to Christianity and religion! I am glad I have met with thee," said I. So I was moved to speak sharply to him of his unchristian carriage, and he slunk away: for he had been a cruel persecutor in Northamptonshire.

Now, after I had visited the meetings of Friends in and about London, I went into BUCKINGHAMSHIRE, and Edward Pyot with me; and in several places in that county many received the truth. Great meetings we had, and the Lord's power was eminently manifested. I passed through Northamptonshire and Nottinghamshire, into LINCOLNSHIRE. After having had several meetings in Lincolnshire, I had at last a meeting where two knights, one called Sir Richard Wrey, and the other Sir John Wrey, with their wives, were at the meeting. One of their wives was convinced, received the truth, and died in it. When the meeting was over we passed away; and it being evening, and dark, a company of wild serving-men encompassed me about, with intent (as I apprehended) to do me some mischief. But I spoke aloud to them, and asked, "What are ye? highwaymen?" Whereupon some Friends and friendly people that were behind, came up to us, and knew some of them. So I reproved them for their uncivil and rude carriage, and exhorted them to fear God; and the Lord's power came over them, and stopped their mischievous design: blessed be his name for ever!

Then I turned into HUNTINGDONSHIRE: and the mayor of HUNTINGDON came to visit me, and was very loving, and his wife received the truth.

Thence I passed into CAMBRIDGESHIRE, and the Fen-country, where I had many meetings, and the Lord's truth spread. Robert Craven (who had been sheriff of Lincoln) and Amor Stoddart, and Alexander Parker were with me. We went to CROWLAND, a very rude place; for the town'speople were collected at the inn we went to, and were half drunk, both priest and people. "I reproved them for their drunkenness, and warned them of the day of the Lord, that was coming upon all the wicked; exhorting them to leave their drunkenness, and turn to the Lord in time." Whilst I was thus speaking to them, and showing the priest the fruits of his ministry, he and the clerk broke out into a rage, and got up the tongs and fireshovel to us; so that had not the Lord's power preserved us, we might have been murdered amongst them. Yet, for all their rudeness and violence, some received the truth then, and have stood in it ever since.

Thence we passed to BOSTON, where most of the chief of the town came to our inn, and the people seemed much satisfied. But there was a raging man in the yard, and Robert Craven was moved to speak to him, and told him he shamed Christianity, which with some few other words so stopped the man, that he went away quiet. Some were convinced there also.

Thus we had large meetings up and down, for I travelled into Yorkshire, and returned out of Holderness, over Humber, visiting Friends; and then returning into Leicestershire, Staffordshire, Worcestershire, and Warwickshire, among Friends, I had a meeting at EDGE-HILL. There came to it Ranters, Baptists, and several sorts of rude people; for I had sent word about three weeks before to have a meeting there, so that hundreds of people were gathered thither, and many Friends came far to it. The

Lord's everlasting truth and word of life reached over all; the rude and unruly spirits were chained down; and many that day were turned to the Lord Jesus Christ, by his power and Spirit, and came to sit under his blessed, free teaching, and to be fed with his eternal, heavenly food. All was peaceable; the people passed quietly away, and some of them said it was a mighty, powerful meeting; for the presence of the Lord was felt, and his power and Spirit amongst them.

From hence I passed to WARWICK and to BAGLEY, having precious meetings; and then into Gloucestershire, and so to OXFORD, where the scholars were very rude; but the Lord's power came over them. Great meetings we had up and down as we travelled. Then I went to Colonel Grimes's, where there was a very large meeting; and thence to Nathaniel Crips's, where came another justice to the meeting, who was also convinced. At CIRENCESTER we had a meeting, which is since much increased; and so we came to EVESHAM again, where I met John Camm.

Thus having travelled over most part of the nation, I returned to LONDON again, having cleared myself of that which lay upon me from the Lord. For after I was released out of Launceston jail, I was moved of the Lord to travel over the nation, the truth being now spread, and finely planted in most places, that I might answer, and remove out of the minds of people some objections, which the envious priests and professors had raised and spread abroad concerning us. For what Christ said of false prophets and antichrists coming in the last days, they applied to us; and said, We were they.

Therefore was I moved to open this through the nation, and to show "That they who said we were the false prophets, antichrists, and deceivers, that should come in the last days, were indeed themselves they. For when Christ told his disciples in the viith and xxivth of Matthew, that false prophets and antichrists should come in the last times, and (if it were possible) should deceive the very elect; he said, 'By their fruits ye shall know them;' for they should be inwardly ravening wolves, having the sheep's clothing. 'And,' said he, 'do men gather grapes of thorns, or figs of thistles?' as much as to say, their nature and spirit should be like a thorn, or like a thistle. And he bid his disciples not go after them. But before the disciples were deceased, the antichrists, false prophets, and deceivers were come. For John in his first epistle said, 'Little children, it is the last time; and as ye have heard that antichrist shall come, even now there are many antichrists, whereby we know that it is the last time.' So here, as Christ said to his disciples they should come, the disciples saw they were come; as may be seen at large in Peter, Jude, John, and other places of Scripture; 'whereby,' says John, 'we know it is the last time.' And this last time began above sixteen hundred years since. John said, 'they went out from us;' the false prophets, antichrists, seducers, and deceivers, went out from the church;' 'but you,' said he, to the church, 'have an anointing, which abideth in you; and you need not that any man teach you, but as the same anointing teacheth you of all things; and as it hath taught you, ye shall abide in him.' Christ said to his disciples, 'Go not after

them, for they are inwardly ravening wolves;' and John exhorts the saints
to the anointing within them; and the rest of the apostles exhort the
churches to the grace, the light, the truth, the Spirit, the word of faith,
and to Christ in their hearts, the hope of glory.   Christ told the saints
that the Spirit of truth, the Holy Ghost, should be their leader into all
truth; and Jude exhorts the church to 'pray in the Holy Ghost,' and 'to
be built up in their most holy faith,' which Christ was the author of.
Christ, by his servant John, 'exhorted the seven churches to hear what
the Spirit said to the churches,' and this was an inward, spiritual hearing.
Christ says, the inwardly ravening wolves should have the sheep's clothing.
Paul speaks of some in his time, that had 'a form of godliness, but denied
the power.'   John said, 'they went out from us.'   Jude said, 'they go in
Cain's way, and in Balaam's, and Corah's way.   By all which it may be
clearly seen, that the false prophets and antichrists, which Christ foretold
should come, the apostles saw were come; and in their day it was the last
time; and these went forth from them into the world, and the world went
after them.   These were the foremen, the leaders of the world, that
brought them into a form of godliness, but inwardly ravened from the
power and Spirit.   These have the sheep's clothing, the words of Christ,
of the prophets, and of the apostles; but are inwardly ravened from the
power and Spirit that they were in, who gave forth the Scriptures.   These
have made up the beast and the whore!   These have got the dragon's
power, the murdering, destroying, persecuting power!   And these are
they that the world wonders after!   These have drunk the blood of the
martyrs, prophets, and saints, and persecuted the true church into the
wilderness!   These have set up the false, compelling worships, and have
drunk the blood of the saints, that will not drink of their cup!   These
have made the cage for the unclean birds, that have their several unclean
notes in their cage; which cage is made up by the power of darkness, and
uncleanness; and the birds of the cage deny the Holy Ghost, and the
power of God, which the apostles were in, to be now manifested in the
saints!   Thus since Christ said, the false prophets and antichrists should
come, and the apostle said, they were come, the beast's and the dragon's
worship hath been set up; and the whore is got up with her false prophets,
and her cage hath been made, and all nations have drunk of her cup of
fornication; the blood of the martyrs and saints they have drunk, and the
true church hath fled into the wilderness; and all this since the apostles'
days.   Yet the blind deceivers, the antichrists and false prophets of our
age, would make us and people believe, that the false prophets, antichrists,
and deceivers are come but now, though John and other of the apostles
tell us they were come above sixteen hundred years ago.   And ye may
see what work and confusion they have made in the world; how much
blood these Cains have drunk that went in Cain's way; which blood cries
to God for vengeance upon Christendom!   And how these Balaams, that
have erred from the power and Spirit which the apostles were in, have
coveted after other men's estates, the many jails, courts, and spoilings of
goods will bear witness.   And how the Corahs have gainsayed the life,
power, and spirit, which the apostles and true church were in, and the free

teaching of Christ and his apostles, and the work of their ministry, which was 'to present every man perfect in Christ Jesus,' hath been evident.

"Therefore in the name and power of the Lord Jesus was I sent to preach again the everlasting gospel, which had been preached before unto Abraham, and in the apostles' days; which was to go over all nations, and be preached to every creature. For as the apostacy hath gone over all nations since the apostles' days, so that the nations are become as waters, unstable, being gone from Christ the foundation; so must the gospel, the power of God, go over all nations again. We find the false prophets, antichrists, deceivers, whore, false church, beast, and his worship in the dragon's power, have got up in the times between the apostles and us. For Christ said, 'they should come;' and the apostles saw 'they were come,' and coming in their days; and that they went forth from them, and the world went after them. And now hath the Lord raised us up beyond them, and set us over them in the everlasting gospel, the power of God; that as all have been darkened by the beast, whore, false prophets, and antichrists, so the everlasting gospel may be preached again by us to all nations, and to every creature, which will bring life and immortality to light in them, that they may see over the devil and his false prophets, antichrists, seducers, and deceivers, and over the whore and beast, and to that which was before they were. This message of the glorious everlasting gospel was I sent forth to declare and publish, and thousands by it are turned to God, having received it; and are come into subjection to it, and into the holy order of it. And since I have declared this message in this part of the world, and in America, and have written books on the same, to spread it universally abroad; the blind prophets, preachers, and deceivers, have given over telling us the false prophets should 'come in the last times;' for a great light is sprung up, and shines over their heads; so that every child in truth sees the folly of their sayings.

"Then they raised other objections against us, and invented shifts to save themselves from truth's stroke. For when we blamed them for taking tithes, which came from the tribe of Levi, and were set up here by the Romish church, they would plead, 'that Christ told the scribes and Pharisees they ought to pay tithes of mint, anise, and cummin, though they had neglected the weightier matters;' and that Christ said, 'the scribes and Pharisees sat in Moses's seat, therefore all that they bid you do, that do and observe.' And when we told them they were envious, persecuting priests, they would reply, that 'some preached Christ of envy, and some of contention, and some of good-will.' Now these Scriptures, and such like they would bring to darken the minds of their hearers, and to persuade them and us, 'that we ought to do as they say, though they themselves were like the Pharisees; and that we should rejoice when envious men and men of strife preached Christ; and that we should give them the tithes, as the Jews did to the tribe of Levi.' These were fair glosses; here was a great heap of husks, but no kernel. Now this was their blindness; for the Levitical priesthood Christ hath ended, and disannulled the commandment that gave them tithes, and the law, by which those priests were made. Christ did not come after that order, neither did he send forth his ministers after that order; for those of that order were to take tithes for their maintenance; but his ministers he sent forth *freely*. And as for hearing that the Pharisees, and the Jews paid tithes of mint, anise, and cummin, that was before Christ was sacrificed and offered up; the Jews were then to do the law, and perform their offerings and sacrifices, which the Jewish priests taught them. But after Christ was offered up, he bid them then, 'go into all nations and preach the gospel; and lo,' said he, 'I will be with you to the end of the world;' and in another place he saith, 'I will be *in* you.' So he did not bid them go to hear the Pharisees then, and pay tithe of mint, anise, and cummin then; but 'Go preach the gospel, and believe in the Lord Jesus, and be saved, and receive the gospel,' which would bring people off from the Jews, the tithes, the Levitical law, and the offerings thereof, to Christ, the one Offering, made once for them all. O what work had the apostle with both the Galatians and the Romans, to bring them off the law to the faith in Christ!

"And as for the apostle's saying, 'Some preached Christ of envy and strife,' &c., that was at the first spreading of Christ's name abroad, when they were in danger not only to be cast out of the synagogues, but to be stoned to death, that confessed the name of Jesus, as may be seen by the uproars that were among the Jews and Diana's worshippers at the preaching of Christ. So the apostle might well rejoice, if the envious, and men of strife and contention, preached Christ at that time, though they thought thereby to add affliction to his bonds; but afterward, when Christ's name was spread abroad, and many had got a form of godliness, but denied the power thereof, 'envious, proud, contentious men, men of strife, covetous teachers for filthy lucre,' the apostles commanded the saints to turn from, and not have any fellowship with them. And the deacons and ministers were first to be proved, to see if they were in the power of godliness, and the Holy Ghost made them overseers and preachers. So it may be seen how the priests have abused these Scriptures for their own ends, and have wrested them to their own destruction, to justify envious, contentious men, and men of strife.' Whereas the apostle says, 'the man of God must be patient, and apt to teach;' and they were to follow Christ, as they had him for their example. The apostle indeed was very tender to people, while he saw them walk in simplicity; as in the case of them that were scrupulous about meats and days; but when the apostle saw that some drew them into the observation of days, and to settle in such things, he then reproves them sharply, and asks them, 'who had bewitched them?' So in the case of marrying he was tender, lest their minds should be drawn from the Lord's joining; but when they came to forbid marriage, and to set up rules for meats and drinks, he called it 'a doctrine of devils,' and an 'erring from the true faith.' So also he was tender concerning circumcision, and in tenderness suffered some to be circumcised; but when he saw they went to make a sect thereby, and set up circumcision as a standing practice, he told them plainly, 'if they were circumcised, Christ would profit them nothing.' In like manner he was tender concerning baptizing with water; but when he saw they began to make sects about it, some crying up Paul, others Apollos, he judged them, and called them carnal, and thanks God he had baptized no more, but such and such; declaring plainly, that 'he was sent to preach the gospel, and not to baptize;' and brought them to the one baptism by the one Spirit, into the one body, which Christ, the spiritual man, is the head of; and exhorted the church 'all to drink into that one Spirit.' For he set up in the church one faith, which Christ was the author of; and one baptism, which was that of the Spirit, into the one body; and one Lord Jesus Christ, the spiritual baptizer, whom John said should come after him. And further the apostle declared, that they who worshipped and served God in the Spirit, were of the circumcision of the Spirit, which was not made with hands; by which 'the body of the sins of the flesh was put off;' which circumcision Christ is the minister of.*

"Another great objection they had, 'That the Quakers denied the sacrament (as they called it) of bread and wine, which,' they said, 'they were to take, and do in remembrance of Christ to the end of the world.' Much work we had with the priests and professors about this, and the several modes of receiving it in Christendom, so called; for some take it kneeling, and some sitting; but none of them all, that ever I could find, take it as the disciples took it. For they took it in a chamber, after supper; but these generally take it before dinner: and some say, after the priest hath blessed it, it is 'Christ's body.' But as to the matter, Christ said, 'Do this in remembrance of me.' He did not tell them how often they should do it, or how long; neither did he enjoin them to do it always, as long as they lived, or that all believers in him should do it to the world's end. The apostle Paul, who was not converted till after Christ's death, tells the Corinthians, that he had received of the Lord that which he delivered unto them concerning this matter: and he relates Christ's words concerning the cup thus; 'This do ye,' as oft as ye drink it, in 'remembrance of me:' and himself adds, 'For [as often as] ye eat this bread, and drink this cup, ye do show the Lord's death till he come.' So according to what the apostle here delivers, neither Christ nor he enjoined people to do this always; but leave it to their liberty [as oft as ye drink it, &c]. Now the Jews used to take a cup, and to break bread, and divide it among them in their feasts; as may be seen in the Jewish Antiquities: so that the breaking of bread, and drinking of wine, were Jewish rites, which were not to last always. They also baptized with water; which made it not seem a strange thing to them when John the Baptist came with his decreasing ministration of water-baptism. But as to the bread and wine, after the disciples had taken it, some of them questioned whether Jesus was the Christ; for some of them said, after he was crucified, 'We trusted that it had been he which should have redeemed Israel,' &c. And though the Corinthians had the bread and wine, and were baptized in water, the apostle told them they were 'reprobates, if Christ was not *in* them;' and bid them 'examine themselves.' And as the apostle said, 'As oft as ye do eat this

---

* For a full declaration of the doctrines of Friends as regards Baptism, "the sacrament of bread and wine," &c., see Bates' *Doctrines*, Barclay's *Apology*, Joseph John Gurney's *Distinguishing Views of Friends*, and Jacob Post's *History and Mystery of those called the Sacraments.*

bread, and drink this cup, ye do show forth the Lord's death [till he come]:' so Christ had said before, that he ' was the bread of life, which came down from heaven ;' and that ' he would come and dwell *in* them ;' which the apostles did witness fulfilled ; and exhorted others to seek for that which comes down from above : but the outward bread and wine, and water, are not from above, but from below. Now ye that eat and drink this outward bread and wine in remembrance of Christ's death, and have your fellowships in that, will ye come no nearer to Christ's death, than to take bread and wine in remembrance of it ? After ye have eaten in remembrance of his death, ye must come *into* his death, and *die* with him, as the apostles did, if ye will *live* with him. This is a nearer and further advanced state, to be with him in the fellowship of his death, than only to take bread and wine in remembrance of his death. You must have fellowship with Christ in his sufferings : if ye will reign with him, ye must suffer with him ; if ye will live with him, ye must die with him ; and if ye die with him, ye must be buried with him : and being buried with him in the true baptism, ye also rise with him. Then having suffered with him, died with him, and been buried with him, if ye are risen with Christ, ' seek those things which are above, where Christ sitteth on the right hand of God.' Eat the bread which comes down from above, which is not outward bread ; and drink the cup of salvation which he gives in his kingdom, which is not outward wine. And then there will not be a looking at the things that are seen (as outward bread and wine, and water are): for, as says the apostle, ' The things that are seen are temporal, but the things that are not seen are eternal.'

"So here are many states and conditions to be gone through, before people come to see and partake of that, which ' cometh down from above.' For first, there was a taking of the outward bread and wine in remembrance of Christ's death : this was temporary, and not of necessity, but at their liberty ; as oft as ye do it, &c. Secondly, there must be a coming into his death, a suffering with Christ ; and this is of necessity to salvation, and not temporary, but continual : there must be a dying daily. Thirdly, a being buried with Christ. Fourthly, a rising with Christ. Fifthly, after they are risen with Christ, then a seeking those things which are above ; a seeking the bread that comes down from heaven, a feeding on and having fellowship in that. For outward bread, wine, and water, are from below, visible and temporal : but saith the apostle, ' We look not at things that are seen ; for the things that are seen are temporal, but the things that are not seen are eternal.' So the fellowship that stands in the use of bread, wine, water, circumcision, outward temple, and things seen, will have an end : but the fellowship which stands in the gospel, the power of God, which was before the Devil was, and which brings life and immortality to light, by which people may see over the Devil, that has darkened them ; this fellowship is eternal, and will stand. And all that are in it seek that which is heavenly and eternal, which comes down from above, and are settled in the eternal mystery of the fellowship of the gospel, which is hid from all eyes, that look only at visible things. The apostle told the Corinthians, who were in disorder about water, bread and wine, that he desired to know nothing amongst them but Jesus Christ, and him crucified."

Thus were the objections, which the priests and professors had raised against Friends, answered and cleared; and the stumbling-blocks, which they had laid in the way of the weak, removed. And as things were thus opened, people came to see over them and through them, and to have their minds settled upon the Lord Jesus Christ, their free teacher: which was the service for which I was moved to travel over the nation after my imprisonment in Launceston jail. In this year the Lord's truth was finely planted over the nation, and many thousands were turned to the Lord; insomuch that there were seldom fewer than one thousand in prison in this nation for truth's testimony; some for tithes, some for going to the steeple-houses, some for contempts (as they called them), some for not swearing, and others for not putting off their hats, &c.

Now after I had visited most parts of the nation, and was come to London again, finding that evil spirit at work, which had drawn J. N. and his followers out from truth, to run Friends into heats about him, I wrote a short epistle to Friends, as follows :—

"To all the elect seed of God called Quakers, where the death is brought into the death, and the elder is servant to the younger, and the elect is known, which cannot be deceived, but obtains victory. This is the word of the Lord God to you all : Go not forth to the aggravating part, to strive with it out of the power of God; lest ye hurt yourselves, and run into the same nature, out of the life. For patience must get the victory; and to answer that of God in every one, it must bring every one to it, to bring them from the contrary. Let your moderation, and temperance, and patience be known unto all men in the Seed of God. For that which reacheth to the aggravating part without life, sets up the aggravating part, and breeds confusion; and hath a life in outward strife, but reacheth not to the witness of God in every one, through which they might come into peace and covenant with God, and fellowship one with another. Therefore that which reacheth this witness of God in yourselves, and in others, is the life and light; which will out-last all, is over all, and will overcome all. And therefore in the Seed of life live, which bruiseth the Seed of death."   G. F.

I also wrote another short epistle to Friends, to encourage them to keep up their meetings in the Lord's power; of which epistle a copy here follows :—

"DEAR FRIENDS,

"Keep your meetings in the power of the Lord, which is over all that is in the fall and must have an end. Therefore be wise in the wisdom of God, which is from above, by which all things were made and created; that that may be justified among you, and you all kept in the solid life, which was before death was; and in the light, which was before the darkness was with all its works. In which light and life ye all may feel, and have the heavenly unity and peace, possessing the gospel fellowship, that is everlasting: which was before that, which doth not last for ever; and will remain when that is gone. For the gospel being the power of God, is pure and everlasting. Know it to be your portion : in which is stability, and life, and immortality, shining over that which darkens the mortal. So be faithful every one to God, in your measures of his power and life, that ye may answer God's love and mercy to you, as obedient children of the Most High ; dwelling in love, unity, and peace, and in innocency of heart towards one another ; that God may be glorified in you, and you kept faithful witnesses for him, and valiant for the truth on earth. God Almighty preserve you all to his glory, that ye may feel his blessing among you, and be possessors thereof."   G. F.

About this time many mouths were opened in our meetings, to declare the goodness of the Lord, and some that were young and tender in the truth would sometimes utter a few words in thanksgiving and praises to God. That no disorder might arise from this in our meetings, I was moved to write an epistle to Friends, by way of advice in that matter. And thus it was :—

"ALL my dear friends in the noble Seed of God, who have known his power, life, and presence among you, let it be your joy to hear or see the springs of life break forth in any ; through which ye have all unity in the same, feeling life and power. And above all things, take heed of judging any one openly in your meetings, except they be openly profane or rebellious, such as be out of the power, life, and wisdom ye may stand over them, and by it answer the witness of God in the world, that such, whom ye bear your testimony against, are none of you : that therein the truth may stand clear and single. But such as are tender, if they should be moved to bubble forth a few words, and speak in the Seed and Lamb's power, suffer and bear that ; that is, the tender. And if they should go beyond their measure, bear it in the meeting for peace and order's sake, and that the spirits of the world be not moved against you. But when the meeting is done, if any be moved to speak to them, between you and them, one or two of you, that feel it in the life, do it in the love and wisdom that is pure and gentle from above : for love is that which edifies, bears all things, suffers long, and fulfils the law. In this ye have order and edification, ye have wisdom to preserve you all wise and in patience ; which takes away the occasion of stumbling the weak, and the occasion of the spirits of the world to get up : but in the royal Seed, the heavy stone, ye keep down all that is wrong ; and by it answer that of God in all. For ye will hear, see, and feel the power of God preaching, as your faith is all in it (when ye do not hear words), to bind, to chain, to limit, to frustrate ; that nothing shall rise, nor come forth but what is in the power : with that ye will hold back, and with that ye will let up, and open every spring, plant, and spark ; in which will be your joy and refreshment in the power of God.

"Now ye that know the power of God, and are come to it, which is the cross of Christ, that crucifies you to the state that Adam and Eve were in, in the fall, and so to the world ; by this power of God ye come to see the state they were in before they fell ; which power of God is the cross, in which stands the everlasting glory ; which brings up into the righteousness, holiness, and image of God, and crucifies to the unrighteousness, unholiness, and image of Satan, that Adam and Eve, and their sons and daughters, are in, in the fall. Through this power of God, ye come to see the state they were in before they fell; yea, I say, and to a higher state, to the Seed Christ, the second Adam, by whom all things were made. For man hath been driven from God: all Adam and Eve's sons and daughters, being in the state of the fall, in the earth, are driven from God. But it is said, The church is *in* God, the Father of our Lord Jesus Christ: so they who come to the church, which is *in* God the Father of Christ, must come to God again; and so out of the state that Adam and Eve, and his children are in, in the fall, out of the image of God, of righteousness and holiness, and they must come into the righteousness, true holiness, and image of God; and so out of the earth, whither man hath been driven, when they come to the church which is *in* God. The way to this, is Christ, the Light, the Life, the Truth, the Saviour, the Redeemer, the Sanctifier, and the Justifier; in and through whose power, light, and life, conversion, regeneration, and translation, are known from death to life, from darkness to light, and from the power of Satan to God again. These are members of the true church, who know the work of regeneration in the operation and feeling of it; and being come to be members of the church in God, they are indeed members one of another in the power of God, which was before the power of darkness was. So they that come to the church, that is *in* God and Christ, must come out of the state that Adam was in, in the fall, driven from God, to know the state that he was in before he fell. But they that live in the state that Adam was in, in the fall, and cannot believe a possibility of coming into the state he was in before he fell, come not to the church, which is *in* God; but are far from that, and are not passed from death to life; but are enemies to the cross of Christ, which is the power of God. For they mind earthly things, and serve not Christ, nor love the power, which should bring them up to the state that Adam was in before he fell, and crucify them to the state that man is in in the fall; that through this power they might see to the beginning, the power that man was in before the heavenly image, and holiness, and righteousness was lost; by which power they might come to know the Seed, Christ, which brings out of the old things, and makes all things new; in which life eternal is felt. For all the poorness, emptiness, and barrenness is in the state that man is in, in the fall, out of God's power; by which power he is made rich, and hath strength again; which power is the cross, in which the mystery of the fellowship stands: and in which is the true glorying, which crucifies to all other gloryings.

"And, Friends, though ye may have been convinced, and tasted of the power, and felt the light; yet afterwards ye may feel a winter storm, tempest and hail, frost and cold, and temptation in the wilderness. Be patient and still in the power, and in the light, that doth convince you, to keep your minds to God; in that be quiet, that ye may come to the summer; that your flight be not in the winter. For if ye sit still in the patience, which overcomes in the power of God, there will be no flying. The husbandman, after he hath sowed his seed, is patient. And by the power, being kept in the patience, ye will come by the light to see through, and feel over winter storms and tempests, and all the coldness, barrenness, and emptiness : and the same light and power will go over the tempter's head ; which power and light was before he was. So standing still in the light, ye will see your salvation, ye will see the Lord's strength, feel the small rain, and the fresh springs, your minds being kept low in the power and light : for that which is out of the power lifts up. But in the power and light ye will feel God, revealing his secrets, inspiring your minds, and his gifts coming in unto you : through which your hearts will be filled with God's love, and praises to him that lives for evermore : for in his light and power his blessing is received. So in that, the eternal power of the Lord Jesus Christ preserve and keep you ! Live every one in the power of God, that ye may all come to be heirs of that, and know it to be your portion ; even the kingdom, that hath no end, and the endless life, which the Seed is heir of. Feel that set over all, which hath the promise and blessing of God for ever." G. F.

About this time I received some lines from a high professor, concerning the way of Christ, to which I returned the following answer :—

"FRIEND,

"It is not circumstances we contend about, but the way of Christ and his light, which are but one ; though the world hath imagined many ways, and all out of the light ; which by the light are condemned. He who preached this light, said, 'He that knoweth God, heareth us ; he that is not of God, heareth us not : hereby know we the Spirit of Truth, and the spirit of error.' It is the same now, with them that know the truth ; though the whole world lies in wickedness. All dispensations and differences, that are not one in the light, we deny ; and by the light, that was before separation, do we see them to be self-separations in the sensual, having not the Spirit. Their fruits and end are weighed in the even balance, and found to be in the dark, the lo-here, and lo-there thou tellest of. The presence of Christ is not with them, though the blind see it not ; who see not with the pure eye, which is single ; but with the many eyes, which lead into the many ways. Nor are any the people of God, but they who are baptized into this principle of light ; by which all the faithful servants of the Lord were ever guided in all ages, since the apostacy, and before. For the apostacy was and is from the light ; and all that oppose the light are apostates. They who contest against the truth, are enemies to it, and are not actuated by the Spirit ; but have another way than the light. All such are in the world, its words, fashions, and customs, though of several forms, as to their worship ; yet all under the god of this world, opposing the light and appearance of Christ, which should lead out from under his power, of what form soever they are : yet are they all joined against the light. All these are of the world ; and fighting against them who are not of the world, but are gathered and gathering out of it ; and so it ever was against the people of God, under what name soever. They only are saints by calling, who are called into the light ; and sons of Sion, who vary not from the light, to which the Spirit is promised, which is not tied to any forms out of the light ; wherein all inherit who are co-heirs with Christ ; which many talk of, who inherit the earthly instead of the heavenly. And whereas thou speakest of Christ and his apostles clothing themselves with the sayings and words of the prophets; and of their being your example in so doing; I say, wolves will take the sheep's clothing; but the light and life finds them out, and judges (not by their stolen words, but) by their works. Nor did Christ cover himself with any words, but what were fulfilled in him; neither do any of Christ's boast in other men's lines made ready without them: to which rule if ye be obedient, fewer words and more life will be seen among you. Then ye will not count it straitness to silence the flesh, and hear what he saith, who speaks peace, 'that his people turn no more to folly.' If ye once know that what is stolen must be restored fourfold, the mouth of the false prophet will be stopped, which builds up in deceit, but not in righteousness. And whereas thou sayest, 'The Spirit of truth affords nothing but endless varieties;' I say, the Spirit of truth thou knowest not: for the Spirit of truth said, 'there is but one thing needful;' and to speak the same thing again, is safe for the hearers. But that spirit, which affords nothing but endless varieties, is not the Spirit of truth; but is gone out into envious notions: and the number of his names and colours is read no-where, but in the unity of the Spirit of truth. All others call truth deceit, and deceit truth, as the blind, that opposed the light, ever did; who are ever learning endless varieties, but never able to come to the knowledge of the truth, nor to an end of their labours: but when they are out of one form, get into another; so long as they can find a green tree without. Thus ye are kept at work all your life, and to the grave in sorrow, as the dumb priests, thou tellest of, have been before you: only ye have got a finer image, but less life. And thou, whose teaching hath no end, art in the horse-mill thou speakest of. I have read the epistles to Timothy, and to the Hebrews; and there I find the duty of all believers is, to see the law of the new covenant written in the heart, whereby all may know God, from the least to the greatest. I know the Holy Scriptures are profitable for the man of God; but what is that to the man of sin, to the first-born, who is out of the light, and being unstable and unlearned, wrest them to his own destruction; but to the life cannot come? And for your two ordinances thou speakest of, I say, upon the same account ye deny the priests of the world therein, we deny you; being both of you not only out of the life, but out of the form too. That command, Matt. xxviii. 19, ye never had, nor its power; which was, 'to baptize into the name of the Father, Son, and Holy Ghost.' What Paul received of the Lord, that body, and that bread, ye know as little, but what ye have found in the chapter; nor the coming of Christ neither, who cannot believe his light. And whereas thou speakest of preaching Christ of envy, and pleadest for it; I say, such preachers we have enough of in these days. What else art thou doing, who sayest, Paul was sent to baptize; though Paul says he was not: and so thou wouldst prove him a liar, if any would believe thee before him. Thou sayest also, 'for ought thou knowest, he might baptize thousands.' Thou mightest as easily have said millions, and as soon have proved it. Thou mayest say the same of circumcision also, and on the same ground. As for the signs that followed those that believed, which thou sayest are ccased; I say, they who cannot receive the light cannot see the signs, nor could believe them if they should see them to carp at; no more than formerly they could do, who opposed the light in former ages. They cannot properly be said to cease to such, who never had them; but have only heard or read, that others long ago had them. But that the power, and signs, and presence of God is not the same that ever it was, in the measure, wherein he is received in the light, that I deny; and declare it to be false, and from a spirit that knows not God, nor his power. And as for the gospel foundation thou speakest of, I say, it is to be laid again in all the world. Ye never were on it, since the man of sin set up his forms without power. Till ye can own the light of Christ, which the saints preached, and their life and practice; for shame cease to talk of their foundation, or glorious work, or quakings and tremblings, which are the saints' experiences, which the world knows not, nor can own: though ye cannot read that ever any came aright to declare how they knew God, or received his word, without them. In thy exhortation thou biddest me 'love Christ, wheresoever I see him:' but hadst thou told me where one might come to see him, or how one might know him, thou hadst showed more of a Christian in that, than in all thou hast spoken. But it seems, ye are not all of one mind: some of you say, 'he is gone, and will be no more seen, till doomsday;' but if ever ye come to see Christ to your comfort, while ye oppose his light, then God hath not spoken by me. This thou shalt remember, when thy time thou hast spent."   G. F.

Great opposition did the priests and professors make about this time against the light of Christ Jesus, denying it to be universally given; and against the pouring forth of the Spirit, and sons and daughters prophesying thereby. Much they laboured to darken the minds of people, that they might keep them still in a dependence on their teaching. Wherefore I was moved of the Lord to give forth the following lines, for the opening of the minds and understandings of people, and to manifest the blindness and darkness of their teachers:—

"To all you professors, priests, and teachers, who are in darkness, and know not the Spirit in prison, nor the light that shines in darkness, and which the darkness doth not comprehend; but are the infidels, whom the god of the world hath blinded, and to whom the gospel is hid. For though ye have the four books, yet the gospel is hid to you; who are now wondering at the work of God, and do not believe that Christ hath enlightened every one that cometh into the world. I offer you some Scriptures to read, which will prove your spirits, and try them, how contrary they are to the apostles' spirit, the Spirit of Christ and of the saints. Christ went and 'preached to the spirits in prison,' 1 Pet. iii. 19. He that readeth, let him understand, whether this was a measure of the Spirit, yea or nay, or the Spirit without measure, which he ministered to? 'For he whom God hath sent, speaketh the words of God; for God giveth not the Spirit by measure unto him,' John iii. 34. Here Christ had not the Spirit given to him by measure. The apostle said, 'We will not boast of things without (or beyond) our measure.' 2 Cor. x. 13. So here was measure, and not by measure. Christ, who received not the Spirit by measure, told his disciples he would 'send them the Comforter, the Spirit of Truth, that should guide them into all truth: for he should not speak of himself, but whatsoever he shall hear, that shall he speak, and he will show you things to come. He shall glorify me: for he shall receive of mine, and show it unto you,' John xvi. 13, 14. Mind, read, and learn; the Comforter shall receive of mine, saith Christ, and shall show it unto you: who hath the measure, receives of his who hath not by measure. The Comforter, when he comes, is to 'reprove the world of sin, and of righteousness, and of judgment,' ver. 8. Now mind the great work of God: the Spirit of Truth, which leads the saints into all truth, which receives of Christ's, and shows it unto the disciples, who are in the measure, he shall reprove the world of sin, because they do not believe, &c. The Comforter, whom Christ will send, takes of his, and shows it to the disciples; the same reproves the world. Mind now, whether this be a measure, yea or nay, which comes from him, who received not the Spirit by measure. He that leads the believer into all truth, reproves the unbeliever in the world, of sin, of righteousness, and of judgment; so he that is led into all truth, sees that which is reproved, by the Spirit of Truth that leads him. Now Christ saith, 'He shall take of mine, and show it unto you.' Is this a measure, yea or nay, from him to whom God gave the Spirit not by measure?

"Again, the Lord said, both by his prophet, Joel ii. 28, and his apostle, Acts ii. 17, 18, 'It shall come to pass in the last days, I will pour out of my Spirit upon all flesh, your sons and your daughters shall prophesy, your young men shall see visions, and your old men shall dream dreams: and on my servants, and handmaidens, I will pour out in those days of my Spirit, and they shall prophesy.' Look, ye deceivers; here the Lord saith, he will pour out of his Spirit; mark the word, or the Lord's Spirit upon all flesh. What! young men, old men, sons and daughters, and maidens, all these to have the Spirit of God poured forth upon them? Here, say they, these deny the means then: nay, that is the means. And the great and notable day of the Lord is coming, wherein it shall come to pass, that whosoever shall call on the name of the Lord shall be saved. The God of the spirits of all flesh is known; 'And,' saith the apostle, who would not boast of things beyond his measure, 'that which may be known of God is manifest in them; for God hath showed it unto them,' Rom. i. 19. By this which was of God manifest in them, they knew covetousness, maliciousness, murder, deceit, and ungodliness; and knew that the judgments of God were upon such things; and that they were worthy of death not only that did the same, but who had pleasure in them that did them. Therefore said the apostle, 'the wrath of God is revealed from heaven against all ungodliness, and unrighteousness of men,' &c. Now this of God manifest in them, which God showed unto them, by which they know unrighteousness, and God's judgments thereupon, and that they which commit such things are worthy of death; whether this be a measure, yea or nay, which is of God, and which he hath showed to them? What was that in them that 'did by nature the things contained in the law, which showed the work of the law written in their heart,' Rom. ii. 14, 15. Mark, 'written!' Shall not this judge them that have the outward law, but are out of the life of it? The apostle saith, 'the manifestation of the Spirit is given to every man to profit withal,' 1 Cor. xii. 7. There are diversities of gifts, but the same Spirit; but 'the manifestation of it is given to every man to profit withal.' Mark, 'to one is given by the Spirit, the word of wisdom; to another the word of knowledge by the same Spirit; to another faith by the same Spirit; to another the gifts of healing by the same Spirit; to another the working of miracles; to another prophecy; to another discerning of spirits; to another divers kinds of tongues; to another the interpretation of tongues: but all these worketh that one and the self-same Spirit, dividing to every man severally as he will.' Mark that, to every man severally as he will.

"Again, the apostle saith, 'the grace of God that bringeth salvation, hath appeared unto all men, teaching us, that denying ungodliness and worldly lusts, we should live soberly, righteously, and godly in this present world,' Tit. ii. 11, 12. Now ye, that turn this grace which bringeth salvation, into lasciviousness, deny it, and say, that which teacheth the saints, who by grace are saved, hath not appeared to all men. Jude saith, 'Behold, the Lord cometh with ten thousands of his saints, to execute judgment upon all, and to convince all that are ungodly among them, of all their ungodly deeds which they have committed, and of all their hard speeches, which ungodly sinners have spoken against him,' ver. 15. Here mark again; him that cometh with ten thousands of his saints, to convince all of their ungodly deeds and hard speeches; here it is, ALL of their ungodly deeds, and ALL of their hard speeches; none left out, but ALL to be convinced and judged, the world reproved by him who comes with ten thousands of his saints, and will reign, and be king and judge. And have not ye all something in you, that doth reprove you for your hard speeches, and your ungodly deeds, the ungodliest of you all, who live in your hard speeches against him, and his light and spiritual appearance in his people?

"Again, the apostle, writing to the Gentiles, saith, 'But unto every one of us is given grace, according to the measure of the gift of Christ,' Eph. iv. 7. Now mark, here is the measure of the gift of Christ, 'who lighteth every man that cometh into the world,' John i. 9, 'that all men through him might believe. He that believeth on him is not condemned, but he that believeth not is condemned, &c. And this is the condemnation, that light is come into the world,' &c., John iii. 18, 19. Now every man that cometh into the world being enlightened, one loves it, and brings his deeds to the light, that with the light he may see whether they be wrought in God; the other hates the light, 'because his deeds are evil;' and he will not bring his deeds to the light, because he knows the light will reprove him. So he that hates the light, wherewith Christ hath enlightened him, knows the light will reprove him for his evil deeds; and, therefore, he will not come to the light.

"Again, the Lord by his prophet said concerning Christ, 'I will give him for a light to the Gentiles, that he may be my salvation to the ends of the earth,' Isa. xlix. 6. And what is that, which the children that walk 'according to the course of this world, according to the prince of the power of the air, the spirit that now worketh in the children of disobedience,'

Eph. ii. 2, are disobedient to? Mark, and read for yourselves, who being disobedient, walk according to the course of the world, according to the power of the prince of the air; mark, I say, what it is that all such are disobedient to? He that hath an ear, let him hear. The apostle saith to the Colossians, 'the wrath of God cometh upon the children of disobedience,' Col. iii. 6. Come, ye professors, let us see, is not this something of God that is disobeyed? Is it not that which is of God manifest *in* them, which God hath shown them, which lets them see God's judgments are upon such, when they act unrighteously? Is not this the measure of God (mark), the Spirit that is in prison? and the Spirit of God that is grieved?

"And ye professors, come, let us read the parable of the talents, and reckon with you, and see who it is that hath hid the Lord's money in the earth? Come, ye that have gained, enter ye into your master's joy. Go, thou that hast hid the Lord's money in the earth, into utter darkness; 'take it from him, and give it to him that hath;' every man shall have his reward. For the Lord hath given 'to every man according to his several ability,' Matt. xxv. 15; mark that, 'to every man according to his several ability?' read this, if you can. Now is the Lord coming to call every man severally to account, to whom he hath given severally according to his ability. Now the wicked and slothful servant, who hid the Lord's money in the earth, will be found out; and the Lord's money will be taken from him, although he hath hidden it. To him the Lord's commands have been grievous; but to us they are not, who love God and keep his commandments. 'And,' saith the apostle to the Romans, 'I say, through the grace given unto me, to every man that is among you, not to think of himself more highly than he ought to think, but to think soberly, according as God hath dealt to every man the measure of faith,' Rom. xii. 3. Read and mark, here is a measure of faith.

"'And,' saith another apostle, 'as every one hath received the gift, even so minister the same one to another, as good stewards of the manifold grace of God,' 1 Pet. iv. 10, 'For the grace of God hath appeared unto all men.' The good stewards can give their account with joy; but ye bad stewards, that turn the grace of God into lasciviousness, now ye will be reckoned withal; now ye shall have your reward. 'But,' say the world, 'must every one minister as he hath received the gift?' 'Yea,' say I, 'but let him speak as the oracles of God; and let him do it as of the ability which God giveth,' ver. 11. John in the Revelation saith, 'They were judged every man according to their works,' Rev. xx. 13. Christ saith, 'Every idle word that men shall speak, they shall give account thereof in the day of judgment,' Matt. xii. 36. So 'ye, that name the name of Christ, depart from iniquity,' 2 Tim. ii. 19. 'The Son of man shall come in the glory of his Father, with his angels; and then he shall reward every one according to his works,' Matt. xvi. 27. He who is gone into a far country, and hath given the talents to every one of you, according to your several ability, 'will render to every man according to his deeds,' Rom. ii. 6. 'And further I say unto you, if any man have not the Spirit of Christ, he is none of his. And if Christ be in you, the body is dead because of sin, but the Spirit is life, because of righteousness,' Rom. viii. 9, 10. So let the light which cometh from Christ examine; for the Lord is appearing. Ye that have received according to your ability, smite not your fellow-servant; and think not that the Lord delayeth the time of his coming. Be not as they that said, 'Let us eat and drink, for to-morrow we shall die.'

"The apostle tells the Ephesians, that unto him 'this grace was given—to make all men see what is the fellowship of the mystery, which from the beginning of the world hath been hid in God, who created all things by Jesus Christ,' Eph. iii. 9. Read and understand every one with the light which comes from Christ, the mystery, which will be your condemnation, if ye believe not in it. This is to all, who stumble at the work of the Spirit of God, the manifestation of it, 'which is given to every man, to profit withal.' Come, ye professors, who stumble at it; let us read the parables. 'A sower went forth to sow; and some seed fell on the highway ground, and some on stony ground, and some on thorny ground; the Seed is the Word, the Son of man is the seedsman. He that hath an ear, let him hear,' Matt. xiii. Now look, all ye professors, what ground ye are? and what ye have brought forth? and whether the wicked seedsman hath not got his seed into your ground? 'He that hath an ear, let him hear.' And come, read another parable, of the householder, hiring labourers to go into the vineyard, and agreeing with every man for a penny, Matt. xx. Every man is to have his penny, the last that went in, as well as the first; and the last shall be first, and the first shall be last; for many are called, but few are chosen. He that hath an ear, let him hear.' There is a promise spoken to Cain, that if he did well he should be accepted, Gen. iv. 7. And Esau had a birthright, but despised it. Yet it is 'not of him that willeth,' Rom. ix. 16; 'but by grace ye are saved,' Eph. ii. 8. And stand still, and see your salvation, Exod. xiv. 13. And ye that are children of light, put on the armour of light, that ye may come into 'the unity of the faith, and of the knowledge of the Son of God, unto a perfect man, unto the measure of the stature of the fulness of Christ; that henceforth ye be no more children tossed to and fro,' Eph. iv. 13.

"And the Lord said, he would make a new covenant, by 'writing his law in people's hearts, and putting his Spirit in their inward parts;' whereby they should all come to know the Lord—Him by whom the world was made. Now every one of you, mind the law written in your hearts, and this Spirit put in your inward parts, that it need not be said to you, 'know the Lord;' but that ye may witness the promise of God fulfilled in you. 'But,' say the world, and professors, 'if every one must come to witness the law of God written in their hearts, and the Spirit put in the inward parts, what must we do with all our teachers?' As we come to witness that, we need not any man to teach us to know the Lord, having his law written in our hearts, and his Spirit put in our inward parts. This is the covenant of life, the everlasting covenant, which decays not, nor changes; and here is the way to the Father, without which no man cometh unto the Father. And here is the everlasting priesthood, the end of the old priesthood, whose lips were to preserve knowledge; but now, saith Christ,

'Learn of me;' who is the high-priest of the new priesthood. 'And,' saith the apostle, 'that ye may grow up in the knowledge of Jesus Christ, in whom are hid the treasures of wisdom and knowledge.' So we are brought off from the old priesthood that changed, to Christ, to the new priesthood, that changeth not; and off from the first covenant, that doth decay, to the everlasting covenant that doth not decay, Christ Jesus, the covenant of Light, from whom every one of you have a light, that ye might believe in the covenant of Light. If ye believe not, ye are condemned; for light is come into the world, and men love darkness rather than light, because their deeds are evil. 'I am come a light into the world,' saith Christ, 'that whosoever believeth in me, should not abide in darkness, but have the light of life,' John xii. 46. And, 'believe in the light, that ye may be children of the light.' But ye who do not believe in the light, but hate it, because it manifests your deeds to be evil, ye are they that are condemned by the light. Therefore, while ye have time, prize it; seek the Lord while he may be found, and call upon him while he is near; lest he say, 'time is past;' for the rich glutton's time was past. Therefore, while time is not quite past, consider, search yourselves, and see if ye be not they that hate the light; and so are builders that stumble at the corner-stone; for they that hated the light, and did not believe in the light, did so in ages past. 'I am the light of the world,' saith Christ, 'who enlighteneth every man that cometh into the world;' and he also saith, 'learn of me;' and of him God saith, 'this is my beloved Son, hear ye him.' Here is your teacher. But ye that hate the light, do not learn of Christ, and will not have him to be your king, to reign over you;—Him, to whom all power in heaven and earth is given, who bears his government upon his shoulders, who is now come to reign; who lighteth every man that cometh into the world, and will give to every man a reward, according to his works, whether they be good or evil. So every man, with the light that comes from Christ, will see his deeds, both he that hates it, and he that loves it. And he that will not bring his deeds to the light, because it will reprove him, that is his condemnation; and he shall have a reward according to his deeds. For the Lord is come to reckon with you. He looks for fruits; now the axe is laid to your root, and every tree of you that bears not good fruit, must be hewn down, and cast into the fire."   G. F.

Having stayed some time in London, and visited the meetings of Friends in and about the city, and cleared myself of what services the Lord had at that time laid upon me there, I travelled into KENT, SUSSEX, and SURREY, visiting Friends, amongst whom I had great meetings; and many times met with opposition from Baptists and other jangling professors; but the Lord's power went over them.

We staid one night at FARNHAM, where we had a little meeting, and the people were exceedingly rude; but at last the Lord's power came over them. After it we went to our inn, and gave notice that any that feared God might come to us: and there came abundance of rude people, the magistrates of the town also, and some professors. I declared the truth unto them; and those of the people that behaved rudely, the magistrates put out of the room. When they were gone, there came another rude company of professors, and some of the chief of the town. They called for faggots and drink, though we forbade them; and were as rude a people as ever I met with. The Lord's power chained them, that they had not power to do us any mischief; but when they went away, they left all their faggots and beer which they had called for into the room, for us to pay for in the morning. We showed the innkeeper what an unworthy thing it was, but he told us, "we must pay it;" and we did. Before we left the town, I wrote a paper to the magistrates and heads of the town, and to the priest, showing them and him how he had taught his people, and laying before them their rude and uncivil conduct to strangers that sought their good.

Leaving that place we came to BASINGSTOKE, a very rude town; where they had formerly very much abused Friends. There I had a meeting in the evening, which was quiet, for the Lord's power chained the unruly. At the close of it I was moved to put off my hat, and pray to the Lord to open their understandings; upon which they raised a report, that "I put off my hat to them, and bid them good night," which was never in my heart. After the meeting, when we came to our inn, I sent for the innkeeper (as I used to do), and he came into the room to us, and showed himself a very rude man. I admonished him to be sober and fear the Lord; but he called for faggots and a pint of wine, and drank it off himself; then called for another, and called up half a dozen men into our chamber. Thereupon I bid him go out of the chamber, and told him he should not drink there, for we sent for him up to speak to him concerning his eternal good. He was exceedingly mad, rude, and drunk. When he continued his rudeness, and would not be gone, I told him the chamber was mine for the time I lodged in it, and I called for the key. Then he went away in great rage. In the morning he would not be seen; but I told his wife of his unchristian and rude behaviour towards us.

After this we came to BRIDPORT, having meetings in the way. We went to an inn, and sent into the town for such as feared God; and there came a shopkeeper, a professor, and put off his hat to us, and seeing we did not the same to him again, but said Thou and Thee to him, he told us, "he was not of our religion;" and after some discourse with him he went away. Then he went and stirred up the priest and magistrates against us, and after a while sent to the inn to desire us to come to his house, for there were some that would speak with us, he said. Thomas Curtis was with me, and he went to the man's house; where, when he came, the man had laid a snare for him, for he had got the priest and magistrate thither, and they boasted much that they had caught George Fox, taking him for me. When they perceived their mistake, they were in great rage; yet the Lord's power came over them, so that they let him go again. Meanwhile I had an opportunity of speaking to some sober people that came to the inn. When Thomas was come back, and we were passing out of the town, some of them came to us, and said, "the officers were coming to fetch me;" but the Lord's power came over them all, so that they had not power to touch me. There were some convinced in the town, who were turned to the Lord, and have stood faithful in their testimony to the truth ever since, and a fine meeting there is there.

Passing hence we visited PORTSMOUTH and POOLE, where we had glorious meetings; and many were turned to the Lord. At RINGWOOD we had a large general meeting, where the Lord's power was over all. At WEYMOUTH we had a meeting; and thence came through DORCHESTER to LYME, where the inn we went to was taken up with mountebanks, so that there was hardly any room for us or our horses. In the evening we drew up some queries concerning the ground of all diseases, and the natures and virtues of medicinal things, and sent them to the mountebanks; letting them know, "if they would not answer them, we would stick them on the cross next day." This brought them down, and made them cool, for they could not answer them; but in the morning they reasoned a little with us. We left the queries with some friendly people, that were convinced in the town, to stick upon the market-cross. The Lord's power reached some of the sober people in that place, who were turned by the Light and Spirit of Christ to his free teaching.

We then travelled to EXETER; and at the sign of the Seven Stars, an inn at the bridge foot, had a general meeting of Friends out of Cornwall and Devonshire; to which came Humphrey Lower, Thomas Lower, and John Ellis* from the Land's End, Henry Pollexfen, and Friends from Plymouth, Elizabeth Trelawny, and divers other Friends. A blessed heavenly meeting we had, and the Lord's everlasting power came over all, in which I saw and said, "that the Lord's power had surrounded this nation round about, as with a wall and bulwark, and his seed reached from sea to sea." Friends were established in the everlasting Seed of life, Christ Jesus, their life, rock, teacher, and shepherd.

Next morning Major Blackmore sent soldiers to apprehend me; but I was gone before they came. As I was riding up the street, I saw the officers going down; so the Lord crossed them in their design, and Friends passed away peaceably and quietly. The soldiers examined some Friends after I was gone, "what they did there;" but when they told them they were in their inn, and had business in the city, they went away without meddling any further with them.

From Exeter I took meetings as I went, till I came to BRISTOL, and was at the meeting there. After which I did not stay in the town, but passed into Wales, and had a meeting at the Stone. Thence going to CARDIFF, a justice of the peace sent to me, desiring I would come with half a

---

* John Ellis, who is only twice mentioned in this journal, was an able gospel minister, preaching in the authority of divine life, to the reaching of God's witness in many hearts. His doctrine was sound, flowing from the living fountain and divine spring of life and heavenly wisdom. His preaching was full of reproof and caution, but in that meekness which made it edifying. Whilst tender of the good in all, he was terrible against the workers of iniquity. He was a man of great kindness, a visitor of the widows and fatherless in their distress, feeding the hungry and clothing the naked, according to his ability. He laboured greatly in the gospel in several counties, often saying, "His Father's business must not be neglected, or done negligently." As he was travelling in the service of Truth, he was taken ill, and died in great peace in 1707, saying, "I am ready, for I have a sure foundation."

dozen of my friends to his house. So I took a friend or two, and went up to him, and he and his wife received us very civilly. The next day we had a meeting at Cardiff in the town-hall, and that justice sent about seventeen of his family to the meeting. There came some disturbers, but the Lord's power was over them, and many were turned to the Lord. To some that had run out with James Nayler, and did not come to meetings, I sent word, that "the day of their visitation was over," and they never prospered after.

We travelled from Cardiff to SWANSEA, where we had a blessed meeting; and a meeting was settled there in the name of Jesus. In our way thither we passed over in a boat, with the high-sheriff of the county, and next day I went to speak with him, but he would not admit me.

We went to another meeting in the country, where the Lord's presence was much with us. Thence to a great man's house, who received us very lovingly; but next morning he would not be seen; one that in the mean time had come to him, had so estranged him, that we could not get to speak with him again.

We still passed on through the countries, having meetings and gathering people, in the name of Christ, to Him their heavenly teacher, till we came to BRECKNOCK; where we set up our horses at an inn. There went with me Thomas Holmes and John-ap-John, who was moved of the Lord to "speak in the streets." I walked out a little into the fields, and when I came in again, the town was in an uproar. When I came into the chamber in the inn, it was full of people, and they were speaking in Welsh; I desired them to speak in English, which they did, and much discourse we had. After a while they went away; but towards night the magistrates gathered together in the streets, with a multitude of people, and they bid them shout, and gathered up the town; so that for about two hours together, there was such a noise, that the like we had not heard; and the magistrates set them on to shout again, when they had given over. We thought it looked like the uproar, which we read was amongst Diana's craftsmen. This tumult continued till night; and if the Lord's power had not limited them, they seemed likely to have pulled down the house, and us to pieces.

At night, the woman of the house would have had us go to supper in another room, but we discerning her plot, refused. Then she would have had half a dozen men come into the room to us, under pretence of discoursing with us. We told her, no persons should come into our room that night, neither would we go to them. Then she said, we should sup in another room; but we told her we would have no supper, if not in our own room. At length, when she saw she could not get us out, she brought up our supper in a great rage. So she and they were crossed in their design, for they had an intent to do us mischief; but the Lord God prevented them. Next morning I wrote a paper to the town concerning their unchristian conduct, showing the fruits of their priests and magistrates; and as I passed out of the town I spoke to the people, and told them, they were a shame to Christianity and religion.

From this place we went to a great meeting in a steeple-house yard, where was a priest, and Walter Jenkin, who had been a justice, and another justice. A blessed glorious meeting we had. There being many professors, I was moved of the Lord "to open the Scriptures to them, and to answer their objections (for I knew them very well); and to turn them to Christ, who had enlightened them; with which light they might see the sins and trespasses they had been dead in, and their Saviour, who came to redeem them out of them, who was to be their way to God, the truth and the life to them, and their priest made higher than the heavens, so that they might come to sit under his teaching." A peaceable meeting we had; many were convinced and settled in the truth that day. After it, I went with Walter Jenkin to the other justice's house; and he said to me, "You have this day given great satisfaction to the people, and answered all the objections that were in their minds." For the people had the Scriptures, but were not turned to the Spirit, which should let them see that, which gave them forth, the Spirit of God, which is the key to open them.

From hence we passed to Richard Hamborow's, at PONTEMOIL, where was a great meeting; to which came another justice of peace, and several great people, whose understandings were opened by the Lord's Spirit and power, and they were turned to the Lord Jesus Christ, from whence it came. A great convincement there was; a large meeting was gathered in those parts, and settled in the name of Jesus.

After this we returned to England, and came to SHREWSBURY, where we had a great meeting, and visited Friends all over the countries in their meetings, till we came to William Gandy's, in CHESHIRE, where we had a meeting of between two and three thousand people, as it was thought; and the everlasting word of life was held forth, and received that day. A blessed meeting it was, for Friends were settled by the power of God upon Christ Jesus, the rock and foundation.

At this time there was a great drought; and after this general meeting was ended, there fell so great a rain, that Friends said, they thought we could not travel, the waters would be so risen. But I believed the rain had not extended so far, as they had come that day to the meeting. Next day in the afternoon, when we turned back into some parts of Wales again, the roads were dusty, and no rain had fallen there.

When Oliver Cromwell sent forth a proclamation for a fast throughout the nation, for rain, when there was a very great drought, it was observed, that as far as truth had spread in the north, there were pleasant showers and rain enough, when in the south, in many places, they were almost spoiled for want of rain. At that time I was moved to write an answer to the Protector's proclamation, wherein I told him, "if he had come to own God's truth, he should have had rain; and that drought was a sign unto them of their barrenness, and want of the water of life." About the same time was written the following paper, to distinguish between true and false fasts :—

"Concerning the true Fast and the false.

"To all you that are keeping fasts, who 'smite with the fist of wickedness, and fast for strife and debate;' against you hath a voice cried

aloud, like a trumpet, that you may come to know the true fast, which is
accepted; and the fast, which is in the strife and the debate, and smiting with
the fists of wickedness; which fast is not required of the Lord. 'Behold,
in the day of your fast, you find pleasure, and exact all your labours.
Behold (mark, take notice), ye fast for strife and debate, and to smite with
the fist of wickedness; ye shall not fast, as ye do this day, to make your
voice heard on high. Is it such a fast, that I have chosen, saith the Lord,
a day for a man to afflict his soul? Is it to bow down his head like a
bulrush, and to spread sackcloth and ashes under him? Wilt thou call
this a fast and an acceptable day to the Lord?'

   "Consider all you that fast, see, if it be not 'hanging down the head
for a day, like a bulrush;' and fasting for 'strife and debate,' and to 'smite
with the fists of wickedness, to make your voice be heard on high?' But
this fast is not accepted of the Lord: but that which leads you from strife,
from debate, from wickedness; which is not to 'bow down the head, as a
bulrush for a day,' and yet live in exacting and pleasure; this is not
accepted of the Lord: but that which separates from all these before-
mentioned. That which separates from 'wickedness, debate, strife, pleasures, smiting with the fist of wickedness,' brings to know the true fast,
which 'breaks the bonds of iniquity, and deals bread to the hungry; brings
the poor that are cast out to his own house, and when he sees any naked,
he covers them, and hides not himself from his own flesh.' Here is the
true fast, which separates from them, where the bonds of iniquity are standing, and the heavy burthens of the oppressed remaining, and the yoke not
broken; who deal not bread to the hungry, and bring not the poor to their
own house; who see the naked, but let him go unclothed, and hide themselves from their own flesh. Yet such will make their voice to be heard
on high, as Christ speaks of the Pharisees, who 'sounded a trumpet before
them, and disfigured their faces,' to appear to men to fast; but the bonds
of iniquity were standing, strife and debate were standing, striking with
the fists of wickedness standing; these made their voice heard on high, who
had their reward.

   "But that which brings to the true fast, which appears not to men to
fast, but unto the Father 'who seeth in secret; the Father that seeth in
secret, shall reward this openly.' This fast separates from the Pharisees'
fast, and them that bow the head for a day, like a bulrush. This is it
which brings 'to deal bread to the hungry, and clothe thine own flesh when
thou seest them naked; to bring the poor to thine house, and to loose the
bonds of wickedness;' mark, this is the fast; and 'to undo every heavy
burthen (mark again), and to let the oppressed go free;' this is the fast:
and 'to break every yoke.' When thou observest this fast, 'then shall thy
light break forth as the morning, and thine health shall spring forth speedily,
and thy righteousness shall go before thee; the glory of the Lord shall be
thy rere-ward. Then shalt thou call, and the Lord shall answer; thou
shalt cry, and he shall say, Here I am: if thou take away from the midst
of thee the yoke, the putting forth of the finger, and speaking vanity; and
if thou draw out thy soul to the hungry, and satisfy the afflicted soul, then
shall thy light arise in obscurity, and thy darkness be as the noon-day.'

The light brings to know this fast; and walking in it this fast is kept: and he that believeth in the light, abides not in darkness. And again; 'the Lord shall guide thee continually, and satisfy thy soul in drought, and make fat thy bones; and thou shalt be like a watered garden, and like a spring of water, whose waters fail not,' Isa. lviii. 11. These are they that are guided by the light which comes from Christ, where the springs are.

"And again; 'they that shall be of thee (that keep this fast), shall build the old waste places, and thou shalt raise up the foundations of many generations; and thou shalt be called The repairer of the breach, The restorer of the paths to dwell in,' Isa. lviii. 12. Now that which gives to see the foundations of many generations, is the light which separates from all, which is out of the light: and they that go out of the light, though they may pretend a fast, and bow down the head for a time, yet they are far from this fast, that doth raise up the foundations of many generations, and is the repairer of the breach, and restorer of the paths to dwell in. That which doth give to see these foundations of many generations, and these breaches that are to be repaired and restored, and paths to dwell in, is the light which brings to know the true fast; and where this fast is known, which is from wickedness, debate, strife, pleasures, from exacting, from the voice that is heard on high, from the speaking of vanity, from the bonds of iniquity, which breaks every yoke, and lets the oppressed go free; here the health grows; here the morning is known, and righteousness goes forth; the glory of the Lord is the rere-ward, and the light riseth; the soul is drawn out to the hungry, and satisfies the afflicted soul; and the springs of living water are known and felt. The waters fail not here; the Lord guides continually, and the foundations of many generations come to be seen and raised up : The repairer of breaches is here witnessed, The restorer of paths to dwell in.

"But all such as are out of the light which the prophets were in, with which they saw Christ, and such as are in fasts, where was strife, wickedness, debate, and bowing down the head like a bulrush for a day, lifting their voice on high, and the bonds of wickedness yet standing, and the burthens unloosed, and the oppressed not let go free, and the yoke not broken, the nakedness not clothed, the bread not dealt to the hungry, and these foundations of many generations not raised up; until these things before-mentioned be broken down,—on such the light breaks not forth as the morning, and the Lord hears them not. Such have their reward; their iniquities have separated them from their God, their sins have hid his face from them, that he will not hear: their hands are defiled with blood, and their fingers with iniquity, whose lips have spoken lies, and tongues mut-tered perverseness. 'None calleth for justice, nor do any plead for truth; they trust in vanity, and speak lies; they conceive mischief, and bring forth iniquity. They hatch cockatrice-eggs, and weave the spider's-web: he that eateth of their eggs, dies; and that which is crushed breaks out into a viper: their webs shall not become garments, neither shall they cover themselves with their works.' Observe; 'their works are works of ini-quity, and the act of violence is in their hands: their feet run to do evil, and they make haste to shed innocent blood. Their thoughts are thoughts

of iniquity; wasting and destruction are in their paths; the way of peace
they know not, and there is no judgment in their doings. They have made
them a crooked path; whosoever goeth therein shall not know peace:'
mark; such go from the light, therefore is judgment far off; neither doth
justice overtake. Here is obscurity, walking in darkness; groping like
blind men, as though they had no eyes, and stumbling at noon-day in
desolat places, like blind men. Here is the roaring like bears, and
mourning sorely like doves; here judgment is looked for, but there is none,
and salvation is put far off: for the light is denied, which gives to see it.
But here are the multiplying of transgression, and their sins testifying
against them; the transgression that was within them, and their iniquities,
which they knew in transgressing and lying against the Lord, speaking the
things they should not, when they knew by that of God in them, that they
should not speak it. So departing from the way of God, speaking oppression,
revolting, conceiving and uttering forth from the heart words of falsehood;
here judgment is turned away backward, and justice stands afar off; truth
is fallen in the streets, and equity cannot enter. Yea, truth faileth; and
he that departeth from evil makes himself a prey. The Lord saw it, and
it displeased him. These are such as are in the fast, which God doth not
accept; not in the true fast, whose 'light breaks forth as the morning:'
but these are such as are in the false fast, who grope, like blind men.

"That which gives to know the true fast, and the false fast, is the
Light, which gives the eye to see each fast, where the true judgment is,
and the iniquity standeth not, nor the transgressor, nor the speaker of lies;
but that is judged and condemned with the Light, which makes it manifest.
And when they who are in this fast call upon the Lord, the Lord will
answer them, Here am I. Here truth is pleaded for, and falsehood flies
away. But they who are out of this fast, in the perverseness, whose
tongues utter perverse things, who are stumbling and groping like blind
men, out of the light, in the iniquity which separates from God, who hides
his face from them that he will not hear;—these going from the light, go
from the Lord and his face. So this is it which must be fasted from; for
it separates from God; and here comes the reward openly, which condemns
all that is contrary to the light; injustice, iniquity, transgression, vanity,
and that which bringeth forth mischief, which hatcheth the cockatrice-eggs,
and weaves the spider's web: he that eateth of these eggs dies. Mark,
'that which is crushed breaks out into a viper;' mark again, 'their webs
shall not become garments, neither shall they cover themselves with their
works of vanity; acts of violence are in their hands.' This is all out of
the light, in the wickedness. 'Their feet run to do evil, and they make
haste to shed innocent blood; their thoughts are thoughts of vanity; wasting and destruction are in their path.' This is all far from the light.
Again, 'the way of peace they know not, there is no judgment in their
goings; they have made them crooked paths, whosoever go therein,
shall not know peace.' Mark; who go in their way, that know not the
way of peace, shall they know peace? 'Whose path is crooked, where
there is no judgment in their goings;' take notice, 'no judgment in their
goings;' this is all from the light, which manifesteth that which is to be

judged; where the covenant of peace is known, where all that wh'ch is contrary to it is kept out. All who live in those things contrary to the light, in the false fast, stumbling and groping like blind men, may mark their path, and behold their reward. They that are in the true fast, are separated from all these; from their words and actions, their fruits, and their fast: but of those whose fast breaks the bonds of iniquity, whom the Lord hears, and to whom righteousness springs forth, and goes before them, the glory of the Lord is the rere-ward."   G. F.

We passed into Wales through MONTGOMERYSHIRE, and so into RADNORSHIRE, where there was a meeting like a leaguer, for multitudes. I walked a little aside, whilst the people were gathering; and there came to me John-ap-John, a Welshman, whom I desired to go to the people; and if he had anything upon him from the Lord to them, he might speak to them in Welsh, and thereby gather them more together. Then came Morgan Watkins * to me, who was then become loving to Friends, and said, "the people lie like a leaguer, and the gentry of the country are come in." I bid him go up also, and leave me, for I had a great travail upon me for the salvation of the people. When they were well gathered, I went into the meeting, and stood upon a chair about three hours. I stood a while before I began to speak; after some time I felt the power of the Lord over the whole assembly; and his everlasting life and truth shone over all. The Scriptures were opened to them, and their objections answered. "They were directed to the light of Christ, the heavenly man; that by it they might all see their sins, and Christ Jesus to be their Saviour, their Redeemer, their Mediator, and come to feed on him, the bread of life from heaven." Many were turned to the Lord Jesus, and his free teaching that day; and all were bowed down under the power of God; so that though the multitude was so great, that many sat on horse-back to hear, there was no opposition. A priest who sat with his wife on horseback, heard attentively, and made no objection. The people parted

* Morgan Watkins, who is only mentioned in this place, became a sufferer for the truth. About eight years from the above date, we find him in the Gatehouse prison, near Westminster abbey, with nineteen others on the same account, being committed by warrant from the Duke of Albemarle, "for being at a meeting in St. John's." This was during the time the plague visited London. In Barclay's *Letters of Early Friends*, are two from Morgan Watkins, one of them dated from the Gatehouse prison, in which he says, "Blessed be His name who hath kept me, and nineteen more in this close place, all in health, above these five weeks; notwithstanding three have been buried out of this prison of the sickness.—Good is the hand of the Lord to his own, whose death is gain."

In a letter written about three months after the above, he mentions the release of himself and Friends, and adds, "I have been weak since I came out into the air, but through the great love of my God, I am wonderfully preserved, to the praise of his name. But the two imprisonments in Newgate, and the one at the Gatehouse, have much weakened my body, in which I have had several battles with death; but the power of my God arising, gave me dominion over the distemper and weakness of the flesh. The day was dreadful to all flesh, and few were able to abide it, and stand in the judgment; but the Lord was very merciful to the remnant of his people, and his blessed seed is arising in many.

peaceably and quietly, with great satisfaction; many of them saying they
never heard such a sermon before, or the Scriptures so opened. For "the
new covenant was opened, and the old, and the nature and terms of each;
and the parables were explained. The state of the church in the apostles'
days was set forth, and the apostacy laid open; and the free teaching of
Christ and the apostles was set over the hireling teachers;" and the Lord
had the praise of all, for many were turned to him that day.

I went back thence to LEOMINSTER, where was a great meeting in a
field; many hundreds of people being gathered together. There were about
six congregational preachers and priests among them; and Thomas Taylor,
who had been a priest, but was now become a minister of Christ, was with
me. I stood up, and declared about three hours; and none of the priests
were able to open their mouths in opposition; the Lord's power and truth
so reached them, and bound them down. At length one priest went off
about a bow-shot from me, drew several of the people after him, and began
to preach to them. So I kept our meeting, and he kept his. After a
while Thomas Taylor was moved to go and speak to him; and he gave
over; and he, and the people he had drawn off, came to us again; and the
Lord's power went over them all. At last a Baptist, that was convinced,
said, "Where's priest Tombs? how chance he doth not come out?" This
Tombs was priest of Leominster. Hereupon some went and told the
priest; who came with the bailiffs and other officers of the town. When
he was come, they set him upon a stool over against me. Now I was
speaking of the heavenly, divine light of Christ, with which he "enlightens
every one that cometh into the world, to give them the knowledge of the
glory of God in the face of Christ Jesus their Saviour." When priest
Tombs heard this, he cried out, "That is a natural light, and a made light."
Then I desired the people to take out their Bibles; and I asked the priest
whether he affirmed that that was a created, natural, made light, which
John, a man that was sent from God, did bear witness to, and spoke of,
when he said, "In him (to wit, in the Word) was life, and that life was
the light of men," John i. 4. "Dost thou affirm and mean," said I, "that
this light here spoken of, was a created, natural, made light?" And he
said, "Yes." Then I showed by the Scriptures, that the natural, created,
made light, is the outward light in the outward firmament, proceeding from
the sun, moon, and stars. "And dost thou affirm," said I, "that God sent
John to bear witness to the light of the sun, moon, and stars?" Then
said he, "Did I say so?" I replied, "Didst thou not say it was a natural,
created, made light, that John bore witness unto? If thou dost not
like thy words, take them again and mend them." Then he said, "That
light which I spoke of, was a natural, created light." I told him, "he
had not at all mended his cause; for that light which I spoke of, was the
very same that John was sent of God to bear witness to, which was the
life in the Word, by which all the natural lights, as sun, moon, and stars,
were made. 'In him (to wit, the Word) was life, and that life was the
light of men.'" So "I directed the people to turn to the place in their
Bibles, and recited to them the words of John, how that 'In the beginning
was the Word, and the Word was with God, and the Word was God.

The same was in the beginning with God; all things were made by him, and without him was not anything made, that was made. (So all natural, created lights were made by Christ the Word.) In him was life, and the life was the light of men; and that was the true light, which lighteth every man that cometh into the world.'" And Christ saith of himself, John viii. 12, "I am the light of the world;" and bids them "believe in the light," John xii. 36. And God said of him by the prophet Isaiah, chap. xlix. 6, "I will also give thee for a light to the Gentiles, that thou mayest be my salvation to the ends of the earth." So Christ in his light is saving. And the apostle said, "The light, which shined in their hearts, was to give them the light of the knowledge of the glory of God in the face of Jesus Christ;" and that was their "treasure in their earthen vessels," 2 Cor. iv. 6, 7.

When I had thus opened the matter to the people, the priest cried to the magistrates, "Take this man away, or else I shall not speak any more." "But," said I, "Priest Tombs, deceive not thyself, thou art not in thy pulpit now, nor in thy old mass-house; but we are in the fields." So he was shuffling to be gone; and Thomas Taylor stood up, and undertook to make out our principle by Christ's parable concerning the sower, Matt. xiii. Then said the priest, "Let that man speak, and not the other." So he got into a little jangling for a while; till the Lord's power stopped and confounded him. Afterwards a Friend stood up and told him, how he had sued him for tithe eggs, and other Friends for other tithes; for he was an Anabaptist preacher, and yet had a parsonage at Leominster, and had several journeymen under him. He said "he had a wife, and he had a concubine; and his wife was the baptized people, and his concubine was the world." But the Lord's power came over him and them all, and the everlasting truth was declared that day; and many were turned by it to the Lord Jesus Christ their teacher and way to God. Of great service that meeting was in those parts. Next day Thomas Taylor went to this priest, and reasoned with him; and overcame him by the power of the Word.

From this place I travelled on in Wales, having several meetings, till I came to TENBY; where, as I rode up the street, a justice of peace came out of his house, desired me to alight, and stay at his house; and I did so. On First-day the mayor and his wife, and several of the chief of the town, came in about ten, and stayed all the time of the meeting. A glorious one it was. John-ap-John being then with me, left it, and went to the steeple-house; and the governor cast him into prison. On the Second-day morning the governor sent one of his officers to the justice's house to fetch me; which grieved the mayor and the justice; for they were both with me in the justice's house when the officer came. So the mayor and the justice went up to the governor before me; and a while after I went up with the officer. When I came in, I said, "Peace be unto this house." And before the governor could examine me, I asked him why he cast my friend into prison. He said, "For standing with his hat on in the church." I said, "Had not the priest two caps on his head, a black one and a white one? Cut off the brims of the hat, and then my friend would have but

one, and the brims of the hat were but to defend him from weather."
"These are frivolous things," said the governor. "Why then," said I, "dost
thou cast my friend into prison for such frivolous things?" Then he
asked me, whether I owned election and reprobation; "Yes," said I, "and
thou art in the reprobation." At that he was in a rage, and said he would
send me to prison till I proved it; but I told him I would prove that
quickly, if he would confess truth. Then I asked him, whether wrath,
fury, rage, and persecution, were not marks of reprobation; for he that
was born of the flesh, persecuted him that was born of the Spirit; but
Christ and his disciples never persecuted nor imprisoned any. Then he
fairly confessed that he had too much wrath, haste, and passion in him.
I told him Esau was up in him, the first birth, not Jacob, the second birth.
The Lord's power so reached and came over him, that he confessed to
truth; and the other justice came, and shook me kindly by the hand.

As I was passing away, I was moved to speak to the governor again,
and he invited me to dine with him, and set my friend at liberty. I went
back to the other justice's house; and after some time the mayor and his
wife, and the justice and his wife, and divers other Friends of the town,
went about half a mile out of town with us, to the water-side, when we
went away; and there, when we parted from them, I was moved of the
Lord to kneel down with them, and pray to the Lord to preserve them.
So after I had recommended them to the Lord Jesus Christ, their Saviour
and free teacher, we passed away in the Lord's power, and the Lord had
the glory. A meeting continues in that town to this day.

We travelled to Pembrokeshire, and in PEMBROKE had some service
for the Lord. Thence we passed to HAVERFORD-WEST, where we had
a great meeting, and all was quiet. The Lord's power came over all,
and many were settled in the new covenant, Christ Jesus, and built upon
him, their rock and foundation; and they stand a precious meeting to this
day. Next day, being their fair-day, we passed through it, and "sounded
the day of the Lord, and his everlasting truth amongst them."

After this we came into another county, and at noon came into
a great market-town, and went into several inns, before we could get any
meat for our horses. At last we came to one where we got some. Then
John-ap-John being with me, went and spoke through the town, declaring
the truth to the people; and when he came to me again, he said he thought
all the town were as people asleep. After a while he was moved to go and
declare truth in the streets again; then the town was all in an uproar, and
cast him into prison. Presently after, several of the chief of the town
came, with others, to the inn where I was, and said, "They have cast your
man into prison." "For what?" said I, "He preached in our streets,"
said they. Then I asked them, "What did he say? had he reproved some
of the drunkards and swearers, and warned them to repent, and leave off
their evil doings, and turn to the Lord?" I asked them, who cast him
into prison? They said, the high-sheriff and justices, and the mayor.
I asked their names, and whether they understood themselves? and whether
that was their conduct to travellers that passed through their town, and
strangers that admonished and exhorted them to fear the Lord, and re-

proved sin in their gates? These went back, and told the officers what I said; and after a while they brought down John-ap-John, guarded with halberts, in order to put him out of the town. Being at the inn door, I bid the officers take their hands off him. They said, "the mayor and justices had commanded them to put him out of town. I told them I would talk with their mayor and justices, concerning their uncivil and unchristian carriage towards him. So I spoke to John to go look after the horses, and get them ready, and charged the officers not to touch him. And after I had declared the truth to them, and showed them the fruits of their priests, and their incivility and unchristian-like carriage, they left us. They were a kind of Independents; a very wicked town, and false. We bid the innkeeper give our horses a peck of oats; and no sooner had we turned our backs, than the oats were stolen from our horses. After we had refreshed ourselves a little, and were ready, we took horse, and rode up to the inn, where the mayor, sheriff, and justices were. I called to speak with them, and asked them why they had imprisoned John-ap-John, and kept him in prison two or three hours? But they would not answer me a word; they only looked out at the windows upon me. So I showed them how unchristian their carriage was to strangers and travellers, and manifested the fruits of their teachers; and I declared the truth unto them, and warned them of the day of the Lord, that was coming upon all evildoers; and the Lord's power came over them, that they looked ashamed; but not a word could I get from them in answer. So when I had warned them to repent, and turn to the Lord, we passed away; and at night came to a little inn, very poor, but very cheap; for our own provision and our two horses, cost but eightpence; but the horses would not eat their oats. We declared the truth to the people of the place, and sounded the day of the Lord through the countries.

Thence, we came to a great town, and went to an inn. Edward Edwards went into the market, and declared the truth amongst the people; and they followed him to the inn, and filled the yard, and were exceedingly rude; yet good service we had for the Lord amongst them; for the life of Christianity and the power of it tormented their chaffy spirits, and came over them, so that some were reached and convinced; and the Lord's power came over all. The magistrates were bound; they had no power to meddle with us.

After this we came to another great town on a market-day; and John-ap John declared the everlasting truth through the streets, and proclaimed the day of the Lord amongst them. In the evening many people gathered about the inn; and some of them, being drunk, would fain have had us into the street again; but seeing their design, I told them, if there were any that feared God, and desired to hear the truth, they might come into our inn; or else we might have a meeting with them next morning. Some service for the Lord we had amongst them, both over night and in the morning; and though the people were hard to receive the truth, yet the seed was sown; and thereabouts the Lord hath a people gathered to himself. In that inn also I turned but my back to the man that was giving oats to my horse; and looking round again, I observed he was filling his pockets with the provender. A wicked, thievish people, to rob the poor dumb creature of his food. I would rather they had robbed me.

Leaving this town and travelling on, a great man overtook us on the way, and he purposed (as he told us afterwards) to take us up at the next town for highwaymen. But before we came to the town, I was moved of the Lord to speak to him. What I spoke reached to the witness of God in the man, who was so affected therewith, that he had us to his house, and entertained us very civilly. He and his wife desired us to give them some Scriptures, both for proof of our principles and against the priests. We were glad of the service, and furnished them with Scriptures enough; and he wrote them down, and was convinced of the truth, both by the Spirit of God in his own heart, and by the Scriptures, which were a confirmation to him. Afterwards he set us on our journey, and as we travelled we came to a hill, which the people of the country say, is two or three miles high; from the side of this hill I could see a great way. And I was moved to set my face several ways, and to sound the day of the Lord there; and I told John-ap-John (a faithful Welsh minister) in what places God would raise up a people to himself, to sit under his own teaching. Those places he took note of, and a great people have since been raised up there. The like I have been moved to do in many other rude places; and yet I have been moved to declare the Lord had a seed in those parts, and afterwards there have been a brave people raised up in the covenant of God, and gathered in the name of Jesus; where they have salvation and free teaching.

From this hill we came to DOLGELLY, and went to an inn. John-ap-John declared through the streets, and the town's people rose and gathered about him. There being two Independent priests in the town, they came out and discoursed with him together. I went up to them, and finding them speaking in Welsh, I asked them, "what was the subject they spoke upon, and why they were not more moderate, and spoke not one by one? For the things of God," I told them, "were weighty, and they should speak of them with fear and reverence." Then I desired them to speak in English, that I might discourse with them, and they did so. They affirmed, "that the light which John came to bear witness of, was a created, natural, made light." But I took the Bible, and showed them (as I had done to others before), "that the natural lights, which were made and created, were the sun, moon, and stars; but this light, which John bare witness to, and which he called 'the true light, that lighteth every man that cometh into the world,' is the life in Christ the Word, by which all things were made and created. The same that is called the life in Christ, is called the light in man; and this is a heavenly divine light, which lets men see their evil words and deeds, shows them all their sins, and, if they would attend unto it, would bring them to Christ, from whom it comes, that they might know him to save them from their sin, and to blot it out. This light, I told them, shone in the darkness of their hearts, and the darkness in them could not comprehend it; but in those hearts where God had commanded it to shine out of darkness, it gave unto such the knowledge of the glory of God, in the face of Christ Jesus their Saviour. Then I opened the Scriptures largely to them, and turned them to the Spirit of God in their hearts, which would reveal the mysteries in the Scriptures to them, and would lead them into all truth as they became subject thereunto. I directed them to that which would give every one of them the knowledge of Christ, who died for them, that he might be their way to God, and make peace between God and them." The people were attentive, and I spoke to John-ap-John to stand up and speak it in Welsh to them, which he did; and they generally received it, and with hands lifted up blessed and praised God. The priests' mouths were stopped, so that they were quiet all the while, for I had brought them to be sober at the first, by telling them that "when they speak of the things of God and of Christ, they should speak with fear and reverence." Thus the meeting broke up in peace in the street, and many of the people accompanied us to our inn, and rejoiced in the truth that had been declared unto them; that they were turned to the light and Spirit in themselves, by which they might see their sin, and know salvation from it. When we went out of the town, the people were so affected, that they lifted up their hands, and blessed the Lord for our coming. A precious seed the Lord hath thereaway, and many people in those parts are since gathered to the Lord Jesus Christ, to sit down under his free teaching; and they have suffered much for him.

From hence we passed to CAERNARVON, a city like a castle. When we had put up our horses at an inn, and refreshed ourselves, John-ap-John went forth, and spoke through the streets; which were so strait and short, that one might stand in the midst of the town and see both the gates. I followed him, and a multitude of people were soon gathered; amongst whom a very dark priest began to babble; but his mouth was soon stopped. When John had cleared himself, I declared the word of life amongst the people; directing them to "the light of Christ in their hearts, that by it they might see all their own ways, religions, and teachers, and might come off from them all, to Christ, the true and living way, and the free teacher." Some of them were rude, but the greater part were civil, and told us they had heard how we had been persecuted and abused in many places, but they would not do so to us there. I commended their moderation and sobriety, and warned them of "the day of the Lord, that was coming upon all sin and wickedness;" testifying unto them, "that Christ was now come to teach his people himself, by his Spirit and by his power."

From hence we went to BEAUMARIS; a town wherein John-ap-John had formerly been preacher. After we had put up our horses at an inn, John went forth and spoke through the street; and there being a garrison in the town, they took him and put him into prison. The innkeeper's wife came and told me that the governor and magistrates were sending for me to commit me to prison also. I told her, they had done more than they could answer already; and had acted contrary to Christianity in imprisoning him for reproving sin in their streets and for declaring the truth. Soon after came other friendly people, and told me, if I went out into the street they would imprison me also; and therefore they desired me to keep at the inn. Upon this I was moved to go and walk up and down the streets; and told the people, "what an uncivil and unchristian thing they had done, in casting my friend into prison." And, they being high professors, I asked them, "if this was the entertainment they had for strangers; if they would willingly be so served themselves; and whether they, who looked upon the Scriptures to be their rule, had any example therein from Christ or his apostles, for what they had done?" So after a while they set John-ap-John at liberty.

Next day, being market-day, we were to cross a great water: and not far from the place where we were to take boat, many of the market-people drew to us; amongst whom we had good service for the Lord, "declaring the word of life and everlasting truth unto them, and proclaiming the day of the Lord amongst them, which was coming upon all wickedness; and directing them to the light of Christ, which he had enlightened them with; by which they might see all their sins, and false ways, religions, worships, and teachers: and by the same light might see Christ Jesus, who was come to save them, and lead them to God. After the Lord's truth had been declared to them in the power of God, and Christ the free teacher set over all the hireling teachers, I bid John-ap-John get his horse into the boat, which was then ready. But there being a company of wild gentlemen, as they called them, got into it, whom we found very rude, and far from gentleness, they, with others, kept his horse out of the boat. I rode to the boat's side and spoke to them, showing them "what unmanly and unchristian conduct it was; and told them they showed an unworthy spirit, below Christianity or humanity." As I spoke, I leaped my horse into the boat amongst them, thinking John's horse would have followed, when he had seen mine go in before him; but the water being deep, John could not get his horse into the boat. Wherefore I leaped out again on horseback into the water, and stayed with John on that side till the boat returned. There we tarried from eleven in the forenoon, to two in the afternoon, before the boat came to fetch us; and then we had forty-two miles to ride that evening: and when we had paid for our passage, we had but one groat left between us in money. We rode about sixteen miles, and then got a little hay for our horses. Setting forward again, we came in the night to a little ale-house, where we intended to stay and bait; but finding we could have neither oats nor hay there, we travelled on all night; and about five in the morning got to a place within six miles of Wrexham; where that day we met with many Friends, and had a glorious meeting; and the Lord's everlasting power and truth was over all: and a meeting is continued there to this day. Very weary we were with travelling so hard up and down in Wales; and in many places we found it difficult to get meat either for our horses or ourselves.

Next day we passed thence into FLINTSHIRE, sounding the day of the Lord through the towns; and came into WREXHAM at night. Here many of Floyd's people came to us; but very rude, wild, and airy they were, and little sense of truth they had: yet some were convinced in that town. Next morning one called a lady sent for me, who kept a preacher in her house. I went, but found both her and her preacher very light and airy; too light to receive the weighty things of God. In her lightness she came and asked me, if she should cut my hair: but I was moved to reprove her, and bid her cut down the corruptions in herself with the sword of the Spirit of God. So after I had admonished her to be more grave and sober, we passed away : and afterwards in her frothy mind, she made her boast that "she came behind me and cut of the curl of my hair ;" but she spoke falsely.

From Wrexham we came to CHESTER ; and being the fair time, we stayed a while, and visited Friends. For I had travelled through every county in Wales, preaching the everlasting gospel of Christ ; and a brave people there is now, who have received it, and sit under Christ's teaching. But before I left Wales, I wrote to the magistrates of Beaumaris concerning the imprisoning of John-ap-John ; letting them see their conditions, and the fruits of their Christianity, and of their teachers. Afterwards I met with some of them near London ; but oh how ashamed they were of their action !

From Chester we came to LIVERPOOL, where was at that time a fair also. As I rode through the fair, there stood a Friend upon the cross, declaring the truth to the people : who seeing me ride by, and knowing I had appointed a meeting next day upon a hill not far off, gave notice to the people "that George Fox, the servant of the Lord, would have a meeting next day upon such hill ; and if any feared the Lord, they might come and hear him declare the word of life to them." We went that night to Richard Cubban's, who himself was convinced, though not his wife ; but at that time she became convinced also.

Next day we went to the meeting on the top of the hill, which was very large. Some rude people with a priest's wife came, and made a noise for a while, but the Lord's power came over them, the meeting became quiet, and the truth of God was declared amongst them. Many were that day settled upon the rock and foundation of Christ Jesus, and under his teaching ; who made peace between God and them.

We had a small meeting, with a few Friends and people at MALPAS. Thence we came to another place, where we had another meeting. There came a bailiff with a sword, and was rude : but the Lord's power came over him, and Friends were established in the truth.

Thence we came to MANCHESTER ; and the sessions being there that day, many rude people were come out of the country. In the meeting they threw at me coals, clods, stones, and water : yet the Lord's power bore me up over them, that they could not strike me down. At last, when they saw they could not prevail by throwing water, stones, and dirt at me, they went and informed the justices in the sessions ; who thereupon sent officers to fetch me before them. The officers came in while I was declaring the word of life to the people, plucked me down, and haled me up into their court. When I came there, all the court was in disorder and noise. Wherefore I asked, where were the magistrates that they did not keep the people civil ? Some of the justices said they were magistrates. I asked them, why then they did not appease the people, and keep them sober ? for one cried, "I'll swear," and another cried, "I'll swear." I declared to the justices how we were abused in our meeting by the rude people, who threw stones, and clods, dirt, and water ; and how I was haled out of the meeting, and brought thither, contrary to the instrument of government, which said, "none should be molested in their meetings that professed God and owned the Lord Jesus Christ;" which I did. So the truth came over them, that when one of the rude fellows cried "he would swear," one of the justices checked him, saying, "What will you swear? hold your tongue." At last they bid the constable take me to my lodging; and there be secured till morning, till they sent for me again. So the constable had me to my lodging; and as we went the people were exceedingly rude; but I let them see "the fruits of their teachers, and how they shamed Christianity, and dishonoured the name of Jesus, which they professed." At night we went to a justice's house in the town, who was pretty moderate; and I had much discourse with him. Next morning we sent to the constable to know if he had anything more to say to us. And he sent us word "he had nothing to say to us, but that we might go whither we would." The Lord hath since raised up a people to stand for his name and truth in that town over those chaffy professors.

We passed from Manchester, having many precious meetings in several places, till we came to PRESTON; between which and Lancaster I had a general meeting: from which I went to LANCASTER. There at our inn I met with Colonel West, who was very glad to see me: who meeting with Judge Fell, told him I was mightily grown in the truth; when indeed he was come nearer to the truth, and so could better discern it.

We came from Lancaster to Robert Widders's. On the First-day after I had a general meeting near SAND-SIDE, of Friends of Westmorland and Lancashire, when the Lord's everlasting power was over all; in which the word of eternal life was declared, and Friends were settled upon the foundation, Christ Jesus, under his free teaching; and many were convinced, and turned to the Lord.

Next day I came over the Sands to SWARTHMORE, where Friends were glad to see me. I stayed there two First-days, visiting Friends in their meetings thereaways. They rejoiced with me in the goodness of the Lord, who by his eternal power had carried me through, and over many difficulties and dangers in his service: to him be the praise for ever!

CHAPTER XI.

1657.—Exhortation to Friends to take heed to the Light of Christ—an expostulation with persecutors—to Friends to be valiant for the truth—in parts of Cumberland the priests are so forsaken that some steeple-houses stand empty—John Wilkinson, the priest, is so deserted, that he sets up a meeting in his own house—then a silent meeting, and at last joins Friends, and becomes an able minister—George Fox travels into Scotland with Col. Osburn and Robert Widders—the latter was a thundering man against the rottenness of the priests' hypocrisy and deceit—Lady Hamilton is convinced—the Scotch priests raise the war-cry, and draw up their curses, which George Fox answers—they are in a rage and panic when he comes there, thinking "that all was gone"—some Baptists, with their logic and syllogisms, are confuted by George Fox's logic—he is banished Scotland by the council, but disregards their order—George Fox and William Osburn are waylaid by thieves, who are admonished by the former, and overawed by the Lord's power—the Highlanders run at them with pitchforks—at Johnstons they are banished the town—on hearing that the council of Edinburgh had issued warrants against him, George Fox goes thither, and is not molested.

Having got a little respite from travel, I was moved to write an epistle to Friends, as follows :—

"All Friends of the Lord everywhere, whose minds are turned in towards the Lord, take heed to the light within you, which is the light of Christ; which, as ye love it, will call your minds inward, that are abroad in the creatures : so your minds may be renewed by it, and turned to God in this which is pure, to worship the living God, the Lord of Hosts over all the creatures. That which calls your minds out of the lusts of the world, will call them out of the affections and desires, and turn you to set your affections above. That which calls the mind out of the world, will give judgment upon the world's affections and lusts, and is the same that calls out your minds from the world's teachers, and the creatures, to have your minds renewed. There is your obedience known and found; there the image of God is renewed in you ; and ye come to grow up in it. That which calls your minds out of the earth, turns them towards God, where the pure Babe is born of the virgin; and the Babe's food is known, the children's bread, which comes from the living God, and nourishes up to eternal life. These babes and children receive their wisdom from above, from the pure living God, and not from the earthly one : for that is trodden under foot with such. All who hate this light, whose minds are abroad in the creatures, in the earth, and in the image of the devil, get the words of the saints, that received their wisdom from above, into the old nature, and their corrupted minds. Such are murderers of the just, enemies to the cross of Christ, in whom the prince of the air lodgeth : sons of perdition, betrayers of the just. Therefore take heed to that light, which is oppressed with that nature ; which light, as it arises, shall condemn all that cursed nature, shall turn it out, and shut it out of the house : and so ye will come to see the candle lighted, and the house sweeping and swept. Then the pure pearl ariseth; then the eternal God is exalted. The same light that calls in your minds out of the world, turns them to God, the Father of lights. Here in the pure mind is the pure God waited upon for wisdom from above; the pure God is seen night and day; and the eternal peace, of which there is no end, enjoyed. People may have openings, and yet their minds go into the lusts of the flesh; but there the affections are not mortified. Therefore hearken to that, and take heed to that, which calls your minds out of the affections and lusts of the world, to have them renewed. The same will turn your minds to God; the same light will set your affections above, and bring you to wait for the pure wisdom of God from on high, that it may be justified in you. Wait all in that, which calls in your minds, and turns them to God; here is the true cross. That mind shall feed upon nothing that is earthly; but be kept in the pure light of God up to God, to feed upon the living food, which comes from the living God. The Lord God Almighty be with you all, dear babes, and keep you all in his strength and power to his glory, over all the world,—you whose minds are called out of it, and turned to God, to worship the Creator, and serve him, and not the creature. The light of God, which calls the mind out of the creatures, and turns it to God, brings into a being of endless joy and peace. Here is always a seeing God present, which is not known to the world, whose hearts are in the creatures, whose knowledge is in the flesh, whose minds are not renewed. Therefore all Friends, the Seed of God mind and dwell in, to reign over the unjust: and the power of the Lord dwell in, to keep you clear in your understandings, that the Seed of God may reign in you all;—the Seed of God, which is but one in all, which is Christ in the male and in the female, which the promise is to. Wait upon the Lord for the just to reign over the unjust, and for the Seed of God to reign over the seed of the serpent, and be the head; and that all that is mortal may die; for out of that will rise presumption. So fare ye well, and God Almighty bless, and guide, and keep you in his wisdom."

G. F.

About this time Friends, that were moved of the Lord to go to the steeple-houses and markets, to "reprove sin, and warn people of the day of the Lord," suffered much hardship from rude people, and also from the magistrates; being commonly pulled down, buffeted, beaten, and frequently sent to prison. Wherefore I was moved to give forth the following expostulation, to be spread amongst people, to show them, how contrary they acted therein to the apostles' doctrine and practice, and to bring them to more moderation. Thus it was:—

"Is it not better for you, that have cast into prison the servants and children of the Lord God, for speaking as they are moved, in steeple-houses or markets? Is it not better, I say, for you to try all things, and hold fast that which is good? Is it not of more honour and credit, to prove all things, and try all things, than to pluck down in the steeple-houses, and pull off the hair of their heads, and cast them into prison? Is this an honour to your truth and gospel you profess? Doth it not show that ye are out of the truth, and are not ready to instruct the gainsayers? Hath not the Lord said, 'He will pour out of his Spirit upon all flesh, and his sons and his daughters shall prophesy; old men shall dream dreams, and young men see visions; and on his handmaids he will pour forth of his Spirit?' Was not this prophecy in past ages stood against by the wise learned men in their own wisdom, and by the synagogue teachers? Were not those haled out of the synagogues and temples, who witnessed the Spirit poured forth upon them? Doth not this show, that ye have not received the pourings forth of this Spirit upon you, who fill the jails with so many sons and daughters, and hold up such teachers as are bred up in learning at Oxford and Cambridge, and are made by the will of man? Doth not this show, that ye, who are bred up there, who are made teachers by the will of man, and who persecute for prophesying, are strangers to the Spirit that is 'poured forth upon sons and daughters,' by which Spirit they come to 'minister to the spirits that are in prison?' The Lord hath a controversy with you, who are found prisoning and persecuting such as the Lord hath poured forth of his Spirit upon. Do not your fruits show, in all the nation where ye come; in towns, cities, villages, and countries, that ye are the seedsmen made by the will of man, who sow to the flesh, of which nothing but corruption is reaped? Ye are looked upon, and your fruits, and that which may be gathered, is seen by all that are in the light, as they pass through your countries, towns, cities, and villages, that ye are all the seedsmen that have sown to the flesh. Mark, and of this take notice, ye who are of that birth that is born of the flesh, sow to your own, persecuting him that is born of the Spirit. Sow to the Spirit, and of the Spirit reap life eternal; such ye cast into prison. Do ye not hale out of the synagogues, persecute and beat in them, and knock down? Are not these the works of the flesh? Have not many been almost murdered and smothered in your synagogues? Have not some been haled out of them, for but looking at the priest, and after cast into prison? Doth not all this make manifest what spirit ye are of, and your fruits to be of the flesh? What pleasures and sports in every town are to be seen among your flocks, that sow to the flesh and are born of it!

"Whereas the ministers of the Spirit cried against such, as 'sported in the day-time;' such as 'ate and drank, and rose up to play;' such as lived wantonly upon earth in pleasures; such as lived in fulness of bread and idleness; such as defile the flesh: such did God overthrow and destroy, and set them forth as examples to all them that after should live ungodly. But are not the fruits of this reaped in every town? Cannot we hence see, that here is sowing to the flesh? Again, what scorning and scoffing, what mocking, derision, and strife! What oaths and drunkenness, uncleanness and cursed speaking! What lust and pride are seen in the streets! These fruits we see are reaped of the flesh. So here we see the seedsman, him that sows to this flesh, of which nothing but corruption is reaped; as the countries, towns, cities, and villages make manifest. But the ministers of the Spirit, who sow to the Spirit, come to reap eternal life. These discern the other seedsman, who sows to the flesh, and of the flesh reaps corruption. For the day hath manifested each seedsman, and what is reaped from each is seen; glory be to the Lord God for ever! The ministers of the Spirit, who are born of the Spirit, sons and daughters, who have the Spirit poured forth upon them, and witness the promise of God fulfilled in them, by the Spirit of God preach and minister to the Spirit in prison in every one, in the sight of God, the Father of Spirits. God's hand is turned against you all, that have destroyed God's creatures upon your lust. God's hand is turned against you that have wronged by unjust dealing, defrauded, and oppressed the poor, and respected the persons of the proud (such as are in gay apparel); and lend not your ear to the cry of the poor. The Lord's hand is turned against you, and his righteous judgment and justice upon you will be accomplished and repaid: who shall have a reward, every one according to his works.

"O! the abomination, the hypocritical profession that is upon the earth, where God and Christ, Faith, Hope, the Holy Spirit, and truth are professed; but the fear of God, and the faith that purifies and gives victory over the world, are not lived in! Doth it not appear, that the wisdom that rules in all those, whom the seedsman that sows to the flesh, sows for, and who are born of the flesh, is from below, earthly, sensual, and devilish; that their understanding is brutish, and their knowledge natural, as the brute beasts? For men and women in that state, have not patience to speak one to the other of the Scriptures, without much corruption and flesh appearing, yet they have a feigned humility, a will-worship, and righteousness of self; but they own not the light, which 'lighteth every man that cometh into the world,' Christ Jesus, the righteousness of God; which being owned, self, and the righteousness of self, come to be denied. Here is the humility that is contrary to the light, that is from below and feigned: here is the wisdom that is earthly, sensual, and devilish; for people can scarce speak one to another, without destroying one another, prisoning and persecuting one another, when they speak of the Scriptures. Now, this is the devilish wisdom, murdering and destroying: this is not the wisdom that is from above, which is pure and peaceable; gentle and easy to be entreated, full of mercy and good fruits. Here all may read each seedsman, which hath each wisdom. He that sows to the flesh, and is born of that, hath the wisdom that is earthly, sensual, and devilish; he that sows to the Spirit, a minister of the Spirit, hath the wisdom from above, which is pure, peaceable, gentle, and easy to be entreated;—the wisdom by which all things were made and created. Now is each wisdom discovered, and each seedsman; the day, which is the light, hath discovered them."　　G. F.

I was also moved to give forth the following epistle to Friends, to stir them up to be bold and valiant for the truth, and to encourage them in their sufferings for it:—

"ALL Friends and brethren everywhere, now is the day of your trial, now is the time for you to be valiant, and to see that the testimony of the Lord doth not fall. Now is the day for the exercise of your gifts, of your patience, and of your faith. Now is the time to be armed with patience, with the light, with righteousness, and with the helmet of salvation. Now is the trial of the slothful servant, who hides his talent, and will judge

Christ hard. Now, happy are they that can say, 'the earth is the Lord's and the fulness thereof, and he gives the increase;' and therefore, who takes it from you? Is it not the Lord still that suffers it? For the Lord can try you as he did Job, whom he made rich, whom he made poor, and whom he made rich again; who still kept his integrity in all conditions. Learn Paul's lesson, 'in all states to be content;' and have his faith, that 'nothing is able to separate us from the love of God, which we have in Christ Jesus.' Therefore be rich in life, and in grace, which will endure, ye who are heirs of life, and born of the womb of eternity, that noble birth, that cannot stoop to that which is born in sin, and conceived in iniquity; who are better bred and born; whose religion is from God, above all the religions that are from below; and who walk by faith, by that which God hath given you, and not by that which men make, who walk by sight, from the Mass-Book to the Directory. Such are subject to stumble and fall, who walk by sight and not by faith. Therefore mind him that destroys the original of sin, the devil and his works, and cuts off the entail of Satan, viz., sin; who would have by entail an inheritance of sin in men and women from generation to generation, and pleads for it by all his lawyers and counsellors. For though the law, which made nothing perfect, did not cut it off; yet Christ being come destroys the devil and his works, and cuts off the entail of sin. This angers all the devil's lawyers and counsellors, that Satan shall not hold sin by entail in thy garden, in thy field, in thy temple, thy tabernacle. So keep your tabernacles, that there ye may see the glory of the Lord appear at the doors thereof. And be faithful; for ye see, what the worthies and valiants of the Lord attained unto by faith. Enoch by faith was translated. Noah by faith was preserved over the waters in his ark. Abraham by faith forsook his father's house and religion, and all the religions of the world. Isaac and Jacob by faith followed his steps. See also how Samuel, with other of the Lord's prophets, and David, by faith were preserved to God, over God's enemies! Daniel and the three children by faith escaped the lions and the fire, and preserved their worship clean, and by it were kept over the worships of the world. The apostles by faith travelled up and down the world, were preserved from all the religions of the world, and held forth the pure religion to the dark world, which they had received from God; and likewise their fellowship was received from above, which is in the gospel that is everlasting. In this, neither powers, principalities, nor thrones, dominions nor angels, things present, nor things to come, nor heights, nor depths, nor death, mockings, nor spoiling of goods, nor prisons, nor fetters, were able to separate them from the love of God, which they had in Christ Jesus. And Friends, 'quench not the Spirit, nor despise prophesying,' where it moves; neither hinder the babes and sucklings from crying Hosanna; for out of their mouths will God ordain strength. There were some in Christ's day that were against such, whom he reproved; and there were some in Moses's day, who would have stopped the prophets in the camp, whom Moses reproved, and said, by way of encouragement to them, 'Would God, that all the Lord's people were prophets!' So I say now to you. Therefore ye, that stop it in yourselves, do not quench it in others, neither in babe nor suckling; for the Lord hears the cries of the needy, and the sighs and groans of the poor. Judge not that, nor the sighs and groans of the Spirit, which cannot be uttered, lest ye judge prayer; for prayer as well lies in sighs and groans to the Lord as otherwise. Let not the sons and daughters, nor the hand-maidens be stopped in their prophesyings, nor the young men in their visions, nor the old men in their dreams; but let the Lord be glorified in and through all, who is over all, God blessed for ever! So every one may improve his talents, every one exercise his gifts, and every one speak as the Spirit gives him utterance. Thus every one may minister as he hath received the grace, as a good steward to him that hath given it him; so that all plants may bud and bring forth fruit to the glory of God; 'for the manifestation of the Spirit is given to every one to profit withal.' See, that every one hath profited in heavenly things: male and female, look into your own vineyards, and see what fruit ye bear to God; look into your own houses, see how they are decked and trimmed, and see what odours, myrrh, and frankincense ye have therein, and what a smell and savour ye have to ascend to God, that he may be glorified. Bring all your deeds to the light, which ye are taught to believe in by Christ, your Head, the heavenly Man; and see how they are wrought in God. Every male and female, let Christ dwell in your hearts by faith, and let your mouths be opened to the glory of God the Father, that he may rule and reign in you. We must not have Christ Jesus, the Lord of life, put any more in a stable, amongst the horses and asses; but he must now have the best chamber, the heart, and the rude, debauched spirit must be turned out. Therefore let Him reign, whose right it is, who was conceived by the Holy Ghost, by which ye call him Lord, in which ye pray, and have comfort and fellowship with the Father and with the Son. Therefore know the triumph in it, and in God and his power (which the devil is out of), and in the seed, which is first and last, the beginning and ending, the top and corner-stone; in which is my love to you, and in which I rest—   Your friend, G. F."

"*Postscript*—And, Friends, be careful how ye set your feet among the tender plants, that are springing up out of God's earth; lest ye tread upon them, hurt, bruise, or crush them in God's vineyard."

After I had tarried two First-days at Swarthmore, and had visited Friends in their meetings thereabouts, I passed into WESTMORLAND, in the same work, till I came to John Audland's, where there was a general meeting. The night before I had a vision of a desperate creature, that was coming to destroy me, but I got victory over it. And next day in meeting-time came one Otway, with some rude fellows. He rode round about the meeting with his sword or rapier, and would fain have got in through the Friends to me; but the meeting being great, the Friends stood close, so that he could not easily come at me. When he had rode about several times raging, and found he could not get in, being limited by the Lord's power, he went away. It was a glorious meeting, ended peaceably, and the Lord's everlasting power came over all. This wild man went home, became distracted, and not long after died. I sent a paper to John Blaykling to read to him, while he lay ill, showing him his wickedness; and he acknowledged something of it.

From hence, I went through KENDAL, where a warrant had long lain to apprehend me; and the constables seeing me, ran to fetch their warrant, as I was riding through the town; but before they could come with it, I was gone past, and so escaped their hands.

I travelled northwards, visiting Friends' meetings, till I came to STRICKLAND-HEAD, where I had a great meeting. Most of the gentry of that country being gathered to a horse-race, not far from the meeting, I was moved to go and declare the truth unto them; and a chief-constable, that was there, also admonished them. Our meeting was quiet, and the Lord was with us; and by his word and power, Friends were settled in the eternal truth.

From hence we passed into CUMBERLAND, where we had many precious living meetings. After we had travelled to GILSLAND, and had a meeting there, we came to CARLISLE, where they used to put Friends out of the town; but there came a great flood while we were there, that they could not put us out; so we had a meeting there on First-day. After which we passed to ABBEY-HOLM, and had a little meeting there. This is a place, where I told Friends long before, a great people would come forth to the Lord; which hath since come to pass, and a large meeting is gathered to the Lord in those parts.

I passed hence to a general meeting at LANGLANDS in Cumberland, which was very large; for most of the people had so forsaken the priests, that the steeple-houses in some places stood empty. And John Wilkinson,* a preacher, I have often named before, who had three steeple-houses, had so few hearers left, that, giving over preaching in them, he first set up a meeting in his house, and preached there to them that were left. Afterwards he set up a silent meeting (like Friends), to which came a few; for most of his hearers were come to Friends. Thus he held on till he had not past half a dozen left; the rest still forsaking him, and coming to Friends. At last, when he had so very few left, he would come to Pardsey Crag (where Friends had a meeting of several hundreds of people, who were all come to sit under the Lord Jesus Christ's teaching), and he would walk about the meeting on First-days, like a man that went about the commons to look for sheep. During this time I came to PARDSEY CRAG meeting, and he with three or four of his followers, that were yet left to him, came to the meeting that day, and were all thoroughly convinced. After the meeting, Wilkinson asked me two or three questions, which I answered him to his satisfaction; and from that time he came amongst Friends, became an able minister, preached the gospel freely, and turned many to Christ's free teaching. And after he had continued many years in the free ministry of Jesus, he died in 1675.

I had for some time felt drawings on my spirit to go into SCOTLAND; and had sent to Colonel William Osburn of Scotland, desiring him to come and meet me; and he, with some others, came out of Scotland to this meeting. After the meeting was over (which, he said, was the most glorious one he ever saw in his life), I passed with him and his company

* This was not that John Wilkinson who joined with Storey in creating a schism in the Society.

into Scotland; having Robert Widders with me, a thundering man against hypocrisy, deceit, and the rottenness of the priests.

The first night we came into Scotland we lodged at an inn. The innkeeper told us, an Earl lived about a quarter of a mile off, who had a desire to see me; and had left word at his house, that if ever I came into Scotland, he should send him word. He told us there were three draw-bridges to his house, and that it would be nine o'clock before the third bridge was drawn. Finding we had time in the evening, we walked to his house. He received us very lovingly; and said, he would have gone with us on our journey, but he was previously engaged to go to a funeral. After we had spent some time with him, we parted very friendly, and re-turned to our inn. Next morning we travelled on, and passing through DUMFRIES came to DOUGLAS, where we met with some Friends; and thence passed to the HEADS, where we had a blessed meeting in the name of Jesus, and felt him in the midst.

Leaving Heads, we went to BADCOW, and had a meeting there; to which abundance of people came, and many were convinced; amongst whom was one, called a lady. From thence we passed towards the HIGH-LANDS to William Osburn's house, where we gathered up the sufferings of Friends, and the principles of the Scotch priests, which may be seen in a book called *The Scotch Priests' Principles*.

Afterwards we returned to Heads, Badcow, and GARSHORE, where the said Lady Margaret Hambleton was convinced; who afterwards went to warn Oliver Cromwell and Charles Fleetwood of the day of the Lord that was coming upon them.

On First-day we had a great meeting, and several professors came to it. Now, the priests had frightened the people with the doctrine of election and reprobation, telling them "that God had ordained the greatest part of men and women for hell; and that, let them pray, or preach, or sing, or do what they could, it was all to no purpose, if they were ordained for hell;—that God had a certain number elected for heaven, let them do what they would, as David an adulterer, and Paul a persecutor, yet elected vessels for heaven. So the fault was not at all in the creature, less or more, but God had ordained it so." I was led to open to the people the falseness and folly of their priests' doctrines, and showed how they had abused those Scriptures they brought and quoted to them, as in Jude, and other places. For whereas they said, there was no fault at all in the creature, I showed them that they whom Jude speaks of, to wit, Cain, Korah, and Balaam, who, he says, were ordained of old to condemnation, the fault was in them. For did not God warn Cain and Balaam, and put the question to Cain, "If thou doest well, shalt thou not be accepted?' And did not the Lord bring Korah out of Egypt and his company? yet did not he gainsay both God and his law, and his prophet Moses? Here people might see that there was a fault in Cain, Korah, and Balaam, and so there is in all that go in their ways. For if they who are called Chris-tians, resist the gospel, as Korah did the law; if they err from the Spirit of God, as Balaam did, and do evil, as Cain did, is not here a fault? Which fault is in themselves, and is the cause of their reprobation, and not God. Doth not Christ say, "Go, preach the gospel to all nations?" Which is the gospel of salvation. He would not have sent them into all nations, to preach the doctrine of salvation, if the greatest part of men had been ordained for hell. Was not Christ a propitiation for the sins of the whole world, for those that become reprobates, as well as for the saints? He died for all men, the ungodly as well as the godly, as the apostle bears witness, 2 Cor. v. 15; Rom. v. 6. And he "enlightens every man that cometh into the world," that through him they might all believe. And Christ bids them believe in the light; but all they that hate the light, which Christ bids all believe in, are reprobated. Again, "the manifestation of the Spirit of God is given to every man to profit withal;" but they that vex, quench, and grieve it, are in the reprobation; and the fault is in them, as it is also in them that hate his light. The apostle says, "The grace of God which brings salvation, hath appeared unto all men, teaching us that, denying ungodliness and worldly lusts, we should live soberly, righteously, and godly, in this present world," Tit. ii. 11, 12. Now when men and women live ungodly, and in the lusts of the world, turn this grace of God into wantonness, and walk despitefully against it, and so deny God, and the Lord Jesus Christ, that bought them; the fault is in all such as thus turn the grace of God into wantonness, and walk despitefully against that which would bring their salvation, and save them out of the reprobation. But the priests, it seems, can see no fault in such as deny God, and the Lord Jesus Christ, that hath bought them—such as deny his light, which they should believe in, and his grace, which should teach them to live godly, and which should bring them their salvation. Now all that believe in the light of Christ, as he commands, are in the election, and sit under the teaching of the grace of God, which brings their salvation. But such as turn this grace into wantonness, are in the reprobation; and such as hate the light, are in the condemnation. Therefore I exhorted all the people to believe in the light, as Christ commands, and own the grace of God, their free teacher; and it would assuredly bring them their salvation; for it is sufficient. Many other Scriptures were opened concerning reprobation, and the eyes of the people were opened; and a spring of life rose up among them.

These things soon came to the priests' ears; for the people that sat under their dark teachings, began to see light, and to come into the covenant of light. The noise was spread over Scotland, amongst the priests, that I was come thither; and a great cry was among them, that all would be spoiled; for, they said, I had spoiled all the honest men and women in England already, so according to their own account, the worst were left to them. Upon this they gathered great assemblies of priests together, and drew up a number of curses to be read in their several steeple-houses, that all the people might say "Amen" to them. Some few of these I will here set down, the rest may be read in the book before mentioned, of *The Scotch Priests' Principles.*

The first was, "Cursed is he that saith, every man hath a light within him sufficient to lead him to salvation; and let all the people say, Amen."

The second, "Cursed is he that saith, faith is without sin; and let all the people say, Amen."

The third, "Cursed is he that denieth the Sabbath-day; and let all the people say, Amen." *

In this last they make the people curse themselves; for on the Sabbath-day (which is the seventh-day of the week, which the Jews kept by the command of God to them) they kept markets and fairs, and so brought the curse upon their own heads.

As to the first, concerning the light, Christ saith, "Believe in the light, that ye may become children of the light;" and "he that believeth shall be saved; he that believeth shall have everlasting life; he that believeth passes from death to life, and is grafted into Christ." And "ye do well," said the apostle, "that ye take heed unto the light that shines in the dark place, until the day dawn, and the day-star arise in your hearts." So the light is sufficient to lead unto the day-star.

And as concerning faith, it is the gift of God; and every gift of God is pure. The faith, which Christ is the author of, is precious, divine, and without sin. This is the faith which gives victory over sin, and access to God; in which faith they please God. But they are reprobates themselves concerning this faith, and are in their dead faith, who charge sin upon this faith under pain of a curse; which faith gives victory over their curse, and returns it into their own bowels.

A company of Scots near BADCOW, challenged a dispute with some of our Scotch Friends, for with me they would not dispute; so some of the Scotch Friends met them at the market-place. The dispute was to be concerning the Sabbath-day, and some other of their principles before-mentioned; and I having got their principles and assertions, showed the Friends where they might easily be overthrown, and a Scotch Friend, a smith, overthrew them clearly.

There were two Independent churches in Scotland, in one of which many were convinced; but the pastor of the other was in a great rage against truth and Friends. They had their elders, who sometimes would exercise their gifts amongst the church-members, and were sometimes pretty tender; but their pastor speaking so much against the light and us, the friends of Christ, he darkened his hearers, so that they grew blind, and dry, and lost their tenderness. He continued preaching against Friends, and against the light of Christ Jesus, calling it natural; at last one day in his preaching, he cursed the light, and fell down, as if dead, in his pulpit. The people carried him out, and laid him upon a grave-stone, and poured strong waters into him, which brought him to life again; and they carried him home, but he was mopish. After a while he stripped off his clothes, put on a Scotch plaid, and went into the country amongst the dairy-women. When he had stayed there about two weeks, he came home, and went into the pulpit again. Whereupon the people expected some great manifestation or revelation from him; but, instead thereof, he began to tell

---

* It is justly observed by a writer, not of the Society of Friends, that these "place the Presbyterian Christianity of that day in a most unfavourable light, and show how deeply it was imbued with a sour persecuting spirit of Popery."

them what entertainment he had met with; how one woman gave him skimmed-milk, another gave him butter-milk, and another gave him good milk; so the people were fain to take him out of the pulpit again, and carry him home. He that gave me this account was Andrew Robinson, one of his chief hearers, who came afterwards to be convinced, and received the truth. He said he never heard that he recovered his senses again. By this people may see what came upon him that cursed the light; which Light is the Life in Christ, the Word; and it may be a warning to all others, that speak evil against the Light of Christ.

Now were the priests in such a rage, that they posted to Edinburgh to Oliver Cromwell's council there, with petitions against me. The noise was, "that all was gone;" for several Friends were come out of England and spread over Scotland, sounding the day of the Lord, preaching the everlasting gospel of salvation, and turning people to Christ Jesus, who died for them, that they might receive his free teaching. After I had gathered the principles of the Scotch priests, and the sufferings of Friends, and had seen the Friends in that part of Scotland settled, by the Lord's power, upon Christ their foundation, I went to Edinburgh, and in the way came to LINLITHGOW; where, lodging at an inn, the innkeeper's wife, who was blind, received the word of life and came under the teaching of Christ Jesus, her Saviour. At night there came in abundance of soldiers and some officers, with whom we had much discourse; some were rude. One of the officers said, "he would obey the Turk's or Pilate's command, if they should command him to guard Christ to crucify him." So far was he from all tenderness, or sense of the Spirit of Christ, that he would rather crucify the just, than suffer for or with the just; whereas many officers and magistrates have lost their places, before they would turn against the Lord and his Just One.

When I had stayed a while at EDINBURGH, I went to LEITH, where many officers of the army came in with their wives, and many were convinced. Among these Edward Billing's wife was one; she brought a great deal of coral in her hand, and threw it on the table before me, to see whether I would speak against it or not. I took no notice of it, but declared the truth to her, and she was reached. There came in many Baptists, who were very rude, but the Lord's power came over them, so that they went away confounded. Then there came in another sort, and one of them said, "he would dispute with me; and for argument's sake, would deny there was a God." I told him, "he might be one of those fools that said in his heart, There is no God, but he should know him in the day of his judgment." So he went his way; and a precious time we had afterwards with several people of account; and the Lord's power came over all. William Osburn was with me. Colonel Lidcot's wife and William Welch's wife, and several of the officers themselves, were convinced. Edward Billing and his wife at that time lived apart; and she being reached by truth, and become loving to Friends, we sent for her husband, who came; and the Lord's power reached unto them both, they joined in it, and agreed to live together in love and unity, as man and wife.

After this we returned to EDINBURGH, where many thousands were

gathered together, with abundance of priests among them, about burning a
witch, and I was moved to declare the day of the Lord amongst them.
When I had done, I went to our meeting, whither many rude people and
Baptists came.   The Baptists began to vaunt with their logic and syllogisms; but I was moved in the Lord's power to thrash their chaffy, light
minds; and showed the people that, after that fallacious way of discoursing,
they might make white seem black, and black white; as, that because a
cock had two legs, and each of them had two legs, therefore they were
all cocks.   Thus they might turn any thing into lightness and vanity; but
it was not the way of Christ or his apostles, to teach, speak, or reason,
after that manner.   Hereupon those Baptists went their way, and after
they were gone, we had a blessed meeting in the Lord's power, which was
over all.

I mentioned before, that many of the Scotch priests, being greatly
disturbed at the spreading of truth, and the loss of their hearers thereby,
were gone to Edinburgh, to petition the council against me.   Now, when
I came from the meeting to the inn where I lodged, an officer belonging to
the council brought me the following order :—

"*Thursday, the 8th of October*, 1657, *at his Highness's Council in Scotland.*

ORDERED,
That George Fox do appear before the Council on Tuesday, the 13th
of October next, in the forenoon.

E. DOWNING, Clerk of the Council."

When he had delivered me the order, he asked me, "whether I would
appear or not?"   I did not tell him whether I would or not; but asked
him "if he had not forged the order:" he said, "no, it was a real order
from the council, and he was sent, as their messenger, with it."   When
the time came I appeared, and was conducted into a large room, where
many great persons came and looked at me.   After a while the door-keeper
had me into the council-chamber; and as I was going in, he took off my
hat.   I asked him "why he did so, and who was there, that I might not
go in with my hat on?" for I told him "I had been before the Protector
with it on."   But he hung it up, and had me in before them.   When I
had stood a while, and they said nothing to me, I was moved of the Lord
to say, "Peace be amongst you; wait in the fear of God, that ye may
receive his wisdom from above, by which all things were made and created;
that by it ye may all be ordered, and may order all things under your hands
to God's glory."   They asked me, "what was the occasion of my coming
into that nation?"   I told them, "I came to visit the seed of God, which
had long lain in bondage under corruption; and the intent of my coming
was, that all in the nation that professed the Scriptures, the words of Christ,
and of the prophets, and apostles, might come to the light, Spirit, and
power, which they were in, who gave them forth; that so in and by the
Spirit they might understand the Scriptures, know Christ and God aright,
and have fellowship with them, and one with another.   They asked me,

"whether I had any outward business there?" I said, "nay." Then they asked me how long I intended to stay in the country? I told them "I should say little to that; my time was not to be long, yet in my freedom in the Lord, I stood in the will of him that sent me." Then they bid me withdraw, and the door-keeper took me by the hand, and led me forth. In a little time they sent for me again, and told me, "I must depart the nation of Scotland by that day seventh night." I asked them, "why, what had I done? What was my transgression, that they passed such a sentence upon me to depart out of the nation?" They told me, "they would not dispute with me." Then I desired them "to hear what I had to say to them;" but they said, "they would not hear me." I told them, Pharaoh heard Moses and Aaron, and yet he was a heathen and no Christian, and Herod heard John the Baptist; and they should not be worse than these. But they cried, "withdraw, withdraw." Whereupon the door-keeper took me again by the hand, and led me out. Then I returned to my inn, and continued still in Edinburgh, visiting Friends there and thereabouts, and strengthening them in the Lord. After a little time, I wrote a letter to the council, to lay before them their unchristian dealing in banishing me, an innocent man, that sought their salvation and eternal good; a copy of which letter here follows:—

"To the Council of Edinburgh,

"YE that sit in council, and bring before your judgment-seat the innocent, the just, without showing the least cause what evil I have done, or convicting me of any breach of law; and afterward banish me out of your nation and country, without telling me why, or what evil I had done; though I told you, when ye asked me how long I would stay in the nation, that my time was not long (I spoke it innocently), and yet ye banish me. Will not all, think ye, that fear God, judge this to be wickedness? Consider, did not they sit in council about Stephen, when they stoned him to death? Did not they sit in council about Peter and John, when they haled them out of the temple, and put them out of their council for a little season, and took council together, and then brought them in again and threatened them, and charged them to speak no more in that name? Was not this to stop the truth from spreading in that time? And had not the priests a hand in these things with the magistrates? and in examining Stephen, when he was stoned to death? Was not the council gathered together against Jesus Christ to put him to death? and had not the chief priests a hand in it? When they go to persecute the just, and crucify the just, do they not then neglect judgment, and mercy, and justice, and the weighty matters of the law, which is just? Was not the apostle Paul tossed up and down by the priests and the rulers? Was not John the Baptist cast into prison? Are not ye doing the same work, showing what spirit ye are of? Now do not ye show the end of your profession, the end of your prayers, the end of your religion, and the end of your teaching, who are now come to banish the truth, and him that is come to declare it unto you? Doth not this show that ye are but in the words, out of the life, of the prophets, Christ, and his apostles? for they did not use such practice as to banish any. How do ye receive strangers, which is a command of God among the prophets, Christ, and the apostles? Some by that means have entertained angels at unawares; but ye banish one that comes to visit the Seed of God, and is not chargeable to any of you. Will not all that fear God, look upon this to be spite and wickedness against the truth? How are ye like to love enemies, that banish your friend? How are ye like to do good to them that hate you, when ye do evil to them that love you? How are ye like to heap coals of fire on their heads that hate you, and to overcome evil with good, when ye banish thus? Do ye not manifest to all that are in the truth, that ye have not the Christian spirit? How did ye do justice to me, when ye could not convict me of any evil, yet banish me? This shows that truth is banished out of your hearts, and ye have taken part against the truth with evil-doers; with the wicked, envious priests, and stoners, strikers, and mockers in the streets; with these, ye that banish, have taken part. Whereas ye should have been a terror to these, and a praise to them that do well, and succourers of them that are in the truth; then might ye have been a blessing to the nation, ye would not have banished him that was moved of the Lord to visit the Seed of God, and thereby have brought your names upon record, and made them to stink in ages to come, among them that fear God. Were not the magistrates stirred up in former ages to persecute or banish, by the corrupt priests? and did not the corrupt priests stir up the rude multitude against the just in other ages? Therefore are your streets like Sodom and Gomorrah. Did not the Jews and the priests make the Gentiles' minds envious against the apostles? Who were they that would not have the prophet Amos to prophesy at the king's chapel; but bid him fly his way? And when Jeremiah was put in the prison, in the dungeon, and in the stocks, had not the priests a hand with the princes in doing it? Now see all that were in this work of banishing, prisoning, persecuting, whether they were not all out of the life of Christ, the prophets, and apostles? To the witness of God in you all I speak. Consider whether they were not always the blind magistrates, who turned their sword backward, that knew not their friends from their foes, and so hit their friends? Such magistrates were deceived by flattery."   G. F.

When this was delivered, and read amongst them, some of them, I heard, were troubled at what they had done, being made sensible that they would not be so served themselves. But it was not long before they that banished me, were banished themselves, or glad to get away; who would not do good in the day when they had power, nor suffer others that would.

After I had spent some time among Friends at Edinburgh, and thereabouts, I passed to HEADS again, where Friends had been in great sufferings; for the Presbyterian priests had excommunicated them, and given charge that none should buy or sell, or eat or drink with them. So they could neither sell their commodities, nor buy what they wanted; which made it go very hard with some of them; for if they had bought bread or other victuals of any of their neighbours, the priests threatened them so with curses, that they would run and fetch it from them again. But

Colonel Ashfield being a justice of peace in that country, put a stop to the priests' proceedings. This Colonel Ashfield was afterwards convinced himself, had a meeting settled at his house, declared the truth, and lived and died in it.

After I had visited Friends at Heads and thereaways, and had encouraged them in the Lord, I went to GLASGOW, where a meeting was appointed; but not one of the town came to it. As I went into the city, the guard at the gates took me before the governor, who was a moderate man. Much discourse I had with him; but he was too light to receive the truth, yet he set me at liberty; so I passed to the meeting. But seeing none of the town's-people came, we declared truth through the town, and so passed away; and having visited Friends in their meetings thereabouts, returned towards BADCOW. Several Friends declared truth in their steeple-houses, and the Lord's power was with them. Once as I was going with William Osburn to his house, there lay a company of rude fellows by the way-side, hid under the hedges and in bushes. Seeing them, I asked him "what they were?" "O," said he, "they are thieves." Robert Widders, being moved to go and speak to a priest, was left behind, intending to come after. So I said to William Osburn, "I will stay here in this valley, and do thou go look after Robert Widders;" but he was unwilling to go, being afraid to leave me there alone, because of those fellows, till I told him, "I feared them not." Then I called to them, asking them, "what they lay lurking there for," and I bid them come to me; but they were loath to come. I charged them to come up to me, or else it might be worse with them; then they came trembling, for the dread of the Lord had struck them. I admonished them to be honest, and directed them to the light of Christ in their hearts, that by it they might see what an evil it was to follow after theft and robbery; and the power of the Lord came over them. I stayed there till William Osburn and Robert Widders came up, and then we passed on together. But it is likely that, if we two had gone away before, they would have robbed Robert Widders when he had come after alone, there being three or four of them.

We went to William Osburn's house, where we had a good opportunity to declare the truth to several people that came in. Then we went among the Highlanders, who were so devilish, they had like to have spoiled us and our horses; for they ran at us with pitch-forks; but through the Lord's goodness we escaped them, being preserved by his power.

Thence we passed to STIRLING, where the soldiers took us up, and had us to the main-guard. After a few words with the officers, the Lord's power coming over them, we were set at liberty: but no meeting could we get amongst them in the town, they were so closed up in darkness. Next morning there came a man with a horse that was to run a race, and most of the town's-people and officers went to see it. As they came back from the race, I had a brave opportunity to declare the day of the Lord and his word of life amongst them. Some confessed to it, and some opposed; but the Lord's truth and power came over them all.

Leaving Stirling, we came to BURNTISLAND, where I had two meetings at one Captain Pool's house; one in the morning, the other in the afternoon. Whilst they went to dine, I walked to the sea-side, not having freedom to eat with them. Both he and his wife were convinced, and became good Friends afterward, and several officers of the army came in and received the truth.

We passed thence through several other places, till we came to JOHN-STONS, where were several Baptists that were very bitter, and came in a rage to dispute with us: vain janglers and disputers indeed they were. When they could not prevail by disputing, they went and informed the governor against us; and next morning raised a whole company of foot, and banished me, and Alexander Parker, also James Lancaster, and Robert Widders out of the town. As they guarded us though the town, James Lancaster was moved to sing with a melodious sound in the power of God; and I was moved to proclaim the day of the Lord, and preach the ever-lasting gospel to the people. For they generally came forth, so that the streets were filled with them: and the soldiers were so ashamed that they said, "they would rather have gone to Jamaica than have guarded us so." But we were put into a boat with our horses, carried over the water, and there left. The Baptists, who were the cause of our being thus put out of this town, were themselves, not long after, turned out of the army; and he that was then governor was discarded also when the king came in.

Being thus thrust out of Johnstons, we went to another market-town, where Edward Billing* and many soldiers quartered. We went to an inn, and desired to have a meeting in the town, that we might preach the ever-lasting gospel amongst them. The officers and soldiers said, we should have it in the town-hall; but the Scotch magistrates in spite appointed a meeting there that day for the business of the town. When the officers of the soldiery understood this, and perceived that it was done in malice, they would have had us to go into the town-hall nevertheless. But we told them, "by no means, for then the magistrates might inform the governor against them, and say, they took the town-hall from them by force, when they were to do their town business therein." We told them, "we would go to the market-place;" they said, "it was market-day;" we replied, "it was so much the better; for we would have all people to hear truth, and

---

* Edward Billing was a faithful sufferer for the truth. Henry Fell, in a letter to Margaret Fell, in 1660, mentions Friends being beat very sore, and exceedingly abused in the streets. "They pulled me out of meeting," he says, "beat me much, knocked me down in the street, and tore all my coat. Edward Billing and his wife were much abused, he especially."

Edward Billing was one of the three Friends, who, in 1659, appeared before the bar of the House of Commons, to present an address describing the sufferings of Friends, and signed by 164 of the Society, wherein they make an offer of their own bodies, person for person, to lie in prison instead of such of their brethren as were then under confinement, and might be in danger of their lives through extreme dur-ance. (See *Letters of Early Friends*, pp. 62–68.) Although little or no apparent effect appeared to be produced at the time in the House from the above-mentioned appeal, it appears, from the journals of the Commons in the month following, a com-mittee was appointed, "to consider of the imprisonment of such persons who continue committed for conscience sake, and how, and in what manner they are, and continue committed, together with the whole cause thereof, and how they may be discharged; and to report the same to the Parliament."

know our principles." Alexander Parker went and stood upon the market-cross with a Bible in his hand, and declared the truth amongst the soldiers and market-people; but the Scots, being a dark, carnal people, gave little heed, and hardly took notice of what was said. After a while I was moved of the Lord to stand up at the cross, and declare with a loud voice the everlasting truth, and the day of the Lord that was coming upon all sin and wickedness. Whereupon the people came running out of the town-hall, and they gathered so together, that at last we had a large meeting; for they sat in the court only for a pretence, to hinder us from having the hall to meet in. When the people were come away, the magistrates followed them. Some walked by, but some stayed and heard; and the Lord's power came over all, and kept all quiet. "The people were turned to the Lord Jesus Christ, who died for them, and had enlightened them, that with his light they might see their evil deeds, be saved from their sins by him, and come to know him to be their teacher. But if they would not receive Christ and own him, it was told them, that this light, which came from him, would be their condemnation."

Several of them were made loving to us, especially the English people, and some came afterwards to be convinced. But there was a soldier that was very envious against us; he hated both us and the truth, spoke evil of it, and very despitefully against the light of Christ Jesus, to which we bore testimony. Mighty zealous he was for the priests and their hearers. As this man was hearing the priest, holding his hat before his face, while the priest prayed, one of the priest's hearers stabbed him to death; so he who had rejected the teachings of the Lord Jesus Christ, and cried down the servants of the Lord, was murdered amongst them whom he had so cried up, and by one of them.

We travelled from this town to LEITH, warning and exhorting people, as we went, to turn to the Lord. At Leith the innkeeper told me, that the council had granted warrants to apprehend me, "because I was not gone out of the nation, after the seven days were expired, that they had ordered me to depart in." Several friendly people also came and told me the same; to whom I said, " What do ye tell me of their warrants against me? if there were a cart-load of them I do not heed them, for the Lord's power is over them all."

I went from Leith to EDINBURGH again, where they said the warrants from the council were out against me. I went to the inn where I had lodged before, and no man offered to meddle with me. After I had visited Friends in the city, I desired those that travelled with me, to get ready their horses in the morning, and we rode out of town together; there were with me at that time Thomas Rawlinson, Alexander Parker, and Robert Widders. When we were out of town, they asked me, " whither I would go?" I told them it was upon me from the Lord to go back again to Johnstons (the town out of which we had been lately thrust), to set the power of God and his truth over them also. Alexander Parker said, " he would go along with me;" and I wished the other two to stay at a town, about three miles from Edinburgh, till we returned. Then Alexander and I got over the water, about three miles across, and rode through the country; but in the afternoon, his horse being weak and not able to hold up with mine, I put on and got into Johnstons just as they were drawing up the bridges; the officers and soldiers never questioning me. I rode up the street to Captain Davenport's house, from which we had been banished. There were many officers with him; and when I came amongst them, they lifted up their hands, wondering that I should come again; but I told them, "the Lord God had sent me amongst them again;" so they went their way. The Baptists sent me a letter, by way of challenge, "to discourse with me next day." I sent them word, "I would meet them at such a house, about half a mile out of the town, at such an hour." For I considered, if I should stay in town to discourse with them, they might, under pretence of discoursing with me, have raised men to put me out of the town again, as they had done before. At the time appointed I went to the place, Captain Davenport and his son accompanying me, where I stayed some hours, but not one of them came. While I stayed there waiting for them, I saw Alexander Parker coming; who, not being able to reach the town, had lain out the night before; and I was exceedingly glad that we were met again.

This Captain Davenport was then loving to Friends; but afterwards coming more into obedience to truth, he was turned out of his place, for not putting off his hat, and for saying Thou and Thee to them.

When we had waited beyond reasonable ground to expect any of them coming, we departed; and Alexander Parker being moved to go again to the town, where we had the meeting at the market-cross, I passed alone to Lieutenant Foster's quarters, where I found several officers that were convinced. From thence I went up to the town, where I had left the other two Friends, and we went back to EDINBURGH together.

When we were come to the city, I bid Robert Widders follow me; and in the dread and power of the Lord we came up to the first two sentries; and the Lord's power came so over them, that we passed by them without any examination. Then we rode up the street to the market-place, by the main-guard out at the gate by the third sentry, and so clear out at the suburbs, and there came to an inn and set up our horses, it being the seventh-day of the week. Now I saw and felt that we had rode, as it were, against the cannon's mouth, or the sword's point; but the Lord's power and immediate hand carried us over the heads of them all. Next day I went to the meeting in the city, Friends having notice that I would attend it. There came many officers and soldiers to it, and a glorious meeting it was; the everlasting power of God was set over the nation, and his Son reigned in his glorious power. All was quiet, and no man offered to meddle with me. When the meeting was ended, and I had visited Friends, I came out of the city to my inn again; and next day, being the second-day of the week, we set forward towards the borders of England.

As we travelled along the country I spied a steeple-house, and it struck at my life. I asked "what steeple-house it was," and was answered, that it was DUNBAR. When I came thither, and had put up at an inn, I walked to the steeple-house, having a friend or two with me. When we came into the yard, one of the chief men of the town was walking there.

I spoke to one of the friends that were with me, to go to him and tell him, "that about nine next morning there would be a meeting there of the people of God called Quakers; of which we desired he would give notice to the people of the town." He sent me word, "that they were to have a lecture there at nine; but that we might have our meeting there at eight, if we would." We concluded so, and desired him to give notice of it. Accordingly in the morning both poor and rich came; and there being a captain of horse quartered in the town, he and his troopers came also, so that we had a large meeting; and a glorious one it was, the Lord's power being over all. After some time the priest came, and went into the steeple-house; but we being in the yard, most of the people stayed with us. Friends were so full, and their voices so high in the power of God, that the priest could do little in the steeple-house, but came quickly out again, stood a while, and then went his way. I opened to the people, "where they might find Christ Jesus, turned them to the light, which he had enlightened them withal, that in the light they might see Christ, that died for them, turn to him, and know him to be their Saviour and free teacher. I let them see, that all the teachers they had hitherto followed, were hirelings, who made the gospel chargeable; showed them the wrong ways they had walked in, in the night of apostacy, directed them to Christ, the new and living way to God; manifested unto them, how they had lost the religion and worship which Christ set up in spirit and truth, and had hitherto been in the religions and worships of men's making and setting up. After I had turned the people to the Spirit of God, which led the holy men of God to give forth the Scriptures; and showed them, that they must also come to receive, and be led by, the same Spirit in themselves (a measure of which was given unto every one of them), if ever they came to know God and Christ, and the Scriptures aright; perceiving the other Friends that were with me to be full of the power and word of the Lord, I stepped down, giving way for them to declare what they had from the Lord unto the people." Towards the latter end of the meeting some professors began to jangle; whereupon I stood up again, and answered their questions, so that they seemed to be satisfied, and our meeting ended in the Lord's power, quiet and peaceable. This was the last meeting I had in Scotland; the truth and the power of God was set over that nation, and many, by the power and Spirit of God, were turned to the Lord Jesus Christ, their Saviour and teacher, whose blood was shed for them; and there is since a great increase, and great there will be in Scotland. For when first I set my horse's feet upon Scottish ground, I felt the Seed of God to sparkle about me, like innumerable sparks of fire. Not but that there is abundance of thick, cloddy earth of hypocrisy and falseness above, and a briery, brambly nature, which is to be burnt up with God's Word, and ploughed up with his spiritual plough, before God's Seed brings forth heavenly and spiritual fruit to his glory. But the husbandman is to wait in patience.

CHAPTER XII.

1657-1659.—George Fox journeys from Scotland to England—dissuades a person from setting up a college at Durham to make ministers—has a meeting with Rice Jones and his people—attends a general Yearly Meeting for the whole nation, held at John Crook's, which continued three days—address to Friends in the ministry —disputes with a Jesuit—writes to Lady Claypole—writes to Cromwell respecting the fast on account of persecution abroad, whilst there was much of it at home—writes a reproof to Parliament for their hypocrisy—speaks to the Protector in Hampton-Court Park about Friends' sufferings—the Protector invites Fox to his house—he goes next day, but the Protector being sick he does not see him— the Protector died soon after—writes to encourage Friends to faithfulness—has a foresight of the King's restoration long before the event occurred, as well as several others—Friends are disseized of their copyhold lands for refusing to swear —cautions Friends to avoid plots, &c.—against bearing arms—great places in the army are offered to Friends, but invariably refused—priest Townsend fails to substantiate his charge of error and blasphemy against George Fox, and is signally defeated—George Fox's vision of the city of London is realized—he gives a final warning to those in authority before their overthrow.

FROM Dunbar we came to BERWICK, where we were questioned a little by the officers; but the governor was loving towards us; and in the evening we had a little meeting, in which the power of the Lord was manifested over all.

Leaving Berwick, we came to MORPETH, and so through the country, visiting Friends, to NEWCASTLE, where I had been once before. The Newcastle priests had written many books against us; and one Ledger, an alderman of the town, was very envious against truth and Friends. He and the priests had said, "the Quakers would not come into any great towns, but lived in the Fells, like butterflies." So I took Anthony Pearson with me, and went to this Ledger, and several others of the aldermen, "desiring to have a meeting amongst them, seeing they had written so many books against us, for we were now come, I told them, into their great town." But they would not allow we should have a meeting, neither would they be spoken to withal, save only this Ledger and one other. I queried, "had they not called Friends butterflies, and said, we would not come into any great towns? and now we were come into their town, they would not hear us, though they had printed books against us; 'Who are the butterflies now?'" said I. Then Ledger began to plead for the Sabbath-day; but I told him they kept markets and fairs on that which was the Sabbath-day, for that was the seventh day of the week; whereas that day, which the professed Christians now met on, and call their Sabbath, is the first day of the week. As we could not have a public meeting among them, we got a little one among Friends and friendly people, at Gateshead; where a meeting is continued to this day, in the name of Jesus. As I was passing by the market-place, the power of the Lord rose in me, "to warn them of the day of the Lord, that was coming upon them." And not long after, all those priests of Newcastle and their profession, were turned out, when the king came in.

From Newcastle we travelled through the countries, having meetings and visiting Friends as we went, in Northumberland and Durham. A very good one we had at Lieutenant Dove's, where many were turned to the Lord and his teaching. After the meeting I went to visit a justice of peace, a very sober, loving man, who confessed to the truth.

Thence we came to DURHAM, where was a man come from London, to set up a college there, to make ministers of Christ, as they said. I went, with some others, to reason with him, and to let him see, "that to teach men Hebrew, Greek, and Latin, and the seven arts, which were all but the teachings of the natural man, was not the way to make them ministers of Christ. For the languages began at Babel; and to the Greeks, that spoke Greek, as their mother-tongue, the preaching of the cross of Christ was foolishness; and to the Jews, that spoke Hebrew as their mother-tongue, Christ was a stumbling-block. The Romans, who had the Latin, persecuted the Christians; and Pilate, one of the Roman governors, set Hebrew, Greek, and Latin over Christ, when he crucified him. So he might see the many languages began at Babel, and they set them above Christ, the Word, when they crucified him. John the divine, who preached the Word, that was in the beginning, said, 'that the beast and the whore have power over tongues and languages, and they are as waters.' Thus I told him he might see, the whore and beast have power over the tongues and the many languages which are in mystery Babylon; for they began at Babel; and the persecutors of Christ Jesus set them over him, when he was crucified by them; but he is risen above them all, who was before them all. 'Now,' said I, to this man, 'dost thou think to make ministers of Christ by these natural, confused languages, which sprung from Babel, are admired in Babylon, and set above Christ, the Life, by a persecutor?' O no!" The man confessed to many of these things. Then we showed him further, "that Christ made his ministers himself, gave gifts unto them, and bid them 'pray to the Lord of the harvest, to send forth labourers.' And Peter and John, though unlearned and ignorant (as to school-learning) preached Christ Jesus, the Word, which was in the beginning, before Babel was. Paul also was made an apostle, not of man, nor by man, neither received he the gospel from man, but from Jesus Christ, who is the same now, and so is his gospel, as it was at that day." When we had thus discoursed with the man, he became very loving and tender; and, after he had considered further of it, declined to set up his college.

From Durham we went to Anthony Pearson's: thence into CLEVE-LAND, passed through Yorkshire to the further end of HOLDERNESS, and had mighty meetings, the Lord's power accompanying us.

After we left Anthony Pearson's, we went by HULL and PONTEFRACT, to George Watkinson's house, and visited most of the meetings in those parts, till we came to SCALE-HOUSE, and so to SWARTHMORE; the everlasting power and arm of God carrying us through and preserving us. After I had visited Friends thereaways, I passed into Yorkshire again, and

Cheshire, and so through other counties into Derbyshire and Nottingham-shire : glorious meetings we had, the Lord's presence being with us.

At NOTTINGHAM I sent to Rice Jones, desiring him to make his people acquainted, that I had something to say to them from the Lord.   He came and told me, "many of them lived in the country, and he could not tell how to send to them."   I told him, "he might acquaint those about the town of it, and send to as many in the country as he could.   Next day we met at the castle, there being about fourscore people, to whom I declared the truth for about two hours ; and the Lord's power was over them all, so that they were not able to open their mouths in opposition.   When I had done, one of them asked me a qustion, which I was loath to answer, for I saw it might lead to dispute, and I was unwilling to go into jangling, for some of the people were tender ; yet I could not well tell how to escape it.   Wherefore I answered the question, and was moved forthwith to speak to Rice Jones, and lay before him, "that he had been the man that had scattered such as had been tender, and some that had been convinced, and had been led out of many vanities of the world, which he had formerly judged ; but now he judged the power of God in them, and they, being simple, turned to him ; and so he and they were turned to be vainer than the world : for many of his followers were become the greatest foot-ball players and wrestlers in the country.   I told him, it was the serpent in him, that had scattered, and done hurt to such as were tender towards the Lord.   Nevertheless, if he waited in the fear of God, for the Seed of the woman, Christ Jesus, to bruise the serpent's head in him, that had scattered and done the hurt, he might come to gather them again by this heavenly Seed ; though it would be a hard work for him to gather them again out of those vanities he had led them into."   At this Rice Jones said, "Thou liest, it is not the Seed of the woman that bruises the serpent's head."   "No !" said I, "what is it then ?"   "I say it is the law," said he.   "But," said I, "the Scripture, speaking of the Seed of the woman, saith, ' It shall bruise thy head, and thou shalt bruise his heel.'   Now, hath the law an heel," said I, "to be bruised ?"   Then Rice Jones and all his company were at a stand, and I was moved in the power of the Lord to speak to him, and say, "This Seed, Jesus Christ, the Seed of the woman, which should bruise the serpent's head, shall bruise thy head, and break you all to pieces."   Thus did I leave on the heads of them the Seed, Christ ; and not long after he and his company scattered to pieces, several of whom came to be Friends, and stand to this day.   Many of them had been convinced about eight years before, but had been led aside by this Rice Jones ; for they denied the inward cross, the power of God, and so went into vanity.   It was about eight years since I had been formerly amongst them ; in which time I was to pass over them, and by them, seeing they had slighted the Lord's truth and power, and the visitation of his love unto them.   But now I was moved to go to them again, and it was of great service, for many of them were brought to the Lord Jesus Christ, and were settled upon him, sitting down under his teaching and feeding, where they were kept fresh and green ; and the others that would not be gathered to him, soon after withered.   This was that Rice Jones who some years before had said, "I was then at the highest, and should fall." But, poor man! he little thought how near his own fall was.

We left Nottingham, and went into WARWICKSHIRE, and thence passing through some parts of NORTHAMPTONSHIRE and LEICESTERSHIRE, visiting Friends, and having meetings with them as we travelled, came into BEDFORDSHIRE, where we had large gatherings in the name of Jesus. After some time we came to John Crook's house, where a general YEARLY MEETING for the whole nation was appointed to be held.* This meeting lasted three days, and many Friends from most parts of the nation came to it; so that the inns and towns around were filled, for many thousands of people were at it. And although there was some disturbance by rude people that had run out from truth; yet the Lord's power came over all, and a glorious meeting it was. The everlasting gospel was preached, and many received it, which brought life and immortality to light in them, and shined over all.

I was moved by the power and Spirit of the Lord, to open unto them "the promise of God, that it was made to the Seed, not to seeds, as many, but to One, which Seed was Christ; and that all people, both male and female, should feel this Seed in them, which was heir of the promise; that so they might all witness Christ in them, the hope of glory, the mystery, which had been hid from ages and generations, which was revealed to the apostles, and is revealed again now, after this long night of apostacy. So that all might come up into this Seed, Christ Jesus, and walk in it, and sit down together in the heavenly places in Christ Jesus, who was the foundation of the prophets and apostles, and the rock of ages; and is our foundation now. All sitting down in him, the substance, the first and the last, that changes not, the Seed that bruises the serpent's head, and was before he was, who ends all types, figures, and shadows, and is the substance of them all; in whom there is no shadow." Now these things were upon me to open unto all, that they might mind and see what it is they sit down in.

"For, First, They that sit down in Adam in the fall, sit down in misery, in death, in darkness, and corruption.

"Secondly, They that sit down in types, figures, and shadows, and

---

* The first Yearly Meeting of the Society appears to have been held in 1658, at Scalehouse, or Scarhouse, about three miles from Skipton. At that meeting, the expenses incurred by the early missions being considerable, the subject of the visits of Friends " beyond the sea," claimed much attention, and it was agreed to recommend a general collection in aid of these gospel missions. An epistle was issued to that effect, and the appeal was liberally responded to, and considering the value of money at that period, a large amount was raised. The epistle, with particulars of the collection and its disbursement, may be seen in Bowden's *History of Friends in America*, vol. i., p. 58–60.

Yearly Meetings were held in different parts of England to the number of twenty-six, at which were reported the number of prisoners; the various sufferings on account of the Truth; those who died for it; and the number of ministers deceased. The affairs of truth were also considered, and the members of the church had blessed opportunities of heavenly correspondence and fellowship, one with another. For full particulars of the setting up of General and Yearly Meetings, and of the institution and objects of the Discipline in the Society, see *Letters, &c. of Early Friends*, part ii., pp. 275–353.

under the first priesthood, law, and covenant, sit down in that which must have an end, and which made nothing perfect.

"Thirdly, They that sit down in the apostacy, that hath got up since the apostles' days, sit down in spiritual Sodom and Egypt, and are drinking of the whore's cup, under the beast's and dragon's power.

"Fourthly, They that sit down in the state in which Adam was before he fell, sit down in that which may be fallen from; for he fell from that state, though it was perfect.

"Fifthly, They that sit down in the prophets, sit down in that which must be fulfilled; and they that sit down in the fellowship of water, bread, and wine, these being temporal things, sit down in that which is short of Christ, and of his baptism.

"Sixthly, To sit down in a profession of all the Scriptures, from Genesis to Revelations, and not to be in the power and Spirit which they were in, that gave them forth; that was to be turned away from, by them that came into the power and Spirit which they were in that gave forth the Scriptures.

"Seventhly, They that sit down in heavenly places in Christ Jesus, sit down in him that never fell nor ever changed. Here is the safe sitting for all his elect, his church, his spiritual members, of which he is the living head, his living stones, the household of faith; of which house he is the corner-stone, that stands and abides all weathers. 'For,' as the apostle said, ' he hath quickened us, who were dead in sins and trespasses, &c. and made us to sit together in heavenly places in Christ Jesus; that in ages to come he might show the exceeding riches of his grace, in his kindness towards us, through Jesus Christ.' Now, the ages are come, that his kindness and exceeding riches towards us through Jesus Christ, are truly manifested in us, as in the apostles' days, even in us, who have been dead in sins and trespasses as they were, but now are quickened, and made to sit together in heavenly places in Christ Jesus, the First and the Last, by whom all things were created; who is ascended above all, and is over all, and whose glorious presence is now known. All that sit down here in Christ Jesus, see where all other people sit, and in what. The promise of God being to the Seed, which is one, Christ Jesus, every man and woman must come to witness this Seed, Christ in them, that they may be heirs of the promise; and inheriting that, they will inherit substance. These things were largely declared of; the state of the church, the state of the false church since the apostles' days, opened; and how the true church fled into the wilderness; and the state of the false prophets, which Christ said should come, and John saw were come, and how all the world wondered after them; how they had filled the world with false doctrines, ways, worships, and religions; and how the everlasting gospel was now preached again to all nations, kindreds, tongues, and people; for all they had drunk the whore's cup, and she was over them, and sat upon them. In this night of apostacy, the pure religion and worship in Spirit, which was in the apostles' days, the way of life and living faith, and the power and Holy Ghost were lost; but now they came to be set up again by Christ Jesus, his messengers and ministers of the gospel, as in the apostles' days. For as Christ

sent his disciples to go and preach the gospel in all the world, and after
that the false prophets and antichrists went over the world, and preached
their false doctrines and traditions, and heathenish and Jewish rudiments :
so now again, the everlasting gospel must be preached to all nations, and
to every creature, that they may come into the pure religion, to worship
God in Spirit and in truth, that they may know Christ Jesus, their way to
God, to be the author of their faith, and receive the gospel from heaven,
and not from men; in which gospel, received from heaven, is the heavenly
fellowship, which is a mystery to all the fellowships in the world." Now
after these things had been largely opened, with many other things concerning Christ Jesus and his kingdom, and the people were turned to the
divine light of Christ, and his Spirit, by which they might come both to
know God and Christ, and the Scriptures, and to have fellowship with
them, and one with another in the same Spirit, I was moved to declare and
open many other things to those Friends who had received a part of the
ministry, concerning the exercise of their spiritual gifts in the church; which,
being taken in writing by one that was present, was after this manner :—

"FRIENDS,

"Take heed of destroying that which ye have begotten; for that which
destroys, goes out, and is the cast-away. And though that be true, yea,
and may be the pure truth which such a one speaks, yet if he doth not
remain in that, and live in that in his own particular, but goes out, the
same which he is gone out from, cometh over him. So that which calms
and cools the spirits, goes over the world, and brings to the Father, to
inherit the life eternal : and reaches to the spirits in prison in all. Therefore in the living, immoveable word of the Lord God dwell, and in the
renown thereof; and remain on the foundation that is pure, and that is
sure: for whosoever goes out from the pure, and ministers not in and from
that, comes to an end, and doth not remain; though he may have had a
time, and may have been serviceable for a time, while he lived in the
thing.

"Take heed of many words; what reacheth to the life, settles in the
life. That which cometh from the life, and is received from God, reaches
to the life, and settles others in the life : for the work is not now as it was
at first; the work now is, to settle and stay in the life. For as Friends
have been led to minister in the power, and the power hath gone through,
so that there hath grown an understanding among both people of the world
and Friends; so Friends must be kept in the life which is pure, that with
that they may answer the pure life of God in others. If Friends do not
live in the pure life which they speak of, to answer the life in those they
speak to, the other part steps in; and so there comes up an outward
acquaintance, and such let that come over them. But as every one is kept
living in the life of God, over all that which is contrary, they are in their
places; then they do not lay hands on any suddenly, which is the danger
now; for if any one do, he may lose his discerning, and may lay hands on
the wrong part, and so let the deceit come too near him; and the deceit
will steal over, so that it will be a hard thing for him to overcome it.
There is no one who strikes his fellow-servants, but first he is gone from

the pure in his own particular; for when he goeth from the light he is enlightened withal, then he strikes; and then he hath his reward; the light which he is gone from, Christ, comes and gives him his reward. This is the state of the evil servants; the boisterous, the hasty, and rash, beget nothing to God; but the life, which doth reach the life, is that which begets to God. When all are settled in the life, they are in that which remains for ever: and what is received there, is received from the Lord; and what one receiveth from the Lord, he keepeth; and so he sitteth still, and cool, and quiet in his own spirit, and gives it forth as he is moved; but to the harlots, judgment.

"Friends, this is the word of the Lord to you all, be watchful and careful in all meetings ye come into; for where Friends are sitting together in silence, they are many times gathered into their own measures. When a man is come newly out of the world, from ministering to the world's people, he cometh out of the mire; and then he had need take heed that he be not rash. For now, when he comes into a silent meeting, that is another state; then he must come, and feel his own spirit, how it is, when he comes to them that sit silent. If he be rash, they will judge him, that having been in the world, and amongst the world, the heat is not yet off him. For he may come in the heat of his spirit out of the world; whereas the others are still and cool; and his condition in that not being agreeable to theirs, he may rather do them hurt, by begetting them out of the cool state into the heating state, if he be not in that which commands his own spirit, and gives him to know it.

"There is a great danger too in travelling abroad in the world. The same power that moves any to go forth, is that which must keep them. For it is the greatest danger to go abroad, except a man be moved of the Lord, and go in the power of the Lord; for then, he keeping in the power, is kept by it in his journey, and in his work; and it will enable him to answer the transgressed, and keep above the transgressor. Every one feeling the danger to his own particular in travelling abroad, there the pure fear of the Lord will be placed, and kept in. Though they that travel may have openings when they are abroad, to minister to others, yet, for their own particular growth, they must dwell in the life which doth open; and that will keep down that which would boast. For the minister comes into the death to that which is in the death and in prison, and so returns up again into the life, and into the power, and into the wisdom, to preserve him clean.

"This is the word of the Lord God to you all; feel that ye stand in the presence of the Lord: for every man's word shall be his burden; but the Word of the Lord is pure, and answers the pure in every one. The Word of the Lord is that which was in the beginning, and brings to the beginning. It is a hammer, to beat down the transgressor (not the transgressed), and as a fire to burn up that which is contrary to it. Friends, come into that which is over all the spirits of the world, fathoms all the spirits of the world, and stands in the patience; with that, ye may see where others stand, and reach that which is of God in every one. Here is no strife, no contention, out of transgression; for he that goeth into strife, and into contention, is from the pure Spirit. For where any goeth into contention, if anything hath been begotten by him before, then that contentious nature doth get a-head, spoileth that which was begotten, and quencheth his own prophesying. So if that which would arise into strife, be not subjected by the power in the particular, that is dangerous.

"If any have a moving to any place, and have spoken what they were moved of the Lord, let them return unto their habitation again, and live in the pure life of God, and in the fear of the Lord; so will ye be kept in the life—in the solid and seasoned spirit, and preach as well in life, as with words (for none must be light or wild). For the Seed of God is weighty, brings to be solid, and leads into the wisdom of God, by which the wisdom of the creation is known. But if that part be up, which runs into imaginations, and that part be standing, in which the imaginations come up, and the pure spirit be not thoroughly come up to rule and reign, then that will run out, that will glory, boast, and vapour; and so will such a one spoil that which opened to him: this is for condemnation. Let every one mind that, which feels through and commands his spirit, whereby every one may know what spirit he is of; for he should first try his own spirit, and then he may try others; he should first know his own spirit, and then he may know others. Therefore that which doth command all these spirits, where the heats and burnings come in and get up, in that wait, which chains them down and cools: that is the elect, the heir of the promise of God. For no hasty, rash, brittle spirits (though they have prophecies) have held out, and gone through, they not being subjected in the prophecy. The earthly will not abide, for it is brittle; and in that state the ministry was another's, not the Son's; for the Son hath life in himself, and the Son hath the power, which man being obedient to, he may be serviceable; but if he go from the pure power, he falls, and abuses it. Therefore let your faith stand in the pure power of the Lord God, and do not abuse it; but let that search through, and work through; and let every one stand in the power of the Lord, which reacheth the Seed of God; which is the heir of the promise of life without end. Let none be hasty to speak; for ye have time enough, and with an eye ye may reach the witness: neither let any be backward when ye are moved; for that brings destruction.

"Now, truth hath an honour in the hearts of those who are not Friends; so that all Friends being kept in the truth, they are kept in the honour, they are honourable, for that will honour them; but if any lose the power, they lose the life, they lose their crown, they lose their honour, they lose the cross, which should crucify them, and they crucify the just; and by losing the power, the Lamb comes to be slain. And as it is here, so will it be in other nations; for all Friends, here and there, are as one family; the seed, the plants, they are as a family. Now all being kept in that which subjects all, and keeps all under, to wit, the Seed itself, the life itself, that is the heir of the promise; that is the bond of peace; for there is the unity in the Spirit with God, and with one another. For he that is kept in the life, hears God, and sees man's condition; and with that he answers the life in others, that hear God also; thus one Friend that is come into that, comprehends the world. But that which Friends speak,

they must live in; so may they expect, that others may come into that
which they speak, to live in the same. For the power of the Lord God
hath been abused by some, and the worth of truth hath not been minded;
there hath been a trampling on, and marring with the feet, and that abuseth
the power. But now every Friend is to keep in the power, and to take
heed to it; for that must be kept down, which would trample and mar with
the feet, and the pure life and power of God is to be lived in over that,
that none with the feet may foul or mar, but every one may be kept in the
pure power and life of the Lord. Then the water of life cometh in; then
he that ministereth, drinketh himself, and giveth others to drink.

"When any shall be moved to go and speak in a steeple-house or
market, turn in to that which moves, and be obedient to it, that that which
would not go, may be kept down; for that which would not go, will be apt
to get up. And take heed on the other hand, that the lavishing part do
not get up, for it is a bad savour; therefore that must be kept down, and
be kept subject. Wait in the light of the Lord, that ye may be all kept
in the wisdom of God. For when the Seed is up in every particular, there
is no danger; but when there is an opening and prophecy, and the power
stirs before the seed comes up, then there is something that will be apt to
run out rashly; there is the danger, and there must be the patience in the
fear. For it is a weighty thing to be in the work of the ministry of the
Lord God, and to go forth in that. It is not as a customary preaching;
but it is to bring people to the end of all outward preaching. For when
ye have declared the truth to the people, and they have received it, and
are come into that which ye speak of, the uttering of many words, and
long declarations out of the life, may beget them into a form. And if any
should run on rashly into words again, without the savour of life, then they
that are come into the thing that he spoke of, will judge him; whereby he
may hurt again that which he had raised up before. So Friends, ye must
all come into the thing that is spoken in the openings of the heavenly
life among you, and walk in the love of God, that ye may answer the thing
spoken to.

'And take heed all of running into inordinate affections; for when
people come to own you, there is danger of the wrong part getting up.
There was a strife among the disciples of Christ, who should be the greatest; Christ told them, 'The heathen exercise lordship, and have dominion
over one another; but it shall not be so among you.' For Christ the Seed
was to come up in every one of them; so then, where is the greatest? for
that part in the disciples which looked to be the greatest, was the same
that was in the Gentiles. But as any one comes here, to live in the word
that sanctified him, having the heart sanctified, the tongue and lips sanctified, living in the word of wisdom that makes clean the heart, and reconciles to God, all things being upheld by the Word and power;—as there
is an abiding in the Word of God, that upholds times and seasons, and
gives all things increase, and a dwelling in the Word of wisdom; if there
be but two or three agreed in this on earth, it shall be done for them in
heaven. So in this must all things be ordered by the Word of wisdom
and power, that upholds all things, the times and the seasons, that are in

the Father's hand, to the glory of God, whereby his blessing may be felt among you; and this brings to the beginning.   So this is the word of the Lord God to you all, Keep down, keep low, that nothing may rule or reign in you, but life itself.

"Now, the power being lived in, the cross is lived in; and wherever Friends come in this, they draw the power and the life over; they leave a witness behind them, answering the witness of God in others.   And where this is lived in, there is no want of wisdom, of power, of knowledge; but he that ministereth in this, seeth with the eye which the Lord openeth in him, what is for the fire, and what for the sword, what must be fed with judgment, and what be nourished.   This brings all down, and to be low, every one keeping to the power; for let a man get up ever so high, yet he must come down again to the power, where he left; what he went from, he must come down again to that.   Before all these wicked spirits be got down, which are rambling abroad, Friends must have patience, must wait in patience, in the cool life; and he who is in this, doing the work of the Lord, hath the tasting and the feeling of the Lamb's power and authority. Therefore all Friends, keep cool and quiet in the power of the Lord God; and all that is contrary will be subjected; the Lamb hath the victory, in the Seed, through the patience.

"If any have been moved to speak, and have quenched that which moved them, let none such go forth afterwards into words, until they feel the power arise and move them thereto again; for after the first motion is quenched, the other part will be apt to get up; and if any go forth in that, he goeth forth in his own, and the betrayer will come into that.   And all Friends, be careful not to meddle with the powers of the earth; but keep out of all such things; and as ye keep in the Lamb's authority, ye will answer that of God in them, and bring them to do justice, which is the end of the law.   Keep out of all jangling; for all that are in the transgression, are out from the law of love, but all that are in the law of love, come to the Lamb's power, in the Lamb's authority, who is the end of the law outward.   For the law being added because of transgression, Christ, who was glorified with the Father, before the world began, is the end of the law, bringing them that live in the law of life, to live over all transgression; which every one must feel in himself."

More was then spoken to many of these particulars, which was not taken at large as delivered.

After this meeting was over, and most of the Friends were gone away, as I was walking in John Crook's garden, there came a party of horse, with a constable, to seize me.   I heard them ask "who was in the house," and somebody answered, "I was there."   They said, "I was the man they looked for;" and went forthwith into the house, where they had many words with John Crook, and some few Friends that were with him.   But the Lord's power so confounded them, that they never came into the garden to look for me, but went their way in a rage.   When I came into the house, Friends were very glad to see them so confounded, and that I had escaped them.   Next day I passed thence, and after I had visited Friends in several places as I went, came to LONDON, the Lord's power accompanying me, and bearing me up in his service.

I had not been long in London, before I heard that a Jesuit, who came over with an ambassador from Spain, had challenged all the Quakers to dispute with them at the Earl of Newport's house :* whereupon Friends let him know that some would meet him.   Then he sent us word "he would meet with twelve of the wisest and most learned men we had :" a while after he sent us word "he would meet with but six ;" and after that, he sent us word again, "he would have but three to come."   We hastened what we could, lest, after all his great boast, he should put it quite off at last.   When we were come to the house, I bid Nicholas Bond and Edward Burrough go up, and enter into discourse with him ; and I would walk a while in the yard, and then come up after them.   I advised them to state this question to him, Whether or not the church of Rome, as it now stood, was not degenerated from the true church, which was in the primitive times, from the life and doctrine, and from the power and Spirit that they were in ?   They stated the question accordingly ; and the Jesuit affirmed, "that the church of Rome now was in the virginity and purity of the primitive church."   By this time I was come to them.   Then we asked him, "whether they had the Holy Ghost poured out upon them, as the apostles had ?"   He said, "No."   "Then," said I, "if ye have not the same Holy Ghost poured forth upon you, and the same power and Spirit that the apostles had, then ye are degenerated from the power and Spirit which the primitive church was in."   There needed little more to be said to that. Then I asked him, "what Scripture they had for setting up cloisters for nuns, abbeys and monasteries for men, for all their several orders ; and for their praying by beads, and to images ; for making crosses, for forbidding meats and marriages, and for putting people to death for religion? If," said I, "ye are in the practice of the primitive church, in its purity and virginity, then let us see by Scriptures, wherever they practised any such things."   (For it was agreed on both hands, that we should make good by Scriptures what we said.)   Then he told us of a written word, and an unwritten word.   I asked him "what he called his unwritten word :" he said, "The written word is the Scriptures, and the unwritten word is that which the apostles spoke by word of mouth ; which," said he, "are all those traditions that we practise."   I bid him prove that by Scripture.   Then he brought the Scripture, where the apostle says (2 Thess. ii. 5), "When I was with you, I told you these things."   "That is," said he, "I told you of nunneries, and monasteries, and of putting to death for religion, and of praying by beads, and to images, and all the rest of the practices of the church of Rome, which," he said, "was the unwritten word of the apostles, which they told then, and have since been continued down by tradition unto

* The Earl of Newport, it would appear, was very favourably inclined towards Friends. In a letter from E. Burrough to F. Howgill, 4th of 7th Month [9th Month] 1658, he observes, "This night, at Woodcock's, at the meeting, was the Earl of Newport ; he is truly loving to us."   In the same letter, E. Burrough says, "Truth spreads and grows. The Earl of Pembroke has been with us ; there is a principle of God stirring in him."

these times." Then "I desired him to read that Scripture again, that he might see how he had perverted the apostle's words; for that which he there tells the Thessalonians 'he had told them before,' is not an unwritten word, but is there written down, namely, that the man of sin, the son of perdition, shall be revealed, before that great and terrible day of Christ, which he was writing of, should come: so this was not telling them any of those things that the church of Rome practises. In like manner the apostle, in the third chapter of that epistle, tells the church of some disorderly persons, he heard were amongst them, busy-bodies, who did not work at all; concerning whom he had commanded them by his unwritten word, when he was among them, that if any would not work, neither should he eat; which now he commands them again in his written word in this epistle, 2 Thess. iii. So this Scripture afforded no proof for their invented traditions; and he had no other Scripture-proof to offer." Therefore I told him, "this was another degeneration of their church into such inventions and traditions as the apostles and primitive saints never practised."

After this he came to his sacrament of the altar, beginning at the paschal-lamb, and the shew-bread; and so came to the words of Christ, "This is my body," and to what the apostle wrote of it to the Corinthians; concluding, "that after the priest had consecrated the bread and wine, it was immortal and divine, and he that received it, received the whole Christ." I followed him through the Scriptures he brought, till I came to Christ's words and the apostle's; and I showed him "that the same apostle told the Corinthians, after they had taken bread and wine in remembrance of Christ's death, that they were reprobates, if Christ was not *in* them: but if the bread they ate was Christ, he must of necessity be in them, after they had eaten it. Besides, if this bread and this wine, which the Corinthians ate and drank, was Christ's body, then how hath Christ a body in heaven?" I observed to him also, "that both the disciples at the supper, and the Corinthians afterwards, were to eat the bread, and drink the wine in 'remembrance of Christ,' and to show forth his death, till he come; which plainly proves, the bread and wine which they took was not his body. For if it had been his real body that they ate, then he had been come, and was then there present; and it had been improper to have done such a thing in remembrance of him, if he had been then present with them; as he must have been, if that bread and wine, which they ate and drank, had been his real body." Then as to those words of Christ, "This is my body," I told him Christ calls himself a vine, and a door, and is called in Scripture, a rock; "Is Christ therefore an outward rock, door, or vine?" "O," said the Jesuit, "those words are to be interpreted:" "So," said I, "are those words of Christ, 'this is my body.'" Now having stopped his mouth as to argument, I made the Jesuit a proposal thus: "That seeing," he said "the bread and wine was immortal and divine, and the very Christ, and that whosoever received it, received the whole Christ; let a meeting be appointed between some of them (whom the Pope and his cardinals should appoint) and some of us; and let a bottle of wine and a loaf of bread be brought, and divided each into two parts, and let them consecrate which of those parts they would. And then set the consecrated and the unconsecrated bread and wine in a safe place, with a sure watch upon it, and let trial thus be made, Whether the consecrated bread and wine would not lose its goodness, and the bread grow dry and mouldy, and the wine turn dead and sour, as well and as soon as that which was unconsecrated. By this means, said I, the truth of this matter may be made manifest. And if the consecrated bread and wine change not, but retain their savour and goodness, this may be a means to draw many to your church: if they change, decay, and lose their goodness, then ought you to confess, and forsake your error, and shed no more blood about it: for much blood hath been shed about these things, as in Queen Mary's days." To this the Jesuit made this reply: "Take," said he, "a piece of new cloth, and cut it into two pieces, and make two garments of it; and put one of them upon king David's back, and the other upon a beggar's, and the one garment shall wear away as well as the other." "Is this thy answer?" said I; "Yes," said he. "Then," said I, "by this the company may all be satisfied that your consecrated bread and wine is not Christ. Have ye told people so long that the consecrated bread and wine was immortal and divine, and that it was the very and real body and blood of Christ, and dost thou now say it will wear away, or decay, as well as the other? I must tell thee, Christ remains the same to-day as yesterday, and never decays; but is the saints' heavenly food in all generations, through which they have life." He replied no more to this, being willing to let it fall; for the people that were present saw his error, and that he could not defend it. Then I asked him "why their church persecuted and put people to death for religion." He replied, "it was not the church that did it, but the magistrates." I asked him "whether those magistrates were not counted and called believers and Christians." He said, "Yes:" "Why then," said I, "are they not members of your church?" "Yes," said he. Then I left it to the people to judge from his own concessions, whether the church of Rome doth not persecute, and put people to death for religion. Thus we parted; and his subtilty was comprehended by simplicity.

During the time I was at London, many services lay upon me; for it was a time of much suffering. I was moved to write to Oliver Cromwell, and lay before him the sufferings of Friends, both in this nation and in Ireland. There was also a rumour about this time of making Cromwell king: whereupon I was moved to go to him, and warned him against it, and of divers dangers; which, if he did not avoid, "he would bring a shame and ruin upon himself and his posterity." He seemed to take well what I said to him, and thanked me: yet afterwards I was moved to write to him more fully concerning that matter.

About this time the Lady Claypole* (so called) was sick and much troubled in mind, and could receive no comfort from any that came to her; which when I heard of, I was moved to write to her the following letter:—

---

* Lady Claypole was the favourite daughter of Oliver Cromwell, who deeply felt her loss, for she died shortly after the period of receiving the letter George Fox addressed to her. Nor was it long before Oliver himself followed her; both he and his daughter dying in the same year.

" Friend,

" Be still and cool in thy own mind and spirit from thy own thoughts, and then thou wilt feel the principle of God to turn thy mind to the Lord, from whom cometh life ; whereby thou mayest receive his strength and power to allay all storms, and tempests. That is it which works up into patience, innocency, soberness, into stillness, staidness, quietness up to God, with his power. Therefore mind ; that is the word of the Lord God unto thee, that thou mayest feel the authority of God, and thy faith in that, to work down that which troubles thee ; for that is it which keeps peace, and brings up the witness in thee, which hath been transgressed, to feel after God with his power and life, who is a God of order and peace. When thou art in the transgression of the life of God in thy own particular, the mind flies up in the air, the creature is led into the night, nature goes out of its course, an old garment goes on, and an uppermost clothing ; and thy nature being led out of its course, it comes to be all on fire, in the transgression ; and that defaceth the glory of the first body. Therefore be still a while from thy own thoughts, searching, seeking, desires, and imaginations, and be staid in the principle of God in thee, that it may raise thy mind up to God, and stay it upon God, and thou wilt find strength from him, and find him to be a God at hand, a present help in the time of trouble, and of need. And thou being come to the principle of God, which hath been transgressed, it will keep thee humble ; and the humble, God will teach his way, which is peace, and such he doth exalt. Now as the principle of God in thee hath been transgressed, come to it, that it may keep thy mind down low to the Lord God ; and deny thyself ; for from thy own will, that is, the earthly, thou must be kept. Then thou wilt feel the power of God, which will bring nature into its course, and give thee to see the glory of the first body. There the wisdom of God will be received, which is Christ, by which all things were made and created, and thou wilt thereby be preserved and ordered to God's glory. There thou wilt come to receive and feel the physician of value, who clothes people in their right mind, whereby they may serve God, and do his will. For all distractions, unruliness, and confusion are in the transgression ; which transgression must be brought down, before the principle of God, which hath been transgressed against, be lifted up : whereby the mind may be seasoned, and stilled, and a right understanding of the Lord may be received ; whereby his blessings enter, and are felt, over all that is contrary, in the power of the Lord God, which raises up the principle of God within, gives a feeling after God, and in time gives dominion. Therefore, keep in the fear of the Lord God ; that is the word of the Lord unto thee. For all these things happen to thee for thy good, and for the good of those concerned for thee, to make you know yourselves, and your own weakness, and that ye may know the Lord's strength and power, and may trust in him. Let the time that is past be sufficient to every one, who in anything hath been lifted up in transgression out of the power of the Lord ; for he can bring down and abase the mighty, and lay them in the dust of the earth. Therefore, all keep low in his fear, that thereby ye may receive the secrets of God and his wisdom, may know the shadow of the Almighty, and sit under it, in all tempests, and storms, and heats. For God is at hand, and the Most High rules in the children of men. This then is the word of the Lord God unto you all; whatever temptations, distractions, confusions, the light doth make manifest and discover, do not look at these temptations, confusions, corruptions; but look at the light, which discovers them, and makes them manifest; and with the same light you may feel over them, to receive power to stand against them. The same light which lets you see sin and transgression, will let you see the covenant of God, which blots out your sin and transgression, which gives victory and dominion over it, and brings into covenant with God. For looking down at sin, and corruption, and distraction, ye are swallowed up in it : but looking at the light, which discovers them, ye will see over them. That will give victory; and ye will find grace and strength : there is the first step to peace. That will bring salvation; by it ye may see to the beginning, and the 'glory that was with the Father before the world began;' and so come to know the Seed of God, which is the heir of the promise of God, and of the world which hath no end; which bruises the head of the serpent, who stops people from coming to God. That ye may feel the power of an endless life, the power of God, which is immortal; which brings the immortal soul up to the immortal God, in whom it doth rejoice. So in the name and power of the Lord Jesus Christ, God Almighty strengthen thee."   G. F.

When the foregoing paper was read to Lady Claypole, she said, it staid her mind for the present. Afterwards many Friends got copies of it, both in England and Ireland, and read it to people that were troubled in mind; and it was made useful for the settling of the minds of several.*

About this time came forth a declaration from Oliver Cromwell, the Protector, for a collection towards the relief of divers Protestant Churches, driven out of Poland; and of twenty Protestant families, driven out of the confines of Bohemia. And there having been a like declaration published some time before, to invite the nation to a day of solemn fasting and humiliation, in order to a contribution being made for the suffering Protestants of the valleys of Lucerne, Angrona, &c. who were persecuted by the Duke of Savoy, I was moved to write to the Protector and chief magistrates on this occasion, both to show them the nature of a true fast (such as God requires and accepts), and to make them sensible of their injustice and self-condemnation, in blaming the Papists for persecuting the Protestants abroad, while they themselves, calling themselves Protestants, were at the same time persecuting their Protestant neighbours and friends at home. That which I wrote to them was after this manner :—

" *To the Heads and Governors of this Nation, who have put forth a Declaration for keeping a day of solemn Fasting and Humiliation, for the persecution (as you say) of divers people beyond the seas, professing the*

---

* The counsels contained in this letter of George Fox's to Lady Claypole, though worded in his own peculiar phraseology, and at first sight not very perspicuous, are such as must be valuable to every spiritual mind, in seasons of trial.

Reformed religion, which, ye say, hath been transmitted unto them from their ancestors.

"A PROFESSION of the Reformed religion may be transmitted to generations, and so holden by tradition; and in that, wherein the profession and tradition are holden, is the day of humiliation kept; which stands in the will of man. This is not the fast that the Lord requires, 'to bow down the head like a bulrush for a day,' and the day following be in the same condition that they were the day before. To the light of Christ Jesus in your consciences do I speak, which testifieth for God every day, and witnesseth against all sin and persecution; which measure of God, if ye be guided by it, doth not limit God to a day, but leads to the fast which the Lord requires, which is, 'To loose the bonds of wickedness, to undo the heavy burdens, to break every yoke, and to let the oppressed go free.' Isa. lviii. 6, 7. This is the fast that the Lord requires; and this stands not in the transmission of times, nor in the traditions of men; but in that which was before times were, which leads out of time, and shall be when time shall be no more. These that teach for doctrine the commandments of men, are they that ever persecuted the life and power when it came. And whereas ye mention a decree or edict that was made against the said persecuted Protestants, all such decrees proceed from the ground of the Pope's religion and supremacy, and therein stands his tyranny and cruelty, acted in that will, which is in that nature which exerciseth lordship over one another (as ye may read, Mark x. 42; Luke xxii. 25), as all the heathen do, and ever did; and in the heathenish nature is all the tyranny and persecution exercised, by them that are out of the obedience to the light of Christ Jesus, which is the guide and leader of all who are tender of that of God in the conscience. But they who are not led by this, know not what it is to suffer for conscience' sake. Now, whereas ye take into your consideration the sad persecution, tyranny, and cruelty exercised upon them, whom ye call your Protestant brethren, and contribute to administer to their wants outwardly; this is good in its place, and we approve it; and see it good to administer to the necessities of others, and to do good to all: and we who are sufferers by a law derived from the Pope, are willing to join and to contribute with you to their outward necessities. For 'the earth is the Lord's, and the fulness thereof;' who is good and gracious to all, willing that all should be saved, and come to the knowledge of the truth. But in the meantime, while ye are doing this, and taking notice of others' cruelty, tyranny, and persecution, turn your eye upon yourselves, and see what ye are doing at home. To the light of Christ Jesus in all your consciences I speak, which cannot lie, nor err, nor bear false witness; but which bears witness for God, and cries for equity, justice, and righteousness to be executed. See what ye are doing, who profess the Scriptures, which were given forth by the saints in light, who dwelt in the light and in the life of them. For them who now witness the same light, life, and power, that gave forth the Scriptures, which ye in words profess, ye persecute;—them ye hale out of your synagogues and markets;—beat, stock, and imprison. Now let that of God in your consciences, which is just, righteous, and equal, examine and try, whether ye have any example or precedent to exercise this persecution, which now many in this nation suffer under, who are a people harmless and innocent, walking in obedience towards God and man. And though ye account the way of truth they walk in, heresy, yet therein do they exercise themselves, to have always 'a conscience void of offence towards God and man,' as ye may read the saints of old did (Acts xxiv. 14, 15, 16); wronging no man, neither giving any just cause of offence; only being obedient to the commands of the Lord, to declare, as they are moved by the Holy Ghost; and standing for the testimony of a good conscience, speaking the truth in Christ, their consciences bearing them witness that they lie not; for this do they suffer under you, who in words profess the same thing for which they suffer. Now see if any age or generation did ever persecute as ye do; for ye profess Christ Jesus, who reveals the Father, and persecute them that witness the revelation of the Father by Christ Jesus unto them. Ye profess Christ Jesus, who is 'the light of the world, that enlightens every man that cometh into the world;' yet persecute them that bear witness and give testimony to this light. Ye profess that the Word is become flesh, yet persecute them that witness it so. Ye profess that whosoever confesseth not that Jesus Christ is come in the flesh, is an antichrist; yet persecute them that do confess him come in the flesh, and call them antichrists and deceivers. Ye profess that the kingdom of Christ is come; yet persecute them that witness it come. Ye profess Christ Jesus, the resurrection and the life; yet persecute them that witness him to be so. If ye say, 'How shall we know that these people, who say they witness these things, do so, or not?' I answer, Turn your minds to the light, which Christ Jesus hath enlightened you withal, which is one in all; and if ye walk in the light, ye shall have the light of life; then ye will know and see what ye have done, who have persecuted the Lord of glory (in his people) in whom is life, and the life is the light of men. To no other touchstone shall we turn you, than into your own consciences; there shall ye find the truth of what we have declared unto you, and of what we bear testimony to, according to the holy Scriptures. When the books of consciences are opened, and all judged out of them, then shall ye witness us to be of God, and our testimony to be true. Though now ye may stop your ears, and harden your hearts, while it is called to-day; but then ye shall know what ye have done, and against whom ye have transgressed;—then ye will see that no persecutors, in any age or generation before you, ever transgressed against that light, and measure of God made manifest, as ye have done. For though Christ and the apostles were persecuted in their times, the Jews, for the most part, did not know that he was the Christ, when he came, notwithstanding they had the Scriptures, which prophesied of him; neither did they believe that he was risen again, when the apostles preached his resurrection. But ye say, 'ye believe he is come; ye believe his resurrection;' yet ye persecute those that witness him come in the flesh, those that are buried with him in baptism, that are conformable to his death, and know the power of his resurrection; these ye persecute, hale before magistrates, and suffer to be beaten in your synagogues; these ye cause to be whipped, and stocked, shamefully entreated, and cast into prison; as many jails in this nation at this day testify to your faces. Therefore honestly consider what ye are doing, while ye are taking notice of others' cruelties, lest ye overlook your own. There is some difference in many things, between the Popish religion and that which ye call the Protestant, but in this persecution of yours there is no difference; for ye will confess that the foundation of your religion is grounded upon the Scriptures; yet ye are persecuting them that are in the same life which they were in, who gave forth the Scriptures, yourselves being the meanwhile under a profession of the words they spoke; and this ye shall one day witness. So ye have a profession and form, and persecute them that are in the possession, life, and power. Therefore know assuredly that ye must come to judgment; for he is made manifest, to whom all judgment is committed. Therefore to the light of Christ Jesus in your own consciences, which searcheth and trieth you, turn your minds; stand still, and wait there to receive the righteous law, which is according to that of God in the conscience, which is now rising, and is bearing witness against all ungodliness and unrighteousness of men; and they whom ye persecute are manifest to God, and that of God in all consciences shall bear witness for us, that we are of God; this ye shall one day witness, whether ye will hear or forbear. Our rejoicing is in the testimony of our consciences, that in simplicity and godly sincerity, not with fleshly wisdom, but by the grace of God, we have had our conversation in the world, not handling the word of God deceitfully, but in the manifestation of the truth, commending ourselves to every man's conscience in the sight of God; and if our gospel be hid, it is hid to them that are lost. For witnessing the holding of the mystery of faith in a pure conscience, do we suffer, and are subject for conscience' sake. This is thankworthy, if a man, for conscience' sake, endure griefs and sufferings wrongfully. In this is our joy and rejoicing, having a good conscience, that whereas we are evil spoken of, as evil-doers, they may be ashamed that falsely accuse our good conversation in Christ; which is not only the putting away of the filth of the flesh, but the answer of a good conscience towards God, by the resurrection of Jesus Christ. This we witness made manifest (eternal praises to the living God!) and bear testimony to that which spoke it in the apostle in life and power. Therefore do we bear witness and testify against those, who, being in a form and profession of it, persecute the life and power. To the eternal light of Christ Jesus, the searcher and trier of all hearts, turn your minds, and see what ye are doing; lest ye overturn your foundation, whereon ye pretend to stand, while ye are professing the Scriptures, and persecuting the life, light, and power, which they were in who gave them forth. For the stone, cut out of the mountains without hands, is now striking at the feet of the image, the profession, which is set up, and stands in the will of man. Now is that made manifest unto which all must answer; all must appear before the judgment-seat of Christ, that every one may receive the things done in the body, according to that he hath done, whether it be good or bad. Knowing therefore the terror of the Lord, we persuade men; but we are made manifest unto God, and shall be made manifest in all your consciences, which ye shall witness." G. F.

Divers times, both in the time of the Long Parliament, and of the Protector (so called) and of the Committee of Safety, when they proclaimed fasts, I was moved to write to them, and tell them, their fasts were like unto Jezebel's; for commonly, when they proclaimed fasts, there was some mischief contrived against us. I knew their fasts were for strife and debate, to smite with the fist of wickedness; as the New England professors soon after did, who, before they put our Friends to death, proclaimed a fast also.

Now it was a time of great sufferings; and many Friends being in prisons, many other Friends were moved to go to the parliament, to offer up themselves to lie in the same dungeon, where their friends lay, that they that were in prison might go out, and not perish in the stinking jails. This we did in love to God and our brethren, that they might not die in prison; and in love to those that cast them in, that they might not bring innocent blood upon their own heads; which we knew would cry to the Lord, and bring his wrath, vengeance, and plagues upon them. But little favour could we find from those professing parliaments; instead thereof they would rage, and sometimes threaten those Friends that thus attended them, that they would whip them, and send them home. Then commonly soon after the Lord would turn them out, and send them home; who had not a heart to do good in the day of their power. But they went not off without being forewarned, for I was moved to write to them, in their several turns, as I did to the Long Parliament, unto whom I declared, before they were broken up, that "thick darkness was coming over them all, even a day of darkness that should be felt."

And because the parliament that now sat was made up mostly of high professors, who, pretending to be more religious than others, were indeed greater prosecutors of them that were truly religious, I was moved to send them the following lines, as a reproof of their hypocrisy:—

"O FRIENDS, do not cloak and cover yourselves; there is a God that knoweth your hearts, and that will uncover you. He seeth your way. 'Woe be to him that covereth, but not with my Spirit, saith the Lord.' Do ye act contrary to the law, and then put it from you? Mercy and true judgment ye neglect. Look, what was spoken against such: my Saviour spoke against such: 'I was sick, and ye visited me not; I was hungry, and ye fed me not; I was a stranger, and ye took me not in; I was in prison, and ye visited me not.' But they said, 'When saw we thee in prison, and did not come to thee?' 'Inasmuch as ye did it not unto one of these little ones, ye did it not unto me.' Friends, ye imprison them that are in the life and power of truth, and yet profess to be the ministers of Christ. But if Christ had sent you, ye would bring out of prison, and bondage, and receive strangers. Ye have lived in pleasure on the earth, and been wanton; ye have nourished your hearts, as in a day of slaughter; ye have condemned, and killed the just, and he doth not resist you."   G. F.

After this, as I was going out of town, having two Friends with me, when we were little more than a mile out of the city, there met us two troopers belonging to Colonel Hacker's regiment, who took me, and the

Friends that were with me, and brought us back to the Mews, and there kept us prisoners. But the Lord's power was so over them, that they did not take us before any officer; but shortly after set us at liberty again. The same day, taking boat, I went to KINGSTON, and thence to HAMPTON COURT, to speak with the Protector about the sufferings of Friends. I met him riding into Hampton-Court Park, and before I came to him, as he rode at the head of his life-guard, I saw and felt a waft (or apparition) of death go forth against him; and when I came to him, he looked like a dead man. After I had laid the sufferings of Friends before him, and had warned him, according as I was moved to speak to him, he bid me come to his house. So I returned to Kingston, and next day went to Hampton Court, to speak further with him. But when I came, he was sick, and ——— Harvey, who was one that waited on him, told me the doctors were not willing I should speak with him. So I passed away, and never saw him more.

From Kingston I went to Isaac Pennington's, in BUCKINGHAMSHIRE, where I had appointed a meeting, and the Lord's truth and power were preciously manifested amongst us. After I had visited Friends in those parts, I returned to LONDON, and soon after went into ESSEX, where I had not been long before I heard that the Protector was dead, and his son Richard made Protector in his room. Whereupon I came up to LONDON again.

Before this time the church-faith (so called) was given forth, which was said to have been made at the Savoy in eleven days' time. I got a copy before it was published, and wrote an answer to it; and when their book of church-faith was sold in the streets, my answer to it was sold also. This angered some of the parliament-men, so that one of them told me, "they must have me to Smithfield." I told him, "I was above their fires, and feared them not." And reasoning with him, I wished him to consider, "Had all people been without a faith these sixteen hundred years, that now the priests must make them one? Did not the apostle say, that Jesus was the author and finisher of their faith? And since Christ Jesus was the author of the apostles' faith, of the church's faith in primitive times, and of the martyrs' faith, should not all people look unto him to be the author and finisher of their faith, and not to the priests?" Much work we had about the priest-made faith; for they called us house-creepers, leading silly women captive, because we met in houses, and would not hold up their priests and temples, which they had made and set up. I told them, that it was they who led silly women captive, and crept into houses, who kept people always learning under them, who were covetous, and had a form of godliness, but denied the power and Spirit which the apostles were in. Such began to creep in the apostles' days; but now they had got the magistrates on their side, who upheld those houses for them, which they had crept into, their temples, with their tithes: whereas the apostles brought people off even from that temple, and those tithes and offerings, which God had for a time commanded. And the apostles met in several private houses, being to preach the gospel to all nations; which they did freely, as Christ had commanded them. Thus do we, who bring people off from these priests, temples, and tithes which God never commanded, to meet in houses, or on mountains, as the saints of old did, who were gathered in the name of Jesus, Christ being their Prophet, Priest, and Shepherd.

Major Wiggan, a very envious man, was present, yet he bridled himself before the parliament-men, and some others that were there in company. He took upon him to make a speech, and said, "Christ had taken away the guilt of sin, but had left the power of sin remaining in us." I told him, that was strange doctrine, for Christ came to destroy the devil and his works, and the power of sin, and so to cleanse men from sin.

So Major Wiggan's mouth was stopped at that time. But next day, desiring to speak with me again, I took a friend or two with me, and went to him. Then he vented much passion and rage, beyond the bounds of a Christian or moral man; whereupon I reproved him; and having brought the Lord's power over him, and let him see what condition he was in, I left him.

After some time I passed out of London, and had a meeting at Serjeant Birkhead's at TWICKENHAM, to which many people came, and some of considerable quality in the world. A glorious meeting it was, wherein the Scriptures were largely and clearly opened, and Christ exalted above all, to the great satisfaction of the hearers.

But there was great persecution in many places, both by imprisoning and breaking up of meetings. At a meeting about seven miles from London, the rude people usually came out of several parishes round about, to abuse Friends, and often beat and bruised them exceedingly. One day they abused about eighty Friends, who went to that meeting out of London, tearing their coats and cloaks off their backs, and throwing them into ditches and ponds; and when they had besmeared them with dirt, they said they looked like witches. The next First-day I was moved of the Lord to go to that meeting, though I was then very weak. When I came there, I bid Friends bring a table, and set it in the field, where they used to meet, to stand upon. According to their wonted course, the rude people came. Having a Bible in my hand, I showed them their and their priests' and teachers' fruits: and the people became ashamed, and were quiet. I opened the Scriptures to them, and our principles agreeing therewith; I turned the people from darkness to the light of Christ and his Spirit, by which they might understand the Scriptures, see themselves and their sins, and know Christ Jesus to be their Saviour. So the meeting ended quietly, and the Lord's power came over all to his glory. But it was a time of great sufferings; for besides the imprisonments (through which many died) our meetings were greatly disturbed. They have thrown rotten eggs and wild-fire into our meetings, and have brought in drums beating, and kettles, to make noises with, that the truth might not be heard; and among these, the priests were as rude as any: as may be seen in the book of the fighting priests, wherein a list is given of some of them that had actually beaten and abused Friends.

Many also of our Friends were brought up to LONDON prisoners, to be tried before the committee; where Henry Vane,* being chairman, would

* Vane was a conspicuous character at this period. He was strongly attached to

not suffer Friends to come in, except they would put off their hats : but at last the Lord's power came over him, so that, through the mediation of others, they were admitted. Many of us having been imprisoned upon contempts (as they called them) for not putting off our hats, it was not a likely thing that Friends, who had suffered so long for it from others, should put off their hats to him. But the Lord's power came over them all, and wrought so, that several Friends were set at liberty by them. Now inasmuch as sufferings grew very sharp, I was moved of the Lord to write a few lines, and send amongst Friends, to encourage them to go on faithfully and boldly, through the exercises of the day ; of which a copy here follows :—

"My dear Friends, wherever scattered abroad, in prison or out of prison ; fear not, because of the reports of sufferings ; let not the evil spies of the good land make you afraid, if they tell you the walls are high, and there are Anakims in the land ; for at the blowing of the rams' horns did the walls of Jericho fall ; and they that brought the evil report, perished in the wilderness. But dwell ye in the faith, patience, and hope, having the Word of Life to keep you, which is beyond the law ; and having the oath of God, his covenant, Christ Jesus, which divides the waters asunder, and makes them to run all on heaps ; in that stand : and ye will see all things work together for good to them that love God. In that triumph, when sufferings come, whatever they may be. Your faith, your shield, your helmet, your armour, you have on ; ye are ready to skip over a mountain, a wall, or a hill, and to walk through the deep waters, though they be as heaps upon heaps. The evil spies of the good land may preach up hardness ; but Caleb, which signifies a heart, and Joshua, a Saviour, triumph over all."

G. F.

After a while I went to READING, where I was under great sufferings and exercises, and in great travail of spirit for about ten weeks. For I saw there was great confusion and distraction amongst the people, and that the powers were plucking each other to pieces. And I saw how many were destroying the simplicity, and betraying the truth. Much hypocrisy, deceit, and strife, was got uppermost in the people, so that they were ready to sheath their swords in one another's bowels. There had been tenderness in many of them formerly, when they were low ; but when they were got up, had killed, and taken possession, they came to be as bad as others ; so that we had much to do with them about our hats, and saying Thou and Thee to them. They turned their profession of patience and moderation into rage and madness ; and many of them were like distracted men for this

---

a republican government, and opposed Cromwell in his progress towards assuming the reins of government as protector. He was said to be one of the leaders of the Independents. Bishop Burnet, the historian, says of him :—" Though he set up a form of religion in a way of his own, yet it consisted rather in a withdrawing from all other forms, than in any new or particular forms and opinions ; from which he and his party were called Seekers, and seemed to wait for some new and clearer manifestations." James Naylor, in a letter to Margaret Fell, speaks of Vane as " very loving to Friends, but drunk with imaginations."

hat-honour. For they had hardened themselves by persecuting the innocent, and were at this time crucifying the Seed, Christ, both in themselves and others; till at last they fell to biting and devouring one another, until they were consumed one of another; who had turned against, and judged, that which God had wrought in them, and showed unto them. So shortly after God overthrew them, turned them upside down, and brought the king over them, who were often surmising that the Quakers met together to bring in King Charles, whereas Friends did not concern themselves with the outward powers, or government. But at last the Lord brought him in, and many of them, when they saw he would be brought in, voted for bringing him in. So with heart and voice praise the name of the Lord, to whom it doth belong; who over all hath the supremacy, and who will rock the nations, for he is over them. I had a sight and sense of the king's return a good while before, and so had some others. I wrote to Oliver several times, and let him know that while he was persecuting God's people, they whom he accounted his enemies were preparing to come upon him. When some forward spirits that came amongst us, would have bought Somerset-House, that we might have meetings in it, I forbade them to do so: for I then foresaw the king's coming in again. Besides, there came a woman to me in the Strand, who had a prophecy concerning King Charles's coming in, three years before he came: and she told me, she must go to him to declare it. I advised her to wait upon the Lord, and keep it to herself; for if it should be known that she went on such a message, they would look upon it to be treason: but she said, she must go, and tell him, that he should be brought into England again. I saw her prophecy was true, and that a great stroke must come upon them in power; for they that had then got possession were so exceeding high, and such great persecution was acted by them, who called themselves saints, that they would take from Friends their copyhold lands, because they could not swear in their courts. Sometimes when we laid these sufferings before Oliver Cromwell, he would not believe it. Wherefore Thomas Aldam* and Anthony Pear-

---

* Thomas Aldam died in 1660, and as this is the last mention of him in this journal, the following particulars may be added:—He resided at Warmsworth, in Yorkshire, and was convinced by George Fox, in 1651, having been previously a great follower of the priests and teachers of the times. But his hungering and thirsting soul not being satisfied amongst them, he left them, and having received the Truth, became valiant for the same, giving up his strength and substance to serve the Lord. Many beatings, reproaches, imprisonments, much spoiling of goods and other sufferings he endured, for Christ's sake. He was one of the first called a Quaker imprisoned in York castle, in 1652, where he was kept two years and six months, not being suffered once to go home, nor permitted to see his wife, children, or relatives, when they went to visit him. He was also fined during that imprisonment £40, at the assize, for appearing before the judge with his hat on, and saying thee and thou to him. During the same imprisonment for tithes, he was sued at law for treble damages, his property being taken to the value of £42, not leaving one cow to give milk for his young children and family. Many other sufferings did he undergo, which made him have a tender sympathy for others who were sufferers for the Truth, whose cause he often pleaded. He wrote several small works in defence of Truth, and his son, Thomas Aldam, who was also a faithful minister, published a testimony concerning him, in 1690. See *Piety Promoted*, vol. i., pp. 25-28; vol. iii., p. 58.

son were moved to go through all the jails in England, and to get copies of Friends' commitments under the jailer's hands, that they might lay the weight of their sufferings upon Oliver Cromwell. And when he would not give order for the releasing of them, Thomas Aldam was moved to take his cap from off his head, and to rend it in pieces before him, and to say unto him, "So shall thy government be rent from thee and thy house." Another Friend also, a woman, was moved to go to the parliament (that was envious against Friends) with a pitcher in her hand, which she broke into pieces before them, and told them, "so should they be broken to pieces:" which came to pass shortly after. And in my great suffering and travail of spirit for the nation, being grievously burdened with their hypocrisy, treachery, and falsehood, I saw God would bring that over them, which they had been above; and that all must be brought down to that which convinced them, before they could get over that bad spirit within and without: for it is the pure, invisible Spirit, that doth and only can work down all deceit in people.

While I was under that sore travail at Reading, by reason of grief and sorrow of mind, and the great exercise that was upon my spirit, my countenance was altered, and I looked poor and thin; and there came a company of unclean spirits to me, and told me, "the plagues of God were upon me." I told them, it was the same spirit spoke that in them, that said so of Christ, when he was stricken and smitten; they hid their face from him. But when I had travailed with the witness of God, which they had quenched, and had got through with it, and over all that hypocrisy which the outside professors were run into, and saw how that would be brought down, and turned under, and that life would rise over it, I came to have ease, and the light, power, and Spirit shone over all. And then having recovered, and got through my travails and sufferings, my body and face swelled, when I came abroad into the air; and then the bad spirits said, "I was grown fat," and they envied at that also. So I saw, that no condition nor state would please that spirit of theirs. But the Lord preserved me by his power and Spirit through and over all, and in his power I came to LONDON again.

Now was there a great pother made about the image or effigies of Oliver Cromwell lying in state; men standing and sounding with trumpets over his image, after he was dead. At this my spirit was greatly grieved, and the Lord, I found, was highly offended. Then did I write the following lines, and sent among them, to reprove their wickedness, and warn them to repent:—

"O friends, what are ye doing! What mean ye to sound before an image! Will not all sober people think ye are like madmen? O, how am I grieved with your abominations! O, how am I wearied! My soul is wearied with you, saith the Lord: will I not be avenged of you, think ye, for your abominations? O, how have ye plucked down and set up! How are your hearts made whole, and not rent! How are ye turned to fooleries! Which things in times past, ye stood over. How have ye left my dread, saith the Lord! Fear therefore, and repent, lest the snare and the pit take you all. The great day of the Lord is come upon all your abominations; the swift hand of the Lord is turned against them. The sober people in these nations stand amazed at your doings, and are ashamed, as if ye would bring in Popery."   G. F.

About this time great stirs were in the nation, the minds of people being unsettled. Much plotting and contriving there was by the several factions, to carry on their several interests. And a great care being upon me, lest any young or ignorant people, that might sometimes come amongst us, should be drawn into that snare, I was moved to give forth the following epistle as a warning unto all such:—

"ALL Friends everywhere, keep out of plots and bustling, and the arm of flesh; for all these are amongst Adam's sons in the fall, where they are destroying men's lives like dogs, beasts, and swine, goring, rending, and biting one another, destroying one another, and wrestling with flesh and blood. Whence arise wars and killing but from the lusts? Now all this is in Adam in the fall, out of Adam that never fell, in whom there is peace and life. Ye are called to peace, therefore follow it; and that peace is in Christ, not in Adam in the fall. All that pretend to fight for Christ, are deceived; for his kingdom is not of this world, therefore his servants do not fight. Fighters are not of Christ's kingdom, but are without Christ's kingdom; his kingdom stands in peace and righteousness, but fighters are in the lust; and all that would destroy men's lives, are not of Christ's mind, who came to save men's lives. Christ's kingdom is not of this world; it is peaceable: and all that are in strife, are not of his kingdom. All that pretend to fight for the gospel, are deceived; for the gospel is the power of God, which was before the devil, or fall of man was; and the gospel of peace was before fighting was. Therefore, they that pretend fighting, are ignorant of the gospel; and all that talk of fighting for Sion, are in darkness; for Sion needs no such helpers. All such as profess themselves to be ministers of Christ, or Christians, and go about to beat down the whore with outward, carnal weapons, the flesh and the whore are got up in themselves, and they are in a blind zeal; for the whore got up by the inward ravening from the Spirit of God; and the beating down thereof, must be by the inward stroke of the sword of the Spirit within. All such as pretend Christ Jesus, and confess him, and yet run into the use of carnal weapons, wrestling with flesh and blood, throw away the spiritual weapons. They that would be wrestlers with flesh and blood, throw away Christ's doctrine; the flesh is got up in them, and they are weary of their sufferings. Such as would revenge themselves, are out of Christ's doctrine. Such as being stricken on one cheek, would not turn the other, are out of Christ's doctrine: and such as do not love one another, nor love enemies, are out of Christ's doctrine. Therefore, ye that are heirs of the blessings of God, which were before the curse and the fall were, come to inherit your portions; and ye that are heirs of the gospel of peace, which was before the devil was, live in the gospel of peace, seeking the peace of all men, and the good of all men; and live in Christ, who came to save men's lives, out of Adam in the fall, where they destroy men's lives, and live not in Christ. The Jews' sword outwardly, by which they cut down the heathen, was a type of the Spirit of God within, which cuts down the heathenish nature within. So live in the peaceable kingdom of Christ Jesus. Live in the peace of God, and not in the lusts, from whence wars arise. Live in Christ, the Prince of Peace, the way of God, who is the second Adam, that never fell; but live not in Adam in the fall, in the destruction, where they destroy one another. Therefore come out of Adam in the fall, into the second Adam that never fell. Live in love and peace with all men; keep out of all the bustlings in the world; meddle not with the powers of the earth; but mind the kingdom, the way of peace. Ye that are heirs of grace, heirs of the kingdom, heirs of the gospel, heirs of salvation, saints of the Most High, and children of God, whose conversation is in heaven, that is, above the combustions of the earth; let your conversation preach to all men, and your innocent lives, that they who speak evil of you, beholding your godly conversation, may glorify your Father which is in heaven. All Friends everywhere, this I charge you, which is the word of the Lord God unto you all, 'Live in peace, in Christ the way of peace,' and therein seek the peace of all men, and no man's hurt. In Adam in the fall, is no peace; but in Adam out of the fall, is peace: so, ye being in Adam which never fell, it is love that overcomes, and not hatred with hatred, nor strife with strife. Therefore live all in the peaceable life, doing good to all men, and seeking the good and welfare of all men."   G. F.

Not long after this, George Booth rose in arms in Cheshire, and Lambert went against him. At which time some foolish, rash spirits, that came sometimes amongst us, were ready to take up arms; but I was moved of the Lord to warn and forbid them, and they were quiet. In the time of the Committee of Safety (so called), we were invited by them to take up arms, and great places and commands were offered some of us; but we denied them all, and declared against it both by word and writing; testifying, that our weapons and armour were not carnal, but spiritual. And lest any that came amongst us, should be drawn into that snare, it came upon me from the Lord, to write a few lines on that occasion, and send them forth, as a caution to all amongst us. Of which this is a copy:

"ALL Friends everywhere, take heed to keep out of the powers of the earth, that run into wars and fightings, which make not for peace, but destroy it; such will not have the kingdom. And, Friends, take heed of joining with this or the other, or meddling with any, or being busy with other men's matters; but mind the Lord, his power, and his service. Let Friends keep out of other men's matters, and keep in that which answers the witness in them all, out of the man's part, where they must expect wars and dishonour. Friends everywhere, dwell in your own, in the power of the Lord God, to keep your minds up to the Lord God, from falling down to the strength of Egypt, or going thither for strength, after ye are come out of it, like the children of Israel after they were come out of outward Egypt. But dwell in the power of the Lord God, that ye may keep over all the powers of the earth, amongst whom the just hand of God is come; for they have turned against the just, disobeyed the just in their own particulars, and so gone on in one against the just; therefore the just sets them one against another. Now he that goes to help among them, is from the just in himself, in the unstaid state, and doth not know, by the All-seeing Eye (that beholdeth), him that recompenseth and rewardeth, and lives not in the hand, in the power, that mangles and overturns, which vexeth the transgressors, that come to be blind, and zealous for they do not know what. Therefore keep in peace, and in the love and power of God, and in unity and love one to another, lest any go out, and fall with the uncircumcised: that is, they that are from the Spirit in themselves, and they that go from it, go into the pit together. Therefore stand (it is the word of the Lord God to you all) in the fear and dread of the Lord God, his power, life, light, seed, and wisdom, by which ye may take away the occasion of wars, and so know a kingdom which hath no end, and fight for that with spiritual weapons, which takes away the occasion of the carnal; and there gather men to war, as many as ye can, and set up as many as ye can with these weapons."   G. F.

After I had stayed some time in London, and had visited Friends' meetings there and thereabouts, and the Lord's power was set over all, I travelled into the counties again, passing through ESSEX and SUFFOLK into NORFOLK, visiting Friends, till I came to NORWICH, where we had a meeting about the time called Christmas. The mayor of Norwich, having got previous notice of the meeting I intended to have there, granted a warrant to apprehend me. When I was come thither, and heard of the warrant, I sent some Friends to the mayor to reason with him about it. His answer was, the soldiers should not meet; and did we think to meet? He would have us to go and meet without the city; for he said, the town's-people were so rude that he could hardly order them, and he feared, that our meeting would make tumults in the town. But our Friends told him, we were a peaceable people, and that he ought to keep the peace; for we could not but meet to worship God, as our manner was. So he became moderate, and did not send his officers to the meeting. A large one it was, and abundance of rude people came, with an intent to do mischief; but the Lord's power came over them, so that they were chained by it, though several priests were there, and professors and Ranters. Among the priests, one, whose name was Townsend, stood up and cried, 'Error, blasphemy, and an ungodly meeting!' I bid him not burden himself with that which he could not make good; and I asked him what was our error and blasphemy; for I told him, he should make good his words, before I had done with him, or be shamed. As for an ungodly meeting, I said, I believed there were many people there that feared God, and therefore it was both unchristian and uncivil in him, to charge civil, godly people with an ungodly meeting. He said, my error and blasphemy was, in that I said, that people must wait upon God by his power and Spirit, and feel his presence when they did not speak words. I asked him then, whether the apostles and holy men of God did not hear God speak to them in their silence, before they spoke forth the Scripture, and before it was written? He replied, Yes, David and the prophets heard God, before they penned the Scriptures, and felt his presence in silence, before they spoke them forth. Then said

I, All people take notice, he said this was error and blasphemy in me to say these words; and now he hath confessed it is no more than the holy men of God in former times witnessed. So I showed them, that as the holy men of God, who gave forth the Scripture as they were moved by the Holy Ghost, heard and learned of God, before they spoke them forth; so must they all hearken and hear what the Spirit saith, which will lead them into all truth, that they may know God and Christ, and may understand the Scriptures. O, said the priest, this is not that George Fox I would speak withal; this is a subtle man, said he. So the Lord's power came over all, and the rude people were made moderate, and were reached by it; and some professors that were there, called to the priests, saying, "Prove the blasphemy and errors which ye have charged them with; ye have spoken much against them behind their backs, but nothing ye can prove now (said they) to their faces." But the priest began to get away; whereupon I told him, we had many things to charge him withal, therefore let him set a time and place to answer them; which he did and went his way. A glorious day this was, for truth came over all, and people were turned to God by his power and Spirit, and to the Lord Jesus Christ, their free teacher, who was exalted over all. And as we passed away, people's hearts were generally filled with love towards us; yea, the ruder sort of them desired another meeting, for the evil intentions they had against us were thrown out of their hearts. At night I passed out of town to a Friend's house, and thence to Colonel Dennis's, where we had a great meeting; and afterwards travelled on, visiting Friends in NORFOLK, HUNTINGDONSHIRE, and CAMBRIDGESHIRE. But George Whitehead and Richard Hubberthorn stayed about Norwich to meet the priest, who was soon confounded, the Lord's power came so over him.

After I had travelled through many counties in the Lord's service, and many were convinced, notwithstanding the people in some places were very rude, I returned to LONDON, when General Monk was come up thither, and the gates and posts of the city were pulling down. Long before this I had a vision, wherein I saw the city lie in heaps and the gates down; and it was then represented to me, just as I saw it several years after, lying in heaps, when it was burned.

Divers times, both by word and writing, had I forewarned the several powers, both in Oliver's time and after, of the day of recompense that was coming upon them; but they rejecting counsel, and slighting those visitations of love to them, I was moved now, before they were quite overturned, to lay their backsliding, hypocrisy, and treacherous dealing before them, thus:

"FRIENDS, now are the prophecies fulfilled and fulfilling upon you, which have been spoken to you by the people of God in your courts, steeple-houses, towns, cities, markets, highways, and at your feasts, when ye were in your pleasures, and puffed up, that ye would neither hear God nor man; when ye were in your height of authority, though raised up from a mean state, none might come nigh you without bowing, or the respect of persons, for ye were in the world's way, compliments, and fashions, which, for conscience' sake towards God they could not go into, being redeemed therefrom; therefore they were hated by you for that cause. But how are ye brought low, who exalted yourselves above your brethren, and threw the just and harmless from among you, until at last God hath thrown you out; and when ye cast the innocent from among you, then ye fell to biting one another until ye were consumed one of another. And so the day is come upon you, which before was told you, though ye would not believe it. And are not your hearts so hardened, that ye will hardly yet believe, though ready to go into captivity? Was it not told you, when ye spilt the blood of the innocent in your steeple-houses, markets, highways, and cities, yea, and even in your courts also, because they said the word 'Thou' to you, and could not put off their hats to you, that if something did not arise up amongst yourselves, to avenge the blood of the innocent, there would come something from beyond the seas, which lay reserved there, which being brought by the arm of God, the arm of flesh and strongest mountain cannot withstand? Yet ye would not consider, regard, or hear; but cried, peace, peace, and feasted yourselves, and sat down in the spoil of your enemies, being treacherous both to God and man; and who will trust you now? Have ye not made covenants and oaths? and broken covenants and oaths between God and man, and made the nations breakers both of covenants and oaths; so that nothing but hypocrisy, rottenness, and falsehood under fair pretence, was amongst you?

"When ye pretended to set up the old cause, it was but yourselves; for which ye long stuck to sober people, who saw ye would do no good. But it was a joy for any of you to get up into authority, that ye might have praise, honour, and respect; and they that were in the self-denial, were a derision to you, from amongst whom that was banished. Thus ye became the nation's masters, and not servants; whereas the greatest of all should be the servants of all. But there ye lost your authority, not considering your estates, from whence ye were, and to what end God had raised you up; but forgot the Lord, and quenched that which was good in yourselves, and persecuted them that lived in it; and so are grown so gross and perverse, that at last ye are fit for neither God nor man. Have not ye called the Quakers the fanatic people, and the giddy heads? But whither now are ye giddying? into Cain's city Nod, which signifies fugitive, or wandering? Have not ye persecuted and imprisoned to death such as God had respect to, and is now reproving you for their sakes, by them whom ye have hated? Were not many amongst you cut off for your persecution, and yet the rest of you would not take warning? Was there not a book of examples sent out unto you, of what sudden and strange deaths happened to the persecutors of the innocent? And yet ye would not take warning, until the overflowing scourge is now coming upon you. Are not ye they that have killed like Cain, who have killed about your sacrifice, and mingled the blood of the innocent with it? Hath not God now vagabonded you, that ye should become a curse upon the earth, who have persecuted Friends to death? Did not the blood of the righteous cry out of the ground for vengeance? And will not the blood of the righteous be required? Could ye think that the Lord would let you sit always with bloody hands and fists of wickedness? Ah! what is become of all your feasts and your fasts, the prayers and blessings of your priests?"

G. F.

CHAPTER XIII.

1659–1660.—Address to the Cornish people, respecting shipwrecks—the soldiers at Bristol are punished for disturbing Friends' meetings—several thousands attend a general meeting at Edward Pyot's—General Monk also restrains his soldiers—great drunkenness at elections for Parliament-men—the Yearly Meeting is held at Balby—and a general meeting of discipline for several counties held at Skipton—a Friend goes naked (divested of the upper garments) through the town, declaring Truth, and is much abused—general meeting at Arnside for three counties—George Fox is committed to Lancaster Castle by Major Porter—writes an answer to his mittimus—Margaret Fell writes to the magistrates thereon—address on true religion—against persecution—to Friends, on the change of government—to Charles II., exhorting him to exercise mercy and forgiveness towards his enemies, and to restrain profaneness—the Sheriff of Lancashire's return to George Fox's writ of *Habeas Corpus*—M. Fell and Ann Curtis speak to the King on the subject—the King orders his removal to London by Habeas Corpus, and there sets him at liberty.

BEING now clear of the city of London, and finding my spirit drawn to visit Friends in the western parts of England, passing first into SURREY and SUSSEX, I came to a great town where there was a large meeting, to which several Friends from Reading came, and a blessed one it was. The priest of the town was in a great rage, but did not come out of his house; wherefore, hearing him make a great noise in his house, as we were passing from the meeting, we bid him come out into the street, and we would discourse with him; but he would not. So the Lord's power being over all, Friends were refreshed therein. Thence I went to another market-town, where in the evening we had a precious meeting, and the fresh sense of the presence of the Lord was sweetly felt amongst us. Then turning into HAMPSHIRE and DORSETSHIRE, I went to RINGWOOD and POOLE visiting Friends in the Lord's power, and had great meetings amongst them.

At DORCHESTER we had a great meeting in the evening at our inn, which many soldiers attended, and were pretty civil. But the constables and officers of the town came, under pretence to look for a Jesuit, whose head (they said) was shaved; and they would have all put off their hats, or they would take them off, to look for the Jesuit's shaven crown. So they took off my hat (for I was the man they aimed at), and looked very narrowly, but not finding any bald or shaven place on my head they went away with shame; and the soldiers, and other sober people, were greatly offended with them. But it was of good service for the Lord, and all things wrought together for good; for it affected the people; and after the officers were gone, we had a fine meeting, and people were turned to the Lord Jesus Christ, their teacher, who had bought them, and would reconcile them to God.

Thence we passed into SOMERSETSHIRE, where the Presbyterians and other professors were very wicked, and often disturbed Friends' meetings.

One time especially (as we were then informed) there was a very wicked man, whom they got to come to the Quakers' meeting; this man put a bear's skin on his back, and undertook with that to play pranks in the meeting. Accordingly, setting himself just opposite to the Friend that was speaking, he lolled his tongue out of his mouth, having his bear's skin on his back, and so made sport to his wicked followers, and caused a great disturbance in the meeting. But an eminent judgment overtook him, and his punishment slumbered not; for as he went back from the meeting, there was a bull-baiting in the way which he stayed to see; and coming within the bull's reach, he struck his horn under the man's chin into his throat, and struck his tongue out of his mouth, so that it hung lolling out, as he had used it before, in derision in the meeting. And the bull's horn running up into the man's head, he swung him about upon his horn in a most remarkable and fearful manner. Thus he that came to do mischief amongst God's people, was mischiefed himself; and well would it be, if such apparent examples of Divine vengeance, would teach others to beware.*

We travelled through SOMERSETSHIRE and DEVONSHIRE, till we came to PLYMOUTH, and so into CORNWALL, visiting the meetings of Friends to the Land's End. Many precious and blessed meetings we had all along as we went, wherein they that were convinced were established, and many others were added to them. At the LAND'S END, there was an honest fisherman convinced, who became a faithful minister of Christ; I took notice of him to Friends, and told them, "he was like Peter."†

While I was in Cornwall, there were great shipwrecks about the Land's End. Now it was the custom of that country, that at such a time both rich and poor went out, to get as much of the wreck as they could, not caring to save the people's lives; and in some places, they call shipwrecks, God's grace. These things troubled me; it grieved my spirit to hear of such unchristian actions, considering how far they were below the heathen at Melita, who received Paul, made him a fire, and were courteous towards him, and them that had suffered shipwreck with him. Wherefore I was moved to write a paper, and send it to all the parishes, priests, and

---

* Many were the judgments which overtook the persecutors of the Early Friends, as related in their journals, and the histories of the Society. The following occurred in Scotland, as related in Jaffray's diary :—" James Skene, who was generally known by the name of 'White James,' to distinguish him from a very abusive and wicked man of the same name, called 'Black James,' took great delight in inventing malicious slanders against Friends. On one occasion, whilst he was repeating some wicked verses, which he had composed on purpose to defame a worthy and innocent person, he was in that instant suddenly struck down as one dead, and was for some time deprived of his senses. When he recovered, he acknowledged the just judgment of God upon him, confessed the offence he had committed against this innocent people, and gave proof of repentance by ever after abstaining from such practices."

† The honest fisherman mentioned here was Nicholas Jose, who was a great sufferer for Christ's sake, both in loss of goods and imprisonments in Launceston jail, Pendennis castle, and other places; indeed scarcely a year passed over without his being called on to suffer severely in some way or other for the testimony of a good conscience. He was imprisoned with twenty-four other Friends, about the year 1682, and continued in confinement till 1685. For an interesting account of this worthy man, see *Select Miscellanies*, vol. iv., 250–255.

magistrates, to reprove them for such greedy actions, and to warn and exhort them that, if they could assist to save people's lives, and preserve their ships and goods, they should use their diligence therein; and consider, if it had been their own condition, they would judge it hard, if they should be upon a wreck, and people should strive to get what they could from them, and not regard their lives. A copy of this paper here follows:—

"FRIENDS AND PEOPLE,

"Take heed of greediness and covetousness, for that is idolatry; and the idolater must not enter into the kingdom of God. Take heed of drunkenness, oaths, and cursings, for such are destroyers of the creation, and make it to groan. Lay aside all fighting, quarreling, brawling, and evil speakings, which are the works of the flesh, and not of the Spirit; for they who follow such things are not likely to inherit the kingdom of God. Put away all corrupt words, which are unsavoury, and misnaming one another; for ye must give an account of every idle word. Lay aside all profession and religion that is vain; and come to the possession, and the pure religion, which is to visit the fatherless, the widow, and the stranger, and receive them; for some thereby may entertain angels, or the servants of the Lord unawares, as Paul was entertained after the shipwreck at Melita. Do not take people's goods from them by force out of their ships, seamen's or others', neither covet ye them; but rather endeavour to preserve their lives, and their goods for them; for that shows a spirit of compassion, and the spirit of a Christian. But if ye be greedy and covetous of other men's goods, not mattering what becomes of the men, would ye be served so yourselves? If ye should have a ship cast away in other places, and the people should come to tear the goods and ship in pieces, not regarding to save the men's lives, but be ready to fight one with another for your goods, do not ye believe such goods would become a curse to them? And may ye not as surely believe, such kind of actions will become a curse unto you? When the spoil of one ship's goods is idly spent, and consumed upon the lusts, in ale-houses, taverns, and otherwise, then ye gape for another. Is this to 'do as ye would be done by,' which is the law and the prophets? Therefore, priest Hull, are these thy fruits? What dost thou take people's labour and goods for? Hast thou taught them no better manners and conversation, who are so brutish and heathenish? Now all such things we judge in whomsoever. But if any Friend, or others, preserve men's lives, and endeavour to save their goods and estates, and restore what they can of a wreck to the owners; if they consider such for their labour, doing in that case unto them what they would have done unto themselves, that we approve. And if they buy or sell, and do not make a prey, that is allowed of still, in the way of 'doing as ye would be done by,' keeping to the law and to the prophets: that is, if ye should be wrecked in another country, ye would have other people to save your lives and goods, and have your goods restored to you again, and you would commend them for so doing. All that do otherwise, that wait for a wreck, and get the goods for themselves, not regarding the lives of the men; but if any of them escape drowning, let them go begging up and down the country; and if any escape with a little, sometimes rob them of it;—all that do so, are not for preserving the creation, but for destroying it; and those goods which are so gotten, shall be a curse, a plague, and a judgment to them, and the judgments of God will follow them for acting such things; the witness in your consciences shall answer it. Therefore, all ye who have done such things, 'do so no more lest a worse thing come unto you.' But that which is good, do; preserve men's lives and estates, and labour to restore the loss and breach; that the Lord requires. Be not like a company of greedy dogs, and worse than heathens, as if ye had never heard of God, nor Christ, nor the Scriptures, nor pure religion.

"And priest Hull, have people spent their money upon thee, for that which is no bread? for a thing of nought, that thou hast such fruits? All such teachers we utterly deny as make a trade of the Scriptures, which are given forth from the Spirit of God, that they may be believed, read, and practised, and that Christ, whom they testify of, may be enjoyed. We own Christ, and are come off from all your steeple-houses, which were the old mass-houses; for there are their bad fruits harboured. Come to the church which is in God (1 Thess. i.), and to the light, which Christ Jesus hath enlightened you withal, which shows you all your ungodly words, ungodly thoughts, and ungodly actions. This will be your teacher, if ye love it; your condemnation, if ye hate it; for the mighty day of the Lord is coming upon all wickedness and ungodliness; therefore lay aside your whoredoms and fornications.

"And ye magistrates, who are to do justice, think ye not, that the hand of the Lord God is against you, and that his judgments will come upon you, who do not look after these things and stop them with the law, which is, 'to do unto all men, as they would have done unto them,' whereby ye might be good savour in your country? Is not the law to preserve men's lives and estates, 'doing unto all men, as they would that men should do unto them?' For all men would have their lives and estates preserved; therefore, should not ye preserve others, and not suffer them to be devoured and destroyed? The evil of these things will lie upon you, both priests and magistrates."   G. F.

"*Postscript.*—All dear Friends who fear the Lord, keep out of the ravenous world's spirit, which leads to destroy, and which is out of the wisdom of God. When ships are wrecked, do not run to destroy and make havoc of ship and goods with the world; but to save the men, and the goods for them; and so deny yourselves, 'and do unto them as ye would that they should do unto you.'"   G. F.

This paper had good service among the people; and Friends have endeavoured much to save the lives of the crews in times of wrecks, and to preserve the ships and goods for them. And when some that have suffered shipwreck, have been almost dead and starved, Friends have taken them to their houses, to succour and recover them; which is an act to be practised by all true Christians.

I had many precious, blessed, living meetings in Cornwall, several eminent people being convinced in that county, whom neither priests nor magistrates, by spoiling goods or imprisonments, could make to forsake their Shepherd, the Lord Jesus, who bought them; and all Friends, who were turned to Christ, their Teacher and Saviour, being settled in peace and quietness upon him, their foundation, we left them to the Lord Jesus Christ's teaching and ordering, fresh and green.   Thomas Lower, who had accompanied me through all that county, brought me over Horse-bridge into DEVONSHIRE again; and after several meetings there, we came into SOMERSETSHIRE, where we had divers large and peaceable meetings; and so passed through the county, visiting Friends, till we came to BRISTOL.

I entered BRISTOL on the seventh day of the week.   The day before, the soldiers came with their muskets into the meeting, and were exceedingly rude, beating and striking Friends with them, and drove them out of the orchard in a great rage, threatening what they would do, if Friends came there again.   For the mayor and the commander of the soldiers had, it seems, combined together to make a disturbance amongst Friends.   When Friends told me what a rage there was in the town, how they were threatened by the mayor and soldiers, and how unruly the soldiers had been the day before, I sent for several Friends, as George Bishop, Thomas Gouldney, Thomas Speed, and Edward Pyot, and desired them to go to the mayor and aldermen, and request them, seeing he and they had broken up our meetings, to let Friends have the town-hall to meet in; and for the use of it Friends would give them twenty pounds a-year, to be distributed amongst the poor; and when the mayor and aldermen had business to do in it, Friends would not meet in it, but only on First-days.   These Friends were astonished at this, and said the mayor and aldermen would think that they were mad.   I said, nay; for this would be a considerable benefit to the poor. And it was upon me from the Lord to bid them go.   At last they consented, and went, though in the cross to their own wills.   When they had laid the thing before the mayor, he said, "for his part he could consent to it, but he was but one:" and he told Friends of another great hall they might have, but that they did not accept, it being inconvenient.   So Friends came away, leaving the mayor in a very loving frame towards them; for they felt the Lord's power had come over him.   When they came back, I spoke to them to go also to the colonel that commanded the soldiers, and lay before him the rude conduct of his soldiers, how they came armed amongst innocent people, who were waiting upon, and worshipping the Lord; but they were backward to go to him.

Next morning, being first day, we went to the meeting in the orchard, where the soldiers had so lately been so rude.   After I had declared the truth some time in the meeting, there came in many rude soldiers and people, some with drawn swords.   The innkeepers had made some of them drunk; and one had bound himself with an oath, to cut down and kill the man that spoke.   He came pressing in, through all the crowd of people, to within two yards of me, and stopped at those four Friends before mentioned (who should have gone to the colonel as I would have had them), and began jangling with them.   Suddenly I saw his sword was put up and gone: for the Lord's power came over all, and chained him with the rest. We had a blessed meeting, and the Lord's everlasting power and presence was felt amongst us. On the day following, the four Friends went and spoke with the colonel, and he sent for the soldiers, and cut and slashed some of them before the Friends' faces; which when I heard of I blamed the Friends for letting him do so, and also that they did not go on the seventh day, as I would have had them, which might have prevented this cutting of the soldiers, and the trouble they gave at our meeting. But thus the Lord's power came over all those persecuting, bloody minds, and the meeting there was held in peace for a good while after without disturbance.

I had then also a general meeting at Edward Pyot's, near Bristol, at which it was supposed were several thousands; for besides Friends from many parts thereabouts, some of the Baptists and Independents, with their teachers, came to it, and many of the sober people of Bristol; insomuch that the people that stayed behind said, "the city looked naked," so many were gone out of it to this meeting. It was very quiet, many glorious truths were opened to the people, and the Lord Jesus Christ was set up, who was the end of all figures and shadows of the law, and the first covenant. It was declared to the people that all figures and shadows were given to man, after he fell; and that all the rudiments and inventions of men, which have been set up in Christendom, many of which were Jewish and heathenish, were not set up by the command of Christ; and all images and likenesses man has made to himself, or for himself, whether of things in heaven or things in earth, have been since he lost the image and likeness of God, which God made him in. But now Christ is come to redeem, translate, convert, and regenerate man out of all these things that he hath set up in the fall, out of the true types, figures, and shadows also, and out of death and darkness, into the light, life, and image of God again, which man and woman were in before they fell. Therefore all now should come, and all might come to receive, Christ Jesus, the substance, by his light, Spirit, grace, and faith; and should live and walk in him, the Redeemer and Saviour.

And as we had much work with priests and professors, who pleaded for imperfection, I was opened to declare and manifest unto them, that Adam and Eve were perfect before they fell; and God saw that all that he had made, was good, and he blessed it. But imperfection came in by the fall, through man and woman's hearkening to the devil, who was out of truth. And though the law made nothing perfect, yet it made way for the bringing in of the better hope, which hope is Christ, who destroys the devil and his works, that made man and woman imperfect. Christ saith to his disciples, "Be ye perfect, even as your heavenly Father is perfect:" and he, who himself was perfect, comes to make man and woman perfect again, and brings them again to the state which God made them in. So he is the maker up of the breach, and the peace between God and man. That this might the better be understood by the lowest capacities, I used a comparison of two old people, that had their house broken down by an enemy, so that they, with all their children, were liable to all storms and tempests. And there came some to them that pretended to be workmen, and offered to build up their house again, if they would give them so much a-year:

but when they had got their money, they left their house as they found it. After this manner came a second, third, fourth, fifth, and sixth, each with his several pretence, to build up the old house, and each got the people's money; and then cried, "they could not rear up the house, nor could the breach be made up; for there is no perfection here, cry they; the house can never be perfectly built up again in this life;" though they had taken the people's money for the doing of it. For all the sect-masters in Christendom (so called) have pretended to build up Adam and Eve's fallen house, and when they have got people's money, they tell them the work cannot be perfectly done here; and so their house lies as it did. But I told the people, Christ was come to do it freely, who, by one offering, hath perfected for ever all them that are sanctified, and renews them into the image of God, which man and woman were in before they fell, and makes man and woman's house as perfect again as God made them at the first: and this, Christ, the heavenly man, doth freely. Therefore all are to look unto him, and all that have received him, are to walk in him, the life, the substance, the first and the last, the rock of ages, and foundation of many generations. Largely were these, and many other things, opened and declared unto the people, the word of life was preached, which doth live and abide; and all were exhorted to hear and obey that which liveth and abideth, that by it all might be born again of the immortal Seed, and feed on the milk of the Word. A glorious meeting there was, wherein the Lord's everlasting Seed, Christ Jesus, was set over all, and Friends parted in the power and Spirit of the Lord, in peace and in his truth, that is over all.

About this time the soldiers under General Monk's command were rude and troublesome at Friends' meetings in many places, whereof complaint being made to him, he gave forth the following order, which somewhat restrained them:—

"*St. James's, the 9th of March*, 1659.

"I do require all officers and soldiers to forbear to disturb the peaceable meetings of the Quakers, they doing nothing prejudicial to the Parliament or Commonwealth of England.   "GEORGE MONK."

After the meeting at Edward Pyot's I passed to OLDESTON, to NAILSWORTH, and to Nathaniel Crisp's; where there was a large meeting, and several soldiers at it, but quiet. From thence we passed to GLOUCESTER, visiting meetings. In Gloucester we had a peaceable meeting, though the town was very rude, and divided; for one part of the soldiers were for the king, and another for the parliament. As I passed out of the town, over the bridge, Edward Pyot being with me, the soldiers there said, "they were for the king;" but after we were past them, and they understood it was I, they were in a great rage that I had escaped them, and said, "had they known it had been I, they would have shot me with hail-shot, rather than I should have escaped them." But the Lord prevented their devilish design, and brought me safe to Colonel Grimes's house, where we had a large general meeting, and the Lord's truth and power was set over all; Friends were established upon the Rock, and settled under the Lord Jesus Christ's teaching.

We passed thence to TEWKESBURY, and so to WORCESTER, visiting Friends in their meetings as we went. And in all my time I never saw the like drunkenness as in the towns, for they had been choosing parliament-men. At Worcester the Lord's truth was set over all, people were finely settled therein, and Friends praised the Lord; nay, I saw the very earth rejoiced. Yet great fears and troubles were in many people, and a looking for the king's coming in, and all things being altered. They would ask me what I thought of times and things. I told them the Lord's power was over all, and his light shone over all; that fear would take hold only on the hypocrites, such as had not been faithful to God, and on our persecutors. For in my travail and sufferings at Reading, when people were at a stand, and could not tell what might come in, and who might rule, I told them the Lord's power was over all (for I had travelled through in it), and his day shined, whosoever should come in; and whether the king came in or not, all would be well to them that loved the Lord, and were faithful to him. Therefore I bid all Friends fear none but the Lord, and keep in his power that was over all.

From Worcester I visited Friends in their meetings, till I came to BADGLEY, and thence I went to DRAYTON, in Leicestershire, to visit my relations. While there, one Burton, a justice, hearing I had a good horse, sent a warrant to search for me and my horse; but I was gone before they came; and so he missed of his wicked end. I passed on to TWY-CROSS, SWANNINGTON, and DERBY, where I visited Friends, and found my old jailer amongst them, who had formerly kept me in the house of correction there, now convinced of the truth, which I then suffered under him for. Passing into Derbyshire and Nottinghamshire, I came to SYNDERHILL-GREEN, visiting Friends through all those parts in their meetings, and so on to BALBY in Yorkshire, where our Yearly Meeting at that time was held in a great orchard of John Killam's, where it was supposed some thousands of people and Friends were gathered together. In the morning I heard that a troop of horse was sent from York, to break up our meeting, and that the militia, newly raised, was to join them. I went into the meeting, and stood up on a great stool, and after I had spoken some time, two trumpeters came up, sounding their trumpets near me, and the captain of the troop cried, "Divide to the right and left, and make way;" then they rode up to me. I was declaring the everlasting truth, and word of life, in the mighty power of the Lord. The captain bid me "come down, for he was come to disperse our meeting." After some time I told him they all knew we were a peaceable people, and used to have such great meetings; but if he apprehended that we met in a hostile way, I desired him to make search among us, and if he found either sword or pistol about any there, let such suffer. He told me, "he must see us dispersed, for he came all night on purpose to disperse us." I asked him, "what honour it would be to him, to ride with swords and pistols amongst so many unarmed men and women as there were?" If he would be still and quiet, our meeting probably might not continue above two or three hours; and when it was done, as we came peaceably together, so we should part; for he might perceive the meeting was so large, that all the country thereabouts could not entertain them, but that they intended to depart towards their homes at night. He said, "he could not stay to see the meeting ended, but must disperse them before he went." I desired him then, if he himself could not stay, that he would let a dozen of his soldiers stay, and see the order and peaceableness of our meeting. He said, "he would permit us an hour's time;" and left half a dozen soldiers with us. Then he went away with his troop, and Friends of the house gave the soldiers that stayed, and their horses, some meat. When the captain was gone, the soldiers that were left told us, "we might stay till night if we would." But we stayed but about three hours after, and had a glorious, powerful meeting; for the presence of the living God was manifest amongst us: the Seed, Christ, was set over all, and Friends were built upon him, the foundation, and settled under his glorious, heavenly teaching. After the meeting, Friends passed away in peace, greatly refreshed with the presence of the Lord, and filled with joy and gladness, that the Lord's power had given them such dominion. Many of the militia soldiers stayed also, and were much vexed that the captain and troopers had not broken up our meeting, and cursed them. It was reported that they intended to do us some mischief that day; but the troopers, instead of assisting them, were rather assistant to us, in not joining with them, as they expected, but preventing them from doing the mischief they designed. Yet this captain was a desperate man, for it was he that had said to me in Scotland, that "he would obey his superior's commands; and if it were to crucify Christ he would do it; or execute the great Turk's commands against the Christians, if he were under him." So that it was an eminent power of the Lord, which chained both him and his troopers, and those envious militia-soldiers also, who went away, not having power to hurt any of us, nor to break up our meeting.

Next day we had a heavenly meeting at WARMSWORTH, of Friends in the ministry and several others; and then Friends parted. As they passed through the country, several were taken up. For the day that our first meeting was held on, Lambert was routed, and it made great confusion in the country; but Friends were not kept long in prison at that time. As I went to this meeting at Balby, there came several to me at Skegby in Nottinghamshire, that were then going to be soldiers under Lambert, and would have bought my horse of me; and because I would not sell him, they were in a great rage against me, using many threatening words; but I told them, "God would confound and scatter them;" and within two or three days after, they were scattered indeed.

From Warmsworth I passed in the Lord's power to BARTON-ABBEY, where I had a great meeting; and thence to Thomas Taylor's, and so to SKIPTON, where there was a general meeting of men Friends out of many counties, concerning the affairs of the church.* A Friend went naked [divested of the upper garments] through the town, declaring truth, and he was much beaten. Some others also came to me all bloody. As I

---

* General Meetings and Yearly Meetings appear to have been somewhat similar in their character. They were held in various parts. The first of which we have any account took place at Swannington, in Leicestershire, in 1654.

walked in the street, a desperate fellow had an intent to do me a mischief; but he was prevented, and our meeting was quiet. To this meeting came many Friends out of most parts of the nation; for it was about business relating to the church, both in this nation and beyond the seas. Several years before, when I was in the North, I was moved to recommend the setting up of this meeting for that service; for many Friends suffered in divers parts of the nation, their goods were taken from them contrary to the law, and they understood not how to help themselves, or where to seek redress. But after this meeting was set up, several Friends who had been magistrates, and others that understood something of the law, came thither, and were able to inform Friends, and to assist them in gathering up the sufferings, that they might be laid before the justices, judges, or Parliament. This meeting had stood several years, and divers justices and captains had come to break it up; but when they understood the business Friends met about, and saw their books and accounts of collections for relief of the poor, how we took care one county to help another, and to help our friends beyond the seas, and provide for our poor, that none of them should be chargeable to their parishes, &c., the justices and officers confessed we did their work, and passed away peaceably and lovingly, commending Friends' practice. Sometimes there would come two hundred of the poor of other people, and wait there till the meeting was done (for all the country knew we met about the poor) and after the meeting, Friends would send to the bakers for bread, and give every one of these poor people a loaf, how many soever there were of them; for we were taught to "do good unto all; though especially to the household of faith."

After this meeting I visited Friends in their meetings, till I came to LANCASTER; whence I went to Robert Widders's, and so to ARNSIDE, where I had a general meeting for all the Friends in Westmorland, Cumberland, and Lancashire. It was quiet and peaceable, and the living presence of the Lord was amongst us. I went back with Robert Widders; and Friends all passed away, fresh in the life and power of Christ, in which they had dominion, being settled upon him, the heavenly rock and foundation. After the meeting, there came several rude fellows, serving-men, belonging to one called Sir George Middleton, a justice that lived near, to make some disturbance, as it was thought. The meeting being ended, they did nothing there; but lighting on three women Friends going from it, they set upon them with impudent scoffs, and one of them carried himself very abusively and immodestly towards them. The same man abused other Friends also, and was so outrageous that he would have cut them with an axe; but was restrained by some of his fellows. Another time the same man set upon six Friends that were going to meeting, at Yelland, and beat and abused them very much, so that he bruised their faces, and shed much of their blood, wounding them very sore, one of them in several parts of his body; yet they lifted not up a hand against him, but gave him their backs and their cheeks to beat.

From Robert Widders's I went next day to SWARTHMORE, Francis Howgill and Thomas Curtis being with me. I had not been long there before Henry Porter, a justice, sent a warrant by the chief constable and three petty constables to apprehend me. I had a sense of this beforehand; and being in the parlour with Richard Richardson and Margaret Fell, her servants came, and told her there were some come to search the house for arms; and they went up into the chambers under that pretence. It came upon me to go out to them; and as I was going by some of them, I spoke to them; whereupon they asked me my name. I readily told them my name; and then they laid hold on me, saying, "I was the man they looked for," and led me away to ULVERSTONE. They kept me all night at the constable's house, and set a guard of fifteen or sixteen men to watch me; some of whom sat in the chimney, for fear I should go up it; such dark imaginations possessed them. They were very rude and uncivil, and would neither suffer me to speak to Friends, nor suffer them to bring me necessaries; but with violence thrust them out, and kept a strong guard upon me. Very wicked and rude they were, and a great noise they made about me. One of the constables, whose name was Ashburnham, said, "He did not think a thousand men could have taken me." Another of the constables, whose name was Mount, a very wicked man, said, "He would have served Judge Fell himself so, if he had been alive, and he had had a warrant for him." Next morning, about six, I was putting on my boots and spurs to go with them before some justice; but they pulled off the latter, took my knife out of my pocket, and hastened me away along the town, with a party of horse and abundance of people, not suffering me to stay till my own horse came down. When I was gone about a quarter of a mile with them, some Friends, with Margaret Fell and her children, came towards me; and then a great party of horse gathered about me in a mad rage and fury, crying out, "Will they rescue him? Will they rescue him?" Whereupon I said unto them, "Here is my hair, here is my back, here are my cheeks, strike on!" With these words their heat was a little assuaged. Then they brought a little horse, and two of them took up one of my legs, and put my foot in the stirrup, and two or three lifting over my other leg, set me upon it behind the saddle, and so led the horse by the halter; but I had nothing to hold by. When they were come some distance out of the town, they beat the little horse, and made him kick and gallop; whereupon I slipped off him, and told them, "They should not abuse the creature." They were much enraged at my getting off, and took me by the legs and feet, and set me upon the same horse, behind the saddle again; and so led it about two miles, till they came to a great water called the CARTER-FORD. By this time my own horse was come to us, and the water being deep, and their little horse scarcely able to carry me through, they let me get upon my own, through the persuasion of some of their own company, leading him through the water. One wicked fellow kneeled down, and lifting up his hands, blessed God, that I was taken. When I was come over the Sands, I told them I heard I had liberty to choose what justice I would go before; but Mount and the other constables cried, "No, I should not." Then they led me to LANCASTER, about fourteen miles, and a great triumph they thought to have had; but as they led me, I was moved "to sing praises to the Lord, in his triumphing power over all."

When I was come to Lancaster, the spirits of the people being mightily up, I stood and looked earnestly upon them; and they cried, "Look at his eyes!" After a while I spoke to them; and then they were pretty sober. Then came a young man, and took me to his house; and after a little time the officers had me to Major Porter's, the justice, and who had sent forth the warrant against me; he had several others with him. When I came in, I said, "Peace be amongst you!" Porter asked me, "Why I came down into the country that troublesome time?" I told him, "To visit my brethren." "Then," said he, "you have great meetings up and down." I told him though we had, our meetings were known throughout the nation to be peaceable, and we were a peaceable people. He said, "We saw the devil in people's faces." I told him, "If I saw a drunkard, or a swearer, or a peevish, heady man, I could not say I saw the Spirit of God in him." And I asked him, "If he could see the Spirit of God?" He said, "We cried against their ministers." I told him, while we were as Saul, sitting under the priests, and running up and down with their packets of letters, we were never called pestilent fellows, nor makers of sects; but when we were come to exercise our consciences towards God and man, we were called pestilent fellows, as Paul was. He said, we could express ourselves well enough, and he would not dispute with me; but he would restrain me. I desired to know, "for what, and by whose order he sent his warrant for me;" and I complained to him of the abuse of the constables and other officers, after they had taken me, and in their bringing me thither. He would not take notice of that, but told me, "He had an order, but would not let me see it; for he would not reveal the king's secrets;" and besides, "a prisoner," he said, "was not to see for what he was committed." I told him, that was not reason; for how should he make his defence then? I said, "I ought to have a copy of it;" but he said, "There was a judge once that fined a man for letting a prisoner have a copy of his mittimus; and," said he, "I have an old clerk, though I am a young justice." Then he called to his clerk, saying, "Is it not ready yet? Bring it," meaning the mittimus; but it not being ready, he said to me, "I was a disturber of the nation." I told him, I had been a blessing to the nation, in and through the Lord's power and truth, and the Spirit of God in all consciences would answer it. Then he charged me as "an enemy to the king; that I endeavoured to raise a new war, and imbrue the nation in blood again." I told him, I had never learned the postures of war, but was clear and innocent as a child concerning those things, and therefore was bold. Then came the clerk with the mittimus, and the jailer was sent for, and commanded to take and put me into the Dark-house, and to let none come to me; but keep me there a close prisoner, till I should be delivered by the king or parliament. Then the justice asked the constables where my horse was; "for I hear," said he, "that he has a good horse; have ye brought it?" I told him where my horse was, but he did not meddle with him. As they took me to the jail, the constable gave me my knife again, and then asked me to give it him; but I told him, nay, he had not been so civil to me. So they put me into the jail, and the under-jailer, one Hardy, a very wicked man, was exceedingly rude and cruel, and many times would not let me have meat brought in, but as I could get it under the door. Many people came to look at me, some in great rage, and very uncivil and rude.   Once there came two young priests, and very abusive they were; the worst of people could not be worse.   Amongst those that came in this manner, old Preston's wife, of Howker, was one.   She used many abusive words, telling me, "My tongue should be cut out," and that "I should be hanged;" showing me the gallows.   But the Lord God cut her off, and she died in a miserable condition.

Being now a close prisoner in the common jail at Lancaster, I desired Thomas Cummins and Thomas Green to go to the jailer, and desire of him a copy of my mittimus, that I might know what I stood committed for. They went; and the jailer answered, "he could not give a copy of it, for another had been fined for so doing;" but he gave them liberty to read it over.   To the best of their remembrance the matters therein charged against me were, "that I was a person generally suspected to be a common disturber of the peace of the nation, an enemy to the king, and a chief upholder of the Quakers' sect; and that, together with others of my fanatic opinion, I have of late endeavoured to raise insurrections in these parts of the country, and to embroil the whole kingdom in blood.   Wherefore the jailer was commanded to keep me in safe custody, until I should be released by order of the king and parliament."

When I had thus got the heads of the charge contained in the mittimus, I wrote a plain answer, in vindication of my innocency in each particular; as follows:—

"I AM a prisoner at Lancaster, committed by Justice Porter.   A copy of the mittimus I cannot get, but such expressions I am told are in it, as are very untrue; as 'that I am generally suspected to be a common disturber of the nation's peace, an enemy to the king, and that I, with others, endeavour to raise insurrections to embroil the nation in blood;' all which is utterly false, and I do, in every part thereof, deny it.   For I am not a person generally suspected to be a disturber of the nation's peace, nor have I given any cause for such suspicion; for through the nation I have been tried for these things formerly.   In the days of Oliver, I was taken up on pretence of raising arms against him, which was also false; for I meddled not with raising arms at all.   Yet I was then carried up a prisoner to London, and brought before him; when I cleared myself, and denied the drawing of a carnal weapon against him, or any man upon the earth; for my weapons are spiritual, which take away the occasion of war, and lead into peace.   Upon my declaring this to Oliver, I was set at liberty by him. After this I was taken, and sent to prison by Major Ceely in Cornwall, who, when I was brought before the judge, informed against me, 'that I took him aside, and told him, that I could raise forty thousand men in an hour's time, to involve the nation in blood, and bring in King Charles.' This also was utterly false, and a lie of his own inventing, as was then proved upon him: for I never spoke any such word to him.   I never was found in any plot; I never took any engagement or oath; nor ever learned war-postures.   As those were false charges against me then, so are these now, which come from Major Porter, who is lately appointed to be justice, but wanted power formerly to exercise his cruelty against us; which is but the wickedness of the old enemy. The peace of the nation I am not a disturber of, nor ever was; but seek the peace of it, and of all men, and stand for all nations' peace, and all men's peace upon the earth, and wish all knew my innocency in these things.

"And whereas Major Porter says, 'I am an enemy to the king:' this is false; for my love is to him and to all men, though they be enemies to God, to themselves, and to me. And I can say, it is of the Lord that he is come in, to bring down many unrighteously set up; of which I had a sight three years before he came in. It is much he should say I am an enemy to the king, for I have no reason so to be, he having done nothing against me. But I have been often imprisoned and persecuted these eleven or twelve years by them that have been against both the king and his father, even the party that Porter was made a major by, and bore arms for; but not by them that were for the king. I was never an enemy to the king, nor to any man's person upon the earth. I am in the love that fulfils the law, which thinks no evil, but loves even enemies, and would have the king saved, and come to the knowledge of the truth, and be brought into the fear of the Lord, to receive his wisdom from above, by which all things were made and created; that with that wisdom he may order all things to the glory of God.

"Whereas he calls me, 'a chief upholder of the Quakers' sect.' I answer: the Quakers are not a sect, but are in the power of God, which was before sects were; they witness the election before the world began, and are come to live in the life, which the prophets and apostles lived in, who gave forth the Scriptures; therefore are we hated by envious, wrathful, wicked, and persecuting men. But God is the upholder of us all by his mighty power, and preserves us from the wrath of the wicked, that would swallow us up.

"And whereas he says, 'that I, together with others of my fanatic opinion, as he calls it, have of late endeavoured to raise insurrections, and to embroil the whole kingdom in blood:' I say this is altogether false; to these things I am as a child, and know nothing of them. The postures of war I never learned: my weapons are spiritual and not carnal: for with carnal weapons I do not fight: I am a follower of him who said, 'My kingdom is not of this world.' And though these lies and slanders are raised upon me, I deny the drawing of any carnal weapon against the king or parliament, or any man upon earth; for I am come to the end of the law, 'to love enemies, and wrestle not with flesh and blood;' but am in that which saves men's lives. A witness I am against all murderers, plotters, and all such as would 'imbrue the nation in blood;' for it is not in my heart to have any man's life destroyed. And as for the word fanatic, which signifies furious, foolish, mad, &c., he might have considered himself, before he had used that word, and have learned the humility which goes before honour. We are not furious, foolish, or mad; but through patience and meekness have borne lies and slanders, and persecutions many years, and have undergone great sufferings. The spiritual man that wrestles not with flesh and blood, and the Spirit, that reproves sin in the gate, which is the Spirit of truth, wisdom, and sound judgment; this is not mad, foolish, furious, which fanatic signifies; but all are of a mad, furious, foolish spirit, that wrestle with flesh and blood, with carnal weapons, in their furiousness, foolishness, and rage. This is not the Spirit of God, but of error, that persecutes in a mad, blind zeal, like Nebuchadnezzar and Saul.

"Now, inasmuch as I am ordered to be kept prisoner, till I be delivered by order from the king or parliament, therefore have I written these things to be laid before you, the king and parliament, that ye may consider of them before ye act any thing therein; that ye may weigh, in the wisdom of God, the intent and end of men's spirits, lest ye act the thing that will bring the hand of the Lord upon you, and against you, as many have done before, who have been in authority, whom God hath overthrown, in whom we trust, whom we fear and cry unto day and night;—who hath heard us, doth, and will hear us, and avenge our cause. For much innocent blood has been shed; and many have been persecuted to death by such as have been in authority before you, whom God hath vomited out, because they turned against the just. Therefore consider your standing, now that ye have the day, and receive this as a warning of love to you.

"From an innocent sufferer in bonds, and close prisoner in Lancaster Castle, called　　　　　　　　　　　　　　"GEORGE FOX."

Upon my being taken and forcibly carried away from Margaret Fell's house, and charged with things of so high a nature, she was concerned, looking upon it to be an injury offered to herself. Whereupon she wrote the following lines, and distributed them :—

" To all Magistrates, concerning the wrong taking up, and imprisoning of
GEORGE FOX at Lancaster.

"I DO inform the governors of this nation, that Henry Porter, mayor of Lancaster, sent a warrant, with four constables, to my house, for which he had no authority or order. They searched my house, and apprehended George Fox in it, who was not guilty of the breach of any law, or of any offence against any in the nation. After they had taken him, and brought him before the said Henry Porter, bail was offered, what he would demand, for his appearance, to answer what could be laid to his charge; but he (contrary to law, if he had taken him lawfully) refused to accept of any bail, and put him in close prison. After he was in prison, a copy of his mittimus was demanded, which ought not to be denied to any prisoner, so that he may see what is laid to his charge; but it was denied him: a copy he could not have, they were suffered only to read it over. Every thing that was there charged against him was utterly false; he was not guilty of any one charge in it, as will be proved and manifested to the nation. Let the governors consider it. I am concerned in this thing, inasmuch as he was apprehended in my house; and if he be guilty, I am too. So I desire to have this searched out.　　　"MARGARET FELL."

After this Margaret Fell determined to go to London, to speak with the king about my being taken, and to show him the manner of it, and the unjust dealing and evil usage I had received. When Justice Porter heard of this, he vapoured, that he would go and meet her in the gap. But when he came before the king, having been a zealous man for the parliament against the king, several of the courtiers spoke to him concerning his plundering their houses; so that he quickly had enough of the court, and soon returned into the country. Meanwhile the jailer seemed very fearful, and said, he was afraid Major Porter would hang him, because he had not put me in the Dark-house. But when the jailer waited on him, after his return from London, he was very blank and down, and asked, "how I did," pretending he would find a way to set me at liberty. But having overshot himself in his mittimus, by ordering me "to be kept a prisoner till I should be delivered by the king or parliament," he had put it out of his power to release me if he would. He was the more down also upon reading a letter which I sent him; for when he was in the height of his rage and threats against me, and thought to ingratiate himself into the king's favour by imprisoning me, I was moved to write to him, and put him in mind, "how fierce he had been against the king and his party, though now he would be thought zealous for the king." Among other things in my letter, I called to his remembrance, that when he held Lancaster Castle for the parliament against the king, he was so rough and fierce against those that favoured the king, that he said, "he would leave them neither dog nor cat, if they did not bring him provision to the castle." I asked him also, "whose great buck's horns those were, that were in his house; and where he had both them and the wainscot from that he ceiled his house withal; had he them not from Hornby Castle?"

About this time Ann Curtis, of Reading, came to see me; and understanding how I stood committed, it was upon her also to go to the king about it. Her father, who had been sheriff of Bristol, had been hung near his own door for endeavouring to bring in the king; on which consideration she had some hopes the king might hear her on my behalf. Accordingly, when she returned to London, she and Margaret Fell went to the king together, who, when he understood whose daughter she was, received her kindly. And her request to him being "to send for me up, and hear the cause himself," he promised her he would, and commanded his secretary to send down an order for bringing me up. But when they came to the secretary for the order, he, being no friend to us, said, "it was not in his power; he must act according to law, and I must be brought up by an *habeas corpus* before the judges." So he wrote to the judge of the King's Bench, signifying that it was the king's pleasure, that I should be sent up by an *habeas corpus*. Accordingly a writ was sent down, and delivered to the sheriff; but because it was directed to the chancellor of Lancaster, the sheriff put it off to him; on the other hand, the chancellor would not make the warrant upon it, but said the sheriff must do that. At length both chancellor and sheriff were got together; but being both enemies to truth, they sought occasion for delay, and found, they said, an error in the writ, which was, that being directed to the chancellor, it stated, "George Fox in prison under *your* custody," whereas the prison I was in was not, they said, in the chancellor's custody, but in the sheriff's; so the word *your* should have been *his*. On this they returned the writ to London, only to have that one word altered. When it was altered, and brought down again, the sheriff refused to carry me up, unless I would seal a writing to him, and become bound to pay for the sealing, and the charge of carrying me up; which I refused, telling them I would not seal anything to them, nor be bound. So the matter rested a while, and I continued in prison. Meanwhile the assize came on; but as there was a writ for removing me up, I was not brought before the judge. At the assize many people came to see me; and I was moved to speak out of the jail window to them, and show them "how uncertain their religion was; and that every sort, when uppermost, had persecuted the rest. When Popery was uppermost, people had been persecuted for not following the mass; and they who then held up the mass cried, 'It was the higher power, and people must be subject to the higher power.' Afterwards, they that set up the Common Prayer persecuted others for not following that; saying, 'It was the higher power then also, and we must be subject to that.' Since that, the Presbyterians and Independents cried each of them, 'We must be subject to the higher power, and submit to the directory of the one, and the church-faith of the other.' Thus all, like the apostate Jews, have cried, 'Help, men of Israel, against the true Christians.' So people might see, how uncertain they are of their religions. But I directed them to Christ Jesus, that they might be built upon him, the rock and foundation, that changeth not." Much on this wise I declared to them, and they were quiet and very attentive. Afterwards I gave forth a paper concerning True Religion, as follows:—

"TRUE RELIGION is the true rule, and right way of serving God; a pure stream of righteousness, flowing from the image of God; the life and power of God planted in the heart and mind by the law of life, which bringeth the soul, mind, spirit, and body to be conformable to God, the Father of spirits, and to Christ; so that they come to have fellowship with the Father and the Son, and with all his holy angels and saints. This religion is from above, pure and undefiled before God, leads to visit the fatherless, widows, and strangers, and keeps from the spots of the world. This religion is above all the defiled, spotted religions in the world, that keep not their professors from defilement, but leave them impure, below, and spotted; whose fatherless, and widows, and strangers beg up and down the streets."　　　　　　　　　　　　　　　　　　　　G. F.

Soon after I gave forth a paper against persecution, as follows:—

"THE Papists, Common-Prayer-men, Presbyterians, Independents, and Baptists persecute one another about their own inventions, their mass, common-prayer, directory, and church-faith, which they have made, and framed, and not for the truth; for they know not what spirit they are of, who persecute, and would have men's lives destroyed about church-worship and religion, as saith Christ; who also said, 'He came not to destroy men's lives, but to save them.' Now we cannot trust our bodies, souls, or spirits into the hands of those that know not what spirit they are of, but will persecute and destroy men's lives, and not save them; they know not what spirit they are of themselves, therefore they are not fit to be trusted with others. They would destroy by a law, as the disciples once would have done by prayer, who would have commanded 'fire to come down from heaven' to destroy them that would not receive Christ. But Christ rebuked them, and told them they did not know what spirit they were of. If they did not know what spirit they were of, do these who have persecuted about church and religion since the apostles' days, who would compel men's bodies, goods, lives, souls, and estates into their hands by a law, or make them suffer? Those that destroy men's lives are not the ministers of Christ, the Saviour; and seeing they know not what spirit they are of, the lives, bodies, and souls of men are not to be trusted in their hands. And ye that persecute shall have no resurrection to life with God, except ye repent. But they that know what spirit they are of themselves, are in the unrebukable zeal, and by the Spirit of God they offer up their spirits, souls, and bodies to the Lord, which are his, to keep them."   G. F.

Whilst I was kept in Lancaster jail, I was moved to give forth the following paper, "for staying the minds of any such as might be hurried or troubled about the change of government:"—

"ALL FRIENDS, let the dread and majesty of God fill you! And as concerning the changing of times and governments, let not that trouble any of you; for God hath a mighty work and hand therein. He will yet change again, until that come up, which must reign; in vain shall powers and armies withstand the Lord, for his determined work shall come to pass. But it is just with the Lord that what is now come up should be so, and he will be served by it. Therefore let none murmur, nor distrust God; for he will provoke many to zeal against unrighteousness, and for righteousness, through things which are suffered now to work for a season; yea many, whose zeal was even dead, shall revive again, shall see their backslidings, and bewail them bitterly. For God shall thunder from heaven, and break forth in a mighty noise; his enemies shall be astonished, the workers of iniquity confounded, and all that have not the garment of righteousness shall be amazed at the mighty and strange work of the Lord, which shall be certainly brought to pass. But, my babes, look ye not out, but be still in the light of the Lamb; and he shall fight for you. The Almighty Hand, which must break and divide your enemies, and take away peace from them, preserve and keep you whole, in unity and peace with itself, and one with another. Amen."   G. F.

I was moved also to write to the king, to "exhort him to exercise mercy and forgiveness towards his enemies, and to warn him to restrain the profaneness and looseness that had got up in the nation on his return." It was thus:—

"To the King.

"KING CHARLES,

"THOU camest not into this nation by sword, nor by victory of war, but by the power of the Lord. Now if thou live not in it, thou wilt not prosper. If the Lord hath showed thee mercy and forgiven thee, and thou dost not show mercy and forgiveness, the Lord God will not hear thy prayers, nor them that pray for thee. If thou stop not persecution and persecutors, and take away all laws that hold up persecution about religion; if thou persist in them, and uphold persecution, that will make thee as blind as those that have gone before thee; for persecution hath always blinded those that have gone into it. Such God by his power overthrows, doth his valiant acts upon, and bringeth salvation to his oppressed ones. If thou bear the sword in vain, and let drunkenness, oaths, plays, may-games, with such like abominations and vanities be encouraged or go unpunished, as setting up may-poles, with the image of the crown on the top of them, &c., the nations will quickly turn like Sodom and Gomorrah, and be as bad as the old world, who grieved the Lord until he overthrew them; and so he will you, if these things be not suppressed. Hardly was there so much wickedness at liberty before, as there is at this day, as though there was no terror nor sword of magistracy; which doth not grace the government, nor is a praise to them that do well. Our prayers are for them that are in authority, that under them we may live a godly life, in which we have peace, and that we may not be brought into ungodliness by them. Hear, and consider, and do good in thy time, whilst thou hast power; be merciful and forgive; this is the way to overcome, and obtain the kingdom of Christ."   G. F.

It was long before the sheriff would yield to remove me to London, unless I would seal a bond to him, and bear their charges; which I still refused to do. Then they consulted how to convey me, and first concluded to send up a party of horse with me. I told them, "If I were such a man as they had represented me to be, they had need send a troop or two of horse to guard me." When they considered what a charge it would be to them to send up a party of horse with me, they altered their purpose, and concluded to send me up guarded only by the jailer and some bailiffs. But, upon further consideration, they found that would be a great charge to them also, and therefore sent for me to the jailer's house, and told me, if I would put in bail, that I would be in London such a day of the term, I should have leave to go up with some of my own friends. I told them, I would neither put in bail, nor give one piece of silver to the jailer; for I was an innocent man, and they had imprisoned me wrongfully, and laid a false charge upon me. Nevertheless, I said, if they would let me go up with one or two of my friends to bear me company, I might go up, and be in London such a day, if the Lord should permit; and if they desired it, I, or any of my friends that went with me, would carry up their charge against myself. At last, when they saw they could do no otherwise with me, the sheriff yielded, consenting that I should come up with some of my friends, without any other engagement than my word, to appear before the judges at London such a day of the term, if the Lord should permit. Whereupon I was let out of prison, and went to SWARTHMORE, where I stayed two or three days, and then to LANCASTER again, and so to PRESTON, having meetings amongst Friends, till I came into CHESHIRE to William

Gandy's, where there was a large meeting out of doors, the house not being sufficient to contain it. That day the Lord's everlasting Seed was set over all, and Friends were turned to it, who is the Heir of the Promise. Thence I came into STAFFORDSHIRE and WARWICKSHIRE, to Anthony Bickliff's; and at NUN-EATON, at the house of a priest's widow, we had a blessed meeting, wherein the everlasting Word of Life was powerfully declared, and many settled in it. Then travelling on, visiting Friends' meetings, in about three weeks from my coming out of prison, I reached LONDON, Richard Hubberthorn and Robert Widders being with me.

When we came to Charing-Cross, multitudes of people were gathered together to see the burning of the bowels of some of the old king's judges, who had been hung, drawn, and quartered.

We went next morning to Judge Mallet's chamber, who was putting on his red gown, to go sit upon some more of the king's judges. He was very peevish and froward, and said I might come another time. We went again to his chamber, when Judge Foster was with him, who was called the lord chief justice of England. With me was one called Esquire Marsh, who was one of the bedchamber to the king. When we had delivered to the judges the charge that was against me, and they had read to those words, "that I and my friends were embroiling the nation in blood," &c., they struck their hands on the table. Whereupon I told them, "I was the man whom that charge was against, but I was as innocent of any such thing as a new-born child, and had brought it up myself; and some of my friends came up with me, without any guard." As yet they had not minded my hat, but now seeing it on, they said, "What, did I stand with my hat on!" I told them I did not so in any contempt of them. Then they commanded it to be taken off; and when they called for the marshal of the King's Bench, they said to him, "You must take this man, and secure him; but let him have a chamber, and not put him amongst the prisoners." "My lord," said the marshal, "I have no chamber to put him into; my house is so full I cannot tell where to provide a room for him but amongst the prisoners." "Nay," said the judge, "you must not put him amongst the prisoners." But when he still answered, he had no other place to put me in, Judge Foster said to me, "Will you appear to-morrow about ten o'clock at the King's Bench bar in Westminster-Hall?" I said, "Yes, if the Lord give me strength." Then said Judge Foster to the other judge, "If he says yes, and promises it, you may take his word;" so I was dismissed. Next day I appeared at the King's Bench bar at the hour appointed, Robert Widders, Richard Hubberthorn, and Esquire Marsh going with me. I was brought into the middle of the court; and as soon as I came in, was moved to look round, and turning to the people, said, "Peace be among you;" and the power of the Lord sprang over the court. The charge against me was read openly. The people were moderate, and the judges cool and loving; and the Lord's mercy was to them. But when they came to that part which said, "that I and my friends were embroiling the nation in blood, and raising a new war, and that I was an enemy to the king," &c., they lifted up their hands. Then, stretching out my arms, I said, "I am the man whom that charge is against; but I am as innocent as a child concerning the charge, and have never learned any war-postures. And," said I, "do ye think that if I and my friends had been such men as the charge declares, that I would have brought it up myself against myself? Or that I should have been suffered to come up with only one or two of my friends with me? Had I been such a man as this charge sets forth, I had need to have been guarded with a troop or two of horse. But the sheriff and magistrates of Lancashire thought fit to let me and my friends come up with it ourselves, nearly two hundred miles, without any guard at all; which, ye may be sure, they would not have done, had they looked upon me to be such a man." Then the judge asked me, whether it should be filed, or what I would do with it. I answered, "Ye are judges, and able. I hope, to judge in this matter, therefore do with it what ye will; for I am the man these charges are against, and here ye see, I have brought them up myself; do ye what ye will with them, I leave it to you." Then Judge Twisden beginning to speak some angry words, I appealed to Judge Foster and Judge Mallet, who had heard me over-night. Whereupon they said, "They did not accuse me, for they had nothing against me." Then stood up Esquire Marsh, who was of the king's bedchamber, and told the judges, "It was the king's pleasure, that I should be set at liberty, seeing no accuser came up against me." They asked me, "Whether I would put it to the king and council?" I said, "Yes, with a good will." Thereupon they sent the sheriff's return, which he made to the writ of *habeas corpus*, containing the matter charged against me in the mittimus, to the king, that he might see for what I was committed. The return of the sheriff of Lancaster was thus:—

"By virtue of his Majesty's writ, to me directed, and hereunto annexed, I certify, that before the receipt of the said writ, George Fox, in the said writ mentioned, was committed to his Majesty's jail at the castle of Lancaster, in my custody, by a warrant from Henry Porter, Esq., one of his Majesty's justices of peace within the county palatine aforesaid, bearing date the fifth of June now last past; for that he, the said George Fox, was generally suspected to be a common disturber of the peace of this nation, an enemy to our sovereign lord the king, and a chief upholder of the Quakers' sect; and that he, together with others of his fanatic opinion, have of late endeavoured to make insurrections in these parts of the country, and to embroil the whole kingdom in blood. And this is the cause of his taking and detaining. Nevertheless, the body of the said George Fox I have ready before Thomas Mallet, knight, one of his Majesty's justices, assigned to hold pleas before his Majesty, at his chamber in Serjeant's Inn, in Fleet-street, to do and receive those things which his Majesty's said justice shall determine concerning him in this behalf, as by the aforesaid writ is required.

'GEORGE CHETHAM, Esq., Sheriff."

On perusal of this, and consideration of the whole matter, the king, being satisfied of my innocency, commanded his secretary to send an order to Judge Mallet for my release; which he did, thus:—

"IT is his Majesty's pleasure, that you give order for releasing, and setting at full liberty, the person of George Fox, late a prisoner in Lancaster jail, and commanded hither by an *habeas corpus*. And this signification of his Majesty's pleasure shall be your sufficient warrant. Dated at Whitehall, the 24th of October, 1660.

"EDWARD NICHOLAS."

For Sir Thomas Mallet, Knight,
one of the Justices of the King's Bench.

When this order was delivered, Judge Mallet forthwith sent his warrant to the marshal of the King's Bench for my release, as follows :—

"BY virtue of a warrant, which this morning I have received from the Right Hon. Sir Edward Nicholas, Knight, one of his Majesty's principal secretaries, for the releasing and setting at liberty of George Fox, late a prisoner in Lancaster jail, and from thence brought hither by *habeas corpus*, and yesterday committed unto your custody; I do hereby require you accordingly to release and set the said prisoner, George Fox, at liberty ; for which this shall be your warrant and discharge. Given under my hand, the 25th day of October, in the year of our Lord God, 1660.

"THOMAS MALLET."

To Sir John Lenthal, Knight,
Marshal of the King's Bench, or his deputy.

Thus, after being a prisoner more than twenty weeks, I was freely set at liberty by the king's command, the Lord's power having wonderfully wrought for the clearing of my innocency; Porter, who committed me, not daring to appear to make good the charge he had falsely suggested against me.

CHAPTER XIV.

1660–1662.—George Fox writes an epistle of consolation to Friends unjustly imprisoned in consequence of the insurrection of the Fifth-Monarchy Men—Friends' declaration against war and plots—John Perrot and Charles Bailey create a schism—some Friends in New England are put to death, a sense whereof is given to George Fox at the time—the King's mandamus to the Governor of New England and others, to restrain them from executing Friends—the *Battledore* is published, showing, by examples from thirty languages, that "Thou" and "Thee" are proper to one person—on true worship—George Fox disputes with some Jesuits, and with *all* other sects—John Perrot's heresy condemned—on judicial swearing—George Fox and Richard Hubberthorn write to the King, showing the number of Friends imprisoned prior to, and during the first year of, the Restoration, and the number who died in prison during the Commonwealth—Thomas Sharman, jailer at Derby, convinced, and writes to George Fox—George Fox applies to Lord D'Aubeny on behalf of two Friends imprisoned in the Inquisition at Malta, who procures their liberation—the ground and rise of persecution set forth—great service at *Bristol*, where also he has a vision—visits Captain Brown and his wife; the former had fled from persecution, and was judged in himself, but afterwards convinced—George Fox and several others are arrested by Lord Beaumont, and sent to Leicester jail—they are suddenly liberated—to Friends on the death of Edward Burrough—escapes from persecutors—Friends established on Christ, the Rock of Ages.

WHEN it was known I was discharged from Lancaster Castle, a company of envious, wicked spirits were troubled, and terror took hold of Justice Porter; for he was afraid I would take advantage of the law against him for my wrong imprisonment, and thereby undo him, his wife, and children. Indeed I was pressed by some in authority to make him and the rest examples; but I said, "I should leave them to the Lord; if the Lord forgave them, I should not trouble myself with them."

Now did I see the end of the travail which I had had in my sore exercise at Reading; for the everlasting power of the Lord was over all, and his blessed truth, life, and light shone over the nation, and great and glorious meetings we had, and very quiet; and many flocked in unto the truth. Richard Hubberthorn had been with the king, who said, "None should molest us, so long as we lived peaceably," and promised this to us upon the word of a king, telling him we might make use of his promise.* Some Friends also were admitted into the House of Lords, and had liberty to declare their reasons, why they could not pay tithes, swear, or go to the steeple-house worship, or join with others in worship, and they heard them moderately. And there being about seven hundred Friends in prison in the nation, who had been committed under Oliver's and Richard's government, upon contempts (as they call them), when the king came in, he set

---

* Some interesting particulars of what passed during Richard Hubberthorn's interview with the king are related in Sewell's *History*, for which see the index of that work.

them all at liberty. There seemed at that time an inclination and intention
in the government to grant Friends liberty, because they were sensible that
we had suffered as well as they under the former powers. But still, when
anything was going forward in order thereto, some dirty spirits or other,
that would seem to be for us, threw something in the way to stop it. It
was said, there was an instrument drawn up for confirming our liberty, and
that it only wanted signing; when suddenly that wicked attempt of the
Fifth-monarchy-people broke out, and put the city and nation in an uproar.
This was on a First-day night, and very glorious meetings we had had that
day, wherein the Lord's truth shone over all, and his power was exalted
above all; but about midnight, or soon after, the drums beat, and the cry
was, "Arm, Arm!" I got up out of bed, and in the morning took boat,
and landing at Whitehall-stairs, walked through Whitehall. They looked
strangely at me there, but I passed through them, and went to Pall-Mall,
where divers Friends came to me, though it had now become dangerous
passing the streets; for by this time the city and suburbs were up in arms,
and exceedingly rude the people and soldiers were; insomuch that Henry
Fell,* going to a Friend's house, the soldiers knocked him down, and he
would have been killed, had not the Duke of York come by. Great mischief was done in the city this week; and when the next First-day came, as
Friends went to their meetings, many were taken prisoners. I stayed at
Pall-Mall, intending to be at the meeting there; but on Seventh-day night,
a company of troopers came and knocked at the door. The servant letting
them in, they rushed into the house, and laid hold of me; and there being
amongst them one that had served under the parliament, he put his hand
to my pocket, and asked, "whether I had any pistols?" I told him, he
knew I did not carry pistols, why therefore ask such a question of me,
whom he knew to be a peaceable man? Others of the soldiers ran into
the chambers, and there found in bed Esquire Marsh, who, though he was
one of the king's bedchamber, out of his love to me, came and lodged where
I did. When they came down again, they said, "Why should we take this
man away with us? We will let him alone." "O," said the parliament
soldier, "he is one of the heads, and a chief ringleader." Upon this the
soldiers were taking me away, but Esquire Marsh hearing of it, sent for
him that commanded the party, and desired him to let me alone, for he
would see me forthcoming in the morning. In the morning before they
could fetch me, and before the meeting was gathered, there came a company
of foot soldiers to the house, and one of them drawing his sword, held it
over my head. I asked him, "why he drew his sword at an unarmed
man?" at which his fellows being ashamed, bid him put up his sword.

---

* Henry Fell was an eminent minister in the Society. In 1656 and 1658 he
visited the West India isles. During the first visit, he was absent from home about
a year. From 1659 to 1662, he was mostly engaged in gospel labours in England,
and from this period we lose all trace of him. He is mentioned in Whiting's Catalogue as having died in America. His home was in Lancashire, and there is reason
to believe he was a near relative of Judge Fell. He appears to have received an
education considerably above most of his day. Some of his letters are given in
Bowden's *History of Friends in America*, and in Barclay's *Letters of Early Friends*.

These foot soldiers took me away to Whitehall, before the troopers came for me. As I was going out, several Friends were coming in to the meeting, whose boldness and cheerfulness I commended, and encouraged them to persevere therein. When I was brought to Whitehall, the soldiers and people were exceedingly rude, yet I declared truth to them; but some great persons coming by, who were very full of envy, "What," said they, "do ye let him preach? Put him into such a place, where he may not stir." So into that place they put me, and the soldiers watched over me. I told them, though they could confine my body and shut that up, yet they could not stop the Word of Life. Some came, and asked me, "What I was?" I told them, "A preacher of righteousness." After I had been kept there two or three hours, Esquire Marsh spoke to Lord Gerrard, and he came and bid them set me at liberty. The marshal, when I was discharged, demanded fees. I told him, I could not give him any, neither was it our practice; and asked him how he could demand fees of me, who was innocent. Then I went through the guards, the Lord's power being over them; and after I had declared truth to the soldiers, I went up the streets with two Irish colonels that came from Whitehall, to an inn, where many Friends were at that time prisoners under a guard. I desired these colonels to speak to the guard to let me go in to visit my friends, that were prisoners there; but they would not. Then I stepped to the sentry, and desired him to let me go up; and he did so. While I was there, the soldiers went to Pall-Mall again to search for me there; but not finding me, they turned towards the inn, and bid all come out that were not prisoners; so they went out. But I asked the soldiers that were within, "Whether I might not stay there a while with my friends?" They said, "Yes." I stayed, and so escaped their hands again. Towards night I went to Pall-Mall, to see how it was with the Friends there; and after I had stayed a while, I went up into the city. Great rifling of houses there was at this time to search for people. I went to a private friend's house, and Richard Hubberthorn was with me. There we drew up a declaration against plots and fightings, to be presented to the king and council; but when finished, and sent to print, it was taken in the press.

On this insurrection of the Fifth-monarchy men, great havoc was made both in city and country, so that it was dangerous for sober people to stir abroad for several weeks after; men or women could hardly go up and down the streets to buy provisions for their families without being abused. In the country they dragged men and women out of their houses, and some sick men out of their beds by the legs. Nay, one man in a fever, the soldiers dragged out of bed to prison, and when he was brought there he died. His name was Thomas Pachyn.

Margaret Fell went to the king, and told him what sad work there was in the city and nation, and showed him we were an innocent, peaceable people, and that we must keep our meetings as heretofore, whatever we suffered; but that it concerned him to see that peace was kept, that no innocent blood might be shed.

The prisons were now everywhere filled with Friends, and others, in the city and country, and the posts were so laid for the searching of letters, that none could pass unsearched. We heard of several thousands of our Friends being cast into prison in several parts of the nation, and Margaret Fell carried an account of them to the king and council. Next week we had an account of several thousands more being cast into prison; and she went and laid them also before the king and council. They wondered how we could have such intelligence, having given strict charge for the intercepting of all letters; but the Lord so ordered it, that we had an account, notwithstanding all their stoppings. In the deep sense I had of the grievous sufferings Friends underwent, and of their innocency towards God and man, I was moved to send the following epistle to them, as a word of consolation, and advised them to send up an account of their sufferings:—

"MY DEAR FRIENDS,

"IN the immortal seed of God, which will plead its own innocency, who are inheritors of an everlasting kingdom that is incorruptible, and of a world and riches that fade not away, peace and mercy be multiplied amongst you in all your sufferings; whose backs were not unready, but your hair and cheeks prepared; who never feared suffering, knowing it is your portion in the world, from the foundation of which the Lamb was slain, who reigns in his glory, which he had with his Father before the world began. He is your rock in all floods and waves, upon which ye can stand safe, with a cheerful countenance, beholding the Lord God of the whole earth on your side. So in the Seed of God, which was before the unrighteous world, in which sufferings are, live and feed; wherein the Bread of Life is felt, and no cause to complain of hunger or cold. Friends, I would have you all, that are or have been lately in prison, to send up an account of your sufferings, and how things are amongst you, that it may be delivered to the king and his council; for things are pretty well here after the storm."   G. F.

London, the 28th of the 11th Month, 1660.

Having lost our former declaration in the press, we hastily drew up another against plots and fighting, got it printed, and sent some copies to the king and council; others were sold in the streets, and at the Exchange. Which declaration was some years after reprinted, and is as follows:—

A DECLARATION from the harmless and innocent people of God, called Quakers, against all sedition, plotters, and fighters in the world: for removing the ground of jealousy and suspicion from magistrates and people concerning wars and fightings.

Presented to the King upon the 21st day of the 11th Month, 1660.

"OUR principle is, and our practices have always been, to seek peace and ensue it; to follow after righteousness and the knowledge of God; seeking the good and welfare, and doing that which tends to the peace of all. We know that wars and fightings proceed from the lusts of men, as James iv. 1—3, out of which the Lord hath redeemed us, and so out of the occasion of war. The occasion of war, and war itself (wherein envious men, who are lovers of themselves more than lovers of God, lust, kill, and desire to have men's lives or estates) ariseth from lust. All bloody principles and practices, as to our own particulars, we utterly deny; with all outward wars and strife, and fightings with outward weapons, for any end, or under any pretence whatsoever; this is our testimony to the whole world.

"And whereas it is objected:

"But although you now say 'that you cannot fight, nor take up arms at all, yet if the Spirit move you, then you will change your principle, and you will sell your coat, and buy a sword, and fight for the kingdom of Christ.'

"To this we answer, Christ said to Peter, 'Put up thy sword in his place;' though he had said before, he that had no sword might sell his coat and buy one (to the fulfilling of the law and the Scripture), yet after, when he had bid him put it up, he said, 'he that taketh the sword, shall perish with the sword.' And further, Christ said to Pilate, 'Thinkest thou, that I cannot now pray to my Father, and he shall presently give me more than twelve legions of angels?' And this might satisfy Peter, Luke xxii. 36, after he had put up his sword, when he said to him, 'He that took it, should perish by it;' which satisfieth us, Matt. xxvi. 51—53. And in the Revelation, it is said, 'He that kills with the sword, shall perish with the sword; and here is the faith and the patience of the saints.' And so Christ's kingdom is not of this world, therefore do not his servants fight, as he told Pilate, the magistrate, who crucified him. And did they not look upon Christ as a raiser of sedition? and did not he pray, 'Forgive them?' But thus it is that we are numbered amongst transgressors, and fighters, that the Scriptures might be fulfilled.

"That the Spirit of Christ, by which we are guided, is not changeable, so as once to command us from a thing as evil, and again to move unto it; and we certainly know, and testify to the world, that the Spirit of Christ, which leads us into all truth, will never move us to fight and war against any man with outward weapons, neither for the kingdom of Christ, nor for the kingdoms of this world.

"First, Because the kingdom of Christ God will exalt, according to his promise, and cause it to grow and flourish in righteousness; 'not by might, nor by power (of outward sword), but by my Spirit, saith the Lord,' Zech. iv. 6. So those that use any weapon to fight for Christ, or for the establishing of his kingdom or government,—their spirit, principle, and practice we deny.

"Secondly, We do earnestly desire and wait, that, by the Word of God's power, and its effectual operation in the hearts of men, the kingdoms of this world may become the kingdoms of the Lord, and of his Christ; that he may rule and reign in men by his Spirit and truth; that thereby all people, out of every profession, may be brought into love and unity with God, and one with another; and that they may all come to witness the prophet's words, who said, 'Nation shall not lift up sword against nation, neither shall they learn war any more,' Isa. ii. 4. Mic. iv. 3.

"So we, whom the Lord hath called into the obedience of his truth, have denied wars and fightings, and cannot more learn them. This is a certain testimony unto all the world, of the truth of our hearts in this particular, that as God persuadeth every man's heart to believe, so they may receive it. For we have not, as some others, gone about with cunningly-devised fables, nor have we ever denied in practice what we have professed in principle; but in sincerity and truth, and by the word of God, have we laboured to manifest unto all men, that both we and our ways might be witnessed in the hearts of all. And whereas all manner of evil hath been falsely spoken of us, we hereby speak the plain truth of our hearts, to take away the occasion of that offence; that so being innocent, we may not suffer for other men's offences, nor be made a prey of by the wills of men for that of which we were never guilty; but in the uprightness of our hearts we may, under the power ordained of God for the punishment of evil-doers, and for the praise of them that do well, live a peaceable and godly life, in all godliness and honesty. For although we have always suffered, and do now more abundantly suffer, yet we know that it is for righteousness' sake; 'for our rejoicing is this, the testimony of our consciences, that in simplicity and godly sincerity, not with fleshly wisdom, but by the grace of God, we have had our conversation in the world,' 2 Cor. i. 12, which for us is a witness for the convincing of our enemies. For this we can say to all the world, we have wronged no man, we have used no force nor violence against any man; we have been found in no plots, nor guilty of sedition. When we have been wronged, we have not sought to revenge ourselves; we have not made resistance against authority; but wherein we could not obey for conscience' sake, we have suffered the most of any people in the nation. We have been counted as sheep for the slaughter, persecuted and despised, beaten, stoned, wounded, stocked, whipped, imprisoned, haled out of synagogues, cast into dungeons and noisome vaults, where many have died in bonds, shut up from our friends, denied needful sustenance for many days together, with other the like cruelties. And the cause of all these sufferings is not for any evil, but for things relating to the worship of our God, and in obedience to his requirings. For which cause we shall freely give up our bodies a sacrifice, rather than disobey the Lord; for we know, as the Lord hath kept us innocent, so he will plead our cause, when there is none in the earth to plead it. So we, in obedience unto his truth, do not love our lives unto death, that we may do his will, and wrong no man in our generation, but seek the good and peace of all men. He who hath commanded us that we shall not swear at all, Matt. v. 34, hath also commanded us that we shall not kill, Matt. v.; so that we can neither kill men, nor swear for or against them. This is both our principle and practice, and has been from the beginning; so that if we suffer, as suspected to take up arms, or make war against any, it is without any ground from us; for it neither is, nor ever was in our hearts, since we owned the truth of God; neither shall we ever do it, because it is contrary to the Spirit of Christ, his doctrine, and the practices of his apostles; even contrary to him, for whom we suffer all things, and endure all things.

"And whereas men come against us with clubs, staves, drawn swords, pistols cocked, and beat, cut, and abuse us, yet we never resisted them; but to them our hair, backs, and cheeks, have been ready. It is not an honour to manhood or nobility to run upon harmless people, who lift not up a hand against them, with arms and weapons.

"Therefore consider these things, ye men of understanding; for plotters, raisers of insurrections, tumultuous ones, and fighters, running with swords, clubs, staves, and pistols, one against another; these, we say, are of the world, and have their foundation from this unrighteous world, from the foundation of which the Lamb hath been slain; which Lamb hath redeemed us from this unrighteous world, and we are not of it, but are heirs of a world of which there is no end, and of a kingdom where no corruptible thing enters. Our weapons are spiritual, and not carnal, yet mighty through God, to the pulling down of the strongholds of sin and Satan, who is the author of wars, fighting, murder, and plots. Our swords are broken into plough-shares, and spears into pruning-hooks, as prophesied of in Micah iv. Therefore we cannot learn war any more, neither rise up against nation or kingdom with outward weapons, though you have numbered us amongst the transgressors and plotters. The Lord knows our innocency herein, and will plead our cause with all people upon earth, at the day of their judgment, when all men shall have a reward according to their works.

"Therefore in love we warn you for your souls' good, not to wrong the innocent, nor the babes of Christ, which he hath in his hand, which he cares for as the apple of his eye; neither seek to destroy the heritage of God, nor turn your swords backward upon such as the law was not made for, i.e., the righteous; but for sinners and transgressors, to keep them down. For those are not peacemakers, nor lovers of enemies, neither can they overcome evil with good, who wrong them that are friends to you and all men, and wish your good, and the good of all people on the earth. If you oppress us, as they did the children of Israel in Egypt, and if you oppress us as they did when Christ was born, and as they did the Christians in the primitive times; we can say, 'The Lord forgive you;' and leave the Lord to deal with you, and not revenge ourselves. If you say, as the council said to Peter and John, 'speak no more in that name;' and if you serve us, as they served the three children spoken of in Daniel, God is the same that ever he was, that lives for ever and ever, who hath the innocent in his arms.

"O, Friends! offend not the Lord and his little ones, neither afflict his people; but consider and be moderate. Do not run on hastily, but consider mercy, justice, and judgment; that is the way for you to prosper, and obtain favour of the Lord. Our meetings were stopped and broken up in the days of Oliver, under pretence of plotting against him; in the days of the Committee of Safety we were looked upon as plotters to bring in King Charles; and now our peaceable meetings are termed seditious. O! that men should lose their reason, and go contrary to their own conscience; knowing that we have suffered all things, and have been accounted plotters from the beginning, though we have declared against them both by word of mouth and printing, and are clear from any such thing! We have suffered all along, because we would not take up carnal weapons to fight, and are thus made a prey, because we are the innocent lambs of Christ, and cannot avenge ourselves! These things are left on your hearts to consider; but we are out of all those things, in the patience of the saints; and we know, as Christ said, 'He that takes the sword, shall perish with the sword;' Matt. xxvi. 52; Rev. xiii. 10.

"This is given forth from the people called Quakers, to satisfy the king and his council, and all those that have any jealousy concerning us, that all occasion of suspicion may be taken away, and our innocency cleared."

"*Postscript.*—Though we are numbered amongst transgressors, and have been given up to rude, merciless men, by whom our meetings are broken up, in which we edified one another in our holy faith, and prayed together to the Lord that lives for ever, yet he is our pleader in this day. The Lord saith, 'They that feared his name spoke often together' (as in Malachi); which were as his jewels. For this cause, and no evil-doing, are we cast into holes, dungeons, houses of correction, prisons (neither old nor young being spared, men nor women), and made a prey of in the sight of all nations, under the pretence of being seditious, &c., so that all rude people run upon us to take possession. For which we say, 'The Lord forgive them that have thus done to us;' who doth, and will enable us to suffer; and never shall we lift up hand against any that thus use us; but desire the Lord may have mercy upon them, that they may consider what they have done. For how is it possible for them to requite us for the wrong they have done to us? Who to all nations have sounded us abroad as seditious, who were never found plotters against any, since we knew the life and power of Jesus Christ manifested in us, who hath redeemed us from the world, all works of darkness, and plotters therein, by which we know the election, before the world began. So we say, the Lord have mercy upon our enemies and forgive them, for what they have done unto us!

"O! do as you would be done by; do unto all men as you would have them do unto you; for this is the law and the prophets.

"All plots, insurrections, and riotous meetings we deny, knowing them to be of the devil, the murderer; which we in Christ, who was before they were, triumph over. And all wars and fightings with carnal weapons we deny, who have the sword of the Spirit; and all that wrong us, we leave to the Lord. This is to clear our innocency from the aspersion cast upon us, that we are seditious or plotters."

Added in the reprinting.

"COURTEOUS READER,

"THIS was our testimony above twenty years ago; since then we have not been found acting contrary to it, nor ever shall; for the truth, that is our guide, is unchangeable. This is now reprinted to the men of this age, many of whom were then children, and doth stand as our certain testimony against all plotting and fighting with carnal weapons. And if any by departing from the truth should do so, this is our testimony in the truth against them, and will stand over them, and the truth will be clear of them."

This declaration somewhat cleared the dark air that was over the city and country. And soon after the king gave forth a proclamation, "That no soldiers should search any house without a constable." But the jails were still full, many thousands of Friends being in prison; which mischief was occasioned by the wicked rising of the Fifth-monarchy-men. But when those that were taken came to be executed, they did us the justice to clear us openly from having any hand in or knowledge of their plot. After that, the king being continually importuned thereunto, issued a declaration, "That Friends should be set at liberty without paying fees." But great labour, travail, and pains were taken, before this was obtained; for Thomas Moor and Margaret Fell went often to the king about it.*

Much blood was shed this year, many of the old king's judges being hung, drawn, and quartered. Amongst them that so suffered, Colonel Hacker was one, who sent me prisoner from Leicester to London in Oliver's time, of which an account is given before. A sad day it was, and a repaying of blood with blood. For in the time of Oliver Cromwell, when several men were put to death by him, being hung, drawn, and quartered for pretended treasons, I felt from the Lord God, that their blood would be required; and I said as much then to several. And now upon the king's return, when several that had been against him were put to death, as the others that were for him had been before by Oliver, this was sad work, destroying people contrary to the nature of Christians, who have the nature of lambs and sheep. But there was a secret hand in bringing this day upon that hypocritical generation of professors, who, being got into power, grew proud, haughty, and cruel beyond others, and persecuted the people of God without pity. Therefore when Friends were under cruel persecutions and sufferings in the Commonwealth's time, I was moved of the Lord to write to Friends to draw up accounts of their sufferings, and lay them before the justices at their sessions; and if they would not do justice, then to lay them before the judges at the assize; and if they would not do justice, then to lay them before the parliament, the protector and his council, that they might all see what was done under their government; and if they would not do justice, then to lay it before the Lord, who would hear the cries of the oppressed, and of the widows and fatherless whom they had made so. For that which we suffered for, and for which our goods were spoiled, was our obedience to the Lord in his Power and in his Spirit, who was able to help and to succour, and we had no helper in the earth but him. And he heard the cries of his people, and brought an overflowing scourge over the heads of all our persecutors, which brought a dread, and a fear amongst and on them all: so that those who had nicknamed us (who are the children of light) and in scorn called us Quakers, the Lord made to quake; and many of them would have been glad to have hid themselves amongst us; and some of them, through the distress that came upon them, did at length come to confess to the truth. O! the daily reproaches, revilings, and beatings we underwent amongst them, even in the highways,

---

* Among the Swarthmore collection of MSS. has been found a narrative of an interview Thomas Moor had with the king, which has been printed in *Letters of Early Friends*, p. 92, to which the reader is referred. It is endorsed by George Fox thus: —"What the king said to T. Moor, 1660, 14th of 10th month." It will be remembered Thomas Moor was formerly a justice of the peace, and was convinced by George Fox, as related in the early part of this journal.

because we could not put off our hats to them, and for saying Thou and Thee to them! O! the havoc and spoil the priests made of our goods, because we could not put into their mouths and give them tithes; besides casting into prisons, and laying great fines upon us, because we could not swear! But for all these things did the Lord God plead with them. Yet some were so hardened in their wickedness, that when they were turned out of their places and offices, they said, "If they had power, they would do the same again." And when this day of overturning was come upon them, they said, "It was all on account of us." Wherefore I was moved to write to them, and ask them, "Did we ever resist them when they took away our ploughs and plough-gears, our carts and horses, our corn and cattle, our kettles and platters from us, whipped us, set us in the stocks, and cast us into prison, and all this only for serving and worshipping God in spirit and truth, and because we could not conform to their religions, manners, customs, and fashions? Did we ever resist them? Did we not give them our backs to beat, and our cheeks to pull off the hair, and our faces to spit on? Had not their priests, that prompted them on to such work, pulled them with themselves into the ditch? Why then would they say, 'It was all through of us,' when it was owing to themselves and their priests, their blind prophets, that followed their own spirits, and could foresee nothing of these times and things that were come upon them, which we had long forewarned them of, as Jeremiah and Christ had forewarned Jerusalem. They had thought to weary us out, and undo us, but they undid themselves. Whereas we could praise God, notwithstanding all their plundering of us, that we had a platter, a horse, and plough still."

Many ways were these professors warned, by word, by writing, and by signs; but they would believe none, till it was too late. William Sympson* was moved of the Lord to go, several times for three years, naked and barefoot before them, as a sign unto them, in markets, courts, towns, cities, to priests' and great men's houses, telling them, "So should they be stripped naked, as he was stripped!" And sometimes he was moved to put on sackcloth, and besmear his face, and tell them, "So would the Lord God besmear all their religion, as he was besmeared." Great sufferings did that poor man undergo, sore whippings with horse-whips and coach-whips on his bare body, grievous stonings and imprisonments, in three years' time, before the king came in, that they might have taken warning; but they would not: they rewarded his love with cruel usage. Only the mayor of Cambridge did nobly to him, for he put his gown about him, and took him into his house.

* This is probably the Friend of whom there is some account in *Piety Promoted*, vol. i., p. 71. He was born in Lancashire, and receiving the Truth, became a faithful minister of it, for which he was often imprisoned, and underwent cruel and hard sufferings. In 1670, he went to Barbadoes with John Burnyeat, to preach the gospel in that island, but after having some service there, he was taken ill of a fever, during which he felt great peace and consolation of spirit, and signified "he should die." He was often praising and glorifying God after this manner: "O! all that is within me praise and magnify the Lord God, who is worthy for ever of all glory; everlasting praises to the God of my life, who only is worthy, and lives over all, and is above all, God blessed for ever. Amen." He died in much peace and quietness.

Another Friend, Robert Huntingdon, was moved of the Lord to go into Carlisle steeple-house, with a white sheet about him, amongst the great Presbyterians and Independents there, to show them that the surplice was coming up again : and he put a halter about his neck, to show them that a halter was coming upon them; which was fulfilled upon some of our persecutors not long after.

Another, Richard Sale, living near Chester, being constable of the place where he lived, had a Friend sent to him with a pass, whom those wicked professors had taken up for a vagabond, because he travelled in the work of the ministry; and this constable being convinced by the Friend, that was thus brought to him, gave him his pass and liberty, and was afterwards himself cast into prison. After this, on a lecture-day, Richard Sale was moved to go to the steeple-house, in the time of their worship, and to carry those persecuting priests and people a lantern and candle, as a figure of their darkness; but they cruelly abused him, and like dark professors as they were, put him into their prison called Little-Ease; and so squeezed his body therein, that not long after he died.* Many warnings of many sorts were Friends moved, in the power of the Lord, to give to that generation; which they not only rejected, but abused Friends, calling us giddy-headed Quakers; but God brought his judgments upon those persecuting priests and magistrates. For when the king came in, most of them were

---

* Richard Sale, the constable who became convinced, was an undaunted reproacher of vice. The place in which he lost his life, called "Little Ease," is described to have been "a hole hewed out in a rock; the breadth across, seventeen inches; from the back to the inside of the great door, at the top, seven inches; at the shoulders, eight inches; at the breast, nine inches and a half; from the top to the bottom, one yard and a half, with a device to lessen the height, as they are minded to torment the persons put in, by draw-boards which shoot over the two sides to a yard height, or thereabout."

In this place they tormented many of those who were induced, with Christian courage, to reprove the vices, either of ministers, magistrates, or people. Richard Costrop, for preaching repentance in the streets, was put in Little Ease till next day, and then, by the Mayor, sent to Bridewell. Thomas Yarwood, who, as the Mayor and Aldermen were going to a customary feast, with music playing before them, dared to remind them wherein real Christianity stood, viz., *in true holiness and the fear of the Lord*, was sent to Little Ease, and kept there five hours; by which he, being but a weak sickly man, was much bruised and hurt. William Sympson, attempting, in Christian love, to exhort the people, after their public preacher had ended his sermon, was first put in the stocks, and afterwards kept in Little Ease nine hours. When, next morning, he complained to the Mayor of his cruel usage, he was sent again to the same place, after the Sheriff, in the Mayor's presence, had struck him in the face, so that he bled very much. Edward Morgan, complaining to the Mayor against a drunken fellow who had grossly abused him, was sent to Little Ease for not putting off his hat when he made that complaint, and the drunkard went unpunished; as did also a servant who had robbed his master, a Friend, the master being, by this same magistrate, imprisoned eleven weeks, because he would not swear to the fact of the robbery.

Into this place was the Friend above named (Richard Sale) put several times, in 1656–1657, for three, four, five, and eight hours together. Being corpulent, it required the strength of four men to thrust him in. In doing which, they crushed him till the blood gushed out of his mouth and nose. He survived the last torture but two months, and died imputing his death to the cruelty of his persecutors.

turned out of their places and benefices, and the spoilers were spoiled: and then we could ask them, "Who were the giddy heads now?" Then many confessed we had been true prophets to the nation, and said, "Had we cried against some priests only, they should have liked us then; but crying against all made them dislike us." But now they saw those priests, which were then looked upon to be the best, were as bad as the rest. For indeed, some of those that were counted the most eminent, were the bitterest and greatest stirrers up of the magistrates to persecution; and it was a judgment upon them to be denied the free liberty of their consciences when the king came in, because when they were uppermost, they would not have liberty of conscience granted to others. One Hewes, of Plymouth, a priest of great note in Oliver's days, when some liberty was granted, prayed "that God would put it into the hearts of the chief magistrates of the nation, to remove this cursed toleration." Others of them prayed against it under the name of Intolerable Toleration. But a while after, when the king was come in, and priest Hewes turned out of his great benefice for not conforming to the Common Prayer, a Friend of Plymouth meeting with him, asked, "Whether he would acount toleration accursed now?" and "Whether he would not now be glad of a toleration?" To which the priest returned no answer, save by the shaking of his head. But as stiff as these men were then against toleration, it is well known that many of them petitioned the king for toleration, and for meeting-places, and paid for licenses too. But to return to the present time, the latter end of the year 1660 and beginning of 1661.

Although those Friends that had been imprisoned on the rising of the Monarchy-men were set at liberty, meetings were much disturbed, and great sufferings Friends underwent. For besides what was done by officers and soldiers, many wild fellows and rude people often came in. There came one time, when I was at Pall-Mall, an ambassador with a company of Irishmen and rude fellows; the meeting was over before they came, and I was gone up into a chamber, where I heard one of them say, "He would kill all the Quakers." I went down to him, and was moved in the power of the Lord to speak to him. I told him, "The law said, 'an eye for an eye, and a tooth for a tooth;' but thou threatenest to kill all the Quakers, though they have done thee no hurt. But," said I, "here is gospel for thee: here is my hair, here is my cheek, and here is my shoulder," turning it to him. This came so over him, that he and his companions stood as men amazed, and said, if that was our principle, and if we were as we said, they never saw the like in their lives. I told them, what I was in words, I was the same in life. Then the ambassador, who had stood without, came in; for he said that Irish colonel was such a desperate man, that he durst not come in with him, for fear he should do us some mischief; but truth came over him, and he carried himself lovingly towards us; as also did the ambassador; for the Lord's power was over them all.

At Mile-End Friends were kept out of their meeting-place by soldiers, but they stood nobly in the truth, valiant for the Lord's name; and at last the truth gave them dominion.

About this time we had an account that John Love, a Friend, that was moved to go and bear testimony against the idolatry of the Papists, was dead in prison at Rome: it was suspected he was privately put to death in prison. John Perrot was also a prisoner there, and being released, came over again; but after his arrival here, he, with Charles Baily and others, turned aside from the unity of Friends and truth. Whereupon I was moved to issue a paper, declaring how the Lord would blast him and his followers, if they did not repent and return, and that they should wither like the grass on the house-top, which many of them did; but others returned and repented.

Also before this time we received account from New England, "that the government there had made a law to banish the Quakers out of their colonies, upon pain of death, in case they returned; and that several Friends, having been so banished, and returning, were taken, and actually hung; and that many more were in prison, in danger of the like sentence being executed upon them.* When those were put to death, I was in prison at Lancaster, and had a perfect sense of their sufferings, as though it had been myself, and as though the halter had been put about my own neck; though we had not at that time heard of it. But as soon as we heard of it, Edward Burrough went to the king, and told him, "There was a vein of innocent blood opened in his dominions, which, if it were not stopped, would overrun all." To which the king replied, "But I will stop that vein." Edward Burrough said, "Then do it speedily, for we do not know

---

* The persecution of the Quakers in New England, by the Puritans and Independents, who had themselves fled from home to enjoy religious liberty, formed a dreadful scene, the very recital of which is revolting to humanity. Some they caused to have their ears cut off; and, amongst many other cruelties, which would fill a volume, they ordered three Quaker women to be stripped to the waist, and flogged through eleven towns, a distance of eighty miles, in all the severity of frost and snow. But, as if this was not enough, they actually hanged three men and one woman for Christ's sake, who all acquitted themselves, at their awful exit, with that firmness and submission which a Christian martyr is enabled to sustain at such an hour of nature's extremity, giving full proof of their sincerity and trust in the goodness and support of Him, who had called them to make a public profession of his name before a wicked and perverse generation. Their names were—William Robinson, Marmaduke Stevenson, William Leddra, and Mary Dyer.

On the day appointed for the execution of these innocent victims, they were led to the gallows by military officers, accompanied by a band of about 200 armed men, besides many horsemen—a measure which plainly indicated that some fear of popular indignation was apprehended; and, that no appeal might be made to the feelings of the multitude, a drummer was appointed to march before the condemned persons, to beat the drum, especially when any of them attempted to speak.

Glorious signs of heavenly joy and gladness were visible in the countenances of these holy martyrs, who walked hand in hand to the place where they were to suffer. "This is to me an honr of the greatest joy," exclaimed Mary Dyer; adding, that no eye could see, no ear could hear, no tongue could utter, no heart could understand, the sweet refreshings of the Spirit of the Lord which she then felt.

Being come to the ladder, and having taken leave of each other with tender affection, they yielded up their lives into the hands of their enemies, Robinson's last words being, "I suffer for Christ, in whom I live, and for whom I die;" and those of Stevenson, "This day shall we be at rest with the Lord." William Leddra, patiently submitting himself whilst the executioner put the halter round his neck, said, "I commit my righteous cause unto thee, O God;" and, as he was turned off, died with

how many may soon be put to death." The king answered, "As speedily as ye will. Call," said he to some present, "the secretary, and I will do it presently." The secretary being called, a mandamus was forthwith granted. A day or two after, Edward Burrough going again to the king, to desire the matter might be expedited, the king said, "He had no occasion at present to send a ship thither, but if we would send one, we might do it as soon as we chose." Edward Burrough then asked the king, "if it would please him to grant his deputation to one called a Quaker, to carry the mandamus to New England?" He said, "Yes, to whom ye will." Whereupon E. B. named Samuel Shattock, who being an inhabitant of New England, was banished by their law, to be hung if he came again; and to him the deputation was granted. Then he sent for Ralph Goldsmith, an honest Friend, who was master of a good ship, and agreed with him for £300, goods or no goods, to sail in ten days. He forthwith prepared to set sail, and, with a prosperous gale, in about six weeks arrived before the town of Boston, in New England, upon a First-day morning. Many passengers went with him, both of New and Old England, Friends, whom the Lord moved to go to bear testimony against those bloody persecutors, who had exceeded all the world in that age in their persecutions.

The townsmen at Boston seeing a ship come into the bay with English colours, soon came on board, and asked for the captain. Ralph Goldsmith told them, he was the commander. They asked him, if he had any

---

these words, "Lord Jesus, receive my spirit!" When Mary Dyer ascended the ladder, she was told by some of the standers-by that even now, if she would obey them, she might come down and save her life. But this magnanimous sufferer shrank not from her doom, well knowing in whom, and for whom she was about to die; she contentedly laid down her life, saying, "In obedience to the will of the Lord, I abide faithful unto death."

> "We, too, have had our martyrs. Such wert thou,
>   Illustrious woman! though the starry crown
> Of martyrdom has sat on many a brow,
>   In the world's eye, of far more wide renown.
>
> Yet the same spirit graced thy fameless end,
>   Which shone in Latimer and his compeers;
> Upon whose hallowed memories still attend
>   Manhood's warm reverence, childhood's guileless tears.
>
> Well did they win them; may they keep them long!
>   Their names require not praise obscure as mine,
> Nor does my muse their cherish'd memories wrong,
>   By this imperfect aim to honour thine.
>
> Heroic martyr of a sect despised!
>   Thy name and memory to my heart are dear:
> Thy fearless zeal (in artless childhood prized)
>   The lapse of years has taught me to revere.
>
> Thy Christian worth demands no poet's lay,
>   Historian's pen, nor sculptor's boasted art;
> What could the proudest tribute these can pay
>   To thy immortal spirit, now impart?
>
> Yet seems it like a sacred debt to give
>   The brief memorial thou may'st well supply;
> Whose life display'd how Christians ought to live,
>   Whose death—how Christian martyrs calmly die."

For further particulars of the New England persecution, the reader is referred to Sewell's *History*; Bowden's *History of Friends in America*; Kelty's *Early Days in the Society of Friends*; Hodgson's *Historical Memoirs, &c.*

letters? He said, "Yes." They asked, if he would deliver them? He said, "No, not to-day." So they went on shore, and reported there was a ship full of Quakers, and that Samuel Shattock was among them, who, they knew, was, by their law, to be put to death, for coming again after banishment; but they knew not his errand, nor his authority. So all being kept close that day, and none of the ship's company suffered to land, next morning, Samuel Shattock, the king's deputy, and Ralph Goldsmith, the commander of the vessel, went on shore; and sending back to the ship the men that landed them, they two went through the town to the governor's (John Endicott) door, and knocked. He sent out a man to know their business. They sent him word, their business was from the king of England, and they would deliver their message to none but the governor himself. They were then admitted, and the governor came to them; and having received the deputation and the mandamus, he put off his hat, and looked upon them. Then going out, he bid the Friends follow him. He went to the deputy-governor, and after a short consultation, came out to the Friends, and said, "We shall obey his Majesty's commands." After this the master gave liberty to the passengers to land; and presently the noise of the business flew about the town, and the Friends of the town and the passengers of the ship met together, to offer up their praises and thanksgivings to God, who had so wonderfully delivered them from the teeth of the devourer. While they were thus met, a poor Friend came in, who, being sentenced by their bloody law to die, had lain some time in irons, expecting execution. This added to their joy, and caused them to lift up their hearts in high praises to God, who is worthy for ever to have the praise, the glory, and the honour; for he only is able to deliver, to save, and to support all that sincerely put their trust in him. Here follows a copy of the mandamus:—

"CHARLES R.

"TRUSTY and well beloved, we greet you well. Having been informed that several of our subjects amongst you, called Quakers, have been and are imprisoned by you, whereof some have been executed, and others, as hath been represented unto us, are in danger to undergo the like, we have thought fit to signify our pleasure in that behalf for the future; and do hereby require, that if there be any of those people called Quakers amongst you, now already condemned to suffer death or other corporal punishment, or that are imprisoned, and obnoxious to the like condemnation, you are to forbear to proceed any further therein; but that you forthwith send the said persons, whether condemned or imprisoned, over into this our kingdom of England, together with the respective crimes or offences laid to their charge: to the end such course may be taken with them here, as shall be agreeable to our laws and their demerits. And for so doing, these our letters shall be your sufficient warrant and discharge. Given at our Court at Whitehall, the 9th day of September, 1661, in the thirteenth year of our reign."

Subscribed: "To our trusty and well beloved John Endicott, Esq., and to all and every other the governor or governors of our plantations of New England, and of all the colonies thereunto belonging, that now

are, or hereafter shall be : and to all and every the ministers and
officers of our plantations and colonies whatsoever, within the continent of New England.   " By his Majesty's command.
                                       " WILLIAM MORRIS."

Some time after this several New England magistrates came over,
with one of their priests. We had several discourses with them concerning their murdering our Friends, the servants of the Lord ; but they were
ashamed to stand to their bloody actions. On one of these occasions I
asked Simon Broadstreet, one of the New England magistrates, " Whether
he had not a hand in putting to death those four servants of God, whom
they hung for being Quakers only, as they had nicknamed them ?" He
confessed he had.   I then asked him and the rest of his associates that
were present, " Whether they would acknowledge themselves to be subject
to the laws of England ; and if they did, by what laws they had put our
Friends to death ?"   They said, " They were subject to the laws of England ; and had put our Friends to death by the same law that the Jesuits
were put to death in England." I asked them then, " Whether they
believed those Friends of ours, whom they had put to death, were Jesuits
or jesuitically affected ?"   They said, nay.   " Then," said I, " ye have
murdered them, if ye have put them to death by the law that Jesuits are
put to death here in England, and yet confess they were no Jesuits.   By
this it plainly appears ye have put them to death in your own wills, without any law."   Then Simon Broadstreet, finding himself and his company
ensnared by their own words, asked, " Did we come to catch them ?"
I told them, they had caught themselves, and they might justly be questioned for their lives ; and if the father of William Robinson, one of them
that were put to death, were in town, it was probable he would question
them, and bring their lives into jeopardy.   Here they began to excuse
themselves, saying, " There was no persecution now amongst them :" but
next morning we had letters from New England, giving us account that
our Friends were persecuted there afresh.   We went again, and showed
them our letters, which put them both to silence and to shame ; and in
great fear they seemed to be, lest some one should call them to account,
and prosecute them for their lives, especially Simon Broadstreet ; for he
had at first, before so many witnesses, confessed he had a hand in putting
our Friends to death, that he could not get off from it ; though he afterwards through fear shuffled, and would have unsaid it again.   After this,
he and the rest soon returned to New England again.
        I went also to Governor Winthrop, and discoursed with him on these
matters ; he assured me, " He had no hand in putting our Friends to death,
or in any way persecuting them ; but was one of them that protested against
it."   These stingy persecutors of New England were a people that fled
thither out of Old England, from the persecution of the bishops here ; but
when they had got power into their own hands, they so far exceeded the
bishops in severity and cruelty, that whereas the bishops had made them
pay twelve pence a Sunday (so called) for not coming to their worship
here, they imposed a fine of five shillings a-day upon such as should not

conform to their will-worship there; and spoiled the goods of Friends that could not pay it. Besides, many they imprisoned, divers they whipped, and that most cruelly; of some they cut off the ears, and some they hanged; as the books of Friends' sufferings in New England largely show, particularly that written by George Bishop, of Bristol, entitled, *New England Judged*. Some of the old royalists were earnest with Friends to prosecute them, but we told them, we left them to the Lord, to whom vengeance belongeth, and he would repay it. And the judgments of God have since fallen heavy on them; for the Indians have been raised up against them, and have cut off many of them.

About this time I lost a very good book, being taken in the printer's hands; it was a useful teaching work, containing the signification and explanation of names, parables, types, and figures in the Scriptures. They who took it were so affected with it, that they were loth to destroy it; but thinking to make a great advantage of it, they would have let us have it again, if we would have given them a great sum of money for it; which we were not free to do.

Before this, while I was prisoner in Lancaster castle, the book called the *Battledore* was published, which was written to show, that in all languages Thou and Thee is the proper and usual form of speech to a single person; and You to more than one. This was set forth in examples or instances taken from the Scriptures, and books of teaching, in about thirty languages. J. Stubbs and Benjamin Furly took great pains in compiling it, which I set them upon; and some things I added to it. When it was finished, copies were presented to the king and his council, to the bishops of Canterbury and London, and to the two universities one each; and many purchased them. The king said, it was the proper language of all nations; and the bishop of Canterbury, being asked what he thought of it, was at a stand, and could not tell what to say to it. For it did so inform and convince people, that few afterwards were so rugged toward us, for saying Thou and Thee to a single person, for which before they were exceedingly fierce against us. Thou and Thee was a sore cut to proud flesh, and them that sought self-honour, who, though they would say it to God and Christ, could not endure to have it said to themselves. So that we were often beaten and abused, and sometimes in danger of our lives, for using those words to some proud men, who would say, "What! you ill-bred clown, do you Thou me?" as though Christian breeding consisted in saying You to one; which is contrary to all their grammars and teaching books, by which they instructed their youth.

Now the bishops and priests being busy and eager to set up their form of worship, and compel all to come to it, I was moved to give forth the following paper, to open the nature of the true worship, which Christ set up, and which God accepts :—

"CHRIST's worship is free in the Spirit to all men; and such as worship in Spirit and in truth, are they whom God seeks to worship him; for he is the God of truth, and is a Spirit, and the God of the spirits of all flesh. He hath given to all nations of men and women breath and life, to live, and move, and have their being in him; and hath put into them an immortal soul. So all are to be temples for him to dwell in; and they that defile his temple will he destroy. Now as the outward Jews, while they had their outward temple at Jerusalem, were to go up thither to worship (which temple God hath long since thrown down, and destroyed that Jerusalem, the vision of peace; and cast off the Jews and their worship; and instead thereof hath set up his gospel-worship in Spirit and in truth), so now all are to worship in Spirit and in truth. This is a free worship; for where the Spirit of the Lord is, and ruleth, there is liberty; the fruits of the Spirit are seen, and will manifest themselves; and the Spirit is not to be limited, but lived and walked in, that its fruits may appear. The tares are such as hang upon the wheat, and thereby draw it down to the earth; yet the tares and the wheat must grow together, till the harvest, lest they that take upon them to pluck up the tares, should pluck up the wheat with the tares. The tares are such as worship not God in Spirit and in truth; but grieve the Spirit, vex and quench it in themselves, and walk not in the truth; yet will hang about the wheat, the true worshippers in the Spirit and in the truth. Christ's church was never established by blood, nor held up by prisons; neither was the foundation of it laid by carnal-weaponed men, nor is it preserved by such. But when men departed from the Spirit and truth, they took up carnal weapons to maintain their outward forms, and yet they cannot preserve them with their carnal weapons; for one plucketh down another's form with his outward weapons. And this work hath been among nominal Christians, since they lost the Spirit, and spiritual weapons, and the true worship which Christ set up, that is in Spirit and in truth, which they that worship in, are over all the tares. All that would be plucking up the tares are forbidden by Christ, who hath all power in heaven and earth given to him; for the tares and the wheat must grow together till the harvest, as Christ hath commanded. The stone that smote the image became a great mountain, and filled the whole earth; now, if the stone fill the whole earth, all nations must be temples for the stone. All that say they travail for the seed, and yet bring forth nothing but a birth of strife, contention, and confusion, their fruit shows their travail to be wrong; for by the fruit, the end of every one's work is seen, of what sort it is."   G. F.

About this time many Papists and Jesuits began to fawn upon Friends, and talked where they came, that of all sects the Quakers were the best and most self-denying people; and said, "It was a great pity they did not return to the holy mother church." Thus they made a buzz among the people, and said, "They would willingly discourse with Friends." But Friends were loth to meddle with them, because they were Jesuits, looking upon it to be both dangerous and scandalous. But when I understood it, I said to Friends, "Let us discourse with them, be they what they will." So a time being appointed at Gerrard Roberts's house, there came two of them like courtiers. When we were met together, they asked our names, which we told them; but we did not ask their names, for we understood they were called Papists, and they knew we were called Quakers. I asked

them the same question that I had formerly asked a Jesuit, namely,
"Whether the church of Rome was not degenerated from the primitive
church, from the Spirit, power, and practice, of the apostles' times?" He
to whom I put this question being subtle, said, "He would not answer it."
I asked him, "Why?" But he would show no reason. His companion
said, he would answer me; and said, "They were not degenerated from
the primitive church times." I asked the other, whether he was of the
same mind? He said, "Yes." Then I told them, that for better understanding one another, and that there might be no mistake, I would repeat my
question over again after this manner, "Whether the church of Rome now
was in the same purity, practice, power, and Spirit, that the church in the
apostles' time was in?" When they saw we would be exact with them,
they flew off, and denied that, saying, "It was presumption in any to say,
they had the same power and Spirit that the apostles had." "But I told
them, it was presumption in them to meddle with the words of Christ and
his apostles, and make people believe they succeeded the apostles, and yet
be forced to confess they were not in the same power and Spirit the apostles
were in. This," said I, "is a spirit of presumption, and rebuked by the
apostles' Spirit." I showed them how different their fruits and practices
were from those of the apostles. Then one of them said, "Ye are a company of dreamers." "Nay," said I, "ye are the filthy dreamers, who
dream ye are the apostles' successors; and yet confess ye have not the
same power and Spirit they were in. And are not they defilers of the
flesh, who say, 'It is presumption in any to say, they have the same power
and Spirit the apostles had?' Now," said I, "if ye have not the same
power and Spirit the apostles had, then it is manifest that ye are led by
another power and spirit than the apostles and primitive church were led
by." Then I began to tell them how that evil spirit, which they were led
by, had led them to pray by beads and images; to set up nunneries, friaries,
and monasteries, and to put people to death for their religion; and this
practice of theirs, I showed them, was below the law, and far short of the
gospel, in which is liberty. They were soon weary of this discourse, went
away, and gave a charge, as we heard, to the Papists, "That they should
not dispute with us, or read any of our books;" so we were rid of them.
But we had reasonings with all the other sects, as Presbyterians, Independents, Seekers, Baptists, Episcopalians, Socinians, Brownists, Lutherans,
Calvinists, Arminians, Fifth-monarchy-men, Familists, Muggletonians, and
Ranters; none of which would affirm they had the same power and Spirit
the apostles had, and were in; so in that power and Spirit the Lord gave
us dominion over them all.

As for the Fifth-monarchy men, I was moved to give forth a paper,
to manifest their error to them; for they looked for Christ's personal
coming in an outward form and manner, and fixed the time to the year
1666; at which time some of them prepared themselves when it thundered
and rained, thinking Christ was then come to set up his kingdom; and
they imagined they were to kill the whore without them. But I told them,
the whore was alive in them, and was not burned with God's fire, nor
judged in them with the same power and Spirit the apostles were in. And

their looking for Christ's coming outwardly to set up his kingdom, was like the Pharisees' "Lo here" and "Lo there." But Christ was come, and had set up his kingdom above sixteen hundred years ago (according to Nebuchadnezzar's dream and Daniel's prophecy), and he had dashed to pieces the four monarchies, the great image, with its head of gold, breast and arms of silver, belly and thighs of brass, legs of iron, and feet part of iron and part of clay; and they were all blown away with God's wind, as the chaff in the summer thrashing-floor. And when Christ was on earth, he said, "His kingdom was not of this world :" if it had been, his servants would have fought, but it was not; therefore his servants did not fight. Therefore all the Fifth-monarchy men, that are fighters with carnal weapons, are none of Christ's servants, but the beast's and the whore's. Christ said, "All power in heaven and in earth is given to me :" so then his kingdom was set up above sixteen hundred years ago, and he reigns. "And we see Jesus Christ reign," said the apostle; and he shall reign, till all things be put under his feet; though all things are not yet put under his feet, nor subdued.

This year several Friends were moved to go beyond the seas, to publish Truth in foreign countries. John Stubbs, and Henry Fell, and Richard Costrop were moved to go towards China and Prester John's country; but no masters of ships would carry them. With much ado they got a warrant from the king; but the East India Company found ways to avoid it, and the masters of their ships would not carry them. Then they went into Holland, hoping to get passage there, but none could they get there either. Then John Stubbs and Henry Fell took shipping for Alexandria in Egypt, intending to go by the caravans from thence. Meanwhile Daniel Baker being to go to Smyrna, drew Richard Costrop,* contrary to his own freedom, to go along with him; and in the passage Richard falling sick, Daniel Baker left him so in the ship, where he died: but that hard-hearted man afterwards lost his own condition.

John Stubbs and Henry Fell reached Alexandria; but they had not been long there before the English consul banished them: yet before they came away, they dispersed many books and papers, for opening the principles and way of truth to the Turks and Grecians. They gave the book called, *The Pope's Strength Broken*, to an old friar, for him to give or send to the Pope; which, when the friar had perused, he placed his hand on his breast, and confessed, "What was written therein was truth; but," said he, "if I should confess it openly, they would burn me." John Stubbs and Henry Fell, not being suffered to go further, returned to England, and

---

* This Richard Costrop (or Scostrop) was born in 1628. He was originally a sore persecutor of Friends, but becoming convinced of the soundness of their principles, he at length joined the Society, and preached the faith which once he destroyed, travelling for this object into various parts of Europe. He seems to have been chiefly instrumental in establishing the meeting at Scalehouse. He appears to have been a man of some estate, but left all, and spent his days in the service of the Gospel. In a document issued by Friends of Settle Monthly Meeting in 1704, it is said of him, "his memory is sweet this day among the brethren." See *Life, &c. of William and Alice Ellis*, by James Backhouse, pp. 278, 279, &c.

came to London again. John had a vision, that the English and Dutch, who had joined together not to carry them, would fall out one with the other : and so it came to pass.

Having now stayed in London some time, I felt drawings to visit Friends in Essex. So I went down to COLCHESTER, where I had very large meetings; and thence to COGGESHALL; not far from which a priest was convinced, and I had a meeting at his house. Travelling a little up and down in those parts, and visiting Friends in their meetings, I returned pretty quickly to LONDON, where I found great service for the Lord; for a large door was opened, many flocked in to our meetings, and the Lord's truth spread mightily this year. Yet Friends had great travail and sore labour, the rude people having been so heightened by the Monarchy-men's rising a little before. But the Lord's power was over all, and in it Friends had dominion; though we had not only those sufferings without, but sufferings within also, by John Perrot and his company; who, giving heed to a spirit of delusion, sought to introduce among Friends that evil and uncomely practice of "keeping on the hat in time of public prayers." Friends had spoken to him and many of his followers about it, and I had written to them concerning it; but he and some others rather strengthened themselves against us.* Wherefore feeling the judgment of truth rise against it, I gave forth the following as a warning to all that were concerned therein :—

"WHOSOEVER is tainted with this spirit of John Perrot, it will perish. Mark his and their end, who are turned into those outward things and janglings about them, and that which is not savoury; all which is for perpetual judgment—is to be swept and cleansed out of the camp of God's elect. This is to that spirit, that is gone into jangling about that which is below (the rotten principle of the old Ranters)—gone from the invisible power of God, in which is the everlasting fellowship; and thus many who now clamour and speak against them that are in the power of God, are become like the untimely figs, and like the corn on the house-top. O ! consider ! the light and power of God goes over you all, and leaves you in the fretting nature, out of the unity which is in the everlasting light, life, and power of God. Consider this, before the day be gone from you ; and take heed, that your memorial be not rooted out from among the righteous."

G. F.

* John Perrot was one who at this time caused great distress and trouble to the faithful members of the Society, from giving way to self-importance and extravagant notions. For particulars, the reader is referred to Sewell's *History;* and to Hodgson's *Historical Memoirs.*

Whilst the Society kept steadily pursuing its path, and increasing in numbers, notwithstanding the persecutions to which its members were everywhere subjected, it was not to be expected that every individual who was found within its precincts should have been rightly prepared for the station which he might have assumed. It would have been indeed remarkable, if, in the multitude of those who went forth in that day of zeal, in the service of the ministry, there had not been instances of men who had taken upon them (perhaps mistakenly) the office of a gospel minister, without waiting for the preparation and the call. And it would have been still more surprising if such forward spirits had proved firm in the day of outward trial, or of inward fascinations and snares of the enemy.

AMONG the exercises and troubles Friends had from without, one was regarding Friends' marriages, which sometimes were called in question. This year there was a cause tried at the assize at Nottingham concerning one. The case was thus. Some years before two Friends were joined together in marriage amongst Friends, and lived together as man and wife about two years. Then the man died, leaving his wife with child, and an estate in lands of copyhold. When the woman was delivered, the jury presented the child heir to its father's lands, and accordingly the child was admitted; afterwards another Friend married the widow. After that, a man that was near of kin to her former husband, brought his action against the Friend that had last married her, endeavouring to dispossess them, and deprive the child of the inheritance, and to possess himself thereof as next heir to the woman's first husband. To effect this, he endeavoured to prove the child illegitimate, alleging, " the marriage was not according to law." In opening the cause, the plaintiff's counsel used unseemly words concerning Friends, saying, "That they went together like brute beasts," with other ill expressions. After the counsels on both sides had pleaded, the judge (viz. Judge Archer) took the matter in hand, and opened it to the jury, telling them, that "There was a marriage in Paradise when Adam took Eve and Eve took Adam, and that it was the consent of the parties that made a marriage. As for the Quakers," he said, "he did not know their opinions, but he did not believe they went together as brute beasts, as had been said of them, but as Christians; and therefore he believed the marriage was lawful, and the child lawful heir." And the better to satisfy the jury, he brought them a case to this purpose:—" A man that was weak of body, and kept his bed, had a desire in that condition to marry, and declared before witnesses that he took such a woman to be his wife, and the woman declared that she took that man to be her husband. This marriage was afterwards called in question; and (as the judge said) all the bishops at that time concluded it to be a lawful marriage." Hereupon the jury gave in their verdict for the Friend's child, against the man that would have deprived it of its inheritance.

About this time the oaths of allegiance and supremacy were tendered to Friends, as a snare, because it was known we could not swear, and thereupon many were imprisoned, and divers premunired. Upon that occasion Friends published in print " The grounds and reasons why they refused to swear;" besides which I was moved to issue these few lines, to be given to the magistrates :—

" THE world saith, ' Kiss the book;' but the book saith, ' Kiss the Son, lest he be angry.' And the Son saith, ' Swear not at all,' but keep to Yea and Nay in all your communications; for whatsoever is more than this cometh of evil. Again, the world saith, ' Lay your hand on the book,' but the book saith, ' Handle the word;' and the word saith, ' Handle not the traditions,' nor the inventions, nor the rudiments of the world. And God saith, ' This is my beloved Son, hear HIM,' who is the life, the truth, the light, and the way to God."   G. F.

Now there being very many Friends in prison in the nation, Richard

Hubberthorn and I drew up a paper concerning them,* and got it delivered to the king, that he might understand how we were dealt with by his officers. It was directed thus :—

" *For the King.*

" FRIEND,

" Who art the chief ruler of these dominions, here is a list of some of the sufferings of the people of God, in scorn called Quakers, that have suffered under the changeable powers before thee, by whom there have been imprisoned, and under whom there have suffered for good conscience' sake, and for bearing testimony to the truth as it is in Jesus, ' three thousand one hundred and seventy-three persons ;' and there lie yet in prison, in the name of the Commonwealth, ' seventy-three persons,' that we know of. And there died in prison in the time of the Commonwealth, and of Oliver and Richard, the protectors, through cruel and hard imprisonments, upon nasty straw and in dungeons, ' thirty-two persons.' There have been also imprisoned in thy name, since thy arrival, by such as thought to ingratiate themselves thereby with thee, ' three thousand sixty and eight persons.' Besides this, our meetings are daily broken up by men with clubs and arms, though we meet peaceably, according to the practice of God's people in the primitive times, and our Friends are thrown into waters, and trod upon, till the very blood gushes out of them ; the number of which abuses can hardly be uttered. Now this we would have of thee, to set them at liberty that lie in prison in the names of the Commonwealth, and of the two Protectors, and them that lie in thy own name, for speaking the truth, and for good conscience' sake, who have not lifted up a hand against thee or any man ; and that the meetings of our Friends, who meet peaceably together in the fear of God, to worship him, may not be broken up by rude people with their clubs, swords, and staves. One of the greatest things that we have suffered for formerly, was, because we could not swear

---

* About this time persecution was very hot, and from estimates deduced from documents of the period, it is probable that, in 1661 or 1662, there were no less than 4500 Friends in prison, in England and Wales, at one time, for meeting to worship God, refusing to swear, &c. And in such prisons too ! They who would know what the miseries of prisoners have been in England, let them read Sewell's *History,* which exhibits such a scene of savage persecution on the one hand, and firmness and patience in suffering on the other, as is not easily paralleled. Little known as these things are, it will hardly be credited now, that to such a length was hatred carried against the Quakers, that few of them, except those below the cognizance of the magistrates, were not in prison, at one time or other, for their religious faith.

The interruption of family ties, the breaking up of households, the loss to many of all means of support, were hard and cruel sufferings for conscience' sake, but they were grievously aggravated at this period by the damp and filthy condition of the prisons, holes, and dungeons in which the sufferers were confined, as well as by their very crowded condition. And to all these circumstances of trial, must be added those of personal abuse, fines, distraints, and, it may strictly be said, of wholesale robberies they endured. Some died of the beatings which they received in the breaking up of their meetings, and many from the filthy and close state of the prisons, in some of which they were so closely packed that they had to take it by turns to stand up, whilst others sat or lay down. They were also often overrun with lice and other vermin.

to the Protectors and all the changeable governments; and now we are imprisoned because we cannot take the oath of allegiance. Now, if our yea be not yea, and nay, nay, to thee, and to all men upon the earth, let us suffer as much for breaking that, as others do for breaking an oath. We have suffered these many years, both in lives and estates, under these changeable governments, because we cannot swear, but obey Christ's doctrine, who commands, 'we should not swear at all' (Matt. v. James v.), and this we seal with our lives and estates, with our yea and nay, according to the doctrine of Christ. Hearken to these things, and so consider them in the wisdom of God, that by it such actions may be stopped; thou that hast the government, and mayest do it. We desire that all that are in prison may be set at liberty, and that for the time to come they may not be imprisoned for conscience and for truth's sake; and if thou question the innocency of their sufferings, let them and their accusers be brought up before thee, and we shall produce a more particular and full account of their sufferings, if required."[*] G. F. and R. H.

I mentioned before, that in the year 1650, I was kept prisoner six months in the house of correction at Derby, and that the keeper of the prison, a cruel man, and one that had dealt very wickedly towards me, was smitten in himself, the plagues and terrors of the Lord falling upon him because thereof. This man, being afterwards convinced of truth, wrote me the following letter:—

    "DEAR FRIEND,

"Having such a convenient messenger, I could do no less than give thee an account of my present condition, remembering, that in the first awakening of me to a sense of life and of the inward principle, God was pleased to make use of thee as an instrument. So that sometimes I am taken with admiration that it should come by such a means as it did; that is to say, that Providence should order thee to be my prisoner, to give me my first real sight of the truth. It makes me many times think of the jailer's conversion by the apostles. O happy George Fox! that first breathed that breath of life within the walls of my habitation! Notwithstanding my outward losses are since that time such, that I am become nothing in the world, yet I hope I shall find that all these light afflictions, which are but for a moment, will work for me a far more exceeding and eternal weight of glory. They have taken all from me, and now, instead of keeping a prison, I am

---

[*] An abruptness of style, and an apparent deficiency of courtesy due from subjects to their sovereign, pervade the foregoing address. When we take into consideration the long catalogue of grievous and unjustifiable wrongs therein enumerated; that these had been reiterated by the suffering party with scarcely a shadow of redress; and that all these evils were now inflicted in direct contradiction to the king's proclamation from Breda, and also of his own royal word of promise to the Quakers after his restoration; it is quite possible the style was intentional on the part of the writers, who, like the rest of his subjects, had by this time found out that the fair promises of Charles II. were not to be relied upon; and therefore, in this instance, felt it their duty to confine themselves to a manly and straightforward statement of the truth of their grievances. It offers an exception to the generally respectful tenor of the addresses of Friends, which are by no means wanting in proper courtesy.—(Marsh.)

rather waiting the time when I shall become a prisoner myself. Pray for me, that my faith fail not, but that I may hold out unto death, that I may receive a crown of life. I earnestly desire to hear from thee, and of thy condition, which would very much rejoice me. Not having else at present but my kind love unto thee, and all Christian Friends with thee, in haste, I rest, thine, in Christ Jesus,   "THOMAS SHARMAN."

Derby, 22d of 4th Month, 1662.

There were two of our Friends in prison in the Inquisition at Malta, both women; Katharine Evans and Sarah Chevers.* I was told that one, called the Lord D'Aubeny [a Roman Catholic priest], could procure their liberty, so I went to him; and having informed him concerning their imprisonment, desired him to write to the magistrates there for their release. He readily promised he would; and, "if I would come again within a month, he would tell me of their discharge." I went again about that time, and he said, "he thought his letters had miscarried, because he had received no answer." But he promised he would write again, and he did so; and they were both set at liberty.

With this great man I had much reasoning about religion, and he confessed that "Christ hath enlightened every man that cometh into the world, with his spiritual light; that he tasted death for every man; that the grace of God, which brings salvation, hath appeared to all men, and

---

* Katharine Evans and Sarah Chevers suffered a dreadful confinement for about four years in the Inquisition at Malta, of which a full account has been published. A more condensed one may be seen in *Select Miscellanies*, v. p. 56–68.

> "——These ministers of Christ did leave
> Their homes in England, faithfully to bear
> The Saviour's message into Eastern lands;
> And here, at Malta, they were seized upon
> By bigoted intolerance, and shut
> Within this fearful engine of the Pope.
> Priests and inquisitors assail them there,
> And urge the claims of Popery. The rack
> And cruel deaths are threatened; and again
> Sweet liberty is offered, as the price
> Of their apostacy. All, all in vain!
> For years these tender women have been thus
> Victims of cruelty. At times apart,
> Confined in gloomy, solitary cells.
> But all these efforts to convert them failed;
> The inquisition had not power enough
> To shake their faith and confidence in Him,
> Whose holy presence anciently was seen
> To save his children from devouring flames;
> He from this furnace of affliction brought
> These persecuted women, who came forth
> Out of the burning, with no smell of fire
> Upon their garments, and again they trod
> Their native land, rejoicing."

Some idea of the sufferings of these poor creatures may be formed from the fact of their *often lying down before the crevice of their prison-door, to inhale what air could be obtained from it.* In this state their skin was parched, the hair fell off their heads, and they frequently fainted; and, in moments when the strength and glory of the Divine presence was not so feelingly experienced as at others, it cannot occasion surprise that, through human weakness, they wished for death; their distress sometimes being such, that when it was day they longed for night, and yet when night came it was only to prompt the constant sigh for returning light. Yet the heavenly

that it would teach them and bring their salvation, if they obeyed it. Then I asked him, "what would they (the Papists) do with all their relics and images, if they should own and believe in this light, and receive the grace to teach them and bring their salvation?" He said, "those things were but policies, to keep people in subjection." He was very free in discourse ; I never heard a Papist confess so much as he did.

Though several about the court began to grow loving to Friends, yet persecution was very hot, and several Friends died in prison. Whereupon I gave forth a little paper concerning the grounds and rise of persecution; which was thus :—

"ALL the sufferings of the people of God in all ages were, because they could not join in the national religions and worships, which men had made and set up ; and because they would not forsake God's religion and his worship, which he had set up. You may see through all chronicles and histories, that the priests joined with the powers of the nation ; the magistrates, soothsayers, and fortune-tellers, all united against the people of God, and imagined vain things against them in their councils. When the Jews did wickedly, they turned against Moses ; and when the Jewish kings transgressed the law of God, they persecuted the prophets, as may be seen in the prophets' writings. When Christ, the substance, came, the Jews

content which, on the whole, was the portion of these sufferers for Christ's sake, in this dark and cloudy day, was remarkable. One of them, in writing to her relatives in England, says, "We are witnesses that the Lord can provide a table in the wilderness, both spiritual and temporal. In all our afflictions and miseries, the Lord remembered mercy, and did not leave nor forsake us, nor suffer his faithfulness to fail; but caused the sweet drops of his mercy to distil upon us, and the brightness of his glorious countenance to shine into our hearts."

The other of these suffering captives writes that she could not, by pen and paper, set forth the extent of the love of God to her soul, in fulfilling his gracious promises to her in the wilderness. They were indeed enabled to "sing the Lord's song in a strange land ;" and, in the midst of heaviness, "their mouths were often filled with laughter, and their tongues with joy," being strong in the faith, giving praises and glory to God.

The following, composed by them in the Inquisition, affords a view of the motives and abilities of these devoted women :—

> "In prisons strong, and dungeons deep,
> To God alone we cry and weep ;
> Our sorrows none can learn nor read,
> But those that in our path do tread.
>   But He whose beauty shineth bright,
> Who turneth darkness into light,
> Makes cedars bow, and oaks to bend,
> To him that's sent to the same end ;
> He is a fountain pure and clear,
> His crystal streams run far and near
> To cleanse all those that come to Him
> For to be healed of their sin :
> All them that patiently abide,
> And never swerve nor go aside,
> The Lord will free them out of all
> Bondage, captivity, and thrall."

It was not in the Inquisition only that these women suffered, but much also in England. In 1657, Katharine Evans was stripped, and tied to a whipping-post in the market-place at Salisbury, and there whipped, for exhorting the people to repentance. Her husband, a man of property, also suffered several imprisonments, and at last died in prison for obeying our Saviour's command, " Swear not at all."

persecuted Christ, his apostles, and disciples. And when the Jews had not power enough of themselves to persecute answerably to their wills, they got the heathen Gentiles to help them against Christ, and against his apostles and disciples, who were in the Spirit and power of Christ." G. F.

After I had made some stay in London, and had cleared myself of those services that at that time lay upon me there, I went into the country, having with me Alexander Parker and John Stubbs. We travelled through the country, visiting Friends' meetings, till we came to Bristol. There we understood the officers were likely to come and break up the meeting; yet on First-day we went to the meeting at Broadmead, and Alexander Parker standing up first, while he was speaking the officers came and took him away. After he was gone, I stood up, and declared the everlasting truth of the Lord God in his eternal power, which came over all; the meeting was quiet the rest of the time, and broke up peaceably. I tarried till the First-day following, visiting Friends, and being visited by them. On First-day morning several Friends came to Edward Pyot's house (where I lay the night before), and used great endeavours to persuade me not to go to the meeting that day, for the magistrates, they said, had threatened to take me, and had raised the trained bands. I wished them to go to the meeting, not telling them what I intended to do; but I told Edward Pyot I intended to go, and he sent his son to show me the way from his house by the fields. As I went I met divers Friends who were coming to me to prevent my going, and did what they could to stop me. "What!" said one, "wilt thou go into the mouth of the beast?" "Wilt thou go into the mouth of the dragon?" said another. I put them by and went on. When I came to the meeting, Margaret Thomas was speaking; and when she had done, I stood up. I saw a concern and fear upon Friends for me; but the power of the Lord, in which I declared, soon struck the fear out of them; life sprang, and a glorious heavenly meeting we had. After I had cleared myself of what was upon me from the Lord to the meeting, I was moved to pray; and after that to stand up again, and tell Friends, "how they might see there was a God in Israel that could deliver." A very large meeting this was, and very hot; but truth was over all, the life was exalted, which carried through all, and the meeting broke up in peace. The officers and soldiers had been breaking up another meeting, which had taken up their time, so that our meeting was ended before they came. But I understood afterwards they were in a great rage, because they had missed me; for they were heard to say one to another before, "I'll warrant we shall have him;" but the Lord prevented them. I went from the meeting to Joan Hily's, where many Friends came to see me, rejoicing and blessing God for our deliverance. In the evening I had a fine fresh meeting among Friends at a Friend's house over the water, where we were much refreshed in the Lord. After this I stayed most part of that week in Bristol, and at Edward Pyot's. Edward was brought so low and weak with an ague, that when I first came, he was looked upon as a dying man; but it pleased the Lord to raise him up again, so that before I went away, his ague left him, and he was finely well.

Having been two First-days together at the meeting at Broadmead, and feeling my spirit clear of Bristol, I went next First-day to a meeting in the country not far distant. And after the meeting, some Friends from Bristol told me, that the soldiers that day had beset the meeting-house round at Bristol, and then went up, saying, "they would be sure to have me now;" but when they came, and found me not there, they were in a great rage, and kept the Friends in the meeting-house most part of the day, before they would let them go home; and queried of them, which way I was gone, and how they might send after me; for the mayor," they said, "would fain have spoken with me." I had a vision of a great mastiff dog, that would have bitten me, but I put one hand above his jaws, and the other hand below, and tore his jaws in pieces. So the Lord by his power tore their power to pieces, and made way for me to escape them. Then I passed through the country, visiting Friends in WILTSHIRE and BERKSHIRE, till I came to LONDON, having great meetings amongst Friends as I went. The Lord's power was over all, and a blessed time it was for the spreading of his glorious truth. It was indeed his immediate hand and power that preserved me out of their hands at Bristol, and over the heads of all our persecutors; and the Lord alone is worthy of all the glory, who did uphold and preserve for his name and truth's sake.

At London I did not stay long, being drawn in spirit to visit Friends northward, as far as LEICESTERSHIRE, John Stubbs being with me. So we travelled, having meetings amongst Friends as we went; at SKEGBY we had a great one. Thence passing on, we came to a place called BARNET-HILLS, where lived Captain Brown, a Baptist, whose wife was convinced of truth. This Captain Brown, after the act for breaking up meetings came forth, being afraid lest his wife should go to meetings, and be cast into prison, left his house at Barrow, and took one on these hills, saying, "his wife should not go to prison." And this being a free place, many, both priests and others, got thither as well as he. But he who would neither stand to truth himself, nor suffer his wife, was in this place where he thought to be safe, found out by the Lord, whose hand fell heavy upon him for his unfaithfulness; so that he was sorely· plagued, and grievously judged in himself for flying, and drawing his wife into that private place. We went to see his wife, and being come into the house, I asked him, "how he did?" "How do I?" said he, "the plagues and vengeance of God are upon me, a runagate, a Cain as I am. God may look for a witness for me, and such as me; for if all were not more faithful than I, God would have no witness left in the earth." In this condition he lived on bread and water, and thought it was too good for him. At length he returned again with his wife to his own house at Barrow, where he afterwards came to be convinced of God's eternal truth, and died in it. A little before his death he said, "though he had not borne a testimony for truth in his life, he would bear a testimony in his death, and would be buried in his orchard;" and he was so. He was an example to all the flying Baptists in the time of persecution, who could not bear persecution themselves, yet persecuted us when they had power.

From Barnet-Hills we came to SWANNINGTON in LEICESTERSHIRE,

where William Smith and some other Friends came to me; but they went away towards night, leaving me at a Friend's house in Swannington. At night, as I was sitting in the hall, speaking to a widow woman and her daughter, there came one called Lord Beaumont with a company of soldiers, who, slapping their swords on the door, rushed into the house with swords and pistols in their hands, crying, "Put out the candles, and make fast the doors." Then they seized upon the Friends in the house, and asked, "if there were no more about the house?" The Friends told them, there was one man more in the hall. There being some Friends out of Derbyshire, one of them was named Thomas Fauks; and this Lord Beaumont, after he had asked all their names, bid his man set down that man's name Thomas Fox; but the Friend said, his name was not Fox, but Fauks. In the meantime some of the soldiers came, and brought me out of the hall to him. He asked me my name; I told him, my name was George Fox, and that I was well known by that name. "Ay," said he, "you are known all the world over." I said, "I was known for no hurt, but for good." Then he put his hands into my pockets to search them, and pulled out my comb-case, and afterwards commanded one of his officers to search further for letters, as he pretended. I told him, I was no letter-carrier, and asked him, Why he came amongst a peaceable people with swords and pistols, without a constable, contrary to the king's proclamation, and to the late act? For he could not say, there was a meeting, I being only talking with a poor widow woman and her daughter. By reasoning thus with him, he came somewhat down; yet sending for the constables, he gave them charge of us, and to bring us before him next morning. Accordingly the constables set a watch of the town's-people upon us that night, and had us next morning to his house, about a mile from Swannington. When we came before him, he told us "we met contrary to the act." I desired him to show us the act. "Why," says he, "you have it in your pocket." I told him, he did not find us in a meeting. Then he asked us, "whether we would take the oaths of allegiance and supremacy?" I told him, I never took any oath in my life, nor engagement, nor covenant. Yet still he would force the oath upon us. I desired him to show us the oath, that we might see whether we were the persons it was to be tendered to, and whether it was not for the discovery of Popish recusants. At length he brought a little book; but we called for the statute-book. He would not show us that, but caused a mittimus to be made, which mentioned, "that we were to have had a meeting." With this he delivered us to the constables to convey us to Leicester jail. But when they had brought us back to Swannington, being harvest time, it was hard to get anybody to go with us; for the people were loath to go with their neighbours to prison, especially in such a busy time. They would have given us our mittimus, to carry it ourselves to the jail; for it had been usual for constables to give Friends their own mittimuses (for they durst trust Friends), and they have gone themselves with them to the jailer. But we told them, though our Friends had sometimes done so, yet we would not take this mittimus, but some of them should go with us to the jail. At last they hired a poor labouring man to go with us, who was loath to go, though hired. So we rode to LEICESTER, being five in number; some carried their Bibles open in their hands, declaring the truth to the people, as we rode, in the fields and through the towns, and telling them, "we were prisoners of the Lord Jesus Christ, going to suffer bonds for his name and truth's sake." One woman Friend carried her wheel on her lap to spin on in prison; and the people were mightily affected.   At Leicester we went to an inn.   The master of the house seemed troubled that we should go to the prison; and being himself in commission, he sent for lawyers in the town to advise with, and would have taken up the mittimus, and kept us in his own house, and not have let us go into the jail.   But I told Friends, it would be a great charge to lie at an inn; and many Friends and people would be coming to visit us, and it might be hard for him to bear our having meetings in his house; besides, we had many Friends in the prison already, and we had rather be with them.   So we let the man know, that we were sensible of his kindness, and to prison we went; the poor man that brought us thither, delivering both the mittimus and us to the jailer.   This jailer had been a very wicked, cruel man.   Six or seven Friends being in prison before we came, he had taken some occasion to quarrel with them, and thrust them into the dungeon amongst the felons, where there was hardly room for them to lie down.   We stayed all that day in the prison-yard, and desired the jailer to let us have some straw.   He surlily answered, "you do not look like men that would lie on straw."   After a while William Smith, a Friend, came to me, and he being acquainted in the house, I asked him, "what rooms there were in it, and what rooms Friends had usually been put into, before they were put into the dungeon?"   I asked him also, Whether the jailer or his wife was master?   He said, The wife was master; and that though she was lame, and sat mostly in her chair, being only able to go on crutches, yet she would beat her husband when he came within her reach, if he did not do as she would have him. I considered, probably many Friends might come to visit us, and that, if we had a room to ourselves, it would be better for them to speak to me, and me to them, as there should be occasion.   Wherefore I desired William Smith to go speak with the woman, and acquaint her, if she would let us have a room, suffer our Friends to come out of the dungeon, and leave it to us, to give her what we would, it might be better for her.   He went, and after some reasoning with her, she consented; and we were had into a room.   Then we were told, that the jailer would not suffer us to have any drink out of the town into the prison, but that what beer we drank, we must take of him.   I told them, I would remedy that, for we would get a pail of water and a little wormwood once a day, and that might serve us; so we should have none of his beer, and the water he could not deny us.

Before we came, when the few Friends that were prisoners there, met together on First-days, if any of them was moved to pray to the Lord, the jailer would come up with his quarter-staff in his hand, and his mastiff dog at his heels, and pluck them down by the hair of the head, and strike them with his staff; but when he struck Friends, the mastiff dog, instead of falling upon them, would take the staff out of his hand.   When the

First-day came, I spoke to one of my fellow-prisoners, to carry a stool and set it in the yard, and give notice to the debtors and felons, that there would be a meeting in the yard, and they that would hear the word of the Lord declared might come thither.   So the debtors and prisoners gathered in the yard, and we went down, and had a very precious meeting, the jailer not meddling.   Thus every First-day we had a meeting as long as we stayed in prison; and several came in out of the town and country.   Many were convinced, and some received the Lord's truth there, who have stood faithful witnesses for it ever since.

When the sessions came, we were brought before the justices, with many more Friends, sent to prison whilst we were there, to the number of about twenty.   Being brought into the court, the jailer put us into the place where the thieves were put, and then some of the justices began to tender the oaths of allegiance and supremacy to us.   I told them, I never took any oath in my life, and they knew we could not swear, because Christ and his apostle forbade it; therefore they put it but as a snare to us.   We told them, if they could prove, that after Christ and the apostle had forbid swearing, they did ever command Christians to swear, then we would take these oaths; otherwise we were resolved to obey Christ's command and the apostle's exhortation.   They said, "we must take the oath, that we might manifest our allegiance to the king."   I told them, I had been formerly sent up a prisoner by Colonel Hacker, from that town to London, under pretence that I held meetings to plot to bring in King Charles.   I also desired them to read our mittimus, which set forth the cause of our commitment to be, that "we were to have a meeting;" and I said, Lord Beaumont could not by that act send us to jail, unless we had been taken at a meeting, and found to be such persons as the act speaks of; therefore we desired they would read the mittimus, and see how wrongfully we were imprisoned.   They would not take notice of the mittimus, but called a jury, and indicted us for refusing to take the oaths of allegiance and supremacy.   When the jury was sworn and instructed, as they were going out, one that had been an alderman of the city, spoke to them, and bid them, "have a good conscience;" and one of the jury, being a peevish man, told the justices, there was one affronted the jury; whereupon they called him up, and tendered him the oath also, and he took it.

While we were standing where the thieves used to stand, a cut-purse had his hand in several Friends' pockets.   Friends declared it to the justices, and showed them the man.   They called him up before them, and upon examination he could not deny it; yet they set him at liberty.*

---

* Cases similar to the above are not rare in the early history of the Society; even thieves being allowed to escape, whilst the party robbed, being unwilling to swear to the known fact, have been made to suffer.   In 1660, the following occurrence took place at Reading assizes:—Henry Hodges, a poor smith, lost three cows, which were found in the possession of the thief who stole them.   He was brought to trial, and Hodges appeared to claim his cows.   The judge told him they must be proved on oath before he could have them again.   He replied that he could not swear for conscience sake.   The judge said, if any of his neighbours would swear they were his, they should be returned to him; upon which one of his neighbours took his oath, and the judge promised that they should be returned.   Thus far, the proceedings appeared

It was not long before the jury returned, and brought us in guilty; and then, after some words, the justices whispered together, and bid the jailer take us down to prison again; but the Lord's power was over them and his everlasting truth, which we declared boldly amongst them. There being a great concourse of people, most of them followed us; so that the cryer and bailiffs were fain to call the people back again to the court. We declared the truth as we went down the streets all along, till we came to the jail, the streets being full of people. When we were in our chamber again, after some time the jailer came to us, and desired all to go forth that were not prisoners. When they were gone, he said, "Gentlemen, it is the court's pleasure, that ye should all be set at liberty, except those that are in for tithes; and you know, there are fees due to me; but I shall leave it to you to give me what you will."

Thus were we all set at liberty suddenly, and passed every one into his service. Leonard Fell stayed with me, and we two went again to SWANNINGTON. I had a letter from Lord Hastings, who hearing of my imprisonment, had written from London to the justices of the sessions to set me at liberty. I had not delivered this letter to the justices, but whether they had any knowledge of his mind from any other hand, which made them discharge us so suddenly, I know not. But this letter I carried to Lord Beaumont who had sent us to prison; and when he had broken it open, and read it, he seemed much troubled; but at last came a little lower; yet threatened us, if we had any more meetings at Swannington, he would break them up and send us to prison again. But notwithstanding his threats, we went to Swannington, and had a meeting with Friends there, and he neither came, nor sent to break it up.

From Swannington we came to TWY-CROSS, where that great man formerly mentioned, whom the Lord God raised up from his sickness in the year 1649 (and whose serving-man came at me with a drawn sword to do me a mischief), and his wife came to see me. Thence we travelled through WARWICKSHIRE, where we had brave meetings; and into NORTHAMPTONSHIRE and BEDFORDSHIRE, visiting Friends till we came to LONDON.

I stayed not long in London, but went into ESSEX, and so into NORFOLK, having great meetings. At NORWICH, when I came to Captain Lawrence's,* there was a great threatening of disturbance; but the meeting was quiet. Passing thence to SUTTON, and so into CAMBRIDGESHIRE, I

just and equal, but many thought the judge too rigorous, when, having observed the sincerity and tenderness of the poor man's conscience, who could not swear in a case of his own property, he caused the oath of allegiance to be tendered him in court; and, for his refusing to take it, sent him to jail.—(Besse.)

* This Captain Lawrence, who has been mentioned before, was a man of some note in the days of the Commonwealth. After he joined Friends, he became a faithful sufferer for Christ. In 1660, with his brother Joseph Lawrence, and George Whitehead, he was imprisoned in Norwich castle, in a small narrow cell called the Vice, where they endured much hardship. In speaking of this imprisonment, George Whitehead says, "I remember one morning, Joseph Lawrence, after his pleasant manner, said to his brother John, 'O, Captain Lawrence, I have seen the day that thou wouldst not have lain there!'"

heard of Edward Burrough's decease. And being sensible how great a grief and exercise it would be to Friends to part with him, I wrote the following lines for the staying and settling of their minds :—

"FRIENDS,

"BE still and quiet in your own conditions, and settled in the Seed of God that doth not change, that in that ye may feel dear E. B. among you in the Seed, in which and by which he begat you to God, with whom he is; and that in the Seed ye may all see and feel him, in which is the unity with him in the life; and so enjoy him in the life that doth not change, which is invisible."

G. F.

Thence I passed to LITTLE PORT and the ISLE OF ELY; where the ex-mayor, with his wife, and the wife of the then mayor of Cambridge, came to the meeting. Travelling into LINCOLNSHIRE and HUNTINGDON-SHIRE, I came to Thomas Parnell's, where the mayor of Huntingdon came to see me, and was very loving. Thence I came into the FEN-COUNTRY, where we had large and quiet meetings. While I was in that country, there came so great a flood that it was dangerous to go out, yet we did get out, and went to LYNN, where we had a blessed meeting. Next morning I went to visit some prisoners there; and then back to the inn, and took horse. As I was riding out of the yard, the officers came to search the inn for me. I knew nothing of it then, only I felt a great burthen come upon me as I rode out of the town, till without the gates. When some Friends that came after, overtook me, they told me, that the officers had been searching for me in the inn, as soon as I was gone out of the yard. So by the good hand of the Lord, I escaped their cruel hands. After this we passed through the countries, visiting Friends in their meetings. The Lord's power carried us over persecuting spirits, and through many dangers; his truth spread and grew, and Friends were established therein; praises and glory to his name for ever.

END OF VOL. I.

Lightning Source UK Ltd.
Milton Keynes UK
UKHW040956250322
400611UK00003B/206